W9-DIV-870

# THE ANNOTATED
# EMERSON

# THE ANNOTATED
# EMERSON

## RALPH WALDO EMERSON

EDITED BY DAVID MIKICS

WITH A FOREWORD BY PHILLIP LOPATE

THE BELKNAP PRESS *of* HARVARD UNIVERSITY PRESS

Cambridge, Massachusetts · London, England

2012

Unless otherwise indicated, Ralph Waldo Emerson texts are reprinted by permission of the publisher from *The Collected Works of Ralph Waldo Emerson*, vols. 1–3, 5–6, 9, Cambridge, Mass.: The Belknap Press of Harvard University Press, Copyright © 1971, 1979, 1983, 1994, 2003, 2011 by the President and Fellows of Harvard College, as detailed on pages 533–535.

Frontispiece: Brook Farm, 1844, by Josiah Wolcott (ca. 1815–1885). Founded by the former Unitarian minister George Ripley in West Roxbury, Massachusetts, in 1841, Brook Farm was a utopian experiment in communal living. Emerson declined to join.

*Library of Congress Cataloging-in-Publication Data*

Emerson, Ralph Waldo, 1803–1882.
  [Selections. 2012]
  The annotated Emerson / edited by David Mikics; with a foreward by Phillip Lopate.
    p.   cm.
  Includes bibliographical references and index.
  ISBN 978-0-674-04923-9 (alk. paper)
  1. Emerson, Ralph Waldo, 1803–1882—Criticism and interpretation.    I. Mikics, David, 1961–   II. Title.
  PS1603.M55   2011
  814'.3—dc23        2011032632

We must learn to reawaken and keep ourselves awake, not by mechanical aids, but by an infinite expectation of the dawn, which does not forsake us in our soundest sleep.

—HENRY DAVID THOREAU
"Where I Lived, and What I Lived For," *Walden*

Not less because in purple I descended
The western day through what you called
The loneliest air, not less was I myself.

—WALLACE STEVENS
"Tea at the Palaz of Hoon"

# CONTENTS

**PHILLIP LOPATE**

Ralph Waldo Emerson is a giant of American literature: perhaps our greatest essayist, certainly one of our finest nonfiction prose writers. Yet his writings are so various and vast that we can hardly take him in at one glance, and so there is a strong impulse on the part of our culture simply to evade him. H. L. Mencken, who, along with his idol Nietzsche, had a healthy respect for Emerson, wrote an essay called "An Unheeded Law-Giver" in which he tried to get at this problem: "Despite the vast mass of writing about him, he remains to be worked out critically; practically all the existing criticism about him is marked by his own mellifluous obscurity. Perhaps a good deal of this obscurity is due to contradictions inherent in the man's character. He was dualism ambulant." Mencken concluded regretfully that Emerson's influence was less than it deserved: "There is, in the true sense, no Emersonian school of American writers." This fact probably would have delighted Emerson, who wrote: "This is my boast that I have no school & no follower. I should account it a measure of the impurity of insight, if it did not create independence."

It would be foolhardy for me to pretend that Emerson has been neglected. He has long been championed by some of our leading critics, such as Richard Poirier, Harold Bloom, and Stanley Cavell; there is also a robust tradition of Emerson scholarship, culminating in Robert D. Richardson's indispensable biography, *Emerson: The Mind of Fire*, and his engaging sequel,

*First We Read, Then We Write.* Still, I sense a resistance to Emerson on the part of the young, a falling out of fashion. One reason, perhaps, is that he was primarily an essayist (though he did write a dozen first-rate poems), and nonfiction has never enjoyed the same cachet as novels and poetry. Another reason Emerson has become almost an afterthought in the American literary canon is that he lacks that outsider romance of our other mid-nineteenth-century giants. We tend to value law-breaking renegades like Thoreau, doomed alcoholics like Poe, recluses like Dickinson, misunderstood visionaries like Melville, expansive gay bards like Whitman.

Ex-schoolmaster, preacher, and family man Emerson was quite aware of his problematic normalcy: "I hate scenes," he confided in his journal. "I think I have not the common degree of sympathy with dark, turbid, mournful, passionate natures. . . . In my strait & decorous way of living, native to my family & to my country, & more strictly proper to me, is nothing extravagant or flowing. I content myself with moderate languid actions, & never transgress the staidness of village manners. Herein I consult the poorness of my powers." Though phrased as inadequacy, it is really stubbornness: he refused to go to extremes. What needs to be understood is that, for Emerson, moderation was a tense, heroic agon. "Very hard it is to keep the middle point. It is a very narrow line," he wrote. And "Between narrow walls we walk—insanity on one side, and fat dullness on the other."

In his journals we see how gradually, hesitantly, incrementally his belief system accrued over decades, how much he took from other writers (he was a synthesizer of Big Ideas, but a true original in his throwaway perceptions), how often he subjected his hunches to testing and self-questioning, and how much he was at the mercy of the intrusions and bonuses of daily life. To over-simplify, the journals show his vulnerable side.

Emerson's journals are one of the most singular and bountiful works of American literature, known mainly to scholars in the sixteen-volume Harvard complete edition, though largely unavailable to the general public because of their unwieldy size. I know of no other text that takes us closer into the mind and psyche of an American writer. Emerson began keeping notebooks as an eighteen-year-old college student, and over the next fifty-seven years filled more than 182 individual volumes. The journals allow us to follow Emerson's progression from a dreamy Harvard student who wanted to write poetry to a penurious schoolteacher and minister; from his marriage to the lovely Ellen Tucker, who died a year later at age nineteen of tuberculosis, his grief-inspired decision to travel in Europe, where he met Carlyle (who became a close friend), Wordsworth, Landor, Mill, and Coleridge; his decision to leave the ministry and dedicate himself solely to writing; his second marriage, to the sturdier Lidian Jackson, which would endure and result in numerous children and grandchildren; his finding kindred spirits nearby who would form the Transcendental circle and the Utopian community of Brook Farm (which Emerson never joined); his career as a roving lecturer and essayist; his eventual celebrity as America's foremost public intellectual, down to his forgetful, twilit old age.

Emerson never published the journals in his lifetime, but he consulted them extensively for his essays, lectures, and poems. He took months at a time to catalog their contents, partly to make self-pillaging easier. Indeed, the notebooks have often been viewed as merely a quarry for his finished work, but they deserve to be considered a fascinating, intentional work in their own right, which Emerson scholar Lawrence Rosenwald has called "his most successful experiment in creating a literary form." I don't know about "creating" the writer's journal as a literary form, but he certainly practiced it with rare devotion and took it to new heights.

At the core of Emerson's journal-keeping was the belief that it was important to record one's fugitive ideas—to note what he called "the meteorology of thought." Not that such note-taking was always comforting: "There is something fearful in coming up against the walls of a mind on every side & learning to describe their invisible circumference." Still: "I notice that I value nothing so much as the threads that spin from a thought to a fact . . . & weaving together into rich webs all solitary observations." Emerson's journals were this web. Underneath his note-taking lay the philosophical, almost mystical conviction that a correspondence existed between nature's patterns and the mind's. As he put it: "Correspondence of the mind to the world . . . the ebb & flow, the pendulum, the alternation, the fits of easy transmission & reception, the pulsation, the undulation which seems to be a fundamental secret of nature, exists in intellect."

Self-study became a goal ("The purpose of life seems to be to acquaint a man with himself") and writing, the technique to achieve that goal ("A poem, a sentence causes us to see ourselves"). This Know Thyself ideal derived partly, of course, from Plato, who was never far from Emerson's thoughts, but also from Montaigne, the essayists' patron saint. In these journals, Emerson cites Montaigne regularly: "In Roxbury, in 1825, I read Cotton's translation of Montaigne. It seemed to me as if I had written the book myself in some former life, so sincerely it spoke to my thought & experience. No book before or since was ever so much to me as that." The young Emerson, spurring himself on, demands: "When will you mend Montaigne? Where are your Essays?" He kept going back to Montaigne, whom he found "full of fun, poetry, business, divinity, philosophy, anecdote, smut . . . of bone & marrow, of cornbarn & flour barrel, of wife, & friend . . ." There is precious little smut in Emerson, but he did take from the French writer permission to reach beyond the staid Unitarianism of his upbringing for an earthier, more inclusive worldliness.

It is useful, up to a point, to think of Emerson as the American Montaigne. Both put enormous faith in tracking their random thoughts and were, in effect, pioneering experimental scientists of consciousness; both believed that everything was flux, transition, uncertainty, undulation; both openly borrowed from older writers yet insisted on being idiosyncratically, freshly honest; both championed tolerance and balance. Their differences were more temperamental than methodological: Montaigne seemed to have arrived at an amused equanimity about his contradictions, while Emerson, descended from puritanical stock, worried his flaws and limitations more. Also, Emerson continued to hunger for a larger philosophical truth (his Transcendentalist notion of the Over-Soul) beneath the concrete material experiences that seemed sufficient for Montaigne. Stylistically, Montaigne's essays meandered, whereas Emerson's were chiseled, hammered out. It was in his journals, more than his essays, that Emerson replicated Montaigne's organic, impromptu approach.

Emerson's essays are dense with thought, requiring one's full attention every second; like a stiff cliff-face, they make purchase difficult. The journals are more conversationally relaxed; there is less strain in them to make every word count. In general, Emerson's literary aesthetic was drawn to the poetically condensed utterance. He advised his wordy friend Bronson Alcott: "He should write that which cannot be omitted, every sentence a cube, standing on its bottom like a die, essential & immortal." Emerson's basic unit of composition *was* the sentence, and he committed one amazing sentence after another. The result was an aphoristic compression in the essays that gives some readers the impression of entering a fog and not remembering after what exactly was said. I doubt that anyone who takes the trouble to go through the journals can continue to dismiss Emerson as "foggy" or "mellifluously obscure." He is too clear there, too candid, as when he says: "I found when I had finished my new lecture that it was a very good house, only the architect had unfortunately omitted the stairs."

No one was more aware of his limitations than Emerson: his modesty, given his achievements, is perhaps the most surprising revelation to me. He criticized himself often for lacking "animal spirits." Though fascinated with genius, he never claimed to possess it. His journals frequently express admiration and envy for others, particularly workmen, who could *do* things, or southern Europeans, who could tell stories in an animated manner: "My only secret was that all men were my masters. I never saw one who was not my superior, & I would so gladly have been his apprentice if his craft had been communicable." For a long while Emerson longed for a spiritual guide: "I carry ever the keys of my castle in my hand ready to throw them at the feet of my lord whenever & in whatever disguise in this great carnival, I may encounter him . . ." But all the candidates who presented themselves proved false, and he concluded that one must seek the god or the truth within.

Emerson's doctrine of self-reliance, arrived at painstakingly, asserted that Americans should stop taking all their cultural cues from Europe, and that those seeking spiritual truth should free themselves from "a historical Christianity. The Belief in Christianity that now prevails is the Unbelief of men. They will have Christ for a lord & not for a brother. Christ preaches the greatness of Man but we hear only the greatness of Christ." After he gave up preaching, he was asked whether he believed in Jesus and the prophets: "[I]t seemed to me an impiety to be listening to one & another, when the pure Heaven was pouring itself into each of us, on the simple condition of obedience. . . . Jesus was Jesus because he refused to listen to another, & listened at home."

He was convinced that every person contained within a vision of the Perfect, and an enormous, if unfulfilled, potential: "he exists as a flint, —he that should be a sun." And: "We are all of us very near to sublimity. . . . Whilst we are waiting we beguile the time, one with jokes, one with sleep, one with eating, one with crimes." Just as we ignore our inner potential, so the outer world brings us a daily abundance that we seemed ill-equipped to harvest. In an especially beautiful sentence he wrote: "The days come & go like muffled & veiled figures sent from a distant friendly party, but they say nothing, & if we do not use the gifts they bring, they carry them as silently away." He expressed dissatisfaction with life like one of Chekhov's characters: "I find no good lives. I would live well. I seem to be free to do so, yet I think with very little respect of my way of living; it is weak, partial, not full & not progressive. But I do not see any other that suits me better." He put it even more succinctly: "We are all dying of miscellany."

One of the main ways Emerson tried to better himself was by reading. In his day he was one of the most widely read men in America. Having devoured the English classics, he taught himself German, French, and Italian, translated Dante's *La Vita Nuova*, and immersed himself in the Bhagavad Gita, the Koran, the Persian poets. Granted, there was an Orientalist vogue among the American educated class at the time that did not go very deep, but Emerson's efforts to embrace those traditions sound sincere: "I set great value in Culture on foreign literature—the farther off the better—much on French, on Italian, on German or Welsh,—more on Persian or Hindu, because if one read & write only English, he soon slides into narrow conventions, & believes there is no other way to write poetry than as Pope or as Milton. But a quite foreign mind born & grown in different latitude & longitude . . . astonishes us with a new nature, gives a fillip to our indolence & we promptly learn that we have faculties which we have never used."

He was curious about everything, and he wished his life were 3,000 years long so that he could dive into what he called the temptations of Egyptian history, Sanskrit literature, and the Chaldaic oracles, as well as astronomy, chemistry, geology, and botany. He admired his idol Goethe as much for the German polymath's study of optics and plants as for writing *Faust*. That nineteenth-century bug of believing one could synthesize all knowledge had bitten Emerson. In Eastern thought he found a model for that integration: "The East is grand,—& makes Europe appear the land of trifles. Identity, identity! friend & foe are of one stuff . . . & the soul is Vishnu; &

animals & stars are transient paintings; & light is whitewash; & durations are deceptive; and form is imprisonment and heaven itself a decoy . . . For Memory, imagination, Reason, sense, are only masks of one power. . . ." While he was ever eager to grasp at a larger pattern, his skepticism kept getting in the way (that walking dualism that Mencken mentioned).

Though his own self-prescription was invariably to work harder, he also believed that we are made for ecstasy, and he chastised himself for not feeling enough joy. Stoicism was his default mode, a trait of all good survivalists. Among his most attractive qualities was that he never exaggerated his sentiments. He took careful note of when indifference or coolness had entered his soul, and as a result his expressions of sympathy were genuinely trustworthy. The one thing he resisted was embracing suffering in order to feel deeper: "We court suffering in the hope that here at least we shall find reality, sharp angular peaks & edges of truth. But it is scene painting, a counterfeit a goblin." His shameful secret, or boast, was to have achieved a gyroscopic equilibrium through all of life's troubles. He confessed: "I told J. V. [the poet Jones Very] that I had never suffered, & that I could scarce bring myself to feel a concern for the safety & life of my nearest friends that would satisfy them: that I saw clearly that if my wife, my child, my mother, should be taken from me, I should still remain whole with the same capacity of cheap enjoyment from all things." This honest, if disturbing, statement seems an admission of shallowness on his part, or at least of the lack of a tragic consciousness.

But he spoke too soon; he would shortly come to know suffering. If it had eluded him after the death of his first wife, whom he incorporated into an angelic myth (his second wife even collaborated in this somewhat maudlin altar worship by suggesting they name their daughter "Ellen"), he had no such protection when he lost his first-born, Waldo. Emerson had delighted in recording the sayings and deeds of this charming son, and when the boy died of a sudden illness at the age of five, it brought only devastation: "the wonderful Boy is gone. What a looking for miracles have I! . . . he most beautiful of the children of men is not here. I comprehend nothing of this fact but its bitterness." In a sense Emerson never fully recovered his optimism or faith after Waldo's death. Decades later, he would recall Waldo at the circus watching the clown's antics and saying, "It makes me want to go home." Emerson added, "I am forced to quote my boy's speech often and often since. I can do so few things, I can see so few companies, that do not remind me of it!" Those who regard Emerson as too cheerful a thinker would do well to ponder his statement: "After thirty a man wakes up sad every morning."

Emerson plunged further into his inner life, recording his thoughts and dreams: "I dreamed that I floated at will in the great Ether, and I saw this world floating also not far off, but diminished to the size of an apple. Then an angel took it in his hand & brought it to me and said 'This must thou eat.' And I ate the world." No wonder he responded so positively to Whitman's omnivorous poems. He dreamt an American intellectual's nightmare, a "city of beheaded men, where the decapitated trunks continued to walk about." There are even dreams of erotic flirtation: "One of the ladies was beautiful, and I, it seemed, had already seen her & was her lover. She looked up from her painting, & saw, but did not recognize me;—which I thought wrong,—unpardonable. Later, I reflected that it was not so criminal in her, since I had not *proposed*." How typical of Emerson: to rationalize a humiliating slight with guilty self-reproach, for not having committed himself enough in advance to the woman!

Emerson was often uneasy about demands of intimacy made on him, worried he might not be able to meet them, either because he was protecting his inner life and writing space, or because he feared he lacked the warmth. Invariably courteous to neighbors and importuning strangers—"Politeness was invented by wise men to keep fools at a distance," he aphorized—it pained him when he cared about someone, a family member or close friend, and still felt his constitutional New England reserve keeping him from honoring these requests. One such crisis occurred when Margaret Fuller, the charismatic feminist and Transcendentalist, taxed him "with inhospitality of soul. She & C. [Caroline Sturgis, another woman friend] would gladly be my friends, yet our intercourse is not friendship, but literary gossip. I count & weigh but do not love. They make no progress with me, but however often we have met, we still meet as strangers. They feel wronged in such relation, & do not wish to be catechized & criticised. I thought of my experience with several persons which resembled this: and confessed that I would not converse with the divinest person more than one week." How refreshingly honest is that! In a later entry, he puzzled over "these strange, cold-warm, attractive-repelling conversations with Margaret, whom I always admire, most revere when I nearest see, and sometimes love, yet whom I freeze, & who freezes me to silence, when we seem to promise to come nearest."

Readers today may wonder whether Fuller had sexual designs on the married Emerson, though that was probably not the case. Rather, when the brilliant members of the Transcendental circle, each of whom had grown up isolated freaks in mercantile, materialistic America, found one another living in the same Boston-Concord area, it must have awakened such hunger for soul-communion as could never be fully slaked.

Part of the problem was that everyone around Emerson sought his approval. He had become a benign father-figure from his late thirties on, like it or not. Compounding the problem was that Emerson felt acutely everyone's essential loneliness and paradoxical need for solitude. Only in solitude could one attempt to free oneself from received opinions or peer pressures, and know one's own mind: "Alone is wisdom. Alone is happiness. Society nowadays makes us lowspirited, hopeless. Alone is heaven." At the same time he was continually made aware of the lack of true communication between people: "Man is insular, and cannot be touched. Every man is an infinitely repellent orb . . ." This melancholy conviction of universal solipsism was the reverse side of Emerson proposing self-reliance and individualism: "Very painful is the discovery we are always making that we can only give to each other a rare & partial sympathy: for, as much time as we have spent in looking over into our neighbor's field & chatting with him is lost to our own, & must be made up by haste & renewed solitude."

In the end Emerson and Fuller did work out a satisfying way to sustain their friendship; and when she drowned, in a ghastly shipwreck off Fire Island on returning from Europe, he wrote a substantial memoir of her and edited a book, *Margaret and Her Friends* (though he was too honest to change his opinion that her genius resided in conversation and not in writing).

The loneliness of the literary endeavor and the brittleness of literary comradeship come through clearly in his journal entry marking Hawthorne's death. "We buried Hawthorne," he writes, remarking on "the painful solitude of the man, which, I suppose, could no longer be endured, & he died of it." Regretting that they never became friends, he says: "It would have been a happiness, doubtless to both of us, to have come into habits of unreserved intercourse. It was easy to talk with him,—there were no barriers,—only, he said so little, that I talked too much. . . . Now it appears that I waited too long."

Talking too little was not Henry David Thoreau's problem. He and Emerson sustained a remarkably close friendship for decades. This in spite of the fact that Thoreau was, according to his friend, almost incessantly combative and self-absorbed: "It is curious that Thoreau goes to a house to say with little preface what he has just read or observed, delivers it in lump, is quite inattentive to any comment or thought which any of the company offer on the matter, nay, is merely interrupted by it, &, when he has finished his report, departs with precipitation." Emerson oscillated between being enchanted and being annoyed by his friend's eccentricities. He admired Thoreau's naturalist ability to wait out each frog and bird, and of course his friend's writing: it was he who urged Thoreau to keep a journal, and he copied pages of Thoreau's journal entries into his own notebook, paying him the compliment that Thoreau went "a step beyond" anything he was capable of doing. Thoreau was the quintessential bachelor, living in the woods ascetically; Emerson was a householder and family man who took Thoreau into his home when the woodsman got tired of camping outdoors. Though they did quarrel for a time, they reconciled with a conversation about "the Eternal loneliness" of everyone they knew, including themselves.

What is perhaps most impressive about Emerson is that, knowing his human limitations, he still tried to stretch himself to accommodate others and become larger-souled. He put up with the quirks of friends like the mad poet Very, he invited Thoreau and Fuller to live with his family in his house for a time, and he even forced himself to abandon his cherished privacy and to engage in political public speaking.

The transition to political activist took a while. At first he was highly suspicious of reformers and their self-righteous, scolding, one-note style. He also felt his task in life was to write, not agitate: "my way to help the government is to write sonnets." He sent an open letter to President Martin Van

Buren deploring the government's ill-treatment of the Cherokees, but he hated writing it. Privately he recorded in journals his liberal views on every issue of the day: he was for abolition of slavery, women's suffrage, and property rights, against the removal of the American Indians from their land, for the new immigrants, unequivocally against U.S. imperialism. Stating that "[n]ationality is babyishness for the most part," he opposed the Mexican War, Texas's annexation, and the expropriation of Hawaii: "Let us wait a thousand years for the Sandwich Islands before we seize them by violence." He thought that capitalism was a form of cannibalism, and that the wealthy always voted for the "worst and meanest things": for tyranny, for slavery, against the ballot, "against schools, colleges, or any high direction of public money." But still, he insisted on clinging to "inaction, this wise passiveness, until my hour comes when I can see how to act with truth. . . ."

His hour finally arrived around 1851, when he became outraged at the Fugitive Slave Act, which stated that runaway slaves must be returned to their owners in the South. He was particularly upset that Daniel Webster, the Massachusetts senator who had been a hero to Emerson, had treacherously compromised with the South by voting for the legislation. He filled dozens of pages with fulmination, horrified that Northerners would no longer defend "a human being who has taken the risks of being shot or burned alive, or cast into the sea, or starved to death or suffocated in a wooden box,—taken all this risk to get away from his driver & recover the rights of man. And this man the Statute says, you men of Massachusetts shall kidnap & send back again a thousand miles across the sea to the dog-hutch he fled from. And this filthy enactment was made in the 19th Century, by people who could read & write. I will not obey it, by God."

Emerson now began speaking widely for abolition of slavery in the United States at public meetings, even getting booed on occasion. He was a born democrat, and his lack of defensiveness, his willingness to learn from personalities very different from his own, made him sought-after. "Better be a nettle in the side of your companion than be his echo," he wrote, and some of his friends were indeed nettles. Trying to balance all the social demands on him, he threatened to close up shop at a certain point: "A man of 45 does not want to open new accounts of friendship. He has said Kitty kitty long enough." Nevertheless, he remained receptive to new acquaintance, helping many younger people get started. The episode with Walt Whitman is legendary. Emerson wrote Whitman not only his famous endorsement but also several letters of recommendation to secure a post in Washington. They met a number of times. Whitman recalled years later: "I think everybody was fascinated by his personality . . . But his usual manner carried with it something penetrating and sweet beyond mere description. There is in some men an indefinable something which flows out and over you like a flood of light —as if they possessed it illimitably—their whole being suffused with it. Being—in fact that is precisely the word. Emerson's whole attitude shed forth such an impression. . . . Never a face more gifted with power to express, fascinate, maintain."

We can stare at his photographs and guess at the power that "the gentle Emerson," as Whitman called him, had for his contemporaries. Or we can turn to the essays, poems, and journals, where his wholeness of being is made manifest. In his latter years he was lionized, awarded, introduced to President Lincoln. Self-mockingly he recorded: "Dull cheerless business this of playing lion & talking down to people. Rather let me be scourged and humiliated." He also said that if the people who were honoring his intellect had read the same books he had, they wouldn't think he was so smart.

When facing the indignities of aging, he saw both sides of the question. On the plus side, he no longer felt the need to prove himself: "It is long already fixed what I can & what I cannot do." On the minus side, he said humorously, "'Tis strange, that it is not in vogue to commit hari-kari as the Japanese do at 60. Nature is *so* insulting in her hints & notices, does not pull you out by the sleeve, but pulls out your teeth, tears off your hair in patches, steals your eyesight, twists your face into an ugly mask, in short, puts all contumelies upon you, without in the least abating your zeal to make a good appearance, and all this at the same time that she is moulding the new figures around you into wonderful beauty which, of course, is only making your plight worse."

I'm sure we could make the case for Emerson's relevance today by molding him into a proto-postmodernist, a covert wild-man with dark imagination, or a progressive fighter for multicultural diversity. My own fondness for him rests on his intelligence and his truthfulness, his questing, nondogmatic sanity. He wrote some of the best reflective prose we have; he was a hero of intellectual labor, a loyal friend, and, taking into account all his flaws and prejudices, a good egg who always tried to do the right thing. True, he was middle-class and wrote increasingly in the wisdom style of middle age. Can we forgive him? Yes; we can even revere him, as a model of how to overcome anxiety and despair, and eloquently wed uncertainty to equanimity.

1803
May 25          Ralph Waldo Emerson born in Boston

1821
August          graduates from Harvard College

1829
March           ordained at Second Church, Boston
September       marries Ellen Tucker

1831
February        death of Ellen Tucker Emerson

1832
December        resigns from Second Church

1832–1833
December–
October         first voyage to Europe

1834
October         brother Edward dies; Emerson moves to Concord

1835
September          marries Lydia Jackson (known as Lidian)

1836
May                brother Charles dies
September          *Nature* published
October            birth of first son, Waldo

1837
August             delivers "The American Scholar"

1838
July               delivers "The Divinity School Address"

1839
February           birth of daughter Ellen

1841
March              *Essays: First Series* published
November           birth of daughter Edith

1842
January            death of Waldo

1844
July               birth of son Edward
August             delivers speech on West Indian Emancipation
October            *Essays: Second Series* published

1847–1848
October–
July               second voyage to Europe

1850
January            *Representative Men* published
July               death of Margaret Fuller Ossoli

**1855**
July                writes to Whitman praising *Leaves of Grass*
September           speaks at Women's Rights Convention, Boston

**1856**
August              *English Traits* published

**1859**
November            speaks at Boston meeting for relief of
                    John Brown's family

**1860**
December            *The Conduct of Life* published

**1861**
April               Civil War begins

**1862**
February            meets Lincoln
May                 death of Thoreau

**1864**
May                 death of Hawthorne

**1865**
April               Confederate surrender; death of Lincoln
                    (Emerson speaks at funeral service in Concord)

**1867**
April               *May-Day and Other Pieces* published

**1872**
July                burning of house

**1882**
April 27            death in Concord

# ABBREVIATIONS

CEC    *The Correspondence of Emerson and Carlyle.* Ed. Joseph Slater. New York: Columbia University Press, 1964.

EL    *Early Lectures of Ralph Waldo Emerson.* Ed. Stephen E. Whicher, Robert E. Spiller, and Wallace E. Williams. 3 vols. Cambridge, MA: Harvard University Press, 1959–1972.

J    Emerson, Ralph Waldo. *Journals and Miscellaneous Notebooks.* Ed. William H. Gilman et al. 16 vols. Cambridge, MA: Harvard University Press, 1960–1982.

L    *Letters of Ralph Waldo Emerson.* Ed. Ralph L. Rusk and Eleanor M. Tilton. 10 vols. New York: Columbia University Press, 1939–1995.

LL    *Later Lectures of Ralph Waldo Emerson, 1843–1871.* Ed. Ronald A. Bosco and Joel Myerson. 2 vols. Athens, GA: University of Georgia Press, 2001.

S    *Complete Sermons of Ralph Waldo Emerson.* Ed. Albert von Frank et al. 4 vols. Columbia, MO: University of Missouri Press, 1989–1992.

THE ANNOTATED
EMERSON

Ralph Waldo Emerson, 1857.

DAVID MIKICS

Equal parts exaltation and grit, Emerson's way of speaking is familiar to all Americans, whether they have ever read him or not. To tell the rude truth, vigorous, in "the swift summary way of boys" (as Emerson says in "Self-Reliance"), and to be proud of it: this is the American manner. Emerson is our Shakespeare, his words woven through American speech, and his character is ours as well, in its changes: volatile, serene, ambitious, and in whatever mood, full of juice. He prizes above all the original and bold, and even contradiction proves healthy—for "a systemgrinder hates the truth."[1] He is a born rebel, itching to damn convention. But he insists, too, on the hard reality that rebels like to defy. The iron law of cause and effect, the work of tooth and claw, cannot be dodged. Emerson the bold warrior against conformity vies with Emerson the grim seer, the man who trusts in unbending facts, however unpalatable. It is just this strange two-sidedness that makes for Emerson's living power, his meaning for us today. Americans are wild idealists; Americans are also tough realists. Is this a mere contradiction, or something more interesting? Emerson asks, and answers, this key question about our nation, in a way no one else has.

America's orators, including its presidents, take after Emerson. After the 2008 presidential election, a new volume, prominently displayed, appeared in bookstores. It bore on its cover the picture of the president elect, Barack Obama. The book itself joined Obama's victory speech with Emerson's "Self-Reliance," and with Lincoln's first and second inaugural addresses and his Gettysburg Address. Hubristic, yes, but the combination has some force behind it. Our politicians and our great reformers like to echo Emerson. When Martin Luther King, Jr., said that "the arc of the moral universe is long, but it bends toward justice," he was remembering Emerson's essays "Compensation" and "Spiritual Laws."

Emerson is the American intellectual founder, a rival to its political founders. James Russell Lowell commented, "We were still socially and intellectually moored to English thought, till Emerson cut the cable and gave us a chance at the dangers and the glories of blue water"; and Oliver Wendell Holmes called "the American Scholar" "our Intellectual Declaration of Independence."[2] Emerson's advice to "read a little proudly" makes the first step toward such independence.[3]

Emerson was far from an unthinking booster of his country. On the one hand he claimed that "America is the idea of emancipation,"[4] the world's courageous, long-needed salvation. On the other hand he spoke freely and earnestly of what he called "my own quarrel with America":

> that the geography is sublime, but the men are not; that the inventions are excellent, but the inventors, one is ashamed of; that the means by which events so grand as the opening of California, Texas, oregon, & the junction of the two Oceans, are effected, are paltry, the filthiest selfishness, fraud, & conspiracy.[5]

For Emerson, in this downcast prophetic mood, "there is nothing of the true democratic element in what is called Democracy; it must fall, being wholly commercial."[6] Emerson was no patriotic cheerleader. "Pray don't read American," he pleaded, for "thought is of no country."[7] Whoever and wherever we are, we all inherit the spark, the genius that wants to show itself in action.

America, Emerson chanted, stands in urgent need of remaking. He refused the standard homages to the founding fathers, whose grand achievements were just a few decades away when Emerson began writing in the 1830s. "What business have Washington or Jefferson in this age?" he groused in his Journal.

You must be a very dull or a very false man if you have not a better
& more advanced policy to offer than they had. They lived in the
greenness & timidity of the political experiment. The kitten's eyes
were not yet opened. They shocked their contemporaries with
their daring wisdom: have you not something which would have
shocked *them?* If not, be silent, for others have.[8]

Emerson appreciated conservatives for the hard-headedness of their
gospel, but he was the very reverse of a conservative. He wanted transformation. He was a romantic visionary who saw a sluggish world about him and
felt compelled to urge it into life. Emerson wrote in a letter:

The first impulse of the newly stricken mind, stricken by light
from heaven is to lament the death with which it is surrounded, as
far as the horizon it can scarcely see anything else than tombs &
ghosts and a sort of Dead-alive population War, war without end
seems then to be its lot . . .[9]

This may sound like Gnostic melodrama, but for Emerson it is no more nor
less than necessary. What we need to become seems unapproachable, hard
to define; but it confronts us, a task to be seen and answered. As we take up
the task, Emerson's words still have the power, more than any others, to spur
us on.

Ralph Waldo Emerson was born on Election Day, May 25, 1803. His
mother was Ruth Haskins, from an old New England family; his father William Emerson, the pastor of Boston's First Church, a grand Unitarian bas-
tion. After William Emerson's death in 1811, the Emerson family fell on
hard times. They took in boarders, and most of the Emerson sons, including
Ralph Waldo Emerson, taught school to finance their own educations.
Emerson went to Boston Latin School and then Harvard College, which
he graduated in 1821. At Harvard, Emerson decided that he wanted to
be called by his middle name, Waldo (an old family name, derived from
Peter Waldo, twelfth-century founder of a heroic proto-Protestant sect, the
Waldensians).

Emerson's aunt, Mary Moody, was his first serious intellectual influence. She was a walking paradox, a strict Calvinist as well as a fervent disciple of the Romantics, especially Byron. In her letters to her nephew, "M. M. E." comes across as a fanatical reader and inventive scholar, a vibrant homemade thinker. Her flights of imagination clearly swayed the young Emerson (and in later years he carefully copied her letters into his notebooks). But Emerson found her barbed critiques and her insistent asceticism less than congenial. "Destitution is the Muse of her genius,—Destitution and Death," he wrote of Aunt Mary.[10] "My aunt had an eye that went through & through you like a needle," Emerson remembered. "'She was endowed,' she said, 'with the *fatal* gift of penetration.' She disgusted every body because she knew them too well." Emerson wrote in his Journal, "If M. M. E. finds out anything is dear & sacred to you, she instantly flings broken crockery at that."[11] Mary Moody Emerson stringently disapproved of her nephew's notably non-Calvinistic essays and was not afraid to tell him so. Her caustic spirit was a stern warning to Emerson as he made his cautious way among illusions and ideals. He recognized his aunt's drive toward dark, skeptical analysis; but he found himself stirred by a stronger sympathy for wish, hope, and dream, even during the hardest times, times of war and oppression.

The family assumed that Emerson would be a preacher like his father. He did become a minister, in Boston's Second Church (Unitarian). But Emerson's relationship to religion was too original, too alive, to be contained within the pastoral vocation. "The profession is antiquated," he confided to his Journal in the summer of 1832. "In an altered age, we worship in the dead forms of our forefathers. Were not a Socratic paganism better than an effete superannuated Christianity?"[12] In 1832 Emerson asked his congregation that he be allowed to celebrate the Lord's Supper without bread and wine. The request was refused, and Emerson left his ministry (though he continued to preach, freelance, for another six years).

The 1830s were, in many ways, a catastrophic decade for Emerson. His adored wife, Ellen Tucker, died of tuberculosis in 1831, after a mere eighteen months of marriage; and he lost two of his brothers to the disease as well, Edward in 1834 and Charles in 1836. (Emerson's biographer Robert Richardson estimates that a third of the population of Boston in these years suffered from tuberculosis.) But he also took a ten-month trip to Europe, just after leaving Second Church; there he met the English Romantic writers he admired, Wordsworth, Coleridge, and Walter Savage Landor, along with a new friend and influence, the Scottish author Thomas Carlyle. Characteristically, he found the limitations of all four, writing, "They would be remembered as sensible well read earnest men—not more."[13] He remarried, to Lydia Jackson (known as Lidian), who seems to have been a perfect companion to him. And he started his career on the public-speaking circuit, developing lectures on topics ranging from natural history, to the biographies of great men, to art and culture. The craze for public lectures had come to America, and Emerson was able to make a good living from it. Since the late 1820s, instructive, entertaining lectures had become wildly popular in America; lecturing halls called Lyceums dotted the landscape, as far west as Oregon. Emerson was probably the most successive Lyceum speaker of his day, followed by the ex-slave and abolitionist Frederick Douglass.

When he married Lidian, Emerson moved from Boston to Concord, a village of two thousand people forty miles away (Boston's population in the 1830s was a little over sixty thousand). Concord had been founded by an Emerson ancestor, Peter Bulkeley (1583–1659), and Emerson's grandfather William had looked on as the minutemen exchanged fire with British soldiers in 1775—the "shot heard round the world," as Emerson unforgettably christened it. The town stood at the center of New England's revolutionary past, and soldiers of the revolution were still alive when Emerson gave Concord's bicentennial address in 1835. Most residents of Concord were farmers, but the town also had sawmills and gristmills, and three busy taverns. The spacious Emerson house, with a white picket fence and a barn (where Henry David Thoreau lodged for months), was on the stage-road to Boston, but only a few fields away from pine woods.

Humble Concord became, rather unexpectedly, a hotbed of intellectual life in the 1840s. Emerson and Thoreau guided each other toward their distinct destinies. With his friend and intellectual comrade, the scintillating Margaret Fuller, who had stayed with the Emersons for a month in 1842, Emerson edited the *Dial*, a magazine of new ideas with a tiny circulation and a large impact. Horace Greeley, the preeminent newspaper editor of the age, said the *Dial* was "like manna in the wilderness."[14] In addition to Thoreau and Margaret Fuller, Sophia and Nathaniel Hawthorne settled in Concord in 1842 (in the Old Manse, the home of Emerson's step-grandfather Ezra Ripley, where Emerson had lived as a child). There was also Emerson's neighbor, the New England rhapsodist and reformer Amos Bronson Alcott (father of Louisa May), a brilliant talker and tedious writer. Alcott had stirred up scandal with his radical "School for Human Culture" in Boston, which featured frank Socratic discussions on topics like the virgin birth. Emerson was dazzled by Alcott's talk, but he noted in his Journal, "He never quotes; he never refers; his only illustration is his own biography."[15] Alcott came to represent for Emerson the looming specter of self-involvement, which had to be distinguished from self-reliance.

Hawthorne's gnarled and gothic universe was not congenial to Emerson, and Hawthorne seems to have been indifferent to the possibilities of Emersonian illumination—especially after their two-day walking trip to the town of Harvard in 1842, an excursion that left Hawthorne silent and miserable. Like Hawthorne, Melville, perhaps the most threatening and sublime of American writers, fought Emerson's influence. It was a fair fight, and still is. "Nay, I do not oscillate in Emerson's rainbow," Melville remarked in a strikingly ambivalent letter to his friend Duyckinck.[16] Melville struck through the masks; he faced the abyss, the nothing behind worldly appearances. Emerson turned such darkness to light, without denying the darkness.

Shortly after Emerson's move to Concord, a crucial event occurred: the first meeting, in 1836, of a group of ardent, innovative thinkers and writers who became known as the Transcendental Club. Emerson was a member, though he never identified himself as a Transcendentalist. George Ripley, one of the circle, said of the Transcendentalists, "Their leading idea is the supremacy of mind over matter. Hence they maintain that the truth of religion does not depend on tradition, or on historical facts, but has an unerring witness in the soul."[17] Controversies about the historical person of Jesus, the facts of his biography, his alleged miracles, swirled in the air of the 1830s. These hotly debated topics spurred the Transcendentalist wave; but the movement often looked beyond Christianity and focused instead on the spiritual truth that all religions point to: the fact that (as Emerson put it) we "want awakening."[18]

Transcendentalism was a great flowering of desire: a quest for meaning, the dimension lacking, the Transcendentalists felt, in both the materialist doctrines of John Locke (a powerful influence in Emerson's era) and the rather wan moral sentiments of Unitarianism at its most respectable. For Locke, the world was a series of sense impressions, and dully, reassuringly predictable; for the Unitarians, the New Testament was a historical record, designed to inspire wholesome moral feeling.[19] To Emerson and his companions in intellectual quest, there was something unreal, even second-hand, about these beliefs. Emerson was looking for reality. He needed to fire back at the useless conformity of his age, to shake people into attention. In an early Journal entry (July 9, 1833), Emerson exclaimed, "How does everybody live on the outside of the world! All young persons thirst for a *real* existence for an object,—for something great & good which they shall do with all their heart."[20] (By the age of thirty, Emerson was writing plentifully in that wonder book, his Journal, the place where he quarried his lectures and essays.)

Emerson and his contemporaries saw that experience was richer, more original and vital, than anything they could find in Unitarian homilies or Lockean empiricism. Emerson turned first to Goethe, in whose writings he exulted; and like Goethe he resolved to become a naturalist, to find pulsating meaning in the web of animal and plant life. On his first trip to Europe in 1833, on a boat between Malta and Sicily, he wrote that "the strong-winged sea gull & striped sheer-water" are better works of art than any made by human hands.[21] He wanted, he said, to throw himself into what he saw in nature, to understand it from the inside.[22] Observing nature, one reads oneself as well: a key insight of Emerson's first book, the extended essay *Nature* (1836). Looking at facts as symbols (as he put it in his essay "History"): this was the overriding necessity. Whether the facts appeared in the natural world, in great historical events, or in private life, was all one. The stunning revelation was that only one's own experience could provide a means—and a reason—for knowing anything at all about the past. First marvel at who and where you are, and then the history of the world will take on meaning: history's true and only significance appears in the manifold illustrations of your life scattered since time began. This is still a shocking thought, and Emerson is its pioneer.

Emerson had been struck by the need for an organic and passionate mode of thinking, an antidote to Locke's mechanistic view. In part, he found what he needed in the enthusiastic and adept summary of German Romantic philosophy offered by Madame Germaine de Staël, one of Emerson's strongest influences. Coleridge, too, was soaked in German thought. He and the American writer Sampson Reed both insisted on a coincidence between mind and nature (though neither considered nature with the eye of the scientist, as Emerson was determined to do in *Nature*); and Coleridge supplied Emerson, along with the rest of the Transcendental Club, with a vocabulary to match their taste for the visionary. Coleridge (along with his American advocate, James Marsh) argued for a distinction between the Understanding, a poor measuring power that judges facts of time and space, cause and effect, and the Reason, which synthesizes, orchestrates, and receives profound insight. Locke's empiricism stayed on the level of Understanding, the mere facts of the world. Reason saw deeper, into the truth of things.

Emerson's next milestone changed everything for him. Invited to give the 1838 address to the graduating class of Harvard Divinity School, Emerson spoke words so upsetting to ordinary Unitarians that he became known as a rebellious firebrand, perhaps an infidel. He lamented the fact that "the divine nature is attributed to one or two persons, and denied to all the rest"; angrily, he charged that Christianity "dwells, with noxious exaggeration about the *person* of Jesus." Emerson was not invited back to Harvard for twenty-nine years. By that time he had become recognized as his country's greatest speaker and man of letters, but he remained, first and last, an iconoclast.

Oliver Wendell Holmes said that Emerson on the lecture podium resembled "a cat picking her footsteps in wet weather." He was judicious in his speech, experimental. With each new sentence, he tested his weight, seeing how much the statement would bear (as Richard Poirier, one of Emerson's best readers, puts it).[23] This delicate effect can be seen in Emerson's essays as well, in which so much depends on the transit from one sentiment to the next. The essays have a logic of their own, one substantially new to prose style, though Emerson's forebear Montaigne anticipated some of it. Emerson's detractors have often seen his style as an airy effusion; but it is hard and precise.

His lecturing career gave Emerson the freedom he needed, though it also meant many long nights in stagecoaches and shabby hotels. To his wife

Lidian he wrote, "A cold raw country this, & plenty of night travelling and arriving at 4 in the morning, to take the last & worst bed in the tavern."[24] But when he was in Concord, he had a dependable repose. He sat at his desk and added to the rich layers of Journal entries that he later culled for his lectures. He wrote to Margaret Fuller (June 7, 1839), "My own habits are much mended this summer. I rise at 6 o'clock, find my coffee in my study, & do not see the family until 12 or 1 o'clock."[25] ("'In the morning,—solitude;' said Pythagoras," Emerson noted with approval.[26])

Early on, Emerson was accused of being an intellectual floater, untethered to the facts: a Luftmensch, like his friends the Transcendentalists, with their calm belief in mind over matter; or like the Swedish prophet Emanuel Swedenborg, whom Emerson read avidly, but with deeply mixed feelings. But was Emerson a Transcendentalist at all? In an 1842 lecture he called Transcendentalism "the Saturnalia or excess of faith";[27] in his Journal, it seemed to him "faith run mad."[28] Transcendentalism was pure speculation: a kind of thinking that dreamed a world without troubling about the limits of practical reality. Emerson by contrast was a man of the real. Yet he faulted the European man of letters he most admired, Goethe, for overpracticality. In September 1836 Emerson called Goethe "the high priest of the age" and "the truest of all writers."[29] A few years later, he lamented that "Goethe must be set down as the poet of the Actual not of the Ideal; the poet of limitation & not of possibility."[30]

Unlike Goethe, Emerson dramatized possibility, the sinews of hope. This was a drama, one with real actors: Emerson shied away from the merely ideal, visions that departed from actual life. He criticized the wild ether of the mystic Swedenborg, and the cadenzas of his friend Alcott (whose mammoth book *Psyche* seemed to Emerson a shimmering and verbose cloud rather than what he wanted, a substantial pillar). Emerson wrote about Goethe and Swedenborg in *Representative Men* (1850), but he also included Napoleon, whom Emerson approached with spectacular ambivalence. Napoleon was a beast, a destroyer; yet his work seemed the work of Fate, awful and admirable at once. But by the end of Emerson's essay on Napoleon, the French emperor looks petty and vindictive rather than sublime: he even cheated at cards. The high turns low, the godlike monarch, base. We must beware of adoring titanic ambition like Napoleon's.

The reality of Napoleon's tyrannic power, and of the crude, arrogant middle-class ambition that Emerson identified with this power (in America as in Europe), spoke against the dreams of reform embodied in utopian communities like George Ripley's Brook Farm or Alcott's Fruitlands. Alcott rejected selling farm products for profit and espoused a strict, eccentric vegetarianism, renouncing even "unaspiring" plants like carrots that grew downward rather than upward. Brook Farm, a joint-stock company based on free choice of labor and cultivation of "spiritual health," was larger, less radical, and attracted mobs of curious visitors. Emerson was invited to join Brook Farm in 1840, an offer he declined. Unlike Hawthorne, he would not pitch hay with his fellow intellectuals. Though Emerson liked the idea of such noble schemes, he knew their prospects were dim, for they shut out too much of human nature. Both Brook Farm and Fruitlands, beset by financial trouble and personal battles, dissolved by the mid-1840s. Our fierce disruptive yearnings could not be tamed by plowing, milking, and dishwashing, however egalitarian. Then again, Emerson knew something else that spoke against utopian idealism: the fact that his own work had to be done alone (like all true work, he was tempted to add).

Emerson had just as much trouble with the other side of the coin, the practicality that faces off against idealism. He saw hard-headed moneymaking incarnated in contemporary England, more than anywhere else. In his book *English Traits* (1856), the result of his second trip to England in 1848, Emerson finds much that is admirable in the English inclination toward trade and profit. But he turns away in disgust from the self-satisfaction that (he says) Englishmen prize. Emerson admired the English tenacity and gusto, but these bluff capabilities seemed wedded to something more troubling. The English idolized staunch, even brute, power; they were aggressive and insular. England knew itself too well; it was not a nation still in the making, like America, but an old, assured one. At its worst, Emerson thought, England dismissed the rest of the world, and the unknown future too, as mere distractions from wealth and home.

Something of the English taste for facts had rubbed off on America, Emerson knew. Emerson's greatest value is that he addresses, and tries to heal, the split in American consciousness between high speculation and hard experience. For more than two centuries in the United States, the cynical realist's business as usual (with the emphasis on business) has battled against a romantic idealism, our desire for a more just and perfect union. Both these trends are equally American. In his late lecture "Fortune of the Republic" (reconstructed after the fact by his daughter Ellen and his literary executor James Elliot Cabot), Emerson lamented, "The American marches with a careless swagger to the height of power, very heedless of his own liberty or of other peoples', in his reckless confidence that he can have all he wants . . ."[31] In place of such ambitious greed, Emerson outlined an ideal: "I wish to see America not like the old powers of the earth, grasping, exclusive and narrow, but a benefactor such as no country ever was": open to all, a welcome source of life and knowledge.[32]

The American character relishes accurate perception and likes best of all to say: make no mistake, that's the way it is.[33] This tough approach can end in swaggering, the arrogant presumption that Emerson denounced: a collaboration, whether tacit or outspoken, with the meanest realities, so long as they have power. But Emerson also recognized, in works like the sublime, disturbing essay "Fate," that cool greed and ambition, however ruthless their work, serve a role in the universe. The law of results cannot be bent. In his wrestling with fact, the idealist had better come armed with something more than mere wish and hope.

Emerson's last masterwork, *The Conduct of Life* (1860), offers an antidote to *English Traits*. Emerson now suggests that pragmatic habits are not grasping and low-minded, but rather a means of coming in tune with the all. The message of *The Conduct of Life* is that "all things ascend"; that even the most mundane efforts to seize one's advantage, to turn a profit, have inscribed within them something of poetry.[34] The roughest worldly person incorporates a hidden dreamer, and every dream that counts is also, unexpectedly, practical.

So Emerson tries mightily to bridge the dichotomy of speculation and experience. He convinces us that there is speculation in experience and, rather more surprisingly, experience in speculation, too. For him, the cruel facts of life must be granted; but idealism, rather than being unrealistic, is just as inevitable as, and infinitely more effective than, the cynic's stance. In his Journal in 1845, Emerson cited with approval "the belief of the Buddhist that no seed will die. Work on, you cannot escape your wages."[35] Truth is a law like gravity. Society's injustices are lies, and therefore bound to fail. "Morals is the science of results," he wrote in 1846, the things that "we cannot but speak, though we shut up our mouths or pluck out our tongues."[36] The law of morals shows itself, insidiously, subtly, within the law of fate. By the end of Emerson's taciturn, finely tuned *Conduct of Life*, published on the eve of the Civil War, he finds moral prospects in even the cruelest of necessities, the punishing facts of war, starvation, death, and disease. But he has to wrestle to get there, and his doubts remain on the page. The doubts, remarkable as they are, testify to Emerson's huge effort to extend his vision.

Emerson was often severe in his verdicts on American politics, especially foreign policy. On the Mexican War of 1846, he wrote, "No act of honor or benevolence or justice is to be expected from the American Government, but only this, that they will be as wicked as they dare."[37] Most shocking of all was slavery. As early as December 1834 he confessed to his Journal the thought that "because every man has within him somewhat really divine therefore is slavery the unpardonable outrage it is."[38] Though from time to time he voiced in his Journal doubts about the prospects of the "African race," by the 1840s he was boldly asserting in public that the Abolition movement had caused "the annihilation of the old indecent nonsense about the nature of the negro": "It now appears, that the negro race is, more than any other, susceptible of rapid civilization."[39] In his Journal he looked forward to "a better species of the genus Homo. The Caucasian is an arrested undertype," he sadly noted—and we sense he was thinking of whites' willingness to accept slavery.[40] Nor did Emerson condescend to slaves, or ex-slaves. Blacks had already freed themselves in Haiti, he noted, and they were working to do so in North America: so "the negro has saved himself, and the white man very patronizingly says, I have saved you."[41]

Emerson struggled for decades against the evil of slaveholding, the central disease of the American polity. He always knew that slavery, by its very nature, was doomed. No institution so thoroughly vicious could possibly last forever. Yet it had lasted too long already. By the 1850s there was only one subject in America, slavery: so Emerson bitterly remarked. "We eat it, we drink it, we breathe it, we trade, we study, we wear it. We are all poisoned with it."[42]

The greatest crisis in Emerson's intellectual career stemmed from the terrible willingness of Americans to accept slavery. The most powerful orator of his day, the representative of staunch New England, independent and rough, was Daniel Webster. In 1850, Webster lent his mighty voice to the support of the Fugitive Slave Law, which bound all Americans, under penalty of law, to return escaped slaves to their masters.

In earlier days, Webster had tempted Emerson with his greatness. "His words are like blows of an axe,"[43] Emerson wrote, in love with Webster's towering attack, the torrent of his speech; and again, "He is no saint, but the wild olive wood, ungrafted yet by grace."[44] Webster was a force of nature, his words undeniable as the wind itself. It was therefore especially horrible that Webster now took it upon himself to incarnate selfishness and greed: that he was willing to accommodate the South at any price, just to keep the two halves of America together, their commerce running smoothly.

When the Fugitive Slave Law passed, Emerson filled dozens of pages in his Journal with condemnations of Webster, whose vote had ensured the law's passage. His anger at Webster's betrayal is, at times, frightening to behold, but it is inspiring, too. "We shall make no more mistakes," Emerson wrote of Webster in his Journal. "He has taught us the ghastly meaning of liberty in his mouth. It is kidnapping & hunting to death men & women . . ."[45] "The fame of Webster ends in this nasty law," he added, "the most detestable law that was ever enacted by a civilized state,"[46] one that had brought Massachusetts down "to the cannibal level."[47]

Emerson soon gave a speech to the citizens of Concord denouncing the "filthy enactment." In the speech, Emerson pursues Webster for whole paragraphs. He is relentless.

Emerson begins by remembering Webster's former grandeur, like that of the old Lucifer in heaven: "Simply, he was the one eminent American of our time, whom we could produce as a finished work of nature." But now Webster's nature had revealed itself more completely. Like Milton's Mammon (to whom Emerson is about to allude), Webster sees only possessions, not spirit:

Mr. Webster is a man who lives by his memory, a man of the past, not a man of faith or of hope. He obeys his powerful animal

nature;—and his finely developed understanding only works truly
and with all its force, when it stands for animal good; that is, for
property. He believes, in so many words, that government exists
for the protection of property.

Then Emerson moves to his climax:

> This is all inevitable from his constitution. All the drops of his
> blood have eyes that look downward. It is neither praise nor blame
> to say that he has no moral perception, no moral sentiment, but,
> in that *region*, to use the phrase of the phrenologists, a hole in the
> head.

"The law is suicidal, and cannot be obeyed," Emerson concluded. "How can
a law be enforced that fines pity, and imprisons charity? . . . You know that
the Act of Congress of September 18, 1850, is a law which every one of you
will break on the earliest occasion." "America, the most prosperous country
in the universe, has the greatest calamity in the universe, negro slavery," he
declared, and America had just passed a law of unparalleled wickedness, or-
dering its Northern citizens to kidnap their fellow men.[48] Sometimes gunpowder smells good, Emerson said when the Civil War finally broke out.

From the mid-1840s, Emerson battled against slavery; he supported
women's rights (after some initial waffling, he championed women's suffrage
and delivered a speech at the Women's Rights Convention in 1855); and he
denounced the horrors of Indian removal in 1838, in a public letter to President Martin Van Buren. He had been moved when he saw, in November
1837, the delegation of two Indian tribes, the Sacs and the Foxes, come to
Boston to plead for their rights. One chief said that "they had no land to put
their words upon, but they were nevertheless true"—so Emerson reported in
his Journal.[49] But Emerson often enough held himself back, out of principle,
from immersion in practical politics. Though he admitted his adherence to
certain political movements, except for his antislavery work he was no fre-
netic activist; he said majestically, "I sit at home with the cause grim or glad.
I think I may never do anything that you shall call a deed again."[50]

As his experience with Webster demonstrated, Emerson was no wor-shipper of greatness. In this matter he departed from his friend and influence Thomas Carlyle. Carlyle was a tormented, brooding prophet, who when Emerson first met him lived in relative isolation with his wife, Jane Welsh, on their Scottish farm, Craigenputtock. (The Carlyles left Craigenputtock for London in 1834.) Unlike Carlyle, author of *On Heroes, Hero-Worship, and the Heroic in History* (1841), Emerson was aware of the dangers posed by he-roes, though he, too, felt their allure. He remarked in his Journal, "The great inspire us: how they beckon, how they animate, and show their legitimate power in nothing more than in their power to misguide us. For, the per-verted great derange & deject us, & perplex ages with their fame. Alexander, Napoleon, Mahomet."[51] Emerson's play with the fine word "legitimate" is razor-sharp: what makes the great legitimate is their underhanded, unlawful nature, their inclination to do the apt but disastrous thing—which in turn tells us something essential and discouraging about the nature of the world, as illicit as it is vigorous.

Emerson wrote after meeting Carlyle in Scotland in 1832, on his first European trip, that "he is a worshipper of strength, heedless much whether its present phase be divine or diabolic."[52] Should he be wary of this learned savage? Emerson helped Carlyle publish his extravagant *Sartor Resartus* in America, but over time the Scottish sage's bitter, embattled nature became sadly evident to Emerson. By 1848 his sense of Carlyle had darkened consid-erably. He wrote in his Journal that Carlyle was "no idealist in opinions": he "goes for slavery, murder, money, punishment by death, & all the pretty abominations, tempering them with epigrams."[53] Emerson was a stranger to Carlyle's insistence (expressed in an 1836 letter to Emerson) that his fellow men were "dreadfully wearisome, unedifying."[54] Unlike Carlyle, Emerson was genial, generous; he possessed a strong and surprising sense of humor far distant from Carlyle's hard satirical vein. The two remained friends, but Emerson knew he needed a higher pitch than Carlyle's.

Emerson's *Representative Men* (1850), called by Emily Dickinson "a little granite book you can lean on," refuses to hold up its seven subjects as objects of adulation.[55] Instead, these men (none of them, incidentally, American) are valuable for their power to receive and focus the force of meaning inherent in their time. In his portraits of Plato, Swedenborg, Shakespeare, Montaigne, Napoleon, and Goethe, Emerson measures their worth for a democracy. *Representative Men* is Emerson's answer not just to Carlyle's encomiums of his heroes but also to his beloved Plutarch's biographies. It is a book engineered for practical use: we may need these men on occasion, but there is a moment in every essay when Emerson comes close to dismissing them.

It is not the grand men but the seemingly ordinary ones who make life a thing of value, Emerson realized. "The world looks poor & mean as long as I think only of its great men," he wrote. "But when I remember how many obscure persons I myself have seen possessing gifts that excited wonder, speculation, & delight in me"—then life discovers its true integrity.[56] The individual, the common man, offers the best rewards; and we are all that man (or woman). "We shall one day talk with the central man," Emerson promises. The central man, however, turns out to be, not some monumental hero, but me myself: "these great secular personalities were only expressions of his face chasing each other like the rack of clouds. Then all will subside, & I find myself alone. I dreamed & did not know my dreams."[57] "All men have Genius if they will," Emerson asserts.[58] Moreover, they seem to know it: they "have a secret persuasion that as little as they pass for in the world, they are immensely rich in expectancy & power."[59]

Such intuition names an openness of the self to cosmic power, not a claim of the ego's virtuous infallibility but a stimulating doubt: do we, can we ever, know ourselves? The individual, for Emerson, is a notably elusive creature. A man "has many enumerable parts," he writes in his Journal: he is "of this or that set & corporation. But," he continues, "there remains as much more which no tongue can tell. And this remainder is that which interests." "For the best part, I repeat, of every mind is not that which he knows, but that which hovers in gleams, suggestions, tantalizing unpossessed before him. His firm recorded knowledge soon loses all interest before him."[60]

The unknown self, then, is Emerson's real object of worship. He first invents what Harold Bloom names the "American religion," a veneration of the self's inwardness, the undeniable and exalted potential that no merely conventional force can gainsay. This is a lonely revelation, as Emerson's friend Thoreau also knew. "There will always be the same gulf between every me & thee as between the original and the picture," Emerson softly announces.[61] The self is original; the others who surround it look and sound like echoes, mere images. They somehow exceed our reach. So each of us remains happily stranded, in a separate world—yet we feel a lack, and burst with restless impulse, eager for something new and other. "Every star in nature is discontented and insatiable," Emerson insisted, and we are like those stars.[62]

In 1846 Emerson wrote, "You must treat the days respectfully, you must be a day yourself, and not interrogate life like a college professor."[63] Days have a rhythm, an integrity worth emulating, that careful analysts never grasp. In his essay "Works and Days," Emerson coasted into Yankee simplicity: "Write it on your heart that every day is the best day in the year."[64]

But all was not full of light. "In the streets I have certain darkenings which I call my nights," Emerson wrote.[65] He is rarely given credit for such understated, harrowing suggestions, as haunting as anything in Hawthorne: he carries his troubles quietly. Emerson was no wide-eyed naïf; he knew depression and death. But he knew intimately, too, the myriad ways we hoist ourselves up, higher than we thought possible.

Emerson is a slyly post-Christian thinker. As a young preacher of thirty, he announced to his shocked listeners, "Christianity is the most emphatic affirmation of spiritual nature. But it is not the only nor the last affirmation. There shall be a thousand more."[66] He outlined the defects of Jesus in a Journal entry from July 1835: "I do not see in him cheerfulness: I do not see in him the love of Natural Science: I see in him no kindness for Art; I see in him nothing of Socrates, of Laplace, of Shakespeare."[67] Most resounding is an 1842 Journal passage. Speaking of Jesus' life, Emerson pronounced, "He did well. . . . But he that shall come shall do better . . . This was a great Defeat; we demand Victory"—a victory of the senses and not just the soul.[68] The detachment of the Church from life, from the vitality of the time, troubled Emerson. "In the dead pond which our church is, no life appears," he remarked, and he spoke of the "corpse-cold Unitarianism of Brattle Street and Boston," the centers of diluted, all-too-liberal Christianity.[69] That which was vital in Christian thought appeared in all other religions too, in the heart of "Stoic & Chinese Mahometan & Hindoo."[70]

Emerson wrote that his ideal form of religion, "Spiritual Religion," "shows the surprizing beauties & terrors of human life. It never scolds &

never sneers. . . . It leaves the dead to bury their dead."[71] This Emersonian religion offered a stark contrast to the "anxious instruction" he saw in the churches around him, and the "periodic shouting about 'atoning blood.'"[72] In reality, "persons are nothing," he concluded—including the person of Jesus.[73] "Cursed is preaching," Emerson insisted, "—the better it is, the worse. A preacher is a bully: I who have preached so much,—by the help of God will never preach more."[74]

Emerson was a thinker of the world—all of it. Nothing was alien to him, from the vast newness of Walt Whitman, nurtured on Emerson's own essays (*Leaves of Grass*, Emerson said, was "a nondescript monster which yet has terrible eyes & buffalo strength, & was indisputably American"), to the farthest reaches of Asia.[75] Like Thoreau, Emerson was a great admirer of the East. He seems to have bought, and studied, a copy of the Koran in 1833, as a young man of thirty.[76] He wrote that Zoroastrianism is "harmonious & sublime," and he adored the Hindu scriptures.[77] In 1848 he wrote of a discussion with Thoreau: "my friend & I,—owed a magnificent day to the Bhagavat Geeta.—It was the first of books; it was as if an empire spake to us nothing small or unworthy but large, serene, consistent."[78] Most of all, he cherished the Persian poets, Hafiz, Saadi, and Rumi, and, relying on German versions, he translated them with enthusiasm. He needed the whole world: not just Concord; not just America and Europe, and Christianity. As Emerson took in the light of the Eastern sages, these more familiar presences began to look, at times, small and partial.

Late in his life, in a manuscript book, Emerson translated one of Saadi's poems on old age. "Now is the time when weakness comes,—& strength goes," he wrote; "The magic of sweet words—I lose." The poem concludes,

> Saadi's whole power lies—in sweet words
> Keep this     all the rest may go to beast & birds[79]

The poem spurs us to reflect on Emerson's encroaching mental twilight, which gradually robbed him of his memory. In the end, at Longfellow's funeral in 1882, Emerson was unable to recall who the "sweet man" was: "Where are we?" he asked, "What house? And who is the sleeper?"[80]

When still in his thirties, Emerson remarked in his Journal, "We are carried by destiny along our life's course looking as grave & knowing as little as the infant who is carried in his wicker coach thro' the street."[81] There is something unreal about our lives. Yet our blithe ignorance, looked at another way, leads to experiments; turns out to be freshness, and more than freshness, originality. We are symbols, and inhabit symbols; our lives are sheer fable—and so they hold the promise of any worthwhile fiction. But we need to trust ourselves rather than the dusty claims that surround us. All those demands for obedience and good sense rely on an unreal regime that, unlike the wholesome and provocative unreality of individual life, harms our prospects. "Ah ye old ghosts! ye builders of dungeons in the air!"[82] Emerson memorably complains. His healing perception is that there is something fatally non-existent about the oppressive claims of power, the proud limitary cherubs insisting on laws of history and human nature, reasons of state and godly doctrine.

Emerson did, though, insist on a truer, more ominous limit, the deep fact of cosmic law that he calls, in his most troubling essay, Fate. To find the moral secret within Fate is not always feasible; even when we don't, we must build altars to the necessity that destroys, and do so in celebration, too. But the constant tension between the destiny that seems utterly alien and inhuman, on the one side, and our demand for justice, on the other, becomes a source of strength for Emerson, rather than a debilitating obstacle. We keep returning to this question, unwilling to loosen our hold on either end of the rope: strangely hopeful, feeling new energy even in the knowledge of doom. Emerson realizes that doom is not the most telling part of the story: that definitive will not do; that the truth of us has not yet been found.

\*   \*   \*

This edition is designed for both the neophyte reader of Emerson and the experienced scholar. *The Annotated Emerson* includes what I consider to be Emerson's most profound essays and poems, and surrounds them with what I hope is a reasonable amount of commentary. Any lover of Emerson will have a different dream book, his or her ideal arrangement of the Concord prophet's writings. Some cherished works will appear in almost every Emersonian's portfolio: "The American Scholar," "Self-Reliance," "Fate," "Uriel." Others, like his memoirs of Margaret Fuller and Thoreau, are less often seen as essential. I have included both, because these two friends, more than any others, helped make Emerson who he was, and because Fuller and Thoreau are exciting, substantial figures in their own right. *The Annotated Emerson* also contains Emerson's letter to President Martin Van Buren protesting the removal of the Cherokee Indians, his watershed speech commemorating the abolition of slavery in the British West Indies, and a speech celebrating John Brown, the antislavery militant who galvanized public opinion on the eve of the Civil War.

Emerson's Journals, all sixteen volumes of them, make up one of the great books of the world. In the late 1830s and the 1840s, especially, Emerson's inspiration is incessant: there is light on every page, and often enough every sentence. In this edition, I set passages from Emerson's Journals (and, less often, his letters) alongside the essays that he fashioned from them. No previous edition juxtaposes essays and Journal entries as I do here (though Stephen Whicher's 1957 *Selections from Ralph Waldo Emerson* took an important step in this direction). The traffic between the Emerson of the study and the Emerson of the lecture platform and finished book is so fascinating, for the new reader of the essays as well as for the seasoned Emersonian, that it deserves to take center stage. (I have relied much less on the Emerson of the lectures, sermons, and later essays, both for lack of space and because I feel the Journals should receive priority.) I hope that readers will go on to explore the thick forest of Emerson's Journals on their own, after they descend from the mountains of his essays. (The two-volume Library of America edition of the Journals, edited by Lawrence Rosenwald, offers a worthy selection, as does Joel Porte's slimmer *Emerson in His Journals.*)

I supply a range of useful contexts in my notations (from history, philosophy, politics, religion) and explain topical references, so that Emerson's erudition will not be an obstacle to the reader. For some of the information in my notes, and for other guidance, I have relied on the ongoing *Collected Works of Ralph Waldo Emerson* (Harvard University Press), edited in its early volumes by Alfred Ferguson, Robert Spiller, Joseph Slater, and Douglas Emory Wilson, and now under the editorship of Ronald A. Bosco (General Editor) and Joel Myerson (Textual Editor). The Harvard *Collected Works* is the source of the texts of Emerson's essays, poems, and lectures published in this volume. Journal passages are cited from Emerson's *Journals and Miscellaneous Notebooks*, also published by Harvard, under the general editorship of William Gilman. Emerson's letters are cited in the version edited by Ralph Rusk and Eleanor Tilton, though I have also consulted the volume of *Selected Letters* edited by Joel Myerson.

The last few decades have seen a revolution in Emerson scholarship spearheaded by Joel Myerson, Ronald Bosco, and Albert von Frank: scholars whose extraordinary talent and diligence have made us see Emerson in a new, radically improved light. This volume, like so many others, rests upon their labors. Among other editors and commentators, I am particularly indebted to (in an earlier era) Edward Everett Emerson, James Elliot Cabot, O. W. Firkins, and John Jay Chapman, and (in a later one) Stephen Whicher, Joel Porte, Harold Bloom, Richard Poirier, Stanley Cavell, Robert Richardson, David Robinson, Lawrence Buell, Philip Gura, Len Gougeon, and the late Barbara Packer. This book would have been impossible without the grand tradition of Emersonians who have prepared its way.

# Notes

1    J 5:75 (1835).

2    Oliver Wendell Holmes, *Ralph Waldo Emerson* (Boston: Houghton Mifflin, 1912), 115.

3    Emerson, "Two Discourses" (1845), in LL 1:100.

4    J 11:406 (1851).

5    J 11:284 (1850); a milder version of the passage is included in Emerson's essay "Considerations by the Way" (1860).

6    J 5:203 (September 1836); "We are an afflicted land, a people not strong in the knees," he wrote in 1846 (J 9:448; also J 15:98 [1861]).

7    J 12:30 (1838).

8    J 8:58 (October 14, 1841).

9    L 2:375 (undated, and addressed only to "My dear friend").

10    J 4:53 (October 1832).

11    J 11:259 (1850).

12    J 4:27 (1832).

13    J 4:79 (September 1, 1833).

14    Horace Greeley, *Autobiography* (New York: 1872 [1st ed. 1868]), 170.

15    J 8:215 (1842).

16    Melville's letter to Evert Duyckinck, March 3, 1849.

17    Cited in Philip Gura, *American Transcendentalism* (New York: Hill and Wang, 2007), 143.

18    J 4:278 (April 20, 1834).

19    See B. L. (Barbara) Packer, *Emerson's Fall* (New York: Continuum, 1982).

20    J 4:76 (July 9, 1833).

21    J 4:104 (January 3, 1833).

22    J 4:285 (April 29, 1834).

23    Richard Poirier, Introduction to *Ralph Waldo Emerson* (Oxford Authors) (New York: Oxford University Press, 1990), x. Poirier cites John Jay Chapman's *Emerson and Other Essays* (1898), in addition to Holmes, for its observations on Emerson's lecturing style.

24    L 5:4 (January 3, 1856).

25    L 2:203 (June 7, 1839).

26    Emerson, "Culture," from *The Conduct of Life*.

27    Emerson, "The Transcendentalist" (1842).

28    J 8:313 (November–December 1842).

29    J 5:202 (September 1836).

30    J 7:365 (June 4, 1840).

31    Emerson, "The Fortune of the Republic" (1863), in *Complete Works*, ed. Edward W. Emerson, vol. 11 (Boston: Houghton Mifflin, 1911), 521.

32    Emerson, "The Fortune of the Republic," in *Complete Works*, vol. 11, 531.

33    See Joel Porte, *Consciousness and Culture* (New Haven: Yale University Press, 2004), 188.

34    Emerson, "Wealth," from *The Conduct of Life*.

35    J 9:330 (1845).

36    J 9:408 (1846).

37    J 10:29 (March–April 1847).

38    J 4:357 (December 1834).

39    J 12:152; Emerson repeated these sentiments in his "Address . . . on . . . the Emancipation of the Negroes in the British West Indies" (in this volume, 320–323). August 1, 1844, in *Emerson's Antislavery Writings*, ed. Len Gougeon and Joel Myerson (New Haven: Yale University Press, 1995), 29–30.

40    J 9:212 (1845).

41    J 9:125 (1844).

42    J 11:361 (1850–1851).

43    J 8:358 (August 17, 1843).

44    J 8:361 (1843).

45    J 11:348 (1851).

46    J 11:351–352 (1851).

47    J 11:355 (1851).

48    See Emerson's "Address to the Citizens of Concord" on the Fugitive Slave Law (May 3, 1851), in Gougeon and Myerson, eds., 57–60.

49    J 5:417 (November 1837).

50    J 7:404 (October 7, 1840).

51    J 9:330 (December 8, 1834).

52    J 5:291 (March 29, 1837).

53    J 11:227 (1850).

54    CEC 152 (November 5, 1836).

55    Robert Richardson, *First We Read, Then We Write* (Iowa City: University of Iowa Press, 2009), 65.

56    J 4:353 (December 1834).

57    J 9:395 (1846).

58    J 12:197 (late 1830s?).

59    J 9:341 (1845).

60    J 9:341 (1845).

61    J 7:467 (September 1842).

62    Emerson, "The Method of Nature" (1841).

63    J 9:361 (1846).

64    Emerson, "Works and Days" (1870).

65    J 11:327 (1850–1851).

66    S 4:213.

67    J 5:72 (July 1835).

68    J 8:228 (1842).

69    J 5:491 (May 1838).

70    J 5:478 (April 23, 1838).

71    J 3:64 (the editors of the Journals note that this entry appears to be in a hand other than Emerson's, but its content seems authentic).

72    J 4:313–314 (August 17, 1834).

73    J 4:383 (1834).

74    J 8:361 (March 23, 1843).

75    Letter to Thomas Carlyle, May 6, 1856, CEC 509.

76    J 4:424.

77    J 4:11 (April 17, 1832).

78    J 10:360 (1848). In a letter to Samuel Gray Ward (July 18?, 1840), Emerson spoke of "the Vedas, the bible of the tropics, which I find I come back upon every three or four years. It is sublime as heat and night and a breathless ocean. It contains every religious sentiment, all the grand ethics . . .," *Letters from Ralph Waldo Emerson to a Friend, 1838–1853*, ed. Charles Eliot Norton (Boston: Houghton Mifflin, 1899), 27–28.

79    From *Collected Poems and Translations*, ed. Harold Bloom and Paul Kane (New York: Library of America, 1994), 491.

80    Emerson's mental decline began in the late 1860s; lecturing and writing became very difficult for him. In 1872, when the family house burned, Emerson threw into the fire the letters of his beloved first wife, Ellen, and the clothes of his dead son, Waldo—a sign of his increasing despondency and psychic torment.

81    J 5:392 (October 1837).

82    J 8:8 (July 6, 1841); the line is altered and used in "Considerations by the Way."

# Nature

A subtle chain of countless rings
The next unto the farthest brings;
The eye reads omens where it goes,
And speaks all languages the rose;
And, striving to be man, the worm
Mounts through all the spires of form.[1]

### ARTICLE I. Introduction

Our age is retrospective. It builds the sepulchres of the fathers.[2] It writes biographies, histories, and criticism. The foregoing generations beheld God and nature face to face; we, through their eyes.[3] Why should not we also enjoy an original relation to the universe?[4] Why should not we have a poetry and philosophy of insight and not of tradition, and a religion by revelation to us, and not the history of theirs? Embosomed for a season in nature, whose floods of life stream around and through us, and invite us by the powers they supply, to action proportioned to nature, why should we grope among the dry bones of the past,[5] or put the living generation into masquerade out of its faded wardrobe?[6] The sun shines to-day also.[7] There is more wool and flax

*Emerson first mentioned* Nature *in his Journal during his homeward voyage from Europe (September 6, 1833: "I like my book about nature, and wish I knew where & how I ought to live. God will show me" [J 4:237]). On June 28, 1836, he revealed in a letter to his brother William that the book was nearly done, and he promised a second volume, on Spirit (L 2:30); in August, as he finished the manuscript, he noted mysteriously that there was "one crack in it not easy to be soldered or welded" (L 2:32). The book was published in September 1836, in an edition of 500 copies. Writing to his friend Thomas Carlyle (1795–1881), Emerson described* Nature *as "an entering wedge, I hope, for something more worthy and significant" (September 17, 1836; CEC 149).*

1    Instead of Emerson's poem, first printed in his edition of 1849, *Nature* originally featured an epigraph from the Neoplatonic philosopher Plotinus (205–270): "Nature is but an image or imitation of wisdom, the last thing of the soul; nature being a thing which doth only do, but not know."

2      In his Sermon CXVI, preached at Second Church on May 29, 1831, Emerson warned that if the Sabbath is not observed, "the children may ride over the sepulchers of their fathers" (S 3:166). By 1836 he had turned the phrase in a different direction, complaining in his Journal, "We build the sepulchers of our fathers: can we never behold the Universe as new" (January 22, 1836, J 5:117). Emerson might have remembered a phrase from Daniel Webster's Bunker Hill oration of 1825, "We are among the sepulchers of our fathers," as well as Jesus' statement to the Pharisees in Luke 11:47, "Woe unto you! For ye build the sepulchers of the prophets, and your fathers killed them."

3      "For now we see through a glass, darkly; but then face to face" (I Corinthians 13:12). In his lecture "The Uses of Natural History"

(1833), Emerson wrote, "The whole of Nature is a metaphor or image of the human Mind. The laws of moral nature answer to those of matter as face to face in a glass"; he uses the passage in Chapter IV (Language), below.

4      There is an irony in Emerson's formulation, with its wry "also": we want to be as original as our fathers. Emerson will balance his opening statements on retrospect with an emphasis on "Prospects" (*Nature*'s final chapter).

5      When the prophet Ezekiel finds himself in a valley full of dry bones, he writes, "Thus saith the Lord GOD unto these bones; Behold, I will cause breath to enter into you, and you shall live" (Ezekiel 37:2–5). In Emerson's *Nature*, natural science and poetic imagination provide the living breath that makes dead bones

*(continued)*

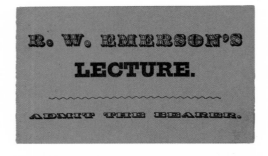

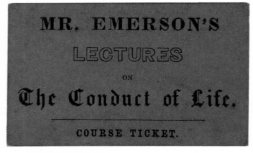

Tickets to Emerson's lectures. "I look on the Lecture Room as the true Church of the coming time . . ." Emerson wrote. "Here, the American orator shall find the theatre he needs; here, he may lay himself out utterly large, prodigal, enormous, on the subject of the hour."

Silhouette of Emerson's aunt, Mary Moody
Emerson.

in the fields.[8] There are new lands, new men, new thoughts. Let us demand
our own works and laws and worship.

Undoubtedly we have no questions to ask which are unanswerable. We
must trust the perfection of the creation so far, as to believe that whatever
curiosity the order of things has awakened in our minds, the order of things
can satisfy. Every man's condition is a solution in hieroglyphic[9] to those inquiries he would put. He acts it as life, before he apprehends it as truth. In
like manner, nature is already, in its forms and tendencies, describing[10] its
own design. Let us interrogate the great apparition, that shines so peacefully
around us. Let us inquire, to what end is nature?

All science has one aim, namely, to find a theory of nature. We have
theories of races and of functions, but scarcely yet a remote approach to an
idea of creation. We are now so far from the road to truth, that religious

come to life. Speaking of religious observance
in his Sermon CXXXIII (October 30, 1831),
Emerson announced, "It is a spirit that must
make these dry bones live, or they are dead"
(S 3:256).

6      "A great deal of life is in masquerade,"
Emerson lamented in Sermon LXXII (April 25,
1830; S 2:174).

7      "The sun also ariseth" (Ecclesiastes 1:5).
In Sermon CLVIII (June 10, 1832), Emerson
announced, "We do not see the sun by the light
which left his orb in the time of Abraham but
the new light that sprang from his globe this
very hour. And so we perceive truth not by what
it was but what it is" (S 4:163).

8      Proverbs 31:13 says of a virtuous woman,
"She seeketh wool, and flax, and worketh willingly with her hands."

9      Egyptian hieroglyphics excited much attention in Emerson's day. They had only become legible in the 1820s, when the French
researcher Jean-François Champollion deciphered the Rosetta Stone (a basalt tablet inscribed in Greek and hieroglyphics). In his Sermon XXXIX from 1829, the young Emerson
remarked, "There is nothing in external nature
but is an emblem, a hieroglyphic of some thing
in us" (S 1:299). *The True Messiah* (1829), by
the French mystic Guillaume Oegger (1790?–
1853?), announces that "Man is the true hieroglyphic of the Divinity"—a sentence Emerson
transcribed in his Journal (J 5:68). In Sermon CLV (May 13, 1832), Emerson described
the "works of nature" as "Hieroglyphicks" to
be read with the aid of man's *"moral nature"*
(S 4:144).

10      Tracing, as well as giving an account of.

11   Early reviews of *Nature* found this a shocking conjunction of terms. Emerson asserted in his Journal (May 3, 1834) that "the true philosophy of man should give a theory of Beasts & Dreams. A German dispatched them both by saying that Beasts are dreams, or 'the nocturnal side of Nature.'" He was referring to a statement of the German artist Johann David Schubert (ca. 1761–ca. 1822) cited by Madame Germaine de Staël (1766–1817) in her book *On Germany* (1813): Schubert called animals the dreams of nature, and man their waking (J 4:289n).

12   Term used by the Scottish author Thomas Carlyle in his extravagant prose work *Sartor Resartus* (1833–1834). In 1836 Emerson wrote the introduction to the first American edition of Carlyle's book. *Sartor Resartus* means "the tailor retailored": see Emerson's reference to the "faded wardrobe" of previous generations in the first paragraph of *Nature*. In his lecture "Demonology" (1839), from his series "Human Life," Emerson remarked, "My dreams are not *me*. They are not Nature, or the *Not Me*. They are both: they have a double consciousness . . ." (EL 3:155).

13   The great American poet Walt Whitman (1819–1892) was influenced by this passage when he wrote "A Clear Midnight": "This is thy hour O Soul, thy free flight into the wordless, / Away from books, away from art, the day erased, the lesson done, / Thee fully forth emerging, silent, gazing, pondering the themes thou lovest best, / Night, sleep, death and the stars." In his Journal (May 11, 1838) Emerson wrote, "Come out of your warm angular house resounding with few voices into the chill grand instantaneous night" (J 5:496).

teachers dispute and hate each other, and speculative men are esteemed unsound and frivolous. But to a sound judgment, the most abstract truth is the most practical. Whenever a true theory appears, it will be its own evidence. Its test is, that it will explain all phenomena. Now many are thought not only unexplained but inexplicable; as language, sleep, madness, dreams, beasts, sex.[11]

Philosophically considered, the universe is composed of Nature and the Soul. Strictly speaking, therefore, all that is separate from us, all which Philosophy distinguishes as the NOT ME,[12] that is, both nature and art, all other men and my own body, must be ranked under this name, NATURE. In enumerating the values of nature and casting up their sum, I shall use the word in both senses;—in its common and in its philosophical import. In inquiries so general as our present one, the inaccuracy is not material; no confusion of thought will occur. *Nature*, in the common sense, refers to essences unchanged by man; space, the air, the river, the leaf. *Art* is applied to the mixture of his will with the same things, as in a house, a canal, a statue, a picture. But his operations taken together are so insignificant, a little chipping, baking, patching, and washing, that in an impression so grand as that of the world on the human mind, they do not vary the result.

ARTICLE II. CHAPTER I. Nature

To go into solitude, a man needs to retire as much from his chamber as from society. I am not solitary whilst I read and write, though nobody is with me. But if a man would be alone, let him look at the stars.[13] The rays that come from those heavenly worlds, will separate between him and vulgar things. One might think the atmosphere was made transparent with this design, to give man, in the heavenly bodies, the perpetual presence of the sublime.[14] Seen in the streets of cities, how great they are! If the stars should appear one night in a thousand years, how would men believe and adore; and preserve for many generations the remembrance of the city of God which had been shown! But every night come out these envoys of beauty, and light the universe with their admonishing smile.

The stars awaken a certain reverence, because though always present, they are always inaccessible; but all natural objects make a kindred impression, when the mind is open to their influence. Nature never wears a mean appearance. Neither does the wisest man extort all her secret, and lose his curiosity by finding out all her perfection. Nature never became a toy to a wise spirit. The flowers, the animals, the mountains, reflected all the wisdom of his best hour, as much as they had delighted the simplicity of his childhood.[15]

When we speak of nature in this manner, we have a distinct but most poetical sense in the mind. We mean the integrity[16] of impression made by manifold natural objects. It is this which distinguishes the stick of timber of the wood-cutter, from the tree of the poet. The charming landscape which I saw this morning, is indubitably made up of some twenty or thirty farms. Miller owns this field, Locke that, and Manning the woodland beyond. But none of them owns the landscape. There is a property in the horizon which no man has but he whose eye can integrate all the parts, that is, the poet. This is the best part of these men's farms, yet to this their warranty-deeds give no title.

To speak truly, few adult persons can see nature. Most persons do not see the sun. At least they have a very superficial seeing. The sun illuminates only the eye of the man, but shines into the eye and the heart of the child. The lover of nature is he whose inward and outward senses are still truly adjusted to each other; who has retained the spirit of infancy even into the era of manhood. His intercourse with heaven and earth, becomes part of his daily food. In the presence of nature, a wild delight runs through the man, in spite of real sorrows. Nature says,—he is my creature, and maugre[17] all his impertinent griefs, he shall be glad with me. Not the sun or the summer alone, but every hour and season yields its tribute of delight; for every hour and change corresponds to and authorizes a different state of the mind, from breathless noon to grimmest midnight. Nature is a setting that fits equally well a comic or a mourning piece. In good health, the air is a cordial[18] of incredible virtue. Crossing a bare common, in snow puddles, at twilight, under a clouded sky, without having in my thoughts any occurrence of special good fortune, I have enjoyed a perfect exhilaration. I am glad to the brink of fear.[19]

14    The sublime is a lofty and powerful aesthetic effect, characterized by greatness of thought and expression. It was first discussed by Longinus (1st century). De Staël wrote in *On Germany*, summarizing the view of the sublime given by the philosopher Immanuel Kant (1724–1804), "The first effect of the sublime is to overwhelm a man, and the second to exalt him."

15    Emerson's connection between nature and the inspired innocence of childhood is indebted to his reading of William Wordsworth (1770–1850).

16    Wholeness.

17    Despite.

18    A drink, usually alcoholic spirits, to cheer or invigorate the heart (*cor* is Latin for heart).

19    Emerson's first version of the sentence (retained by the Harvard editors) was "Almost I fear to think how glad I am." This is the most famous passage in *Nature*. In the journal entry that forms the basis for this paragraph (March 26, 1835), Emerson wrote, "The wild delight runs through the man in spite of real sorrows. Nature says he is my creature & spite of all his impertinent griefs he shall be glad with me. Almost I fear to think how glad I am" (J 5:24–25). A few months earlier (December 1834), he exclaimed, "I rejoice in Time. I do not cross the common without a wild poetic delight notwithstanding the prose of my demeanour" (J 4:337).

20     After beginning his studies at Harvard Divinity School in 1825, Emerson found his eyesight failing. Unable for a time to read or write, he withdrew from school. Emerson reflects on the blindness of the scientist Galileo Galilei (1564–1642) and the poet John Milton (1608–1674) in Sermon CLI (April 1832; S 4:118).

21     In the Journal entry that provided the basis for this passage (March 1835), Emerson added, "I become happy in my universal relations. . . . I am the heir of uncontained beauty & power" (J 5:18).

22     This image rapidly became famous when the artist and writer Christopher Cranch (1813–1892), a friend of the Transcendentalists, caricatured Emerson as an enormous eyeball precariously perched in stalking posture on a rather spindly yet supple pair of legs.

23     Emerson evokes the high praise of beauty in the *Symposium* and other dialogues by Plato (429–347 BCE).

Caricature of Emerson by Christopher Cranch (1813–1892).

In the woods too, a man casts off his years, as the snake his slough, and at what period soever of life, is always a child. In the woods, is perpetual youth. Within these plantations of God, a decorum and sanctity reign, a perennial festival is dressed, and the guest sees not how he should tire of them in a thousand years. In the woods, we return to reason and faith. There I feel that nothing can befal me in life,—no disgrace, no calamity, (leaving me my eyes,)[20] which nature cannot repair. Standing on the bare ground,—my head bathed by the blithe air, and uplifted into infinite space,—all mean egotism vanishes.[21] I become a transparent eye-ball.[22] I am nothing. I see all. The currents of the Universal Being circulate through me; I am part or particle of God. The name of the nearest friend sounds then foreign and accidental. To be brothers, to be acquaintances,—master or servant, is then a trifle and a disturbance. I am the lover of uncontained and immortal beauty.[23] In the wilderness, I find something more dear and connate[24] than in streets or villages. In the tranquil landscape, and especially in the distant line of the horizon, man beholds somewhat as beautiful as his own nature.

The greatest delight which the fields and woods minister,[25] is the suggestion of an occult[26] relation between man and the vegetable.[27] I am not alone and unacknowledged. They nod to me and I to them. The waving of the boughs in the storm, is new to me and old.[28] It takes me by surprise, and yet is not unknown. Its effect is like that of a higher thought or a better emotion coming over me, when I deemed I was thinking justly or doing right.

Yet it is certain that the power to produce this delight, does not reside in nature, but in man, or in a harmony of both. It is necessary to use these pleasures with great temperance. For, nature is not always tricked in holiday attire, but the same scene which yesterday breathed perfume and glittered as for the frolic of the nymphs, is overspread with melancholy today. Nature always wears the colors of the spirit. To a man laboring under calamity, the heat of his own fire hath sadness in it. Then, there is a kind of contempt of the landscape felt by him who has just lost by death a dear friend.[29] The sky is less grand as it shuts down over less worth in the population.

ARTICLE III. CHAPTER II. Commodity

Whoever considers the final cause of the world, will discern a multitude of uses that enter as parts into that result. They all admit of being thrown into one of the following classes: Commodity; Beauty; Language; and Discipline.

24    Allied, related (literally "born together with").

25    Supply (though Emerson suggests that they preach as well).

26    In his lecture "The Uses of Natural History" (1833) Emerson asserted, "We feel that there is an occult relation between very worm, the crawling scorpions, and man. I am moved by strange sympathies. I say I will listen to this invitation. I will be a Naturalist" (EL 1:10).

27    Organic nature.

28    In the Journal passage that provides the source for this paragraph, Emerson noted, "I love the wood god. I love the mighty PAN. Yesterday I walked in the storm. And truly in the fields I am not alone or unacknowledged. They nod to me & I to them" (June 22, 1836; J 5:179).

29    Emerson's brother Charles died in May 1836, while he was finishing *Nature*. In his Journal for May 16, 1836, Emerson wrote, "The eye is closed that was to see Nature for me, and give me leave to see" (J 5:152).

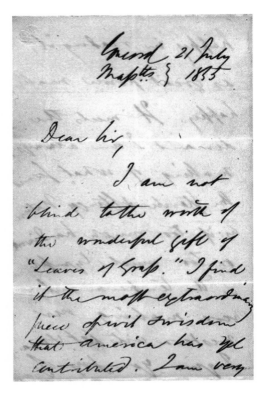

First page of Emerson's 1855 letter to Walt Whitman.

30    Lavish. De Staël remarked in *On Germany* that "Nature often displays her magnificence without any aim, and often with a profuseness, which the partisans of utility would call prodigal."

31    In Genesis 1:6–8, God divides the universe between the seas or waters (Hebrew *maim*) and the heavens (*shamaim*, "seas there").

32    Lines from "Man" by the seventeenth-century poet George Herbert (1593–1633). Emerson will quote Herbert again in a later section of Nature, "Prospects."

Under the general name of Commodity, I rank all those advantages which our senses owe to nature. This, of course, is a benefit which is temporary and mediate, not ultimate, like its service to the soul. Yet although low, it is perfect in its kind, and is the only use of nature which all men apprehend. The misery of man appears like childish petulance, when we explore the steady and prodigal[30] provision that has been made for his support and delight on this green ball which floats him through the heavens. What angels invented these splendid ornaments, these rich conveniences, this ocean of air above, this ocean of water beneath,[31] this firmament of earth between? this zodiac of lights, this tent of dropping clouds, this striped coat of climates, this fourfold year? Beasts, fire, water, stones, and corn serve him. The field is at once his floor, his work-yard, his play-ground, his garden, and his bed.

"More servants wait on man
Than he'll take notice of."[32]_____

Nature, in its ministry to man, is not only the material, but is also the process and the result. All the parts incessantly work into each other's hands for the profit of man. The wind sows the seed; the sun evaporates the sea; the wind blows the vapor to the field; the ice, on the other side of the planet, condenses rain on this; the rain feeds the plant; the plant feeds the animal; and thus the endless circulations of the divine charity nourish man.

The useful arts are but reproductions or new combinations by the wit[33] of man, of the same natural benefactors. He no longer waits for favoring gales, but by means of steam, he realizes the fable of Æolus's bag,[34] and carries the two and thirty winds in the boiler of his boat.[35] To diminish friction, he paves the road with iron bars, and, mounting a coach with a ship-load of men, animals, and merchandise behind him, he darts through the country, from town to town, like an eagle or a swallow through the air.[36] By the aggregate of these aids, how is the face of the world changed, from the era of Noah to that of Napoleon![37] The private poor man hath cities, ships, canals, bridges, built for him. He goes to the post-office, and the human race run on his errands; to the book-shop, and the human race read and write of all that happens, for him; to the court-house, and nations repair his wrongs. He sets his house upon the road, and the human race go forth every morning, and shovel out the snow, and cut a path for him.

But there is no need of specifying particulars in this class of uses. The catalogue is endless, and the examples so obvious, that I shall leave them to the reader's reflection, with the general remark, that this mercenary[38] benefit is one which has respect to a farther good. A man is fed, not that he may be fed, but that he may work.

Amos Bronson Alcott (1799–1888).

33    Ingenuity, resourceful cleverness. In his lecture "Humanity of Science" (1836) Emerson argued that arranging by "occult resemblances" is "the habit of wit," whereas science discovers "intrinsic likeness" (EL 2:23).

34    The story of Aeolus, guardian of the winds in Greek myth, is told in Bk. 10 of Homer's *Odyssey* (ca. 9th century BCE). He gives the winds in a bag to Odysseus to aid his journey; disastrously, Odysseus's men open the bag, causing their ship to be blown off course.

35    In 1807, Robert Fulton's steamboat began regular service on the Hudson River between New York City and Albany; by the 1830s, steamboats were common on the Ohio and Mississippi rivers.

36    Emerson remarked in a Journal entry (May 31, 1834) that one has "confirmation of the ideal philosophy that matter is phenomenal, when riding on the rail road, & seeing trees & men whiz by you as fast as the leaves of a dictionary as you hiss by them in your tea kettle" (J 4:293). Railroads were a recent development in the 1830s. The freight railroad between Boston and Lowell, a textile-manufacturing center, began in 1835. Passengers could make the journey as well, in forty-five minutes (at a bumpy sixty miles an hour). The rail line from Concord to Boston opened in 1845. Emerson wrote in his Journal in 1843, "Fear haunts the building railroad but it will be American power & beauty, when it is done" (J 9:23).

37    Napoleon Bonaparte (1769–1821), the French emperor, is the subject of an essay in Emerson's *Representative Men* (1850).

38    Motivated by personal gain rather than by ethics.

39　　In Greek, *kosmos* means order and, in a secondary sense, beauty (as in the English word "cosmetic"). In his Journal, Emerson commented on the German author and sage J. W. von Goethe (1749–1832), whom he first read in 1828, "It were life enough to one man merely to lift his hands & say Kosmos! Beauty! Well, this he did" (J 5:133).

40　　Shaping, creating. The British Romantic poet and theorist Samuel Taylor Coleridge (1772–1834), a major influence on Emerson, described the imagination as an "esemplastic power" (esemplastic is Coleridge's neologism, used to describe a unifying creativity). Coleridge in "Dejection: An Ode" (1802) lamented the loss of "what nature gave me at birth, / my shaping spirit of imagination."

41　　Not used as a musical term here; Emerson refers to the composition (that is, arrangement) of objects in a painting.

42　　Emerson wrote in his later essay "Spiritual Laws," "We discover that our life is embosomed in beauty. . . . Even the corpse that has lain in the chambers has added a solemn ornament to the house." On March 29, 1832, Emerson remarked in his Journal, "I visited Ellen's tomb and opened the coffin" (J 4:7); his wife had been dead for a little more than a year. Emerson's biographer Robert Richardson notes that opening the coffin of one's beloved was not unheard of in his day; Emerson's act was curious and affectionate rather than gruesome.

43　　John Ruskin (1819–1900) in *The Stones of Venice* (1851–1853) discussed the natural forms that provide the basis for architectural ornament, from the lines of waves to the wings of birds. Ruskin acknowledged his debt to Emerson in *Time and Tide* (1867), writing, "Next to Carlyle, for my own immediate help and teaching, I nearly always look to Emerson."

## ARTICLE IV. CHAPTER III. Beauty

A nobler want of man is served by nature, namely, the love of Beauty.

　　The ancient Greeks called the world kosmos,[39] beauty. Such is the constitution of all things, or such the plastic[40] power of the human eye, that the primary forms, as the sky, the mountain, the tree, the animal, give us a delight *in and for themselves;* a pleasure arising from outline, color, motion, and grouping. This seems partly owing to the eye itself. The eye is the best of artists. By the mutual action of its structure and of the laws of light, perspective is produced, which integrates every mass of objects, of what character soever, into a well colored and shaded globe, so that where the particular objects are mean and unaffecting, the landscape which they compose, is round and symmetrical. And as the eye is the best composer,[41] so light is the first of painters. There is no object so foul that intense light will not make beautiful. And the stimulus it affords to the sense, and a sort of infinitude which it hath, like space and time, make all matter gay. Even the corpse hath its own beauty.[42] But beside this general grace diffused over nature, almost all the individual forms are agreeable to the eye, as is proved by our endless imitations of some of them, as the acorn, the grape, the pine-cone, the wheat-ear, the egg, the wings and forms of most birds, the lion's claw, the serpent, the butterfly, sea-shells, flames, clouds, buds, leaves, and the forms of many trees, as the palm.[43]

　　For better consideration, we may distribute the aspects of Beauty in a threefold manner.

　　1. First, the simple perception of natural forms is a delight. The influence of the forms and actions in nature, is so needful to man, that, in its lowest functions, it seems to lie on the confines of commodity and beauty. To the body and mind which have been cramped by noxious work or company, nature is medicinal and restores their tone. The tradesman, the attorney comes out of the din and craft of the street, and sees the sky and the woods, and is a man again. In their eternal calm, he finds himself. The health of the eye seems to demand a horizon.[44] We are never tired, so long as we can see far enough.[45]

　　But in other hours, Nature satisfies the soul purely by its loveliness, and without any mixture of corporeal benefit. I have seen the spectacle of morning from the hill-top over against my house, from day-break to sunrise, with emotions which an angel might share. The long slender bars of cloud float like fishes in the sea of crimson light. From the earth, as a shore, I look out into that silent sea. I seem to partake its rapid transformations: the active enchantment reaches my dust, and I dilate and conspire[46] with the morning wind. How does Nature deify us with a few and cheap elements! Give me health and a day, and I will make the pomp of emperors ridiculous. The dawn is my Assyria; the sun-set and moon-rise my Paphos, and unimaginable realms of faerie; broad noon shall be my England of the senses and the understanding; the night shall be my Germany of mystic philosophy and dreams.[47]

Not less excellent, except for our less susceptibility in the afternoon, was the charm, last evening, of a January sunset. The western clouds divided and subdivided themselves into pink flakes modulated with tints of unspeakable softness; and the air had so much life and sweetness, that it was a pain to come within doors. What was it that nature would say? Was there no meaning in the live repose of the valley behind the mill, and which Homer or Shakspeare could not re-form for me in words? The leafless trees become spires of flame in the sunset, with the blue east for their background, and the stars of the dead calices[48] of flowers, and every withered stem and stubble rimed with frost, contribute something to the mute music.

The inhabitants of cities suppose that the country landscape is pleasant only half the year. I please myself with observing the graces of the winter scenery, and believe that we are as much touched by it as by the genial influences of summer. To the attentive eye, each moment of the year has its own beauty, and in the same field, it beholds, every hour, a picture which was never seen before, and which shall never be seen again. The heavens change every moment, and reflect their glory or gloom on the plains beneath. The state of the crop in the surrounding farms alters the expression of the earth from week to week. The succession of native plants in the pastures and roadsides, which make the silent clock by which time tells the summer hours, will make even the divisions of the day sensible to a keen observer. The tribes of birds and insects, like the plants punctual to their time, follow each other, and the year has room for all. By water-courses, the variety is greater. In July, the blue pontederia or pickerel-weed[49] blooms in large beds in the shallow

44   Emerson begins his essay "Circles," "The eye is the first circle; the horizon which it forms is the second . . ."

45   Emerson ascribed this phrase to his brother Charles (J 5:45, 6:198).

46   Here and elsewhere in *Nature*, Emerson plays on the Latin etymology of "conspire," from Latin *con*, with, and *spirare*, to breathe. The American religious thinker Sampson Reed (1800–1880) remarked in his *Observations on the Growth of the Mind* (1826) that "the poet . . . makes bare his bosom for the reception of nature, and presents her breathing with his own life and soul."

47   In his Journal (January 15, 1835), Emerson wrote, "The Morning sky before sunrise is my Assyria; the sunset my Paphos & unimaginable realms of Faerie the night is my Germany" (J 5:13). (Paphos is the home island of the Greek goddess Aphrodite.) Emerson's association of Germany with "mystic philosophy" was cemented by his reading of Madame de Staël's *On Germany*. De Staël credits German thinkers with "a philosophy more comprehensive, which would embrace the universe in its *collective character*, and which would not despise the *nocturnal side of nature*."

48   Plural of calix, the cup of a flower.

49   A common aquatic plant, native to the Americas.

So fare ye well gay Powers & Princedoms! To you
the sheets were inscribed. Light thanks for your tutelary
smiles. Grim witches from Valhalla, & courteous
dames from Faery-land, whose protection was implored,
& whose dreams were invoked to furnish forth
the scroll. adieu to you all; —You have the
laughing poet's benison & malison, his wish
& his forgetfulness.    Abandoning your
allegiance he throws you to the winds, recklessly
defying your malice & fun.    Pinch the red nose;
lead him astray after will-o'the-wisp over wilderness
& fen; fright him with ghastly hobgoblins— wreak
your vengeance as you will — He gives you free
leave, on this sole condition, — if you can. —

Junio.

August 24.
1820.

Page from the seventeen-year-old Emerson's Journal.

parts of our pleasant river, and swarms with yellow butterflies in continual motion. Art cannot rival this pomp of purple and gold. Indeed the river is a perpetual gala, and boasts each month a new ornament.

But this beauty of Nature which is seen and felt as beauty, is the least part. The shows of day, the dewy morning, the rainbow, mountains, orchards in blossom, stars, moonlight, shadows in still water, and the like, if too eagerly hunted, become shows merely, and mock us with their unreality. Go out of the house to see the moon, and 't is mere tinsel; it will not please as when its light shines upon your necessary journey. The beauty that shimmers in the yellow afternoons of October, who ever could clutch it?[50] Go forth to find it, and it is gone: 't is only a mirage as you look from the windows of diligence.[51]

2. The presence of a higher, namely, of the spiritual element is essential to its perfection. The high and divine beauty which can be loved without effeminacy, is that which is found in combination with the human will, and never separate. Beauty is the mark God sets upon virtue. Every natural action is graceful. Every heroic act is also decent,[52] and causes the place and the bystanders to shine. We are taught by great actions that the universe is the property of every individual in it. Every rational creature has all nature for his dowry and estate. It is his, if he will. He may divest himself of it; he may creep into a corner, and abdicate his kingdom, as most men do, but he is entitled to the world by his constitution. In proportion to the energy of his thought and will, he takes up the world into himself. "All those things for which men plough, build, or sail, obey virtue;" said an ancient historian. "The winds and waves," said Gibbon, "are always on the side of the ablest navigators."[53] So are the sun and moon and all the stars of heaven. When a noble act is done,—perchance in a scene of great natural beauty; when Leonidas and his three hundred martyrs consume one day in dying, and the sun and moon come each and look at them once in the steep defile of Thermopylæ;[54] when Arnold Winkelried, in the high Alps, under the shadow of the avalanche, gathers in his side a sheaf of Austrian spears to break the line for his comrades;[55] are not these heroes entitled to add the beauty of the scene to the beauty of the deed? When the bark of Columbus nears the shore of America;—before it, the beach lined with savages, fleeing out of all their huts of cane; the sea behind; and the purple mountains of the Indian Archi-

50    In October 1835 Emerson commented in his Journal, "What a Tantalus cup this life is! The beauty that shimmers on these yellow afternoons who ever could clutch it?" (J 5:96–97).

51    The word has its current meaning, but a secondary one hovers: in Emerson's day, a diligence is a stagecoach (note "necessary journey" and "windows").

52    Handsome, becoming.

53    The ancient historian is the acerbic, insightful Roman writer Sallust (86–34 BCE); Emerson probably remembered the Sallust quotation from *An Apology for Smectymnuus* (1642) by John Milton. Edward Gibbon (1737–1794) wrote *The Decline and Fall of the Roman Empire* (1776–1788).

54    Leonidas was the Spartan hero who led three hundred men against the vastly larger Persian forces at the "defile" (narrow pass) of Thermopylae in 480 BCE.

55    Arnold Winkelried fought with his fellow Swiss against the Habsburgs at the Battle of Sempach in 1386. According to legend, he breached the Austrian lines by throwing his body against the enemy's pikes. Wordsworth's poem "The Church of San Salvador" (1820) culminates with a depiction of Winkelried "gathering with a wide embrace, / Into his single breast, a sheaf / Of fatal Austrian spears."

56    In his Journal (1840) Emerson announced, "A man is a compendium of nature an
indomitable savage. Take the smoothest curled
courtier in London or Paris . . . he has a physique which . . . is directly related there amid essences & billets doux to Himmaleh mountain
chains, wild cedar swamps, & the interior fires,
the molten core of the globe" (J 7:540).

57    Sir Henry Vane (1613–1662) was an English Puritan politician who briefly governed
Massachusetts in the 1630s. After returning
from America, he served in the Parliament of
the Lord Protector Oliver Cromwell (1599–
1658). Led to the scaffold during the Restoration, he "died justifying himself and the cause
he had stood for" (so Samuel Pepys reported).

58    The Whig politician William Russell
(1639–1683) was tried and executed for the Rye
House Plot, an alleged plan to assassinate King
Charles II (1630–1685).

59    Homer, author of the *Iliad* and the *Odyssey*, probably lived in the ninth century BCE; the
philosopher Socrates (469–399 BCE) was condemned to death by an Athenian jury in 399
BCE. Pindar (ca. 520–ca. 438 BCE), the Greek
poet, wrote sublime odes that praised the victors in athletic contests. Phocion, an Athenian
general and statesman, governed the city between 322 and 318 BCE. Emerson, who had a
high regard for Phocion's independence and
courage, was influenced by the account of him
in *Parallel Lives* by Plutarch (ca. 46–ca. 122).
See Emerson's Sermon CXVII (May 29, 1831),
in which he refers to "the virtuous Phocion of
Athens": "when on one occasion the crowd
applauded him in the midst of his speech; he
stopped and inquired, 'What have I said
*(continued)*

pelago around, can we separate the man from the living picture?[56] Does not
the New World clothe his form with her palm-groves and savannahs as fit
drapery? Ever does natural beauty steal in like air, and envelope great actions. When Sir Harry Vane[57] was dragged up the Tower-hill, sitting on a
sled, to suffer death, as the champion of the English laws, one of the multitude cried out to him, "You never sate on so glorious a seat." Charles II., to
intimidate the citizens of London, caused the patriot Lord Russell[58] to be
drawn in an open coach, through the principal streets of the city, on his way
to the scaffold. "But," to use the simple narrative of his biographer, "the
multitude imagined they saw liberty and virtue sitting by his side." In private
places, among sordid objects, an act of truth or heroism seems at once to
draw to itself the sky as its temple, the sun as its candle. Nature stretcheth
out her arms to embrace man, only let his thoughts be of equal greatness.
Willingly does she follow his steps with the rose and the violet, and bend her
lines of grandeur and grace to the decoration of her darling child. Only let
his thoughts be of equal scope, and the frame will suit the picture. A virtuous
man is in unison with her works, and makes the central figure of the visible
sphere. Homer, Pindar, Socrates, Phocion,[59] associate themselves fitly in our
memory with the whole geography and climate of Greece. The visible heavens and earth sympathize with Jesus. And in common life, whosoever has
seen a person of powerful character and happy genius, will have remarked
how easily he took all things along with him,—the persons, the opinions,
and the day, and nature became ancillary[60] to a man.

3. There is still another aspect under which the beauty of the world
may be viewed, namely, as it becomes an object of the intellect. Beside the
relation of things to virtue, they have a relation to thought. The intellect
searches out the absolute order of things as they stand in the mind of God,
and without the colors of affection. The intellectual and the active powers
seem to succeed each other in man, and the exclusive activity of the one,
generates the exclusive activity of the other. There is something unfriendly
in each to the other, but they are like the alternate periods of feeding and
working in animals; each prepares and certainly will be followed by the other.
Therefore does beauty, which, in relation to actions, as we have seen, comes
unsought, and comes because it is unsought, remain for the apprehension

and pursuit of the intellect; and then again, in its turn, of the active power. Nothing divine dies. All good is eternally reproductive.[61] The beauty of nature reforms itself in the mind, and not for barren contemplation, but for new creation.

All men are in some degree impressed by the face of the world; some men even to delight. This love of beauty is Taste. Others have the same love in such excess, that, not content with admiring, they seek to embody it in new forms. The creation of beauty is Art.

The production of a work of art throws a light upon the mystery of humanity. A work of art is an abstract or epitome of the world. It is the result or expression of nature, in miniature. For although the works of nature are innumerable and all different, the result or the expression of them all is similar and single. Nature is a sea of forms radically alike and even unique. A leaf, a sun-beam, a landscape, the ocean, make an analogous impression on the mind. What is common to them all,—that perfectness and harmony, is beauty.[62] Therefore the standard of beauty is the entire circuit of natural forms,—the totality of nature; which the Italians expressed by defining beauty "il piu nell' uno."[63] Nothing is quite beautiful alone: nothing but is beautiful in the whole. A single object is only so far beautiful as it suggests this universal grace. The poet, the painter, the sculptor, the musician, the architect, seek each to concentrate this radiance of the world on one point, and each in his several work to satisfy the love of beauty which stimulates him to produce. Thus is Art, a nature passed through the alembic[64] of man. Thus in art, does nature work through the will of a man filled with the beauty of her first works.

The world thus exists to the soul to satisfy the desire of beauty. Extend this element to the uttermost, and I call it an ultimate end. No reason can be asked or given why the soul seeks beauty. Beauty, in its largest and profoundest sense, is one expression for the universe. God is the all-fair. Truth, and goodness, and beauty, are but different faces of the same All. But beauty in nature is not ultimate. It is the herald of inward and eternal beauty, and is not alone a solid and satisfactory good. It must therefore stand as a part and not as yet the last or highest expression of the final cause of Nature.

wrong?'" (S 3:172). In his Journal he commented, "The mob ought to be treated only with contempt. Phocion even Jesus cannot otherwise regard it in so far as it is mob" (October 1835; J 5:101).

60    Accessory (from Latin *ancilla*, handmaid).

61    From the rhapsodic speech given by Plato's character Diotima in the *Symposium:* beauty gives birth to itself, and to more beauty in its admirers.

62    "A leaf is a compend of Nature, and Nature a colossal leaf," Emerson wrote in his Journal (5:137).

63    Emerson took this Italian phrase, meaning "many (or much) in one," from Coleridge's *Table Talk* (1836). Coleridge remarked that "the old definition of beauty in the Roman school of painting was, *il piu nell' uno*—multitude in unity . . ." In his Journal Emerson wrote of the scholar's "power to stand *beside* his thoughts, or, to hold off his thoughts at arm's length & give them perspective; to form piu nell' uno" (January 22, 1836; J 5:116).

64    A device used for distilling by both chemists and alchemists.

65    Emerson follows the insistence of the Swedish mystical writer Emanuel Swedenborg (1688–1772) that nature is a language with an abundant spiritual sense. Reed in his Swedenborgian *Observations on the Growth of the Mind*, an influential book for the young Emerson, argued that "there is a language not of words, but of things. . . . everything which is, whether animal or vegetable, is full of the expression of that use for which it is designed, as of its own existence."

66    Ruskin in his *Sesame and Lilies* (1865) also considers how etymology influences meaning; his examples are similar to Emerson's.

67    An emblem is an explanatory image, accompanied (in Renaissance emblem books) by a motto. In a Journal entry of August 1, 1835, Emerson wrote, "The Imagination is Vision, regards the world as symbolical & pierces the emblem for the real sense, sees all external objects as types" (J 5:76; for *type* see note 69, below). Guillaume Oegger's *True Messiah* comments, "Every mortal must voluntarily or involuntarily continually furnish in his life & death emblems capable of characterizing the depth of his being" (transcribed by Emerson in his Journal, July 1835, J 5:69). Emerson's later version of this thought, in the essay "Self-Reliance," is "character teaches above our wills."

68    In *Aids to Reflection* (1825), one of Emerson's favorite books, Coleridge wrote, "Is anger an inconsiderable beast, when it barks in your heart? What is deceit, when it lies hid in a cunning mind; is it not a fox? Is not the man who is furiously bent upon calumny, a scorpion?" Emerson noted in Sermon CLV (May 13, 1832), "all the beasts appear to be expressions of particular qualities, good or bad, which are attributes of man" (S 4:144).

ARTICLE V. CHAPTER IV. Language

A third use which Nature subserves to man is that of Language. Nature is the vehicle of thought, and in a simple, double, and threefold degree.

1. Words are signs of natural facts.

2. Particular natural facts are symbols of particular spiritual facts.

3. Nature is the symbol of spirit.[65]

1. Words are signs of natural facts. The use of natural history is to give us aid in supernatural history. The use of the outer creation is to give us language for the beings and changes of the inward creation. Every word which is used to express a moral or intellectual fact, if traced to its root, is found to be borrowed from some material appearance. *Right* originally means *straight*; *wrong* means *twisted*. *Spirit* primarily means *wind*; *transgression*, the crossing of a *line*; *supercilious*, the *raising of the eye-brow*.[66] We say the *heart* to express emotion, the *head* to denote thought; and *thought* and *emotion* are, in their turn, words borrowed from sensible things, and now appropriated to spiritual nature. Most of the process by which this transformation is made, is hidden from us in the remote time when language was framed; but the same tendency may be daily observed in children. Children and savages use only nouns or names of things, which they continually convert into verbs, and apply to analogous mental acts.

2. But this origin of all words that convey a spiritual import,—so conspicuous a fact in the history of language,—is our least debt to nature. It is not words only that are emblematic;[67] it is things which are emblematic. Every natural fact is a symbol of some spiritual fact. Every appearance in nature corresponds to some state of the mind, and that state of the mind can only be described by presenting that natural appearance as its picture. An enraged man is a lion, a cunning man is a fox, a firm man is a rock, a learned man is a torch.[68] A lamb is innocence; a snake is subtle spite; flowers express to us the delicate affections. Light and darkness are our familiar expression for knowledge and ignorance; and heat for love. Visible distance behind and before us, is respectively our image of memory and hope.

Emerson's study. "My own habits are much mended this summer. I rise at 6 o'clock, find my coffee in my study, & do not see the family until 12 or 1 o'clock," Emerson wrote in a letter to Margaret Fuller on June 7, 1839.

Who looks upon a river in a meditative hour, and is not reminded of the flux of all things? Throw a stone into the stream, and the circles that propagate themselves are the beautiful type of all influence.[69] Man is conscious of a universal soul within or behind his individual life, wherein, as in a firmament, the natures of Justice, Truth, Love, Freedom, arise and shine. This universal soul, he calls Reason:[70] it is not mine or thine or his, but we are its; we are its property and men. And the blue sky in which the private earth is buried, the sky with its eternal calm, and full of everlasting orbs, is

69  A type is a figure for, or premonitory image of, something more significant. In Christian theology, events and characters in the Old Testament were considered types; the Gospels provided the antitype, or fulfillment. So Christ (for example) completes, and supersedes, the liberating mission of Moses. Emerson remarked in his Sermon CLI (April 8, 1832) that "the outward world and all that it contains, was designed in God's plan only as a shadow or type of the world within" (S 4:120).

70  Emerson's term "Reason," denoting our higher intuition, is often opposed in his work to the "Understanding," which works from the evidence of the senses and draws limited conclusions. He was influenced in this usage by Coleridge, for whom truth (arrived at by Reason) cannot be approached by the Understanding. (The 1831 American edition of Coleridge's *Aids to Reflection*, persuasively introduced by James Marsh [1794–1842], first clarified this distinction for Emerson and his contemporaries.) The Understanding tends to translate spiritual questions into terms of physical demonstration and historical proof. Emerson wrote in his Journal in 1835 that the Understanding "works in time & space, & therefore successively. It divides, compares, reasons, invents. It lives from the Reason, yet disobeys it. . . . The Ideas of the Reason assume a new appearance as they descend into the Understanding. Invested with space & time they walk in masquerade. . . . Thus the gods of the ancient Greeks are all Ideas (as Cupid, Apollo, the Muse, &c or Love, Poesy, Wisdom, &c) but make an awkward appearance joined with the appetites of beasts. . . ." (J 5:272–273).

*(continued)*

In his Journal entry for June 22, 1836, Emerson commented, "Now all man's power over nature is by the understanding; as by manure, steam, the economic use of the wind & water & needle. . . . But Animal Magnetism, the Miracles of enthusiasts as Hohenlohe & the Shakers & the Swedenborgian, prayer, eloquence, self-healing . . . the achievements of a principle as in Revolutions & in the abolition of Slave Trade—& the wisdom (often observed) of children—these are the examples of the Reason's momentary grasp of the scepter" (J 5:180).

71    On March 27, 1836, Emerson wrote in his Journal, "Man is an analogist. He cannot help seeing every thing under its relations to all other things & to himself. The most conspicuous example of this habit of his mind is his naming the Deity father" (J 5:146).

72    George Louis Leclerc, Comte de Buffon (1707–1788) was a French naturalist; the Swede Carl Linnaeus (1707–1778) invented taxonomy, the scientific classification of plants and animals. A flora is a guide to plants.

73    I Corinthians 15:44.

the type of Reason. That which, intellectually considered, we call Reason, considered in relation to nature, we call Spirit. Spirit is the Creator. Spirit hath life in itself. And man in all ages and countries, embodies it in his language, as the FATHER.[71]

It is easily seen that there is nothing lucky or capricious in these analogies, but that they are constant, and pervade nature. These are not the dreams of a few poets, here and there, but man is an analogist, and studies relations in all objects. He is placed in the centre of beings, and a ray of relation passes from every other being to him. And neither can man be understood without these objects, nor these objects without man. All the facts in natural history taken by themselves, have no value, but are barren like a single sex. But marry it to human history, and it is full of life. Whole Floras, all Linnæus' and Buffon's[72] volumes, are but dry catalogues of facts; but the most trivial of these facts, the habit of a plant, the organs, or work, or noise of an insect, applied to the illustration of a fact in intellectual philosophy, or, in any way associated to human nature, affects us in the most lively and agreeable manner. The seed of a plant,—to what affecting analogies in the nature of man, is that little fruit made use of, in all discourse, up to the voice of Paul, who calls the human corpse a seed,—"It is sown a natural body; it is raised a spiritual body."[73] The motion of the earth round its axis, and round the sun, makes the day, and the year. These are certain amounts of brute light and heat. But is there no intent of an analogy between man's life and the seasons? And do the seasons gain no grandeur or pathos from that analogy? The instincts of the ant are very unimportant considered as the ant's; but the moment a ray of relation is seen to extend from it to man, and the little drudge is seen to be a monitor, a little body with a mighty heart, then all its habits, even that said to be recently observed, that it never sleeps, become sublime.

Because of this radical correspondence between visible things and human thoughts, savages, who have only what is necessary, converse in figures. As we go back in history, language becomes more picturesque, until its infancy, when it is all poetry; or, all spiritual facts are represented by natural symbols. The same symbols are found to make the original elements of all languages. It has moreover been observed, that the idioms of all languages approach each other in passages of the greatest eloquence and power. And as this is the first language, so is it the last. This immediate dependence of language upon nature, this conversion of an outward phenomenon into a type of somewhat in human life, never loses its power to affect us. It is this which gives that piquancy to the conversation of a strong-natured farmer or backwoodsman, which all men relish.

Thus is nature an interpreter, by whose means man converses with his fellow men. A man's power to connect his thought with its proper symbol, and so to utter it, depends on the simplicity of his character, that is, upon his love of truth and his desire to communicate it without loss. The corruption of man is followed by the corruption of language. When simplicity of character and the sovereignty of ideas is broken up by the prevalence of secondary desires, the desire of riches, the desire of pleasure, the desire of power, the desire of praise,—and duplicity and falsehood take place of simplicity and truth, the power over nature as an interpreter of the will, is in a degree lost; new imagery ceases to be created, and old words are perverted to stand for things which are not; a paper currency is employed when there is no bullion in the vaults. In due time, the fraud is manifest, and words lose all power to stimulate the understanding or the affections. Hundreds of writers may be found in every long-civilized nation, who for a short time believe, and make others believe, that they see and utter truths, who do not of themselves clothe one thought in its natural garment, but who feed unconsciously upon the language created by the primary writers of the country, those, namely, who hold primarily on nature.

But wise men pierce this rotten diction and fasten words again to visible things; so that picturesque language is at once a commanding certificate that he who employs it, is a man in alliance with truth and God. The moment our discourse rises above the ground line of familiar facts, and is inflamed with passion or exalted by thought, it clothes itself in images. A man conversing in earnest, if he watch his intellectual processes, will find that always a material image, more or less luminous, arises in his mind, cotemporaneous with every thought, which furnishes the vestment of the thought. Hence, good writing and brilliant discourse are perpetual allegories. This imagery is spontaneous. It is the blending of experience with the present action of the mind. It is proper creation. It is the working of the Original Cause through the instruments he has already made.

74    For Wordsworth in his Preface to *Lyrical Ballads* (1800), rural life was a more favorable object for poetry than urban existence, with its hectic superficiality.

75    Turmoil.

76    Brilliance, splendor.

77    Echoing Wordsworth's *Immortality Ode* (1807), one of Emerson's favorite poems. In Sermon LXXII (April 25, 1830), Emerson expounded the "simplicity which belongs to infancy" (S 2:173).

78    Trifling, trivial. In his essay "Worship," Emerson writes of "peppercorn aims."

79    The sentence is from Swedenborg. Emerson wrote in an 1845 Journal entry, "Lord Bacon & Swedenborg & Plato have this superb speculation as from a tower over nature without ever losing the sequence of things" (J 9:187). The next year, 1846, he wrote in a contrasting vein, "Swedenborg, how strange, that he should have persuaded men & drawn a church after him this enchanter with his mob of dreams! . . . the combination of verity & of moonshine, dreams in the costume of science" (J 9:362).

80    Emerson varies the statement of de Staël in *On Germany*, "Almost all the axioms of physics correspond with the maxims of morals."

81    The philosopher Plotinus (205–270), quoted by Coleridge in his *Biographia Literaria* (1817).

82    *Macbeth* 3.4.110–112.

83    The Brahmins, the elite Hindu caste, included priests, lawmakers, and scholars. Pythagoras (ca. 575–ca. 495 BCE) was a legendary Greek philosopher; Francis Bacon (1561–1626),
*(continued)*

These facts may suggest the advantage which the country-life possesses for a powerful mind, over the artificial and curtailed life of cities.[74] We know more from nature than we can at will communicate. Its light flows into the mind evermore, and we forget its presence. The poet, the orator, bred in the woods, whose senses have been nourished by their fair and appeasing changes, year after year, without design and without heed,—shall not lose their lesson altogether, in the roar of cities or the broil[75] of politics. Long hereafter, amidst agitation and terror in national councils,—in the hour of revolution,—these solemn images shall reappear in their morning lustre,[76] as fit symbols and words of the thoughts which the passing events shall awaken. At the call of a noble sentiment, again the woods wave, the pines murmur, the river rolls and shines, and the cattle low upon the mountains, as he saw and heard them in his infancy.[77] And with these forms, the spells of persuasion, the keys of power are put into his hands.

3. We are thus assisted by natural objects in the expression of particular meanings. But how great a language to convey such pepper-corn[78] informations! Did it need such noble races of creatures, this profusion of forms, this host of orbs in heaven, to furnish man with the dictionary and grammar of his municipal speech? Whilst we use this grand cipher to expedite the affairs of our pot and kettle, we feel that we have not yet put it to its use, neither are able. We are like travellers using the cinders of a volcano to roast their eggs. Whilst we see that it always stands ready to clothe what we would say, we cannot avoid the question, whether the characters are not significant of themselves. Have mountains, and waves, and skies, no significance but what we consciously give them, when we employ them as emblems of our thoughts? The world is emblematic. Parts of speech are metaphors because the whole of nature is a metaphor of the human mind. The laws of moral nature answer to those of matter as face to face in a glass. "The visible world and the relation of its parts, is the dial plate of the invisible."[79] The axioms of physics translate the laws of ethics.[80] Thus, "the whole is greater than its part;" "reaction is equal to action;" "the smallest weight may be made to lift the greatest, the difference of weight being compensated by time;" and many the like propositions, which have an ethical as well as physical sense. These propositions have a much more extensive and universal sense when applied to human life, than when confined to technical use.

In like manner, the memorable words of history, and the proverbs of nations, consist usually of a natural fact, selected as a picture or parable of a moral truth. Thus; A rolling stone gathers no moss; A bird in the hand is worth two in the bush; A cripple in the right way, will beat a racer in the wrong; Make hay whilst the sun shines; 'T is hard to carry a full cup even; Vinegar is the son of wine; The last ounce broke the camel's back; Long-lived trees make roots first;—and the like. In their primary sense these are trivial facts, but we repeat them for the value of their analogical import. What is true of proverbs, is true of all fables, parables, and allegories.

This relation between the mind and matter is not fancied by some poet, but stands in the will of God, and so is free to be known by all men. It appears to men, or it does not appear.[81] When in fortunate hours we ponder this miracle, the wise man doubts, if, at all other times, he is not blind and deaf;

> _____ "Can these things be,
> And overcome us like a summer's cloud,
> Without our special wonder?"[82]

for the universe becomes transparent, and the light of higher laws than its own, shines through it. It is the standing problem which has exercised the wonder and the study of every fine genius since the world began; from the era of the Egyptians and the Brahmins, to that of Pythagoras, of Plato, of Bacon, of Leibnitz,[83] of Swedenborg. There sits the Sphinx[84] at the roadside, and from age to age, as each prophet comes by, he tries his fortune at reading her riddle. There seems to be a necessity in spirit to manifest itself in material forms; and day and night, river and storm, beast and bird, acid and alkali, preëxist in necessary Ideas in the mind of God, and are what they are by virtue of preceding affections, in the world of spirit. A Fact is the end or last issue of spirit. The visible creation is the terminus or the circumference of the invisible world. "Material objects," said a French philosopher,[85] "are necessarily kinds of *scoriae*[86] of the substantial thoughts of the Creator, which must always preserve an exact relation to their first origin; in other words, visible nature must have a spiritual and moral side."

English scientist and essayist; and G. W. von Leibniz (1646–1716), German philosopher. De Staël in *On Germany* judged that Leibniz "pushed his abstractions too far." Swedenborg's mystical speculations created great excitement among Emerson's contemporaries; Emerson devotes an essay to him in *Representative Men*.

84   Legendary monster in Greek (and, earlier, Egyptian) myth. In her Greek version she had wings and the head of a lion and would devour any traveler who could not answer her riddles. She was finally defeated by Oedipus. De Staël in *On Germany* writes, "The aenigma of ourselves swallows up, like the sphinx, thousands of systems which pretend to the glory of having guessed its meaning." Bacon in his "Critique upon the Mythology of the Ancients" sees the Sphinx as representative of science itself. According to Bacon she bears two kinds of riddles: one concerning the nature of man, the other concerning the nature of things.

85   Guillaume Oegger; Emerson quotes again from Oegger's *True Messiah*.

86   Scoriae are ashen or cinder-like traces, the results of industrial smelting or volcanic fire. In July 1835 Emerson transcribed in his journal the passages from Guillaume Oegger that he quotes here (J 5:66). He wrote in his Journal, referring to Oegger and similar mystics, "The ethical doctrines of these theosophists are true & exalting, but straightway they run upon their Divine Transformation the Death of God &c. & become horn mad" (J 5:61).

87    Quoted from George Fox (1624–1691), founder of the Society of Friends (Quakers). Emerson called Fox "a consistent reformer" (J 4:32).

88    Emerson suggests that nature is a holy scripture; to study it properly is to experience revelation. In his essay on Swedenborg, Emerson quotes Swedenborg's statement that the "physical world" is "purely symbolic of the spiritual world": every natural fact corresponds to a spiritual one.

89    From Coleridge's *Aids to Reflection*.

90    Perceptible.

This doctrine is abstruse, and though the images of "garment," "scoriæ," "mirror," &c., may stimulate the fancy, we must summon the aid of subtler and more vital expositors to make it plain. "Every scripture is to be interpreted by the same spirit which gave it forth,"[87]—is the fundamental law of criticism. A life in harmony with nature, the love of truth and of virtue, will purge the eyes to understand her text. By degrees we may come to know the primitive sense of the permanent objects of nature, so that the world shall be to us an open book, and every form significant of its hidden life and final cause.[88]

A new interest surprises us, whilst, under the view now suggested, we contemplate the fearful extent and multitude of objects; since "every object rightly seen, unlocks a new faculty of the soul."[89] That which was unconscious truth, becomes, when interpreted and defined in an object, a part of the domain of knowledge,—a new weapon in the magazine of power.

ARTICLE VI. CHAPTER V. Discipline

In view of this significance of nature, we arrive at once at a new fact, that nature is a discipline. This use of the world includes the preceding uses, as parts of itself.

Space, time, society, labor, climate, food, locomotion, the animals, the mechanical forces, give us sincerest lessons, day by day, whose meaning is unlimited. They educate both the Understanding and the Reason. Every property of matter is a school for the understanding,—its solidity or resistance, its inertia, its extension, its figure, its divisibility. The understanding adds, divides, combines, measures, and finds everlasting nutriment and room for its activity in this worthy scene. Meantime, Reason transfers all these lessons into its own world of thought, by perceiving the analogy that marries Matter and Mind.

1. Nature is a discipline of the understanding in intellectual truths. Our dealing with sensible[90] objects is a constant exercise in the necessary lessons of difference, of likeness, of order, of being and seeming, of progressive arrangement; of ascent from particular to general; of combination to one end of manifold forces. Proportioned to the importance of the organ to be

formed, is the extreme care with which its tuition is provided,—a care pretermitted in no single case. What tedious training, day after day, year after year, never ending, to form the common sense; what continual reproduction of annoyances, inconveniences, dilemmas; what rejoicing over us of little men; what disputing of prices, what reckonings of interest,—and all to form the Hand of the mind;—to instruct us that "good thoughts are no better than good dreams, unless they be executed!"[91]

The same good office is performed by Property and its filial systems of debt and credit. Debt, grinding debt, whose iron face the widow, the orphan, and the sons of genius fear and hate;—debt, which consumes so much time, which so cripples and disheartens a great spirit with cares that seem so base, is a preceptor[92] whose lessons cannot be foregone, and is needed most by those who suffer from it most. Moreover, property, which has been well compared to snow,—"if it fall level to-day, it will be blown into drifts to-morrow,"—is merely the surface action of internal machinery, like the index on the face of a clock. Whilst now it is the gymnastics of the understanding, it is hiving[93] in the foresight of the spirit, experience in profounder laws.

The whole character and fortune of the individual are affected by the least inequalities in the culture of the understanding; for example, in the perception of differences. Therefore is Space, and therefore Time, that man may know that things are not huddled and lumped, but sundered and individual. A bell and a plough have each their use, and neither can do the office of the other. Water is good to drink, coal to burn, wool to wear; but wool cannot be drunk, nor water spun, nor coal eaten. The wise man shows his wisdom in separation, in gradation, and his scale of creatures and of merits, is as wide as nature. The foolish have no range in their scale, but suppose every man is as every other man. What is not good they call the worst, and what is not hateful, they call the best.

In like manner, what good heed, nature forms in us! She pardons no mistakes. Her yea is yea, and her nay, nay.[94]

The first steps in Agriculture, Astronomy, Zoölogy, (those first steps which the farmer, the hunter, and the sailor take,) teach that nature's dice are always loaded;[95] that in her heaps and rubbish are concealed sure and useful results.

91    Francis Bacon wrote in his essay "Of Great Place" (1625), "For good thoughts (though God accept them) yet, towards men, are little better than good dreams, except they be put in act . . ."

92    Teacher, tutor.

93    Accumulating, as bees store honey in a hive: "hiving wisdom with each studious year" (George Gordon, Lord Byron [1788–1824], *Childe Harold* [1812–1818], 3:107).

94    From Jesus' Sermon on the Mount (Matthew 5:37): "Let your communication be yea, yea, nay, nay." Alluding to a similar passage, James 5:12, Emerson said of children in his Sermon LXXII (April 25, 1830), "Their yea is yea, their nay is nay. They speak the truth" (S 2:172). In his Journal (May 6, 1838) Emerson wrote, "Wherever a man comes, there comes revolution. The old is for slaves. When a man comes, all books are legible, all things transparent, all religions are forms. . . . All men bless & curse. He saith yea & nay only" (J 5:492).

95    Emerson wrote in his Journal on February 24, 1836: "For the education of the Understanding the earth & worlds serve. It takes the first steps by geology, astronomy, zoology, to learn that natures dice are always loaded; that in the most promiscuous heaps & rubbish, an informed eye can find harmonious, inevitable, & beneficial results . . ." (J 5:124). Emerson's essay "Compensation" cites a line from a fragmentary play by Sophocles, *aei gar eu piptousin hoi dios kuboi* (the god's dice always fall well), and adds, "The dice of God are always loaded." Emerson also alludes to Sophocles' words in another essay, "Worship."

96    Ascribed to Bishop Joseph Butler (1692–1752).

97    Phrase spoken by Jesus in the Lord's Prayer and later during the Agony in the Garden (Matthew 6:10, 26:42).

98    Jesus entered Jerusalem on an ass (John 12:14).

99    Legendary Greek hero known for his strength and courage.

100   In his essay "Prudence," Emerson wrote, "The world of manners and actions is wrought of one stuff, and begin where we will, we are pretty sure in a short space, to be mumbling our ten commandments." De Staël, summarizing Kant in *On Germany*, wrote that "the feeling of right and wrong is, according to his ideas, the primitive law of the heart, as space and time are of the understanding."

How calmly and genially the mind apprehends one after another the laws of physics! What noble emotions dilate the mortal as he enters into the counsels of the creation, and feels by knowledge the privilege to Be! His insight refines him. The beauty of nature shines in his own breast. Man is greater that he can see this, and the universe less, because Time and Space relations vanish as laws are known.

Here again we are impressed and even daunted by the immense Universe to be explored. 'What we know, is a point to what we do not know.'[96] Open any recent journal of science, and weigh the problems suggested concerning Light, Heat, Electricity, Magnetism, Physiology, Geology, and judge whether the interest of natural science is likely to be soon exhausted.

Passing by many particulars of the discipline of nature we must not omit to specify two.

The exercise of the Will or the lesson of power is taught in every event. From the child's successive possession of his several senses up to the hour when he saith, "thy will be done!"[97] he is learning the secret, that he can reduce under his will, not only particular events, but great classes, nay the whole series of events, and so conform all facts to his character. Nature is thoroughly mediate. It is made to serve. It receives the dominion of man as meekly as the ass on which the Saviour rode.[98] It offers all its kingdoms to man as the raw material which he may mould into what is useful. Man is never weary of working it up. He forges the subtile and delicate air into wise and melodious words, and gives them wing as angels of persuasion and command. More and more, with every thought, does his kingdom stretch over things, until the world becomes, at last, only a realized will,—the double of the man.

2. Sensible objects conform to the premonitions of Reason and reflect the conscience. All things are moral; and in their boundless changes have an unceasing reference to spiritual nature. Therefore is nature glorious with form, color, and motion, that every globe in the remotest heaven; every chemical change from the rudest crystal up to the laws of life; every change of vegetation from the first principle of growth in the eye of a leaf, to the tropical forest and antediluvian coal-mine; every animal function from the sponge up to Hercules,[99] shall hint or thunder to man the laws of right and wrong, and echo the Ten Commandments.[100] Therefore is nature ever

the ally of Religion: lends all her pomp and riches to the religious sentiment. Prophet and priest, David, Isaiah,[101] Jesus, have drawn deeply from
this source.

This ethical character so penetrates the bone and marrow of nature, as
to seem the end for which it was made. Whatever private purpose is answered by any member or part, this is its public and universal function, and
is never omitted. Nothing in nature is exhausted in its first use. When a thing
has served an end to the uttermost, it is wholly new for an ulterior service. In
God, every end is converted into a new means. Thus the use of Commodity,
regarded by itself, is mean and squalid. But it is to the mind an education in
the great doctrine of Use, namely, that a thing is good only so far as it serves;
that a conspiring of parts and efforts to the production of an end, is essential
to any being. The first and gross manifestation of this truth, is our inevitable
and hated training in values and wants, in corn and meat.

It has already been illustrated, in treating of the significance of material
things, that every natural process is but a version of a moral sentence. The
moral law lies at the centre of nature and radiates to the circumference. It is
the pith and marrow of every substance, every relation, and every process.
All things with which we deal, preach to us. What is a farm but a mute gospel? The chaff and the wheat, weeds and plants, blight, rain, insects, sun,—it
is a sacred emblem from the first furrow of spring to the last stack which the
snow of winter overtakes in the fields. But the sailor, the shepherd, the miner,
the merchant, in their several resorts, have each an experience precisely parallel and leading to the same conclusion: because all organizations are radically alike. Nor can it be doubted that this moral sentiment which thus scents
the air, and grows in the grain, and impregnates the waters of the world, is
caught by man and sinks into his soul. The moral influence of nature upon
every individual is that amount of truth which it illustrates to him. Who can
estimate this? Who can guess how much firmness the sea-beaten rock has
taught the fisherman? how much tranquillity has been reflected to man from
the azure sky, over whose unspotted deeps the winds forevermore drive
flocks of stormy clouds,[102] and leave no wrinkle or stain? how much industry
and providence and affection we have caught from the pantomime of brutes?
What a searching preacher of self-command is the varying phenomenon
of Health!

101  David (11th–10th century BCE), king of
Judah and Israel, traditionally credited with authorship of the book of Psalms; Isaiah (8th century BCE), Hebrew prophet.

102  Emerson recalls the "Ode to the West
Wind" (1820) by the English Romantic poet
Percy Bysshe Shelley (1792–1822), with its
tranquil yet ominous atmosphere; Shelley pictures the wind "driving sweet buds like flocks to
feed in air."

Lidian Emerson with
son Edward.

Herein is especially apprehended the Unity of Nature,—the Unity in Variety,—which meets us everywhere. All the endless variety of things make a unique, an identical impression. Xenophanes[103] complained in his old age, that, look where he would, all things hastened back to Unity. He was weary of seeing the same entity in the tedious variety of forms. The fable of Proteus[104] has a cordial truth. Every particular in nature, a leaf, a drop, a crystal, a moment of time is related to the whole, and partakes of the perfection of the whole. Each particle is a microcosm, and faithfully renders the likeness of the world.

Not only resemblances exist in things whose analogy is obvious, as when we detect the type of the human hand in the flipper of the fossil saurus,[105] but also in objects wherein there is great superficial unlikeness.[106] Thus architecture is called "frozen music,"[107] by De Stael and Goethe. Vitruvius thought an architect should be a musician. "A Gothic church," said Coleridge, "is a petrified religion." Michael Angelo[108] maintained, that, to an architect, a knowledge of anatomy is essential. In Haydn's[109] oratorios, the notes present to the imagination not only motions, as, of the snake, the stag, and the elephant, but colors also; as the green grass. The law of harmonic sounds reappears in the harmonic colors. The granite is differenced in its laws only by the more or less of heat, from the river that wears it away. The river, as it flows, resembles the air that flows over it; the air resembles the light which traverses it with more subtile currents; the light resembles the heat which rides with it through Space. Each creature is only a modification of the other; the likeness in them is more than the difference, and their radical law is one and the same. Hence it is, that a rule of one art, or a law of one organization, holds true throughout nature. So intimate is this Unity, that, it is easily seen, it lies under the undermost garment of nature, and betrays its source in universal Spirit. For, it pervades Thought also. Every universal truth which we express in words, implies or supposes every other truth. *Omne verum vero consonat.*[110] It is like a great circle on a sphere, comprising all possible circles; which, however, may be drawn, and comprise it, in like manner. Every such truth is the absolute Ens[111] seen from one side. But it has innumerable sides.

The same central Unity is still more conspicuous in actions. Words are finite organs of the infinite mind. They cannot cover the dimensions of what

103   Xenophanes of Elea, Greek philosopher (570–480 BCE). In his poem "Xenophanes," Emerson described the philosopher's insight that "universal Nature . . . repeats one note."

104   Proteus, the "old man of the sea," could turn himself into various forms, both animal and inanimate; but when held to his true shape by Menelaus, he spoke the truth (Homer, *Odyssey*, Bk. 4). Emerson draws on the image of Proteus in "History" and elsewhere.

105   Prehistoric reptile, dinosaur. Emerson in his lecture "Humanity of Science" remarked that the French naturalist Georges Dagobert, Baron Cuvier (1769–1832), "not long since from a fragment of a fossil bone succeeded in restoring correctly the true skeleton and outline of a saurian" (EL 2:33). In his Journal (1840–1841) Emerson exclaimed, "What nimble gigantic creatures our thoughts are! What saurians . . ." (J 7:487).

106   In his lecture "Demonology" (1839) from the series "Human Life," Emerson remarked, "The universe is pervaded with secret analogies that tie together its remotest parts" (EL 3:158).

107   The idea originates with Vitruvius, first-century BCE Roman writer on architecture.

108   Michelangelo Buonarroti, Renaissance painter and sculptor (1475–1564).

109   Joseph Haydn (1732–1809), Austrian composer.

110   "Every true thing is in harmony with truth" (Latin). In the Journal entry from which Emerson drew this passage (March 11, 1836), he added, "Hence Goethe's striving to find the Arch-plant" (J 5:138).

111   Being (philosophical term).

112   From Carlyle's translation of Goethe's *Wilhelm Meister's Travels*, which Emerson read avidly.

is in truth. They break, chop, and impoverish it. An action is the perfection and publication of thought. A right action seems to fill the eye, and to be related to all nature. "The wise man, in doing one thing, does all; or, in the one thing he does rightly, he sees the likeness of all which is done rightly."[112]

Words and actions are not the attributes of mute and brute nature. They introduce us to the human form, of which all other organizations appear to be degradations. When this organization appears among so many that surround it, the spirit prefers it to all others. It says, 'From such as this, have I drawn joy and knowledge. In such as this, have I found and beheld myself. I will speak to it. It can speak again. It can yield me thought already formed and alive.' In fact, the eye,—the mind,—is always accompanied by these forms, male and female; and these are incomparably the richest informations of the power and order that lie at the heart of things. Unfortunately, every one of them bears the marks as of some injury; is marred and superficially defective. Nevertheless, far different from the deaf and dumb nature around them, these all rest like fountain-pipes on the unfathomed sea of

Boston Latin School, which Emerson attended from the age of nine to fourteen (1812–1817).

thought and virtue whereto they alone, of all organizations, are the entrances.

It were a pleasant inquiry to follow into detail their ministry to our education, but where would it stop? We are associated in adolescent and adult life with some friends, who, like skies and waters, are coextensive with our idea; who, answering each to a certain affection of the soul, satisfy our desire on that side; whom we lack power to put at such focal distance from us, that we can mend or even analyze them. We cannot chuse but love them. When much intercourse with a friend has supplied us with a standard of excellence, and has increased our respect for the resources of God who thus sends a real person to outgo our ideal; when he has, moreover, become an object of thought, and, whilst his character retains all its unconscious effect, is converted in the mind into solid and sweet wisdom,—it is a sign to us that his office is closing, and he is commonly withdrawn from our sight in a short time.

ARTICLE VII. CHAPTER VI. Idealism

Thus is the unspeakable but intelligible and practicable meaning of the world conveyed to man, the immortal pupil, in every object of sense. To this one end of Discipline, all parts of nature conspire.

A noble doubt perpetually suggests itself, whether this end be not the Final Cause of the Universe; and whether nature outwardly exists. It is a sufficient account of that Appearance we call the World, that God will teach a human mind, and so makes it the receiver of a certain number of congruent sensations, which we call sun and moon, man and woman, house and trade. In my utter impotence to test the authenticity of the report of my senses, to know whether the impressions they make on me correspond with outlying objects, what difference does it make, whether Orion is up there in heaven, or some god paints the image in the firmament of the soul? The relations of parts and the end of the whole remaining the same, what is the difference, whether land and sea interact, and worlds revolve and intermingle without number or end,—deep yawning under deep, and galaxy balancing galaxy, throughout absolute space, or, whether, without relations of time and space,

Louis Agassiz (1807–1873). Emerson wrote in his Journal on September 21, 1864, "Agassiz is really a man of great ability, breadth & resources, a rare & rich *Nature*, and always maintains himself,—in all companies, & on all occasions."

113    Nitrogen.

the same appearances are inscribed in the constant faith of man? Whether nature enjoy a substantial existence without, or is only in the apocalypse of the mind, it is alike useful and alike venerable to me. Be it what it may, it is ideal to me, so long as I cannot try the accuracy of my senses.

The frivolous make themselves merry with the Ideal theory, as if its consequences were burlesque; as if it affected the stability of nature. It surely does not. God never jests with us, and will not compromise the end of nature, by permitting any inconsequence in its procession. Any distrust of the permanence of laws, would paralyze the faculties of man. Their permanence is sacredly respected, and his faith therein is perfect. The wheels and springs of man are all set to the hypothesis of the permanence of nature. We are not built like a ship to be tossed, but like a house to stand. It is a natural consequence of this structure, that, so long as the active powers predominate over the reflective, we resist with indignation any hint that nature is more short-lived or mutable than spirit. The broker, the wheelwright, the carpenter, the toll-man, are much displeased at the intimation.

But whilst we acquiesce entirely in the permanence of natural laws, the question of the absolute existence of nature, still remains open. It is the uniform effect of culture on the human mind, not to shake our faith in the stability of particular phenomena, as of heat, water, azote;[113] but to lead us to regard nature as a phenomenon, not a substance; to attribute necessary existence to spirit; to esteem nature as an accident and an effect.

To the senses and the unrenewed understanding, belongs a sort of instinctive belief in the absolute existence of nature. In their view, man and nature are indissolubly joined. Things are ultimates, and they never look beyond their sphere. The presence of Reason mars this faith. The first effort of thought tends to relax this despotism of the senses, which binds us to nature as if we were a part of it, and shows us nature aloof, and, as it were, afloat. Until this higher agency intervened, the animal eye sees, with wonderful accuracy, sharp outlines and colored surfaces. When the eye of Reason opens, to outline and surface are at once added, grace and expression. These proceed from imagination and affection, and abate somewhat of the angular distinctness of objects. If the Reason be stimulated to more earnest vision, outlines and surfaces become transparent, and are no longer seen; causes and spirits are seen through them. The best, the happiest moments of life, are these delicious awakenings of the higher powers, and the reverential withdrawing of nature before its God.

Let us proceed to indicate the effects of culture. 1. Our first institution in the Ideal philosophy is a hint from nature herself.

Nature is made to conspire with spirit to emancipate us.[114] Certain mechanical changes, a small alteration in our local position apprizes us of a dualism. We are strangely affected by seeing the shore from a moving ship, from a balloon, or through the tints of an unusual sky. The least change in our point of view, gives the whole world a pictorial air. A man who seldom rides, needs only to get into a coach and traverse his own town, to turn the street into a puppet-show. The men, the women,—talking, running, bartering, fighting,—the earnest mechanic, the lounger, the beggar, the boys, the dogs, are unrealized at once, or, at least, wholly detached from all relation to the observer, and seen as apparent, not substantial beings. What new thoughts are suggested by seeing a face of country quite familiar, in the rapid movement of the rail-road car! Nay, the most wonted objects, (make a very slight change in the point of vision,) please us most. In a camera obscura,[115] the butcher's cart, and the figure of one of our own family amuse us. So a portrait of a well-known face gratifies us. Turn the eyes upside down, by looking at the landscape through your legs, and how agreeable is the picture, though you have seen it any time these twenty years!

In these cases, by mechanical means, is suggested the difference between the observer and the spectacle,—between man and nature. Hence arises a pleasure mixed with awe; I may say, a low degree of the sublime is felt from the fact, probably, that man is hereby apprized, that, whilst the world is a spectacle, something in himself is stable.[116]

2. In a higher manner, the poet communicates the same pleasure. By a few strokes he delineates, as on air, the sun, the mountain, the camp, the city, the hero, the maiden, not different from what we know them, but only lifted from the ground and afloat before the eye. He unfixes the land and the sea, makes them revolve around the axis of his primary thought, and disposes them anew. Possessed himself by a heroic passion, he uses matter as symbols of it. The sensual man conforms thoughts to things; the poet conforms things to his thoughts. The one esteems nature as rooted and fast; the other, as fluid, and impresses his being thereon. To him, the refractory world is

114  Reed, in *The Growth of the Mind*, wrote that when "phenomena . . . become gradually classified," "at length all things . . . all events . . . shall at once conspire to form one stupendous miracle."

115  Dark chamber (Latin): the precursor of the camera. A box with a lens or pinhole on one side, it projects images from the outside world onto a surface inside the box; the images appear upside down and reversed from left to right.

116  Next to this passage in his copy of *Nature*, Emerson's young friend the talented and mentally unstable poet Jones Very (1813–1880) wrote, "Rev XX:II"—"And I saw a great white throne, and him that sat on it, from whose face the earth and the heaven fled away" (Revelation 20:11). Emerson wrote in his Journal on November 19, 1848, "'Tis a pretty revolution which is effected in the landscape by simply turning your head upside down, or, looking through your legs: an infinite softness & loveliness is added to the picture" (J 11:15).

117   Shakespeare, Sonnet 70 (slightly mis-quoted).

118   Shakespeare, Sonnet 124 (misquoted).

119   Shakespeare, *Measure for Measure*, 4.1.1–4 (slightly inaccurate). In a letter of December 1838 to the American preacher James Freeman Clarke (1810–1888), Emerson remarked on the "starry gleam" of Shakespeare's lines.

ductile and flexible; he invests dust and stones with humanity, and makes them the words of the Reason. The imagination may be defined to be, the use which the Reason makes of the material world. Shakspeare possesses the power of subordinating nature for the purposes of expression, beyond all poets. His imperial muse tosses the creation like a bauble from hand to hand, and uses it to embody any capricious shade of thought that is uppermost in his mind. The remotest spaces of nature are visited, and the farthest sundered things are brought together, by a subtile spiritual connexion. We are made aware that magnitude of material things is merely relative, and all objects shrink and expand to serve the passion of the poet. Thus, in his sonnets, the lays of birds, the scents and dyes of flowers, he finds to be the *shadow* of his beloved; time, which keeps her from him, is his *chest;* the suspicion she has awakened, is her *ornament;*

> The ornament of beauty is Suspect,
> A crow which flies in heaven's sweetest air.[117]

His passion is not the fruit of chance; it swells, as he speaks, to a city, or a state.

> No, it was builded far from accident;
> It suffers not in smiling pomp, nor falls
> Under the brow of thralling discontent;
> It fears not policy, that heretic,
> That works on leases of short numbered hours,
> But all alone stands hugely politic.[118]

In the strength of his constancy, the Pyramids seem to him recent and transitory. And the freshness of youth and love dazzles him with its resemblance to morning.

> Take those lips away
> Which so sweetly were forsworn;
> And those eyes,—the break of day,
> Lights that do mislead the morn.[119]

The wild beauty of this hyperbole, I may say, in passing, it would not be easy to match in literature.

This transfiguration which all material objects undergo through the passion of the poet,—this power which he exerts, at any moment, to magnify the small, to micrify the great,—might be illustrated by a thousand examples from his Plays. I have before me the Tempest, and will cite only these few lines.

> ARIEL. The strong based promontory
> Have I made shake, and by the spurs plucked up
> The pine and cedar.

Prospero calls for music to sooth the frantic Alonzo, and his companions;

> A solemn air, and the best comforter
> To an unsettled fancy, cure thy brains
> Now useless, boiled within thy skull.

Again;

> The charm dissolves apace
> And, as the morning steals upon the night,
> Melting the darkness, so their rising senses
> Begin to chase the ignorant fumes that mantle
> Their clearer reason.
> Their understanding
> Begins to swell: and the approaching tide
> Will shortly fill the reasonable shores
> That now lie foul and muddy.[120]

The perception of real affinities between events, (that is to say, of *ideal* affinities, for those only are real,) enables the poet thus to make free with the most imposing forms and phenomena of the world, and to assert the predominance of the soul.

120   Shakespeare, *The Tempest*, 5.1.46–82.

121   As adapted by Coleridge in *The Friend* (1818).

122   Aristotle (384–322 BCE), ancient Greek philosopher.

123   *Antigone* (441 BCE?), Greek tragic drama by Sophocles (497–406 BCE). Emerson read *Antigone* in Greek with his brother Charles in November 1835.

124   Weighty, encumbering.

125   Leonhard Euler (1707–1783), Swiss mathematician, physicist, and philosopher. Catherine the Great (1684–1727) sent for him to teach in St. Petersburg, and Frederick the Great (1712–1786) in Berlin. Emerson found Euler's remark in Coleridge's *Aids to Reflection*.

126   Anne Robert Jacques Turgot (1727–1781), French politician and economist.

127   Mt. Olympus was the home of the Greek gods.

3. Whilst thus the poet delights us by animating nature like a creator, with his own thoughts, he differs from the philosopher only herein, that the one proposes Beauty as his main end; the other Truth. But, the philosopher, not less than the poet, postpones the apparent order and relations of things to the empire of thought. "The problem of philosophy," according to Plato, "is, for all that exists conditionally, to find a ground unconditioned and absolute."[121] It proceeds on the faith that a law determines all phenomena, which being known, the phenomena can be predicted. That law, when in the mind, is an idea. Its beauty is infinite. The true philosopher and the true poet are one, and a beauty, which is truth, and a truth, which is beauty, is the aim of both. Is not the charm of one of Plato's or Aristotle's[122] definitions, strictly like that of the Antigone of Sophocles?[123] It is, in both cases, that a spiritual life has been imparted to nature; that the solid seeming block of matter has been pervaded and dissolved by a thought; that this feeble human being has penetrated the vast masses of nature with an informing soul, and recognised itself in their harmony, that is, seized their law. In physics, when this is attained, the memory disburthens itself of its cumbrous[124] catalogues of particulars, and carries centuries of observation in a single formula.

Thus even in physics, the material is ever degraded before the spiritual. The astronomer, the geometer, rely on their irrefragable analysis, and disdain the results of observation. The sublime remark of Euler[125] on his law of arches, "This will be found contrary to all experience, yet is true;" had already transferred nature into the mind, and left matter like an outcast corpse.

4. Intellectual science has been observed to beget invariably a doubt of the existence of matter. Turgot[126] said, "He that has never doubted the existence of matter, may be assured he has no aptitude for metaphysical inquiries." It fastens the attention upon immortal necessary uncreated natures, that is, upon Ideas; and in their beautiful and majestic presence, we feel that our outward being is a dream and a shade. Whilst we wait in this Olympus[127] of gods, we think of nature as an appendix to the soul. We ascend into their region, and know that these are the thoughts of the Supreme Being. "These are they who were set up from everlasting, from the beginning, or ever the earth was. When he prepared the heavens, they were there; when

he established the clouds above, when he strengthened the fountains of the deep. Then they were by him, as one brought up with him. Of them took he counsel."[128]

Their influence is proportionate. As objects of science, they are accessible to few men. Yet all men are capable of being raised by piety or by passion, into their region. And no man touches these divine natures, without becoming, in some degree, himself divine. Like a new soul, they renew the body. We become physically nimble and lightsome; we tread on air; life is no longer irksome, and we think it will never be so. No man fears age or misfortune or death, in their serene company, for he is transported out of the district of change. Whilst we behold unveiled the nature of Justice and Truth, we learn the difference between the absolute and the conditional or relative. We apprehend the absolute. As it were, for the first time, *we exist*. We become immortal, for we learn that time and space are relations of matter; that, with a perception of truth, or a virtuous will, they have no affinity.

5. Finally, religion and ethics, which may be fitly called,—the practice of ideas, or the introduction of ideas into life,—have an analogous effect with all lower culture, in degrading nature and suggesting its dependence on spirit. Ethics and religion differ herein; that the one is the system of human duties commencing from man; the other, from God. Religion includes the personality of God; Ethics does not. They are one to our present design. They both put nature under foot. The first and last lesson of religion is, "The things that are seen, are temporal; the things that are unseen are eternal."[129] It puts an affront upon nature. It does that for the unschooled, which philosophy does for Berkeley and Viasa.[130] The uniform language that may be heard in the churches of the most ignorant sects, is,—'Contemn the unsubstantial shows of the world; they are vanities, dreams, shadows, unrealities; seek the realities of religion.' The devotee flouts nature. Some theosophists have arrived at a certain hostility and indignation towards matter, as the Manichean[131] and Plotinus. They distrusted in themselves any looking back to these flesh-pots of Egypt.[132] Plotinus was ashamed of his body.[133] In short, they might all better say of matter, what Michael Angelo said of external beauty, "it is the frail and weary weed, in which God dresses the soul, which he has called into time."[134]

128   Emerson quotes from Proverbs 8:23–30.

129   Adapted from II Corinthians 4:18.

130   George Berkeley (1685–1753) was an idealist philosopher; Viasa or Viyasa, the legendary arranger of the Vedas, Hindu scriptures.

131   Manicheans believe that two warring principles govern the universe (good and evil, light and dark). Manes was a third-century CE mystic in Babylonia.

132   Exodus 16:2–3.

133   The *Life of Plotinus* by Porphyry (ca. 234–ca. 305) begins with the remark that Plotinus seemed ashamed of being in his body, never discussed his parents or his birthplace, and was reluctant to sit for a portrait (J 3:251). In his essay "Heroism," Emerson wrote, "Heroism, like Plotinus, is almost ashamed of its body."

134   From Sonnet 51 by Michelangelo Buonarroti, genius of the Italian Renaissance better known for his painting and sculpture.

A certificate issued in New York several years after the short-lived Hungarian Revolution of 1848, from Emerson's collection. In May 1852, the leader of the Hungarian Revolution, Louis Kossuth (1802–1894, depicted at lower left of the certificate), visited Lexington and Concord, where he received a hero's welcome. Emerson told Kossuth in his speech on this occasion, "The man of freedom, you are also the man of fate. . . . you are elected by God and your genius to your task."

It appears that motion, poetry, physical and intellectual science, and religion, all tend to affect our convictions of the reality of the external world. But I own there is something ungrateful in expanding too curiously the particulars of the general proposition, that all culture tends to imbue us with idealism. I have no hostility to nature, but a child's love to it. I expand and live in the warm day like corn and melons. Let us speak her fair. I do not wish to fling stones at my beautiful mother, nor soil my gentle nest. I only wish to indicate the true position of nature in regard to man, wherein to establish man, all right education tends; as the ground which to attain is the object of human life, that is, of man's connexion with nature. Culture inverts the vulgar views of nature, and brings the mind to call that apparent, which it uses to call real, and that real, which it uses to call visionary. Children, it is true, believe in the external world. The belief that it appears only, is an afterthought, but with culture, this faith will as surely arise on the mind as did the first.

The advantage of the ideal theory over the popular faith, is this, that it presents the world in precisely that view which is most desirable to the mind. It is, in fact, the view which Reason, both speculative and practical, that is, philosophy and virtue, take. For, seen in the light of thought, the world always is phenomenal; and virtue subordinates it to the mind. Idealism sees the world in God. It beholds the whole circle of persons and things, of actions and events, of country and religion, not as painfully accumulated, atom after atom, act after act, in an aged creeping Past, but as one vast picture, which God paints on the instant eternity, for the contemplation of the soul. Therefore the soul holds itself off from a too trivial and microscopic study of the universal tablet. It respects the end too much, to immerse itself in the means. It sees something more important in Christianity, than the scandals of ecclesiastical history or the niceties of criticism; and, very incurious concerning persons or miracles, and not at all disturbed by chasms of historical evidence, it accepts from God the phenomenon, as it finds it, as the pure and awful form of religion in the world. It is not hot and passionate at the appearance of what it calls its own good or bad fortune, at the union or opposition of other persons. No man is its enemy. It accepts whatsoever befals, as part of its lesson. It is a watcher more than a doer, and it is a doer, only that it may the better watch.

### ARTICLE VIII. CHAPTER VII. Spirit[135]

It is essential to a true theory of nature and of man, that it should contain somewhat progressive. Uses that are exhausted or that may be, and facts that end in the statement, cannot be all that is true of this brave lodging wherein man is harbored, and wherein all his faculties find appropriate and endless exercise. And all the uses of nature admit of being summed in one, which yields the activity of man an infinite scope. Through all its kingdoms, to the suburbs and outskirts of things, it is faithful to the cause whence it had its origin. It always speaks of Spirit. It suggests the absolute. It is a perpetual effect. It is a great shadow pointing always to the sun behind us.

The aspect of nature is devout. Like the figure of Jesus, she stands with bended head, and hands folded upon the breast. The happiest man is he who learns from nature the lesson of worship.

Of that ineffable essence which we call Spirit, he that thinks most, will say least. We can foresee God in the course and, as it were, distant phenom-

135    Emerson wrote in his Journal on January 16, 1837, four months after *Nature* was published, "How evanescent is the idea of Spirit, how incomprehensible!" (J 5:282).

ena of matter; but when we try to define and describe himself, both language
and thought desert us, and we are as helpless as fools and savages. That essence refuses to be recorded in propositions, but when man has worshipped
him intellectually, the noblest ministry of nature is to stand as the apparition
of God. It is the great organ through which the universal spirit speaks to the
individual, and strives to lead back the individual to it.

When we consider Spirit, we see that the views already presented do
not include the whole circumference of man. We must add some related
thoughts.

Three problems are put by nature to the mind; What is matter?
Whence is it? and Whereto? The first of these questions only, the ideal
theory answers. Idealism saith: matter is a phenomenon, not a substance.
Idealism acquaints us with the total disparity between the evidence of
our own being, and the evidence of the world's being. The one is perfect;
the other, incapable of any assurance; the mind is a part of the nature
of things; the world is a divine dream, from which we may presently awake
to the glories and certainties of day. Idealism is a hypothesis to account
for nature by other principles than those of carpentry and chemistry. Yet,
if it only deny the existence of matter, it does not satisfy the demands
of the spirit. It leaves God out of me. It leaves me in the splendid labyrinth of my perceptions, to wander without end. Then the heart resists it,
because it baulks the affections in denying substantive being to men and
women. Nature is so pervaded with human life, that there is something
of humanity in all, and in every particular. But this theory makes nature foreign to me, and does not account for that consanguinity which we acknowledge to it.

Let it stand then, in the present state of our knowledge, merely as a
useful introductory hypothesis, serving to apprize us of the eternal distinction between the soul and the world.

But when, following the invisible steps of thought, we come to inquire,
Whence is matter? and Whereto? many truths arise to us out of the recesses
of consciousness. We learn that the highest is present to the soul of man,
that the dread universal essence, which is not wisdom, or love, or beauty, or
power, but all in one, and each entirely, is that for which all things exist, and

that by which they are; that spirit creates; that behind nature, throughout nature, spirit is present; that spirit is one and not compound; that spirit does not act upon us from without, that is, in space and time, but spiritually, or through ourselves. Therefore, that spirit, that is, the Supreme Being, does not build up nature around us, but puts it forth through us, as the life of the tree puts forth new branches and leaves through the pores of the old. As a plant upon the earth, so a man rests upon the bosom of God; he is nourished by unfailing fountains, and draws, at his need, inexhaustible power. Who can set bounds to the possibilities of man? Once inhale the upper air, being admitted to behold the absolute natures of justice and truth, and we learn that man has access to the entire mind of the Creator, is himself the creator in the finite. This view, which admonishes me where the sources of wisdom and power lie, and points to virtue as to

> "The golden key
> Which opes the palace of eternity,"[136]

carries upon its face the highest certificate of truth, because it animates me to create my own world through the purification of my soul.

The world proceeds from the same spirit as the body of man. It is a remoter and inferior incarnation of God, a projection of God in the unconscious. But it differs from the body in one important respect. It is not, like that, now subjected to the human will. Its serene order is inviolable by us. It is therefore, to us, the present expositor of the divine mind. It is a fixed point whereby we may measure our departure. As we degenerate, the contrast between us and our house is more evident. We are as much strangers in nature, as we are aliens from God. We do not understand the notes of birds. The fox and the deer run away from us; the bear and tiger rend us. We do not know the uses of more than a few plants, as corn and the apple, the potato and the vine. Is not the landscape, every glimpse of which hath a grandeur, a face of him? Yet this may show us what discord is between man and nature, for you cannot freely admire a noble landscape, if laborers are digging in the field hard by. The poet finds something ridiculous in his delight, until he is out of the sight of men.

136   From the opening speech in Milton's *Comus* (1634).

137   Emerson here remembers his visit to the Jardin des Plantes, the natural history museum in Paris. Afterward, on July 13, 1833, he wrote in his Journal, "The Universe is a more amazing puzzle than ever as you glance along this bewildering series of animated forms,—the hazy butterflies, the carved shells, the birds, beasts, fishes, insects, snakes,—& the upheaving principle of life everywhere incipient in the very rock aping organized forms. Not a form so grotesque, so savage, nor so beautiful but is an expression of some property inherent in man the observer,—an occult relation between the very scorpions and man. I feel the centipede in me—cayman, carp, eagle, & fox. I am moved by strange sympathies, I say continually 'I will be a naturalist'" (J 4:199).

ARTICLE IX. CHAPTER VIII. Prospects

In inquiries respecting the laws of the world and the frame of things, the highest reason is always the truest. That which seems faintly possible—it is so refined, is often faint and dim because it is deepest seated in the mind among the eternal verities. Empirical science is apt to cloud the sight, and, by the very knowledge of functions and processes, to bereave the student of the manly contemplation of the whole. The savant becomes unpoetic. But the best read naturalist who lends an entire and devout attention to truth, will see that there remains much to learn of his relation to the world, and that it is not to be learned by any addition or subtraction or other comparison of known quantities, but is arrived at by untaught sallies of the spirit, by a continual self-recovery, and by entire humility. He will perceive that there are far more excellent qualities in the student than preciseness and infallibility; that a guess is often more fruitful than an indisputable affirmation, and that a dream may let us deeper into the secret of nature than a hundred concerted experiments.

For, the problems to be solved are precisely those which the physiologist and the naturalist omit to state. It is not so pertinent to man to know all the individuals of the animal kingdom, as it is to know whence and whereto is this tyrannizing unity in his constitution, which evermore separates and classifies things, endeavoring to reduce the most diverse to one form. When I behold a rich landscape, it is less to my purpose to recite correctly the order and superposition of the strata, than to know why all thought of multitude is lost in a tranquil sense of unity. I cannot greatly honor minuteness in details, so long as there is no hint to explain the relation between things and thoughts; no ray upon the *metaphysics* of conchology, of botany, of the arts, to show the relation of the forms of flowers, shells, animals, architecture, to the mind, and build science upon ideas. In a cabinet of natural history,[137] we become sensible of a certain occult recognition and sympathy in regard to the most unwieldy and eccentric forms of beast, fish, and insect. The American who has been confined, in his own country, to the sight of buildings designed after foreign models, is surprised on entering York Minster or St. Peter's at Rome, by the feeling that these structures are imitations also,—faint copies of an invisible archetype. Nor has science sufficient humanity, so long as the naturalist overlooks that wonderful congruity which subsists between man and the world; of which he is lord, not because he is the most subtile inhabitant, but because he is its head and heart, and finds something of himself in every great and small thing, in every mountain stratum, in every new law of color, fact of astronomy, or atmospheric influence which observation or analysis lay open.[138] A perception of this mystery inspires the muse of George Herbert, the beautiful psalmist of the seventeenth century. The following lines are part of his little poem on Man.

> "Man is all symmetry,
> Full of proportions, one limb to another,
> And to all the world besides.
> Each part may call the farthest, brother;
> For head with foot hath private amity,
> And both with moons and tides.
>
> "Nothing hath got so far
> But man hath caught and kept it as his prey;
> His eyes dismount the highest star;
> He is in little all the sphere.
> Herbs gladly cure our flesh, because that they
> Find their acquaintance there.
>
> "For us, the winds do blow,
> The earth doth rest, heaven move, and fountains flow;
> Nothing we see, but means our good,
> As our delight, or as our treasure;
> The whole is either our cupboard of food,
> Or cabinet of pleasure.
>
> "The stars have us to bed:
> Night draws the curtain; which the sun withdraws.
> Music and light attend our head.
> All things unto our flesh are kind,
> In their descent and being; to our mind,
> In their ascent and cause.

138   In *The Growth of the Mind*, Reed wrote that "Reason is beginning to learn the necessity of simply tracing the relations which exist between created things, and of not even touching what it examines, lest it disturb the arrangement in the cabinet of creation" (a cabinet is a collection of remarkable objects, like the Cabinet of Natural History at the Jardin des Plantes in Paris, which Emerson visited in 1833).

139   Emerson's quotation from Herbert's "Man" omits several passages.

140   Paraphrased from Aristotle's *Poetics* (9.3); Emerson mistakenly ascribed the line to Plato.

141   Premonition, prophecy (from the Latin *vates*, divinely inspired bard).

142   Sluggish.

143   Emerson himself.

144   Nebuchadnezzar, the king of Babylon, is told in a prophecy, "thy dwelling shall be with the beasts of the field, and they shall make thee to eat grass as oxen" (Daniel 4:25; the prophecy is fulfilled in 4:33).

"More servants wait on man
Than he'll take notice of. In every path,
He treads down that which doth befriend him
When sickness makes him pale and wan.
Oh mighty love! Man is one world, and hath
Another to attend him."[139]

The perception of this class of truths makes the eternal attraction which draws men to science, but the end is lost sight of in attention to the means. In view of this half-sight of science, we accept the sentence of Plato, that, "poetry comes nearer to vital truth than history."[140] Every surmise and vaticination[141] of the mind is entitled to a certain respect, and we learn to prefer imperfect theories, and sentences, which contain glimpses of truth, to digested systems which have no one valuable suggestion. A wise writer will feel that the ends of study and composition are best answered by announcing undiscovered regions of thought, and so communicating, through hope, new activity to the torpid[142] spirit.

I shall therefore conclude this essay with some traditions of man and nature, which a certain poet[143] sang to me; and which, as they have always been in the world, and perhaps reappear to every bard, may be both history and prophecy.

'The foundations of man are not in matter, but in spirit. But the element of spirit is eternity. To it, therefore, the longest series of events, the oldest chronologies are young and recent. In the cycle of the universal man, from whom the known individuals proceed, centuries are points, and all history is but the epoch of one degradation.

'We distrust and deny inwardly our sympathy with nature. We own and disown our relation to it, by turns. We are, like Nebuchadnezzar, dethroned, bereft of reason, and eating grass like an ox.[144] But who can set limits to the remedial force of spirit?

'A man is a god in ruins. When men are innocent, life shall be longer, and shall pass into the immortal, as gently as we awake from dreams. Now, the world would be insane and rabid, if these disorganizations should last for hundreds of years. It is kept in check by death and infancy. Infancy is the perpetual Messiah, which comes into the arms of fallen men, and pleads with them to return to paradise.

'Man is the dwarf of himself. Once he was permeated and dissolved by spirit. He filled nature with his overflowing currents. Out from him sprang the sun and moon; from man, the sun; from woman, the moon. The laws of his mind, the periods of his actions externized themselves into day and night, into the year and the seasons. But, having made for himself this huge shell, his waters retired; he no longer fills the veins and veinlets; he is shrunk to a drop. He sees, that the structure still fits him, but fits him colossally. Say, rather, once it fitted him, now it corresponds to him from far and on high. He adores timidly his own work. Now is man the follower of the sun, and woman the follower of the moon. Yet sometimes he starts in his slumber, and wonders at himself and his house, and muses strangely at the resemblance betwixt him and it. He perceives that if his law is still paramount, if still he have elemental power, "if his word is sterling yet in nature,"[145] it is not conscious power, it is not inferior but superior to his will. It is Instinct.' Thus my Orphic[146] poet sang.

At present, man applies to nature but half his force. He works on the world with his understanding alone. He lives in it, and masters it by a penny-wisdom; and he that works most in it, is but a half-man, and whilst his arms are strong and his digestion good, his mind is imbruted and he is a selfish savage. His relation to nature, his power over it, is through the understanding; as by manure; the economic use of fire, wind, water, and the mariner's needle; steam, coal, chemical agriculture; the repairs of the human body by the dentist and the surgeon. This is such a resumption of power, as if a banished king should buy his territories inch by inch, instead of vaulting at once into his throne. Meantime, in the thick darkness, there are not wanting gleams of a better light,[147]—occasional examples of the action of man upon nature with his entire force,—with reason as well as understanding. Such examples are; the traditions of miracles in the earliest antiquity of all nations; the history of Jesus Christ; the achievements of a principle, as in religious and political revolutions, and in the abolition of the Slave-trade; the miracles of enthusiasm, as those reported of Swedenborg, Hohenlohe,[148] and the Shakers; many obscure and yet contested facts, now arranged under the

145 Variation on a phrase in Shakespeare's *Richard II*, 4.1.264 ("And if my word be sterling yet in England").

146 Orpheus was the legendary Greek poet and seer, credited with supernatural powers; in antiquity, Orphic cults practiced secret religious rituals. Emerson's son Edward Emerson cites a comment from the *Theology of Plato* by Proclus (ca. 410–485): "He who desires to signify divine concerns through symbols is orphic."

147 Emerson is about to introduce an ethical perspective absent in his reference a few pages earlier (end of Chapter 7) to the difficulty of admiring a landscape if laborers are digging in the field nearby. Reed may have influenced him here when he remarked (in *The Growth of the Mind*) that "it is the natural world from which the philosopher draws his knowledge; it is the natural world in which the slave toils for his bread. Alas! When will they be one? When we are willing to practise what we learn, and religion makes our duty our delight."

148 Prince Alexander Leopold of Hohenlohe-Waldenberg-Schillingsfürst (1794–1849), German bishop and writer known for his miraculous cures.

149  Variety of hypnotism, also called mesmerism after its inventor, Friedrich Anton Mesmer (1733–1815).

150  The distinction derives from *The City of God* (11.7) by St. Augustine (354–430), and was developed further by the schoolmen (medieval theologians also known as scholastics) (J 5:141, 6:179).

151  John Milton described his blindness in *Paradise Lost* (1667) as "a universal blank / Of Nature's works to me expunged and rased" (an image of writing scraped off, the original method of erasure: 3.48–49); Coleridge in "Dejection: An Ode" wrote, "Still I gaze—and with how blank an eye!"

152  Psalms 42:7: "Deep calleth unto deep at the noise of thy waterspouts: all thy waves and thy billows are gone over me."

153  The passage originally expressed Emerson's disagreement with Goethe. In June 1836 Emerson wrote in his Journal, "Monsters & aberrations give us glimpses of the higher law;—let us into the secret of Nature, thought Goethe. Well. We fable to conform things better to our higher law, but when by & by we see the true cause, the fable fades & shrivels up. We see then the true higher law. To the wise therefore a fact is true poetry & the most beautiful of fables" (J 5:175).

name of Animal Magnetism;[149] prayer; eloquence; self-healing; and the wisdom of children. These are examples of Reason's momentary grasp of the sceptre; the exertions of a power which exists not in time or space, but an instantaneous in-streaming causing power. The difference between the actual and the ideal force of man is happily figured by the schoolmen, in saying, that the knowledge of man is an evening knowledge, *vespertina cognitio*, but that of God is a morning knowledge, *matutina cognitio*.[150]

The problem of restoring to the world original and eternal beauty, is solved by the redemption of the soul. The ruin or the blank, that we see when we look at nature, is in our own eye.[151] The axis of vision is not coincident with the axis of things, and so they appear not transparent but opake. The reason why the world lacks unity, and lies broken and in heaps, is, because man is disunited with himself. He cannot be a naturalist, until he satisfies all the demands of the spirit. Love is as much its demand, as perception. Indeed, neither can be perfect without the other. In the uttermost meaning of the words, thought is devout, and devotion is thought. Deep calls unto deep.[152] But in actual life, the marriage is not celebrated. There are innocent men who worship God after the tradition of their fathers, but their sense of duty has not yet extended to the use of all their faculties. And there are patient naturalists, but they freeze their subject under the wintry light of the understanding. Is not prayer also a study of truth,—a sally of the soul into the unfound infinite? No man ever prayed heartily, without learning something. But when a faithful thinker, resolute to detach every object from personal relations, and see it in the light of thought, shall, at the same time, kindle science with the fire of the holiest affections, then will God go forth anew into the creation.

It will not need, when the mind is prepared for study, to search for objects. The invariable mark of wisdom is to see the miraculous in the common. What is a day? What is a year? What is summer? What is woman? What is a child? What is sleep? To our blindness, these things seem unaffecting. We make fables to hide the baldness of the fact and conform it, as we say, to the higher law of the mind. But when the fact is seen under the light of an idea, the gaudy fable fades and shrivels. We behold the real higher law. To the wise, therefore, a fact is true poetry, and the most beautiful of fables.[153] These wonders are brought to our own door. You also are a man.

Man and woman, and their social life, poverty, labor, sleep, fear, fortune, are known to you. Learn that none of these things is superficial, but that each phenomenon hath its roots in the faculties and affections of the mind. Whilst the abstract question occupies your intellect, nature brings it in the concrete to be solved by your hands. It were a wise inquiry for the closet, to compare, point by point, especially at remarkable crises in life, our daily history, with the rise and progress of ideas in the mind.

So shall we come to look at the world with new eyes. It shall answer the endless inquiry of the intellect,—What is truth? and of the affections,—What is good? by yielding itself passive to the educated Will. Then shall come to pass what my poet said; 'Nature is not fixed but fluid. Spirit alters, moulds, makes it. The immobility or bruteness of nature, is the absence of spirit; to pure spirit, it is fluid, it is volatile, it is obedient. Every spirit builds itself a house; and beyond its house, a world; and beyond its world, a heaven. Know then, that the world exists for you. For you is the phenomenon perfect. What we are, that only can we see. All that Adam had, all that Cæsar could, you have and can do. Adam called his house, heaven and earth; Cæsar called his house, Rome; you perhaps call yours, a cobler's trade; a hundred acres of ploughed land; or a scholar's garret. Yet line for line and point for point, your dominion is as great as theirs, though without fine names. Build, therefore, your own world. As fast as you conform your life to the pure idea in your mind, that will unfold its great proportions. A correspondent revolution in things will attend the influx of the spirit. So fast will disagreeable appearances, swine, spiders, snakes, pests, mad-houses, prisons, enemies, vanish; they are temporary and shall be no more seen. The sordor[154] and filths of nature, the sun shall dry up, and the wind exhale. As when the summer comes from the south, the snow-banks melt, and the face of the earth becomes green before it, so shall the advancing spirit create its ornaments along its path, and carry with it the beauty it visits, and the song which enchants it; it shall draw beautiful faces, and warm hearts, and wise discourse, and heroic acts, around its way, until evil is no more seen.[155] The kingdom of man over nature, which cometh not with observation,—a dominion such as now is beyond his dream of God,—he shall enter without more wonder than the blind man feels who is gradually restored to perfect sight.'[156]

154 Squalor, sordidness.

155 A strangely assured prophecy! The critic Harold Bloom characterizes *Nature* as "a blandly dissociative apocalypse, in which everything is a cheerful error, indeed a misreading, starting with the title, which says 'Nature' but means 'Man.'"

156 Emerson alludes to Luke 17:20: when Jesus is asked by the Pharisees "when the kingdom of God should come, he answered them and said, The kingdom of God cometh not with observation." He also has in mind Jesus' miraculous healing of the blind (Mark 8:22–25 and 10:51–52, Luke 18:35–43, John 9:1–41), as well as his own earlier allusions to eyes and blindness.

# The American Scholar

*An Oration Delivered before the Phi Beta Kappa Society,
at Cambridge, August 31, 1837*

*In August 1837 Emerson delivered the Phi Beta Kappa Society address, given annually by a distinguished citizen, and usually concerned with some aspect of scholarship or letters. His audience included a number of prominent authors, orators, and social thinkers: James Russell Lowell (1819–1891), Richard Henry Dana (1815–1882), Wendell Phillips (1811–1884), Edward Everett (1794–1865), Oliver Wendell Holmes, Sr. (1809–1894); as well as Emerson's teacher Edward Tyrrel Channing (1790–1856) and U.S. Supreme Court Justice Joseph Story (1779–1845). Holmes later called Emerson's address "America's intellectual Declaration of Independence." Emerson (the second choice for the occasion after an Episcopalian minister, Jonathan Wainwright [1792–1854], declined the invitation) gave his address in First Parish Church across from Harvard Yard, called by Emerson's biographer Robert Richardson "an awkward monument of Carpenter Gothic that never seems able to hold a coat of paint through the winter." The Scottish author Thomas Carlyle (1795–1881) wrote to Emerson after reading "The American Scholar," "My friend!*
(continued)

Mr. President, and Gentlemen,

I greet you on the re-commencement of our literary year. Our anniversary is one of hope, and, perhaps, not enough of labor. We do not meet for games of strength or skill, for the recitation of histories, tragedies and odes, like the ancient Greeks; for parliaments of love and poesy, like the Troubadours;[1] nor for the advancement of science, like our cotemporaries in the British and European capitals. Thus far, our holiday has been simply a friendly sign of the survival of the love of letters amongst a people too busy to give to letters any more. As such, it is precious as the sign of an indestructible instinct. Perhaps the time is already come, when it ought to be, and will be something else; when the sluggard[2] intellect of this continent will look from under its iron lids and fill the postponed expectation of the world with something better than the exertions of mechanical skill. Our day of dependence, our long apprenticeship to the learning of other lands, draws to a close. The millions that around us are rushing into life, cannot always be fed on the sere[3] remains of foreign harvests. Events, actions arise, that must be sung, that will sing themselves. Who can doubt that poetry will revive and lead in a new age, as the star in the constellation Harp which now flames in our zenith, astronomers announce, shall one day be the pole-star for a thousand years?[4]

In the light of this hope, I accept the topic which not only usage, but the nature of our association, seem to prescribe to this day,—the AMERICAN SCHOLAR. Year by year, we come up hither to read one more chapter of his biography. Let us inquire what light new days and events have thrown on his character, his duties and his hopes.

It is one of those fables, which out of an unknown antiquity, convey an unlooked-for wisdom, that the gods, in the beginning, divided Man into men, that he might be more helpful to himself; just as the hand was divided into fingers, the better to answer its end.

The old fable covers a doctrine ever new and sublime; that there is One Man,—present to all particular men only partially, or through one faculty; and that you must take the whole society to find the whole man.[5] Man is not a farmer, or a professor, or an engineer, but he is all. Man is priest, and scholar, and statesman, and producer, and soldier. In the *divided* or social

Emerson's father, Reverend William Emerson.

*You know not what you have done for me there. . . . Lo, out of the West comes a clear utterance, clearly recognizable as a* man's *voice, and I have a kinsman and brother . . ."* In Heroes and Hero-Worship *(1841), Carlyle, following Emerson, wrote that the "Man-of-Letters Hero must be regarded as our most important modern person."*

*In 1837 Emerson received the final portion of the estate of his first wife, Ellen, giving him an annual income of about $1,200, which he supplemented with lecturing fees.*

1      The troubadour poets of southern France in the twelfth and thirteenth centuries celebrated courtly love (*parliament* here means a competition or concert of poet-singers).

2      Lazy.

3      Withered, dry.

4      The constellation Lyra depicts a lyre or harp, associated with poetry. Travelers rely on the pole star (the North Star, currently Polaris in Ursa Minor) for orientation. As Emerson writes, the star Vega, in Lyra, was the pole star about 12,000 BCE and will be again in 13,727 CE. In the Journal entry from which the passage derives, Emerson described "an enchanting night of southwind & clouds. . . . All the trees are windharps. Blessed be light & darkness, ebb & flow, cold & heat, these restless pulsations of Nature which by & by will throb no more" (August 2, 1837, J 5:350).

5      Emerson may be thinking of the Fable of the Belly attributed to Aesop (ca. 6th century BCE) and used in Shakespeare's *Coriolanus* (and, earlier, in "Life of Coriolanus" by the Greek historian Plutarch [ca. 46–ca. 122]) to suggest that the parts of the body are interdependent just as different social classes are.

6      The Greek philosopher Empedocles (ca. 492–ca. 432 BCE) wrote, "Here sprang up many faces without necks, arms wandered without shoulders, unattached, and eyes strayed alone, in need of foreheads" (fragment 443). Emerson might also be alluding to the adaptation of the Empedocles passage in *Hyperion* (1797–1799) by the German author Friedrich Hölderlin (1770–1843): "I can think of no people more disintegrated than the Germans . . . is it not like a battlefield, where hands and arms and limbs lie everywhere in pieces, while the life blood flows out into the sand?" Similarly, the philosopher Friedrich Nietzsche (1844–1900) in *Thus Spake Zarathustra* (1883–1885) sees "fragments and limbs and fearful chances—but no human beings."

In his Journal (November 1834) Emerson wrote of mismatched traits as "anomalous unpaired creatures, who are but partially developed, wizzeled apples, as if you should seek to match monsters, one of whom has a leg, another an arm, another two heads" (J 4:337).

7      In his "Ode, Inscribed to W. H. Channing," Emerson remarked, "Things are in the saddle, and ride mankind."

8      From the *Enchiridion*, or handbook, of the Greek Stoic Epictetus (ca. 55–ca. 135): "Everything has two handles, one by which it may be carried, the other not." Henry James, Sr. (1811–1882), thinking of Emerson, exclaimed, "O you man without a handle!"

9      Advantage or right granted because of one's rank or status.

10     In his Journal (August 3, 1837), Emerson commented, "A Scholar is one attuned to nature & life so that heaven & earth traverse freely with their influences his heart and meet in him" (J 5:351).

state, these functions are parcelled out to individuals, each of whom aims to do his stint of the joint work, whilst each other performs his. The fable implies that the individual to possess himself, must sometimes return from his own labor to embrace all the other laborers. But unfortunately, this original unit, this fountain of power, has been so distributed to multitudes, has been so minutely subdivided and peddled out, that it is spilled into drops, and cannot be gathered. The state of society is one in which the members have suffered amputation from the trunk, and strut about so many walking monsters, —a good finger, a neck, a stomach, an elbow, but never a man.[6]

Man is thus metamorphosed into a thing, into many things. The planter, who is Man sent out into the field to gather food, is seldom cheered by any idea of the true dignity of his ministry. He sees his bushel and his cart, and nothing beyond, and sinks into the farmer, instead of Man on the farm. The tradesman scarcely ever gives an ideal worth to his work, but is ridden by the routine of his craft, and the soul is subject to dollars.[7] The priest becomes a form; the attorney, a statute-book; the mechanic, a machine; the sailor, a rope of a ship.

In this distribution of functions, the scholar is the delegated intellect. In the right state, he is, *Man Thinking*. In the degenerate state, when the victim of society, he tends to become a mere thinker, or, still worse, the parrot of other men's thinking.

In this view of him, as Man Thinking, the whole theory of his office is contained. Him nature solicits, with all her placid, all her monitory pictures. Him the past instructs. Him the future invites. Is not, indeed, every man a student, and do not all things exist for the student's behoof? And, finally, is not the true scholar the only true master? But, as the old oracle said, "All things have two handles. Beware of the wrong one."[8] In life, too often, the scholar errs with mankind and forfeits his privilege.[9] Let us see him in his school, and consider him in reference to the main influences he receives.[10]

I. The first in time and the first in importance of the influences upon the mind is that of nature. Every day, the sun; and, after sunset, night and her stars. Ever the winds blow; ever the grass grows. Every day, men and women, conversing, beholding and beholden.[11] The scholar must needs stand wistful and admiring before this great spectacle. He must settle its value in his mind. What is nature to him? There is never a beginning, there is never an end to the inexplicable continuity of this web of God, but always circular power returning into itself.[12] Therein it resembles his own spirit, whose beginning, whose ending he never can find—so entire, so boundless. Far, too, as her splendors shine, system on system shooting like rays, upward, downward, without centre, without circumference,—in the mass and in the particle nature hastens to render account of herself to the mind. Classification begins. To the young mind, every thing is individual, stands by itself. By and by, it finds how to join two things, and see in them one nature; then three, then three thousand; and so, tyrannized over by its own unifying instinct, it goes on tying things together, diminishing anomalies, discovering roots running under ground, whereby contrary and remote things cohere, and flower out from one stem.[13] It presently learns, that, since the dawn of history, there has been a constant accumulation and classifying of facts. But what is classification but the perceiving that these objects are not chaotic, and are not foreign, but have a law which is also a law of the human mind? The astronomer discovers that geometry, a pure abstraction of the human mind, is the measure of planetary motion. The chemist finds proportions and intelligible method throughout matter: and science is nothing but the finding of analogy, identity in the most remote parts. The ambitious soul sits down before each refractory fact; one after another, reduces all strange constitutions, all new powers, to their class and their law, and goes on forever to animate the last fibre of organization, the outskirts of nature, by insight.[14]

Thus to him, to this school-boy under the bending dome of day, is suggested, that he and it proceed from one root; one is leaf and one is flower; relation, sympathy, stirring in every vein. And what is that Root? Is not that the soul of his soul?[15]—A thought too bold—a dream too wild. Yet when this spiritual light shall have revealed the law of more earthly natures,—when he has learned to worship the soul, and to see that the natural philosophy that now is, is only the first gropings of its gigantic hand, he shall look forward to an ever expanding knowledge as to a becoming creator. He shall see that nature is the opposite of the soul, answering to it part for part. One is seal, and one is print. Its beauty is the beauty of his own mind. Its laws are the laws of his own mind. Nature then becomes to him the measure of his attainments. So much of nature as he is ignorant of, so much of his own mind does he not

11    In May 1837 Emerson wrote in his Journal, "I am a surprised spectator & learner of all my life. This is the habitual posture of the mind,—beholding" (J:337). Beholden means "indebted," an idea that Emerson joins to perceiving (beholding).

12    In Emerson's poem "Uriel," the rebel angel Uriel proclaims, "Line in nature is not found; / Unit and universe are round; / In vain produced, all rays return; / Evil will bless, and ice will burn." In the next paragraph, Emerson transforms the image of circular power into the scholar's "ever expanding" progressive knowledge.

13    In his Journal (October 15, 1836), Emerson wrote, "It is the constant tendency of the mind to Unify all it beholds, or to reduce the remotest facts to a single law. Hence all endeavors at classification." He added that "there is a tendency in the mind to separate particulars & in magnifying them to lose sight of the connexion of the object with the whole. Hence all false views, Sects; . . ." (J 5:221).

14    "Observe this invincible tendency of the mind to unify," Emerson noted in his Journal (October 13, 1836; J 5:219).

15    As he prepared for his "American Scholar" lecture, Emerson wrote in his Journal (August 19, 1837), "The secret of the scholar or intellectual man is that all nature is only the foliage, the flowering, & the fruit of the Soul and that every part therefore exists as emblem & sign, of some fact in the soul. Instantly rags & offal are elevated into hieroglyphics . . ." (J 5:366; Emerson had used the image of hieroglyphics in *Nature*).

16    Know thyself (in Greek, *Gnôthi seauton*) is the motto inscribed on the oracle at Delphi, and attributed to the Athenian poet and lawgiver Solon (638–558 BCE). "Study nature" is Emerson's phrase for the emphasis on scientific discovery during the Enlightenment, and in thinkers such as J. W. von Goethe (1749–1832).

17    Misguided.

18    In Emerson's vocabulary, Reason is a higher, more comprehensive, and intuitive kind of knowledge, and the Understanding a lower, manipulative power. The distinction derives from German idealist philosophy, as adapted by Samuel Taylor Coleridge (1772–1834), a major influence on Emerson. In a letter to his brother Edward (May 31, 1834) Emerson wrote, "Reason is the highest faculty of the soul—what we mean often by the soul itself; it never *reasons*, never proves, it simply perceives; it is vision" (L 1:412–413).

yet possess. And, in fine, the ancient precept, "Know thyself," and the modern precept, "Study nature," become at last one maxim.[16]

II. The next great influence into the spirit of the scholar, is, the mind of the Past,—in whatever form, whether of literature, of art, of institutions, that mind is inscribed. Books are the best type of the influence of the past, and perhaps we shall get at the truth—learn the amount of this influence more conveniently—by considering their value alone.

The theory of books is noble. The scholar of the first age received into him the world around; brooded thereon; gave it the new arrangement of his own mind, and uttered it again. It came into him—life; it went out from him—truth. It came to him—short-lived actions; it went out from him—immortal thoughts. It came to him—business; it went from him—poetry. It was—dead fact; now, it is quick thought. It can stand, and it can go. It now endures, it now flies, it now inspires. Precisely in proportion to the depth of mind from which it issued, so high does it soar, so long does it sing.

Or, I might say, it depends on how far the process had gone, of transmuting life into truth. In proportion to the completeness of the distillation, so will the purity and imperishableness of the product be. But none is quite perfect. As no air-pump can by any means make a perfect vacuum, so neither can any artist entirely exclude the conventional, the local, the perishable from his book, or write a book of pure thought that shall be as efficient, in all respects, to a remote posterity, as to cotemporaries, or rather to the second age. Each age, it is found, must write its own books; or rather, each generation for the next succeeding. The books of an older period will not fit this.

Yet hence arises a grave mischief. The sacredness which attaches to the act of creation,—the act of thought,—is instantly transferred to the record. The poet chanting, was felt to be a divine man. Henceforth the chant is divine also. The writer was a just and wise spirit. Henceforward it is settled, the book is perfect; as love of the hero corrupts into worship of his statue. Instantly, the book becomes noxious. The guide is a tyrant. We sought a brother, and lo, a governor. The sluggish and perverted[17] mind of the multitude, always slow to open to the incursions of Reason,[18] having once so opened, having once received this book, stands upon it, and makes an outcry, if it is disparaged. Colleges are built on it. Books are written on it by thinkers, not by Man Thinking; by men of talent, that is, who start wrong, who set out from accepted dogmas, not from their own sight of principles. Meek young men grow up in libraries, believing it their duty to accept the views which Cicero, which Locke, which Bacon[19] have given, forgetful that Cicero, Locke and Bacon were only young men in libraries when they wrote these books.

Hence, instead of Man Thinking, we have the bookworm. Hence, the book-learned class, who value books, as such; not as related to nature and the human constitution, but as making a sort of Third Estate with the world and the soul. Hence, the restorers of readings, the emendators, the bibliomaniacs of all degrees.[20]

This is bad; this is worse than it seems. Books are the best of things, well used; abused, among the worst. What is the right use? What is the one end which all means go to effect? They are for nothing but to inspire. I had better never see a book than to be warped by its attraction clean out of my own orbit, and made a satellite instead of a system.[21] The one thing in the world of value, is, the active soul,—the soul, free, sovereign, active. This every man is entitled to; this every man contains within him, although in almost all men, obstructed, and as yet unborn. The soul active sees absolute truth; and utters truth, or creates. In this action, it is genius; not the privilege of here and there a favorite, but the sound estate of every man. In its essence, it is progressive.[22] The book, the college, the school of art, the institution of any kind, stop with some past utterance of genius. This is good, say they,— let us hold by this. They pin me down. They look backward and not forward. But genius always looks forward. The eyes of man are set in his forehead, not in his hindhead. Man hopes. Genius creates.[23] To create,—to create,—is the proof of a divine presence. Whatever talents may be, if the man create not, the pure efflux of the Deity is not his:—cinders and smoke, there may be, but not yet flame. There are creative manners, there are creative actions, and creative words; manners, actions, words, that is, indicative of no custom or authority, but springing spontaneous from the mind's own sense of good and fair.

On the other part, instead of being its own seer, let it receive always from another mind its truth, though it were in torrents of light, without

19    Marcus Tullius Cicero (106–43 BCE), Roman orator and statesman; John Locke (1632–1704), English philosopher; Sir Francis Bacon (1561–1626), English scientist and essayist. Emerson and his Transcendentalist circle considered Locke's empiricism mundane and anticreative; like Cicero and Bacon, Locke stood for methodical, structured thinking. In a Journal entry of August 18, 1837, written while he was preparing "The American Scholar," Emerson wrote, "Now the young are oppressed by their instructors. Bacon or Locke saw and thought . . . now all must be pinned to their thinking which a year after was already too narrow for them. The coverlet is too narrow & too short" (J 5:365).

20    In this paragraph Emerson strikes out against scholarship as it is traditionally defined: his scholar does not occupy himself with the study of textual minutiae.

21    See the image of the pole star in the first paragraph of "The American Scholar." In a letter to his aunt Mary Moody Emerson from Rome (April 18, 1833), Emerson wrote, "I never get used to men. They always awaken expectations in me which they always disappoint, and I am a poor asteroid in the great system subject to disturbances in my orbit not only from all the planets but from all their moons" (L 1:375).

22    Emerson underlines his theme of progress, prominent in the opening paragraphs of "The American Scholar."

23    Genius comes from the Latin *generare*, "to create or beget"; it signifies the inborn power of the individual, a personal creative spark.

24 In his Journal (June 22, 1836) Emerson wrote, "Each new mind we approach seems to require an abdication of all our past & present empire. . . . Take thankfully & heartily all they can give, exhaust them, leave father & mother & goods, wrestle with them, let them not go until their blessing be won, & after a short season the dismay will be overpast, the excess of influence will be withdrawn . . ." (J 5:178–179). (Emerson here alludes to Matthew 10:37 and 19:29, and to Genesis 32:24–30, Jacob's struggle with the angel.)

25 Emerson later developed this observation in his essay "Shakspeare."

26 Nietzsche in his *Ecce Homo* (1888) developed Emerson's thought: "Early in the morning, at break of day, in all the freshness and dawn of one's strength, to read a book—I call that vicious!" Nathaniel Hawthorne (1804–1864) in his short story "Earth's Holocaust" (1844) savagely mocks Emerson's stance when he describes a "modern philosopher" who consigns books to a bonfire, announcing, "Now we shall get rid of the weight of dead men's thought, which has hitherto pressed so heavily on the living intellect . . . Well done, my lads! Into the fire with them! Now you are enlightening the world indeed!"

27 See the Bible's book of Joel 2:10 ("the sun and the moon shall be dark, and the stars shall withdraw their shining"). Emerson makes Joel's apocalyptic image a remarkable but day-to-day event; he also returns to the image of stars, introduced in his first paragraph.

28 In a Notebook from 1835, Emerson exclaimed, "What a benefit if a rule could be given whereby the mind dreaming amidst the gross fogs of matter, could at any moment east itself

*(continued)*

Emerson in lecturing stance, 1869. John Jay Chapman (1862–1933) described Emerson's lecturing style: "The pauses and hesitations, the abstraction, the searching, the balancing, the turning forward and back of the leaves of his lecture, and then the discovery, the illumination, the gleam of lightning which you saw before your eyes descend into a man of genius—all this was Emerson. He invented this style of speaking."

periods of solitude, inquest and self-recovery, and a fatal disservice is done. Genius is always sufficiently the enemy of genius by over-influence.[24] The literature of every nation bear me witness. The English dramatic poets have Shakspearized now for two hundred years.[25]

Undoubtedly there is a right way of reading,—so it be sternly subordinated. Man Thinking must not be subdued by his instruments. Books are for the scholar's idle times. When he can read God directly, the hour is too precious to be wasted in other men's transcripts of their readings.[26] But when the intervals of darkness come, as come they must,—when the soul seeth not, when the sun is hid, and the stars withdraw their shining,[27]—we repair to the lamps which were kindled by their ray to guide our steps to the East again, where the dawn is.[28] We hear that we may speak.[29] The Arabian proverb says, "A fig tree looking on a fig tree, becometh fruitful."

It is remarkable, the character of the pleasure we derive from the best books. They impress us ever with the conviction that one nature wrote and the same reads. We read the verses of one of the great English poets, of Chaucer, of Marvell, of Dryden,[30] with the most modern joy,—with a pleasure, I mean, which is in great part caused by the abstraction of all *time* from their verses. There is some awe mixed with the joy of our surprise, when this poet, who lived in some past world, two or three hundred years ago, says that which lies close to my own soul, that which I also had wellnigh thought and said. But for the evidence thence afforded to the philosophical doctrine of the identity of all minds, we should suppose some pre-established harmony, some foresight of souls that were to be, and some preparation of stores for their future wants, like the fact observed in insects, who lay up food before death for the young grub they shall never see.

I would not be hurried by any love of system, by any exaggeration of instincts, to underrate the Book. We all know, that as the human body can be nourished on any food, though it were boiled grass and the broth of shoes, so the human mind can be fed by any knowledge.[31] And great and heroic men have existed, who had almost no other information than by the printed page. I only would say, that it needs a strong head to bear that diet. One must be an inventor to read well.[32] As the proverb says, "He that would bring home the wealth of the Indies, must carry out the wealth of the Indies." There is then creative reading, as well as creative writing.[33] When the mind

and find the Sun. But the common life is an endless succession of phantasms" (J 5:275–276).

29  A variation on "beholding and beholden" (see note 11 above).

30  Geoffrey Chaucer (ca. 1342–1400), Andrew Marvell (1621–1678), and John Dryden (1631–1700): English poets from (respectively) the Middle Ages, the Renaissance, and the Restoration. Emerson gave a lecture on Chaucer in his 1835 lecture series on the history of English literature.

31  In his Journal (November 1837), Emerson varied the image: "A few kernels of corn will support life as well as tables groaning with meats & sauces from every zone of the globe . . . in the barroom of a country tavern, we find information, & suggestion in every shipping-list & auctioneer's advertisement in a newspaper. A few coals to kindle the fire are as good as a ton" (J 5:429).

32  Emerson relies on the etymology of "inventor," from Latin *invenire* (which means to come upon or discover by chance, often while reading, as well as to invent). In rhetoric, *inventio* (or invention) means the marshalling of persuasive devices.

33  Emerson wrote in his Journal (1845), "It is sad to see people reading again their old books, merely because they don't know what new books they want" (J 9:343). In contrast, he announced in 1847, "Centrality Centrality. 'Your reading is irrelevant.' Yes, for you, but not for me. It makes no difference what I read. If it is irrelevant, I read it deeper. I read it until it is pertinent to me & mine, to nature & to the hour that now passes" (J 10:34–35).

34    Made firm and steady, girded in resolute preparation for a task.

35    Plato, Greek philosopher (429–347 BCE). In his Journal Emerson remarked, "Plato is the articulate speaker, who no longer needs a barbaric paint & tattoo & whooping, for he can define. He leaves with Asia the vast & superlative: he is the arrival of accuracy & intelligence. He is the unrivalled definer" (1845; J 9:325).

36    In 1851, Emerson noted in his Journal that "it is absurd to rail at books: it is as certain that there will always be books, as that there will be clothes" (J 11:428).

37    Emerson often, as here, attacks the tendency to assume a division between speculation and experience. In at least one Journal passage from 1845, however, he expressed pessimism about the scholar's life, writing, "The scholar is led on by the sweet opium of reading to pallor & squalor, to anxiety & timorousness, to a life as dry & thin as his paper, to coldness & hardness & inefficiency" (J 9:275).

38    Henry James (1843–1916), in his 1887 review of James Elliot Cabot's (1821–1903) memoir of Emerson, was bemused by Emerson's "frequent invocation of the 'scholar': there is such a friendly vagueness and convenience in it. It is of the scholar that he expects all the heroic and uncomfortable things," James wrote.

39    Rather than judging the scholar on whether his thoughts result in action, Emerson makes action the preamble (introduction or presage) of thought.

40    Not just heaped, but charged (like a gun) with powerful implication; biased (like a loaded question or loaded dice).

is braced[34] by labor and invention, the page of whatever book we read becomes luminous with manifold allusion. Every sentence is doubly significant, and the sense of our author is as broad as the world. We then see, what is always true, that as the seer's hour of vision is short and rare among heavy days and months, so is its record, perchance, the least part of his volume. The discerning will read in his Plato[35] or Shakspeare, only that least part,—only the authentic utterances of the oracle,—and all the rest he rejects, were it never so many times Plato's and Shakspeare's.

Of course, there is a portion of reading quite indispensable to a wise man.[36] History and exact science he must learn by laborious reading. Colleges, in like manner, have their indispensable office,—to teach elements. But they can only highly serve us, when they aim not to drill, but to create; when they gather from far every ray of various genius to their hospitable halls, and, by the concentrated fires, set the hearts of their youth on flame. Thought and knowledge are natures in which apparatus and pretension avail nothing. Gowns, and pecuniary foundations, though of towns of gold, can never countervail the least sentence or syllable of wit. Forget this, and our American colleges will recede in their public importance whilst they grow richer every year.

III. There goes in the world a notion that the scholar should be a recluse, a valetudinarian,—as unfit for any handiwork or public labor, as a penknife for an axe. The so-called "practical men" sneer at speculative men, as if, because they speculate or *see*, they could do nothing.[37] I have heard it said that the clergy,—who are always more universally than any other class, the scholars of their day,—are addressed as women: that the rough, spontaneous conversation of men they do not hear, but only a mincing and diluted speech. They are often virtually disfranchised; and, indeed, there are advocates for their celibacy. As far as this is true of the studious classes, it is not just and wise. Action is with the scholar subordinate, but it is essential. Without it, he is not yet man. Without it, thought can never ripen into truth. Whilst the world hangs before the eye as a cloud of beauty, we cannot even see its beauty. Inaction is cowardice, but there can be no scholar without the heroic mind.[38] The preamble of thought, the transition through which it passes from the unconscious to the conscious, is action.[39] Only so much do I know, as I have lived. Instantly we know whose words are loaded[40] with life, and whose not.

The world,—this shadow of the soul, or *other me*, lies wide around. Its attractions are the keys which unlock my thoughts and make me acquainted with myself. I run eagerly into this resounding tumult. I grasp the hands of those next me, and take my place in the ring to suffer and to work, taught by an instinct that so shall the dumb abyss be vocal with speech. I pierce its order; I dissipate its fear; I dispose of it within the circuit of my expanding life. So much only of life as I know by experience, so much of the wilderness have I vanquished and planted, or so far have I extended my being, my dominion. I do not see how any man can afford, for the sake of his nerves and his nap, to spare any action in which he can partake. It is pearls and rubies to his discourse.[41] Drudgery, calamity, exasperation, want, are instructers in eloquence and wisdom. The true scholar grudges every opportunity of action past by, as a loss of power.

It is the raw material out of which the intellect moulds her splendid products. A strange process too, this, by which experience is converted into thought, as a mulberry leaf is converted into satin.[42] The manufacture goes forward at all hours.

The actions and events of our childhood and youth are now matters of calmest observation. They lie like fair pictures in the air. Not so with our recent actions,—with the business which we now have in hand. On this we are quite unable to speculate. Our affections as yet circulate through it. We no more feel or know it, than we feel the feet, or the hand, or the brain of our body. The new deed is yet a part of life,—remains for a time immersed in our unconscious life. In some contemplative hour, it detaches itself from the life like a ripe fruit, to become a thought of the mind. Instantly, it is raised, transfigured; the corruptible has put on incorruption.[43] Always now it is an object of beauty, however base its origin and neighborhood. Observe, too, the impossibility of antedating this act. In its grub state, it cannot fly, it cannot shine,—it is a dull grub. But suddenly, without observation, the selfsame thing unfurls beautiful wings, and is an angel of wisdom.[44] So is there no fact, no event, in our private history, which shall not, sooner or later, lose its adhesive inert form, and astonish us by soaring from our body into the empyrean.[45] Cradle and infancy, school and playground, the fear of boys, and dogs, and ferules,[46] the love of little maids and berries, and many another fact that once filled the whole sky, are gone already; friend and relative, pro-

41 Action becomes a lavish, even regal sign of the scholar's discursive power (rather than the purpose or end of his discourse).

42 With a glance back at the "bookworm" from earlier in his lecture (silkworms munch mulberry leaves as bookworms devour the leaves of books). Emerson also looks back to the image of eating "boiled grass and the broth of shoes."

43 I Corinthians 15:53: "For this corruptible must put on incorruption, and this mortal must put on immortality."

44 The ancient Greek word for soul, *psuche*, also means "butterfly or moth"; the mythological character Psyche was often depicted with wings.

45 Heavens, sky.

46 Cane or rod used to beat children in school.

47    Inhabitants of Savoy, Alpine region of Northwest Italy and Southeast France; in Emerson's day part of the kingdom of Sardinia. Emerson's explanation is fanciful: Savoy had suffered from deforestation for hundreds of years, but the shortage of timber was due to house and shipbuilding, not woodcarving. In Emerson's original Journal passage, he wrote, "I sometimes fear that like those Savoyards . . . so I careless of action, intent on composition, have exhausted already all my stock of experience, have fairly written it out" (J 5:353).

48    The French essayist Michel de Montaigne (1533–1592), one of Emerson's key influences, writes in his essay "On the Education of Children," "A mere bookish learning is both troublesom and ungrateful . . . whatsoever presents itself before us, is Book sufficient: An arch or waggish Trick of a Page, a sottish Mistake of a Servant, or a Jest at the Table, are so many new Subjects."

49    "Polarity is a law of all being," Emerson noted in his Journal (April 22, 1837; J 5:304).

50    In Emerson's Journal (May 1837) this sentence was joined to a disappointed reflection on the orator and politician Daniel Webster (1782–1852): "Webster in his speech does but half engage himself" (J 5:318).

fession and party, town and country, nation and world, must also soar and sing.

Of course, he who has put forth his total strength in fit actions, has the richest return of wisdom. I will not shut myself out of this globe of action and transplant an oak into a flower pot, there to hunger and pine; nor trust the revenue of some single faculty, and exhaust one vein of thought, much like those Savoyards,[47] who, getting their livelihood by carving shepherds, shepherdesses, and smoking Dutchmen, for all Europe, went out one day to the mountain to find stock, and discovered that they had whittled up the last of their pine trees. Authors we have in numbers, who have written out their vein, and who, moved by a commendable prudence, sail for Greece or Palestine, follow the trapper into the prairie, or ramble round Algiers to replenish their merchantable stock.

If it were only for a vocabulary the scholar would be covetous of action. Life is our dictionary. Years are well spent in country labors; in town—in the insight into trades and manufactures; in frank intercourse with many men and women; in science; in art; to the one end of mastering in all their facts a language, by which to illustrate and embody our perceptions. I learn immediately from any speaker how much he has already lived, through the poverty or the splendor of his speech. Life lies behind us as the quarry from whence we get tiles and copestones for the masonry of to-day. This is the way to learn grammar. Colleges and books only copy the language which the field and the work-yard made.[48]

But the final value of action, like that of books, and better than books, is, that it is a resource. That great principle of Undulation in nature, that shows itself in the inspiring and expiring of the breath; in desire and satiety; in the ebb and flow of the sea, in day and night, in heat and cold, and as yet more deeply ingrained in every atom and every fluid, is known to us under the name of Polarity,[49]—these "fits of easy transmission and reflection," as Newton called them, are the law of nature because they are the law of spirit.

The mind now thinks; now acts; and each fit reproduces the other. When the artist has exhausted his materials, when the fancy no longer paints, when thoughts are no longer apprehended, and books are a weariness,—he has always the resource *to live*. Character is higher than intellect.[50] Thinking is the function. Living is the functionary. The stream retreats to its source. A great soul will be strong to live, as well as strong to think. Does he lack organ or medium to impart his truths? He can still fall back on this elemental force of living them. This is a total act. Thinking is a partial act. Let the grandeur of justice shine in his affairs. Let the beauty of affection cheer his lowly roof. Those "far from fame" who dwell and act with him, will feel the force of his constitution in the doings and passages of the day better than it can be measured by any public and designed display. Time shall teach him that the scholar loses no hour which the man lives. Herein he unfolds the sacred germ of his instinct, screened from influence. What is lost in seemliness is gained in strength. Not out of those on whom systems of education have exhausted their culture, comes the helpful giant to destroy the old or to build the new, but out of unhandselled savage nature, out of terrible Druids and Berserkirs, come at last Alfred and Shakspear.[51]

I hear therefore with joy whatever is beginning to be said of the dignity and necessity of labor to every citizen. There is virtue yet in the hoe and the spade, for learned as well as for unlearned hands. And labor is every where welcome; always we are invited to work; only be this limitation observed, that a man shall not for the sake of wider activity sacrifice any opinion to the popular judgments and modes of action.

I have now spoken of the education of the scholar by nature, by books, and by action. It remains to say somewhat of his duties.

They are such as become Man Thinking.[52] They may all be comprised in self-trust. The office of the scholar is to cheer, to raise, and to guide men by showing them facts amidst appearances. He plies the slow, unhonored, and unpaid task of observation. Flamsteed and Herschel,[53] in their glazed observatories, may catalogue the stars with the praise of all men, and, the results being splendid and useful, honor is sure. But he, in his private observatory, cataloguing obscure and nebulous stars of the human mind,[54] which as yet no man has thought of as such,—watching days and months, sometimes, for a few facts; correcting still his old records;—must relinquish display and immediate fame. In the long period of his preparation, he must betray often an ignorance and shiftlessness in popular arts, incurring the disdain of the able who shoulder him aside. Long he must stammer in his speech; often forego the living for the dead. Worse yet, he must accept—how often! poverty and solitude.[55] For the ease and pleasure of treading the

51 The Berserkirs were raging, frenzied Norse warriors, described in medieval sagas; the Druids, ancient pagan priests of the British Isles, thought to practice human sacrifice. King Alfred (847–899) was a learned king of the Anglo-Saxons who reformed law and education. On September 30, 1836, Emerson wrote in his Journal, "Genius hurts us by its excessive influence, hurts the freedom & inborn faculty of the individual . . . But by this screen of porcupine quills, of bad manners & hatred, is the sacred germ of individual genius concealed & guarded in Secular darkness. After centuries, will it be born a god. Out of Druids & Berserkirs were Alfred & Shakspear made" (J 5:217). Emerson read in the English historian Sharon Turner's (1768–1847) *History of the Anglo-Saxons* (1799–1805) a depiction of the ancient Britons as a savage, primitive race.

52 Here and elsewhere, Emerson defines the scholar in broader terms than we are used to: as a public intellectual and an exemplary figure and guide, rather than as a mere researcher.

53 John Flamsteed (1646–1719) and Sir William Herschel (1738–1822), English astronomers.

54 Emerson continues the star imagery that runs throughout "The American Scholar."

55 Emerson remarked in his Journal (January 1836), "The Scholar works with invisible tools to invisible ends. So passes for an idler or worse; brain sick; defenceless . . . he studies the art of solitude. . . ." (J 5:116–117).

56    In contrast to the scholar's progress. Emerson delivered "The American Scholar" in the
first year of a banking crisis: the Panic of 1837,
which led to a five-year depression and enormous financial hardship. America was far from
prosperous in August 1837.

57    In the Journal remarks from August 1837
that provide the basis for this passage, Emerson
added, "The wisdom that he painfully gathers
sweetens his own life" (J 5:360).

58    Object irrationally venerated; idol.

59    See note 27, on the apocalyptic image
from Joel.

old road, accepting the fashions, the education, the religion of society, he takes the cross of making his own, and, of course, the self-accusation, the faint heart, the frequent uncertainty and loss of time which are the nettles and tangling vines in the way of the self-relying and self-directed; and the state of virtual hostility in which he seems to stand to society, and especially to educated society. For all this loss and scorn, what offset? He is to find consolation in exercising the highest functions of human nature. He is one who raises himself from private considerations, and breathes and lives on public and illustrious thoughts. He is the world's eye. He is the world's heart. He is to resist the vulgar prosperity that retrogrades ever to barbarism,[56] by preserving and communicating heroic sentiments, noble biographies, melodious verse, and the conclusions of history. Whatsoever oracles the human heart in all emergencies, in all solemn hours has uttered as its commentary on the world of actions,—these he shall receive and impart.[57] And whatsoever new verdict Reason from her inviolable seat pronounces on the passing men and events of to-day,—this he shall hear and promulgate.

These being his functions, it becomes him to feel all confidence in himself, and to defer never to the popular cry. He and he only knows the world. The world of any moment is the merest appearance. Some great decorum, some fetish[58] of a government, some ephemeral trade, or war, or man, is cried up by half mankind and cried down by the other half, as if all depended on this particular up or down. The odds are that the whole question is not worth the poorest thought which the scholar has lost in listening to the controversy. Let him not quit his belief that a popgun is a popgun, though the ancient and honorable of the earth affirm it to be the crack of doom.[59] In silence, in steadiness, in severe abstraction, let him hold by himself; add observation to observation, patient of neglect, patient of reproach; and bide his own time,—happy enough if he can satisfy himself alone that this day he has seen something truly. Success treads on every right step. For the instinct is sure that prompts him to tell his brother what he thinks. He then learns that in going down into the secrets of his own mind, he has descended into the secrets of all minds. He learns that he who has mastered any law in his private thoughts, is master to that extent of all men whose language he speaks, and of all into whose language his own can be translated. The poet in utter solitude remembering his spontaneous thoughts and

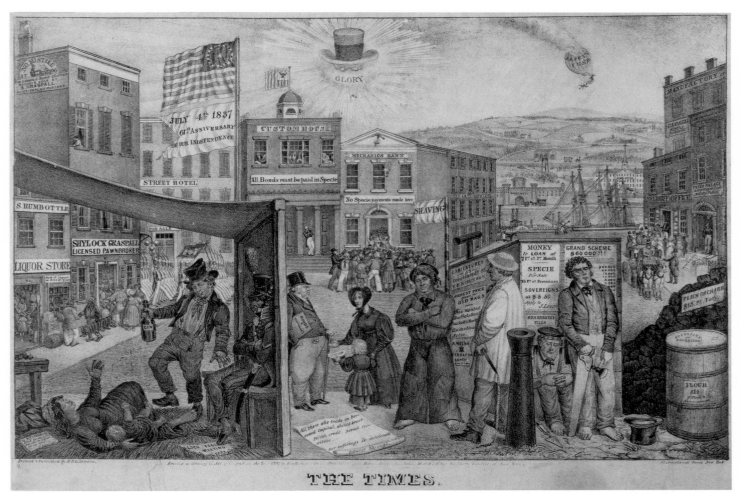

The Panic of 1837. The hat, glasses, and clay pipe in the sky belong to President Andrew Jackson (1767–1845), who is blamed for the crisis in this contemporary caricature.

Ralph Waldo Emerson.

recording them, is found to have recorded that which men in crowded cities find true for them also. The orator distrusts at first the fitness of his frank confessions,—his want of knowledge of the persons he addresses,—until he finds that he is the complement of his hearers;—that they drink his words because he fulfils for them their own nature; the deeper he dives into his privatest secretest presentiment,—to his wonder he finds, this is the most acceptable, most public, and universally true. The people delight in it; the better part of every man feels, This is my music: this is myself.

In self-trust, all the virtues are comprehended. Free should the scholar be,—free and brave. Free even to the definition of freedom, "without any hindrance that does not arise out of his own constitution." Brave; for fear is a thing which a scholar by his very function puts behind him. Fear always springs from ignorance. It is a shame to him if his tranquillity, amid dangerous times, arise from the presumption that like children and women, his is a protected class; or if he seek a temporary peace by the diversion of his thoughts from politics or vexed questions, hiding his head like an ostrich in the flowering bushes, peeping into microscopes, and turning rhymes, as a boy whistles to keep his courage up. So is the danger a danger still: so is the fear worse. Manlike let him turn and face it. Let him look into its eye and search its nature, inspect its origin,—see the whelping of this lion,—which lies no great way back; he will then find in himself a perfect comprehension of its nature and extent; he will have made his hands meet on the other side, and can henceforth defy it, and pass on superior. The world is his who can see through its pretension. What deafness, what stone-blind custom, what overgrown error you behold, is there only by sufferance,—by your sufferance. See it to be a lie, and you have already dealt it its mortal blow.

Yes, we are the cowed,—we the trustless. It is a mischievous notion that we are come late into nature; that the world was finished a long time ago. As the world was plastic and fluid in the hands of God, so it is ever to so much of his attributes as we bring to it. To ignorance and sin, it is flint. They adapt themselves to it as they may; but in proportion as a man has anything in him divine, the firmament flows before him, and takes his signet and form. Not he is great who can alter matter, but he who can alter my state of mind. They are the kings of the world who give the color of their present thought to all

nature and all art, and persuade men by the cheerful serenity of their carrying the matter, that this thing which they do, is the apple which the ages
have desired to pluck, now at last ripe, and inviting nations to the harvest.
The great man makes the great thing. Wherever Macdonald sits, there is the
head of the table.[60] Linnæus makes botany the most alluring of studies and
wins it from the farmer and the herb-woman. Davy, chemistry: and Cuvier,
fossils.[61] The day is always his, who works in it with serenity and great aims.
The unstable estimates of men crowd to him whose mind is filled with a
truth, as the heaped waves of the Atlantic follow the moon.

For this self-trust, the reason is deeper than can be fathomed,—darker
than can be enlightened. I might not carry with me the feeling of my audience in stating my own belief. But I have already shown the ground of my
hope, in adverting to the doctrine that man is one. I believe man has been
wronged: he has wronged himself. He has almost lost the light that can lead
him back to his prerogatives. Men are become of no account. Men in history,
men in the world of to-day are bugs, are spawn, and are called "the mass"
and "the herd." In a century, in a millenium, one or two men; that is to say—
one or two approximations to the right state of every man. All the rest behold in the hero or the poet their own green and crude being—ripened; yes,
and are content to be less, so *that* may attain to its full stature. What a testimony—full of grandeur, full of pity, is borne to the demands of his own nature, by the poor clansman, the poor partisan, who rejoices in the glory of
his chief. The poor and the low find some amends to their immense moral
capacity, for their acquiescence in a political and social inferiority.[62] They are
content to be brushed like flies from the path of a great person, so that justice shall be done by him to that common nature which it is the dearest desire of all to see enlarged and glorified. They sun themselves in the great
man's light, and feel it to be their own element. They cast the dignity of man
from their downtrod selves upon the shoulders of a hero, and will perish to
add one drop of blood to make that great heart beat, those giant sinews combat and conquer. He lives for us, and we live in him.

Men such as they are, very naturally seek money or power; and power
because it is as good as money,—the "spoils," so called, "of office." And why
not? for they aspire to the highest, and this, in their sleep-walking, they

60    "Where MacGregor sits, there is the
head of the table": attributed to Robert "Rob
Roy" MacGregor (1671–1734), the Scottish
hero featured in *Rob Roy* (1817) by Sir Walter
Scott (1771–1832). Emerson alters the name to
Macdonald. The American poet Wallace Stevens (1879–1955) in *Notes toward a Supreme Fiction* (1942) depicts "the MacCullough" as "major man."

61    Carl Linnaeus (1707–1778), Swedish
botanist; Sir Humphry Davy (1778–1829), English chemist; and Georges Dagobert, Baron
Cuvier (1769–1832), French paleontologist.

62    In the Journal entry from which Emerson derived this passage (August 1837), he
added, "This is the principle of Aristocracy in
history, its foundation in human nature . . ."
(J 5:354).

63    Emerson plays on the German word for
education, *Bildung*. In a Notebook passage
(probably from the late 1830s), he lamented, "A
man esteems himself as a mere circumstance &
not as the solid adamant mundane ground plan
of a universal man" (J 12:195).

dream is highest. Wake them, and they shall quit the false good and leap to
the true, and leave governments to clerks and desks. This revolution is to be
wrought by the gradual domestication of the idea of Culture. The main enterprise of the world for splendor, for extent, is the upbuilding of a man.
Here are the materials strown along the ground.[63] The private life of one
man shall be a more illustrious monarchy,—more formidable to its enemy,
more sweet and serene in its influence to its friend, than any kingdom in history. For a man, rightly viewed, comprehendeth the particular natures of all
men. Each philosopher, each bard, each actor, has only done for me, as by a
delegate, what one day I can do for myself. The books which once we valued
more than the apple of the eye, we have quite exhausted. What is that but
saying that we have come up with the point of view which the universal mind
took through the eyes of that one scribe; we have been that man, and have
passed on. First, one; then, another; we drain all cisterns, and waxing greater
by all these supplies, we crave a better and more abundant food. The man
has never lived that can feed us ever. The human mind cannot be enshrined
in a person who shall set a barrier on any one side to this unbounded, un-
boundable empire. It is one central fire which flaming now out of the lips of
Etna, lightens the capes of Sicily; and now out of the throat of Vesuvius, illuminates the towers and vineyards of Naples. It is one light which beams
out of a thousand stars. It is one soul which animates all men.

But I have dwelt perhaps tediously upon this abstraction of the Scholar.
I ought not to delay longer to add what I have to say, of nearer reference to
the time and to this country.

Historically, there is thought to be a difference in the ideas which predominate over successive epochs, and there are data for marking the genius
of the Classic, of the Romantic, and now of the Reflective or Philosophical
age. With the views I have intimated of the oneness or the identity of the
mind through all individuals, I do not much dwell on these differences. In
fact, I believe each individual passes through all three. The boy is a Greek;
the youth, romantic; the adult, reflective. I deny not, however, that a revolution in the leading idea may be distinctly enough traced.

Our age is bewailed as the age of Introversion. Must that needs be evil?
We, it seems, are critical. We are embarrassed with second thoughts. We

cannot enjoy any thing for hankering to know whereof the pleasure consists. We are lined with eyes. We see with our feet.[64] The time is infected with Hamlet's unhappiness,[65]—

"Sicklied o'er with the pale cast of thought."[66]

Is it so bad then? Sight is the last thing to be pitied. Would we be blind? Do we fear lest we should outsee nature and God, and drink truth dry? I look upon the discontent of the literary class as a mere announcement of the fact that they find themselves not in the state of mind of their fathers, and regret the coming state as untried; as a boy dreads the water before he has learned that he can swim. If there is any period one would desire to be born in,—is it not the age of Revolution; when the old and the new stand side by side, and admit of being compared; when the energies of all men are searched by fear and by hope; when the historic glories of the old, can be compensated by the rich possibilities of the new era? This time, like all times, is a very good one, if we but know what to do with it.

I read with joy some of the auspicious signs of the coming days as they glimmer already through poetry and art, through philosophy and science, through church and state.

One of these signs is the fact that the same movement which effected the elevation of what was called the lowest class in the state, assumed in literature a very marked and as benign an aspect. Instead of the sublime and beautiful, the near, the low, the common, was explored and poetized. That which had been negligently trodden under foot by those who were harnessing and provisioning themselves for long journeys into far countries, is suddenly found to be richer than all foreign parts. The literature of the poor, the feelings of the child, the philosophy of the street, the meaning of household life, are the topics of the time. It is a great stride. It is a sign—is it not? of new vigor, when the extremities are made active, when currents of warm life run into the hands and the feet.[67] I ask not for the great, the remote, the romantic; what is doing in Italy or Arabia; what is Greek art, or Provencal Minstrelsy; I embrace the common, I explore and sit at the feet of the familiar, the low.[68] Give me insight into to-day, and you may have the antique and

64    Obliquely echoes Hamlet's words to his mother, Gertrude (3.4.79–80), "Eyes without feeling, feeling without sight / Ears without hands or eyes, smelling sans all." Emerson reminds us of the image of isolated body parts from early on in his lecture (see note 6, above). On August 19, 1834, he exclaimed in his Journal, "What mischief is in this art of Writing. An unlettered man considers a fact to learn what it means; the lettered man does not sooner see it than it occurs to him how it can be told. . . . He has a morbid growth of eyes; he sees with his feet" (J 4:314).

65    "Unhappiness" has something of its etymological sense of mischance or untimeliness (a hap is a chance event).

66    *Hamlet* (3.1.85).

67    See the contrasting image at the top of this page: "We are lined with eyes. We see with our feet."

68    In his Journal (January 1836) Emerson exclaimed, "Meanest life a thread of empyrean light. Scholar converts for them the dishonored facts which they know, into trees of life" (J 5:117).

69    In the Journal entry that provided the basis of this passage (August 4, 1837), Emerson wrote, "the meal in the firkin, the milk in the pan, the beggar and the insane man, aunts & cousins" (L 5:352). In "Large Red Man Reading" (1950) by Wallace Stevens, Stevens writes of "ghosts that returned to earth to hear his phrases": "There were those that returned to hear him read from the poem of life, / Of the pans above the stove, the pots on the table, the tulips among them. / They were those that would have wept to step barefoot into reality . . ."

70    Room in a house filled with old furniture.

71    Oliver Goldsmith (1730?–1774), English poet and prose writer; Robert Burns (1759–1796), Scottish poet; William Cowper (1731–1800), English poet.

72    William Wordsworth (1770–1850), English poet, like Goethe and Carlyle a champion of imagination's power to connect the ordinary and the sublime. Emerson wrote to his aunt Mary Moody Emerson about Goethe (August 19, 1832), "The Germans regard him as the restorer of Faith & Love after the desolations of Hume & the French. that he married Faith & Reason, for the world" (L 1:354; Emerson refers to David Hume [1711–1776], the Scottish skeptical philosopher). On August 8, 1836, Emerson wrote to his brother William that "Goethe is a wonderful man. I read little else than his books lately" (L 2:33).

73    Alexander Pope (1688–1744), English Neoclassical poet; Dr. Samuel Johnson (1709–1784), imposing literary critic and man of letters; Edward Gibbon (1737–1794), historian of ancient Rome.

future worlds. What would we really know the meaning of? The meal in the firkin; the milk in the pan;[69] the ballad in the street; the news of the boat; the glance of the eye; the form and the gait of the body;—show me the ultimate reason of these matters;—show me the sublime presence of the highest spiritual cause lurking, as always it does lurk, in these suburbs and extremities of nature; let me see every trifle bristling with the polarity that ranges it instantly on an eternal law; and the shop, the plough, and the leger, referred to the like cause by which light undulates and poets sing;—and the world lies no longer a dull miscellany and lumber room,[70] but has form and order; there is no trifle; there is no puzzle; but one design unites and animates the farthest pinnacle and the lowest trench.

This idea has inspired the genius of Goldsmith, Burns, Cowper,[71] and, in a newer time, of Goethe, Wordsworth, and Carlyle.[72] This idea they have differently followed and with various success. In contrast with their writing, the style of Pope, of Johnson, of Gibbon,[73] looks cold and pedantic. This writing is blood-warm. Man is surprised to find that things near are not less beautiful and wondrous than things remote. The near explains the far. The drop is a small ocean. A man is related to all nature. This perception of the worth of the vulgar, is fruitful in discoveries. Goethe, in this very thing the most modern of the moderns, has shown us, as none ever did, the genius of the ancients.

There is one man of genius who has done much for this philosophy of life, whose literary value has never yet been rightly estimated;—I mean Emanuel Swedenborg.[74] The most imaginative of men, yet writing with the precision of a mathematician, he endeavored to engraft a purely philosophical Ethics on the popular Christianity of his time. Such an attempt, of course, must have difficulty which no genius could surmount. But he saw and showed the connexion between nature and the affections of the soul. He pierced the emblematic or spiritual character of the visible, audible, tangible world. Especially did his shade-loving muse hover over and interpret the lower parts of nature; he showed the mysterious bond that allies moral evil to the foul material forms, and has given in epical parables a theory of insanity, of beasts, of unclean and fearful things.

Another sign of our times, also marked by an analogous political movement is, the new importance given to the single person. Every thing that tends to insulate the individual,—to surround him with barriers of natural respect, so that each man shall feel the world is his, and man shall treat with man as a sovereign state with a sovereign state;—tends to true union as well as greatness. "I learned," said the melancholy Pestalozzi,[75] "that no man in God's wide earth is either willing or able to help any other man." Help must come from the bosom alone. The scholar is that man who must take up into himself all the ability of the time, all the contributions of the past, all the hopes of the future. He must be an university of knowledges. If there be one lesson more than another which should pierce his ear, it is, The world is nothing, the man is all; in yourself is the law of all nature, and you know not yet how a globule of sap ascends; in yourself slumbers the whole of Reason; it is for you to know all, it is for you to dare all. Mr. President and Gentlemen, this confidence in the unsearched might of man, belongs by all motives, by all prophecy, by all preparation, to the American Scholar. We have listened too long to the courtly muses of Europe. The spirit of the American freeman is already suspected to be timid, imitative, tame. Public and private avarice make the air we breathe thick and fat. The scholar is decent, indolent, complaisant. See already the tragic consequence. The mind of this country taught to aim at low objects, eats upon itself. There is no work for any but the decorous and the complaisant. Young men of the fairest promise, who begin life upon our shores, inflated by the mountain winds, shined upon by all the stars of God, find the earth below not in unison with these,—but are hindered from action by the disgust which the principles on which business is managed inspire, and turn drudges, or die of disgust,—some of them suicides.[76] What is the remedy? They did not yet see, and thousands of young men as hopeful now crowding to the barriers for the career, do not yet see, that if the single man plant himself indomitably on his instincts, and there abide, the huge world will come round to him. Patience—patience;—with the shades of all the good and great for company; and for solace, the perspective of your own infinite life; and for work, the study and the communication of principles, the making those instincts prevalent, the conversion of the world. Is it not the chief disgrace in the world, not to be an unit;—not to be reckoned one character;—not to yield that peculiar fruit[77] which each man was created to bear, but to be reckoned in the gross, in the hundred, or the thousand, of the party, the section, to which we belong; and our opinion

74   Swedish mystic and philosopher (1688–1772).

75   Johann Heinrich Pestalozzi (1746–1827) was a Swiss educational reformer and an influence on Emerson's friends Bronson Alcott (1799–1888), founder of the Temple School in Boston, and Elizabeth Peabody (1804–1894), who opened the first American kindergarten.

76   The Panic of 1837 had already led to suicides. On April 22, 1837, Emerson commented on the crisis in his Journal, "Cold April; hard times; men breaking who ought not to break . . . all the newspapers a chorus of owls. . . . Loud cracks in the social edifice" (J 5:304). The financial crisis hit on May 10, 1837, when banks in New York announced that they would accept payment only in specie (gold or silver coins). Many blamed the Panic on the economic policies of President Andrew Jackson (1767–1845), who had left office in March; but feverish speculation in land during the 1830s—an unsustainable "bubble"—was the deeper cause.

77   Result. In "Experience," Emerson writes, "I find a private fruit sufficient."

78    In "Self-Reliance" Emerson complains, "If I know your sect, I anticipate your argument."

79    Emerson again draws on the image of the body and its parts that recurs often in "The American Scholar."

80    "We must have society, provocation, a whip for the top. A Scholar is a candle which the love & desire of all men will light. Let it not lie in a dark box. But here I am with so much all ready to be revealed to me as to others if only I could be set aglow" (March–April 1847; J 10:28).

predicted geographically, as the north, or the south.[78] Not so, brothers and friends,—please God, ours shall not be so. We will walk on our own feet; we will work with our own hands; we will speak our own minds.[79] The study of letters shall be no longer a name for pity, for doubt, and for sensual indulgence. The dread of man and the love of man shall be a wall of defence and a wreath of joy around all. A nation of men will for the first time exist, because each believes himself inspired by the Divine Soul which also inspires all men.[80]

Alumni procession from the First Parish Meeting House, Cambridge, Massachusetts, where Emerson delivered "The American Scholar."

# Letter to Martin Van Buren, President of the United States, Concord, Mass., April 23, 1838

SIR: The seat you fill places you in a relation of credit and dearness to every citizen. By right and natural position, every citizen is your friend. Before any acts, contrary to his own judgment or interest, have repelled the affections of any man, each may look with trust and living anticipations to your government. Each has the highest right to call your attention to such subjects as are of a public nature, and properly belong to the Chief Magistrate; and the good magistrate will feel a joy in meeting such confidence. In this belief, and at the instance of a few of my friends and neighbors,[1] I crave of your patience, through the medium of the press, a short hearing for their sentiments and my own; and the circumstance that my name will be utterly unknown to you will only give the fairer chance to your equitable construction of what I have to say.

Sir, my communication respects the sinister rumors that fill this part of the country concerning the Cherokee people. The interest always felt in the aboriginal population—an interest naturally growing as that decays—has been heightened in regard to this tribe. Even in our distant State, some good rumor of their worth and civility has arrived. We have learned with joy their improvement in social arts. We have read their newspapers. We have seen some of them in our schools and colleges. In common with the great body of the American People, we have witnessed with sympathy the painful labors of these red men to redeem their own race from the doom of eternal inferiority,

*Van Buren (1782–1862), much disliked by Emerson, became president in 1837. He had been vice president under Andrew Jackson (1767–1845) and continued Jackson's policy of Indian removal.*

*In 1827 the state of Georgia refused to recognize the sovereignty of the Cherokee Nation, announced in their written constitution of that year. The dispute continued until 1831, when the Supreme Court decided in favor of the Cherokee, declaring that they were not bound by Georgia state law (though the Court denied the tribe full sovereignty). But Georgia would not abide by the Supreme Court decision, and President Jackson supported Georgia against the Cherokee. Jackson was the architect of the Indian Removal Act of 1830, designed to transfer the Indians to lands west of the Mississippi to make room for white settlers. A small group of Cherokee signed a removal agreement, the Treaty of New Echota, in 1835. The Senate ratified the treaty by a margin of one vote in May 1836. This time, the Supreme Court upheld the treaty. By late April, U.S. soldiers were preparing for the roundup of the Cherokee; the removal began in October. The Cherokee were marched westward under brutal conditions to*

*(continued)*

*Arkansas and Oklahoma territories. About four thousand died on what became known as the Trail of Tears.*

*Emerson composed the final version of his letter on April 18, 1838. The next day he wrote in his Journal about "this disaster of the Cherokees. . . . I can do nothing; why shriek? why strike ineffectual blows? I stir in it for the sad reason that no other mortal will move, and if I do not, why, it is left undone. The amount of it, to be sure, is merely a scream; but sometimes a scream is better than a thesis." He went on to describe his letter to Van Buren as "a letter hated of me, a deliverance that does not deliver the soul. I write my journal, I read my lecture with joy, but this stirring in the philanthropic mud gives me no peace" (J 5:479).*

*Emerson sent his letter to Massachusetts Congressman John Reed, who published it in the Washington Daily National Intelligencer on May 14, 1838. Over the next few months it appeared in four other newspapers, including the Liberator (June 22, 1838), edited by the fiery abolitionist William Lloyd Garrison (1805–1879). The Intelligencer text is reprinted here.*

1       Emerson's wife Lidian was a prominent defender of the Cherokee against the government. Emerson was the first speaker at Concord's meeting in opposition to the government's Cherokee policy (on April 22, 1838). At this meeting, Emerson seems to have read the "Appeal of the Cherokees" (of July 17, 1830), in which they said, "If we are compelled to leave our country, we see nothing but ruin before us. The country west of the Arkansas territory is unknown to us. . . . The original possessors of that region are now wandering savages lurking for prey in the neighborhood. They have always been at war, and would be easily tempted to turn their arms against peaceful emigrants. Were the country to which we are urged much

*(continued)*

and to borrow and domesticate in the tribe the inventions and customs of the Caucasian race.[2] And notwithstanding the unaccountable apathy with which, of late years, the Indians have been sometimes abandoned to their enemies,[3] it is not to be doubted that it is the good pleasure and the understanding of all humane persons in the Republic, of the men and the matrons sitting in thriving independent families all over the land, that they shall be duly cared for, that they shall taste justice and love from all to whom we have delegated the office of dealing with them.

Sequoyah (1776–1843), inventor of a writing system for the Cherokee language.

Antiremoval tract by the
Cherokee Nation (1831).

THE CASE

OF

# THE CHEROKEE NATION

*against*

THE STATE OF GEORGIA:

ARGUED AND DETERMINED AT

THE SUPREME COURT OF THE UNITED STATES,

JANUARY TERM 1831.

WITH

AN APPENDIX,

Containing the Opinion of Chancellor Kent on the Case ; the Treaties between
the United States and the Cherokee Indians ; the Act of Congress of
1802, entitled 'An Act to regulate intercourse with the Indian
tribes, &c.'; and the Laws of Georgia relative to the
country occupied by the Cherokee Indians,
within the boundary of that State.

BY RICHARD PETERS,

COUNSELLOR AT LAW.

Philadelphia:

JOHN GRIGG, 9 NORTH FOURTH STREET.

1831.

better than it is represented to be, and were it free from the objections which we have made to it, still it is not the land of our birth, nor of our affections. It contains neither the scenes of our childhood, nor the graves of our fathers." After the removal to the west, the Cherokee suffered a lengthy civil war, which Chief John Ross (1790–1866), the leader of the Cherokee in Georgia and a fervent opponent of removal, eventually won. They contended as well with a slave revolt and a war with the Republic of Texas.

2    The Cherokee were skilled farmers, and over half could read in their native language. The Cherokee scholar Sequoyah (1776–1843) developed the Cherokee alphabet in 1821; within four years, books were translated into Cherokee, and a newspaper began in 1828. Prominent Cherokee were well-educated; some, like Ross, were wealthy slaveowners.

3    The president who preceded Jackson, John Quincy Adams (1767–1848, president 1825–1829), was sympathetic to Indian rights.

4    Among them Major Ridge (ca. 1771–1839), his son John Ridge (1792–1839), and Elias Boudinot (1802–1839). Ross's faction killed all three after the tribe arrived in the west.

5    The actual number was even higher: 15,964. Ross presented the petition to Congress in February 1838.

The newspapers now inform us that in December, 1835, a treaty, contracting for the exchange of the entire Cherokee territory, was pre-tended to be made by an agent on the part of the United States with some persons appearing on the part of the Cherokees;[4] that the fact afterwards transpired that these individual Indians did by no means represent the will of the nation; and that, out of eighteen thousand souls composing the nation, fifteen thousand six hundred and sixty-eight have protested against the so-called treaty.[5] It now appears that the government of the United States choose to hold the Cherokees to this sham treaty, and the proceeding to execute the

6    In his original, unsent version of the letter (April 10, 1838), Emerson wrote, "And the
American President, the Senate, & the House
neither hear nor see. Their eyes are nailed to
the question of finance their ears hear only of
the currency & they are proceeding to put this
nation into carts & rafts & drag them over
mountains & rivers" (J 12:26).

7    The removal, led by General Winfield
Scott (1786–1866), began on May 23.

8    In his first version of the letter Emerson
continued, "Do they forget in the zeal of business the majesty of principles?" (J 12:27).

9    Curses.

10   Deceit.

same. Almost the entire Cherokee Nation stand up and say, "This is not our
act. Behold us. Here are we. Do not mistake that handful of deserters for
us." And the American President and the Cabinet, the Senate and the House
of Representatives, neither hear these men nor see them,[6] and are contracting to put this nation into carts and boats, and to drag them over mountains
and rivers to a wilderness at a vast distance beyond the Mississippi. And a
paper purporting to be an army order fixes a month from this day as the hour
for this doleful removal.[7]

In the name of God, sir, we ask you if this be so. Do the newspapers
rightly inform us? Men and women, with pale and perplexed faces, meet one
another in streets and churches here, and ask if this be so? We have inquired
if this be a gross misrepresentation from the party opposed to the government and anxious to blacken it with the People. We have looked in the newspapers of different parties and find a horrid confirmation of the tale. We are
slow to believe it. We hoped the Indians were misinformed, and their remonstrance was premature, and would turn out to be a needless act of terror.
The piety, the principle, that is left in these United States—if only its coarsest form, a regard to the speech of men—forbid us to entertain it as a fact.
Such a dereliction of all faith and virtue, such a denial of justice, and such
deafness to screams for mercy were never heard of in times of peace, and in
the dealing of a nation with its own allies and wards, since the earth was
made. Sir, does the Government think that the People of the United States
are become savage and mad?[8] From their mind are the sentiments of love
and of a good nature wiped clean out? The soul of man, the justice, the
mercy, that is the heart's heart in all men, from Maine to Georgia, does ab-
hor this business.

In speaking thus the sentiments of my neighbors and my own, perhaps
I overstep the bounds of decorum. But would it not be a higher indecorum
coldly to argue a matter like this? We only state the fact, that a crime is projected that confounds our understandings by its magnitude,—a crime that
really deprives us as well as the Cherokees of a country; for how could we
call the conspiracy that should crush these poor Indians our Government, or
the land that was cursed by their parting and dying imprecations[9] our country, any more? You, sir, will bring down that renowned chair in which you
sit into infamy if your seal is set to this instrument of perfidy;[10] and the name

President Martin Van Buren (1782–1862).

11    Specks. In his first draft Emerson wrote "the prostration of currency, the good & evil of banks, the vicissitudes of exchange, the questions of territory, are dust & ashes in the comparison" (J 12:28).

12    The last half of this sentence originally ran "& they shall assume the attitude & do the deed of devils by the Cherokee Nation" (J 12:28).

13    Lack of confidence in.

14    Protest against.

15    There was considerable opposition to Jackson's program for Indian removal, beginning with a famous six-hour speech in the Senate by Theodore Frelinghuysen (1787–1862), senator of New Jersey (April 7–9, 1830).

of this nation, hitherto the sweet omen of religion and liberty, will stink to the world.

You will not do us the injustice of connecting this remonstrance with any sectional and party feeling. It is in our hearts the simplest commandment of brotherly love. We will not have this great and solemn claim upon national and human justice huddled aside under the flimsy plea of its being a party act. Sir, to us the questions upon which the government and the people have been agitated during the past year, touching the prostration of the currency and of trade, seem motes[11] in comparison. These hard times, it is true, have brought this discussion home to every farmhouse and poor man's table in this town, but it is the chirping of grasshoppers, beside the immortal question whether justice shall be done by the race of civilized to the race of savage man; whether all the attributes of reason, of civility, of justice, and even of mercy, shall be put off by the American People, and so vast an outrage upon the Cherokee nation, and upon human nature, shall be consummated.[12]

One circumstance lessens the reluctance with which I intrude on your attention: my conviction that the Government ought to be admonished of a new historical fact, which the discussion of this question has disclosed, namely, that there exists in a great part of the Northern People a gloomy diffidence of[13] the *moral* character of the Government. On the broaching of this question, a general expression of despondency, of disbelief that any good will accrue from a remonstrance on[14] an act of fraud and robbery, appeared in those men to whom we naturally turn for aid and counsel. Will the American Government steal? will it lie? will it kill? We asked triumphantly. Our wise men shake their heads dubiously. Our counsellors and old statesmen here say that, ten years ago, they would have staked their life on the affirmation that the proposed Indian measures could not be executed; that the unanimous country would put them down.[15] And now the steps of this crime follow each other so fast, at such fatally quick time, that the millions of virtuous citizens whose agents the government are, have no place to interpose, and must shut their eyes until the last howl and wailing of these tormented villages and tribes shall afflict the ear of the world.

I will not hide from you as an indication of the alarming distrust, that a letter addressed as mine is, and suggesting to the mind of the Executive the plain obligations of man, has a burlesque character in the apprehension of some of my friends.[16] I, sir, will not beforehand treat you with the contumely[17] of this distrust. I will at least state to you this fact, and show you how plain and humane people whose love would be honor regard the policy of the Government and what injurious inferences they draw as to the mind of the governors. A man with your experience in affairs must have seen cause to appreciate the futility of opposition to the moral sentiment. However feeble the sufferer, and however great the oppressor, it is in the nature of things that the blow should recoil on the aggressor. For, God is in the sentiment, and it cannot be withstood. The potentate and the People perish before it; but with it and as its executors, they are omnipotent.

I write thus, sir, to inform you of the state of mind these Indian tidings have awakened here, and to pray with one voice more, that you, whose hands are strong with the delegated power of fifteen millions of men, will avert, with that might, the terrific injury which threatens the Cherokee tribe.[18]

With great respect, sir, I am, your fellow-citizen,

*Ralph Waldo Emerson.*

16   In Emerson's first draft he began this paragraph with these (cancelled) words: "I have tried to sit still but I have not been able" (J 12:28).

17   Rude scorn.

18   In his earlier draft of the letter Emerson ended with these severe and prophetic words: "I would suggest to your mind the futility of opposition to a moral sentiment. God is in it & it cannot be opposed. Your chair is rottenness, & this nation but a name against it & both will be annihilated. With it & in it they are immeasurably strong" (J 12:29).

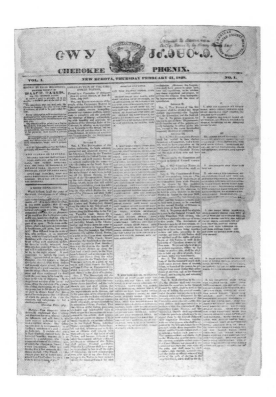

Front page of the *Cherokee Phoenix* (February 21, 1828).

## An Address Delivered before the Senior Class in Divinity College, Cambridge, Sunday Evening, 15 July, 1838

*Known as "The Divinity School Address," Emerson's oration caused a storm of controversy. Emerson delivered it to the Harvard Divinity School senior class (six students along with their families and teachers). It was a direct attack on the "Unitarian pope," the theologian Andrews Norton (1786–1853), a central figure at Harvard; and it condemned much of the religious observance of its day as lifeless and misguided. Friends begged Emerson not to print the Address, but he did so in August 1838. Norton condemned Emerson's speech (in the title of his 1839 pamphlet) as* The Latest Form of Infidelity. *The Divinity School Address marked the end of Emerson's preaching career and his definitive turn toward his true vocation of lecturer. He was not invited back to Harvard for nearly thirty years (1866).*

1    Radiant, brilliant. In his Sermon CLX (September 2, 1832), Emerson envisioned "our whole soul becom[ing] one refulgent mirror of the presence and power and love of God" (S 4:177).

2    "The hardest ascetic may inhale delighted this breath of June," Emerson wrote in his Journal (1836; J 5:139).

In this refulgent[1] summer it has been a luxury to draw the breath of life.[2] The grass grows, the buds burst, the meadow is spotted with fire and gold in the tint of flowers. The air is full of birds, and sweet with the breath of the pine, the balm-of-Gilead,[3] and the new hay. Night brings no gloom to the heart with its welcome shade. Through the transparent darkness the stars pour their almost spiritual rays. Man under them seems a young child, and his huge globe a toy. The cool night bathes the world as with a river, and prepares[4] his eyes again for the crimson dawn. The mystery of nature was never displayed more happily. The corn and the wine have been freely dealt to all creatures,[5] and the never-broken silence with which the old bounty goes forward, has not yielded yet one word of explanation. One is constrained to respect the perfection of this world, in which our senses converse. How wide; how rich; what invitation from every property it gives to every faculty of man! In its fruitful soils; in its navigable sea; in its mountains of metal and stone; in its forests of all woods; in its animals; in its chemical ingredients; in the powers and path of light, heat, attraction, and life, it is well worth the pith[6] and heart of great men to subdue and enjoy it. The planters, the mechanics, the inventors, the astronomers, the builders of cities, and the captains, history delights to honor.

But the moment the mind opens, and reveals the laws which traverse the universe, and make things what they are, then shrinks the great world at once into a mere illustration and fable of this mind. What am I? and What is? asks the human spirit with a curiosity new-kindled, but never to be quenched. Behold these outrunning laws, which our imperfect apprehension can see tend this way and that, but not come full circle. Behold these infinite relations, so like, so unlike; many, yet one. I would study, I would know, I would admire forever. These works of thought have been the entertainments of the human spirit in all ages.

A more secret, sweet, and overpowering beauty appears to man when his heart and mind open to the sentiment of virtue. Then instantly he is instructed in what is above him. He learns that his being is without bound; that, to the good, to the perfect, he is born, low as he now lies in evil and weakness. That which he venerates is still his own, though he has not realized it yet. *He ought*. He knows the sense of that grand word, though his analysis fails entirely to render account of it. When in innocency, or when by intellectual perception, he attains to say,—'I love the Right; Truth is beautiful within and without, forevermore. Virtue, I am thine: save me: use me: thee will I serve, day and night, in great, in small, that I may be not virtuous, but virtue;'—then is the end of the creation answered, and God is well pleased.[7]

The sentiment of virtue is a reverence and delight in the presence of certain divine laws. It perceives that this homely game of life we play, covers, under what seem foolish details, principles that astonish. The child amidst his baubles, is learning the action of light, motion, gravity, muscular force; and in the game of human life, love, fear, justice, appetite, man, and God, interact.[8] These laws refuse to be adequately stated. They will not by us or for us be written out on paper, or spoken by the tongue. They elude, evade our persevering thought, and yet we read them hourly in each other's faces, in each other's actions, in our own remorse. The moral traits which are all globed into every virtuous act and thought,—in speech, we must sever, and describe or suggest by painful enumeration of many particulars. Yet, as this sentiment is the essence of all religion, let me guide your eye to the precise objects of the sentiment, by an enumeration of some of those classes of facts in which this element is conspicuous.

The intuition of the moral sentiment is an insight of the perfection of the laws of the soul. These laws execute themselves. They are out of time,

3    A variety of North American poplar, used to make a soothing, aromatic cough syrup.

4    In Christianity, to prepare means "to bring into spiritual readiness."

5    The corn (wheat or grain) and the wine represent the bread and wine of the Eucharist or holy communion ceremony, which Emerson had refused to perform since 1832. Emerson adapts religious language to show the sacramental powers of nature.

6    Vital, succinct power.

7    Matthew 3:17: "And lo a voice from heaven, saying, This is my beloved Son, in whom I am well pleased."

8    Emerson continues his themes of the child and of play.

9    Alludes to I Corinthians 15:53: "For this corruptible must put on incorruption, and this mortal must put on immortality." St. Paul's passage refers to an otherworldly transformation; Emerson's, a worldly and practical one. See also "The American Scholar," note 43.

10    That is, evil is an absence of good, rather than a separate, substantial force. St. Augustine (354–430) advocated this view against the Manichaeans.

out of space, and not subject to circumstance. Thus; in the soul of man there is a justice whose retributions are instant and entire. He who does a good deed, is instantly ennobled himself. He who does a mean deed, is by the action itself contracted. He who puts off impurity, thereby puts on purity.[9] If a man is at heart just, then in so far is he God; the safety of God, the immortality of God, the majesty of God do enter into that man with justice. If a man dissemble, deceive, he deceives himself, and goes out of acquaintance with his own being. A man in the view of absolute goodness, adores, with total humility. Every step so downward, is a step upward. The man who renounces himself, comes to himself by so doing.

See how this rapid intrinsic energy worketh everywhere, righting wrongs, correcting appearances, and bringing up facts to a harmony with thoughts. Its operation in life, though slow to the senses, is, at last, as sure as in the soul. By it, a man is made the Providence to himself, dispensing good to his goodness, and evil to his sin. Character is always known. Thefts never enrich; alms never impoverish; murder will speak out of stone walls. The least admixture of a lie,—for example, the smallest mixture of vanity, the least attempt to make a good impression, a favorable appearance,—will instantly vitiate the effect. But speak the truth, and all nature and all spirits help you with unexpected furtherance. Speak the truth, and all things alive or brute are vouchers, and the very roots of the grass underground there, do seem to stir and move to bear you witness. See again the perfection of the Law as it applies itself to the affections, and becomes the law of society. As we are, so we associate. The good, by affinity, seek the good; the vile, by affinity, the vile. Thus of their own volition, souls proceed into heaven, into hell.

These facts have always suggested to man the sublime creed, that the world is not the product of manifold power, but of one will, of one mind; and that one mind is everywhere active, in each ray of the star, in each wavelet of the pool; and whatever opposes that will, is everywhere baulked and baffled, because things are made so, and not otherwise. Good is positive. Evil is merely privative, not absolute.[10] It is like cold, which is the privation of heat. All evil is so much death or nonentity. Benevolence is absolute and real. So much benevolence as a man hath, so much life hath he. For all things proceed out of this same spirit, which is differently named love, justice, temper-

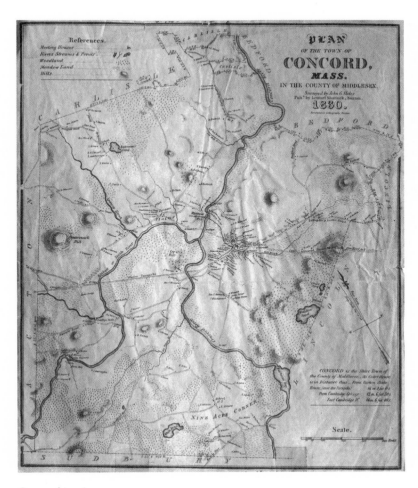

Concord in 1830.

ance, in its different applications, just as the ocean receives different names on the several shores which it washes. All things proceed out of the same spirit, and all things conspire with it. Whilst a man seeks good ends, he is strong by the whole strength of nature. In so far as he roves from these ends, he bereaves himself of power, of auxiliaries; his being shrinks out of all remote channels, he becomes less and less, a mote, a point, until absolute badness is absolute death.

11    Utter suddenly and fervently; often used in respect to prayer.

12    Emerson probably alludes here to the parable of the sower from Matthew 13:1–23; some of the sower's seeds (that is, Jesus' words) "fell into good ground, and brought forth fruit," while others fell among stones or thorns. Jesus' image of his yoke (Matthew 11:29–30) also suggests plowing.

The perception of this law of laws always awakens in the mind a sentiment which we call the religious sentiment, and which makes our highest happiness. Wonderful is its power to charm and to command. It is a mountain air. It is the embalmer of the world. It is myrrh and storax, and chlorine and rosemary. It makes the sky and the hills sublime, and the silent song of the stars is it. By it, is the universe made safe and habitable, not by science or power. Thought may work cold and intransitive in things, and find no end or unity. But the dawn of the sentiment of virtue on the heart, gives and is the assurance that Law is sovereign over all natures; and the worlds, time, space, eternity, do seem to break out into joy.

This sentiment is divine and deifying. It is the beatitude of man. It makes him illimitable. Through it, the soul first knows itself. It corrects the capital mistake of the infant man, who seeks to be great by following the great, and hopes to derive advantages *from another*;—by showing the fountain of all good to be in himself, and that he, equally with every man, is an inlet into the deeps of Reason. When he says, "I ought;" when love warms him; when he chooses, warned from on high, the good and great deed; then, deep melodies wander through his soul from Supreme Wisdom. Then he can worship, and be enlarged by his worship; for he can never go behind this sentiment. In the sublimest flights of the soul, rectitude is never surmounted, love is never outgrown.

This sentiment lies at the foundation of society, and successively creates all forms of worship. The principle of veneration never dies out. Man fallen into superstition, into sensuality, is never wholly without the visions of the moral sentiment. In like manner, all the expressions of this sentiment are sacred and permanent in proportion to their purity. The expressions of this sentiment affect us deeper, greatlier, than all other compositions. The sentences of the oldest time, which ejaculate[11] this piety, are still fresh and fragrant. This thought dwelled always deepest in the minds of men in the devout and contemplative East; not alone in Palestine, where it reached its purest expression, but in Egypt, in Persia, in India, in China. Europe has always owed to oriental genius, its divine impulses. What these holy bards said, all sane men found agreeable and true. And the unique impression of Jesus upon mankind, whose name is not so much written as ploughed[12] into the history of this world, is proof of the subtle virtue of this infusion.

Meantime, whilst the doors of the temple stand open, night and day, before every man, and the oracles of this truth cease never, it is guarded by one stern condition; this, namely; It is an intuition. It cannot be received at second hand.[13] Truly speaking, it is not instruction, but provocation,[14] that I can receive from another soul. What he announces, I must find true in me, or wholly reject; and on his word, or as his second, be he who he may, I can accept nothing. On the contrary, the absence of this primary faith is the presence of degradation. As is the flood so is the ebb. Let this faith depart, and the very words it spake, and the things it made, become false and hurtful. Then falls the church, the state, art, letters, life. The doctrine of the divine nature being forgotten, a sickness infects and dwarfs the constitution. Once man was all; now he is an appendage, a nuisance. And because the indwelling Supreme Spirit cannot wholly be got rid of, the doctrine of it suffers this perversion, that the divine nature is attributed to one or two persons, and denied to all the rest, and denied with fury. The doctrine of inspiration is lost; the base doctrine of the majority of voices, usurps the place of the doctrine of the soul. Miracles, prophecy, poetry, the ideal life, the holy life, exist as ancient history merely; they are not in the belief, nor in the aspiration of society; but, when suggested, seem ridiculous. Life is comic or pitiful, as soon as the high ends of being fade out of sight, and man becomes nearsighted, and can only attend to what addresses the senses.

These general views, which, whilst they are general, none will contest, find abundant illustration in the history of religion, and especially in the history of the Christian church. In that, all of us have had our birth and nurture. The truth contained in that, you, my young friends, are now setting forth to teach. As the Cultus,[15] or established worship of the civilized world, it has great historical interest for us. Of its blessed words, which have been the consolation of humanity, you need not that I should speak. I shall endeavor to discharge my duty to you, on this occasion, by pointing out two errors in its administration, which daily appear more gross from the point of view we have just now taken.

Jesus Christ belonged to the true race of prophets. He saw with open eye the mystery of the soul. Drawn by its severe harmony, ravished with its beauty, he lived in it, and had his being there. Alone in all history, he estimated the greatness of man. One man was true to what is in you and me. He saw that God incarnates himself in man, and evermore goes forth anew to take possession of his world. He said, in this jubilee of sublime emotion, 'I

13 As in "The American Scholar," Emerson appears to reject the work of institutions, including divinity schools; he is about to declare himself against instruction. The philosopher Stanley Cavell notes an implied contrast between the intuition that Emerson values and the tuition demanded by colleges. In "The Transcendentalist," a lecture from December 1841, Emerson identified transcendentalism with "the tendency to respect the intuitions, and to give them, at least in our creed, all authority over our experience."

14 Calling forth or summoning.

15 Religious ceremony or worship; the Latin *cultus* (the care owed to a god) is a form of the verb *colere*, to till or cultivate. Earlier, Emerson says that Christ's name is "ploughed" into history (see note 12).

16    Emerson wrote in his Journal in August 1837, "If Jesus came now into the world, he would say—You, YOU! He said to his age, I" (J 5:362).

17    Reason is higher intuition; Understanding, a lower, more literal-minded power. Emerson draws the distinction (common in his essays) from Samuel Taylor Coleridge (1772–1834) and others. In his Journal in April 1835, Emerson wrote, "Why must always the philosopher mince his words & fatigue us with explanation? He speaks from the Reason & being of course contradicted word for word by the Understanding he stops like a cogwheel at every notch to explain. Let him say, *I idealize*, & let that be once for all; or *I sensualize*, & then the Rationalist may stop his ears" (J 5:31).

18    Poetic or figurative usages of language. The word comes from the Greek *trephein*, "to turn": thus the expression "turns of phrase." In the late essay "Poetry and Imagination," assembled from various Emerson manuscripts by his daughter Ellen and James Elliot Cabot (1821–1903), Emerson asserted that "Nature itself is a vast trope."

19    Fable or myth.

20    For Emerson and the Transcendentalists, miracles spoke only to the literal-minded Understanding, whereas Christ's words addressed the inward power of Reason (see note 17). They argued that miraculous deeds could not be the primary basis for Jesus' importance, and opposed the attempt of the Unitarian Church to establish the historical reality of the miracles described in the Gospels. The main polemicists on the Transcendentalist side were George Ripley (1802–1880) and William Henry Furness (1802–1896). They were influenced by two sensational German books, *On the Spirit of Hebrew Poetry* (1782) by Johann Gottfried von Herder (1744–1803) and *The Life of Jesus, Critically Examined* (1835–1836) by David Friedrich Strauss (1808–1874), which argued that the Gospel versions of Jesus' life offered a powerful spiritual myth rather than a historical account. The Transcendentalists, like Emerson, followed Strauss, evading any impulse to establish the historical facts of Jesus' life and study the implications of these facts for faith. Instead, they severed the connection between Jesus' factual biography and the inward power he represented, and chose the latter.

21    Prodigy, marvel, or amazing event (archaic)—a sense that Emerson combines with the usual one of "deformed creature."

22    In November 1838 Emerson exclaimed in his journal, "'Miracles have ceased.' Have they indeed? When? They had not ceased this afternoon when I walked into the wood & got into bright miraculous sunshine in shelter from the roaring wind" (J 5:423).

23    In Sermon CLVIII (June 10, 1832), Emerson criticized "this error of searching traces of the divine mind in other ages and other worlds." He proclaimed, "Men make their religion a historical religion; they do not transfer it from their bibles to their own life; they see God in Judea and Egypt, in Moses and in Jesus, but not around them and within them. . . . We want a living religion" (S 4:161).

24    In the notes he made for the Address, Emerson added, "Be Christians. There have never been any" (J 12:9).

25    Unwholesome, harmful.

am divine. Through me, God acts; through me, speaks. Would you see God, see me; or, see thee, when thou also thinkest as I now think.'[16] But what a distortion did his doctrine and memory suffer in the same, in the next, and the following ages! There is no doctrine of the Reason which will bear to be taught by the Understanding.[17] The understanding caught this high chant from the poet's lips, and said, in the next age, "This was Jehovah come down out of heaven. I will kill you, if you say he was a man." The idioms of his language, and the figures of his rhetoric, have usurped the place of his truth; and churches are not built on his principles, but on his tropes.[18] Christianity became a Mythus,[19] as the poetic teaching of Greece and of Egypt, before. He spoke of miracles; for he felt that man's life was a miracle, and all that man doth, and he knew that this daily miracle shines, as the man is diviner. But the very word Miracle,[20] as pronounced by Christian churches, gives a false impression; it is Monster.[21] It is not one with the blowing clover and the falling rain.[22]

He felt respect for Moses and the prophets; but no unfit tenderness at postponing their initial revelations, to the hour and the man that now is; to the eternal revelation in the heart. Thus was he a true man. Having seen that the law in us is commanding, he would not suffer it to be commanded. Boldly, with hand, and heart, and life, he declared it was God. Thus was he a true man. Thus is he, as I think, the only soul in history who has appreciated the worth of a man.

1. In thus contemplating Jesus, we become very sensible of the first defect of historical Christianity.[23] Historical Christianity has fallen into the error that corrupts all attempts to communicate religion. As it appears to us, and as it has appeared for ages, it is not the doctrine of the soul, but an exaggeration of the personal, the positive, the ritual.[24] It has dwelt, it dwells, with noxious[25] exaggeration about the *person* of Jesus.[26] The soul knows no persons. It invites every man to expand to the full circle of the universe, and will have no preferences but those of spontaneous love. But by this eastern monarchy of a Christianity,[27] which indolence and fear have built, the friend of man is made the injurer of man. The manner in which his name is surrounded with expressions, which were once sallies of admiration and love, but are now petrified into official titles, kills all generous sympathy and liking. All who hear me, feel, that the language that describes Christ to Europe

26 Speaking in defense of God against the Boston atheist Abner Kneeland, Emerson wrote in his Journal (July 30, 1835), "Oft I have doubted of his person, never that truth is divine" (J 5:71). In his essay "Nominalist and Realist," he asserted bluntly, "there are no such men as we fable; no Jesus . . . such as we have made." Emerson disliked thinking of God as a person, and (along with the Unitarians) he denied Jesus' divinity.

27 Alludes to the lavish pomp and authoritarian practices that characterized the monarchies of Asia, according to ancient Greek and later writers.

28    Osiris is the Egyptian god who judges the dead, Apollo the Greek god of poetry.

29    The catechism is a manual for doctrinal instruction in Christianity, taking the form of a series of questions and answers.

30    From the sonnet beginning "The world is too much with us" (1807), by William Wordsworth (1770–1850). Emerson took to heart Wordsworth's sentiment elsewhere in his sonnet: "Getting and spending, we lay waste our powers."

31    Crowd, mob.

32    A year earlier, in "The American Scholar," Emerson emphasized "Know thyself," another ancient Greek motto. The Stoics were ascetic philosophers who preached self-sufficiency and reduction of one's desires to what was strictly necessary. In the essay "The Over-Soul," Emerson asserted that "all reform aims, in some one particular, to let the soul have its way through us; in other words, to engage us to obey."

33    Lump, tumor.

34    In Acts 26:14–19, St. Paul recounts his illumination on the road to Damascus and adds, "I was not disobedient unto the heavenly vision."

35    "To invite" is a secondary meaning of *provoke*.

and America, is not the style of friendship and enthusiasm to a good and noble heart, but is appropriated and formal,—paints a demigod, as the Orientals or the Greeks would describe Osiris or Apollo.[28] Accept the injurious impositions of our early catechetical[29] instruction, and even honesty and self-denial were but splendid sins, if they did not wear the Christian name. One would rather be

'A pagan suckled in a creed outworn,'[30]

than to be defrauded of his manly right in coming into nature, and finding not names and places, not land and professions, but even virtue and truth foreclosed and monopolized. You shall not be a man even. You shall not own the world; you shall not dare, and live after the infinite Law that is in you, and in company with the infinite Beauty which heaven and earth reflect to you in all lovely forms; but you must subordinate your nature to Christ's nature; you must accept our interpretations; and take his portrait as the vulgar[31] draw it.

That is always best which gives me to myself. The sublime is excited in me by the great stoical doctrine, Obey thyself.[32] That which shows God in me, fortifies me. That which shows God out of me, makes me a wart and a wen.[33] There is no longer a necessary reason for my being. Already the long shadows of untimely oblivion creep over me, and I shall decease forever.

The divine bards are the friends of my virtue, of my intellect, of my strength. They admonish me, that the gleams which flash across my mind, are not mine, but God's; that they had the like, and were not disobedient to the heavenly vision.[34] So I love them. Noble provocations[35] go out from them, inviting me also to emancipate myself; to resist evil; to subdue the world; and to Be. And thus by his holy thoughts, Jesus serves us, and thus only. To aim to convert a man by miracles, is a profanation of the soul. A true conversion, a true Christ, is now, as always, to be made, by the reception of beautiful sentiments. It is true that a great and rich soul, like his, falling among the simple, does so preponderate, that, as his did, it names the world. The world seems to them to exist for him, and they have not yet drunk so deeply of his sense, as to see that only by coming again to themselves, or to God in themselves, can they grow forevermore. It is a low benefit to give me something; it is a high benefit to enable me to do somewhat of myself. The time is coming when all men will see, that the gift of God to the soul is not a vaunting, overpowering, excluding sanctity, but a sweet, natural goodness, a goodness like thine and mine, and that so invites thine and mine to be and to grow.

The injustice of the vulgar tone of preaching is not less flagrant to Jesus, than it is to the souls which it profanes. The preachers do not see that they make his gospel not glad, and shear him of the locks of beauty and the attributes of heaven. When I see a majestic Epaminondas,[36] or Washington; when I see among my contemporaries, a true orator, an upright judge, a dear friend; when I vibrate to the melody and fancy of a poem; I see beauty that is to be desired. And so lovely, and with yet more entire consent of my human being, sounds in my ear the severe music of the bards that have sung of the true God in all ages. Now do not degrade the life and dialogues of Christ out of the circle of this charm, by insulation and peculiarity. Let them lie as they befel, alive and warm, part of human life, and of the landscape, and of the cheerful day.

2. The second defect of the traditional and limited way of using the mind of Christ is a consequence of the first; this, namely; that the Moral Nature, that Law of laws, whose revelations introduce greatness,—yea, God himself, into the open soul, is not explored as the fountain of the established teaching in society. Men have come to speak of the revelation as somewhat long ago given and done, as if God were dead. The injury to faith throttles the preacher; and the goodliest of institutions becomes an uncertain and inarticulate voice.[37]

It is very certain that it is the effect of conversation with the beauty of the soul, to beget a desire and need to impart to others the same knowledge and love. If utterance is denied, the thought lies like a burden on the man. Always the seer is a sayer. Somehow his dream is told. Somehow he publishes it with solemn joy. Sometimes with pencil on canvas; sometimes with chisel on stone; sometimes in towers and aisles of granite, his soul's worship is builded; sometimes in anthems of indefinite music; but clearest and most permanent, in words.

The man enamored of this excellency, becomes its priest or poet. The office is coeval[38] with the world. But observe the condition, the spiritual lim-

36    Brilliant Theban general (ca. 410–362 BCE) who liberated Thebes from Spartan control, and therefore analogous to George Washington (1732–1799).

37    On April 1, 1838, Emerson recorded in his Journal an encounter with Harvard Divinity School students: "I told them that the preacher should be a poet smit with love of the harmonies of moral nature: and yet look at the Unitarian Association & see if its aspect is poetic. They all smiled No. A minister nowadays is plainest prose, the prose of prose. He is a Warming-pan, a Night-chair at sick beds & rheumatic souls; and the fire of the minstrel's eye & the vivacity of his word is exchanged for intense grumbling enunciation of the Cambridge sort, & for scripture phraseology" (J 5:471). The insistence that "the preacher should be a poet," assigned to reveal beauty and joy, is at the core of Emerson's address.

38    Sharing the same time.

39    Unholy, secular.

40    Ecclesiastical assemblies.

41    The vocation of preaching.

itation of the office. The spirit only can teach. Not any profane[39] man, not any sensual, not any liar, not any slave can teach, but only he can give, who has; he only can create, who is. The man on whom the soul descends, through whom the soul speaks, alone can teach. Courage, piety, love, wisdom, can teach; and every man can open his door to these angels, and they shall bring him the gift of tongues. But the man who aims to speak as books enable, as synods[40] use, as the fashion guides, and as interest commands, babbles. Let him hush.

To this holy office,[41] you propose to devote yourselves. I wish you may feel your call in throbs of desire and hope. The office is the first in the world. It is of that reality, that it cannot suffer the deduction of any falsehood. And it is my duty to say to you, that the need was never greater of new revelation than now. From the views I have already expressed, you will infer the sad conviction, which I share, I believe, with numbers, of the universal decay and now almost death of faith in society. The soul is not preached. The Church seems to totter to its fall, almost all life extinct. On this occasion, any complaisance, would be criminal, which told you, whose hope and commission it is to preach the faith of Christ, that the faith of Christ is preached.

It is time that this ill-suppressed murmur of all thoughtful men against the famine of our churches; this moaning of the heart because it is bereaved of the consolation, the hope, the grandeur, that come alone out of the culture of the moral nature; should be heard through the sleep of indolence, and over the din of routine. This great and perpetual office of the preacher is not discharged. Preaching is the expression of the moral sentiment in application to the duties of life. In how many churches, by how many prophets, tell me, is man made sensible that he is an infinite Soul; that the earth and heavens are passing into his mind; that he is drinking forever the soul of God? Where now sounds the persuasion, that by its very melody imparadises my heart, and so affirms its own origin in heaven? Where shall I hear words such as in elder ages drew men to leave all and follow,—father and mother, house and land, wife and child? Where shall I hear these august laws of moral being so pronounced, as to fill my ear, and I feel ennobled by the offer of my uttermost action and passion? The test of the true faith, certainly, should be its power to charm and command the soul, as the laws of nature control the activity of the hands,—so commanding that we find pleasure and honor in obeying. The faith should blend with the light of rising and of setting suns, with the flying cloud, the singing bird, and the breath of flowers. But now the priest's Sabbath has lost the splendor of nature; it is unlovely; we are glad when it is done; we can make, we do make, even sitting in our pews, a far better, holier, sweeter, for ourselves.

Whenever the pulpit is usurped by a formalist,[42] then is the worshipper defrauded and disconsolate. We shrink as soon as the prayers begin, which do not uplift, but smite and offend us. We are fain to wrap our cloaks about us, and secure, as best we can, a solitude that hears not. I once heard a preacher who sorely tempted me to say, I would go to church no more. Men go, thought I, where they are wont to go, else had no soul entered the temple in the afternoon. A snowstorm was falling around us. The snowstorm was real; the preacher merely spectral; and the eye felt the sad contrast in looking at him, and then out of the window behind him, into the beautiful meteor of the snow.[43] He had lived in vain. He had no one word intimating that he had laughed or wept, was married or in love, had been commended, or cheated, or chagrined. If he had ever lived and acted, we were none the wiser for it. The capital secret of his profession, namely, to convert life into truth, he had not learned. Not one fact in all his experience, had he yet imported into his doctrine. This man had ploughed, and planted, and talked, and bought, and sold; he had read books; he had eaten and drunken; his head aches; his heart throbs; he smiles and suffers; yet was there not a surmise, a hint, in all the discourse, that he had ever lived at all. Not a line did he draw out of real history. The true preacher can always be known by this, that he deals out to the people his life,—life passed through the fire of thought. But of the bad preacher, it could not be told from his sermon, what age of the world he fell in; whether he had a father or a child; whether he was a freeholder or a pauper; whether he was a citizen or a countryman; or any other fact of his biography.[44]

It seemed strange that the people should come to church. It seemed as if their houses were very unentertaining, that they should prefer this thoughtless clamor. It shows that there is a commanding attraction in the moral sentiment, that can lend a faint tint of light to dulness and ignorance, coming in its name and place. The good hearer is sure he has been touched sometimes; is sure there is somewhat to be reached, and some word that can reach it.

42  One who merely adheres to the forms of religion, rather than to its inward substance. In his Journal (July 6, 1832) Emerson wrote, "Religion in the mind is not credulity & in practice is not form. It is life. It is the order & soundness of a man" (J 4:27).

43  Emerson hints mockingly at the cold speech of Barzillai Frost (1804–1858), the junior pastor at the Unitarian Church in Concord (see J 5:463–464). Edward Everett Hale (1822–1909) recalled that Frost "would not go a hair's breadth beyond what he was sure of, for any effect of rhetoric."

44  In September–October 1837, Emerson remembered a bad sermon in his Journal: "The young preacher preached from his ears & his memory, & never a word from his soul. His sermon was loud & hollow. . . . A solemn conclusion of a Calvinistic discourse imitated at the end of a Unitarian sermon, is purely ludicrous like grandfather's hat & spectacles on a rogue of six years" (J 5:380).

45    Bas-relief (1st century BCE) found in a temple dedicated to Osiris at Denderah, in Egypt. The Denderah zodiac was transported to Paris in 1821.

46    Emerson confided to his Journal in December 1846, "I think that the whole modus loquendi [way of talking] about believing Xy is vicious. It has no pertinence to the state of the case. It grows out of the Calvinistic nonsense of a Gospel-Scheme a dogmatic Architecture" (J 5:267).

47    Communion. Emerson declared his personal opposition to this rite in 1832, when he resigned his position as pastor of Boston's Second Church. He announced, "I cannot bring myself to believe" that Jesus "meant to impose a memorial feast upon the whole world"; and said later on in his sermon, "I have no hostility to this institution. I am only stating my want of sympathy with it. . . . That is the end of my opposition, that I am not interested in it" (Sermon CLXII, S 4:194).

When he listens to these vain words, he comforts himself by their relation to his remembrance of better hours, and so they clatter and echo unchallenged.

I am not ignorant that when we preach unworthily, it is not always quite in vain. There is a good ear, in some men, that draws supplies to virtue out of very indifferent nutriment. There is poetic truth concealed in all the common-places of prayer and of sermons, and though foolishly spoken, they may be wisely heard; for, each is some select expression that broke out in a moment of piety from some stricken or jubilant soul, and its excellency made it remembered. The prayers and even the dogmas of our church, are like the zodiac of Denderah,[45] and the astronomical monuments of the Hindoos, wholly insulated from anything now extant in the life and business of the people.[46] They mark the height to which the waters once rose. But this docility is a check upon the mischief from the good and devout. In a large portion of the community, the religious service gives rise to quite other thoughts and emotions. We need not chide the negligent servant. We are struck with pity, rather, at the swift retribution of his sloth. Alas for the unhappy man that is called to stand in the pulpit, and *not* give bread of life. Everything that befals, accuses him. Would he ask contributions for the missions, foreign or domestic? Instantly his face is suffused with shame, to propose to his parish, that they should send money a hundred or a thousand miles, to furnish such poor fare as they have at home, and would do well to go the hundred or the thousand miles, to escape. Would he urge people to a godly way of living;— and can he ask a fellow creature to come to Sabbath meetings, when he and they all know what is the poor uttermost they can hope for therein? Will he invite them privately to the Lord's Supper?[47] He dares not. If no heart warm this rite, the hollow, dry, creaking formality is too plain, than that he can face a man of wit and energy, and put the invitation without terror. In the street, what has he to say to the bold village blasphemer? The village blasphemer sees fear in the face, form, and gait of the minister.

Let me not taint the sincerity of this plea by any oversight of the claims of good men. I know and honor the purity and strict conscience of numbers of the clergy. What life the public worship retains, it owes to the scattered company of pious men, who minister here and there in the churches, and

Oliver Wendell Holmes (1809–1894).

who, sometimes accepting with too great tenderness the tenet of the elders, have not accepted from others, but from their own heart, the genuine impulses of virtue, and so still command our love and awe, to the sanctity of character. Moreover, the exceptions are not so much to be found in a few eminent preachers, as in the better hours, the truer inspirations of all,—nay, in the sincere moments of every man. But with whatever exception, it is still true, that tradition characterizes the preaching of this country; that it comes out of the memory, and not out of the soul; that it aims at what is usual, and not at what is necessary and eternal; that thus, historical Christianity destroys the power of preaching, by withdrawing it from the exploration of the moral nature of man, where the sublime is, where are the resources of astonishment and power. What a cruel injustice it is to that Law, the joy of the whole earth, which alone can make thought dear and rich; that Law whose fatal sureness the astronomical orbits poorly emulate, that it is travestied and depreciated, that it is behooted and behowled, and not a trait, not a word of it articulated. The pulpit in losing sight of this Law, loses all its inspiration, and gropes after it knows not what. And for want of this culture, the soul of the community is sick and faithless. It wants nothing so much as a stern, high, stoical, Christian discipline, to make it know itself and the divinity that speaks through it. Now man is ashamed of himself; he skulks and sneaks through the world, to be tolerated, to be pitied, and scarcely in a thousand years does any man dare to be wise and good, and so draw after him the tears and blessings of his kind.

Certainly there have been periods when, from the inactivity of the intellect on certain truths, a greater faith was possible in names and persons. The Puritans in England and America, found in the Christ of the Catholic Church, and in the dogmas inherited from Rome, scope for their austere piety, and their longings for civil freedom. But their creed is passing away, and none arises in its room. I think no man can go with his thoughts about him, into one of our churches, without feeling that what hold the public worship had on men, is gone or going. It has lost its grasp on the affection of the good, and the fear of the bad. In the country,—neighborhoods, half parishes are *signing off,*—to use the local term. It is already beginning to indicate character and religion to withdraw from the religious meetings. I have heard a devout person, who prized the Sabbath, say in bitterness of heart, "On Sundays, it seems wicked to go to church." And the motive, that holds the best there, is now only a hope and a waiting. What was once a mere circumstance, that the best and the worst men in the parish, the poor and the rich, the learned and the ignorant, young and old, should meet one day as fellows in one house, in sign of an equal right in the soul,—has come to be a paramount motive for going thither.

My friends, in these two errors, I think, I find the causes of that calamity of a decaying church and a wasting unbelief, which are casting malignant influences around us, and making the hearts of good men sad. And what greater calamity can fall upon a nation, than the loss of worship? Then all things go to decay. Genius leaves the temple, to haunt the senate, or the market. Literature becomes frivolous. Science is cold. The eye of youth is not lighted by the hope of other worlds, and age is without honor. Society lives to trifles, and when men die, we do not mention them.

And now, my brothers, you will ask, What in these desponding days can be done by us? The remedy is already declared in the ground of our complaint of the Church. We have contrasted the Church with the Soul. In the soul, then, let the redemption be sought. In one soul, in your soul, there are resources for the world. Wherever a man comes, there comes revolution. The old is for slaves. When a man comes, all books are legible, all things transparent, all religions are forms. He is religious. Man is the wonder-worker. He is seen amid miracles. All men bless and curse. He saith yea and nay, only.[48] The stationariness of religion; the assumption that the age of inspiration is past, that the Bible is closed; the fear of degrading the character of Jesus by representing him as a man; indicate with sufficient clearness the falsehood of our theology. It is the office of a true teacher to show us that God is, not was; that He speaketh, not spake. The true Christianity,—a faith like Christ's in the infinitude of man,—is lost. None believeth in the soul of man, but only in some man or person old and departed. Ah me! no man goeth alone. All men go in flocks to this saint or that poet, avoiding the God who seeth in secret.[49] They cannot see in secret; they love to be blind in public. They think society wiser than their soul, and know not that one soul, and their soul, is wiser than the whole world. See how nations and races flit by on the sea of time, and leave no ripple to tell where they floated or sunk, and one good soul shall make the name of Moses, or of Zeno, or of Zoroaster,[50] reverend forever. None assayeth the stern ambition to be the Self of the nation, and of nature, but each would be an easy secondary to some Christian scheme, or sectarian connexion, or some eminent man. Once leave your own knowledge of God, your own sentiment, and take secondary knowledge, as St. Paul's, or George Fox's,[51] or Swedenborg's, and you get wide from God with every year this secondary form lasts, and if, as now, for centuries,—the chasm yawns to that breadth, that men can scarcely be convinced there is in them anything divine.

48  Matthew 5:37: "Let your communication be yea, yea, nay, nay."

49  Jesus in the Sermon on the Mount warns his audience to pray or fast not in public but for the benefit of "thy Father which seeth in secret" (Matthew 6:4, 6:18).

50  Zeno of Elea (ca. 488–ca. 430 BCE), Greek philosopher; Zoroaster (ca. 11th century BCE), Iranian founder of the Zoroastrian religion. In his Journal (April 17, 1832) Emerson compared Zoroaster to Plato and Swedenborg: "A strange poem is Zoroastrism. It is a system as separate & harmonious & sublime as Swedenborgianism. congruent. One would be glad to behold the truth which they all shadow forth" (J 4:11; for Swedenborg, see note 51 below).

51  St. Paul (d. ca. 65), apostle of Jesus and author of New Testament letters. George Fox (1624–1691) founded the Society of Friends (Quakers). Emanuel Swedenborg (1688–1772), Swedish mystic whom Emerson read avidly.

52    John Wesley (1704–1791) was the founder of Methodism; Jean-Frédéric Oberlin (1740–1826), an Alsatian religious reformer.

53    A term that Emerson reflects on at length in "Self-Reliance."

Let me admonish you, first of all, to go alone; to refuse the good models, even those most sacred in the imagination of men, and dare to love God without mediator or veil. Friends enough you shall find who will hold up to your emulation Wesleys and Oberlins,[52] Saints and Prophets. Thank God for these good men, but say, 'I also am a man.' Imitation cannot go above its model. The imitator dooms himself to hopeless mediocrity. The inventor did it, because it was natural to him, and so in him it has a charm. In the imitator, something else is natural, and he bereaves himself of his own beauty, to come short of another man's.

Yourself a newborn bard of the Holy Ghost,—cast behind you all conformity,[53] and acquaint men at first hand with Deity. Be to them a man. Look to it first and only, that you are such; that fashion, custom, authority, pleasure, and money are nothing to you,—are not bandages over your eyes, that you cannot see,—but live with the privilege of the immeasurable mind. Not too anxious to visit periodically all families and each family in your parish connexion,—when you meet one of these men or women, be to them a divine man; be to them thought and virtue; let their timid aspirations find in you a friend; let their trampled instincts be genially tempted out in your atmosphere; let their doubts know that you have doubted, and their wonder feel that you have wondered. By trusting your own soul, you shall gain a greater confidence in other men. For all our penny-wisdom, for all our soul-destroying slavery to habit, it is not to be doubted, that all men have sublime thoughts; that all men do value the few real hours of life; they love to be heard; they love to be caught up into the vision of principles. We mark with light in the memory the few interviews, we have had in the dreary years of routine and of sin, with souls that made our souls wiser; that spoke what we thought; that told us what we knew; that gave us leave to be what we inly were. Discharge to men the priestly office, and, present or absent, you shall be followed with their love as by an angel.

And, to this end, let us not aim at common degrees of merit. Can we not leave, to such as love it, the virtue that glitters for the commendation of society, and ourselves pierce the deep solitudes of absolute ability and worth? We easily come up to the standard of goodness in society. Society's praise can be cheaply secured, and almost all men are content with those easy merits; but the instant effect of conversing with God, will be, to put them away.

There are sublime merits; persons who are not actors, not speakers, but influences; persons too great for fame, for display; who disdain eloquence; to whom all we call art and artist, seems too nearly allied to show and by-ends, to the exaggeration of the finite and selfish, and loss of the universal. The orators, the poets, the commanders encroach on us only as fair women do, by our allowance and homage. Slight them by preoccupation of mind, slight them, as you can well afford to do, by high and universal aims, and they instantly feel that you have right, and that it is in lower places that they must shine. They also feel your right; for they with you are open to the influx of the all-knowing Spirit, which annihilates before its broad noon the little shades and gradations of intelligence in the compositions we call wiser and wisest.

In such high communion, let us study the grand strokes of rectitude: a bold benevolence, an independence of friends, so that not the unjust wishes of those who love us, shall impair our freedom, but we shall resist for truth's sake the freest flow of kindness, and appeal to sympathies far in advance; and,—what is the highest form in which we know this beautiful element,—a certain solidity of merit, that has nothing to do with opinion, and which is so essentially and manifestly virtue, that it is taken for granted, that the right, the brave, the generous step will be taken by it, and nobody thinks of commending it. You would compliment a coxcomb[54] doing a good act, but you would not praise an angel. The silence that accepts merit as the most natural thing in the world, is the highest applause. Such souls, when they appear, are the Imperial Guard of Virtue, the perpetual reserve, the dictators of fortune. One needs not praise their courage,—they are the heart and soul of nature. O my friends, there are resources in us on which we have not drawn. There are men who rise refreshed on hearing a threat; men to whom a crisis which intimidates and paralyzes the majority—demanding not the faculties of prudence and thrift, but comprehension, immovableness, the readiness of sacrifice,—comes graceful and beloved as a bride. Napoleon said of Massena,[55] that he was not himself until the battle began to go against him; then, when the dead began to fall in ranks around him, awoke his powers of combination, and he put on terror and victory as a robe. So it is in rugged crises, in unweariable endurance, and in aims which put sympathy out of question, that the angel is shown. But these are heights that we can scarce remember

54   Fool (originally, the fool's cap).

55   Napoleon Bonaparte (1769–1821), French emperor; André Masséna, duc de Rivoli (1758–1817), was one of his marshals. Emerson relied on Barry O'Meara's (d. 1836) interview with Napoleon, recorded in O'Meara's *Napoleon in Exile* (1823).

56    Jewelry worked with intricate metal threads, resembling lace.

57    Malleable, well-formed.

and look up to, without contrition and shame. Let us thank God that such things exist.

And now let us do what we can to rekindle the smouldering, nigh quenched fire on the altar. The evils of the church that now is, are manifest. The question returns, What shall we do? I confess, all attempts to project and establish a Cultus with new rites and forms, seem to me vain. Faith makes us, and not we it, and faith makes its own forms. All attempts to contrive a system, are as cold as the new worship introduced by the French to the goddess of Reason,—to-day, pasteboard and fillagree,[56] and ending to-morrow in madness and murder. Rather let the breath of new life be breathed by you through the forms already existing. For, if once you are alive, you shall find they shall become plastic[57] and new. The remedy to their

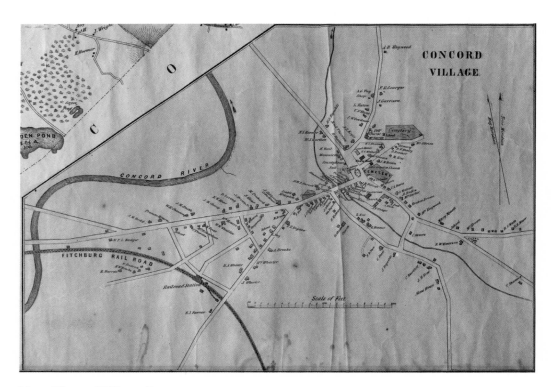

Map of Concord Village, 1852.

deformity is, first, soul, and second, soul, and evermore, soul. A whole pope-dom of forms, one pulsation of virtue can uplift and vivify. Two inestimable advantages Christianity has given us; first; the Sabbath, the jubilee[58] of the whole world; whose light dawns welcome alike into the closet of the philoso-pher, into the garret of toil, and into prison cells, and everywhere suggests, even to the vile, a thought of the dignity of spiritual being. Let it stand for-evermore, a temple, which new love, new faith, new sight shall restore to more than its first splendor to mankind. And secondly, the institution of preaching,—the speech of man to men,—essentially the most flexible of all organs, of all forms. What hinders that now, everywhere, in pulpits, in lecture-rooms, in houses, in fields, wherever the invitation of men or your own occasions lead you, you speak the very truth, as your life and conscience teach it, and cheer the waiting, fainting hearts of men with new hope and new revelation?

I look for the hour when that supreme Beauty, which ravished the souls of those Eastern men, and chiefly of those Hebrews, and through their lips spoke oracles to all time, shall speak in the West also. The Hebrew and Greek Scriptures contain immortal sentences, that have been bread of life to millions. But they have no epical integrity; are fragmentary;[59] are not shown in their order to the intellect. I look for the new Teacher, that shall follow so far those shining laws, that he shall see them come full circle;[60] shall see their rounding complete grace; shall see the world to be the mirror of the soul; shall see the identity of the law of gravitation with purity of heart; and shall show that the Ought, that Duty, is one thing with Science, with Beauty, and with Joy.[61]

58   The jubilee year occurs every fifty years, according to the book of Leviticus (25:9); dur-ing the jubilee, the land would be given a sab-bath (or rest) from harvesting and each person would be released from debt. Earlier in the Di-vinity School Address, Emerson refers to Jesus' "jubilee of sublime emotion."

59   The Higher Criticism of the Bible, pio-neered by the German scholar Johann Gott-fried Eichhorn (1753–1827), was influential in Emerson's day. The Higher Critics often saw scripture as incomplete or contradictory; they detected different source-texts in the Bible, for them a literary artifact composed of separate strands. In Emerson's day, most of the Higher Critics wished to support rather than to under-mine Christian faith. But their revelation that the Bible was a humanly constructed book, rather than one simply given by God, fostered doubt in many.

60   The image of circular power also occurs in Emerson's poem "Uriel" and his essay "Cir-cles."

61   The Address concludes with an imagina-tive portrait of a "new teacher" who will over-shadow even the Jesus of the Gospels ("the Greek scriptures") in his will to reconcile beauty and the moral Ought. This prophetic figure presents a resounding contrast to the ineffectual "spectral" preacher described midway through Emerson's speech.

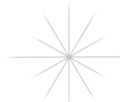

# Literary Ethics

*An Oration Delivered before the Literary Societies of*
*Dartmouth College, July 24, 1838*

*Emerson gave almost fifteen hundred lectures over the course of fifty years, between 1833 and 1881. He was thirty-five years old when he addressed the students of Dartmouth College in Hanover, New Hampshire (at their invitation) for their commencement in July 1838, just nine days after the bombshell Divinity School Address. On the way to Hanover he wrote to his wife Lidian, then pregnant with their second child, "I have had a very good journey seeing Monadnoc in its glory & Auscutney in its pride & Bellows Falls in its fury, & this blessed Connecticutt river in its lovely intervales." After the address he wrote to her again: "I have no doubt some of it found ears in the crowd. It is very pleasant to me to see these young men. They look strong & hopeful & college audiences are as yet uncommitted" (July 23 and 25, 1838, L 2:144–146). The speech, like the better-known "American Scholar," gives a call to arms and a portrait of the scholar. It was printed in September 1838.*

1    Job says of himself, "I was eyes to the blind, and feet was I to the lame" (Job 29:15).

Gentlemen,

The invitation to address you this day, with which you have honored me, was a call so welcome, that I made haste to obey it. A summons to celebrate with scholars a literary festival, is so alluring to me, as to overcome the doubts I might well entertain of my ability to bring you any thought worthy of your attention. I have reached the middle age of man; yet I believe I am not less glad or sanguine at the meeting of scholars, than when, a boy, I first saw the graduates of my own College assembled at their anniversary. Neither years nor books have yet availed to extirpate a prejudice then rooted in me, that a scholar is the favorite of Heaven and earth, the excellency of his country, the happiest of men. His duties lead him directly into the holy ground where other men's aspirations only point. His successes are occasions of the purest joy to all men. Eyes is he to the blind; feet is he to the lame.[1] His failures, if he is worthy, are inlets to higher advantages. And because the scholar, by every thought he thinks, extends his dominion into the general mind of men, he is not one, but many. The few scholars in each country, whose genius I know, seem to me not individuals, but societies; and, when events occur of great import, I count over these representatives of opinion, whom they will affect, as if I were counting nations. And, even if his results were incommunicable; if they abode in his own spirit; the intellect hath somewhat so sacred in its possessions, that the fact of his existence and pursuits would not be without joy.

Meantime I know that a very different estimate of the scholar's profession prevails in this country, and the importunity, with which society presses its claim upon young men, tends always to pervert the views of the youth in respect to the culture of the intellect. Somewhat mediocre and sordid has polluted the image of this great duty. It is not sought with enthusiasm. Its higher courts,—of philosophy, of poetry,—are thinly peopled, and the intellect still wants the voice that shall say to it, 'Sleep no more.'[2]

Hence the historical failure on which Europe and America have so freely commented. This country has not fulfilled what seemed the reasonable expectation of mankind. Men looked, when all feudal straps and bandages were snapped asunder, that nature, too long the mother of dwarfs, should reimburse itself by a brood of Titans,[3] who should laugh and leap in the continent, and run up the mountains of the West with the errand of genius and of love. But the mark of American merit in painting, in sculpture, in poetry, in fiction, in eloquence, seems to be a certain grace without grandeur, and itself not new but derivative; a vase of fair outline, but empty,—which whoso sees, may fill with what wit and character is in him, but which does not, like the charged cloud, overflow with terrible beauty and emit lightnings on all beholders;[4] a muse, which does not lay the grasp of despotic genius on us, and chain an age to its thought and emotion.

I will not lose myself in the desultory[5] questions, what are the limitations, and what the causes of the fact. It suffices me to say, in general, that all particular reasons merge themselves in this, that the diffidence of mankind in the soul has crept over the American mind; that men here, as elsewhere, are indisposed to innovation, and prefer any antiquity, any usage, any livery[6] productive of ease or profit, to the unproductive service of thought.

Yet, in every sane hour, the service of thought appears reasonable, the despotism of the senses insane. The scholar may, and does, lose himself in schools, in words, and become a pedant; but when he comprehends his duties, he above all men is a realist, and converses with things. For, the scholar is the student of the world, and of what worth the world is, and with

2    Oddly, Emerson echoes *Macbeth* 2.2.32–33: "Methought I heard a voice cry 'Sleep no more! / Macbeth does murder sleep.'"

3    In Greek mythology, giant race of gods overthrown by the Olympians, headed by Zeus.

4    Emerson accuses American artistry of being beautiful but not sublime. According to the critic Edmund Burke (1729–1797), the beautiful is smooth and harmonious; the sublime rough, overwhelming, and exalted.

5    Leaping from one thing to another.

6    The distinguishing uniform, showing rank and affiliation, worn by household servants, soldiers, and others (analogous to "service" in the final phrase of the sentence).

7    Challenges.

8    Island in the South Atlantic where the French emperor Napoleon Bonaparte (1769–1821) lived during the last six years of his life after his defeat by the British.

what emphasis it accosts[7] the soul of man, such is the worth, such the call of the scholar.

The want of the times, and the propriety of this anniversary, concur to draw attention to the doctrine of Literary Ethics. On that doctrine, I wish to offer you a few thoughts. What I have to say, distributes itself under the topics of the resources, the subject, and the discipline of the scholar.

*    *    *

I. The resources of the scholar are proportioned to his confidence in the attributes of the Intellect. The resources of the scholar are coextensive with nature and truth, yet can never be his, unless claimed by him with an equal greatness of mind. He cannot know them until he has beheld with awe the infinitude and impersonality of the intellectual power, and worshipped that great light. When he has seen, that it is not his, nor any man's, but that it is the soul which made the world, and that it is all accessible to him, he will then see, that he, as its minister, may rightfully hold all things subordinate and answerable to it. When he stands in the world, he feels himself its native king. A divine pilgrim in nature, all things attend his steps. Over him stream the flying constellations; over him streams Time, as they, scarcely divided into months and years. He inhales the year as a vapor: its fragrant midsummer breath, its sparkling January heaven. And so pass into his mind, in bright transfiguration, the grand events of history, to take a new order and scale from him. He is the world; and the epochs and heroes of chronology are pictorial images, in which his thoughts are told. There is no event but sprung somewhere from the soul of man; and therefore there is none but the soul of man can interpret. Every presentiment of the mind is executed somewhere in some gigantic fact. What else is Greece, Rome, England, France, St. Helena?[8] What else are churches, and literatures, and empires?

But the soul, so feeling its right, must exercise the same, or it surrenders itself to the usurpation of facts. Essential to our riches is the unsleeping assertion of spiritual independence, as all the history of literature may teach. The new man must feel that he is new, and has not come into the world mortgaged to the opinions and usages of Europe, and Asia, and Egypt. The sense of spiritual independence is like the lovely varnish of the dew, whereby the old, hard, peaked earth, and its old self-same productions, are made new every morning, and shining with the last touch of the artist's hand. A false humility, a complaisance to reigning schools, or to the wisdom of antiquity, must not defraud me of supreme possession of this hour. If any person have less love of liberty, and less jealousy to guard his integrity, shall he therefore dictate to you and me? Say to such doctors, We are thankful to you, as we are to history, to the pyramids, and the authors; but now our day is come; we have been born out of the eternal silence; and now will we live,—live for ourselves,—and not as the pall-bearers of a funeral, but as the upholders and creators of our age; and neither Greece nor Rome, nor the three Unities of Aristotle, nor the three Kings of Cologne, nor the College of the Sorbonne, nor the Edinburgh Review,[9] is to command any longer. Now that we are here, we will put our own interpretation on things, and, moreover, our own things for interpretation. Please himself with complaisance who will,—for me, things must take my scale, not I theirs. I will say with the warlike king, "God gave me this crown, and the whole world shall not take it away."[10]

The whole value of history, of biography, is to increase my self-trust, by demonstrating what man can be and do. This is the moral of the Plutarchs, the Cudworths, the Tennemanns,[11] who give us the story of men or of opinions. Any history of philosophy fortifies my faith in the treasuries of the soul, by showing me, that what high dogmas I had supposed were the rare and late fruit of a cumulative culture, and only now possible to some recent Kant or Fichte,[12]—were the prompt improvisations of the earliest inquirers; of Parmenides, Heraclitus, and Xenophanes.[13] In view of these students, the soul seems to whisper, 'There is a better way than this indolent learning of another. Leave me alone; do not teach me out of Leibnitz or Schelling,[14] and I shall find it all out myself.'

Still more do we owe to biography the fortification of our hope. If you would know the power of character, see how much you would impoverish the world, if you could take clean out of history the life of Milton, of Shakspeare, of Plato,—these three, and cause them not to be. See you not, instantly, how much less the power of man would be? I console myself in the poverty of my present thoughts, in the paucity of great men, in the malignity and dulness of the nations, by falling back on these sublime recollections, and seeing what the prolific soul could beget on actual nature;—seeing that

9    The unities of time, place, and action, from the *Poetics* of Aristotle (384–322 BCE), became principles of playwriting in the Neoclassical drama; the shrine of the three kings in Cologne Cathedral, Germany, a lavish gilded sarcophagus from the thirteenth century, is said to contain the bones of the three wise men (or Magi) who visited the infant Jesus; the Sorbonne is the central institution of higher learning in France. Emerson avidly read the *Edinburgh Review*, an influential intellectual journal founded in 1802.

10   Words of Napoleon, who crowned himself king of Italy in 1805 (J 7:8).

11   Plutarch (ca. 46–ca. 122), Greek biographer and moralist often cited by Emerson; Ralph Cudworth (1617–1688), English philosopher, one of the Cambridge Platonists; Wilhelm Gottlieb Tennemann (1761–1819), German historian of philosophy.

12   Immanuel Kant (1724–1804) and J. G. Fichte (1762–1814), German philosophers.

13   Parmenides (early 5th century BCE), Heraclitus (6th century BCE), and Xenophanes (ca. 560–ca. 478 BCE), early Greek philosophers.

14   G. W. von Leibniz (1646–1716) and F. W. J. von Schelling (1775–1854), German philosophers.

15    Allusion to *Hamlet* 1.1.116, describing the portents presaging the death of Julius Caesar (100–44 BCE): "The sheeted dead / Did squeak and gibber in the Roman streets").

16    Charles V (1500–1558), Holy Roman Emperor. Emerson had read William Robertson's (1721–1793) *History of the Reign of Charles V* (1792).

17    Spanish; the court of Spain had an elaborate code of manners.

18    The phrase "born of women" is used in Matthew 11:11 and Luke 7:28. William Pitt (the Elder), first Earl of Chatham (1708–1778), British leader; John Hampden (ca. 1595–1643), politician who played a central role in the English Civil War; Pierre Terrail Le Vieux, seigneur de Bayard (1473–1524), heroic exemplar of French knighthood; Alfred the Great (849–899), king of Wessex who defended the Anglo-Saxon peoples against Vikings and revived education; Cornelius Scipio (235–183 BCE), known as Africanus after his famous victory over the Carthaginian general Hannibal (248–ca. 183 BCE) at Zama (202 BCE); Pericles (ca. 495–429 BCE), Athenian general and leader during its Golden Age.

Plato was, and Shakspeare, and Milton,—three irrefragable facts. Then I dare; I also will essay to be. The humblest, the most hopeless, in view of these radiant facts, may now theorize and hope. In spite of all the rueful abortions that squeak and gibber in the street,[15] in spite of slumber and guilt, in spite of the army, the bar-room, and the jail, *have been* these glorious manifestations of the mind; and I will thank my great brothers so truly for the admonition of their being, as to endeavor also to be just and brave, to aspire and to speak. Plotinus too, and Spinoza, and the immortal bards of philosophy,—that which they have written out with patient courage, makes me bold. No more will I dismiss, with haste, the visions which flash and sparkle across my sky; but observe them, approach them, domesticate them, brood on them, and thus draw out of the past, genuine life for the present hour.

To feel the full value of these facts, of these lives, as occasions of hope and provocation, one must rightly ponder the mystery of our common soul. You must come to know, that each admirable genius is but a successful diver in that sea whose floor of pearls is all your own. The impoverishing philosophy of ages has laid stress on the distinctions of the individual, and not on the universal attributes of man. The youth, intoxicated with his admiration of a hero, fails to see, that it is only a projection of his own soul, which he admires. In solitude, in a remote village, the ardent youth loiters and mourns. With inflamed eye, in this sleeping wilderness, he has read the story of the Emperor Charles the Fifth,[16] until his fancy has brought home to the surrounding woods, the faint roar of cannonades in the Milanese, and marches in Germany. He is curious concerning that man's day. What filled it? the crowded orders, the stern decisions, the foreign despatches, the Castilian[17] etiquette? The soul answers—Behold his day here! In the sighing of these woods, in the quiet of these gray fields, in the cool breeze that sings out of these northern mountains; in the workmen, the boys, the maidens, you meet,—in the hopes of the morning, the ennui of noon, and sauntering of the afternoon; in the disquieting comparisons; in the regrets at want of vigor; in the great idea, and the puny execution;—behold Charles the Fifth's day; another, yet the same; behold Chatham's, Hampden's, Bayard's, Alfred's, Scipio's, Pericles's day,—day of all that are born of women.[18] The difference of circumstance is merely costume. I am tasting the self-same life,—its sweetness, its greatness, its pain, which I so admire in other men. Do not foolishly ask of the inscrutable, obliterated past, what it cannot tell,—the details of that nature, of that day, called Byron, or Burke;[19]—but ask it of the enveloping Now; the more quaintly you inspect its evanescent beauties, its wonderful details, its spiritual causes, its astounding whole,—so much the more you master the biography of this hero, and that, and every hero. Be lord of a day, through wisdom and justice, and you can put up your history books.

An intimation of these broad rights is familiar in the sense of injury which men feel in the assumption of any man to limit their possible progress. We resent all criticism, which denies us any thing that lies in our line of advance. Say to the man of letters, that he cannot paint a Transfiguration,[20] or build a steamboat, or be a grand-marshal,—and he will not seem to himself depreciated. But deny to him any quality of literary or metaphysical power, and he is piqued. Concede to him genius, which is a sort of Stoical *plenum*[21] annulling the comparative, and he is content; but concede him talents never so rare, denying him genius, and he is aggrieved. What does this mean? Why simply, that the soul has assurance, by instincts and presentiments, of *all* power in the direction of its ray, as well as of the special skills it has already acquired.

In order to a knowledge of the resources of the scholar, we must not rest in the use of slender accomplishments,—of faculties to do this and that other feat with words; but we must pay our vows to the highest power, and pass, if it be possible, by assiduous love and watching, into the visions of absolute truth. The growth of the intellect is strictly analogous in all individuals. It is larger reception of a common soul. Able men, in general, have good dispositions, and a respect for justice; because an able man is nothing else than a good, free, vascular organization, whereinto the universal spirit freely flows; so that his fund of justice is not only vast, but infinite. All men, in the abstract, are just and good; what hinders them, in the particular, is, the momentary predominance of the finite and individual over the general truth. The condition of our incarnation in a private self, seems to be, a perpetual tendency to prefer the private law, to obey the private impulse, to the exclu-

19   George Gordon, Lord Byron (1788–1824), English Romantic poet.

20   Painting by Raphael Sanzio (1483–1520) that Emerson had admired in the Vatican on his trip to Europe in 1833 (J 4:150).

21   The Stoics, a Greek philosophical school that flourished in the third century BCE, thought that the universe was a *plenum* (full of matter, without empty space).

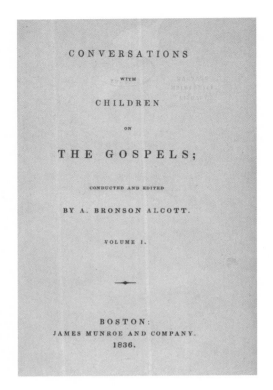

Title page of Amos Bronson Alcott's *Conversations with Children on the Gospels.*

sion of the law of universal being. The great man is great by means of the predominance of the universal nature; he has only to open his mouth, and it speaks; he has only to be forced to act, and it acts. All men catch the word, or embrace the deed, with the heart, for it is verily theirs as much as his; but in them this disease of an excess of organization cheats them of equal issues. Nothing is more simple than greatness; indeed, to be simple is to be great. All vision, all genius, comes by renouncing the too officious activity of the understanding, and giving leave and amplest privilege to the spontaneous sentiment. Out of this must all that is alive and genial in thought go. Men grind and grind in the mill of a truism, and nothing comes out but what was put in. But the moment they desert the tradition, and speak a spontaneous thought, instantly poetry, wit, hope, virtue, learning, anecdote, all flock to their aid. Observe the phenomenon of extempore debate. A man of cultivated mind, but reserved habits, sitting silent, admires the miracle of free, impassioned, picturesque speech, in the man addressing an assembly;—a state of being and power, how unlike his own! Presently his own emotion rises to his lips, and overflows in speech. He must also rise and say somewhat. Once embarked, once having overcome the novelty of the situation, he finds it just as easy and natural to speak,—to speak with thoughts, with pictures, with rhythmical balance of sentences,—as it was to sit silent; for, it needs not to do, but to suffer; he only adjusts himself to the free spirit which gladly utters itself through him; and motion is as easy as rest.

\* \* \*

II. I pass now to consider the task offered to the intellect of this country. The view I have taken of the resources of the scholar, presupposes a subject as broad. We do not seem to have imagined its riches. We have not heeded the invitation it holds out. To be as good a scholar as Englishmen are; to have as much learning as our contemporaries; to have written a book that is read; satisfies us. We assume, that all thought is already long ago adequately set down in books,—all imaginations in poems; and what we say, we only throw in as confirmatory of this supposed complete body of literature. A very shallow assumption. A true man will think rather, all literature is yet to be written. Poetry has scarce chanted its first song. The perpetual admonition of nature to us, is, 'The world is new, untried. Do not believe the past. I give you the universe a virgin to-day.'

By Latin and English poetry, we were born and bred in an oratorio of praises of nature,—flowers, birds, mountains, sun, and moon,—yet the naturalist of this hour finds that he knows nothing, by all their poems, of any of these fine things; that he has conversed with the merest surface and show of them all; and of their essence, or of their history, knows nothing. Further inquiry will discover that nobody,—that not these chanting poets themselves, knew any thing sincere of these handsome natures they so commended; that they contented themselves with the passing chirp of a bird, that they saw one or two mornings, and listlessly looked at sunsets, and repeated idly these few glimpses in their song. But go into the forest, you shall find all new and undescribed. The honking of the wild geese flying by night; the thin note of the companionable titmouse, in the winter day; the fall of swarms of flies, in autumn, from combats high in the air, pattering down on the leaves like rain; the angry hiss of the wood-birds; the pine throwing out its pollen for the benefit of the next century; the turpentine exuding from the tree;—and, indeed, any vegetation; any animation; any and all, are alike unattempted. The man who stands on the seashore, or who rambles in the woods, seems to be the first man that ever stood on the shore, or entered a grove, his sensations and his world are so novel and strange. Whilst I read the poets, I think that nothing new can be said about morning and evening. But when I see the daybreak, I am not reminded of these Homeric, or Shakspearian, or Miltonic, or Chaucerian pictures. No; but I feel perhaps the pain of an alien world; a world not yet subdued by the thought; or, I am cheered by the moist, warm, glittering, budding, melodious hour, that takes down the narrow walls of my soul, and extends its life and pulsation to the very horizon. *That* is morning, to cease for a bright hour to be a prisoner of this sickly body, and to become as large as nature.

The noonday darkness of the American forest, the deep, echoing, aboriginal woods, where the living columns of the oak and fir tower up from the ruins of the trees of the last millennium; where, from year to year, the eagle and the crow see no intruder; the pines, bearded with savage moss, yet

Emerson, 1847.

22    In his copy of *The Prelude* (1850) by the English Romantic poet William Wordsworth (1770–1850), Emerson marked as *to deinon* (Greek: sublimely powerful) Wordsworth's description of "*that* beauty which, as Milton sings, / Hath terror in it."

23    Native American name for New Hampshire's White Mountains.

24    The Pelasgi were early inhabitants of Greece; Athens its most famous city; and the Etrurians, ancient inhabitants of west-central Italy (now Tuscany and Umbria).

25    Unyielding, unbreakable stone.

26    The French philosopher Victor Cousin (1792–1867) espoused Eclecticism, according to which truth resides not in one particular philosophical system but in the best of each system, selected by a discerning reader. Cousin's philosophy was popular in New England, and was embraced for a time by Emerson's friends Amos Bronson Alcott (1799–1888) and George Ripley (1802–1880).

touched with grace by the violets at their feet; the broad, cold lowland, which forms its coat of vapor with the stillness of subterranean crystallization; and where the traveller, amid the repulsive plants that are native in the swamp, thinks with pleasing terror of the distant town; this beauty,—haggard and desert beauty,[22] which the sun and the moon, the snow and the rain repaint and vary, has never been recorded by art, yet is not indifferent to any passenger. All men are poets at heart. They serve nature for bread, but her loveliness overcomes them sometimes. What mean these journeys to Niagara; these pilgrims to the White Hills? Men believe in the adaptations of utility, always. In the mountains, they may believe in the adaptations of the eye. Undoubtedly, the changes of geology have a relation to the prosperous sprouting of the corn and peas in my kitchen garden; but not less is there a relation of beauty between my soul and the dim crags of Agiocochook[23] up there in the clouds. Every man, when this is told, hearkens with joy, and yet his own conversation with nature is still unsung.

Is it otherwise with civil history? Is it not the lesson of our experience that every man, were life long enough, would write history for himself? What else do these volumes of extracts and manuscript commentaries, that every scholar writes, indicate? Greek history is one thing to me; another to you. Since the birth of Niebuhr and Wolf, Roman and Greek History have been written anew. Since Carlyle wrote French History, we see that no history, that we have, is safe, but a new classifier shall give it new and more philosophical arrangement. Thucydides, Livy, have only provided materials. The moment a man of genius pronounces the name of the Pelasgi, of Athens, of the Etrurian,[24] of the Roman people, instantly we see their state under a new aspect. As in poetry and history, so in the other departments. There are few masters or none. Religion is yet to be settled on its fast foundations in the breast of man; and politics, and philosophy, and letters, and art. As yet we have nothing but tendency and indication.

This starting, this warping of the best literary works from the adamant[25] of nature, is especially observable in philosophy. Let it take what tone of pretension it will, to this complexion must it come, at last. Take, for example, the French Eclecticism, which Cousin esteems so conclusive;[26] there is an optical illusion in it. It avows great pretensions. It looks as if they had got all truth, in taking all the systems, and had nothing to do, but to sift and wash and strain, and the gold and diamonds would remain in the last colander. But, in fact, this is not so; for Truth is such a flyaway, such a slyboots,[27] so untransportable and unbarrelable a commodity, that it is as bad to catch as light. Shut the shutters never so quick, to keep all the light in, it is all in vain; it is gone before you can cry, Hold.[28] And so it happens with our philosophy. Translate, collate, distil all the systems, it steads[29] you nothing; for truth will not be compelled, in any mechanical manner. But the first observation you make, in the sincere act of your nature, though on the veriest trifle, may open a new view of nature and of man, that, like a menstruum,[30] shall dissolve all theories in it; shall take up Greece, Rome, Stoicism, Eclecticism, and what not, as mere data and food for analysis, and dispose of your world-containing system, as a very little unit. A profound thought, anywhere, classifies all things. A profound thought will lift Olympus. The book of philosophy is only a fact, and no more inspiring fact than another, and no less; but a wise man will never esteem it any thing final and transcending. Go and talk with a man of genius, and the first word he utters, sets all your so-called knowledge afloat and at large. Then Plato, Bacon,[31] Kant, and the Eclectic Cousin, condescend instantly to be men and mere facts.

I by no means aim, in these remarks, to disparage the merit of these or of any existing compositions; I only say that such is the dread statute of Nature, which they all underlie, that any particular portraiture does not in any manner exclude or forestall a new attempt, but, when considered by the soul, warps and shrinks away. The inundation of the spirit sweeps away before it all our little architecture of wit and memory, as straws and straw-huts before the torrent. Works of the intellect are great only by comparison with each other; Ivanhoe and Waverley compared with Castle Radcliffe and the Porter novels;[32] but nothing is great,—not mighty Homer and Milton,[33]—beside the infinite Reason. It carries them away as a flood. They are as a sleep.[34]

Thus is justice done to each generation and individual,—wisdom teaching man that he shall not hate, or fear, or mimic his ancestors; that he shall not bewail himself, as if the world was old, and thought was spent, and he was born into the dotage of things; for, by virtue of the Deity, thought renews

27    Shrewd person.

28    A reference to Shakespeare's *Macbeth* (5.7.34): "Damned be him that first cries, 'Hold, enough!'"

29    Avails, profits.

30    Solvent.

31    Francis Bacon (1561–1626), pioneering English scientist and essayist.

32    Emerson esteems the Waverley novels and *Ivanhoe* (1819) by Sir Walter Scott (1771–1832) over the historical fiction of the sisters Anna Maria (1780–1832) and Jane Porter (1776–1850), such as Jane's *Scottish Chiefs* (1810). "Castle Radcliffe" is probably a misremembering and conflation of *Castle Rackrent* (1800) by Maria Edgeworth (1768–1849) with the works of Anne Radcliffe (1764–1823).

33    Homer (ca. 9th century BCE), legendary author of the *Iliad* and the *Odyssey*; John Milton (1608–1674), author of *Paradise Lost*.

34    Psalms 90:5 ("Thou carriest them away as with a flood; they are as a sleep: in the morning they are like grass which groweth up"); also Revelation 12:15.

35    In his Journal (1846), Emerson wrote, "I see not how we can live except alone. Trenchant manners, a sharp decided way will prove a lasting convenience. Society will coo & claw & caress. You must curse & swear a little: They will remember it, & it will do them good. . . . Understand me when I say, I love you, it is your genius & not you. I like man, but not men" (J 9:377).

36    Pindar (ca. 518–ca. 438 BCE), Greek author of sublime odes; Michelangelo Buonnaroti (1475–1564), Italian Renaissance painter, sculptor, and architect; John Dryden (1631–1700), English Restoration poet; Madame Germaine de Staël (1766–1817), French woman of letters and major influence on Emerson.

itself inexhaustibly every day, and the thing whereon it shines, though it were dust and sand, is a new subject with countless relations.

* * *

III. Having thus spoken of the resources and the subject of the scholar, out of the same faith proceeds also the rule of his ambition and life. Let him know that the world is his, but he must possess it by putting himself into harmony with the constitution of things. He must be a solitary, laborious, modest, and charitable soul.

He must embrace solitude as a bride. He must have his glees and his glooms alone.[35] His own estimate must be measure enough, his own praise reward enough for him. And why must the student be solitary and silent? That he may become acquainted with his thoughts. If he pines in a lonely place, hankering for the crowd, for display, he is not in the lonely place; his heart is in the market; he does not see; he does not hear; he does not think. But go cherish your soul; expel companions; set your habits to a life of solitude; then, will the faculties rise fair and full within, like forest trees and field flowers; you will have results, which, when you meet your fellow men, you can communicate, and they will gladly receive. Do not go into solitude only that you may presently come to the public. Such solitude denies itself; is public and stale. The public can get public experience, but they wish the scholar to replace to them those private, sincere, divine experiences, of which they have been defrauded by dwelling in the street. It is the noble, manlike, just thought, which is the superiority demanded of you, and not crowds but solitude confers this elevation. See distinctly, that it is not insulation of place, but independence of spirit that is essential, and it is only as the garden, the cottage, the forest, and the rock are a sort of mechanical aids to this, that they are of value. Think alone, and all places are friendly and sacred. The poets who have lived in cities have been hermits still. Inspiration makes solitude anywhere. Pindar, Raphael, Angelo, Dryden, De Staël,[36] dwell in crowds, it may be, but the instant thought comes, the crowd grows dim to their eye; their eye fixes on the horizon,—on vacant space; they forget the bystanders; they spurn personal relations; they deal with abstractions, with verities, with ideas. They are alone with the mind.

Of course, I would not have any superstition about solitude. Let the youth study the uses of solitude and of society. Let him use both, not serve either. The reason why an ingenious soul shuns society, is to the end of finding society. It repudiates the false, out of love of the true. You can very soon learn all that society can teach you for one while. Its foolish routine, an indefinite multiplication of balls, concerts, rides, theatres, can teach you no more than a few can. Then accept the hint of shame, of spiritual emptiness and waste, which true Nature gives you, and retire, and hide; lock the door; shut the shutters; then welcome falls the imprisoning rain,—dear hermitage of nature. Re-collect the spirits. Have solitary prayer and praise. Digest and correct the past experience. Blend it with the new and divine life, and grow with God.

You will pardon me, Gentlemen, if I say, I think that we have need of a more rigorous scholastic rule; such an asceticism, I mean, as only the hardihood and devotion of the scholar himself can enforce. We live in the sun and on the surface,—a thin, plausible, superficial existence, and talk of muse and prophet, of art and creation. But out of our shallow and frivolous way of life, how can greatness ever grow? Come now, let us go and be dumb. Let us sit with our hands on our mouths, a long, austere, Pythagorean lustrum.[37] Let us live in corners, and do chares, and suffer, and weep, and drudge, with eyes and hearts that love the Lord. Silence, seclusion, austerity, may pierce deep into the grandeur and secret of our being, and so diving, bring up out of secular darkness, the sublimities of the moral constitution. How mean to go blazing, a gaudy butterfly, in fashionable or political saloons, the fool of society, the fool of notoriety, a topic for newspapers, a piece of the street, and forfeiting the real prerogative of the russet coat, the privacy, and the true and warm heart of the citizen!

Fatal to the man of letters, fatal to man, is the lust of display, the seeming that unmakes our being. A mistake of the main end to which they labor, is incident to literary men, who, dealing with the organ of language,—the subtlest, strongest, and longest-lived of man's creations, and only fitly used as the weapon of thought and of justice,—learn to enjoy the pride of playing with this splendid engine, but rob it of its almightiness by failing to work with it. Extricating themselves from all the tasks of the world, the world revenges itself by exposing, at every turn, the folly of these incomplete, pedan-

37    A lustrum (Latin) is a five-year period; Pythagoras (ca. 570–ca. 495 BCE), the Greek philosopher, was well known for his prizing of silence. In 1829, Emerson quoted Pythagoras in his Journal: "We ought either to be silent or to speak things better than silence" (J 6:93).

38    On July 15, 1815, after losing the Battle of Waterloo, Napoleon surrendered to the British aboard the *HMS Bellerophon*. Emerson took the anecdote from the *Memorial of St. Helena* (1823) by Emmanuel de las Cases (1766–1842), who interviewed Napoleon at length.

tic, useless, ghostly creatures. The true scholar will feel, that the richest romance,—the noblest fiction that was ever woven,—the heart and soul of beauty,—lies enclosed in human life. Itself of surpassing value, it is also the richest material for his creations. How shall he know its secrets of tenderness, of terror, of will, and of fate? How can he catch and keep the strain of upper music that peals from it? Its laws are concealed under the details of daily action. All action is an experiment upon them. He must bear his share of the common load. He must work with men in houses, and not with their names in books. His needs, appetites, talents, affections, accomplishments, are keys that open to him the beautiful museum of human life. Why should he read it as an Arabian tale, and not know, in his own beating bosom, its sweet and smart? Out of love and hatred, out of earnings and borrowings, and lendings and losses; out of sickness and pain; out of wooing and worshipping; out of travelling, and voting, and watching, and caring; out of disgrace and contempt, comes our tuition in the serene and beautiful laws. Let him not slur his lesson; let him learn it by heart. Let him endeavor exactly, bravely, and cheerfully, to solve the problem of that life which is set before *him*. And this, by punctual action, and not by promises or dreams. Believing, as in God, in the presence and favor of the grandest influences, let him deserve that favor, and learn how to receive and use it, by fidelity also to the lower observances.

This lesson is taught with emphasis in the life of the great actor of this age, and affords the explanation of his success. Bonaparte represents truly a great recent revolution, which we in this country, please God, shall carry to its farthest consummation. Not the least instructive passage in modern history, seems to me a trait of Napoleon, exhibited to the English when he became their prisoner. On coming on board the Bellerophon, a file of English soldiers, drawn up on deck, gave him a military salute. Napoleon observed, that their manner of handling their arms differed from the French exercise, and, putting aside the guns of those nearest him, walked up to a soldier, took his gun, and himself went through the motion in the French mode. The English officers and men looked on with astonishment, and inquired if such familiarity was usual with the Emperor.[38]

In this instance, as always, that man, with whatever defects or vices, represented performance in lieu of pretension. Feudalism and Orientalism

East Boston, 1879.

had long enough thought it majestic to do nothing; the modern majesty consists in work. He belonged to a class, fast growing in the world, who think, that what a man can do is his greatest ornament, and that he always consults his dignity by doing it. He was not a believer in luck; he had a faith, like sight, in the application of means to ends. Means to ends, is the motto of all his behaviour. He believed that all the great captains of antiquity performed their exploits only by correct combinations, and by justly comparing the relation between means and consequences; efforts and obstacles. The vulgar call good fortune that which really is produced by the calculations of genius. But Napoleon, thus faithful to facts, had also this crowning merit; that, whilst he believed in number and weight, and omitted no part of prudence, he believed also in the freedom and quite incalculable force of the soul. A man of infinite caution, he neglected never the least particular of preparation, of patient adaptation; yet nevertheless he had a sublime confidence, as in his all, in the sallies of the courage, and the faith in his destiny, which, at the right moment, repaired all losses, and demolished cavalry, infantry, king, and kaisar, as with irresistible thunderbolts. As they say the bough of the tree has the character of the leaf, and the whole tree of the bough, so, it is curious to remark, Bonaparte's army partook of this double strength of the captain; for, whilst strictly supplied in all its appointments, and every thing expected from the valor and discipline of every platoon, in flank and centre, yet always remained his total trust in the prodigious revolutions of fortune, which his reserved Imperial Guard were capable of working, if, in all else, the day was lost. Here he was sublime. He no longer calculated the chance of the cannon-ball. He was faithful to tactics to the uttermost,—and when all tactics had come to an end, then, he dilated, and availed himself of the mighty saltations[39] of the most formidable soldiers in nature.

Let the scholar appreciate this combination of gifts, which, applied to better purpose, make true wisdom. He is a revealer of things. Let him first learn the things. Let him not, too eager to grasp some badge of reward, omit the work to be done. Let him know, that, though the success of the market is in the reward, true success is the doing; that, in the private obedience to his mind; in the sedulous inquiry, day after day, year after year, to know how the thing stands; in the use of all means, and most in the reverence of the humble commerce and humble needs of life,—to hearken what *they* say, and so, by mutual reaction of thought and life, to make thought solid, and life wise; and in a contempt for the gabble of to-day's opinions, the secret of the world is to be learned, and the skill truly to unfold it is acquired. Or, rather, is it not, that, by this discipline, the refractoriness of the usurping senses and of the perverted will is overcome, and the lower faculties of man are subdued to docility; through which, as an unobstructed channel, the soul now easily and gladly flows?

The good scholar will not refuse to bear the yoke in his youth; to know, if he can, the uttermost secret of toil and endurance; to make his own hands acquainted with the soil by which he is fed, and the sweat that goes before comfort and luxury. Let him pay his tithe, and serve the world as a true and noble man; never forgetting to worship the immortal divinities, who whisper to the poet, and make him the utterer of melodies that pierce the ear of eternal time. If he have this twofold goodness,—the drill and the inspiration,—then he has health; then he is a whole, and not a fragment; and the perfection of his endowment will appear in his compositions. Indeed, this twofold merit characterizes ever the productions of great masters. The man of genius should occupy the whole space between God or pure mind, and the multitude of uneducated men. He must draw from the infinite Reason, on one side; and he must penetrate into the heart and sense of the crowd, on the other. From one, he must draw his strength; to the other, he must owe his aim. The one yokes him to the real; the other, to the apparent. At one pole, is Reason; at the other, Common Sense. If he be defective at either extreme of the scale, his philosophy will seem low and utilitarian; or it will appear too vague and indefinite for the uses of life.

The student, as we all along insist, is great only by being passive to the superincumbent spirit. Let this faith, then, dictate all his action. Snares and bribes abound to mislead him; let him be true nevertheless. His success has its perils too. There is somewhat inconvenient and injurious in his position. They whom his thoughts have entertained or inflamed, seek him before yet they have learned the hard conditions of thought. They seek him, that he may turn his lamp upon the dark riddles whose solution they think is inscribed on the walls of their being. They find that he is a poor, ignorant man, in a white-seamed, rusty coat, like themselves, no wise emitting a continuous stream of light, but now and then a jet of luminous thought, followed by to-

40     Crude soda ash, used in glassmaking.

41     Equipped and ready for action (girded, as with a belt).

tal darkness; moreover, that he cannot make of his infrequent illumination a portable taper to carry whither he would, and explain now this dark riddle, now that, Sorrow ensues. The scholar regrets to damp the hope of ingenuous boys; and the youth has lost a star out of his new flaming firmament. Hence the temptation to the scholar to mystify; to hear the question; to sit upon it; to make an answer of words, in lack of the oracle of things. Not the less let him be cold and true, and wait in patience, knowing that truth can make even silence eloquent and memorable. Always truth is policy enough for him. Let him open his breast to all honest inquiry, and be an artist superior to tricks of art. Show frankly as a saint would do, all your experience, your methods, tools, and means. Welcome all comers to the freest use of the same. And out of this superior frankness and charity, you shall learn higher secrets of your nature, which gods will bend and aid you to communicate.

If, with a high trust, he can thus submit himself to the supreme soul, he will find that ample returns are poured into his bosom, out of what seemed hours of obstruction and loss. Let him not grieve too much on account of unfit associates. When he sees how much thought he owes to the disagreeable antagonism of various persons who pass and cross him, he can easily think that in a society of perfect sympathy, no word, no act, no record, would be. He will learn, that it is not much matter what he reads, what he does. Be a scholar, and he shall have the scholar's part of every thing. As, in the counting-room, the merchant cares little whether the cargo be hides or barilla;[40] the transaction, a letter of credit or a transfer of stocks; be it what it may, his commission comes gently out of it; so you shall get your lesson out of the hour, and the object, whether it be a concentrated or a wasteful employment, even in reading a dull book, or working off a stint of mechanical day labor, which your necessities or the necessities of others impose.

Gentlemen, I have ventured to offer you these considerations upon the scholar's place, and hope, because I thought, that, standing, as many of you now do, on the threshold of this College, girt[41] and ready to go and assume tasks, public and private, in your country, you would not be sorry to be admonished of those primary duties of the intellect, whereof you will seldom hear from the lips of your new companions. You will hear every day the maxims of a low prudence. You will hear, that the first duty is to get land and money, place and name. 'What is this Truth you seek? What is this Beauty?' men will ask, with derision. If, nevertheless, God have called any of you to explore truth and beauty, be bold, be firm, be true. When you shall say, 'As others do, so will I. I renounce, I am sorry for it, my early visions; I must eat the good of the land,[42] and let learning and romantic expectations go, until a more convenient season;'—then dies the man in you; then once more perish the buds of art, and poetry, and science, as they have died already in a thousand thousand men.[43] The hour of that choice is the crisis of your history; and see that you hold yourself fast by the intellect. Feel that it is this domineering temper of the sensual world, that creates the extreme need of the priests of science; and that it is the office and right of the intellect to make and not take its estimate. Bend to the persuasion which is flowing to you from every object in nature, to be its tongue to the heart of man, and to show the besotted world how passing fair is wisdom. Forewarned that the vice of the times and the country is an excessive pretension, let us seek the shade, and find wisdom in neglect. Be content with a little light, so it be your own. Explore, and explore, and explore. Be neither chided nor flattered out of your position of perpetual inquiry. Neither dogmatize yourself, nor accept another's dogmatism. Why should you renounce your right to traverse the star-lit deserts of truth, for the premature comforts of an acre, house, and barn? Truth also has its roof, and bed, and board. Make yourself necessary to the world, and mankind will give you bread, and if not store of it, yet such as shall not take away your property in all men's possessions, in all men's affections, in art, in nature, and in hope.

You will not fear, that I am enjoining too stern an asceticism. Ask not, Of what use is a scholarship that systematically retreats? or, Who is the better for the philosopher who conceals his accomplishments, and hides his thoughts from the waiting world? Hides his thoughts! Hide the sun and moon. Thought is all light, and publishes itself to the universe. It will speak, though you were dumb, by its own miraculous organ. It will flow out of your actions, your manners, and your face. It will bring you friendships. It will impledge you to truth by the love and expectation of generous minds. By virtue of the laws of that Nature, which is one and perfect, it shall yield every sincere good that is in the soul, to the scholar beloved of earth and heaven.

42    Isaiah 1:19: "If ye be willing and obedient, ye shall eat the good of the land."

43    In his lecture "The Method of Nature" (1841), Emerson quoted the book of Proverbs (29:18): "Where there is no vision, the people perish."

# History

*This is the opening essay in Emerson's* Essays *(1841), his second book. Emerson composed his essays from the rich quarry of journal entries and from his public lectures (especially the lecture series on "The Philosophy of History" that he gave at Boston's Masonic Temple in 1836–1837). The essays share ideas with the journals and lectures, but they add much that is new, and they establish a form that is Emerson's own: wandering yet precise, experimental and cumulative. Emerson's friend Thomas Carlyle (1795–1881) wrote in his Preface to the English edition of* Essays, *"That this little Book has no 'system,' and points or stretches far beyond all systems, is one of its merits." Emerson begins with "History," perhaps, to clear the field for the self (the theme of the collection's second essay, "Self-Reliance").*

*In March 1841, when* Essays *appeared, Emerson's son Waldo was four years old and his daughter Ellen two; in November Lidian gave birth to another daughter, Edith.*

1    Emerson joins a military hero, Julius Caesar (100–44 BCE), and a philosopher, Plato (429–347 BCE), to Jesus and William Shake-
*(continued)*

There is no great and no small
To the Soul that maketh all:
And where it cometh, all things are;
And it cometh everywhere.

I am owner of the sphere,
Of the seven stars and the solar year,
Of Cæsar's hand, and Plato's brain,
Of Lord Christ's heart, and Shakspeare's strain.[1]

There is one mind common to all individual men. Every man is an inlet to the same and to all of the same. He that is once admitted to the right of reason is made a freeman of the whole estate. What Plato has thought, he may think; what a saint has felt, he may feel; what at any time has befallen any man, he can understand. Who hath access to this universal mind, is a party to all that is or can be done, for this is the only and sovereign agent.

Of the works of this mind history is the record. Its genius is illustrated by the entire series of days. Man is explicable by nothing less than all his history. Without hurry, without rest,[2] the human spirit goes forth from the beginning to embody every faculty, every thought, every emotion, which belongs to it in appropriate events. But the thought is always prior to the fact;

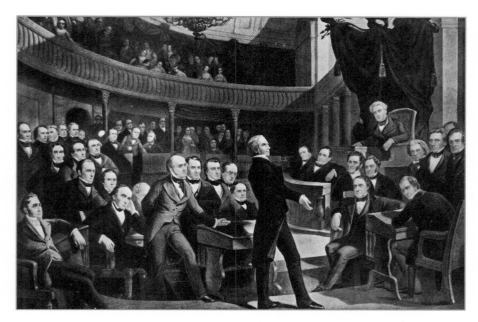

Senator Henry Clay (1777–1852) speaking to Congress in January 1850, urging compromise over slavery.

all the facts of history preëxist in the mind as laws. Each law in turn is made by circumstances predominant, and the limits of nature give power to but one at a time. A man is the whole encyclopædia of facts. The creation of a thousand forests is in one acorn, and Egypt, Greece, Rome, Gaul, Britain, America, lie folded already in the first man.[3] Epoch after epoch, camp, kingdom, empire, republic, democracy, are the application of his manifold spirit to the manifold world.[4]

This human mind wrote history and this must read it. The Sphinx[5] must solve her own riddle. If the whole of history is in one man, it is all to be explained from individual experience. There is a relation between the hours of our life and the centuries of time. As the air I breathe is drawn from the great repositories of nature, as the light on my book is yielded by a star a hundred millions of miles distant, as the poise of my body depends on the equilibrium of centrifugal and centripetal forces, so the hours should be in-

speare (1564–1616), who represent religion and literature—a fourfold assemblage of extraordinary human talents. The seven stars are the five planets visible to the naked eye along with the sun and the moon.

2    The German poet and thinker J. W. von Goethe (1749–1832) in "Zahme Xenien II" wrote, "Wie das Gestirn / Ohne Hast, / Aber ohne Rast" (like the stars, without haste, but without rest).

3    In his lecture "The Individual" (1837), from the series "The Philosophy of History," Emerson said, "Give me one man, and uncover for me his pleasures and pains . . . and you may travel all round the world and visit the Chinese, the Malay, the Esquimaux, the Arab. I travel faster than you. In my closet I see more and anticipate all your wonders" (EL 2:178–179; "closet" here means room).

4    In this paragraph Emerson plays on the words *explicable*, *folded*, and *manifold:* to explicate is (in its root meaning) to unfold.

5    The Sphinx, depicted with wings, a lion body, and the head of a woman, posed a riddle: what walks on four legs in the morning, two at noon, and three at evening? (Oedipus gave the answer: man.) In Emerson's poem "The Sphinx," she "broods on the world" and asks, "'Who'll tell me my secret, / The ages have kept?'" Thomas Taylor (1758–1835) in a comment on the *Treatise on Providence* by Synesius (ca. 373–ca. 414; one of Emerson's favorite books) wrote that the Sphinx "represents the nature of phantasy or imagination" (*Select Works of Plotinus*, trans. Taylor); Emerson marked the passage.

6    In his essay "Works and Days," Emerson wrote, "The use of history is to give value to the present hour and its duty."

7    Asdrubal or Hasdrubal (d. 207 BCE) was a daring, imaginative Carthaginian general in the Second Punic War against Rome, and younger brother of the more famous Hannibal (248–ca. 183 BCE). Cesare Borgia (ca. 1475–1507) was an Italian political leader known for his bold and ruthless tactics, and admired by Niccolò Machiavelli (1469–1527) in *The Prince* (publ. 1532).

8    Proteus, in Greek mythology, was the old man of the sea, who turned himself into various shapes to avoid being questioned, but when captured would reveal the truth. Emerson often drew on the myth of Proteus. In his essay on Goethe, he wrote, "Amid littleness and detail, he detected the Genius of life, the old cunning Proteus, nestling close beside us." In his Journal (December 6, 1836) he remarked that, when studying history, one should "stand before each of its tablets with the faith, Here is one of the coverings: Under this heavy & odious mask did my Proteus nature hide itself, but look there & see the effort it made to be a god again" (J 5:262).

9    Solomon, king of Israel (ca. 10th century BCE), was tempted by his wives into idolatry; the Athenian general Alcibiades (ca. 450–404 BCE) defected from Athens to Sparta and then to Persia; and Catiline (108–62 BCE) tried to overthrow the Roman Republic.

10   Emerson noted in his Journal (November 8, 1836) that "the Greek had, it seems, the same fellow beings as I; the sun & moon water & fire met his eye & heart as they do mine, precisely"; *(continued)*

structed by the ages, and the ages explained by the hours. Of the universal mind each individual man is one more incarnation. All its properties consist in him. Each new fact in his private experience flashes a light on what great bodies of men have done, and the crises of his life refer to national crises. Every revolution was first a thought in one man's mind, and when the same thought occurs to another man, it is the key to that era. Every reform was once a private opinion, and when it shall be a private opinion again, it will solve the problem of the age. The fact narrated must correspond to something in me to be credible or intelligible.[6] We as we read must become Greeks, Romans, Turks, priest and king, martyr and executioner, must fasten these images to some reality in our secret experience, or we shall learn nothing rightly. What befell Asdrubal or Cæsar Borgia,[7] is as much an illustration of the mind's powers and depravations as what has befallen us. Each new law and political movement has meaning for you. Stand before each of its tablets and say, 'Under this mask did my Proteus nature hide itself.'[8] This remedies the defect of our too great nearness to ourselves. This throws our actions into perspective: and as crabs, goats, scorpions, the balance and the water-pot, lose their meanness when hung as signs in the zodiack, so I can see my own vices without heat in the distant persons of Solomon, Alcibiades, and Catiline.[9]

It is the universal nature which gives worth to particular men and things.[10] Human life as containing this is mysterious and inviolable, and we hedge it round with penalties and laws. All laws derive hence their ultimate reason; all express more or less distinctly some command of this supreme illimitable essence. Property also holds of the soul, covers great spiritual facts, and instinctively we at first hold to it with swords and laws, and wide and complex combinations. The obscure consciousness of this fact is the light of all our day, the claim of claims; the plea for education, for justice, for charity, the foundation of friendship and love, and of the heroism and grandeur which belong to acts of self-reliance. It is remarkable that involuntarily we always read as superior beings. Universal history, the poets, the romancers, do not in their stateliest pictures—in the sacerdotal, the imperial palaces, in the triumphs of will, or of genius—anywhere lose our ear, anywhere make us feel that we intrude, that this is for better men; but rather is it true that in their grandest strokes we feel most at home. All that Shakspeare says of the king, yonder slip of a boy that reads in the corner, feels to be true of himself. We sympathize in the great moments of history, in the great discoveries, the great resistances, the great prosperities of men;—because there law was enacted, the sea was searched, the land was found, or the blow was struck *for us*, as we ourselves in that place would have done or applauded.

We have the same interest in condition and character. We honor the rich because they have externally the freedom, power and grace which we feel to be proper to man, proper to us. So all that is said of the wise man by stoic or oriental or modern essayist, describes to each reader his own idea, describes his unattained but attainable self. All literature writes the character of the wise man. Books, monuments, pictures, conversation, are portraits in which he finds the lineaments he is forming. The silent and the eloquent praise him, and accost him,[11] and he is stimulated wherever he moves as by personal allusions. A true aspirant, therefore, never needs look for allusions personal and laudatory in discourse. He hears the commendation, not of himself, but more sweet, of that character he seeks, in every word that is said concerning character, yea, further, in every fact and circumstance,—in the running river, and the rustling corn. Praise is looked, homage tendered, love flows from mute nature, from the mountains and the lights of the firmament.

These hints, dropped as it were from sleep and night, let us use in broad day. The student is to read history actively and not passively; to esteem his own life the text, and books the commentary. Thus compelled, the muse of history will utter oracles, as never to those who do not respect themselves. I have no expectation that any man will read history aright, who thinks that what was done in a remote age, by men whose names have resounded far, has any deeper sense than what he is doing to-day.

The world exists for the education of each man. There is no age or state of society or mode of action in history, to which there is not somewhat corresponding in his life. Every thing tends in a wonderful manner to abbreviate itself and yield its own virtue to him. He should see that he can live all history in his own person. He must sit solidly at home, and not suffer himself to be bullied by kings or empires, but know that he is greater than all the

and more somberly, "A wife, a babe, a brother, poverty, & a country, which the Greek had, I have" (J 5:244–245).

11    Approach with an air of challenge.

12    Ancient Phoenician city, now in Leba-non.

13    Town where Joshua made the sun stand still (Joshua 10:12–13).

14    Napoleon Bonaparte, French emperor (1769–1821), was reported in the *Memorial of St. Helena* (1823) by Emmanuel de las Cases (1766–1842) to have said, "What then is, generally speaking, the truth of history? A fable agreed upon."

15    Roman name for the region of Europe encompassing present-day France and Belgium.

16    The Isles of the Blessed, where Greek heroes enjoyed a paradisal existence after death.

17    In a letter of October 12, 1840, to the reformer Elizabeth Palmer Peabody (1804–1894), Emerson wrote, "it is too plain tht the modern scholar begins with the fact of his own nature & is only willing to hear any result you can bring him from these old dead men by way of illustration or ornament of his own biography" (L 2:345).

18    The Scottish astronomer James Ferguson (1710–1776) made these discoveries in mechanics (not astronomy, as Emerson claims) when he was a young shepherd.

19    Edmund Burke (1729–1797), Anglo-Irish statesman and author; Sir Thomas More (1478–1535) was executed by King Henry VIII (1491–1547), and Algernon Sidney (1622–1683) by Charles II (1630–1685). Marmaduke Stevenson and William Robinson were Quakers executed by the Puritans in Boston in 1659 (Emerson
*(continued)*

geography and all the government of the world; he must transfer the point of view from which history is commonly read, from Rome and Athens and London to himself, and not deny his conviction that he is the Court, and if England or Egypt have any thing to say to him, he will try the case; if not, let them forever be silent. He must attain and maintain that lofty sight where facts yield their secret sense, and poetry and annals are alike. The instinct of the mind, the purpose of nature betrays itself in the use we make of the signal narrations of history. Time dissipates to shining ether the solid angularity of facts. No anchor, no cable, no fences avail to keep a fact a fact. Babylon, Troy, Tyre,[12] Palestine, and even early Rome, have passed or are passing into fiction. The Garden of Eden, the Sun standing still in Gibeon,[13] is poetry thenceforward to all nations. Who cares what the fact was, when we have made a constellation of it to hang in heaven an immortal sign? London and Paris and New York must go the same way. "What is History," said Napoleon, "but a fable agreed upon?"[14] This life of ours is stuck round with Egypt, Greece, Gaul,[15] England, War, Colonization, Church, Court, and Commerce, as with so many flowers and wild ornaments grave and gay. I will not make more account of them. I believe in Eternity. I can find Greece, Asia, Italy, Spain, and the Islands,[16]—the genius and creative principle of each and of all eras in my own mind.

We are always coming up with the emphatic facts of history in our private experience, and verifying them here. All history becomes subjective; in other words, there is properly no History; only Biography.[17] Every mind must know the whole lesson for itself—must go over the whole ground. What it does not see, what it does not live, it will not know. What the former age has epitomized into a formula or rule for manipular convenience, it will lose all the good of verifying for itself, by means of the wall of that rule. Somewhere, sometime, it will demand and find compensation for that loss by doing the work itself. Ferguson discovered many things in astronomy which had long been known.[18] The better for him.

History must be this or it is nothing. Every law which the state enacts, indicates a fact in human nature; that is all. We must in ourselves see the necessary reason of every fact,—see how it could and must be. So stand before every public and private work; before an oration of Burke, before a victory of Napoleon, before a martyrdom of Sir Thomas More, of Sidney, of Marmaduke Robinson, before a French Reign of Terror, and a Salem hanging of witches, before a fanatic Revival, and the Animal Magnetism in Paris, or in Providence.[19] We assume that we under like influence should be alike affected, and should achieve the like; and we aim to master intellectually the steps, and reach the same height or the same degradation that our fellow, our proxy has done.

All inquiry into antiquity,—all curiosity respecting the pyramids, the excavated cities, Stonehenge, the Ohio Circles, Mexico, Memphis,[20]—is the desire to do away this wild, savage and preposterous There or Then, and introduce in its place the Here and the Now. Belzoni digs and measures in the mummy-pits and pyramids of Thebes,[21] until he can see the end of the difference between the monstrous work and himself. When he has satisfied himself, in general and in detail, that it was made by such a person as he, so armed and so motived, and to ends to which he himself should also have worked, the problem is solved; his thought lives along the whole line of temples and sphinxes and catacombs, passes through them all with satisfaction, and they live again to the mind, or are *now*.

A Gothic cathedral affirms that it was done by us, and not done by us.[22] Surely it was by man, but we find it not in our man. But we apply ourselves to the history of its production. We put ourselves into the place and state of the builder. We remember the forest dwellers, the first temples, the adherence to the first type, and the decoration of it as the wealth of the nation increased; the value which is given to wood by carving led to the carving over the whole mountain of stone of a cathedral. When we have gone through this process, and added thereto the Catholic Church, its cross, its music, its processions, its Saints' days and image-worship, we have, as it were, been the man that made the minster;[23] we have seen how it could and must be. We have the sufficient reason.[24]

The difference between men is in their principle of association. Some men classify objects by color and size and other accidents of appearance; others by intrinsic likeness, or by the relation of cause and effect. The progress of the intellect is to the clearer vision of causes, which neglects surface differences. To the poet, to the philosopher, to the saint, all things are

misremembered and conflated the two names); in a lecture from the 1830s, he said that these hangings "entitle our town to the name of that bloody town of Boston" which it bears in Quaker history (EL 1:179). The Reign of Terror (1793–1794) was a time of tyrannical revolutionary bloodshed during the French Revolution. Famous witch trials occurred in 1692 in Salem, Massachusetts. Animal magnetism was a form of hypnosis, and a serious nineteenth-century fad. In a letter to his brother William (January 13, 1837), Emerson wrote, "The gossip of the city is of Animal Magnetism. Three weeks ago I went to see the magnetic sleep. & saw the wonder" (L 2:55).

20    Emerson refers to the mysterious prehistoric monument at Stonehenge, in England; the ancient Indian earthworks in southern Ohio; the vast buildings of the Mexican empires; and the ancient Egyptian ruins at Memphis.

21    Giovanni Battista Belzoni (1778–1823), Italian archeologist who excavated the Egyptian city of Thebes and the pyramid at Giza.

22    The Gothic cathedrals of medieval Europe are often vast, sublime works of collective artistry, made by anonymous craftsmen.

23    Church or monastery.

24    The logical principle of sufficient reason states that every event or fact must have a cause; often, this cause is transformed into an explanation or ground (in Emerson's terms, "how it could be" becomes how it "must be").

25    The German philosopher Friedrich Nietzsche (1844–1900) used this sentence as epigraph to *The Gay Science* (1882), a work substantially influenced by Emerson.

26    In the Pythagorean philosophy of ancient Greece, the monad was the first thing in existence; from it evolved the variety of elements and worldly objects.

27    Cycle of reincarnation.

28    In Greek mythology, Zeus seduces the priestess Io and then transforms her into a cow. She wanders through the world until she arrives in Egypt. Io is sometimes identified with the Egyptian goddess Isis, since Io's heifer's horns resemble the horns of the curved moon that adorn Isis. The Greek tragic playwright Aeschylus (525–456 BCE) draws on the story of Io in *Prometheus Bound* (ca. 430 BCE). Emerson wrote to Margaret Fuller (1810–1850), "Nothing is to me more welcome nor to my recent speculation more familiar than the Protean energy by which the brute horns of Io become the crescent moon of Isis, and nature lifts itself through everlasting transition to the higher & the highest. Whoever lives must rise & grow" (September 25, 1840; L 2:337). Emerson was remembering the essay "Of Isis and Osiris" by Plutarch (ca. 46– ca. 122), one of his cherished authors.

29    Herodotus and Thucydides were pioneering Greek historians from the fifth century BCE; Xenophon (ca. 430–ca. 354 BCE), Greek historian and philosopher who continued Thucydides' history of the Peloponnesian War; Plutarch composed biographies of Greek and Roman political figures. Emerson remarked in his Journal, "Plutarch's heroes cheer exalt," in contrast to the work of the "German Weimarish Art friends": "The voice of Nature they bring
*(continued)*

friendly and sacred, all events profitable, all days holy, all men divine.[25] For the eye is fastened on the life, and slights the circumstance. Every chemical substance, every plant, every animal in its growth, teaches the unity of cause, the variety of appearance.

Upborne and surrounded as we are by this all-creating nature, soft and fluid as a cloud or the air, why should we be such hard pedants, and magnify a few forms? Why should we make account of time, or of magnitude, or of figure? The soul knows them not, and genius, obeying its law, knows how to play with them as a young child plays with greybeards and in churches. Genius studies the causal thought, and far back in the womb of things, sees the rays parting from one orb, that diverge ere they fall by infinite diameters. Genius watches the monad[26] through all his masks as he performs the metempsychosis[27] of nature. Genius detects through the fly, through the caterpillar, through the grub, through the egg, the constant individual; through countless individuals the fixed species; through many species the genus;

Ralph Waldo and Lidian Emerson with children and grandchildren, on the steps of Bush, their home in Concord (1879).

through all genera the steadfast type; through all the kingdoms of organized life the eternal unity. Nature is a mutable cloud, which is always and never the same. She casts the same thought into troops of forms, as a poet makes twenty fables with one moral. Through the bruteness and toughness of matter, a subtle spirit bends all things to its own will. The adamant streams into soft but precise form before it, and, whilst I look at it, its outline and texture are changed again. Nothing is so fleeting as form; yet never does it quite deny itself. In man we still trace the remains or hints of all that we esteem badges of servitude in the lower races, yet in him they enhance his nobleness and grace; as Io, in Æschylus, transformed to a cow, offends the imagination, but how changed when as Isis in Egypt she meets Osiris-Jove, a beautiful woman, with nothing of the metamorphosis left but the lunar horns as the splendid ornament of her brows.[28]

The identity of history is equally intrinsic, the diversity equally obvious. There is at the surface infinite variety of things; at the centre there is simplicity of cause. How many are the acts of one man in which we recognize the same character. Observe the sources of our information in respect to the Greek genius. We have the *civil history* of that people, as Herodotus, Thucydides, Xenophon, and Plutarch have given it[29]—a very sufficient account of what manner of persons they were, and what they did. We have the same national mind expressed for us again in their *literature*, in epic and lyric poems, drama, and philosophy; a very complete form. Then we have it once more in their *architecture*, a beauty as of temperance itself, limited to the straight line and the square,—a builded geometry. Then we have it once again in *sculpture*, the "tongue on the balance of expression,"[30] a multitude of forms in the utmost freedom of action, and never transgressing the ideal serenity; like votaries[31] performing some religious dance before the gods, and, though in convulsive pain or mortal combat, never daring to break the figure and decorum of their dance. Thus, of the genius of one remarkable people, we have a fourfold representation: and to the senses what more unlike than an ode of Pindar, a marble Centaur, the Peristyle of the Parthenon, and the last actions of Phocion?[32]

Every one must have observed faces and forms which, without any resembling feature, make a like impression on the beholder. A particular picture or copy of verses, if it do not awaken the same train of images, will yet

me to hear is not divine, but ghastly hard & ironical" (J 5:306, April 26, 1837). In his lecture "Manners" (1837), from his series "The Philosophy of History," Emerson said, "Xenophon arose naked and taking an ax began to split wood [during the miserable retreat of the Ten Thousand]. . . . Xenophon is as sharp-tongued as any . . . and so gives as good as he gets" (EL 2:134).

30    Phrase describing the ancient ideal of beauty by the German art historian J. J. Winckelmann (1717–1768). ("Tongue" here means the index on a balance.) In a lecture on English literature from 1835, Emerson cites Winckelmann's comment and adds as elucidation lines by the poet Robert Herrick (1591–1674), "Beauty no other thing is than a beam / Flashed out between the middle and extreme" (EL 1:348).

31    Those devoted to a god.

32    Pindar (ca. 522–443 BCE) was the Greek writer of sublime odes celebrating Olympic heroes; the Parthenon, the temple of Athena that became the emblem of classical Athens (its peristyle is its long series of columns); and Phocion (ca. 402–ca. 318 BCE), Athenian statesman famous for his honesty and austerity. Accused of treachery, he was sentenced to death by the Athenian assembly. Plutarch in his *Life of Phocion* describes the latter's calm defiance of the crowd that condemned him.

33    North American Indian chief. Emerson admired the portrait of the Indian Joseph Brant (1742–1807) by the American painter George Catlin (1796–1872). He wrote in his Journal (March 1839) that Brant's head "reminded me instantly of a mountain head & the furrows of the brow suggest the strata of the summit. Gladly I perceive this fine resemblance for we like to reconcile man & the world in all ways" (J 7:171–72).

34    Awe-inspiring.

35    Guido Reni (1575–1642), Italian painter. His *Aurora* (Dawn; 1613–14) is a large, luminous ceiling fresco in the Casino Rospigliosi in Rome. In 1839 Thomas Carlyle sent a print of the painting to Emerson's wife Lidian, who hung it in the Emerson parlor in Concord.

36    The painter was Emerson's friend Caroline Sturgis (1819–1888; J 7:214).

37    Emerson probably refers to Johann Heinrich Roos (1631–1685), German artist, who made many drawings of sheep and cattle in idealized Italian landscapes. In *Conversations with Goethe, 1823–32* (1836–1848) by J. P. Eckermann (1792–1854), Goethe, looking at Roos's etchings, asked, "How could he enter so into the inmost character of these creatures? For their very soul looks through the bodies he has drawn" (J 7:214).

superinduce the same sentiment as some wild mountain walk, although the resemblance is nowise obvious to the senses, but is occult and out of the reach of the understanding. Nature is an endless combination and repetition of a very few laws. She hums the old well known air through innumerable variations.

Nature is full of a sublime family likeness throughout her works; and delights in startling us with resemblances in the most unexpected quarters. I have seen the head of an old sachem[33] of the forest, which at once reminded the eye of a bald mountain summit, and the furrows of the brow suggested the strata of the rock. There are men whose manners have the same essential splendor as the simple and awful[34] sculpture on the friezes of the Parthenon, and the remains of the earliest Greek art. And there are compositions of the same strain to be found in the books of all ages. What is Guido's Rospigliosi Aurora but a morning thought, as the horses in it are only a morning cloud.[35] If any one will but take pains to observe the variety of actions to which he is equally inclined in certain moods of mind, and those to which he is averse, he will see how deep is the chain of affinity.

A painter told me that nobody could draw a tree without in some sort becoming a tree;[36] or draw a child by studying the outlines of its form merely,—but, by watching for a time his motions and plays, the painter enters into his nature, and can then draw him at will in every attitude. So Roos "entered into the inmost nature of a sheep."[37] I knew a draughtsman employed in a public survey, who found that he could not sketch the rocks until their geological structure was first explained to him. In a certain state of thought is the common origin of very diverse works. It is the spirit and not the fact that is identical. By a deeper apprehension, and not primarily by a painful acquisition of many manual skills, the artist attains the power of awakening other souls to a given activity.

It has been said that "common souls pay with what they do; nobler souls with that which they are." And why? Because a profound nature awakens in us by its actions and words, by its very looks and manners, the same power and beauty that a gallery of sculpture, or of pictures, addresses.

Civil and natural history, the history of art and of literature, must be explained from individual history, or must remain words. There is nothing but is related to us, nothing that does not interest us—kingdom, college, tree, horse, or iron shoe, the roots of all things are in man. Santa Croce and the Dome of St. Peter's[38] are lame copies after a divine model. Strasburg Cathedral is a material counterpart of the soul of Erwin of Steinbach.[39] The true poem is the poet's mind; the true ship is the ship-builder. In the man, could we lay him open, we should see the reason for the last flourish and tendril of his work, as every spine and tint in the sea-shell preëxist in the secreting organs of the fish. The whole of heraldry and of chivalry is in courtesy.[40] A man of fine manners shall pronounce your name with all the ornament that titles of nobility could ever add.

The trivial experience of every day is always verifying some old prediction to us, and converting into things the words and signs which we had heard and seen without heed. A lady, with whom I was riding in the forest, said to me, that the woods always seemed to her *to wait*, as if the genii who inhabit them suspended their deeds until the wayfarer has passed onward: a thought which poetry has celebrated in the dance of the fairies which breaks off on the approach of human feet.[41] The man who has seen the rising moon break out of the clouds at midnight, has been present like an archangel at the creation of light and of the world. I remember one summer day, in the fields, my companion pointed out to me a broad cloud, which might extend a quarter of a mile parallel to the horizon, quite accurately in the form of a cherub as painted over churches,—a round block in the centre which it was easy to animate with eyes and mouth, supported on either side by wide-stretched symmetrical wings.[42] What appears once in the atmosphere may appear often, and it was undoubtedly the archetype of that familiar ornament. I have seen in the sky a chain of summer lightning which at once showed to me that the Greeks drew from nature when they painted the thunderbolt in the hand of Jove.[43] I have seen a snow-drift along the sides of the stone wall which obviously gave the idea of the common architectural scroll to abut a tower.

By surrounding ourselves with the original circumstances, we invent anew the orders and the ornaments of architecture, as we see how each people merely decorated its primitive abodes. The Doric temple preserves the semblance of the wooden cabin in which the Dorian dwelt. The Chinese pagoda is plainly a Tartar tent. The Indian and Egyptian temples still betray

38   Santa Croce is a magnificent Franciscan church in Florence, Italy; the enormous Dome of St. Peter's (designed by Michelangelo Buonarroti (1546–1564)) is the central architectural presence in Rome's Vatican City.

39   Erwin von Steinbach (ca. 1244–1318) played a key role in the construction of the Cathedral of Notre-Dame de Strasbourg. Goethe in his essay *Of German Architecture* (1772) celebrates Erwin's creative brilliance, comparing him to Muhammad and Prometheus (J 6:307).

40   Emerson here compares a biological process (the shellfish's secretions) to the animating, essential role of manners in life. Medieval Europe, with its practices of gallant knighthood (chivalry) and its coats of arms (heraldry), depended on courtesy, he implies; but so does contemporary society.

41   The genii (plural of genius) are the spirits of the place; fairies are traditionally skittish of human contact. The lady Emerson mentions was Elizabeth Hoar (1814–1878), who had been engaged to Emerson's brother Charles before Charles's death in 1836. Emerson rode with her from Waltham to Concord (J 7:61, August 31, 1838).

42   Emerson here remembers a day in May 1838 with John Sullivan Dwight (1813–1893), a youthful minister (J 5:504).

43   Jove or Jupiter is the Roman name for the Greek Zeus, who was often imagined as a hurler of thunderbolts.

44 The Doric order is the simplest of the three types of classical Greek architecture; it was named after the Dorians, an archaic people who came to Greece centuries earlier. The Tartars were a migratory people of Central Asia; they held the Chinese throne from 907 to 1260.

45 From Arnold H. L. Heeren (1760–1842), German historian. The Nubians, from southern Egypt, conquered that country and ruled as pharaohs during the Twenty-fifth Dynasty (ca. 750–655 BCE).

46 Germanic tribe that settled Britain in the fifth century and later.

47 Ecbatana, in present-day Iran, was a city built by the Medes and conquered by Persia in the sixth century BCE; Susa, the ancient city of the Elamite empire, was taken by Persia in the same period. Xenophon (followed by Plutarch and Heeren, Emerson's source) was the first to claim that the Persian emperors divided their time among these two cities and Babylon. It seems likely that Ecbatana was the summer residence, and that the court occupied Susa for the rest of the year.

the mounds and subterranean houses of their forefathers.[44] "The custom of making houses and tombs in the living rock," (says Heeren, in his Researches on the Ethiopians) "determined very naturally the principal character of the Nubian Egyptian architecture to the colossal form which it assumed. In these caverns already prepared by nature, the eye was accustomed to dwell on huge shapes and masses, so that when art came to the assistance of nature, it could not move on a small scale without degrading itself. What would statues of the usual size, or neat porches and wings have been, associated with those gigantic halls before which only Colossi could sit as watchmen, or lean on the pillars of the interior?"[45]

The Gothic church plainly originated in a rude adaptation of the forest trees with all their boughs to a festal or solemn arcade, as the bands about the cleft pillars still indicate the green withes that tied them. No one can walk in a road cut through pine woods, without being struck with the architectural appearance of the grove, especially in winter, when the bareness of all other trees shows the low arch of the Saxons.[46] In the woods in a winter afternoon one will see as readily the origin of the stained glass window with which the Gothic cathedrals are adorned, in the colors of the western sky seen through the bare and crossing branches of the forest. Nor can any lover of nature enter the old piles of Oxford and the English cathedrals without feeling that the forest overpowered the mind of the builder, and that his chisel, his saw, and plane still reproduced its ferns, its spikes of flowers, its locust, elm, oak, pine, fir, and spruce.

The Gothic cathedral is a blossoming in stone subdued by the insatiable demand of harmony in man. The mountain of granite blooms into an eternal flower with the lightness and delicate finish as well as the aerial proportions and perspective of vegetable beauty.

In like manner all public facts are to be individualized, all private facts are to be generalized. Then at once History becomes fluid and true, and Biography deep and sublime. As the Persian imitated in the slender shafts and capitals of his architecture the stem and flower of the lotus and palm, so the Persian Court in its magnificent era never gave over the Nomadism of its barbarous tribes, but travelled from Ecbatana, where the spring was spent, to Susa in summer, and to Babylon for the winter.[47]

In the early history of Asia and Africa, Nomadism and Agriculture are the two antagonist facts. The geography of Asia and of Africa necessitated a nomadic life. But the nomads were the terror of all those whom the soil or the advantages of a market had induced to build towns. Agriculture therefore was a religious injunction because of the perils of the state from nomadism. And in these late and civil countries of England and America, these propensities still fight out the old battle in the nation and in the individual. The nomads of Africa were constrained to wander by the attacks of the gadfly, which drives the cattle mad, and so compels the tribe to emigrate in the rainy season and to drive off the cattle to the higher sandy regions.[48] The nomads of Asia follow the pasturage from month to month. In America and Europe the nomadism is of trade and curiosity; a progress certainly from the gadfly of Astaboras[49] to the Anglo and Italo-mania of Boston Bay. Sacred cities, to which a periodical religious pilgrimage was enjoined, or stringent laws and customs, tending to invigorate the national bond, were the check on the old rovers; and the cumulative values of long residence are the restraints on the itineracy of the present day. The antagonism of the two tendencies is not less active in individuals, as the love of adventure or the love of repose happens to predominate. A man of rude health and flowing spirits has the faculty of rapid domestication, lives in his wagon, and roams through all latitudes as easily as a Calmuc.[50] At sea, or in the forest, or in the snow, he sleeps as warm, dines with as good appetite, and associates as happily, as beside his own chimneys. Or perhaps his facility is deeper seated, in the increased range of his faculties of observation, which yield him points of interest wherever fresh objects meet his eyes. The pastoral nations were needy and hungry to desperation; and this intellectual nomadism, in its excess, bankrupts the mind, through the dissipation of power on a miscellany of objects. The home-keeping wit,[51] on the other hand, is that continence or content which finds all the elements of life in its own soil; and which has its own perils of monotony and deterioration, if not stimulated by foreign infusions.

Every thing the individual sees without him, corresponds to his states of mind, and every thing is in turn intelligible to him, as his onward thinking leads him into the truth to which that fact or series belongs.

48    Again derived from Heeren's histories.

49    River in Ethiopia and Sudan.

50    The Calmucs or Kalmucks were Mongolian nomads who roamed between China and the Upper Volga region of Russia. Emerson's inheritor the American poet Walt Whitman (1819–1892) pictured himself as such a "man of rude health and flowing spirits."

51    Wit here means sense or perceptive skill.

52    *Vorwelt* (German): the primitive or ancestral world.

53    Emerson is here influenced by Winckelmann's description of the Greek ideal.

54    Phoebus is Apollo, the radiant sun god;
Hercules, the muscle-bound Greek hero who
faced twelve labors.

55    Agamemnon and Diomed (Diomedes)
are characters in Homer's *Iliad* (ca. 9th century
BCE). Xenophon's *Anabasis* (ca. 400 BCE) describes the heroic journey of a Greek army of
ten thousand mercenaries, hired by Cyrus the
Younger of Persia (d. 401 BCE), through mountains and desert to the Black Sea.

The primeval world,—the Fore-World, as the Germans say,[52]—I can
dive to it in myself as well as grope for it with researching fingers in catacombs, libraries, and the broken reliefs and torsos of ruined villas.

What is the foundation of that interest all men feel in Greek history,
letters, art and poetry, in all its periods, from the heroic or Homeric age,
down to the domestic life of the Athenians and Spartans, four or five centuries later? What but this, that every man passes personally through a Grecian period. The Grecian state is the era of the bodily nature, the perfection of the senses,—of the spiritual nature unfolded in strict unity with the
body.[53] In it existed those human forms which supplied the sculptor with his
models of Hercules, Phœbus, and Jove;[54] not like the forms abounding in the
streets of modern cities, wherein the face is a confused blur of features, but
composed of incorrupt, sharply defined and symmetrical features, whose
eye-sockets are so formed that it would be impossible for such eyes to squint,
and take furtive glances on this side and on that, but they must turn the
whole head. The manners of that period are plain and fierce. The reverence
exhibited is for personal qualities, courage, address, self-command, justice,
strength, swiftness, a loud voice, a broad chest. Luxury and elegance are not
known. A sparse population and want make every man his own valet, cook,
butcher, and soldier, and the habit of supplying his own needs educates
the body to wonderful performances. Such are the Agamemnon and Diomed
of Homer, and not far different is the picture Xenophon gives of himself and
his compatriots in the Retreat of the Ten Thousand.[55] "After the army had
crossed the river Teleboas in Armenia, there fell much snow, and the troops
lay miserably on the ground covered with it. But Xenophon arose naked, and
taking an axe, began to split wood; whereupon others rose and did the like."
Throughout his army exists a boundless liberty of speech. They quarrel for
plunder, they wrangle with the generals on each new order, and Xenophon is
as sharp-tongued as any, and sharper-tongued than most, and so gives as
good as he gets. Who does not see that this is a gang of great boys with such
a code of honor and such lax discipline as great boys have?

The costly charm of the ancient tragedy and indeed of all the old literature is, that the persons speak simply,—speak as persons who have great
good sense without knowing it, before yet the reflective habit has become

the predominant habit of the mind. Our admiration of the antique is not admiration of the old, but of the natural. The Greeks are not reflective, but perfect in their senses and in their health, with the finest physical organization in the world. Adults acted with the simplicity and grace of children.[56] They made vases, tragedies, and statues such as healthy senses should—that is, in good taste. Such things have continued to be made in all ages, and are now, wherever a healthy physique exists; but, as a class, from their superior organization, they have surpassed all. They combine the energy of manhood with the engaging unconsciousness of childhood. The attraction of these manners is, that they belong to man, and are known to every man in virtue of his being once a child; besides that there are always individuals who retain these characteristics. A person of childlike genius and inborn energy is still a Greek, and revives our love of the muse of Hellas. I admire the love of nature in the Philoctetes.[57] In reading those fine apostrophes to sleep, to the stars, rocks, mountains, and waves, I feel time passing away as an ebbing sea. I feel the eternity of man, the identity of his thought. The Greek had, it seems, the same fellow beings as I. The sun and moon, water and fire, met his heart precisely as they meet mine. Then the vaunted distinction between Greek and English, between Classic and Romantic schools seems superficial and pedantic. When a thought of Plato becomes a thought to me,—when a truth that fired the soul of Pindar fires mine, time is no more. When I feel that we two meet in a perception, that our two souls are tinged with the same hue, and do, as it were, run into one, why should I measure degrees of latitude, why should I count Egyptian years?[58]

The student interprets the age of chivalry by his own age of chivalry, and the days of maritime adventure and circumnavigation by quite parallel miniature experiences of his own. To the sacred history of the world, he has the same key. When the voice of a prophet out of the deeps of antiquity merely echoes to him a sentiment of his infancy, a prayer of his youth, he then pierces to the truth through all the confusion of tradition and the caricature of institutions.

Rare, extravagant spirits come by us at intervals, who disclose to us new facts in nature. I see that men of God have, from time to time, walked among men and made their commission felt in the heart and soul of the commonest

56    According to Friedrich Schiller (1759–1805) in *On Naive and Sentimental Poetry* (1795–1796), ancient Greek literature and culture were naive and childlike. In the *Commentaries on Plato's Timaeus* by Proclus (412–485), a book known to Emerson, Proclus claimed that "the Greeks are always children," and that their youthfulness was "analogous to renovation of life."

57    Tragic drama by Sophocles (ca. 496–406 BCE). Emerson was thinking of the play's final speech, in which the hero bids farewell to the landscape and seas of Lemnos, the island where he has been marooned.

58    The ancient Egyptian year, like ours, had 365 days and was divided into twelve months; but the Egyptians' method of counting the years (based on the reigns of their kings) was cumbersome.

59    The Pythian priestess or Sibyl sat on the tripod of Delphi while she gave her oracular responses. The afflatus is the divine breath or impulse that possesses a priest or prophet. The English Romantic writer Samuel Taylor Coleridge (1772–1834) in *The Statesman's Manual* (1816) wrote that "the SIBYLL with wild enthusiastic mouth shrilling forth unmirthful, inornate, and unperfumed truths reaches to a thousand years with her voice through the power of God."

60    Along with Moses, who transmitted the Ten Commandments to the Israelites, and Socrates (ca. 469–399 BCE), who questioned the laws of Athens, Emerson mentions the Iranian prophet Zoroaster (ca. 11th century BCE) and Menu (or Manu), the legendary Hindu lawgiver. When still a teenager (1821), Emerson noted in his Journal that "as long ago as Menu enlightened morality was taught in India" (J 1:340); when he was editor of the *Dial*, in 1843, he published the *Laws of Menu* in a selection made by Henry David Thoreau (1817–1862).

61    Anchorite (ascetic Christian hermit or monk).

62    The Magians were Zoroastrian priests, the Brahmins the Hindu priestly caste, and the Druids the priests of ancient Britain and Gaul; the Inca empire in South America was a theocracy headed by the king and the high priest.

63    Scrupulous adherent to fixed forms.

64    Belus was a legendary king of Egypt sometimes identified with Bel Marduk, the patron god of ancient Babylon. The French scholar Jean-François Champollion (1790–1832) deciphered Egyptian hieroglyphics.

hearer. Hence, evidently, the tripod, the priest, the priestess inspired by the divine afflatus.[59]

Jesus astonishes and overpowers sensual people. They cannot unite him to history or reconcile him with themselves. As they come to revere their intuitions and aspire to live holily, their own piety explains every fact, every word.

How easily these old worships of Moses, of Zoroaster, of Menu, of Socrates,[60] domesticate themselves in the mind. I cannot find any antiquity in them. They are mine as much as theirs.

I have seen the first monks and anchorets[61] without crossing seas or centuries. More than once some individual has appeared to me with such negligence of labor and such commanding contemplation, a haughty beneficiary, begging in the name of God, as made good to the nineteenth century Simeon the Stylite, the Thebais, and the first Capuchins.

The priestcraft of the East and West, of the Magian, Brahmin, Druid and Inca,[62] is expounded in the individual's private life. The cramping influence of a hard formalist[63] on a young child in repressing his spirits and courage, paralyzing the understanding, and that without producing indignation, but only fear and obedience, and even much sympathy with the tyranny,—is a familiar fact explained to the child when he becomes a man, only by seeing that the oppressor of his youth is himself a child tyrannized over by those names and words and forms, of whose influence he was merely the organ to the youth. The fact teaches him how Belus was worshipped, and how the pyramids were built, better than the discovery by Champollion of the names of all the workmen and the cost of every tile.[64] He finds Assyria and the Mounds of Cholula[65] at his door, and himself has laid the courses.

Again, in that protest which each considerate person makes against the superstition of his times, he repeats step for step the part of old reformers, and in the search after truth finds like them new perils to virtue. He learns again what moral vigor is needed to supply the girdle[66] of a superstition. A great licentiousness treads on the heels of a reformation. How many times in the history of the world has the Luther of the day had to lament the decay of piety in his own household. "Doctor," said his wife to Martin Luther one day, "how is it that whilst subject to papacy, we prayed so often and with such fervor, whilst now we pray with the utmost coldness and very seldom?"[67]

## A PUBLIC RECEPTION
### —OF—
### Mr. R. W. EMERSON
#### ON HIS
### Return Home from Europe
#### Will be given by the Citizens of Concord, on

### A Procession of Citizens
#### AND SCHOOL CHILDREN

will be formed at the Railroad Station, to escort Mr. Emerson to his home.
All are invited to attend.

MR. EMERSON may be expected in one of the afternoon Trains Monday, Tuesday or Wednesday next. Notice of his arrival in Boston will be given by ringing the bells for fifteen minutes, as soon as the Steamer Olympus comes in. Notice of the train on which he comes will be given by striking the bell TWELVE times for the noon train; THREE times for the 3 o'clock; FIVE for the 5 o'clock; SIX for the 6 o'clock, and SEVEN for the 7 o'clock trains.

Concord, May 24, 1873.

65 The ruins of Cholula, the sacred city of the Toltecs in Mexico, feature spectacular mounds made of adobe bricks. Assyria was the ancient kingdom that controlled Upper Mesopotamia from the twentieth to the fifteenth centuries BCE and, in the late eighth century BCE, conquered Israel.

66 Supplant the constraint.

67 The anecdote about the German Protestant Reformer Martin Luther (1483–1546) and his wife occurs in Luther's *Table Talk* (1566).

Announcement of a reception
for Emerson on his return
from Europe, 1873.

68    Aesop (6th century BCE), Greek writer of fables; Hafiz (ca. 1320–ca. 1389), Persian poet; Ludovico Ariosto (1474–1533), Italian author of *Orlando Furioso*, extravagant epic romance. Geoffrey Chaucer (ca. 1343–1400), English poet who wrote *The Canterbury Tales* (ca. 1387–1400); Sir Walter Scott (1771–1832), Scottish novelist.

69    Emerson follows Coleridge in his distinction between the Imagination, the creative power that "struggles to idealize and to unify," and the Fancy, which manipulates already existing objects. A strong admirer of Coleridge, Emerson wrote that "every opinion he expresses is a canon of criticism that should be writ in steel, & his italics are italics of the mind" (J 5:252, November 24, 1836).

70    In Greek mythology, Prometheus stole fire from the gods for the benefit of mankind. Zeus carried him to Mt. Caucasus and bound him to a rock. "A vulture stood by him which in the daytime gnawed his liver, but in the nighttime the wasted parts were supplied again, whence matter for his pain was never wanting" (from Emerson's lecture "The Age of Fable" [1835], EL 1:258). The story is recounted in Aeschylus's *Prometheus Bound* as well as *Prometheus Unbound* (1820) by Percy Bysshe Shelley (1792–1822).

71    *Prometheus Bound.*

72    The story is recounted in *Alcestis* (438 BCE) by the Athenian playwright Euripides (ca. 480–406 BCE).

73    The struggle between Antaeus and Hercules was taken to suggest the strength that accrues from being firmly located in one's place.
*(continued)*

The advancing man discovers how deep a property he has in literature, —in all fable as well as in all history. He finds that the poet was no odd fellow who described strange and impossible situations, but that universal man wrote by his pen a confession true for one and true for all. His own secret biography he finds in lines wonderfully intelligible to him, dotted down before he was born. One after another he comes up in his private adventures with every fable of Æsop, of Homer, of Hafiz, of Ariosto, of Chaucer, of Scott,[68] and verifies them with his own head and hands.

The beautiful fables of the Greeks, being proper creations of the Imagination and not of the Fancy,[69] are universal verities. What a range of meanings and what perpetual pertinence has the story of Prometheus! Beside its primary value as the first chapter of the history of Europe, (the mythology thinly veiling authentic facts, the invention of the mechanic arts, and the migration of colonies,) it gives the history of religion with some closeness to the faith of later ages. Prometheus is the Jesus of the old mythology. He is the friend of man; stands between the unjust 'justice' of the Eternal Father, and the race of mortals; and readily suffers all things on their account.[70] But where it departs from the Calvinistic Christianity, and exhibits him as the defier of Jove, it represents a state of mind which readily appears wherever the doctrine of Theism is taught in a crude, objective form, and which seems the self-defence of man against this untruth, namely, a discontent with the believed fact that a God exists, and a feeling that the obligation of reverence is onerous. It would steal, if it could, the fire of the Creator, and live apart from him, and independent of him. The Prometheus Vinctus[71] is the romance of skepticism. Not less true to all time are the details of that stately apologue. Apollo kept the flocks of Admetus, said the poets.[72] When the gods come among men, they are not known. Jesus was not; Socrates and Shakspeare were not. Antæus was suffocated by the gripe of Hercules, but every time he touched his mother earth, his strength was renewed.[73] Man is the broken giant, and in all his weakness, both his body and his mind are invigorated by habits of conversation with nature. The power of music, the power of poetry to unfix, and as it were, clap wings to solid nature, interprets the riddle of Orpheus.[74] The philosophical perception of identity through endless mutations of form, makes him know the Proteus. What else am I who laughed or wept yesterday, who slept last night like a corpse, and this morning stood and ran? And what see I on any side but the transmigrations of Proteus? I can symbolize my thought by using the name of any creature, of any fact, because every creature is man agent or patient.[75] Tantalus[76] is but a name for you and me. Tantalus means the impossibility of drinking the waters of thought which are always gleaming and waving within sight of the soul. The transmigration of souls is no fable. I would it were; but men and women are only half human. Every animal of the barn-yard, the field and the forest, of the earth and of the waters that are under the earth, has contrived to get a footing and to leave the print of its features and form in some one or other of these upright, heaven-facing speakers. Ah! brother, stop the ebb of thy soul—ebbing downward into the forms into whose habits thou hast now for many years slid. As near and proper to us is also that old fable of the Sphinx, who was said to sit in the roadside and put riddles to every passenger. If the man could not answer she swallowed him alive. If he could solve the riddle, the Sphinx was slain.[77] What is our life but an endless flight of winged facts or events! In splendid variety these changes come, all putting questions to the human spirit. Those men who cannot answer by a superior wisdom these facts or questions of time, serve them. Facts encumber them, tyrannize over them, and make the men of routine, the men of *sense*, in whom a literal obedience to facts has extinguished every spark of that light by which man is truly man.[78] But if the man is true to his better instincts or sentiments, and refuses the dominion of facts, as one that comes of a higher race, remains fast by the soul and sees the principle, then the facts fall aptly and supple into their places; they know their master, and the meanest of them glorifies him.

See in Goethe's Helena[79] the same desire that every word should be a thing. These figures, he would say, these Chirons, Griffins, Phorkyas, Helen, and Leda,[80] are somewhat, and do exert a specific influence on the mind. So far then are they eternal entities, as real to-day as in the first Olympiad.[81] Much revolving them, he writes out freely his humor, and gives them body to his own imagination. And although that poem be as vague and fantastic as a dream, yet is it much more attractive than the more regular dramatic pieces of the same author, for the reason that it operates a wonderful relief to

In *Walden* (1854), Emerson's friend Thoreau says of the beans that he planted, "They attached me to the earth, and so I got strength like Antaeus."

74    Orpheus, legendary Greek poet, was able to make stones and trees respond to his songs.

75    Acting or suffering (from Latin *ago* and *patior*).

76    Son of Zeus punished in the underworld by being unable to reach the water below him or the fruit hanging above.

77    The riddle of the Sphinx was finally solved by Oedipus, whereupon the monster killed herself.

78    In his introductory lecture to his series "Human Culture" (1837), Emerson lamented, "A universal principle of compromise has crept into use. A Routine which no man made and for whose abuses no man holds himself accountable tyrannizes over the spontaneous will and character of all the individuals."

79    Helena (Helen of Troy) is a character in the second part of Goethe's *Faust* (1832).

80    Chiron was the centaur who tutored Achilles and other Greek heroes; the Griffin (or Griffon), a beast half eagle and half lion; Phorkyas, in Goethe's Helen episode (from *Faust*, Part II), the devil Mephistopheles transformed into a woman. Helen, the great beauty, was the cause of the Trojan War; Zeus ravished her mother, Leda, in the form of a swan. All these characters appear in Part II of *Faust*.

81    Four-year period marking the Olympic games; the first one was 776–772 BCE.

82    From the *Apology*, Plato's version of Soc-rates's speech at his trial—but whereas Socrates criticizes poets for their ignorance, Emerson grants them a higher knowledge.

83    According to Francis Bacon (1561–1626) in his *Advancement of Learning* (1605), "poesy . . . was ever thought to have some participation of divineness, because it doth raise and erect the mind, by submitting the shows of things to the desires of the mind." This sentence of Bacon was one of Emerson's favorites.

84    Tales of romance and magic: the anony-mous French *Perceforest* (ca. 1340), the Spanish *Amadis of Gaul* (1508), and the English fable of a boy who uses a magic mantle to expose the false ladies of Arthur's court (which Emerson confused with a German fairy tale, "The Short Mantle," featuring a girl named Genelas).

85    Regions of England and France that were prime territory for stories of chivalric romance.

86    Celebrated novel (1819) by Sir Walter Scott.

the mind from the routine of customary images,—awakens the reader's in-vention and fancy by the wild freedom of the design, and by the unceasing succession of brisk shocks of surprise.

The universal nature, too strong for the petty nature of the bard, sits on his neck and writes through his hand; so that when he seems to vent a mere caprice and wild romance, the issue is an exact allegory. Hence Plato said that "poets utter great and wise things which they do not themselves understand."[82] All the fictions of the Middle Age explain themselves as a masked or frolic expression of that which in grave earnest the mind of that period toiled to achieve. Magic, and all that is ascribed to it, is a deep presen-timent of the powers of science. The shoes of swiftness, the sword of sharp-ness, the power of subduing the elements, of using the secret virtues of min-erals, of understanding the voices of birds, are the obscure efforts of the mind in a right direction. The preternatural prowess of the hero, the gift of perpetual youth, and the like, are alike the endeavor of the human spirit "to bend the shows of things to the desires of the mind."[83]

In Perceforest and Amadis de Gaul, a garland and a rose bloom on the head of her who is faithful, and fade on the brow of the inconstant. In the story of the Boy and the Mantle, even a mature reader may be surprised with a glow of virtuous pleasure at the triumph of the gentle Genelas;[84] and in-deed, all the postulates of elfin annals,—that the Fairies do not like to be named; that their gifts are capricious and not to be trusted; that who seeks a treasure must not speak; and the like,—I find true in Concord, however they might be in Cornwall or Bretagne.[85]

Is it otherwise in the newest romance? I read the Bride of Lammer-moor.[86] Sir William Ashton is a mask for a vulgar temptation, Ravenswood Castle a fine name for proud poverty, and the foreign mission of state only a Bunyan disguise for honest industry. We may all shoot a wild bull that would toss the good and beautiful, by fighting down the unjust and sensual. Lucy Ashton is another name for fidelity, which is always beautiful and always lia-ble to calamity in this world.

But along with the civil and metaphysical history of man, another his-tory goes daily forward—that of the external world,—in which he is not less strictly implicated. He is the compend of time: he is also the correlative of nature. His power consists in the multitude of his affinities, in the fact that his life is intertwined with the whole chain of organic and inorganic being. In old Rome the public roads beginning at the Forum proceeded north, south, east, west, to the centre of every province of the empire, making each market-town of Persia, Spain and Britain, pervious to the soldiers of the capital: so out of the human heart go, as it were, highways to the heart of every object in nature, to reduce it under the dominion of man. A man is a bundle of relations, a knot of roots, whose flower and fruitage is the world. His faculties refer to natures out of him, and predict the world he is to inhabit, as the fins of the fish foreshow that water exists, or the wings of an eagle in the egg presuppose air. He cannot live without a world.[87] Put Napoleon in an island prison,[88] let his faculties find no men to act on, no Alps to climb, no stake to play for, and he would beat the air and appear stupid. Transport him to large countries, dense population, complex interests, and antagonist power, and you shall see that the man Napoleon, bounded, that is, by such a profile and outline, is not the virtual Napoleon. This is but Talbot's shadow;

> "His substance is not here:
> For what you see is but the smallest part,
> And least proportion of humanity;
> But were the whole frame here,
> It is of such a spacious, lofty pitch,
> Your roof were not sufficient to contain it."
>
> *Henry VI.*[89]

Columbus needs a planet to shape his course upon. Newton and Laplace need myriads of ages and thick-strown celestial areas.[90] One may say a gravitating solar system is already prophesied in the nature of Newton's mind. Not less does the brain of Davy or of Gay-Lussac,[91] from childhood exploring the affinities and repulsions of particles, anticipate the laws of organization. Does not the eye of the human embryo predict the light? the ear of Handel[92] predict the witchcraft of harmonic sound? Do not the constructive fingers of Watt, Fulton, Whittemore, Arkwright[93] predict the fusible, hard, and temperable texture of metals, the properties of stone, water and wood? Do not the lovely attributes of the maiden child predict the refine-

87    In the original version of this passage, from the introductory lecture to Emerson's series on the philosophy of history (1836), he continued, "Insulate a man and you annihilate him. He cannot unfold—he cannot live without a world" (EL 2:17; Emerson was playing on the Latin *insula*, "island").

88    Napoleon was twice exiled, to two islands: Elba (1814) and St. Helena (1815).

89    From Shakespeare's *Henry VI*, Part 1 (2.3.50–56).

90    Christopher Columbus (ca. 1451–1506), explorer of the New World; Isaac Newton (1643–1727), English mathematician and physicist; Pierre-Simon Laplace, French mathematician and astronomer (1749–1827).

91    Humphry Davy (1778–1829), British chemist and inventor; J.-L. Gay-Lussac (1778–1850), French chemist whom Emerson heard lecture at the Sorbonne in 1833 (J 4:197).

92    G. F. Handel (1685–1759), English Baroque composer born in Germany.

93    All four of the men Emerson names transformed society by means of their revolutionary ingenuity. James Watt (1736–1819) was a British inventor who decisively improved the steam engine and played a key role in the Industrial Revolution; Robert Fulton (1765–1815) was an American inventor of the commercial steamboat. Amos Whittemore (1759–1828) of Massachusetts developed a machine for making cotton and wool cards, called by the Virginia statesman John Randolph (1773–1833) "the only machine which ever had a soul." The Englishman Sir Richard Arkwright (1732–1792) was an inventor of spinning machinery and developer of the textile industry.

94    Chaucer's *House of Fame* (ca. 1379–1380), like earlier works by Greek and Latin writers, describes the embellished house of the goddess Fame; but her robe is not mentioned.

95    In this sentence Emerson presents a marvelous capsule version of history: the paradisal Golden Age described by classical authors; the Garden of the Hesperides, with its golden apples bestowing immortality; the quest of Jason and the Argonauts for the Golden Fleece; the journey of Abraham from Chaldea to Canaan in the book of Genesis; the building of Solomon's temple in Jerusalem; the Christian era, Middle Ages, Renaissance, Reformation, Age of Discovery, and Enlightenment—and, finally, the spiritual adventure of Emerson's own day, with its search for "new regions in man."

96    Goat-footed, pipe-playing Greek god of the woodlands, whose name means "all."

ments and decorations of civil society? Here also we are reminded of the action of man on man. A mind might ponder its thought for ages, and not gain so much self-knowledge as the passion of love shall teach it in a day. Who knows himself before he has been thrilled with indignation at an outrage, or has heard an eloquent tongue, or has shared the throb of thousands in a national exultation or alarm? No man can antedate his experience, or guess what faculty or feeling a new object shall unlock, any more than he can draw to-day the face of a person whom he shall see to-morrow for the first time.

I will not now go behind the general statement to explore the reason of this correspondency. Let it suffice that in the light of these two facts, namely, that the mind is One, and that nature is its correlative, history is to be read and written.

Thus in all ways does the soul concentrate and reproduce its treasures for each pupil. He, too, shall pass through the whole cycle of experience. He shall collect into a focus the rays of nature. History no longer shall be a dull book. It shall walk incarnate in every just and wise man. You shall not tell me by languages and titles a catalogue of the volumes you have read. You shall make me feel what periods you have lived. A man shall be the Temple of Fame. He shall walk, as the poets have described that goddess, in a robe painted all over with wonderful events and experiences;[94]—his own form and features by their exalted intelligence shall be that variegated vest. I shall find in him the Foreworld; in his childhood the Age of Gold; the Apples of Knowledge; the Argonautic Expedition; the calling of Abraham; the building of the Temple; the Advent of Christ; Dark Ages; the Revival of Letters; the Reformation; the discovery of new lands, the opening of new sciences, and new regions in man.[95] He shall be the priest of Pan,[96] and bring with him into humble cottages the blessing of the morning stars and all the recorded benefits of heaven and earth.

Is there somewhat overweening in this claim? Then I reject all I have written, for what is the use of pretending to know what we know not? But it is the fault of our rhetoric that we cannot strongly state one fact without seeming to belie some other. I hold our actual knowledge very cheap. Hear the rats in the wall, see the lizard on the fence, the fungus under foot, the lichen on the log. What do I know sympathetically, morally, of either of these worlds of life? As old as the Caucasian man,—perhaps older,—these creatures have kept their counsel beside him, and there is no record of any word or sign that has passed from one to the other. What connection do the books show between the fifty or sixty chemical elements, and the historical eras? Nay, what does history yet record of the metaphysical annals of man? What light does it shed on those mysteries which we hide under the names Death and Immortality? Yet every history should be written in a wisdom which divined the range of our affinities and looked at facts as symbols. I am ashamed to see what a shallow village tale our so-called History is. How many times we must say Rome, and Paris, and Constantinople. What does Rome know of rat and lizard?[97] What are Olympiads and Consulates to these neighboring systems of being? Nay, what food or experience or succor have they for the Esquimaux seal-hunter, for the Kanàka in his canoe, for the fisherman, the stevedore, the porter?[98]

Broader and deeper we must write our annals—from an ethical reformation, from an influx of the ever new, ever sanative[99] conscience,—if we would truelier express our central and wide-related nature, instead of this old chronology of selfishness and pride to which we have too long lent our eyes. Already that day exists for us, shines in on us at unawares, but the path of science and of letters is not the way into nature. The idiot, the Indian, the child, and unschooled farmer's boy, stand nearer to the light by which nature is to be read, than the dissector or the antiquary.

97    Emerson wrote in his Journal (April 26, 1834) that "the knowledge of nature is *most permanent*, clouds & grass are older antiquities than pyramids or Athens . . ." (J 4:282).

98    Kanaka, Hawaiian, or other Pacific Islander; stevedore, a longshoreman or dockworker. In his Journal (October 1837), Emerson expanded his point to include contemporary, as well as ancient, history: "What a dream our Boston is, and New York will one day be an ancient illustration" (J 5:398).

99    Curative.

# Self-Reliance

*This is Emerson's best-known essay, the second in* Essays *(1841). Its roots go back to the early 1830s. In Sermon CXLV (February 26, 1832), Emerson said, "Your own reason is the voice of God himself which speaks to you and to all mankind without an interpreter" (S 4:79); and he added, "Does any one fear that a too great reliance on one's self and an obstinate questioning of every practice and institution might beget danger to faith and to virtue? Oh no" (S 4:82). Emerson wrote to Benjamin Hunt in 1835, "You used to talk of self-Reverence That word indeed contains the whole of Philosophy & the whole of Religion" (L 1:433).*

1    "Do not seek yourself beyond [yourself]," line adapted from the *Satires* (1.7) of the Roman poet and Stoic Persius (34–62; J 4:318).

2    From *The Honest Man's Fortune* (1613, publ. 1647) by the Renaissance playwrights Francis Beaumont (ca. 1584–1616) and John Fletcher (1579–1625). Emerson's essay will pursue the idea of the "perfect man" in terms of his ability to command influence, as well as the *(continued)*

Ne te quæsiveris extra.[1]
Man is his own star; and the soul that can
Render an honest and a perfect man,
Commands all light, all influence, all fate;
Nothing to him falls early or too late.
Our acts our angels are, or good or ill,
Our fatal shadows that walk by us still.[2]

Epilogue to Beaumont and Fletcher's *Honest Man's Fortune.*


Cast the bantling on the rocks,
Suckle him with the she-wolf's teat;
Wintered with the hawk and fox,
Power and speed be hands and feet.[3]


I read the other day some verses written by an eminent painter[4] which were original and not conventional. The soul always hears an admonition in such lines, let the subject be what it may. The sentiment they instil is of more value than any thought they may contain. To believe your own thought, to believe that what is true for you in your private heart, is true for all men,—

that is genius. Speak your latent conviction and it shall be the universal sense;[5] for the inmost in due time becomes the outmost,—and our first thought is rendered back to us by the trumpets of the Last Judgment. Familiar as the voice of the mind is to each, the highest merit we ascribe to Moses, Plato, and Milton,[6] is that they set at naught books and traditions, and spoke not what men but what they thought. A man should learn to detect and watch that gleam of light which flashes across his mind from within, more than the lustre of the firmament of bards and sages. Yet he dismisses without notice his thought, because it is his. In every work of genius we recognize our own rejected thoughts: they come back to us with a certain alienated majesty.[7] Great works of art have no more affecting lesson for us than this. They teach us to abide by our spontaneous impression with good-humored inflexibility then most when the whole cry of voices is on the other side. Else, to-morrow a stranger will say with masterly good sense precisely what we have thought and felt all the time, and we shall be forced to take with shame our own opinion from another.

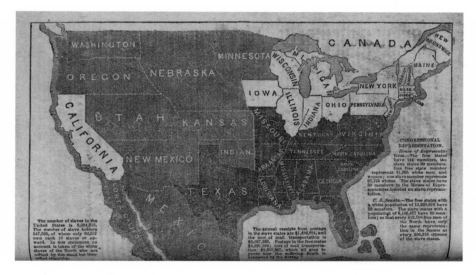

Page from "The Border Ruffian Code in Kansas," antislavery publication (1856).

relation between self-reliance and time ("Nothing to him falls early or too late").

3    A bantling is a young child. Emerson evokes the ancient Spartan ritual of training boys for military service by casting them into the wilderness.

4    Washington Allston (1779–1843), known for painting biblical subjects in romantic landscape settings. In 1837 Emerson recorded in his Journal that he found one of Allston's poems "very good & entirely self-taught, original, not conventional" (J 5:377).

5    In *The Friend* (1809–1810), the English Romantic poet S. T. Coleridge (1772–1834) wrote (in a passage noted by Emerson), "For that must appear to each man to be *his* reason which produces in him the highest sense of certainty, and yet it is *not* reason, except as far as it is of universal validity and obligatory on all mankind. . . . What is of permanent and essential interest to one man must needs be so to all . . ." (Volume 1, Essay 13).

6    This triad brings together the religious, the philosophical, and the literary. Moses's leading of the Israelites out of bondage in Egypt will figure later in "Self-Reliance," as will the ideas of Plato (429–347 BCE) and the poetry of John Milton (1608–1674).

7    A famous line. Emerson implies that each of us is a commanding presence—our thoughts, like kings, have majesty—but that we only recognize our authority, and accept these thoughts, when they come to us from another. Such dependence on the words of others is not, however, conformity, but its opposite. In his Journal (summer 1845), Emerson noted, "You cannot hear what I say until it is yours. Who of all of

*(continued)*

you dare take home to himself this that he need not seek anything" (J 9:225). And ten years earlier, in October 1835, he remarked, "In every work of genius you recognize your own rejected thoughts. It is here as in science, that the true chemist collects what every body else throws away. Our own thoughts come back to us in unexpected majesty" (J 5:92). Alienated, in Emerson's sentence, combines its two senses of "estranged" and "transferred to another's ownership."

8    The rather desperate tone of such epigrammatic commands ("envy is ignorance . . . imitation is suicide") is intended to reflect "every man's" harsh awakening. These phrases will find their refinements later. In "Self-Reliance," epigrams—pointed, compact, and intensely memorable—are the signatures of Emerson's thought; they sink like darts in our ears, and raise us to thought and action.

9    Emerson substitutes "trust thyself" for the Delphic oracle's admonition "know thyself," which guided Socrates. The string is iron both because it is unbreakable, and because its music is harsh and real. This is another epigram, followed by a commentary that deepens and even perplexes its meaning: self-trust turns out to mean "accept[ing] the place" that has been given to you.

10    In Milton's *Paradise Lost* (1667), the fallen angels' shout "frighted the reign of Chaos and old Night" (1.543).

11    "If therefore thine eye be single, thy whole body shall be full of light" (Matthew 6:22). In *The Friend*, Coleridge associated "GENIUS, as originality in intellectual construction," with "the carrying on of the freshness and
*(continued)*

There is a time in every man's education when he arrives at the conviction that envy is ignorance; that imitation is suicide;[8] that he must take himself for better, for worse, as his portion; that though the wide universe is full of good, no kernel of nourishing corn can come to him but through his toil bestowed on that plot of ground which is given to him to till. The power which resides in him is new in nature, and none but he knows what that is which he can do, nor does he know until he has tried. Not for nothing one face, one character, one fact makes much impression on him, and another none. This sculpture in the memory is not without preëstablished harmony. The eye was placed where one ray should fall, that it might testify of that particular ray. We but half express ourselves, and are ashamed of that divine idea which each of us represents. It may be safely trusted as proportionate and of good issues, so it be faithfully imparted, but God will not have his work made manifest by cowards. A man is relieved and gay when he has put his heart into his work and done his best; but what he has said or done otherwise, shall give him no peace. It is a deliverance which does not deliver. In the attempt his genius deserts him; no muse befriends; no invention, no hope.

Trust thyself: every heart vibrates to that iron string.[9] Accept the place the divine Providence has found for you; the society of your contemporaries, the connexion of events. Great men have always done so and confided themselves childlike to the genius of their age, betraying their perception that the absolutely trustworthy was seated at their heart, working through their hands, predominating in all their being. And we are now men, and must accept in the highest mind the same transcendent destiny; and not minors and invalids in a protected corner, not cowards fleeing before a revolution, but guides, redeemers, and benefactors, obeying the Almighty effort, and advancing on Chaos and the Dark.[10]

What pretty oracles nature yields us on this text in the face and behavior of children, babes and even brutes. That divided and rebel mind, that distrust of a sentiment because our arithmetic has computed the strength and means opposed to our purpose, these have not. Their mind being whole, their eye is as yet unconquered,[11] and when we look in their faces, we are disconcerted. Infancy conforms to nobody: all conform to it, so that one babe commonly makes four or five out of the adults who prattle and play to it. So God has armed youth and puberty and manhood no less with its own piquancy and charm, and made it enviable and gracious and its claims not to be put by, if it will stand by itself. Do not think the youth has no force because he cannot speak to you and me. Hark! in the next room his voice is sufficiently clear and emphatic. It seems he knows how to speak to his contemporaries. Bashful or bold, then, he will know how to make us seniors very unnecessary.

The nonchalance of boys who are sure of a dinner, and would disdain as much as a lord to do or say aught to conciliate one, is the healthy attitude of human nature. A boy is in the parlour what the pit[12] is in the playhouse; independent, irresponsible, looking out from his corner on such people and facts as pass by, he tries and sentences them on their merits, in the swift summary way of boys, as good, bad, interesting, silly, eloquent, troublesome. He cumbers himself never about consequences, about interests: he gives an independent, genuine verdict.[13]

You must court him: he does not court you. But the man is, as it were, clapped into jail by his consciousness.[14] As soon as he has once acted or spoken with eclat, he is a committed person, watched by the sympathy or the hatred of hundreds whose affections must now enter into his account. There is no Lethe[15] for this. Ah, that he could pass again into his neutrality! Who can thus avoid all pledges, and having observed, observe again from the same unaffected, unbiassed, unbribable, unaffrighted innocence, must always be formidable. He would utter opinions on all passing affairs, which being seen to be not private but necessary, would sink like darts into the ear of men, and put them in fear.[16]

These are the voices which we hear in solitude, but they grow faint and inaudible as we enter into the world. Society everywhere is in conspiracy against the manhood of every one of its members. Society is a joint-stock company in which the members agree for the better securing of his bread to each shareholder, to surrender the liberty and culture of the eater. The virtue in most request is conformity. Self-reliance is its aversion.[17] It loves not realities and creators, but names and customs.

Whoso would be a man must be a nonconformist. He who would gather immortal palms[18] must not be hindered by the name of goodness, but

feelings of childhood into the powers of manhood" (Volume 3 [Section 2], Essay 1; Emerson marked the passage).

12    In Shakespeare's day, a spectator could pay the cheap price of one penny to stand in the pit, an area directly below and in front of the stage. These groundlings (as they were called) often responded vociferously to the play.

In his lecture "Manners" (1837), from the series on "The Philosophy of History," Emerson said, "Bard or hero cannot look down upon the word or gesture of a child. It is as great as they" (EL 2:135).

13    Emerson wrote in his Journal (1852–1853), "At St Louis they say that there is no difference between a boy & a man. As soon as a boy is 'that high,' high as the table, he contradicts his father" (J 13:32).

14    In his Journal Emerson noted, "The reason we like simplicity of character, the reason why grown men listen with untiring interest to a lively child is the same, viz it is something more than man above man & we hearken with a curiosity that has something of awe. We should so listen to every man if his soul spake, but it does not; his fears speak, his senses speak, & he himself seldom" (July 1832; J 4:29).

15    In Greek and Roman myth, river of forgetfulness in the underworld.

16    Years later Emerson noted in his Journal, "The staple figure in novels is the man of aplomb, who sits among the young aspirants & desperates, quite sure & compact, &, never sharing their affections or debilities, hurls his word like a bullet, when occasion requires; knows his way, & carries his points" (J 10:289).

17 The root meaning of aversion is "turning away"; variations on the word will occur frequently in "Self-Reliance."

18 The palm represents victory; Emerson alludes to the *Immortality Ode* (1802–1804) by the English Romantic poet William Wordsworth (1770–1850): "Another race hath been, and other palms are won." In his Journal (February 1838), Emerson spoke of the self-reliance of Wordsworth's writing (referring to a poem of 1809, "Growth of Genius from the Influences of Natural Objects, on the Imagination in Boyhood, and Early Youth," later better known as the ice-skating scene in Bk. 1 of the *Prelude* [1850]): "How much self reliance it implies to write a true description of anything For example Wordsworth's picture of skating; that leaning back on your heels & stopping in mid career. So simple a fact no common man would have trusted himself to detach as a thought" (J 5:454).

19 In the Roman Catholic Church, priests grant absolution for sins. By contrast, Emerson proposes self-absolution.

20 "Away with this succumbing & servility forever. I will not be warned of the sacredness of traditions. I will live wholly from within," Emerson proclaimed in his Journal (June 1835; J 5:48–49).

21 Emerson brooded in his Journal (February 10, 1833), "As self means Devil so it means God" (J 4:68).

22 Raw, unpolished.

23 In 1834 Britain abolished slavery in the West Indies.

24 Unbelievable.

25 To Margaret Fuller (1810–1850), the first editor of the *Dial* magazine, Emerson wrote (July 21, 1840), "I hope our Dial will get to be a little *bad*. This first number is not enough so to scare the tenderest bantling of Conformity" (L 2:316). In his Journal (June 23, 1838) he remarked, "I hate goodies. I hate goodness that preaches. Goodness that preaches undoes itself" (J 7:31).

26 Whimpers. Emerson may have been thinking of John 12:25: "He that loveth his life shall lose it; and he that hates his life in this world shall keep it unto life eternal." But Emerson, unlike John's Jesus, has no brief against this world. In his Journal (1846), Emerson remarked, "Society will coo & claw & caress. You must curse & swear a little: They will remember it, & it will do them good" (J 9:377).

27 See Matthew 10:36–37 ("And a man's foes shall be they of his own household. He that loveth father or mother more than me is not worthy of me"), along with Matthew 19:29, in which Jesus praises "every one that hath forsaken houses, or brethren, or sisters, or father, or mother, or wife, or children, or lands, for my name's sake." In his Journal (June 22, 1836), Emerson wrote, "Jesus says, Leave father & mother, house & lands & follow me. There is no man who hath left all but he receives more. This is as true intellectually as morally" (J 5:178–179). (Genius here means guiding, personal spirit.)

28 Refers to Exodus 12:23, where the Angel of Death spares the first-born of the Israelites, who have smeared the lintels and side posts of their doors with blood. As Stanley Cavell suggests, Emerson may also have in mind the Jewish custom of affixing to one's door a mezuzah,

*(continued)*

must explore if it be goodness. Nothing is at last sacred but the integrity of your own mind. Absolve[19] you to yourself, and you shall have the suffrage of the world. I remember an answer which when quite young I was prompted to make to a valued adviser who was wont to importune me with the dear old doctrines of the church. On my saying, What have I to do with the sacredness of traditions, if I live wholly from within?[20] my friend suggested—"But these impulses may be from below, not from above." I replied, "They do not seem to me to be such; but if I am the Devil's child, I will live then from the Devil."[21] No law can be sacred to me but that of my nature. Good and bad are but names very readily transferable to that or this; the only right is what is after my constitution, the only wrong what is against it. A man is to carry himself in the presence of all opposition as if every thing were titular and ephemeral but he. I am ashamed to think how easily we capitulate to badges and names, to large societies and dead institutions. Every decent and well-spoken individual affects and sways me more than is right. I ought to go upright and vital, and speak the rude[22] truth in all ways. If malice and vanity wear the coat of philanthropy, shall that pass? If an angry bigot assumes this bountiful cause of Abolition, and comes to me with his last news from Barbadoes,[23] why should I not say to him, 'Go love thy infant; love thy woodchopper: be good-natured and modest: have that grace; and never varnish your hard, uncharitable ambition with this incredible[24] tenderness for black folk a thousand miles off. Thy love afar is spite at home.' Rough and graceless would be such greeting, but truth is handsomer than the affectation of love. Your goodness must have some edge to it—else it is none.[25] The doctrine of hatred must be preached as the counteraction of the doctrine of love when that pules[26] and whines. I shun father and mother and wife and brother, when my genius calls me.[27] I would write on the lintels of the door-post, *Whim*.[28] I hope it is somewhat better than whim at last, but we cannot spend the day in explanation. Expect me not to show cause why I seek or why I exclude company. Then, again, do not tell me, as a good man did to-day, of my obligation to put all poor men in good situations. Are they *my* poor? I tell thee, thou foolish philanthropist, that I grudge the dollar, the dime, the cent I give to such men as do not belong to me and to whom I do not belong. There is a class of persons to whom by all spiritual affinity I am bought and

a small box containing passages from the books of Deuteronomy and Numbers. In place of the law written on the door of the Jewish home, Emerson writes "whim" (his own way of replacing the Hebrew commandments with a new gospel, as Christianity claims that Jesus has done).

29    In Concord, Emerson was surrounded by an array of charitable projects. In a notebook (1836–1840), he complained, "Our benevolence is unhappy. Our Sunday Schools and churches & Pauper societies are yokes to the neck. We pain ourselves to pleasure nobody. But be a good man & you help by looking, by speaking, by acting, Virtue goes out of you: you make humanity lovely. Why should all give dollars?" (J 12:123).

30    Later in "Self-Reliance," Emerson will allude to the statement of the philosopher René Descartes (1596–1650), "I think, therefore I am."

sold; for them I will go to prison, if need be; but your miscellaneous popular charities; the education at college of fools; the building of meeting-houses to the vain end to which many now stand; alms to sots; and the thousandfold Relief Societies;—though I confess with shame I sometimes succumb and give the dollar, it is a wicked dollar which by and by I shall have the manhood to withhold.[29]

Virtues are in the popular estimate rather the exception than the rule. There is the man *and* his virtues. Men do what is called a good action, as some piece of courage or charity, much as they would pay a fine in expiation of daily non-appearance on parade. Their works are done as an apology or extenuation of their living in the world,—as invalids and the insane pay a high board. Their virtues are penances. I do not wish to expiate, but to live. My life is for itself and not for a spectacle. I much prefer that it should be of a lower strain, so it be genuine and equal, than that it should be glittering and unsteady. I wish it to be sound and sweet, and not to need diet and bleeding. I ask primary evidence that you are a man, and refuse this appeal from the man to his actions. I know that for myself it makes no difference whether I do or forbear those actions which are reckoned excellent. I cannot consent to pay for a privilege where I have intrinsic right. Few and mean as my gifts may be, I actually am,[30] and do not need for my own assurance or the assurance of my fellows any secondary testimony.

What I must do, is all that concerns me, not what the people think. This rule, equally arduous in actual and in intellectual life, may serve for the whole distinction between greatness and meanness. It is the harder, because you will always find those who think they know what is your duty better than you know it. It is easy in the world to live after the world's opinion; it is easy in solitude to live after our own; but the great man is he who in the midst of the crowd keeps with perfect sweetness the independence of solitude.

The objection to conforming to usages that have become dead to you, is, that it scatters your force. It loses your time and blurs the impression of your character. If you maintain a dead church, contribute to a dead Bible-Society, vote with a great party either for the Government or against it, spread your table like base housekeepers,—under all these screens, I have difficulty to detect the precise man you are. And, of course, so much force is withdrawn from your proper life. But do your work, and I shall know you.

Do your work, and you shall reinforce yourself.[31] A man must consider what a blindman's-buff[32] is this game of conformity. If I know your sect, I anticipate your argument. I hear a preacher announce for his text and topic the expediency of one of the institutions of his church. Do I not know beforehand that not possibly can he say a new and spontaneous word? Do I not know that with all this ostentation of examining the grounds of the institution, he will do no such thing? Do I not know that he is pledged to himself not to look but at one side,—the permitted side, not as a man, but as a parish minister? He is a retained attorney, and these airs of the bench are the emptiest affectation. Well, most men have bound their eyes with one or another handkerchief, and attached themselves to some one of these communities of opinion. This conformity makes them not false in a few particulars, authors of a few lies, but false in all particulars. Their every truth is not quite true. Their two is not the real two, their four not the real four: so that every word they say chagrins us, and we know not where to begin to set them right. Meantime nature is not slow to equip us in the prison-uniform of the party to which we adhere. We come to wear one cut of face and figure, and acquire by degrees the gentlest asinine expression. There is a mortifying experience in particular which does not fail to wreak itself also in the general history; I mean "the foolish face of praise,"[33] the forced smile which we put on in company where we do not feel at ease in answer to conversation which does not interest us. The muscles, not spontaneously moved, but moved by a low usurping wilfulness, grow tight about the outline of the face with the most disagreeable sensation.[34]

For nonconformity the world whips you with its displeasure.[35] And therefore a man must know how to estimate a sour face. The bystanders look askance on him in the public street or in the friend's parlor. If this aversation had its origin in contempt and resistance like his own, he might well go home with a sad countenance; but the sour faces of the multitude, like their sweet faces, have no deep cause, but are put on and off as the wind blows, and a newspaper directs. Yet is the discontent of the multitude more formidable than that of the senate and the college. It is easy enough for a firm man who knows the world to brook[36] the rage of the cultivated classes. Their rage is decorous and prudent, for they are timid as being very vulnerable themselves. But when to their feminine rage the indignation of the people is

31    In his later essay "Behavior" (in *The Conduct of Life*), Emerson asserted, "Self-reliance is the basis of behavior, as it is the guaranty that the powers are not squandered in too much demonstration."

32    A game in which one person is blindfolded and tries to catch and identify one of the others (who jostle and shove the blindfolded one).

33    Phrase from the *Epistle to Dr. Arbuthnot* (1735) by the British poet Alexander Pope (1688–1744).

34    Emerson's original Journal passage (September 19, 1937) added, "A sensation of rebuke & warning which no young man ought to suffer more than once."

35    Plutarch (ca. 46–ca. 122) in his *Moralia* (187f) wrote that "an oracle was given to the Athenians telling them there was one man in the city contrary to the opinions of all; they ordered a search for him and shouted. Phocion said that he was the man, for he alone disliked everything that the crowd did and said." The Athenian statesman Phocion (ca. 402–ca. 318 BCE) was one of Emerson's heroes.

36    Endure.

37    Emerson remarked in his Journal (March 1839), "I meet men whose faces instantly assure me they are where I left them; no new thoughts, new books, new facts, but facts old & decrepit by the inaction of the soul. Others I know, who are new men in new regions with faint memory of their own words & deeds on past occasions" (J 7:178).

38    In Genesis, the young Joseph flees the sexual advances of his master Potiphar's wife: "And she caught him by his garment, saying, Lie with me: and he left his garment in her hand, and fled, and got him out" (Genesis 39:12). In his Journal (November 27, 1838) Emerson wrote, "The brilliant young student . . . should dread his own theories. They are snares for his own feet" (J 7:161; Emerson alludes to Jeremiah 18:22).

39    Another famous sentence. Hobgoblin: a spirit inspiring superstitious dread; the bad counterpart of the daemon or genius. Arthur McGiffert, Jr., the editor of Emerson's sermons, recounts the story that Emerson once paused as he was delivering a sermon to say to the congregation, "The sentence which I have just read I do not now believe," and then calmly went on.

40    The philosopher Pythagoras (ca. 570–ca. 490 BCE), when he returned to Greece after studying in Egypt, was spurned by his countrymen; Socrates (469–399 BCE) was condemned to death by his fellow Athenians; Nicolaus Copernicus (1473–1543) and Galileo Galilei (1564–1642) defied the doctrines of the church by proposing that the earth is not the center of the universe. Isaac Newton (1643–1727) developed the theory of gravity, calculus, and the theory of optics; he was attacked by his fellow scientists Robert Hooke (1635–1703) and G. W. Leibniz (1646–1716).

added, when the ignorant and the poor are aroused, when the unintelligent brute force that lies at the bottom of society is made to growl and mow, it needs the habit of magnanimity and religion to treat it godlike as a trifle of no concernment.

The other terror that scares us from self-trust is our consistency; a reverence for our past act or word, because the eyes of others have no other data for computing our orbit than our past acts, and we are loath to disappoint them.

But why should you keep your head over your shoulder? Why drag about this corpse of your memory, lest you contradict somewhat you have stated in this or that public place? Suppose you should contradict yourself; what then?[37] It seems to be a rule of wisdom never to rely on your memory alone, scarcely even in acts of pure memory, but to bring the past for judgment into the thousand-eyed present, and live ever in a new day. In your metaphysics you have denied personality to the Deity: yet when the devout motions of the soul come, yield to them heart and life, though they should clothe God with shape and color. Leave your theory as Joseph his coat in the hand of the harlot, and flee.[38]

A foolish consistency is the hobgoblin of little minds,[39] adored by little statesmen and philosophers and divines. With consistency a great soul has simply nothing to do. He may as well concern himself with his shadow on the wall. Speak what you think now in hard words, and to-morrow speak what to-morrow thinks in hard words again, though it contradict every thing you said to-day.—'Ah, so you shall be sure to be misunderstood.'—Is it so bad then to be misunderstood? Pythagoras was misunderstood, and Socrates, and Jesus, and Luther, and Copernicus, and Galileo, and Newton,[40] and every pure and wise spirit that ever took flesh. To be great is to be misunderstood.

I suppose no man can violate his nature. All the sallies of his will are rounded in by the law of his being as the inequalities of Andes and Himmaleh are insignificant in the curve of the sphere. Nor does it matter how you gauge and try him. A character is like an acrostic or Alexandrian stanza;[41] —read it forward, backward, or across, it still spells the same thing. In this pleasing contrite wood-life which God allows me, let me record day by day my honest thought without prospect or retrospect, and, I cannot doubt, it will be found symmetrical, though I mean it not, and see it not. My book should smell of pines and resound with the hum of insects.[42] The swallow over my window should interweave that thread or straw he carries in his bill into my web also. We pass for what we are. Character teaches above our wills. Men imagine that they communicate their virtue or vice only by overt actions and do not see that virtue or vice emit a breath every moment.[43]

There will be an agreement in whatever variety of actions, so they be each honest and natural in their hour. For of one will, the actions will be harmonious, however unlike they seem. These varieties are lost sight of at a little distance, at a little height of thought. One tendency unites them all. The voyage of the best ship is a zigzag line of a hundred tacks. See the line from a sufficient distance, and it straightens itself to the average tendency. Your genuine action will explain itself and will explain your other genuine actions. Your conformity explains nothing. Act singly, and what you have already done singly, will justify you now. Greatness appeals to the future. If I can be firm enough to-day to do right and scorn eyes, I must have done so much right before, as to defend me now. Be it how it will, do right now. Always scorn appearances, and you always may. The force of character is cumulative. All the foregone days of virtue work their health into this. What makes the majesty of the heroes of the senate and the field, which so fills the imagination? The consciousness of a train of great days and victories behind. They shed an united light on the advancing actor. He is attended as by a visible escort of angels. That is it which throws thunder into Chatham's voice, and dignity into Washington's port, and America into Adams's eye.[44] Honor is venerable to us because it is no ephemeris.[45] It is always ancient virtue. We worship it to-day, because it is not of to-day. We love it and pay it homage, because it is not a trap for our love and homage, but is self-dependent, self-derived, and therefore of an old immaculate pedigree, even if shown in a young person.

I hope in these days we have heard the last of conformity and consistency. Let the words be gazetted[46] and ridiculous henceforward. Instead of the gong for dinner, let us hear a whistle from the Spartan fife.[47] Let us never bow and apologize more. A great man is coming to eat at my house. I do not wish to please him: I wish that he should wish to please me. I will stand here for humanity, and though I would make it kind, I would make it true. Let

41   The Greek poets of the city of Alexandria in Egypt were known for their ingenuity; they sometimes wrote acrostics (poems in which the initial letter of each line spells out—for example—the author's name). Palindromes, in which lines can be read both forward and backward, flourished later, in the Byzantine empire (324–1453).

42   In his Journal (March 27, 1838) Emerson wrote, "Every man that goes into the wood seems to be the first man that ever went into a wood. His sensations & his World are new. You really think that nothing new can be said about morning & evening. And the fact is morning & evening have not yet begun to be described" (J 5:469).

43   In the essay "Behavior," Emerson remarked, "Men are like Geneva watches with crystal faces which expose the whole movement. They carry the liquor of life flowing up and down in these beautiful bodies, and announcing to the curious how it is with them."

44   William Pitt (the Elder), Earl of Chatham (1708–1778), British leader during the Seven Years' War (1756–1763); George Washington (1732–1799) and John Adams (1735–1826), first and second presidents of the United States.

45   Calendar (implying transience).

46   An officer whose resignation was announced in an official gazette was said to be "gazetted out."

47   Sparta was famous for its austere, military character. Emerson commented in his Journal in 1845 that Spartans "wrote to be read, & spoke to be understood," but "alas for the poor Helots" (the Spartans' slaves), "the price with which this grandeur was bought" (J 9:298).

48    St. Antony (3rd–4th century), founder of a monastic order in the deserts of Egypt; Martin Luther (1483–1546), central Protestant reformer; George Fox (1624–1691), English founder of the Society of Friends (Quakers); John Wesley (1703–1791), founder of Methodism; Thomas Clarkson (1769–1846), British abolitionist. In *Paradise Lost* (9.510) Satan, tempting Eve, resembles the great Roman military leader Cornelius Scipio Africanus (235–183 BCE).

49    Outfit; equipment. Note the contrast between this "alien . . . air" and the "alienated majesty" Emerson invokes earlier.

50    In the introductory lecture of his series "Human Culture" (1837), Emerson remarked, "The great works of art are unable to check our criticism. They create a want they do not gratify. They instantly point us to somewhat better than themselves" (EL 2:217). In another lecture, "The Protest" (1839), he asked, "Why then do you so overestimate a book? You are yourself the book's book. Its worth is always your worth. It is but an echo, a mirror, a shadow. I will read myself and there find the libraries" (EL 3:97).

51    A well-known version of this folktale motif occurs in the Introduction to Shakespeare's *Taming of the Shrew*.

us affront and reprimand the smooth mediocrity and squalid contentment of the times, and hurl in the face of custom, and trade, and office, the fact which is the upshot of all history, that there is a great responsible Thinker and Actor working wherever a man works; that a true man belongs to no other time or place, but is the centre of things. Where he is, there is nature. He measures you, and all men, and all events. Ordinarily every body in society reminds us of somewhat else or of some other person. Character, reality, reminds you of nothing else; it takes place of the whole creation. The man must be so much that he must make all circumstances indifferent. Every true man is a cause, a country, and an age; requires infinite spaces and numbers and time fully to accomplish his design;—and posterity seem to follow his steps as a train of clients. A man Cæsar is born, and for ages after, we have a Roman Empire. Christ is born, and millions of minds so grow and cleave to his genius, that he is confounded with virtue and the possible of man. An institution is the lengthened shadow of one man; as, Monachism, of the Hermit Antony; the Reformation, of Luther; Quakerism, of Fox; Methodism, of Wesley; Abolition, of Clarkson. Scipio, Milton called "the height of Rome;"[48] and all history resolves itself very easily into the biography of a few stout and earnest persons.

Let a man then know his worth, and keep things under his feet. Let him not peep or steal, or skulk up and down with the air of a charity-boy, a bastard, or an interloper, in the world which exists for him. But the man in the street finding no worth in himself which corresponds to the force which built a tower or sculptured a marble god, feels poor when he looks on these. To him a palace, a statue, or a costly book have an alien and forbidding air, much like a gay equipage,[49] and seem to say like that, 'Who are you, sir?' Yet they all are his, suitors for his notice, petitioners to his faculties that they will come out and take possession. The picture waits for my verdict: it is not to command me, but I am to settle its claims to praise.[50] That popular fable of the sot who was picked up dead drunk in the street, carried to the duke's house, washed and dressed and laid in the duke's bed, and, on his waking, treated with all obsequious ceremony like the duke, and assured that he had been insane, owes its popularity to the fact, that it symbolizes so well the state of man, who is in the world a sort of sot, but now and then wakes up, exercises his reason, and finds himself a true prince.[51]

Our reading is mendicant and sycophantic. In history, our imagination plays us false. Kingdom and lordship, power and estate are a gaudier vocabulary than private John and Edward in a small house and common day's work: but the things of life are the same to both: the sum total of both is the same. Why all this deference to Alfred, and Scanderbeg, and Gustavus?[52] Suppose they were virtuous: did they wear out virtue? As great a stake depends on your private act to-day, as followed their public and renowned steps. When private men shall act with original views, the lustre will be transferred from the actions of kings to those of gentlemen.

The world has been instructed by its kings, who have so magnetized the eyes of nations. It has been taught by this colossal symbol the mutual reverence that is due from man to man. The joyful loyalty with which men have everywhere suffered the king, the noble, or the great proprietor to walk among them by a law of his own, make his own scale of men and things, and reverse theirs, pay for benefits not with money but with honor, and represent the Law in his person, was the hieroglyphic by which they obscurely signified their consciousness of their own right and comeliness, the right of every man.

The magnetism which all original action exerts is explained when we inquire the reason of self-trust. Who is the Trustee? What is the aboriginal[53] Self on which a universal reliance may be grounded? What is the nature and power of that science-baffling star, without parallax,[54] without calculable elements, which shoots a ray of beauty even into trivial and impure actions, if the least mark of independence appear? The inquiry leads us to that source, at once the essence of genius, of virtue, and of life, which we call Spontaneity or Instinct. We denote this primary wisdom as Intuition, whilst all later teachings are tuitions. In that deep force, the last fact behind which analysis cannot go, all things find their common origin. For the sense of being which in calm hours rises, we know not how, in the soul, is not diverse from things, from space, from light, from time, from man, but one with them, and proceeds obviously from the same source whence their life and being also proceed. We first share the life by which things exist, and afterwards see them as appearances in nature, and forget that we have shared their cause. Here is the fountain of action and of thought. Here are the lungs of that inspiration which giveth man wisdom, and which cannot be denied without impiety and

52    Alfred the Great, king of Wessex (849–899); George Castriota (1405–1468), who led the Albanian rebels against the Turks, known by the title Iskander Bey (Emerson's "Skanderbeg"); Gustavus Adolphus (1594–1632), king of Sweden during the Thirty Years' War.

53    Primitive, original.

54    Used by astronomers to measure the position of a star (or other heavenly body).

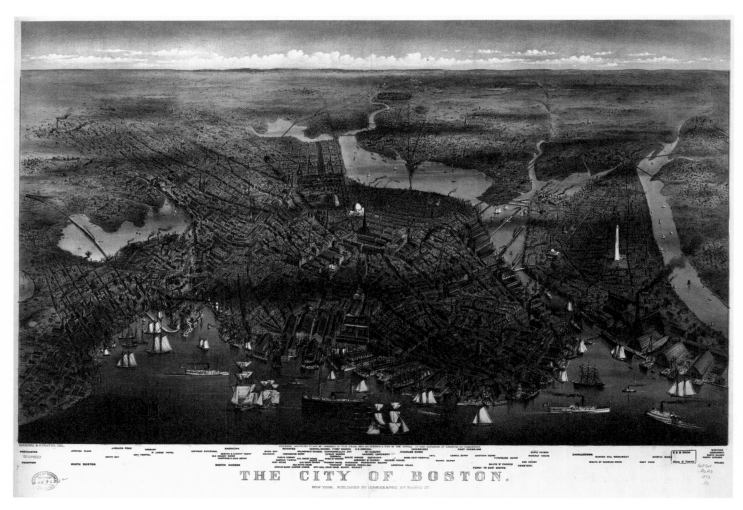

City of Boston, 1873.

atheism. We lie in the lap of immense intelligence, which makes us receivers of its truth and organs of its activity. When we discern justice, when we discern truth, we do nothing of ourselves, but allow a passage to its beams. If we ask whence this comes, if we seek to pry into the soul that causes, all philosophy is at fault. Its presence or its absence is all we can affirm. Every man discriminates between the voluntary acts of his mind, and his involuntary perceptions, and knows that to his involuntary perceptions a perfect faith is due.[55] He may err in the expression of them, but he knows that these things are so, like day and night, not to be disputed. My wilful actions and acquisitions are but roving;—the idlest reverie, the faintest native emotion, command my curiosity and respect. Thoughtless people contradict as readily the statement of perceptions as of opinions, or rather much more readily; for, they do not distinguish between perception and notion. They fancy that I choose to see this or that thing. But perception is not whimsical, but fatal.[56] If I see a trait, my children will see it after me, and in course of time, all mankind,—although it may chance that no one has seen it before me. For my perception of it is as much a fact as the sun.

The relations of the soul to the divine spirit are so pure that it is profane to seek to interpose helps. It must be that when God speaketh, he should communicate not one thing, but all things; should fill the world with his voice; should scatter forth light, nature, time, souls, from the centre of the present thought; and new date and new create the whole. Whenever a mind is simple, and receives a divine wisdom, old things pass away,—means, teachers, texts, temples fall; it lives now and absorbs past and future into the present hour. All things are made sacred by relation to it,—one as much as another. All things are dissolved to their centre by their cause, and in the universal miracle petty and particular miracles disappear. If, therefore, a man claims to know and speak of God, and carries you backward to the phraseology of some old mouldered nation in another country, in another world, believe him not. Is the acorn better than the oak which is its fulness and completion? Is the parent better than the child into whom he has cast his ripened being? Whence then this worship of the past? The centuries are conspirators against the sanity and authority of the soul. Time and space are but physiological colors which the eye makes, but the soul is light; where it is, is day; where it was, is night; and history is an impertinence and an injury, if

55  In his Journal Emerson asked, "Can you believe, Waldo Emerson, that you may relieve yourself of this perpetual perplexity of choosing? by putting your ear close to the soul, learn always the true way" (J 4:264).

56  Emerson revises his earlier reliance on the word *whim* (which he wrote above his door); *fatal* here means guided by fate (as in the essay's epigraph from Beaumont and Fletcher).

57    King of Israel (David), Hebrew prophet (Jeremiah), and Christian saint (Paul).

58    A new, deliberately elusive movement of "Self-Reliance" begins here. Emerson suggests that any statement of a credo (such as he has been giving) is necessarily inadequate; that, as the critic Richard Poirier argues, self-reliance is by its nature indefinable, rather than a doctrine to be followed: intuition, not tuition.

it be anything more than a cheerful apologue or parable of my being and becoming.

Man is timid and apologetic; he is no longer upright; he dares not say 'I think,' 'I am,' but quotes some saint or sage. He is ashamed before the blade of grass or the blowing rose. These roses under my window make no reference to former roses or to better ones; they are for what they are; they exist with God to-day. There is no time to them. There is simply the rose; it is perfect in every moment of its existence. Before a leaf-bud has burst, its whole life acts; in the full-blown flower, there is no more; in the leafless root, there is no less. Its nature is satisfied, and it satisfies nature, in all moments alike. But man postpones or remembers; he does not live in the present, but with reverted eye laments the past, or, heedless of the riches that surround him, stands on tiptoe to foresee the future. He cannot be happy and strong until he too lives with nature in the present, above time.

This should be plain enough. Yet see what strong intellects dare not yet hear God himself, unless he speak the phraseology of I know not what David, or Jeremiah, or Paul.[57] We shall not always set so great a price on a few texts, on a few lives. We are like children who repeat by rote the sentences of grandames and tutors, and, as they grow older, of the men of talents and character they chance to see,—painfully recollecting the exact words they spoke; afterwards, when they come into the point of view which those had who uttered these sayings, they understand them, and are willing to let the words go; for, at any time, they can use words as good, when occasion comes. If we live truly, we shall see truly. It is as easy for the strong man to be strong, as it is for the weak to be weak. When we have new perception, we shall gladly disburden the memory of its hoarded treasures as old rubbish. When a man lives with God, his voice shall be as sweet as the murmur of the brook and the rustle of the corn.

And now at last the highest truth on this subject remains unsaid; probably, cannot be said; for all that we say is the far off remembering of the intuition.[58] That thought, by what I can now nearest approach to say it, is this. When good is near you, when you have life in yourself, it is not by any known or accustomed way; you shall not discern the foot-prints of any other; you shall not see the face of man; you shall not hear any name;—the way, the thought, the good shall be wholly strange and new. It shall exclude example and experience.[59] You take the way from man, not to man. All persons that ever existed are its forgotten ministers. Fear and hope are alike beneath it. There is somewhat low even in hope. In the hour of vision, there is nothing that can be called gratitude, nor properly joy. The soul raised over passion beholds identity and eternal causation, perceives the self-existence of Truth and Right, and calms itself with knowing that all things go well.[60] Vast spaces of nature, the Atlantic Ocean, the South Sea,—long intervals of time, years, centuries,—are of no account. This which I think and feel underlay every former state of life and circumstances, as it does underlie my present, and what is called life, and what is called death.

Life only avails, not the having lived. Power ceases in the instant of repose; it resides in the moment of transition from a past to a new state, in the shooting of the gulf, in the darting to an aim.[61] This one fact the world hates, that the soul *becomes;* for, that forever degrades the past, turns all riches to poverty, all reputation to a shame, confounds the saint with the rogue, shoves Jesus and Judas equally aside. Why then do we prate of self-reliance? Inasmuch as the soul is present, there will be power not confident but agent.[62] To talk of reliance, is a poor external way of speaking. Speak rather of that which relies, because it works and is.[63] Who has more obedience than I, masters me, though he should not raise his finger. Round him I must revolve by the gravitation of spirits. We fancy it rhetoric when we speak of eminent virtue. We do not yet see that virtue is Height, and that a man or a company of men plastic and permeable to principles, by the law of nature must overpower and ride all cities, nations, kings, rich men, poets, who are not.

This is the ultimate fact which we so quickly reach on this as on every topic, the resolution of all into the ever blessed ONE. Self-existence is the attribute of the Supreme Cause, and it constitutes the measure of good by the degree in which it enters into all lower forms. All things real are so by so much virtue as they contain. Commerce, husbandry, hunting, whaling, war, eloquence, personal weight, are somewhat, and engage my respect as examples of its presence and impure action. I see the same law working in nature for conservation and growth. Power is in nature the essential measure of right. Nature suffers nothing to remain in her kingdoms which cannot help itself. The genesis and maturation of a planet, its poise and orbit, the bended tree recovering itself from the strong wind, the vital resources of every ani-

59  In his original Journal passage (November 14, 1838), Emerson wrote, "It shall exclude all other being. There shall be no fear in it. To climb that most holy mountain, you must tread on Fear. You take the way *from* man not *to* man. Quit the shore & go out to sea. Christian, Jew, Pagan, leave all behind you & rush" (the sentence breaks off; J 7:151).

60  Reminiscent of Plato's invocations of the soul (especially in his *Symposium*).

61  Emerson remembered this passage when he wrote in his Journal (1849) that "the Universe is only in transit, or, we behold it shooting the gulf from the past to the future" (J 11:187).

62  Not dependent on someone or something, but acting of itself.

63  Because it works and (therefore) is: an Emersonian response to Descartes's statement "I think, therefore I am."

64    In Exodus 3:5, God tells Moses at the burning bush, "Draw not nigh hither: put off thy shoes from off thy feet, for the place whereon thou standest is holy ground."

65    Isaiah 36:16: "Thus saith the king of Assyria, Make an agreement with me by a present, and come out to me."

66    Variation on lines by Friedrich Schiller (1759–1805) in his epigram "Love and Desire." Schiller wrote that "man loves, what he has; man desires, what he has not; / And only the rich spirit loves, only the poor one desires."

67    Thor was the god of thunder and Woden (or Odin) king of the gods in Norse legend. Emerson wrote of the Saxons, one of the early tribes of Britain, in *English Traits*, "These Saxons are the hands of mankind. They have the taste for toil, a distaste for pleasure or repose, and the telescopic appreciation of distant gain."

mal and vegetable, are demonstrations of the self-sufficing, and therefore self-relying soul.

Thus all concentrates; let us not rove; let us sit at home with the cause. Let us stun and astonish the intruding rabble of men and books and institutions by a simple declaration of the divine fact. Bid the invaders take the shoes from off their feet, for God is here within.[64] Let our simplicity judge them, and our docility to our own law demonstrate the poverty of nature and fortune beside our native riches.

But now we are a mob. Man does not stand in awe of man, nor is his genius admonished to stay at home, to put itself in communication with the internal ocean, but it goes abroad to beg a cup of water of the urns of other men. We must go alone. I like the silent church before the service begins, better than any preaching. How far off, how cool, how chaste the persons look, begirt each one with a precinct or sanctuary. So let us always sit. Why should we assume the faults of our friend, or wife, or father, or child, because they sit around our hearth, or are said to have the same blood? All men have my blood, and I have all men's. Not for that will I adopt their petulance or folly, even to the extent of being ashamed of it. But your isolation must not be mechanical, but spiritual, that is, must be elevation. At times the whole world seems to be in conspiracy to importune you with emphatic trifles. Friend, client, child, sickness, fear, want, charity, all knock at once at thy closet door and say,—'Come out unto us.'[65] But keep thy state; come not into their confusion. The power men possess to annoy me, I give them by a weak curiosity. No man can come near me but through my act. "What we love that we have, but by desire we bereave ourselves of the love."[66]

If we cannot at once rise to the sanctities of obedience and faith, let us at least resist our temptations; let us enter into the state of war, and wake Thor and Woden, courage and constancy, in our Saxon breasts.[67] This is to be done in our smooth times by speaking the truth. Check this lying hospitality and lying affection. Live no longer to the expectation of these deceived and deceiving people with whom we converse. Say to them, O father, O mother, O wife, O brother, O friend, I have lived with you after appearances hitherto. Henceforward I am the truth's. Be it known unto you that henceforward I obey no law less than the eternal law. I will have no covenants but proximities.[68] I shall endeavor to nourish my parents, to support my family, to be the chaste husband of one wife,—but these relations I must fill after a new and unprecedented way. I appeal from your customs. I must be myself. I cannot break myself any longer for you, or you. If you can love me for what I am, we shall be the happier. If you cannot, I will still seek to deserve that you should. I will not hide my tastes or aversions. I will so trust that what is deep is holy, that I will do strongly before the sun and moon whatever inly rejoices me, and the heart appoints. If you are noble, I will love you; if you are not, I will not hurt you and myself by hypocritical attentions. If you are true, but not in the same truth with me, cleave to your companions; I will seek my own. I do this not selfishly, but humbly and truly. It is alike your interest and mine and all men's, however long we have dwelt in lies, to live in truth. Does this sound harsh to-day? You will soon love what is dictated by your nature as well as mine, and if we follow the truth, it will bring us out safe at last.— But so you may give these friends pain. Yes, but I cannot sell my liberty and my power, to save their sensibility. Besides, all persons have their moments of reason when they look out into the region of absolute truth; then will they justify me and do the same thing.

The populace think that your rejection of popular standards is a rejection of all standard, and mere antinomianism; and the bold sensualist will use the name of philosophy to gild his crimes. But the law of consciousness abides. There are two confessionals, in one or the other of which we must be shriven. You may fulfil your round of duties by clearing yourself in the *direct*, or, in the *reflex* way. Consider whether you have satisfied your relations to father, mother, cousin, neighbor, town, cat, and dog; whether any of these can upbraid you. But I may also neglect this reflex standard, and absolve me to myself. I have my own stern claims and perfect circle. It denies the name of duty to many offices that are called duties. But if I can discharge its debts, it enables me to dispense with the popular code. If any one imagines that this law is lax, let him keep its commandment one day.

And truly it demands something godlike in him who has cast off the common motives of humanity, and has ventured to trust himself for a task-master. High be his heart, faithful his will, clear his sight, that he may in good earnest be doctrine, society, law to himself, that a simple purpose may be to him as strong as iron necessity is to others.

68    Perhaps a glance back at the reminder of the covenant, the words of the law affixed to the door (see note 28 above).

69   In September 1833, in Liverpool waiting to sail back to America, Emerson wrote in his Journal, "Let us hear this new thing. It is very old. . . . A man contains all that is needful to his government within himself. He is made a law unto himself. All real good or evil that can befall him must be from himself. He only can do himself any good or any harm. . . . The purpose of life seems to be to acquaint a man with himself. . . . The highest revelation is that God is in every man" (J 4:84).

If any man consider the present aspects of what is called by distinction *society*, he will see the need of these ethics. The sinew and heart of man seem to be drawn out, and we are become timorous desponding whimperers. We are afraid of truth, afraid of fortune, afraid of death, and afraid of each other. Our age yields no great and perfect persons. We want men and women who shall renovate life and our social state, but we see that most natures are insolvent, cannot satisfy their own wants, have an ambition out of all proportion to their practical force, and do lean and beg day and night continually. Our housekeeping is mendicant, our arts, our occupations, our marriages, our religion we have not chosen, but society has chosen for us. We are parlor soldiers. We shun the rugged battle of fate, where strength is born.

If our young men miscarry in their first enterprizes, they lose all heart. If the young merchant fails, men say he is *ruined*. If the finest genius studies at one of our colleges, and is not installed in an office within one year afterwards in the cities or suburbs of Boston or New York, it seems to his friends and to himself that he is right in being disheartened and in complaining the rest of his life. A sturdy lad from New Hampshire or Vermont, who in turn tries all the professions, who *teams it, farms it, peddles*, keeps a school, preaches, edits a newspaper, goes to Congress, buys a township, and so forth, in successive years, and always, like a cat, falls on his feet, is worth a hundred of these city dolls. He walks abreast with his days, and feels no shame in not 'studying a profession,' for he does not postpone his life, but lives already. He has not one chance, but a hundred chances. Let a Stoic open the resources of man, and tell men they are not leaning willows, but can and must detach themselves; that with the exercise of self-trust, new powers shall appear; that a man is the word made flesh, born to shed healing to the nations, that he should be ashamed of our compassion, and that the moment he acts from himself, tossing the laws, the books, idolatries, and customs out of the window, we pity him no more but thank and revere him,—and that teacher shall restore the life of man to splendor, and make his name dear to all History.[69]

It is easy to see that a greater self-reliance must work a revolution in all the offices and relations of men; in their religion; in their education; in their pursuits; their modes of living; their association; in their property; in their speculative views.

1. In what prayers do men allow themselves! That which they call a holy office, is not so much as brave and manly. Prayer looks abroad and asks for some foreign addition to come through some foreign virtue, and loses itself in endless mazes of natural and supernatural, and mediatorial and miraculous. Prayer that craves a particular commodity,—any thing less than all good,—is vicious. Prayer is the contemplation of the facts of life from the highest point of view. It is the soliloquy of a beholding and jubilant soul. It is the spirit of God pronouncing his works good.[70] But prayer as a means to effect a private end, is meanness and theft. It supposes dualism and not unity in nature and consciousness. As soon as the man is at one with God, he will not beg. He will then see prayer in all action. The prayer of the farmer kneeling in his field to weed it, the prayer of the rower kneeling with the stroke of his oar, are true prayers heard throughout nature, though for cheap[71] ends. Caratach, in Fletcher's *Bonduca*, when admonished to inquire the mind of the god Audate,[72] replies,—

"His hidden meaning lies in our endeavors,
Our valors are our best gods."

Another sort of false prayers are our regrets. Discontent is the want of self-reliance: it is infirmity of will. Regret calamities, if you can thereby help the sufferer; if not, attend your own work, and already the evil begins to be repaired. Our sympathy is just as base. We come to them who weep foolishly, and sit down and cry for company, instead of imparting to them truth and health in rough electric shocks, putting them once more in communication with their own reason. The secret of fortune is joy in our hands. Welcome evermore to gods and men is the self-helping man. For him all doors are flung wide: him all tongues greet, all honors crown, all eyes follow with desire. Our love goes out to him and embraces him, because he did not need it. We solicitously and apologetically caress and celebrate him, because he held on his way and scorned our disapprobation. The gods love him because men hated him. "To the persevering mortal," said Zoroaster, "the blessed Immortals are swift."[73]

As men's prayers are a disease of the will, so are their creeds a disease of the intellect. They say with those foolish Israelites, 'Let not God speak to us,

70    God in Genesis 1 blesses his own creation; Emerson implies an identification between the human being and God. In Thomas Taylor's translation of Iamblichus (ca. 250–ca. 330), *On the Mysteries of the Egyptians, Chaldeans, and Assyrians* (1821), Emerson noted this passage: "The third and most perfect species of prayer is *the seal of ineffable union with the divinities*," which "causes the soul to repose in the Gods, as in a never failing port."

71    Lowly. Emerson's son Edward remembered that his father had worked in his uncle's hayfield alongside a Methodist farmhand who insisted "that men are always praying."

72    British war god. Emerson quotes from Fletcher's play *Bonduca* (staged ca. 1613), about a British queen and warrior who rebelled against the Romans.

73    Zoroaster (ca. 11th century BCE), Iranian prophet and founder of the Zoroastrian religion. Emerson found the sentence in Isaac Cory's *Ancient Fragments of the Phoenician, Chaldaean . . . and Other Writers* (1832).

74    Exodus 20:18: with thunder and smoke engulfing Mt. Sinai, the Israelites beg that Moses, rather than God, speak to them.

75    John Locke (1632–1704), English philosopher whose doctrine of materialism was influential in Emerson's day (and opposed by the Transcendentalists); Antoine Lavoisier (1743–1794), pioneering French chemist; James Hutton (1726–1797), whose theories of the earth's evolution were later developed by Emerson's contemporary Charles Lyell (1797–1875); Jeremy Bentham (1748–1832), English Utilitarian philosopher; Charles Fourier (1772–1837), French utopian theorist.

76    Calvinists were the Protestant followers of John Calvin (1509–1564); Emmanuel Swedenborg (1688–1772) was a Swedish mystic whose readers started a religious movement.

77    Gentleman's manservant. In his essay "Culture," Emerson lamented the fact that "all educated Americans, first or last, go to Europe": "You do not think you will find anything there which you have not seen at home? The stuff of all countries is just the same." He added, though, that "as a medical remedy, travel seems one of the best."

78    Thebes, city in upper Egypt founded ca. 3200 BCE; Palmyra (Tadmor), ancient Aramaic city in Syria.

79    Henry David Thoreau (1817–1862), influenced by Emerson, redefines traveling, giving it an inward sense. In *Walden* (1854) he remarks, "I have travelled a great deal in Concord," and in his Journal (1:171), "The deepest and most original thinker is the farthest travelled."

lest we die. Speak thou, speak any man with us, and we will obey.'[74] Everywhere I am hindered of meeting God in my brother, because he has shut his own temple doors, and recites fables merely of his brother's, or his brother's brother's God. Every new mind is a new classification. If it prove a mind of uncommon activity and power, a Locke, a Lavoisier, a Hutton, a Bentham, a Fourier,[75] it imposes its classification on other men, and lo! a new system. In proportion to the depth of the thought, and so to the number of the objects it touches and brings within reach of the pupil, is his complacency. But chiefly is this apparent in creeds and churches, which are also classifications of some powerful mind acting on the elemental thought of Duty, and man's relation to the Highest. Such is Calvinism, Quakerism, Swedenborgianism.[76] The pupil takes the same delight in subordinating every thing to the new terminology, as a girl who has just learned botany in seeing a new earth and new seasons thereby. It will happen for a time, that the pupil will find his intellectual power has grown by the study of his master's mind. But in all unbalanced minds, the classification is idolized, passes for the end, and not for a speedily exhaustible means, so that the walls of the system blend to their eye in the remote horizon with the walls of the universe; the luminaries of heaven seem to them hung on the arch their master built. They cannot imagine how you aliens have any right to see,—how you can see; 'It must be somehow that you stole the light from us.' They do not yet perceive, that light, unsystematic, indomitable, will break into any cabin, even into theirs. Let them chirp awhile and call it their own. If they are honest and do well, presently their neat new pinfold will be too strait and low, will crack, will lean, will rot and vanish, and the immortal light, all young and joyful, million-orbed, million-colored, will beam over the universe as on the first morning.

2. It is for want of self-culture that the superstition of Travelling, whose idols are Italy, England, Egypt, retains its fascination for all educated Americans. They who made England, Italy, or Greece venerable in the imagination, did so by sticking fast where they were, like an axis of the earth. In manly hours, we feel that duty is our place. The soul is no traveller: the wise man stays at home, and when his necessities, his duties, on any occasion call him from his house, or into foreign lands, he is at home still, and shall make men sensible by the expression of his countenance, that he goes the mission-

ary of wisdom and virtue, and visits cities and men like a sovereign, and not like an interloper or a valet.[77]

I have no churlish objection to the circumnavigation of the globe, for the purposes of art, of study, and benevolence, so that the man is first domesticated, or does not go abroad with the hope of finding somewhat greater than he knows. He who travels to be amused, or to get somewhat which he does not carry, travels away from himself, and grows old even in youth among old things. In Thebes, in Palmyra,[78] his will and mind have become old and dilapidated as they. He carries ruins to ruins.

Travelling is a fool's paradise.[79] Our first journeys discover to us the indifference of places. At home I dream that at Naples, at Rome, I can be intoxicated with beauty, and lose my sadness. I pack my trunk, embrace my friends, embark on the sea, and at last wake up in Naples, and there beside me is the stern Fact, the sad self, unrelenting, identical, that I fled from.[80] I seek the Vatican, and the palaces. I affect to be intoxicated with sights and suggestions, but I am not intoxicated. My giant[81] goes with me wherever I go.

3. But the rage of travelling is a symptom of a deeper unsoundness affecting the whole intellectual action. The intellect is vagabond, and our system of education fosters restlessness.[82] Our minds travel when our bodies are forced to stay at home. We imitate; and what is imitation but the travelling of the mind? Our houses are built with foreign taste; our shelves are garnished with foreign ornaments; our opinions, our tastes, our faculties, lean, and follow the Past and the Distant. The soul created the arts wherever they have flourished. It was in his own mind that the artist sought his model. It was an application of his own thought to the thing to be done and the conditions to be observed. And why need we copy the Doric or the Gothic[83] model? Beauty, convenience, grandeur of thought, and quaint expression are as near to us as to any, and if the American artist will study with hope and love the precise thing to be done by him, considering the climate, the soil, the length of the day, the wants of the people, the habit and form of the government, he will create a house in which all these will find themselves fitted, and taste and sentiment will be satisfied also.

Insist on yourself; never imitate.[84] Your own gift you can present every moment with the cumulative force of a whole life's cultivation; but of the

80 When he reached Italy on his first trip to Europe, Emerson wrote in his Journal (March 12, 1833), "And what if it is Naples, it is only the same world of cake & ale—of man & truth & folly. I won't be imposed upon by a name. . . . Here's for the plain old Adam, the simple genuine self against the whole world" (J 4:141). In the "Self-Reliance" passage, this vigorous Adam becomes a "sad self, unrelenting, identical."

In 1835 Emerson remarked, "So I read the history of all men in myself . . . I travel faster than you. In my chimney corner I see more, & anticipate all your wonders" (J 5:107).

81 "Some influence or agency of enormous power" (OED).

82 Emerson remarked in his Journal (October 1838), "In my weak hours I look fondly to Europe & think how gladly I would live in Florence & Rome"; but then he added, "I defy these leanings, these lingering looks *behind*, these fleshpots of Egypt, & feel that my duty is my place . . . In peace, in ease, in custom, in tradition, the soul sleeps, & lets itself be mastered & enslaved by the biggest tradition, the oldest city" (J 7:118).

83 Doric, order of classical Greek architecture (exemplified by the Parthenon); Gothic, major form of medieval architecture, seen in many monumental European cathedrals.

84 In his lecture "Ethics" (1837), from his series "The Philosophy of History," Emerson followed this command (after a few sentences) with "Be true to yourself. I have seen boys in their play put a shovel under the feet of one of their mates and trip him up. The boy standing on the shovel resembles the man's state who does not rely upon himself" (EL 2:151–152).

85    Benjamin Franklin (1706–1790), American founder, scientist, author, and politician; Francis Bacon (1561–1626), Renaissance scientist and author.

86    Phidias (5th century BCE), the greatest sculptor of classical Greece, directed the work on the Parthenon; the Egyptians were known for their massive building projects; Moses is said to have written the Torah, the first five books of the Hebrew Bible; Dante Alighieri (1265–1321) wrote the *Divine Comedy* (1307–1321), an epic journey through hell, purgatory, and heaven.

87    Alludes to the "cloven tongues" of fire that cause the disciples of Jesus to speak in different languages miraculously understood by all (Acts 2:1–8).

88    Emerson's adaptation of the German *Vorwelt* ("preworld"; often, archaic or ancestral past).

adopted talent of another, you have only an extemporaneous, half possession. That which each can do best, none but his Maker can teach him. No man yet knows what it is, nor can, till that person has exhibited it. Where is the master who could have taught Shakspeare? Where is the master who could have instructed Franklin, or Washington, or Bacon, or Newton?[85] Every great man is a unique. The Scipionism of Scipio is precisely that part he could not borrow. Shakspeare will never be made by the study of Shakspeare. Do that which is assigned you, and you cannot hope too much or dare too much. There is at this moment for you an utterance brave and grand as that of the colossal chisel of Phidias, or trowel of the Egyptians, or the pen of Moses, or Dante,[86] but different from all these. Not possibly will the soul all rich, all eloquent, with thousand-cloven tongue,[87] deign to repeat itself; but if you can hear what these patriarchs say, surely you can reply to them in the same pitch of voice: for the ear and the tongue are two organs of one nature. Abide in the simple and noble regions of thy life, obey thy heart, and thou shalt reproduce the Foreworld[88] again.

4. As our Religion, our Education, our Art look abroad, so does our spirit of society. All men plume themselves on the improvement of society, and no man improves.

Society never advances. It recedes as fast on one side as it gains on the other. It undergoes continual changes: it is barbarous, it is civilized, it is christianized, it is rich, it is scientific; but this change is not amelioration. For every thing that is given, something is taken. Society acquires new arts and loses old instincts. What a contrast between the well-clad, reading, writing, thinking American, with a watch, a pencil, and a bill of exchange in his pocket, and the naked New Zealander, whose property is a club, a spear, a mat, and an undivided twentieth of a shed to sleep under. But compare the health of the two men, and you shall see that the white man has lost his aboriginal strength. If the traveller tell us truly, strike the savage with a broad axe, and in a day or two the flesh shall unite and heal as if you struck the blow into soft pitch, and the same blow shall send the white to his grave.

The civilized man has built a coach, but has lost the use of his feet. He is supported on crutches, but lacks so much support of muscle. He has a fine Geneva watch, but he fails of the skill to tell the hour by the sun. A Greenwich nautical almanac he has, and so being sure of the information when he wants it, the man in the street does not know a star in the sky. The solstice he does not observe; the equinox he knows as little; and the whole bright calendar of the year is without a dial in his mind. His note-books impair his memory; his libraries overload his wit; the insurance office increases the number of accidents; and it may be a question whether machinery does not encumber; whether we have not lost by refinement some energy, by a christianity entrenched in establishments and forms, some vigor of wild virtue. For every stoic was a stoic; but in Christendom where is the Christian?

There is no more deviation in the moral standard than in the standard of height or bulk. No greater men are now than ever were. A singular equality may be observed between the great men of the first and of the last ages; nor can all the science, art, religion and philosophy of the nineteenth century avail to educate greater men than Plutarch's heroes, three or four and twenty centuries ago. Not in time is the race progressive. Phocion, Socrates, Anaxagoras, Diogenes,[89] are great men, but they leave no class. He who is really of their class will not be called by their name, but will be his own man, and, in his turn the founder of a sect. The arts and inventions of each period are only its costume, and do not invigorate men. The harm of the improved machinery may compensate its good. Hudson and Behring accomplished so much in their fishing-boats, as to astonish Parry and Franklin,[90] whose equipment exhausted the resources of science and art. Galileo, with an opera-glass, discovered a more splendid series of celestial phenomena than any one since. Columbus found the New World in an undecked boat. It is curious to see the periodical disuse and perishing of means and machinery which were introduced with loud laudation, a few years or centuries before. The great genius returns to essential man. We reckoned the improvements of the art of war among the triumphs of science, and yet Napoleon conquered Europe by the Bivouac, which consisted of falling back on naked valor, and disencumbering it of all aids. The Emperor held it impossible to make a perfect army, says Las Cases, "without abolishing our arms, magazines, commissaries, and carriages, until in imitation of the Roman custom, the soldier should receive his supply of corn, grind it in his hand-mill, and bake his bread himself."[91]

89    Anaxagoras (b. ca. 490 BCE), Greek Presocratic thinker; Diogenes the Cynic (ca. 404–323 BCE), iconoclastic Greek philosopher.

90    William Parry (1790–1855) and John Franklin (1786–1847), British explorers of the Arctic; Henry Hudson (d. ca. 1611), navigator and explorer of the Hudson River; Vitus Bering (1681–1741), Danish navigator who discovered the Bering Strait.

91    Emerson enthusiastically read the *Memorial of St. Helena* (1823) by Emmanuel de Las Cases (1766–1842), based on his talks with Napoleon.

92    Merely apparent.

93    Ali (ca. 599–661), son-in-law of the
prophet Muhammad, and leader of Islam; he
became a central figure for Shi'ite Muslims and
for Sufis. In his Journal (September 1840), Emerson cited "a noble sentence of Ali": "Thy lot
or portion of life is seeking after thee; therefore
be at rest from seeking after it" (J 7:400).

94    The Whigs were an American political
party between 1833 and 1856, formed in opposition to President Andrew Jackson (1767–1845)
and his Democratic party.

Society is a wave. The wave moves onward, but the water of which it is
composed, does not. The same particle does not rise from the valley to the
ridge. Its unity is only phenomenal.[92] The persons who make up a nation to-
day, next year die, and their experience with them.

And so the reliance on Property, including the reliance on governments
which protect it, is the want of self-reliance. Men have looked away from
themselves and at things so long, that they have come to esteem the religious, learned, and civil institutions, as guards of property, and they depre-
cate assaults on these, because they feel them to be assaults on property.
They measure their esteem of each other, by what each has, and not by what
each is. But a cultivated man becomes ashamed of his property, out of new
respect for his nature. Especially he hates what he has, if he see that it is
accidental,—came to him by inheritance, or gift, or crime; then he feels that
it is not having; it does not belong to him, has no root in him, and merely lies
there, because no revolution or no robber takes it away. But that which a
man is, does always by necessity acquire, and what the man acquires is living
property, which does not wait the beck of rulers, or mobs, or revolutions, or
fire, or storm, or bankruptcies, but perpetually renews itself wherever the
man breathes. "Thy lot or portion of life," said the Caliph Ali,[93] "is seeking
after thee; therefore be at rest from seeking after it." Our dependence on
these foreign goods leads us to our slavish respect for numbers. The political
parties meet in numerous conventions; the greater the concourse, and with
each new uproar of announcement, The delegation from Essex! The Democrats from New Hampshire! The Whigs[94] of Maine! the young patriot feels
himself stronger than before by a new thousand of eyes and arms. In like
manner the reformers summon conventions, and vote and resolve in multitude. Not so, O friends! will the God deign to enter and inhabit you, but by
a method precisely the reverse. It is only as a man puts off all foreign support, and stands alone, that I see him to be strong and to prevail. He is weaker
by every recruit to his banner. Is not a man better than a town? Ask nothing
of men, and in the endless mutation, thou only firm column must presently
appear the upholder of all that surrounds thee. He who knows that power is
inborn, that he is weak because he has looked for good out of him and elsewhere, and so perceiving, throws himself unhesitatingly on his thought, instantly rights himself, stands in the erect position, commands his limbs,

works miracles; just as a man who stands on his feet is stronger than a man who stands on his head.

So use all that is called Fortune. Most men gamble with her, and gain all, and lose all, as her wheel[95] rolls. But do thou leave as unlawful these winnings, and deal with Cause and Effect, the chancellors of God. In the Will work and acquire, and thou hast chained the wheel of Chance, and shalt sit hereafter out of fear from her rotations. A political victory, a rise of rents, the recovery of your sick, or the return of your absent friend, or some other favorable event, raises your spirits, and you think good days are preparing for you. Do not believe it. Nothing can bring you peace but yourself. Nothing can bring you peace but the triumph of principles.[96]

95    The Middle Ages and Renaissance pictured the goddess Fortune holding a wheel.

96    "Self-Reliance," studded with epigrams, turns in its last line to aphorism, a more mysterious genre. In this final sentence, Emerson suggests that the essay has been concerned with peace rather than with victory, in contrast to his earlier statement that "a man or a company of men plastic and permeable to principles, by the law of nature must overpower and ride all cities, nations, kings, rich men, poets, who are not." Now, the aim is not overpowering achievement but rather recognition of fortune's law—and through such recognition, immunity from fortune.

Thomas Carlyle (1795–1881). "He is a worshipper of strength, heedless much whether its present phase be divine or diabolic," wrote Emerson.

# Circles

*The tenth essay in Emerson's* Essays, *published in 1841. "Circles" is the most radical and far-reaching of the essays in the book. Emerson's assertion that "the universe is fluid and volatile" presages later statements by the German philosopher Friedrich Nietzsche (1844–1900), an admirer of Emerson and an aggressive questioner of our desire for fixed and final truths. In our day, Emerson has been claimed as a poststructuralist intent on dissolving all certainties, as well as a pragmatist who celebrates the human capacity to grasp and manipulate the world (however unreliable the world may be).*

1    Emerson pictures human beings, who are "fast" (adherent) to the world's surface, as "ephemerals" (creatures of a day). Stuck to the "outside," they see only external features.

2    Their act of scanning. Emerson's prefatory poem was added in the 1847 edition of the *Essays.*

3    The American thinker Sampson Reed (1800–1880) in *The Growth of the Mind* (1826), one of Emerson's favorite books, commented

*(continued)*

Nature centres into balls,
And her proud ephemerals,
Fast to surface and outside,[1]
Scan the profile of the sphere;
Knew they what that[2] signified,
A new genesis were here.

The eye is the first circle; the horizon which it forms is the second; and throughout nature this primary figure is repeated without end.[3] It is the highest emblem[4] in the cipher of the world. St. Augustine described the nature of God as a circle whose centre was everywhere, and its circumference nowhere.[5] We are all our lifetime reading the copious sense of this first of forms. One moral we have already deduced in considering the circular or compensatory[6] character of every human action. Another analogy we shall now trace; that every action admits of being outdone. Our life is an apprenticeship to the truth, that around every circle another can be drawn; that there is no end in nature, but every end is a beginning; that there is always another dawn risen on mid-noon, and under every deep a lower deep opens.[7]

   This fact, as far as it symbolizes the moral fact of the Unattainable, the flying Perfect, around which the hands of man can never meet, at once the

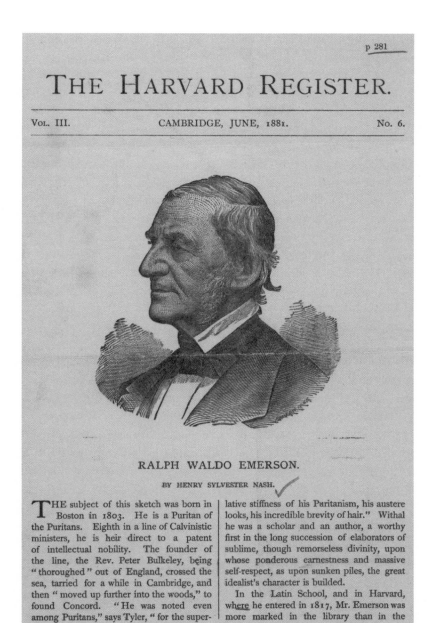

Article on Emerson by Henry Sylvester Nash, from the *Harvard Register* (1881).

that "the eye appears to be the point at which the united rays of the sun within and the sun without, converge to an expression of unity." "Circles" assiduously links the eye and the I: the engine of perception and the self that, in a certain mood, can be reduced to its ruling perspective.

4 Significant pictorial device, often requiring decoding, like a cipher.

5 This idea actually appears, not in the works of St. Augustine (354–430), but in a twelfth-century treatise attributed to a legendary author, Hermes Trismegistus; it appears as well in the texts of Alain de Lille (ca. 1128–1203) and many later authors, including Nicholas of Cusa (1401–1464) and Blaise Pascal (1623–1662). Emerson wrote in his Journal (July 2, 1835), "Can never go out of the sphere of truth whose centre is every where & whose circumference is nowhere" (J 5:57); he had found this variant formula in the *Theory of the Ideal or Intelligible World* (1701) by the English Platonist John Norris (1657–1711).

6 In the essay "Compensation," Emerson describes "the perfect compensation of the universe": "The absolute balance of Give and Take, the doctrine that every thing has its price."

7 In the essay "Politics," Emerson wrote, "We think our civilization near its meridian, but we are yet only at the cock-crowing and the morning star." Here, in "Circles," Emerson draws on John Milton's (1608–1674) *Paradise Lost* (1667): Milton's Satan, convinced of his damnation, laments, "Myself am hell; / And in the lowest deep a lower deep / Still threatning to devour me opens wide" (4:55–57); and the angel Raphael, sent to counsel the unfallen Adam and Eve, blazes in Eden like "another

*(continued)*

morn / Risen on mid-noon" (5:310–311). In his Bunker Hill oration (1825), the American orator Daniel Webster (1782–1852) exclaimed, "On the light of Liberty you saw arise the light of Peace, 'like another morn, / Risen on mid-noon.'" Emerson used the lines from *Paradise Lost* at the end of his essay "Montaigne," and in his Journal as well: "What a benefit if a rule could be given whereby the mind could at any moment *east* itself, & find the sun. But long after we have thought we were recovered & sane, light breaks in upon us & we find we have yet had no sane moment. Another morn rises on mid noon" (May 13, 1835, J 5:38).

8       In a letter to Sarah Ann Clarke (October 9, 1840), Emerson outlined a more conservative circular theory: "Nature—what is it but the circumference of which I am the centre, the outside of my inside, object whereof I am subject? . . . This external unity & kindred of production and producer is the account of that feeling of self recognition we always find in the landscape. Strange if we were not domesticated in the house we have built, in the child we have begotten" (L 7:417–418).

9       Lasting for centuries.

10      Emerson wrote in his Journal (1838), "Who can see the river in a meditative hour, & not be reminded of the flux of all things? Heat & Light answer to Love & Knowledge. The circles in the disturbed water, are the beautiful type of all influence" (J 12:46).

inspirer and the condemner of every success, may conveniently serve us to connect many illustrations of human power in every department.

There are no fixtures in nature. The universe is fluid and volatile. Permanence is but a word of degrees. Our globe seen by God, is a transparent law, not a mass of facts. The law dissolves the fact and holds it fluid.[8] Our culture is the predominance of an idea which draws after it this train of cities and institutions. Let us rise into another idea: they will disappear. The Greek sculpture is all melted away, as if it had been statues of ice: here and there a solitary figure or fragment remaining, as we see flecks and scraps of snow left in cold dells and mountain clefts, in June and July. For, the genius that created it, creates now somewhat else. The Greek letters last a little longer, but are already passing under the same sentence, and tumbling into the inevitable pit which the creation of new thought opens for all that is old. The new continents are built out of the ruins of an old planet: the new races fed out of the decomposition of the foregoing. New arts destroy the old. See the investment of capital in aqueducts, made useless by hydraulics; fortifications, by gunpowder; roads and canals, by railways; sails, by steam; steam by electricity.

You admire this tower of granite, weathering the hurts of so many ages. Yet a little waving hand built this huge wall, and that which builds, is better than that which is built. The hand that built, can topple it down much faster. Better than the hand, and nimbler, was the invisible thought which wrought through it, and thus ever behind the coarse effect, is a fine cause, which, being narrowly seen, is itself the effect of a finer cause. Every thing looks permanent until its secret is known. A rich estate appears to women a firm and lasting fact; to a merchant, one easily created out of any materials, and easily lost. An orchard, good tillage, good grounds, seem a fixture, like a gold mine, or a river, to a citizen; but to a large farmer, not much more fixed than the state of the crop. Nature looks provokingly stable and secular,[9] but it has a cause like all the rest; and when once I comprehend that, will these fields stretch so immovably wide, these leaves hang so individually considerable? Permanence is a word of degrees. Every thing is medial. Moons are no more bounds to spiritual power than bat-balls.[10]

The key to every man is his thought. Sturdy and defying though he look, he has a helm which he obeys, which is, the idea after which all his facts are classified. He can only be reformed by showing him a new idea which commands his own.[11] The life of man is a self-evolving circle, which, from a ring imperceptibly small, rushes on all sides outwards to new and larger circles, and that without end. The extent to which this generation of circles, wheel without wheel will go, depends on the force or truth of the individual soul. For, it is the inert effort of each thought having formed itself into a circular wave of circumstance,—as, for instance, an empire, rules of an art, a local usage, a religious rite,—to heap itself on that ridge, and to solidify, and hem in the life. But if the soul is quick and strong, it bursts over that boundary on all sides, and expands another orbit on the great deep, which also runs up into a high wave, with attempt again to stop and to bind. But the heart refuses to be imprisoned; in its first and narrowest pulses, it already tends outward with a vast force, and to immense and innumerable expansions.

Every ultimate fact is only the first of a new series. Every general law only a particular fact of some more general law presently to disclose itself.[12] There is no outside, no enclosing wall, no circumference to us. The man finishes his story,—how good! how final! how it puts a new face on all things! He fills the sky. Lo! on the other side rises also a man, and draws a circle around the circle we had just pronounced the outline of the sphere. Then already is our first speaker, not man, but only a first speaker. His only redress is forthwith to draw a circle outside of his antagonist. And so men do by themselves. The result of to-day which haunts the mind and cannot be escaped, will presently be abridged into a word, and the principle that seemed to explain nature, will itself be included as one example of a bolder generalization. In the thought of to-morrow there is a power to upheave all thy creed, all the creeds, all the literatures of the nations, and marshal thee to a heaven which no epic dream has yet depicted. Every man is not so much a workman in the world, as he is a suggestion of that he should be. Men walk as prophecies of the next age.

Step by step we scale this mysterious ladder: the steps are actions; the new prospect is power. Every several result is threatened and judged by that which follows. Every one seems to be contradicted by the new; it is only limited by the new. The new statement is always hated by the old, and, to those dwelling in the old, comes like an abyss of skepticism. But the eye soon gets wonted to it, for the eye and it are effects of one cause; then its innocency

11    Emerson wrote in his Journal (1840–1841), "What avail marble brows & inscrutable purposes? Bring in a new man with a truth that commands the last & the marble brow becomes a rippled wave the inscrutable purposes are exposed & scattered" (J 7:531).

12    In his Journal (1845–1846), Emerson noted, "Every generalization shows the way to a larger generalization. What is that game called which we play with children, piling hand upon hand? Generalizing? It is a trick very quickly taught" (J 9:323).

13    In his Journal (1851), Emerson wrote, "Mediator mediation There is nothing else; there is no Immediate known to us. Cloud on cloud, degree on degree, remove one coat, one lamina, and another coat or lamina just like it is the result,—to be also removed. When the symbol is explained the new truth turns out to be only a symbol of ulterior truth. The Judgment Day is in reality the Past" (J 11:424).

14    Residue.

15    A mood is, by definition, a temporary state. After a time it must yield to other moods; but for now, intent on itself, it resists, or disbelieves, in them. Such blindness, Emerson suggests, is also a form of strength. Emerson may also be thinking of the archaic sense of mood: "mind, thought, will" (OED); for him, a mood seems to have a mind of its own. The novel *Moods* (1864) by Louisa May Alcott (1832–1888), who knew Emerson as a girl in Concord, contains an epigraph from Emerson's "Experience": "Life is a train of moods like a string of beads; and as we pass through them they prove to be many colored lenses, which paint the world their own hue, and each shows us only what lies in its own focus."

16    Summit.

17    A double meaning: reveals itself; proves false to itself.

18    In his Journal (1845), Emerson wrote, "Nearness is the aim of all love. An exchange of nobleness, is it also. But if you would sublimate it, I think you must keep it hard & cold, and with a Dantean leanness. We strangely stand, —souls do,—on the very edges of their own spheres, leaning tiptoe towards & into the adjoining sphere" (J 9:228; Dante Alighieri [ca. 1265–1321], Italian poet, author of the *Divine Comedy* [1308–1321]) .

and benefit appear, and, presently, all its energy spent, it pales and dwindles before the revelation of the new hour.[13]

Fear not the new generalization. Does the fact look crass and material, threatening to degrade thy theory of spirit? Resist it not; it goes to refine and raise thy theory of matter just as much.

There are no fixtures to men, if we appeal to consciousness. Every man supposes himself not to be fully understood; and if there is any truth in him, if he rests at last on the divine soul, I see not how it can be otherwise. The last chamber, the last closet, he must feel, was never opened; there is always a residuum[14] unknown, unanalyzable. That is, every man believes that he has a greater possibility.

Our moods do not believe in each other.[15] To-day, I am full of thoughts, and can write what I please. I see no reason why I should not have the same thought, the same power of expression to-morrow. What I write, whilst I write it, seems the most natural thing in the world: but, yesterday, I saw a dreary vacuity in this direction in which now I see so much; and a month hence, I doubt not, I shall wonder who he was that wrote so many continuous pages. Alas for this infirm faith, this will not strenuous, this vast ebb of a vast flow! I am God in nature; I am a weed by the wall.

The continual effort to raise himself above himself, to work a pitch[16] above his last height, betrays itself[17] in a man's relations. We thirst for approbation, yet cannot forgive the approver. The sweet of nature is love; yet if I have a friend, I am tormented by my imperfections. The love of me accuses the other party. If he were high enough to slight me, then could I love him, and rise by my affection to new heights.[18] A man's growth is seen in the successive choirs of his friends. For every friend whom he loses for truth, he gains a better. I thought, as I walked in the woods and mused on my friends, why should I play with them this game of idolatry? I know and see too well, when not voluntarily blind, the speedy limits of persons called high and worthy. Rich, noble, and great they are by the liberality of our speech, but truth is sad. O blessed Spirit, whom I forsake for these, they are not thou! Every personal consideration that we allow, costs us heavenly state. We sell the thrones of angels for a short and turbulent pleasure.

How often must we learn this lesson? Men cease to interest us when we find their limitations. The only sin is limitation. As soon as you once come up with a man's limitations, it is all over with him. Has he talents? has he enterprises? has he knowledge? it boots not. Infinitely alluring and attractive was he to you yesterday, a great hope, a sea to swim in; now, you have found his shores, found it a pond, and you care not if you never see it again.[19]

Each new step we take in thought reconciles twenty seemingly discordant facts, as expressions of one law. Aristotle and Plato are reckoned the respective heads of two schools. A wise man will see that Aristotle Platonizes.[20] By going one step farther back in thought, discordant opinions are reconciled, by being seen to be two extremes of one principle, and we can never go so far back as to preclude a still higher vision.

Beware when the great God lets loose a thinker on this planet. Then all things are at risk. It is as when a conflagration[21] has broken out in a great city, and no man knows what is safe, or where it will end. There is not a piece of science, but its flank may be turned to-morrow; there is not any literary reputation, not the so-called eternal names of fame, that may not be revised and condemned. The very hopes of man, the thoughts of his heart, the religion of nations, the manners and morals of mankind, are all at the mercy of a new generalization. Generalization is always a new influx of the divinity into the mind. Hence the thrill that attends it.

Valor consists in the power of self-recovery, so that a man cannot have his flank turned, cannot be outgeneralled, but put him where you will, he stands. This can only be by his preferring truth to his past apprehension of truth; and his alert acceptance of it from whatever quarter; the intrepid conviction that his laws, his relations to society, his christianity, his world, may at any time be superseded and decease.[22]

There are degrees in idealism. We learn first to play with it academically, as the magnet was once a toy. Then we see in the heyday of youth and poetry that it may be true, that it is true in gleams and fragments. Then, its countenance waxes stern and grand, and we see that it must be true. It now shows itself ethical and practical. We learn that God IS; that he is in me; and that all things are shadows of him. The idealism of Berkeley[23] is only a crude statement of the idealism of Jesus, and that, again, is a crude statement of the fact that all nature is the rapid efflux of goodness executing and organizing itself. Much more obviously is history and the state of the world at any one time, directly dependent on the intellectual classification then existing in the

19    In his essay "The Poet," Emerson expresses a similar rhythm of expectation and disappointment in the new talent.

20    Aristotle (384–322 BCE) was the student of Plato (429–347 BCE), and often seen as his opposite, with Plato being the heaven-bent idealist and Aristotle the this-worldly thinker. In the Journal passage from which these sentences are drawn, Emerson also commented, "For these two years back, I incline more to show the insignificance of these differences as they melt into the Unity which is the base of them all" (August 20, 1837, J 5:370).

21    Vast, ruinous fire.

22    In his Journal (1863?) Emerson wrote, "The Arabs measure distance by horizons, & scholars must" (J 15:30), and in July 1843, "'Tis high time we should have a bible that should be no provincial record, but should open the history of the planet, and bind all tendencies and dwarf all the Epics & philosophies we have. It will have no Books of Ruth & Esther, no Song of Solomon, nor excellent, sophistical Pauls." He added, "As if any taste or imagination could supply fidelity. The old duty is the old God" (J 8:438).

23    George Berkeley, bishop of Cloyne (1685–1753), Anglo-Irish philosopher who argued that things exist only insofar as they are perceived; that there are no material objects as such, only ideas of them in the mind. This doctrine is known as idealism (in contrast to materialism).

192

CIRCLES

24    Limits.

25    Communal land.

26    During Pentecost (Acts 2:1–8), the Holy Spirit descended upon Jesus' followers (in the "cloven flame" that Emerson mentions); each began speaking in his native tongue, yet all were understood.

27    Daily.

28    From the ancient empire of Carthage.

minds of men. The things which are dear to men at this hour, are so on account of the ideas which have emerged on their mental horizon, and which cause the present order of things as a tree bears its apples. A new degree of culture would instantly revolutionize the entire system of human pursuits.

Conversation is a game of circles. In conversation we pluck up the *termini*[24] which bound the common[25] of silence on every side. The parties are not to be judged by the spirit they partake and even express under this Pentecost.[26] To-morrow they will have receded from this high-water mark. To-morrow you shall find them stooping under the old packsaddles. Yet let us enjoy the cloven flame whilst it glows on our walls. When each new speaker strikes a new light, emancipates us from the oppression of the last speaker, to oppress us with the greatness and exclusiveness of his own thought, then yields us to another redeemer, we seem to recover our rights, to become men. O what truths profound and executable only in ages and orbs, are supposed in the announcement of every truth! In common hours, society sits cold and statuesque. We all stand waiting, empty,—knowing, possibly, that we can be full, surrounded by mighty symbols which are not symbols to us, but prose and trivial toys. Then cometh the god, and converts the statues into fiery men, and by a flash of his eye burns up the veil which shrouded all things, and the meaning of the very furniture, of cup and saucer, of chair and clock and tester, is manifest. The facts which loomed so large in the fogs of yesterday,—property, climate, breeding, personal beauty, and the like, have strangely changed their proportions. All that we reckoned settled, shakes and rattles; and literatures, cities, climates, religions, leave their foundations, and dance before our eyes. And yet here again see the swift circumscription. Good as is discourse, silence is better, and shames it. The length of the discourse indicates the distance of thought betwixt the speaker and the hearer. If they were at a perfect understanding in any part, no words would be necessary thereon. If at one in all parts, no words would be suffered.

Literature is a point outside of our hodiernal[27] circle, through which a new one may be described. The use of literature is to afford us a platform whence we may command a view of our present life, a purchase by which we may move it. We fill ourselves with ancient learning; install ourselves the best we can in Greek, in Punic,[28] in Roman houses, only that we may wiselier see French, English, and American houses and modes of living. In like manner, we see literature best from the midst of wild nature, or from the din of affairs, or from a high religion. The field cannot be well seen from within the field. The astronomer must have his diameter of the earth's orbit as a base to find the parallax[29] of any star.

Therefore, we value the poet. All the argument, and all the wisdom, is not in the encyclopedia, or the treatise on metaphysics, or the Body of Divinity, but in the sonnet or the play. In my daily work I incline to repeat my old steps, and do not believe in remedial force, in the power of change and reform. But some Petrarch or Ariosto,[30] filled with the new wine of his imagination, writes me an ode, or a brisk romance, full of daring thought and action. He smites and arouses me with his shrill tones, breaks up my whole chain of habits, and I open my eye on my own possibilities. He claps wings to the sides of all the solid old lumber of the world, and I am capable once more of choosing a straight path in theory and practice.

We have the same need to command a view of the religion of the world. We can never see christianity from the catechism:—from the pastures, from a boat in the pond, from amidst the songs of wood-birds, we possibly may. Cleansed by the elemental light and wind, steeped in the sea of beautiful forms which the field offers us, we may chance to cast a right glance back upon biography. Christianity is rightly dear to the best of mankind; yet was there never a young philosopher whose breeding had fallen into the christian church, by whom that brave text of Paul's, was not specially prized:— "Then shall also the Son be subject unto Him who put all things under him, that God may be all in all."[31] Let the claims and virtues of persons be never so great and welcome, the instinct of man presses eagerly onward to the impersonal and illimitable, and gladly arms itself against the dogmatism of bigots with this generous word, out of the book itself.

The natural world may be conceived of as a system of concentric circles, and we now and then detect in nature slight dislocations, which apprize us that this surface on which we now stand, is not fixed, but sliding. These manifold tenacious qualities, this chemistry and vegetation, these metals and animals, which seem to stand there for their own sake, are means and methods only,—are words of God, and as fugitive as other words. Has the naturalist or chemist learned his craft, who has explored the gravity of atoms and the elective affinities,[32] who has not yet discerned the deeper law whereof

29   True position. In his Journal (1832) Emerson referred to the "great *parallax* in human nature ascertained by observing it from different states of mind" (J 4:22).

30   Italian poets: Francesco Petrarca, known as Petrarch (1304–1374), and Ludovico Ariosto (1474–1533).

31   I Corinthians 15:28.

32   Chemical bonds.

this is only a partial or approximate statement, namely, that like draws to like; and that the goods which belong to you, gravitate to you, and need not be pursued with pains and cost? Yet is that statement approximate also, and not final. Omnipresence is a higher fact. Not through subtle, subterranean channels, need friend and fact be drawn to their counterpart, but, rightly considered, these things proceed from the eternal generation of the soul. Cause and effect are two sides of one fact.

The same law of eternal procession ranges all that we call the virtues, and extinguishes each in the light of a better. The great man will not be prudent in the popular sense; all his prudence will be so much deduction from his grandeur. But it behoves each to see when he sacrifices prudence, to what

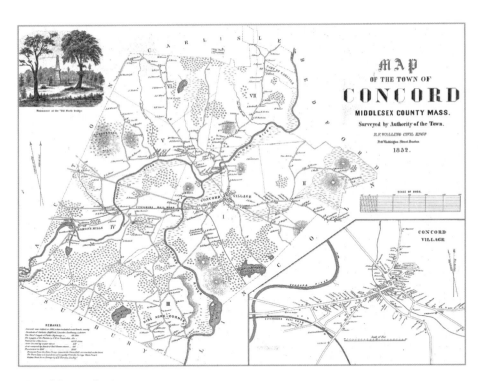

Map of Concord, 1852.

god he devotes it; if to ease and pleasure, he had better be prudent still: if to a great trust, he can well spare his mule and panniers,[33] who has a winged chariot instead. Geoffrey draws on his boots to go through the woods, that his feet may be safer from the bite of snakes; Aaron never thinks of such a peril. In many years, neither is harmed by such an accident. Yet it seems to me that with every precaution you take against such an evil, you put yourself into the power of the evil. I suppose that the highest prudence is the lowest prudence. Is this too sudden a rushing from the centre to the verge of our orbit? Think how many times we shall fall back into pitiful calculations, before we take up our rest in the great sentiment, or make the verge of to-day the new centre. Besides, your bravest sentiment is familiar to the humblest men. The poor and the low have their way of expressing the last facts of philosophy as well as you. "Blessed be nothing," and "the worse things are, the better they are," are proverbs which express the transcendentalism of common life.

One man's justice is another's injustice; one man's beauty, another's ugliness; one man's wisdom, another's folly; as one beholds the same objects from a higher point. One man thinks justice consists in paying debts, and has no measure in his abhorrence of another who is very remiss in this duty, and makes the creditor wait tediously. But that second man has his own way of looking at things; asks himself, which debt must I pay first, the debt to the rich, or the debt to the poor? the debt of money, or the debt of thought to mankind, of genius to nature? For you, O broker, there is no other principle but arithmetic. For me, commerce is of trivial import; love, faith, truth of character, the aspiration of man, these are sacred: nor can I detach one duty, like you, from all other duties, and concentrate my forces mechanically on the payment of moneys. Let me live onward: you shall find that, though slower, the progress of my character will liquidate all these debts without injustice to higher claims. If a man should dedicate himself to the payment of notes, would not this be injustice? Does he owe no debt but money? And are all claims on him to be postponed to a landlord's or a banker's?

There is no virtue which is final; all are initial. The virtues of society are vices of the saint. The terror of reform is the discovery that we must cast

33    Baskets carried on the sides of a pack animal.

34    From *Night Thoughts* (1742–1746) by the
English poet Edward Young (1683–1765).

35    Skepticism: the ancient doctrine that
since certainty is impossible, we must suspend
judgment.

36    Emerson probably remembers the saying
of Jesus (Luke 20:17), "The stone which the
builders rejected, the same is become the head
of the corner" (quoting Psalm 118:22). The
critic Barbara Packer observes that "there is
something alien in the tone of this passage;
its strangely hearty mockery reminds one of
Carlyle" (Emerson's friend the Scottish writer
Thomas Carlyle [1795–1881]).

37    Saccharine: sweet and optimistic in sentiment; vegetable: live, growing. In his lecture
"The Method of Nature" (1841), Emerson remarked that "total nature is growing like a field
of maize in July; is becoming somewhat else; is
in rapid metamorphosis."

38    A defiantly evasive response to the reader's objection in the previous paragraph. Emerson also considers the strength of whims in
"Self-Reliance," where he announces, "I would
write on the lintels of the door-post, Whim."

away our virtues, or what we have always esteemed such, into the same pit
that has consumed our grosser vices.

> "Forgive his crimes, forgive his virtues too,
> Those smaller faults, half converts to the right."[34]

It is the highest power of divine moments that they abolish our contritions also. I accuse myself of sloth and unprofitableness, day by day; but
when these waves of God flow into me, I no longer reckon lost time. I no
longer poorly compute my possible achievement by what remains to me of
the month or the year; for these moments confer a sort of omnipresence and
omnipotence, which asks nothing of duration, but sees that the energy of the
mind is commensurate with the work to be done, without time.

And thus, O circular philosopher, I hear some reader exclaim, you
have arrived at a fine pyrrhonism,[35] at an equivalence and indifferency of all
actions, and would fain teach us, that, *if we are true*, forsooth, our crimes may
be lively stones out of which we shall construct the temple of the true
God.[36]

I am not careful to justify myself. I own I am gladdened by seeing the
predominance of the saccharine principle throughout vegetable[37] nature, and
not less by beholding in morals that unrestrained inundation of the principle
of good into every chink and hole that selfishness has left open, yea, into
selfishness and sin itself; so that no evil is pure, nor hell itself without its extreme satisfactions. But lest I should mislead any when I have my own head,
and obey my whims, let me remind the reader that I am only an experimenter. Do not set the least value on what I do, or the least discredit on what
I do not, as if I pretended to settle anything as true or false. I unsettle all
things. No facts are to me sacred; none are profane; I simply experiment, an
endless seeker, with no Past at my back.[38]

Yet this incessant movement and progression, which all things partake, could never become sensible to us, but by contrast to some principle of
fixture or stability in the soul. Whilst the eternal generation of circles proceeds, the eternal generator abides. That central life is somewhat superior
to creation, superior to knowledge and thought, and contains all its circles.
Forever it labors to create a life and thought as large and excellent as itself,

suggesting to our thought a certain development, as if that which is made, instructs how to make a better.

Thus there is no sleep, no pause, no preservation, but all things renew, germinate, and spring. Why should we import rags and relics into the new hour? Nature abhors the old, and old age seems the only disease: all others run into this one. We call it by many names,—fever, intemperance, insanity, stupidity, and crime: they are all forms of old age: they are rest, conservatism, appropriation, inertia, not newness, not the way onward. We grizzle every day. I see no need of it. Whilst we converse with what is above us, we do not grow old, but grow young. Infancy, youth, receptive, aspiring, with religious eye looking upward, counts itself nothing, and abandons itself to the instruction flowing from all sides. But the man and woman of seventy[39] assume to know all, they have outlived their hope, they renounce aspiration, accept the actual for the necessary, and talk down to the young. Let them then become organs of the Holy Ghost; let them be lovers; let them behold truth; and their eyes are uplifted, their wrinkles smoothed, they are perfumed again with hope and power. This old age ought not to creep on a human mind. In nature, every moment is new; the past is always swallowed and forgotten; the coming only is sacred. Nothing is secure but life, transition, the energizing spirit. No love can be bound by oath or covenant to secure it against a higher love. No truth so sublime but it may be trivial tomorrow in the light of new thoughts. People wish to be settled: only as far as they are unsettled, is there any hope for them.

Life is a series of surprises. We do not guess to-day the mood, the pleasure, the power of to-morrow, when we are building up our being. Of lower states,—of acts of routine and sense,—we can tell somewhat; but the masterpieces of God, the total growths and universal movements of the soul, he hideth; they are incalculable. I can know that truth is divine and helpful, but how it shall help me, I can have no guess, for, *so to be* is the sole inlet of *so to know*. The new position of the advancing man has all the powers of the old, yet has them all new. It carries in its bosom all the energies of the past, yet is itself an exhalation of the morning. I cast away in this new moment all my once hoarded knowledge, as vacant and vain. Now, for the first time, seem I to know any thing rightly. The simplest words,—we do not know what they mean, except when we love and aspire.

39    Seventy years was often considered the allotted span of human life, because of Psalm 90:10: "The days of our years are threescore years and ten."

40    Eternal.

41    Oliver Cromwell (1599–1658) ruled
England as Lord Protector (1653–1658). Cromwell's statement, made to the French statesman
Pompone de Bellièvre (1606–1657), is recorded
in the *Memoirs* of Jean François Paul de Gondi,
cardinal de Retz (1613–1679).

42    An odd and stimulating conclusion, as
Emerson recognizes the trivial and the merely
imitative forms of intoxication that may take
the place of the truly creative ones. Emerson
also discusses such forms of "animal exhilaration" in "The Poet."

The difference between talents and character is adroitness to keep the
old and trodden round, and power and courage to make a new road to new
and better goals. Character makes an overpowering present, a cheerful, determined hour, which fortifies all the company, by making them see that
much is possible and excellent, that was not thought of. Character dulls the
impression of particular events. When we see the conqueror, we do not think
much of any one battle or success. We see that we had exaggerated the difficulty. It was easy to him. The great man is not convulsible or tormentable;
events pass over him without much impression. People say sometimes, "See
what I have overcome; see how cheerful I am; see how completely I have
triumphed over these black events." Not if they still remind me of the black
event. True conquest is the causing the calamity to fade and disappear as an
early cloud of insignificant result in a history so large and advancing.

The one thing which we seek with insatiable desire, is to forget ourselves, to be surprised out of our propriety, to lose our sempiternal[40] memory,
and to do something without knowing how or why; in short, to draw a new
circle. Nothing great was ever achieved without enthusiasm. The way of life
is wonderful: it is by abandonment. The great moments of history are the
facilities of performance through the strength of ideas, as the works of genius and religion. "A man," said Oliver Cromwell, "never rises so high as
when he knows not whither he is going."[41] Dreams and drunkenness, the use
of opium and alcohol are the semblance and counterfeit of this oracular genius, and hence their dangerous attraction for men. For the like reason, they
ask the aid of wild passions, as in gaming and war, to ape in some manner
these flames and generosities of the heart.[42]

# The Poet

A moody child and wildly wise[1]
Pursued the game with joyful eyes,
Which chose, like meteors, their way,
And rived the dark with private ray:
They overleapt the horizon's edge,
Searched with Apollo's privilege;[2]
Through man, and woman, and sea, and star,
Saw the dance of nature forward far;
Through worlds, and races, and terms, and times,
Saw musical order, and pairing rhymes.

Olympian bards who sung
   Divine ideas below,[3]
Which always find us young,
   And always keep us so.

Those who are esteemed umpires[4] of taste, are often persons who have acquired some knowledge of admired pictures or sculptures, and have an inclination for whatever is elegant;[5] but if you inquire whether they are beautiful souls, and whether their own acts are like fair pictures, you learn that they are selfish and sensual. Their cultivation is local, as if you should rub a log of

*"The Poet" was an influential essay for American authors, including Walt Whitman (1819–1892) and Wallace Stevens (1879–1955). It opens Emerson's* Essays: Second Series (1844), *a book that is darker, more searching, and more skeptical than Emerson's first volume of essays. The death of Emerson's beloved five-year-old son, Waldo, in January 1842 contributed to the at times disillusioned mood of* Essays: Second Series, *which appeared on October 19, 1844 (that spring Lidian had given birth to a new Emerson son, Edward). "The Poet," with its radiant energy, belongs in spirit to the earlier book. The central figure of the essay represents a pervasive principle of our lives: expressiveness. On June 7, 1844, Emerson sent the essay to the poet Christopher Cranch (1813–1892) and wrote in his accompanying letter that it was "[a] topic so subtle & defying. . . . He must be the best mixed man in the Universe, or the universe will drive him crazy when he comes too near its secret" (L 7:599). "The Poet" began as a lecture in Emerson's 1841–1842 series on "The Times"; he revised it substantially in the next few years.*

   *Walt Whitman took from Emerson's essay the*
*(continued)*

*idea that the poet "stands among partial men for the complete man" and that "America is a poem in our eyes" (as Emerson put it). Whitman added an incarnational drive that made the profane holy, a sense that, if you "dismiss whatever insults your own soul . . . your very flesh shall be a great poem," along with a riotous spirit, a determination to "stand up for the stupid and crazy" (in the words of his 1855 Preface to* Leaves of Grass.

*In October 1844, when the second volume of Emerson's essays appeared, his daughter Ellen was almost six years old, Edith was three, and his infant son Edward about three months old.*

1    Compare the child in the epigraph to "Experience" (also in Emerson's 1844 *Essays*). In his Journal (November 1874?) Emerson wrote, "The secret of poetry is never explained, —is always new. . . . In every house a child that in mere play utters oracles, & knows not that they are such, 'Tis as easy as breath. 'Tis like this gravity, which holds the Universe together, & none knows what it is" (J 16:302).

2    Apollo was the Greek god of poetry; his privilege is the hereditary right passed down to the "moody child" (the adjective connotes feeling and state of mind, but also musical mode, since music accompanied Greek poetry).

3    To sing "divine ideas below" is to translate them from the realm of the Olympian gods to earthly terms; Emerson pictures this descent as a perpetual rejuvenation.

4    Judges.

5    Cultivated, select.

6    Lovers (of beauty): from the Latin *amare*, to love.

7    Pressing: from the Latin *instare*.

dry wood in one spot to produce fire, all the rest remaining cold. Their knowledge of the fine arts is some study of rules and particulars, or some limited judgment of color or form, which is exercised for amusement or for show. It is a proof of the shallowness of the doctrine of beauty, as it lies in the minds of our amateurs,[6] that men seem to have lost the perception of the instant[7] dependence of form upon soul. There is no doctrine of forms[8] in our philosophy. We were put into our bodies, as fire is put into a pan, to be carried about;[9] but there is no accurate adjustment between the spirit and the organ, much less is the latter the germination of the former. So in regard to other forms, the intellectual men do not believe in any essential dependence of the material world on thought and volition. Theologians think it a pretty air-castle to talk of the spiritual meaning of a ship or a cloud, of a city or a contract, but they prefer to come again to the solid ground of historical evidence; and even the poets are contented with a civil and conformed manner of living, and to write poems from the fancy,[10] at a safe distance from their own experience.[11] But the highest minds of the world have never ceased to explore the double meaning, or, shall I say, the quadruple, or the centuple, or much more manifold meaning, of every sensuous fact: Orpheus, Empedocles, Heraclitus, Plato, Plutarch, Dante, Swedenborg,[12] and the masters of sculpture, picture, and poetry. For we are not pans and barrows,[13] nor even porters of the fire and torch-bearers, but children of the fire, made of it, and only the same divinity transmuted, and at two or three removes, when we know least about it. And this hidden truth, that the fountains whence all this river of Time, and its creatures, floweth, are intrinsically ideal and beautiful, draws us to the consideration of the nature and functions of the Poet, or the man of Beauty, to the means and materials he uses, and to the general aspect of the art in the present time.

The breadth of the problem is great, for the poet is representative.[14] He stands among partial men for the complete man, and apprises us not of his wealth, but of the commonwealth. The young man reveres men of genius, because, to speak truly, they are more himself than he is. They receive of the soul as he also receives, but they more. Nature enhances her beauty to the eye of loving men, from their belief that the poet is beholding her shows at the same time. He is isolated among his contemporaries, by truth and by his art, but with this consolation in his pursuits, that they will draw all men

Walt Whitman (1819–1892).

8    The Greek philosopher Plato (429–347 BCE) argued that forms or ideas, not the material world, are the ultimate reality and source of knowledge.

9    Such fire-pans are still used by campers.

10    A lower faculty of mere invention (as in the adjective "fanciful"), in contrast to the high imagination, which creates (Emerson frequently cites this distinction, adopted from the English poet and critic S. T. Coleridge [1772–1834]).

11    In his Journal (1845) Emerson wrote, "Is the solar system good art & architecture? . . . the poetic gift we want, but not the poetic profession . . . not cold spying & authorship. A poet who suffers the man to sit in him with the poet, as a charioteer with the hero in the Iliad" (J 9:268–269).

12    Orpheus, legendary Greek poet and founder of a religious cult; Empedocles (ca. 490–430 BCE), Greek philosopher who believed in two cosmic principles, love and strife—and who, according to legend, threw himself into an active volcano; Heraclitus (late 6th century BCE), Greek philosopher who argued for the unity of opposites (for example, that "strife is justice") and who believed that the cosmos is "ever-living fire"; Plutarch (ca. 46–ca. 122), Greek historian and essayist passionately admired by Emerson; Dante Alighieri (1265–1321), Italian poet, author of the *Divine Comedy* (1308–1321); Emanuel Swedenborg (1688–1772), Swedish mystic influential in Emerson's circle.

13    Wheelbarrows.

14    In his late, synthetic essay "Poetry and Imagination," assembled from fragments by Emerson's editor James Elliot Cabot (1821–1903), Emerson wrote, "The poet is represen-

*(continued)*

tative,—whole man, diamond-merchant, symbolizer, emancipator; in him the world projects a scribe's hand and writes adequate genesis."

15    Publicly announced.

16    More than merely material.

17    Distinctive, special. Emerson plays on the line from Sonnet 19 by the English poet John Milton (1608–1674): "They also serve who only stand and wait."

18    The phlegmatic type (one of the four classical humors, or temperaments) harbors an excess of moisture, and is rather sluggish—so antithetical to the fiery impulse that Emerson values.

19    Driving motions toward (us).

20    The living, sensing part.

21    Emerson here equates the Christian Trinity of Father, Son, and Holy Ghost with the classical gods who preside over the earth and sky (Jove), the underworld (Pluto), and the sea (Neptune)—and then to his own invented triad.

22    Exposed, visible (opposed to latent, or hidden).

23    Emerson wrote in his Journal (June–July 1846), "The Poet should instal himself & shove all usurpers from their chairs by electrifying mankind with the right tone, long wished for, never heard. The true centre thus appearing, all false centres are suddenly superseded, and grass grows in the Capitol" (J 9:432).

24    Ruler subject to a greater power (like a Persian satrap, or the governor of an American state).

sooner or later. For all men live by truth, and stand in need of expression. In love, in art, in avarice, in politics, in labor, in games, we study to utter our painful secret. The man is only half himself, the other half is his expression.

Notwithstanding this necessity to be published,[15] adequate expression is rare. I know not how it is that we need an interpreter; but the great majority of men seem to be minors, who have not yet come into possession of their own, or mutes, who cannot report the conversation they have had with nature. There is no man who does not anticipate a supersensual[16] utility in the sun, and stars, earth, and water. These stand and wait to render him a peculiar[17] service. But there is some obstruction, or some excess of phlegm[18] in our constitution, which does not suffer them to yield the due effect. Too feeble fall the impressions of nature on us to make us artists. Every touch should thrill. Every man should be so much an artist, that he could report in conversation what had befallen him. Yet, in our experience, the rays or appulses[19] have sufficient force to arrive at the senses, but not enough to reach the quick,[20] and compel the reproduction of themselves in speech. The poet is the person in whom these powers are in balance, the man without impediment, who sees and handles that which others dream of, traverses the whole scale of experience, and is representative of man, in virtue of being the largest power to receive and to impart.

For the Universe has three children, born at one time, which reappear, under different names, in every system of thought, whether they be called cause, operation, and effect; or, more poetically, Jove, Pluto, Neptune; or, theologically, the Father, the Spirit, and the Son; but which we will call here, the Knower, the Doer, and the Sayer.[21] These stand respectively for the love of truth, for the love of good, and for the love of beauty. These three are equal. Each is that which he is essentially, so that he cannot be surmounted or analyzed, and each of these three has the power of the others latent in him, and his own patent.[22]

The poet is the sayer, the namer, and represents beauty. He is a sovereign, and stands on the centre.[23] For the world is not painted, or adorned, but is from the beginning beautiful; and God has not made some beautiful things, but Beauty is the creator of the universe. Therefore the poet is not any permissive potentate,[24] but is emperor in his own right. Criticism is infested with a cant of materialism, which assumes that manual skill and activity is the first merit of all men, and disparages such as say and do not, over-looking the fact, that some men, namely, poets, are natural sayers, sent into the world to the end of expression, and confounds them with those whose province is action, but who quit it to imitate the sayers. But Homer's words are as costly and admirable to Homer, as Agamemnon's victories are to Agamemnon.[25] The poet does not wait for the hero or the sage, but, as they act and think primarily, so he writes primarily what will and must be spoken, reckoning the others, though primaries also, yet, in respect to him, second-aries and servants; as sitters or models in the studio of a painter, or as assis-tants who bring building materials to an architect.[26]

For poetry was all written before time was,[27] and whenever we are so finely organized that we can penetrate into that region where the air is mu-sic, we hear those primal warblings, and attempt to write them down, but we lose ever and anon a word, or a verse, and substitute something of our own, and thus miswrite the poem. The men of more delicate ear write down these cadences more faithfully, and these transcripts, though imperfect, become the songs of the nations.[28] For nature is as truly beautiful as it is good, or as it is reasonable, and must as much appear, as it must be done, or be known. Words and deeds are quite indifferent[29] modes of the divine energy. Words are also actions, and actions are a kind of words.

The sign and credentials of the poet are, that he announces that which no man foretold. He is the true and only doctor;[30] he knows and tells; he is the only teller of news, for he was present and privy to the appearance which he describes. He is a beholder of ideas, and an utterer of the necessary and causal. For we do not speak now of men of poetical talents, or of industry[31] and skill in metre, but of the true poet. I took part in a conversation the other day, concerning a recent writer of lyrics, a man of subtle mind, whose head appeared to be a music-box of delicate tunes and rhythms, and whose skill, and command of language, we could not sufficiently praise. But when the question arose, whether he was not only a lyrist, but a poet, we were obliged to confess that he is plainly a contemporary, not an eternal man. He does not stand out of our low limitations, like a Chimborazo under the line,[32] running up from the torrid base through all the climates of the globe, with belts of the herbage of every latitude on its high and mottled sides; but this genius is the landscape-garden of a modern house, adorned with foun-

25   Homer (ca. 9th century BCE), legendary author of Greek epics; Agamemnon, king of Mycenae featured in Homer's *Iliad*.

26   Emerson daringly envisions the poet or artist preceding and new-creating his subject.

27   Analogy to the Jewish idea, of which Emerson may have been aware, that the Torah (the first five books of the Bible) was written before the creation of the universe.

28   In his Journal (1844–1845) Emerson wrote, "A poet is so rare because he must be exquisitely fine & vital in his tissue, & at the same time immoveably centred" (J 9:179).

29   Not different.

30   Learned man.

31   Diligence. "Yes, we want a poet, the genuine poet of our time, no parrot, & no child," Emerson exclaimed in his Journal (1846; J 9:378).

32   Highest mountain in Ecuador, located below the equator ("under the line"). In his Journal (September 1836), Emerson wrote, "A great wit is, at any time, great solitude. A barn-yard is full of chirping & cackle, but no fowl claps wings on Chimborazo" (J 5:194).

33    A repeated bass line over which compos-
ers created new melodies in Renaissance and
Baroque music.

34    A famous statement; "argument" here
means subject-matter. In his later essay "Poetry
and Imagination," Emerson wrote, "Ask the
fact for the form. For a verse is not a vehicle to
carry a sentence as a jewel is carried in a case:
the verse must be alive, and inseparable from its
contents."

35    Ready to believe.

36    Shakespeare's Macbeth says, "My way of
life / Is fall'n into the sere, the yellow leaf"
(5.3.23): here this autumnal dryness afflicts the
author of *Macbeth*.

37    Northern lights.

38    A contrast similar to the one between
fancy and imagination (see note 10).

tains and statues, with well-bred men and women standing and sitting in
the walks and terraces. We hear, through all the varied music, the ground-
tone[33] of conventional life. Our poets are men of talents who sing, and not
the children of music. The argument is secondary, the finish of the verses is
primary.

For it is not metres, but a metre-making argument, that makes a
poem,[34]—a thought so passionate and alive, that, like the spirit of a plant or
an animal, it has an architecture of its own, and adorns nature with a new
thing. The thought and the form are equal in the order of time, but in the order of genesis the thought is prior to the form. The poet has a new thought:
he has a whole new experience to unfold; he will tell us how it was with him,
and all men will be the richer in his fortune. For, the experience of each new
age requires a new confession, and the world seems always waiting for its
poet. I remember, when I was young, how much I was moved one morning
by tidings that genius had appeared in a youth who sat near me at table. He
had left his work, and gone rambling none knew whither, and had written
hundreds of lines, but could not tell whether that which was in him was
therein told: he could tell nothing but that all was changed,—man, beast,
heaven, earth, and sea. How gladly we listened! how credulous![35] Society
seemed to be compromised. We sat in the aurora of a sunrise which was to
put out all the stars. Boston seemed to be at twice the distance it had the
night before, or was much farther than that. Rome,—what was Rome? Plutarch and Shakspeare were in the yellow leaf, and Homer no more should be
heard of.[36] It is much to know that poetry has been written this very day, under this very roof, by your side. What! that wonderful spirit has not expired!
these stony moments are still sparkling and animated! I had fancied that the
oracles were all silent, and nature had spent her fires, and behold! all night,
from every pore, these fine auroras[37] have been streaming. Every one has
some interest in the advent of the poet, and no one knows how much it may
concern him. We know that the secret of the world is profound, but who or
what shall be our interpreter, we know not. A mountain ramble, a new style
of face, a new person, may put the key into our hands. Of course, the value of
genius to us is in the veracity of its report. Talent may frolic and juggle; genius realizes and adds.[38] Mankind, in good earnest, have arrived so far in understanding themselves and their work, that the foremost watchman on the

peak announces his news. It is the truest word ever spoken, and the phrase will be the fittest, most musical, and the unerring voice of the world for that time.

All that we call sacred history attests that the birth of a poet is the principal event in chronology. Man, never so often deceived, still watches for the arrival of a brother who can hold him steady to a truth, until he has made it his own. With what joy I begin to read a poem, which I confide in as an inspiration! And now my chains are to be broken; I shall mount above these clouds and opaque airs in which I live,—opaque, though they seem transparent,—and from the heaven of truth I shall see and comprehend my relations. That will reconcile me to life, and renovate nature, to see trifles animated by a tendency, and to know what I am doing. Life will no more be a noise; now I shall see men and women, and know the signs by which they may be discerned from fools and satans.[39] This day shall be better than my birthday: then I became an animal: now I am invited into the science[40] of the real. Such is the hope, but the fruition is postponed. Oftener it falls, that this winged man, who will carry me into the heaven, whirls me into mists, then leaps and frisks about with me as it were from cloud to cloud, still affirming that he is bound heavenward; and I, being myself a novice, am slow in perceiving that he does not know the way into the heavens, and is merely bent that I should admire his skill to rise, like a fowl or a flying fish, a little way from the ground or the water; but the all-piercing, all-feeding, and ocular air of heaven, that man shall never inhabit. I tumble down again soon into my old nooks, and lead the life of exaggerations as before, and have lost some faith in the possibility of any guide who can lead me thither where I would be.[41]

But leaving these victims of vanity, let us, with new hope, observe how nature, by worthier impulses, has ensured the poet's fidelity to his office of announcement and affirming, namely, by the beauty of things, which becomes a new, and higher beauty, when expressed. Nature offers all her creatures to him as a picture-language. Being used as a type,[42] a second wonderful value appears in the object, far better than its old value, as the carpenter's stretched cord, if you hold your ear close enough, is musical in the breeze.[43] "Things more excellent than every image," says Jamblichus, "are expressed through images."[44] Things admit of being used as symbols, because nature is

39    Tempting adversaries (as in the Bible's book of Job).

40    Knowledge.

41    Emerson's imagined, abortive flight resembles that of the legendary Icarus, whose wings melted when he flew too close to the sun.

42    Significant emblem.

43    A play on the Aeolian harp beloved of Romantic poets (a stringed instrument set in a window and sounded by the breeze).

44    Jamblichus (or Iamblichus) (ca. 250–ca. 330) was a Neoplatonic philosopher.

45    From "An Hymne in Honour of Beau-
tie," by the English poet Edmund Spenser (ca.
1552–1599), author of *The Faerie Queene* (1590–
1596).

46    Based on sensory perception.

47    Line (train) of people following a royal or
noble person.

48    Greek Neoplatonic philosopher (412–
485), one of Emerson's favorite authors.

49    At the beginning of Genesis, God's spirit
or breath hovers over the face of the waters.

a symbol, in the whole, and in every part. Every line we can draw in the sand, has expression; and there is no body without its spirit or genius. All form is an effect of character; all condition, of the quality of the life; all harmony, of health; (and, for this reason, a perception of beauty should be sympathetic, or proper only to the good.) The beautiful rests on the foundations of the necessary. The soul makes the body, as the wise Spenser teaches:—

> "So every spirit, as it is most pure,
> And hath in it the more of heavenly light,
> So it the fairer body doth procure
> To habit in, and it more fairly dight,
> With cheerful grace and amiable sight.
> For, of the soul, the body form doth take,
> For soul is form, and doth the body make."[45]

Here we find ourselves, suddenly, not in a critical speculation, but in a holy place, and should go very warily and reverently. We stand before the secret of the world, there where Being passes into Appearance, and Unity into Variety.

The Universe is the externization of the soul. Wherever the life is, that bursts into appearance around it. Our science is sensual,[46] and therefore superficial. The earth, and the heavenly bodies, physics, and chemistry, we sensually treat, as if they were self-existent; but these are the retinue[47] of that Being we have. "The mighty heaven," said Proclus,[48] "exhibits, in its transfigurations, clear images of the splendor of intellectual perceptions; being moved in conjunction with the unapparent periods of intellectual natures." Therefore, science always goes abreast with the just elevation of the man, keeping step with religion and metaphysics; or, the state of science is an index of our self-knowledge. Since everything in nature answers to a moral power, if any phenomenon remains brute and dark, it is because the corresponding faculty in the observer is not yet active.

No wonder, then, if these waters be so deep, that we hover over them with a religious regard.[49] The beauty of the fable proves the importance of the sense; to the poet, and to all others; or, if you please, every man is so far a poet as to be susceptible of these enchantments of nature: for all men have the thoughts whereof the universe is the celebration. I find that the fascination resides in the symbol. Who loves nature? Who does not? Is it only poets, and men of leisure and cultivation, who live with her? No; but also hunters, farmers, grooms,[50] and butchers, though they express their affection in their choice of life, and not in their choice of words. The writer wonders what the coachman or the hunter values in riding, in horses, and dogs. It is not superficial qualities. When you talk with him, he holds these at as slight a rate as you. His worship is sympathetic; he has no definitions, but he is commanded in nature, by the living power which he feels to be there present. No imitation, or playing of these things, would content him; he loves the earnest[51] of the north wind, of rain, of stone, and wood, and iron. A beauty not explicable, is dearer than a beauty which we can see to the end of. It is nature the symbol, nature certifying the supernatural, body overflowed by life, which he worships, with coarse, but sincere rites.[52]

The inwardness, and mystery, of this attachment, drive men of every class to the use of emblems. The schools of poets, and philosophers, are not more intoxicated with their symbols, than the populace with theirs. In our political parties, compute the power of badges and emblems. See the huge wooden ball rolled by successive ardent crowds from Baltimore to Bunker hill![53] In the political processions, Lowell goes in a loom, and Lynn in a shoe, and Salem in a ship. Witness the cider-barrel, the log-cabin, the hickory-stick, the palmetto, and all the cognizances[54] of party. See the power of national emblems. Some stars, lilies, leopards, a crescent, a lion, an eagle, or other figure, which came into credit God knows how, on an old rag of bunting,[55] blowing in the wind, on a fort, at the ends of the earth, shall make the blood tingle under the rudest, or the most conventional exterior. The people fancy they hate poetry, and they are all poets and mystics!

Beyond this universality of the symbolic language, we are apprised of the divineness of this superior use of things, whereby the world is a temple, whose walls are covered with emblems, pictures, and commandments of the Deity, in this, that there is no fact in nature which does not carry the whole sense of nature; and the distinctions which we make in events, and in affairs, of low and high, honest and base, disappear when nature is used as a symbol. Thought makes everything fit for use. The vocabulary of an omniscient man would embrace words and images excluded from polite conversation. What

50   Servants who tend horses.

51   Serious intent, ardor.

52   This passage must have inspired Whitman, who announced himself as the poet Emerson was seeking. In his Journal (1845) Emerson wrote, "The good of doing with one's own hands is the honouring of the symbol. My own cooking, my own cobbling, fencebuilding, digging of a well, building of a house, twisting of a rope, forging of a hoe & shovel,—is poetic" (J 9:226).

53   During the 1840 presidential campaign of the Whig William Henry Harrison (1773–1841), enthusiastic crowds rolled a ten-foot ball covered with political slogans from town to town—and chanted, "Keep the ball rolling!"

54   Badges, emblems. Harrison's 1840 campaign relied on the cider-barrel and log cabin; the hickory stick was associated with President Andrew Jackson (1767–1845), known as "Old Hickory"; and the palmetto is the symbol of South Carolina.

55   Fabric used for flags.

Los Señores Mason y Compañia, amigos del difunto D. EDUARDO B. EMERZON (Q. G. G.), suplican á V. se digne asistir al entierro de su cadáver, cuyos oficios se celebrarán en la Santa Iglesia Catedral donde se halla depositado, hoy primero de Octubre entre cuatro y cinco de la tarde; de cuyo favor vivirán eternamente reconocidos.

Sr. D.

Funeral notice for Emerson's brother Edward, who died in Puerto Rico in 1834.

would be base, or even obscene, to the obscene, becomes illustrious, spoken in a new connexion of thought. The piety of the Hebrew prophets purges their grossness. The circumcision is an example of the power of poetry to raise the low and offensive. Small and mean things serve as well as great symbols. The meaner the type by which a law is expressed, the more pungent it is, and the more lasting in the memories of men: just as we choose the smallest box, or case, in which any needful utensil can be carried. Bare lists of words are found suggestive, to an imaginative and excited mind; as it is related of Lord Chatham, that he was accustomed to read in Bailey's Dictionary,[56] when he was preparing to speak in Parliament. The poorest experience is rich enough for all the purposes of expressing thought. Why covet a knowledge of new facts? Day and night, house and garden, a few books, a few actions, serve us as well as would all trades and all spectacles. We are far from having exhausted the significance of the few symbols we use. We can come to use them yet with a terrible simplicity. It does not need that a poem should be long. Every word was once a poem.[57] Every new relation is a new word. Also, we use defects and deformities to a sacred purpose, so expressing our sense that the evils of the world are such only to the evil eye. In the old mythology, mythologists observe, defects are ascribed to divine natures, as lameness to Vulcan, blindness to Cupid,[58] and the like, to signify exuberances.

For, as it is dislocation and detachment from the life of God, that makes things ugly, the poet, who re-attaches things to nature and the Whole,— re-attaching even artificial things, and violations of nature, to nature, by a deeper insight,—disposes very easily of the most disagreeable facts. Readers of poetry see the factory-village, and the railway, and fancy that the poetry of the landscape is broken up by these; for these works of art are not yet consecrated in their reading; but the poet sees them fall within the great Order not less than the bee-hive, or the spider's geometrical web. Nature adopts them very fast into her vital circles, and the gliding train of cars she loves like her own. Besides, in a centred mind, it signifies nothing how many mechanical inventions you exhibit. Though you add millions, and never so surprising, the fact of mechanics has not gained a grain's weight. The spiritual fact remains unalterable, by many or by few particulars; as no mountain is of any

56 Poets from Homer to Whitman and beyond have relied on the list (catalog); the British poet W. H. Auden (1907–1973) wrote that "proper names are poetry in the raw." William Pitt (the Elder), Earl of Chatham (1708–1778), British political leader; in 1721, Nathan Bailey (d. 1742) published the most popular English dictionary of the eighteenth century.

57 Emerson dwells on the power of even the plainest, most familiar faces of life, finding poetry where it is least expected. He also alludes to the theory presented in "Language," Chapter IV of *Nature:* abstract words were once startlingly tangible (so that "wrong" originally meant "twisted," for example). As Emerson comments later on in "The Poet," "Language is fossil poetry."

58 Deities also known as Hephaestus, the lame Greek smith-god, and Eros or Amor, the son of Aphrodite (Venus) who makes humans fall in love.

59    Threaded beads used as currency by North American Indians.

60    Fleeting nature.

61    Lyncaeus (or Lynceus), one of the legendary Argonauts who accompanied Jason on his quest for the Golden Fleece, was said to be able to see through the earth.

62    Emerson wrote in his Journal (1846), "The poet can class things so audaciously because he is sensible of the celestial flowing from which nothing is exempt: his own body also is a fleeing apparition, his personality as fugitive as any type, as fugitive as the trope he employs" (J 9:370).

appreciable height to break the curve of the sphere. A shrewd country-boy goes to the city for the first time, and the complacent citizen is not satisfied with his little wonder. It is not that he does not see all the fine houses, and know that he never saw such before, but he disposes of them as easily as the poet finds place for the railway. The chief value of the new fact, is to enhance the great and constant fact of Life, which can dwarf any and every circumstance, and to which the belt of wampum,[59] and the commerce of America, are alike.

The world being thus put under the mind for verb and noun, the poet is he who can articulate it. For, though life is great, and fascinates, and absorbs,—and though all men are intelligent of the symbols through which it is named,—yet they cannot originally use them. We are symbols, and inhabit symbols; workmen, work, and tools, words and things, birth and death, all are emblems; but we sympathize with the symbols, and, being infatuated with the economical uses of things, we do not know that they are thoughts. The poet, by an ulterior intellectual perception, gives them a power which makes their old use forgotten, and puts eyes, and a tongue, into every dumb and inanimate object. He perceives the thought's independence of the symbol, the stability of the thought, the accidency and fugacity[60] of the symbol. As the eyes of Lyncæus were said to see through the earth, so the poet turns the world to glass,[61] and shows us all things in their right series and procession. For, through that better perception, he stands one step nearer to things, and sees the flowing or metamorphosis; perceives that thought is multiform; that within the form of every creature is a force impelling it to ascend into a higher form; and, following with his eyes the life, uses the forms which express that life, and so his speech flows with the flowing of nature.[62] All the facts of the animal economy,—sex, nutriment, gestation, birth, growth—are symbols of the passage of the world into the soul of man, to suffer there a change, and reappear a new and higher fact. He uses forms according to the life, and not according to the form. This is true science. The poet alone knows astronomy, chemistry, vegetation, and animation, for he does not stop at these facts, but employs them as signs. He knows why the plain, or meadow of space, was strown with these flowers we call suns, and moons, and stars; why the great deep is adorned with animals, with men, and gods; for, in every word he speaks he rides on them as the horses of thought.

By virtue of this science the poet is the Namer, or Language-maker, naming things sometimes after their appearance, sometimes after their essence, and giving to every one its own name and not another's, thereby rejoicing the intellect, which delights in detachment or boundary. The poets made all the words, and therefore language is the archives of history, and, if we must say it, a sort of tomb of the muses. For, though the origin of most of our words is forgotten, each word was at first a stroke of genius, and obtained currency, because for the moment it symbolized the world to the first speaker and to the hearer. The etymologist finds the deadest word to have been once a brilliant picture. Language is fossil poetry. As the limestone of the continent consists of infinite masses of the shells of animalcules, so language is made up of images, or tropes, which now, in their secondary use, have long ceased to remind us of their poetic origin. But the poet names the thing because he sees it, or comes one step nearer to it than any other. This expression, or naming, is not art, but a second nature, grown out of the first, as a leaf out of a tree.[63] What we call nature, is a certain self-regulated motion, or change; and nature does all things by her own hands, and does not leave another to baptize her, but baptizes herself; and this through the metamorphosis again. I remember that a certain poet described it to me thus:

\*   \*   \*

Genius is the activity which repairs the decays of things, whether wholly or partly of a material and finite kind. Nature, through all her kingdoms, insures herself. Nobody cares for planting the poor fungus: so she shakes down from the gills of one agaric[64] countless spores, any one of which, being preserved, transmits new billions of spores to-morrow or next day. The new agaric of this hour has a chance which the old one had not. This atom of seed is thrown into a new place, not subject to the accidents which destroyed its parent two rods off. She makes a man; and having brought him to ripe age, she will no longer run the risk of losing this wonder at a blow, but she detaches from him a new self, that the kind may be safe from accidents to

63    Sir Philip Sidney (1554–1586) in his *Apology for Poetry* (publ. 1595) praised the poet who, "lifted up with the vigor of his own invention, doth grow in effect another nature," and added that nature's "world is brazen, the poets only deliver a golden."

64    Mushroom.

65    In his essay "Culture," Emerson sounded a more cautionary note: "Beware of the man who says, 'I am on the eve of a revelation.'"

66    Another, yet the same (Latin).

67    Indwelling power, genius.

which the individual is exposed. So when the soul of the poet has come to ripeness of thought, she detaches and sends away from it its poems or songs, —a fearless, sleepless, deathless progeny, which is not exposed to the accidents of the weary kingdom of time: a fearless, vivacious offspring, clad with wings (such was the virtue of the soul out of which they came), which carry them fast and far, and infix them irrecoverably into the hearts of men. These wings are the beauty of the poet's soul. The songs, thus flying immortal from their mortal parent, are pursued by clamorous flights of censures, which swarm in far greater numbers, and threaten to devour them; but these last are not winged. At the end of a very short leap they fall plump down, and rot, having received from the souls out of which they came no beautiful wings. But the melodies of the poet ascend, and leap, and pierce into the deeps of infinite time.[65]

\* \* \*

So far the bard taught me, using his freer speech. But nature has a higher end, in the production of new individuals, than security, namely, *ascension*, or, the passage of the soul into higher forms. I knew, in my younger days, the sculptor who made the statue of the youth which stands in the public garden. He was, as I remember, unable to tell, directly, what made him happy, or unhappy, but by wonderful indirections he could tell. He rose one day, according to his habit, before the dawn, and saw the morning break, grand as the eternity out of which it came, and, for many days after, he strove to express this tranquillity, and, lo! his chisel had fashioned out of marble the form of a beautiful youth, Phosphor, whose aspect is such, that, it is said, all persons who look on it become silent. The poet also resigns himself to his mood, and that thought which agitated him is expressed, but *alter idem*,[66] in a manner totally new. The expression is organic, or, the new type which things themselves take when liberated. As, in the sun, objects paint their images on the retina of the eye, so they, sharing the aspiration of the whole universe, tend to paint a far more delicate copy of their essence in his mind. Like the metamorphosis of things into higher organic forms, is their change into melodies. Over everything stands its dæmon,[67] or soul, and, as the form of the thing is reflected by the eye, so the soul of the thing is reflected by a melody. The sea, the mountain-ridge, Niagara, and every flower-bed, pre-exist, or super-exist, in pre-cantations, which sail like odors in the air, and when any man goes by with an ear sufficiently fine, he overhears them, and endeavors to write down the notes, without diluting or depraving them. And herein is the legitimation of criticism, in the mind's faith, that the poems are a corrupt version of some text in nature, with which they ought to be made to tally.[68] A rhyme in one of our sonnets should not be less pleasing than the iterated nodes of a sea-shell, or the resembling difference of a group of flowers. The pairing of the birds is an idyl,[69] not tedious as our idyls are; a tempest is a rough ode without falsehood or rant; a summer, with its harvest sown, reaped, and stored, is an epic song, subordinating how many admirably executed parts. Why should not the symmetry and truth that modulate these, glide into our spirits, and we participate the invention of nature?[70]

This insight, which expresses itself by what is called Imagination, is a very high sort of seeing, which does not come by study, but by the intellect being where and what it sees, by sharing the path, or circuit of things through forms, and so making them translucid to others. The path of things is silent. Will they suffer a speaker to go with them? A spy they will not suffer; a lover, a poet, is the transcendency of their own nature,—him they will suffer. The condition of true naming, on the poet's part, is his resigning himself to the divine *aura*[71] which breathes through forms, and accompanying that.

It is a secret which every intellectual man quickly learns, that, beyond the energy of his possessed and conscious intellect, he is capable of a new energy (as of an intellect doubled on itself), by abandonment to the nature of things; that, beside his privacy of power as an individual man, there is a great public power, on which he can draw, by unlocking, at all risks, his human doors, and suffering the ethereal tides to roll and circulate through him: then he is caught up into the life of the Universe, his speech is thunder,[72] his thought is law, and his words are universally intelligible as the plants and animals. The poet knows that he speaks adequately, then only when he speaks somewhat wildly, or, "with the flower of the mind;"[73] not with the intellect,

68   In his Journal (1844–1845), Emerson remarked, "A true melody like Ben Jonson's good songs & all Milton's is of eternity already. Verses of true poets are hickory nuts so fresh & sound" (J 9:179; Ben Jonson, English poet [1572–1637]).

69   Pastoral scene depicted in idealized, paradisal terms.

70   Here as elsewhere in "The Poet," Emerson downgrades literary tradition and elevates nature. In his Journal (1847) he wrote, "I may well ask when men wanted their bard & prophet as now? They have a Quixote gallery of old romances & mythologies, Norse, Greek, Persian, Jewish, & Indian, but nothing that will fit them, and they go without music or symbol to their day labor" (J 10:83). Emerson refers to the multifarious novel *Don Quixote* (1605, 1615) by Miguel de Cervantes Saavedra (1547–1616).

71   Distinctive atmosphere.

72   Emerson's Journal, August 1846: "A poet is all we want. He acts on us like a thunder clap" (J 9:449).

73   Phrase associated with Zoroaster, the Iranian religious founder (ca. 11th century BCE).

74    Here, as with his earlier image of the "horses of thought," Emerson is thinking of the myth of the charioteer in Plato's dialogue *Phaedrus*. The last few pages of "The Poet" mime the Platonic myth, with its motions of yearning, ascent, and disappointment. In his later essay "Fate," Emerson remarks, "A man must ride alternately on the horses of his private and his public nature."

75    Nectar was the food of the Greek gods. In his Journal in 1843 Emerson remarked, "I take many stimulants & often make an art of my inebriation. I read Proclus for my opium, it excites my imagination to let sail before me the pleasing & grand figures of gods & daemons & demoniacal men" (J 8:378). In a Notebook, Emerson wrote, "This is the wine, this freedom, we are slugs & snails half-entombed already, pawing to get free; all partialists, one a brandy-sot, & one an order-sot, or precisian; & one a fact-sot or practical man; date hunter; every one mad with some madness, sot of some bottle" (J 12:349). Here Emerson alludes to the Creation in Milton's *Paradise Lost* (1667), with its description of the "tawny lion, pawing to get free / His hinder parts" (7.464–465). In his essay "Culture," Emerson wrote, "Half-engaged in the soil, pawing to get free, man needs all the music that can be brought to disengage him."

76    The Greek poet Pindar (ca. 522–443 BCE) famously asserted "water is best." Milton echoes the sentiment in his *Elegy 6* (1629) and elsewhere.

used as an organ, but with the intellect released from all service, and suffered to take its direction from its celestial life; or, as the ancients were wont to express themselves, not with intellect alone, but with the intellect inebriated by nectar. As the traveller who has lost his way, throws his reins on his horse's neck, and trusts to the instinct of the animal to find his road, so must we do with the divine animal who carries us through this world.[74] For if in any manner we can stimulate this instinct, new passages are opened for us into nature, the mind flows into and through things hardest and highest, and the metamorphosis is possible.

This is the reason why bards love wine, mead, narcotics, coffee, tea, opium, the fumes of sandal-wood and tobacco, or whatever other procurers of animal exhilaration. All men avail themselves of such means as they can, to add this extraordinary power to their normal powers; and to this end they prize conversation, music, pictures, sculpture, dancing, theatres, travelling, war, mobs, fires, gaming, politics, or love, or science, or animal intoxication, which are several coarser or finer *quasi*-mechanical substitutes for the true nectar, which is the ravishment of the intellect by coming nearer to the fact.[75] These are auxiliaries to the centrifugal tendency of a man, to his passage out into free space, and they help him to escape the custody of that body in which he is pent up, and of that jail-yard of individual relations in which he is enclosed. Hence a great number of such as were professionally expressors of Beauty, as painters, poets, musicians, and actors, have been more than others wont to lead a life of pleasure and indulgence; all but the few who received the true nectar; and, as it was a spurious mode of attaining freedom, as it was an emancipation not into the heavens, but into the freedom of baser places, they were punished for that advantage they won, by a dissipation and deterioration. But never can any advantage be taken of nature by a trick. The spirit of the world, the great calm presence of the creator, comes not forth to the sorceries of opium or of wine. The sublime vision comes to the pure and simple soul in a clean and chaste body. That is not an inspiration which we owe to narcotics, but some counterfeit excitement and fury. Milton says, that the lyric poet may drink wine and live generously, but the epic poet, he who shall sing of the gods, and their descent unto men, must drink water out of a wooden bowl.[76] For poetry is not "Devil's wine," but God's wine.[77] It is with this as it is with toys. We fill the hands and nurseries of our children with all manner of dolls, drums, and horses, withdrawing their eyes from the plain face and sufficing objects of nature, the sun, and moon, the animals, the water, and stones, which should be their toys. So the poet's habit of living should be set on a key so low, that the common influences should delight him. His cheerfulness should be the gift of the sunlight; the air should suffice for his inspiration, and he should be tipsy with water. That spirit which suffices quiet hearts, which seems to come forth to such from every dry knoll of sere grass, from every pine-stump, and half-imbedded stone, on which the dull March sun shines, comes forth to the poor and hungry, and such as are of simple taste. If thou fill thy brain with Boston and New York, with fashion and covetousness, and wilt stimulate thy jaded senses with wine and French coffee, thou shalt find no radiance of wisdom in the lonely waste of the pinewoods.[78]

If the imagination intoxicates the poet, it is not inactive in other men. The metamorphosis excites in the beholder an emotion of joy. The use of symbols has a certain power of emancipation and exhilaration for all men. We seem to be touched by a wand, which makes us dance and run about happily, like children. We are like persons who come out of a cave or cellar into the open air. This is the effect on us of tropes,[79] fables, oracles, and all poetic forms. Poets are thus liberating gods. Men have really got a new sense, and found within their world, another world, or nest of worlds; for, the metamorphosis once seen, we divine that it does not stop. I will not now consider how much this makes the charm of algebra and the mathematics, which also have their tropes, but it is felt in every definition; as, when Aristotle defines *space* to be an immovable vessel, in which things are contained;—or, when Plato defines a *line* to be a flowing point; or, *figure* to be a bound of solid; and many the like. What a joyful sense of freedom we have, when Vitruvius announces the old opinion of artists, that no architect can build any house well, who does not know something of anatomy. When Socrates, in Charmides, tells us that the soul is cured of its maladies by certain incantations, and that these incantations are beautiful reasons, from which temperance is generated in souls; when Plato calls the world an animal; and Timæus[80] affirms that the plants also are animals; or affirms a man to be a heavenly tree, grow-

77   Emerson remarked in his notebook that "the Church Fathers" called poetry "Vinum daemonum devils' wine" (J 12:349).

78   To Margaret Fuller (1810–1850) Emerson wrote (February 21, 1840), "Let us surrender ourselves for fifteen minutes to the slightest of these nameless influences—these nymphs or imps of wood & flood of pasture & roadside, and we shall quickly find out what an ignorant pretending old Dummy is Literature who has quite omitted all that we care to know . . ." (L 2:255).

79   Figures of speech or of thought. In Bk. 7 of his *Republic*, Plato describes the allegory of the cave, in which people take the shadows cast on the cave's wall for reality; the philosopher, Plato implies, ascends from the cave into the light above.

80   Aristotle (384–322 BCE), Greek philosopher. The *Charmides* and the *Timaeus* are Platonic dialogues, both of them featuring Socrates (469–399 BCE), Plato's teacher. Vitruvius (ca. 75–ca. 15 BCE), influential Roman writer on architecture.

81    George Chapman (ca. 1559–1634), English dramatist and poet; the quoted lines are from the Epistle Dedicatory to Chapman's translation of Homer's *Iliad*. Orpheus, legendary Greek poet; Geoffrey Chaucer (ca. 1343–1400) in the Wife of Bath's Tale from *The Canterbury Tales* (1387–1400) writes that fire, like gentility, burns whether or not anyone is watching it. The Caucasus mountains lie between the Black Sea and the Caspian Sea. The book of Revelation, or Apocalypse of St. John, is the final book of the New Testament: "And the stars of heaven fell unto the earth, even as a fig tree casteth her untimely figs, when she is shaken of a mighty wind" (Rev. 6:13). Aesop (6th century BCE), legendary author, was thought to be the author of a famous collection of beast fables.

82    Pythagoras (6th century BCE), Greek thinker and mathematician; Paracelsus (1493–1541), Swiss alchemist and physician; Cornelius Agrippa (1486–1535), German mystic; Jerome Cardan, or Girolamo Cardano (1501–1576), Italian mathematician; Johannes Kepler (1571–1630), founder of modern astronomy; Lorenz Oken (1779–1851), German naturalist. All of these men held to occult beliefs.

ing with his root, which is his head, upward; and, as George Chapman, following him, writes,—

"So in our tree of man, whose nervie root
Springs in his top;"

when Orpheus speaks of hoariness as "that white flower which marks extreme old age;" when Proclus calls the universe the statue of the intellect; when Chaucer, in his praise of 'Gentilesse,' compares good blood in mean condition to fire, which, though carried to the darkest house betwixt this and the mount of Caucasus, will yet hold its natural office, and burn as bright as if twenty thousand men did it behold; when John saw, in the apocalypse, the ruin of the world through evil, and the stars fall from heaven, as the figtree casteth her untimely fruit; when Æsop[81] reports the whole catalogue of common daily relations through the masquerade of birds and beasts;—we take the cheerful hint of the immortality of our essence, and its versatile habit and escapes, as when the gypsies say of themselves, "it is in vain to hang them, they cannot die."

The poets are thus liberating gods. The ancient British bards had for the title of their order, "Those who are free throughout the world." They are free, and they make free. An imaginative book renders us much more service at first, by stimulating us through its tropes, than afterward, when we arrive at the precise sense of the author. I think nothing is of any value in books, excepting the transcendental and extraordinary. If a man is inflamed and carried away by his thought, to that degree that he forgets the authors and the public, and heeds only this one dream, which holds him like an insanity, let me read his paper, and you may have all the arguments and histories and criticism. All the value which attaches to Pythagoras, Paracelsus, Cornelius Agrippa, Cardan, Kepler, Swedenborg, Schelling, Oken,[82] or any other who introduces questionable facts into his cosmogony, as angels, devils, magic, astrology, palmistry, mesmerism, and so on, is the certificate we have of departure from routine, and that here is a new witness. That also is the best success in conversation, the magic of liberty, which puts the world, like a ball, in our hands. How cheap even the liberty then seems; how mean to study, when an emotion communicates to the intellect the power to sap and upheave nature: how great the perspective! nations, times, systems, enter and disappear, like threads in tapestry of large figure and many colors; dream delivers us to dream,[83] and, while the drunkenness lasts, we will sell our bed, our philosophy, our religion, in our opulence.

There is good reason why we should prize this liberation. The fate of the poor shepherd, who, blinded and lost in the snowstorm, perishes in a drift within a few feet of his cottage door, is an emblem of the state of man. On the brink of the waters of life and truth, we are miserably dying.[84] The inaccessibleness of every thought but that we are in, is wonderful. What if you come near to it,—you are as remote, when you are nearest, as when you are farthest. Every thought is also a prison; every heaven is also a prison. Therefore we love the poet, the inventor, who in any form, whether in an ode, or in an action, or in looks and behavior, has yielded us a new thought. He unlocks our chains, and admits us to a new scene.

This emancipation is dear to all men, and the power to impart it, as it must come from greater depth and scope of thought, is a measure of intellect. Therefore all books of the imagination endure, all which ascend to that truth, that the writer sees nature beneath him, and uses it as his exponent. Every verse or sentence, possessing this virtue, will take care of its own immortality. The religions of the world are the ejaculations[85] of a few imaginative men.

But the quality of the imagination is to flow, and not to freeze. The poet did not stop at the color, or the form, but read their meaning; neither may he rest in this meaning, but he makes the same objects exponents of his new thought. Here is the difference betwixt the poet and the mystic, that the last nails a symbol to one sense, which was a true sense for a moment, but soon becomes old and false. For all symbols are fluxional; all language is vehicular and transitive, and is good, as ferries and horses are, for conveyance, not as farms and houses are, for homestead. Mysticism consists in the mistake of an accidental and individual symbol for an universal one. The morning-redness happens to be the favorite meteor to the eyes of Jacob Behmen,[86] and comes to stand to him for truth and faith; and he believes should stand for the same realities to every reader. But the first reader prefers as naturally the symbol of a mother and child, or a gardener and his bulb, or a jeweller polishing a gem. Either of these, or of a myriad more, are equally

83   A phrase that also occurs in Emerson's essay "Experience."

84   In a letter of March 12, 1835, to Thomas Carlyle (1795–1881), Emerson lamented, "Men live on the brink of mysteries & harmonies into which yet they never enter, and with their hand on the doorlatch they die outside" (CEC 121). In his Journal, a year earlier, he had written, "We are always on the brink of an ocean of thought into which we do not yet swim" (April 12, 1834, J 4:274).

85   Expressions, outpourings.

86   Jakob Behmen, or Boehme (1575–1624), was a German mystic writer.

87    In a notebook entry Emerson wrote, "The poet should read the symbol of nature but for its own beauty or in other words for joy. Then his moral is pure & winged as is the moral of nature. But Swedenborg, though he reads the symbol, yet he reads it for good not for beauty; & the impression corresponds;—it is sad & is preaching. Shakspeare is pure Poet" (J 12:351).

88    The Bramins, or Brahmins, were the Hindu priestly caste; like Pythagoras, they produced a theory of reincarnation.

89    In his Journal (1846), Emerson lamented, "The poets that we praise, or try to, are all abortive Homers. . . . We do not wish to make-believe be instructed; we wish to be ravished, inspired, & taught" (J 9:378–379). In a letter of January 30, 1840, to William Ellery Channing (1818–1901), he commented, "My quarrel with our poets is that they are secondary & mimetic but you may thank the god for intuition & experience" (L 2:253).

      Whitman proclaimed himself the poet Emerson was looking for, and Emerson's famous letter to Whitman after reading *Leaves of Grass* (1855) ("I greet you at the beginning of a great career . . .") seems to reciprocate the feeling. Though Emerson later voiced reservations about Whitman's rough frankness, the two remained friends. In his 1855 Preface to *Leaves of Grass*, Whitman wrote, "The known universe has one complete lover and that is the greatest poet." Whitman's insistence on an erotic embrace and recognition of the world takes Emerson's idea of poetry even further, making it more kinetic and more committed to entering the lives of the people Whitman observes.

90    In the *Divine Comedy* (1308–1321), Dante is the pilgrim remembering his own life, traveling through a hell, purgatory, and heaven of his own making.

good to the person to whom they are significant. Only they must be held lightly, and be very willingly translated into the equivalent terms which others use. And the mystic must be steadily told,—All that you say is just as true without the tedious use of that symbol as with it. Let us have a little algebra, instead of this trite rhetoric,—universal signs, instead of these village symbols,—and we shall both be gainers. The history of hierarchies seems to show, that all religious error consisted in making the symbol too stark and solid, and, at last, nothing but an excess of the organ of language.

Swedenborg,[87] of all men in the recent ages, stands eminently for the translator of nature into thought. I do not know the man in history to whom things stood so uniformly for words. Before him the metamorphosis continually plays. Everything on which his eye rests, obeys the impulses of moral nature. The figs become grapes whilst he eats them. When some of his angels affirmed a truth, the laurel twig which they held blossomed in their hands. The noise which, at a distance, appeared like gnashing and thumping, on coming nearer was found to be the voice of disputants. The men, in one of his visions, seen in heavenly light, appeared like dragons, and seemed in darkness; but, to each other, they appeared as men, and, when the light from heaven shone into their cabin, they complained of the darkness, and were compelled to shut the window that they might see.

There was this perception in him, which makes the poet or seer an object of awe and terror, namely, that the same man, or society of men, may wear one aspect to themselves and their companions, and a different aspect to higher intelligences. Certain priests, whom he describes as conversing very learnedly together, appeared to the children, who were at some distance, like dead horses; and many the like misappearances. And instantly the mind inquires, whether these fishes under the bridge, yonder oxen in the pasture, those dogs in the yard, are immutably fishes, oxen, and dogs, or only so appear to me, and perchance to themselves appear upright men; and whether I appear as a man to all eyes. The Bramins and Pythagoras[88] propounded the same question, and if any poet has witnessed the transformation, he doubtless found it in harmony with various experiences. We have all seen changes as considerable in wheat and caterpillars. He is the poet, and shall draw us with love and terror, who sees, through the flowing vest, the firm nature, and can declare it.

I look in vain for the poet whom I describe.[89] We do not, with sufficient plainness, or sufficient profoundness, address ourselves to life, nor dare we chaunt our own times and social circumstance. If we filled the day with bravery, we should not shrink from celebrating it. Time and nature yield us many gifts, but not yet the timely man, the new religion, the reconciler, whom all things await. Dante's praise is, that he dared to write his autobiography in colossal cipher, or into universality.[90] We have yet had no genius in America, with tyrannous eye, which knew the value of our incomparable materials, and saw, in the barbarism and materialism of the times, another carnival of the same gods whose picture he so much admires in Homer; then in the middle age; then in Calvinism.[91] Banks and tariffs, the newspaper and caucus, methodism and unitarianism, are flat and dull to dull people, but rest on the same foundations of wonder as the town of Troy, and the temple of Delphi,[92] and are as swiftly passing away. Our logrolling,[93] our stumps and their politics, our fisheries, our Negroes, and Indians, our boasts, and our repudiations,[94] the wrath of rogues, and the pusillanimity of honest men, the north-

91   Calvinism, austere form of Protestantism founded by the Genevan reformer John Calvin (1509–1564), and influential in early America.

92   Troy, site of the Trojan War immortalized in Homer; Delphi, Greek town where the most important ancient oracle was located. Emerson commented in his Journal (December 1839), "Every thing should be treated poetically —law, politics, housekeeping, money. A judge and a banker must drive their craft poetically as well as a dancer or a scribe. That is, they must exert that higher vision which causes the object to become fluid & plastic. Then they are inventive, they detect its capabilities" (J 7:329).

93   Trading of favors in the state or national legislature (from the practice of neighbors' helping one another to move logs). The term was probably coined by American frontiersman and congressman Davy Crockett (1786–1836) in 1835.

94   Certain American states refused to pay (repudiated) their debts, causing understandable anxiety in investors.

Card of the passenger agent Edward Whineray, captain of the steamer *S. S. Wyoming* when Emerson and his daughter Ellen sailed to Liverpool on the ship in 1872.

95    In 1843, settlers formed an autonomous government in Oregon Country; Texas became an independent republic in 1836 (and joined the United States in 1845, the year after Emerson's essay).

96    The Scottish scholar Alexander Chalmers (1759–1834) edited a multivolume collection of English poetry.

97    Spirits.

98    Desire to.

99    Liquid that flows through the Greek gods' veins, instead of blood.

ern trade, the southern planting, the western clearing, Oregon, and Texas,[95] are yet unsung. Yet America is a poem in our eyes; its ample geography dazzles the imagination, and it will not wait long for metres. If I have not found that excellent combination of gifts in my countrymen which I seek, neither could I aid myself to fix the idea of the poet by reading now and then in Chalmers's[96] collection of five centuries of English poets. These are wits, more than poets, though there have been poets among them. But when we adhere to the ideal of the poet, we have our difficulties even with Milton and Homer. Milton is too literary, and Homer too literal and historical.

But I am not wise enough for a national criticism, and must use the old largeness a little longer, to discharge my errand from the muse to the poet concerning his art.

Art is the path of the creator to his work. The paths, or methods, are ideal and eternal, though few men ever see them, not the artist himself for years, or for a lifetime, unless he come into the conditions. The painter, the sculptor, the composer, the epic rhapsodist, the orator, all partake one desire, namely, to express themselves symmetrically and abundantly, not dwarfishly and fragmentarily. They found or put themselves in certain conditions, as, the painter and sculptor before some impressive human figures; the orator, into the assembly of the people; and the others, in such scenes as each has found exciting to his intellect; and each presently feels the new desire. He hears a voice, he sees a beckoning. Then he is apprised, with wonder, what herds of dæmons[97] hem him in. He can no more rest; he says, with the old painter, "By God, it is in me, and must go forth of me." He pursues a beauty, half seen, which flies before him. The poet pours out verses in every solitude. Most of the things he says are conventional, no doubt; but by and by he says something which is original and beautiful. That charms him. He would say nothing else but such things. In our way of talking, we say, 'That is yours, this is mine;' but the poet knows well that it is not his; that it is as strange and beautiful to him as to you; he would fain[98] hear the like eloquence at length. Once having tasted this immortal ichor,[99] he cannot have enough of it, and, as an admirable creative power exists in these intellections, it is of the last importance that these things get spoken. What a little of all we know is said! What drops of all the sea of our science are baled up! and by what accident it is that these are exposed, when so many secrets sleep in nature! Hence the necessity of speech and song; hence these throbs and heart-beatings in the orator, at the door of the assembly, to the end, namely, that thought may be ejaculated as Logos, or Word.[100]

Doubt not, O poet, but persist. Say, "It is in me, and shall out." Stand there, baulked and dumb, stuttering and stammering, hissed and hooted, stand and strive, until, at last, rage draw out of thee that *dream*-power which every night shows thee is thine own; a power transcending all limit and privacy, and by virtue of which a man is the conductor of the whole river of electricity.[101] Nothing walks, or creeps, or grows, or exists, which must not in turn arise and walk before him as exponent of his meaning. Comes he to that power, his genius is no longer exhaustible. All the creatures, by pairs and by tribes, pour into his mind as into a Noah's ark, to come forth again to people a new world. This is like the stock of air for our respiration, or for the combustion of our fireplace, not a measure of gallons, but the entire atmosphere if wanted. And therefore the rich poets, as Homer, Chaucer, Shakspeare, and Raphael, have obviously no limits to their works, except the limits of their lifetime, and resemble a mirror carried through the street,[102] ready to render an image of every created thing.

O poet! a new nobility is conferred in groves and pastures, and not in castles, or by the sword-blade, any longer. The conditions are hard, but equal. Thou shalt leave the world, and know the muse only. Thou shalt not know any longer the times, customs, graces, politics, or opinions of men, but shalt take all from the muse. For the time of towns is tolled from the world by funereal chimes, but in nature the universal hours are counted by succeeding tribes of animals and plants, and by growth of joy on joy. God wills also that thou abdicate a duplex and manifold life, and that thou be content that others speak for thee. Others shall be thy gentlemen, and shall represent all courtesy and worldly life for thee; others shall do the great and resounding actions also.[103] Thou shalt lie close hid with nature, and canst not be afforded to the Capitol or the Exchange. The world is full of renunciations and apprenticeships, and this is thine; thou must pass for a fool and a churl for a long season. This is the screen and sheath in which Pan[104] has protected his well-beloved flower, and thou shalt be known only to thine own, and they

100  "Ejaculated" means expressed. The Gospel of John (1:1) begins by identifying Jesus with the Word (in Greek, *logos*).

101  Emerson proclaimed in his Journal, "The Poet should install himself & shove all usurpers from their chairs by electrifying mankind . . . The true centre thus appearing, all false centres are suddenly superseded, and grass grows in the Capitol" (June 27, 1846; J 9:432).

102  Raphael Sanzio (1483–1520), Italian Renaissance painter. In *The Red and the Black* (1830) by the French novelist Stendhal (Henri Beyle; 1783–1842), the image of a mirror carried through the street conveys Stendhal's realist method. The American poet Wallace Stevens (1879–1955), in his poem "Asides on the Oboe" (1940), portrays an Emersonian figure who is himself transparent: "the central man, the human globe, responsive / As a mirror with a voice, the man of glass, / Who in a million diamonds sums us up." This is "the man without impediment" (as Emerson calls him earlier in "The Poet").

103  Emerson noted a passage in Thomas Taylor's (1758–1835) translation of Hermeas's scholia on the *Phaedrus:* "The musical mania, therefore, causes us to speak in verse, and to act and be moved rhythmically, and to sing in metre, the splendid deeds of divine men, and their virtues and pursuits; and through these, to discipline our life."

104  The pagan woodland god (whose name means "all" in Greek).

shall console thee with tenderest love. And thou shalt not be able to rehearse the names of thy friends in thy verse, for an old shame before the holy ideal. And this is the reward: that the ideal shall be real to thee, and the impressions of the actual world shall fall like summer rain, copious, but not troublesome, to thy invulnerable essence. Thou shalt have the whole land for thy park and manor, the sea for thy bath and navigation, without tax and without envy; the woods and the rivers thou shalt own; and thou shalt possess that wherein others are only tenants and boarders. Thou true land-lord! sea-lord! air-lord! Wherever snow falls, or water flows, or birds fly, wherever day and night meet in twilight, wherever the blue heaven is hung by clouds, or sown with stars, wherever are forms with transparent boundaries, wherever are outlets into celestial space, wherever is danger, and awe, and love, there is Beauty, plenteous as rain, shed for thee, and though thou shouldst walk the world over, thou shalt not be able to find a condition inopportune or ignoble.

Exterior of the Emerson House in Concord.

# Experience

The lords of life, the lords of life,—
I saw them pass,
In their own guise,
Like and unlike,
Portly and grim,
Use and Surprise,
Surface and Dream,
Succession swift, and spectral Wrong,
Temperament without a tongue,
And the inventor of the game
Omnipresent without name;—[1]
Some to see, some to be guessed,
They marched from east to west:
Little man, least of all,[2]
Among the legs of his guardians tall,
Walked about with puzzled look:—
Him by the hand dear nature took;
Dearest nature, strong and kind,
Whispered, 'Darling, never mind!
Tomorrow they will wear another face,
The founder thou! these are thy race!'[3]

"Experience" is the second essay in Essays: Second Series (1844). The title derives from the Latin experiri, "to try"—also the origin of "experiment." "To make experience of" something is to make trial of it, to put it into practice. In Emerson's day, "experience-meetings" were fervent religious gatherings, sometimes known as "love-feasts." Emerson refers in his essay "The Over-Soul" to "the experiences of the Methodists." The word experience also brings to mind the skeptical thought of the Scottish philosopher David Hume (1711–1776), whose philosophical works Emerson read with great and troubled interest (as the critic Barbara Packer notes). According to Hume, experience is the only source of our knowledge, and if we consider experience carefully, we may find ourselves doubtful about the stability of personal identity, the connection between cause and effect, and even the material world itself. Emerson here addresses the relativism and skeptical doubt associated in our day with claims that the human self is performed or constructed, rather than a reliable fact.

1       Playing on familiar ideas of God, who is said by Christians to be omnipresent, and whose name is unpronounceable in Judaism. Emerson's deity, practical and tricky rather than solemn, is an "inventor" (from the Latin *invenire*, to contrive or discover), not a creator.

2       Emerson may have in mind an image from the *Immortality Ode* (1807) by the English Romantic poet William Wordsworth (1770–1850), a poem that Emerson described in his Journal (1856) as "the high-water mark which the intellect has reached in this age. A new step has been taken new means have been employed. No courage has surpassed that, & a way made through the void by this finer Columbus" (J 14:99). In Wordsworth the child, seen somewhat grotesquely as a "six years' darling of a pygmy size," experiences a "dream of human life" featuring the various roles played by mankind. Immortality, who "broods like the day, a Master o'er a Slave," presides over Wordsworth's child. By contrast, a maternal nature, "strong and kind," inducts Emerson's "little man" into his maturity.

3       The philosopher Stanley Cavell argues that the essay that follows, beginning with its first line ("Where do we find ourselves?"), will reflect on the connection between finding and founding: that is, between invention (coming upon a scene, contriving a solution) and establishment (of a world and a future).

4       Emerson's prefatory poem pictured the "lords of life" "march[ing] from east to west" (from Europe to America?), and then the little man "walk[ing] about." The essay's first page converts these horizontal images into a vertical one, perhaps echoing Jacob's visionary ladder in Genesis (28:12).

5       Emerson writes in his essay "Beauty," "The ancients believed that a genius or demon took possession at birth of each mortal, to guide him." In the myth of Er at the end of the *Republic*, by the Greek philosopher Plato (429–347 BCE), the Genius or presiding spirit (in Greek, *daimon*) leads dead souls to the river of Lethe. They drink from the river before their next incarnation, and as a result forget their previous lives. Emerson wrote to his wife Lidian on March 6, 1843, "The Genius of Life, you know, is said to give to every soul that enters this world, at birth, a cup of oblivion. I think it would add to the power & peace somewhat of these parties, if each guest could forget his days to pictures, could forget all the particulars of yesterday & the day before, & all the expectations of tomorrow, & be driven to suck the deep life of the present hour" (L 3:156). In his Notebook Emerson wrote, "Souls entering this life drink of oblivion before they enter into bodies, from the demon who is above this ingress. *Plato*" (J 6:378).

6       In his Journal (1840), Emerson wrote, "Sleeps lurks all day about the corners of my eyes as night lurks all day about the stem of a pinetree."

7       The image comes from Psalm 103, which compares man to "a flower of the field": "For the wind passeth over it, and it is gone; and the place thereof shall know it no more." Emerson may also be thinking of Job 7:10: "He shall return no more to his house, neither shall his place know him any more." The great English critic Walter Pater (1839–1894) in his Conclusion to *The Renaissance* (1873) noted the transience and intensity of human life in terms similar to Emerson's: "We have an interval, and then our place knows us no more."

Where do we find ourselves? In a series, of which we do not know the extremes, and believe that it has none. We wake and find ourselves on a stair:[4] there are stairs below us, which we seem to have ascended; there are stairs above us, many a one, which go upward and out of sight. But the Genius which, according to the old belief, stands at the door by which we enter, and gives us the lethe to drink,[5] that we may tell no tales, mixed the cup too strongly, and we cannot shake off the lethargy now at noonday. Sleep lingers all our lifetime about our eyes, as night hovers all day in the boughs of the fir-tree.[6] All things swim and glimmer. Our life is not so much threatened as our perception. Ghostlike we glide through nature, and should not know our place again.[7] Did our birth fall in some fit of indigence and frugality in nature, that she was so sparing of her fire and so liberal of her earth, that it appears to us that we lack the affirmative principle, and though we have health and reason, yet we have no superfluity of spirit for new creation? We have enough to live and bring the year about, but not an ounce to impart or to invest. Ah that our Genius were a little more of a genius! We are like millers on the lower levels of a stream, when the factories above them have exhausted the water. We too fancy that the upper people must have raised their dams.[8]

If any of us knew what we were doing, or where we are going, then when we think we best know! We do not know today whether we are busy or idle. In times when we thought ourselves indolent, we have afterwards discovered, that much was accomplished, and much was begun in us. All our days are so unprofitable while they pass,[9] that 'tis wonderful where or when we ever got anything of this which we call wisdom, poetry, virtue. We never got it on any dated calendar day. Some heavenly days must have been intercalated somewhere, like those that Hermes won with dice of the Moon, that Osiris might be born.[10] It is said, all martyrdoms looked mean when they were suffered.[11] Every ship is a romantic object, except that we sail in. Embark, and the romance quits our vessel, and hangs on every other sail in the horizon. Our life looks trivial, and we shun to record it. Men seem to have learned of the horizon the art of perpetual retreating and reference. 'Yonder uplands are rich pasturage, and my neighbor has fertile meadow, but my field,' says the querulous farmer, 'only holds the world together.' I quote another man's saying; unluckily, that other withdraws himself in the same way,

8    In his Journal Emerson reflected on marriage in terms reminiscent of this paragraph from "Experience": "We live amid hallucinations & illusions, & this especial trap is laid for us to trip up our feet with & all are tripped up, first or last. But the Mighty Mother who had been so sly with us, feels that she owes us some indemnity, & insinuates into the Pandora-box of marriage, amidst dyspepsia, nervousness, screams, Christianity, 'help,' poverty, & all kinds of music, some deep & serious benefits & some great joys" (September–October 1848; J 10:351).

9    Emerson wrote in his Journal in May 1843, "All intercourse is random & remote, yet what fiery & consoling friendships we have, the Ideal journeying always with us the heaven without rent or seam. We never know while the days pass which day is valuable. The surface is vexation but the serene lies underneath" (J 8:397).

10    Added to the calendar. Emerson knew the story about the birth of the Egyptian god Osiris from the essay *Of Isis and Osiris* by the Greek writer Plutarch (ca. 46–ca. 122). Emerson wrote in his Journal (October 16, 1839), "Hermes played at dice with the moon & won of her the seventieth part of each of her revolutions with which he made five new days & added to the year that Osiris might be born. Plut. *Isis & Osiris*" (J 7:270).

11    Emerson commented in his Journal (January–February 1841) on "that which Harriet Martineau well noted, that all martyrdoms at the moment when they were suffered, appeared mean" (J 7:418). Emerson refers to the novel *Deerbrook* (1839) by Martineau (1802–1876), the pioneering British sociologist and feminist.

12    Sound of busy activity or overlapping conversations; rumor.

13    Emerson combines two senses of "pith": "the true nature or essence of something" and a "vigorous and concise expression" (OED).

14    Girolamo Tiraboschi (1731–1794) was the author of a thirteen-volume history of Italian literature (publ. 1771–1782); Thomas Warton (1728–1790) wrote a *History of English Poetry* (1774–1781) that Emerson treasured; and Friedrich von Schlegel (1772–1829), along with his brother, August Wilhelm von Schlegel (1767–1845), was an influential German romantic critic. Emerson is probably thinking of Schlegel's *History of Ancient and Modern Literature* (1812).

15    Emerson quotes from *The Anatomy of Melancholy* (1621) by the grandly idiosyncratic English writer Robert Burton (1577–1640). Burton here translates some lines of the Greek satirist Lucian (2nd century). *Ate Dea* means, in Greek, the goddess of blind destiny who torments humanity. She is credited in Homer's *Iliad* (ca. 9th century BCE) with making Helen choose Paris over Menelaus.

16    Emerson is thinking of his first wife, Ellen, as well as the recent loss of his son Waldo (see note 18). In addition, lover can mean friend (as in Shakespeare's *Julius Caesar* [3.2.49]: "I slew my best lover for the good of Rome").

17    R. J. Boscovich (1711–1787), a Jesuit mathematician, claimed in his *Theory of Natural Philosophy* (1758) that matter is composed of mutually repellent atoms that never touch one another. Emerson referred to "Boscovich's researches" in his Journal as early as 1823 (J 2:167).

and quotes me. 'Tis the trick of nature thus to degrade today; a good deal of buzz,[12] and somewhere a result slipped magically in. Every roof is agreeable to the eye, until it is lifted; then we find tragedy and moaning women, and hard-eyed husbands, and deluges of lethe, and the men ask, 'What's the news?' as if the old were so bad. How many individuals can we count in society? how many actions? how many opinions? So much of our time is preparation, so much is routine, and so much retrospect, that the pith[13] of each man's genius contracts itself to a very few hours. The history of literature—take the net result of Tiraboschi, Warton, or Schlegel,[14]—is a sum of very few ideas, and of very few original tales,—all the rest being variation of these. So in this great society wide lying around us, a critical analysis would find very few spontaneous actions. It is almost all custom and gross sense. There are even few opinions, and these seem organic in the speakers, and do not disturb the universal necessity.

What opium is instilled into all disaster! It shows formidable as we approach it, but there is at last no rough rasping friction, but the most slippery sliding surfaces: we fall soft on a thought: *Ate Dea* is gentle,[15]

"Over men's heads walking aloft,
With tender feet treading so soft."

People grieve and bemoan themselves, but it is not half so bad with them as they say. There are moods in which we court suffering, in the hope that here, at least, we shall find reality, sharp peaks and edges of truth. But it turns out to be scene-painting and counterfeit. The only thing grief has taught me, is to know how shallow it is. That, like all the rest, plays about the surface, and never introduces me into the reality, for contact with which, we would even pay the costly price of sons and lovers.[16] Was it Boscovich who found out that bodies never come in contact?[17] Well, souls never touch their objects. An innavigable sea washes with silent waves between us and the things we aim at and converse with. Grief too will make us idealists. In the death of my son,[18] now more than two years ago, I seem to have lost a beautiful estate,—no more.[19] I cannot get it nearer to me. If tomorrow I should be informed of the bankruptcy of my principal debtors, the loss of my property would be a great inconvenience to me, perhaps, for many years; but it would

## CONCORD LYCEUM.

### SEASON OF 1873 and 1874.

Arrangements have been made for the following Course of Lectures and Entertainments for the present season:

Mrs. MARY A. LIVERMORE will lecture on Wednesday Evening, December 3d, 1873. Subject, "THE BATTLE OF MONEY."

Mrs. LIVERMORE's lecture in the course last winter gave universal satisfaction. The new lecture she offers this season cannot fail to interest all hearers.

Dr. ISAAC I. HAYES will lecture on Wednesday Evening, Dec. 10th, 1873, upon "ARCTIC DISCOVERY."

Dr. HAYES bears a reputation second to that of no living man, as an Arctic traveller, and is also highly spoken of as a lecturer.

Hon. WILLIAM PARSONS, of Ireland, will lecture on Wednesday Evening, Dec. 17th, 1873, upon "CHRISTOPHER COLUMBUS."

This gentleman will be favorably remembered by all who heard his lecture upon George Stephenson three years ago.

Mr. WENDELL PHILLIPS will lecture on Thursday Evening, Jan. 1st, 1874.

A general desire has been expressed to hear MR. PHILLIPS's lecture on the "LOST ARTS." Due notice will be given of his subject.

On Wednesday Evening, Jan. 7th, 1874, there will be an Exhibition of BLACK'S STEREOPTICON.

Mr. BLACK's apparatus is the most perfect of its kind in the country, and the exhibition will be a very pleasant feature of the course. If necessary, a programme of the entertainment will be printed.

Mr. WM. R. EMERSON will lecture on Wednesday Evening, Jan. 14th, 1874. Subject, "AMERICA IN 1900."

Mr. EMERSON is highly spoken of by those who have heard him, and seldom fails to interest his audience.

The MENDELSSOHN QUINTETTE CLUB will give a CONCERT on Wednesday Evening, Jan. 21st, 1874.

The concert will be wholly instrumental, and programmes will be in readiness in proper season.

Prof. WM. H. NILES will lecture on Wednesday Evening, Jan. 28, 1874. Subject, "CORAL AND CORAL ISLANDS," with illustrations.

REV. H. C. SPAULDING, will lecture on Wednesday Evening, Feb. 4, 1874. Subject, "WALKS IN ROME," with illustrations.

This lecture has been very highly praised by the Boston press, and is said to be a truthful and interesting account of the Eternal City.

Mr. RALPH WALDO EMERSON will lecture on Wednesday Evening, Feb. 11th, 1874.

The Lectures and Entertainments will be in the TOWN HALL on the evenings named, commencing promptly at quarter before eight o'clock.

### TICKETS.

The tickets for the present course are furnished in slips of ten, at $2.00 for the course. Each Ticket must be detached from the slip and given up at the door, upon entering. No ticket will be good for any other evening than the one for which it is issued, and no person will be admitted without a ticket.

Single tickets to the CONCERT 50 cents. Other evenings 35 cents.

It is hoped that the expense attending this Course will be wholly met by the sale of tickets.

ALBERT TOLMAN, Curator.

CONCORD, Nov. 15, 1873.

Tolman & White, Printers, 221 Washington Street, Boston.

Lyceum Program, 1863.

18    In 1842, a sudden attack of scarlet fever killed Emerson's five-year-old son Waldo (known as "little Waldo"; Emerson himself was called Waldo by his friends and family). Three days after Waldo's death, Emerson wrote in his Journal that his son made the world real, for himself and for others: "What he looked upon is better, what he looked not upon is insignificant" (J 8:163). He added, "Sorrow makes us all children again destroys all differences of intellect The wisest knows nothing" (J 8:165). Emerson commented several times that Waldo's death seemed unreal to him. On February 4, in a letter to Caroline Sturgis (1819–1888), he wrote, "Alas! I chiefly grieve that I cannot grieve; that this fact takes no more deep hold than other facts, is as dreamlike as they" (L 3:9). In January 1844, Margaret Fuller (1810–1850) reminded Emerson of the anniversary of Waldo's death. He wrote to her, "My divine temple which all angels seemed to love to build and which was shattered in a night, I can never rebuild,—and is the facility of entertainment from thought or friendship or affairs, an amends? Rather it seems like a cup of Somnus or of Momus" (L 3:235; among the ancients, Somnus was the god of sleep, and Momus ridiculed the gods).

19    Plato (429–347 BCE) in his *Republic* wrote that "a good man . . . will least of all think it a misfortune to lose a son, a brother, or some money" (387d–388a).

20    Part of an organism that falls off naturally when it has served its purpose. The term is often used in botany. Describing the romantic history of a couple, Emerson wrote in his Journal (April 16, 1837), "At last they discover that all that at first drew them together was wholly caducous . . ." (J 5:298). On August 17, 1837, he added, "These caducous relations are in the soul as leaves, flowers, & fruits are in the arboreous nature, and wherever it is put & how often soever they are lopped off, yet still it renews them ever" (J 5:363).

21    A type is a pattern or model. In *The Curse of Kehama* (1820) by English poet Robert Southey (1774–1843), the evil sorcerer Kehama puts a spell on a peasant named Ladurlad. Ladurlad will be safe "from fire and from flood. / From the serpent's tooth, / and the beasts of blood," but also deprived of "earth's fruits," water, winds, and dew. Ladurlad calls on death for release from the spell. In his Journal (December 22, 1839), Emerson remarked, "It is the necessity of my nature to shed all influences. Who can come near to Kehama? Neither the rain, neither the warm ray of love, nor the touch of human hand" (J 7:326–327). Emerson had already read Southey's poem by 1821 (J 1:340).

22    Raincoats made of Brazilian rubber and imported from the city of Para (now known as Belèm). Emerson wrote in his Journal (May–June 1843), "Man sheds grief as his skin sheds rain. A preoccupied mind an immense protection" (J 8:407).

23    The critic Lawrence Buell notes that Henry David Thoreau (1817–1862) responds to Emerson in *Walden* (1854). Thoreau writes, "Be it life or death, we crave only reality. If we are really dying, let us hear the rattle in our throats and feel cold in the extremities; if we are alive, let us go about our business."

leave me as it found me,—neither better nor worse. So is it with this calamity: it does not touch me: something which I fancied was a part of me, which could not be torn away without tearing me, nor enlarged without enriching me, falls off from me, and leaves no scar. It was caducous.[20] I grieve that grief can teach me nothing, nor carry me one step into real nature. The Indian who was laid under a curse, that the wind should not blow on him, nor water flow to him, nor fire burn him, is a type of us all.[21] The dearest events are summer-rain, and we the Para coats[22] that shed every drop. Nothing is left us now but death.[23] We look to that with a grim satisfaction, saying, there at least is reality that will not dodge us.

I take this evanescence and lubricity of all objects, which lets them slip through our fingers then when we clutch hardest, to be the most unhandsome part of our condition.[24] Nature does not like to be observed, and likes that we should be her fools and playmates. We may have the sphere for our cricket-ball, but not a berry for our philosophy. Direct strokes she never gave us power to make; all our blows glance, all our hits are accidents. Our relations to each other are oblique and casual.[25]

\* \* \*

Dream delivers us to dream, and there is no end to illusion. Life is a train of moods like a string of beads, and, as we pass through them, they prove to be many-colored lenses which paint the world their own hue, and each shows only what lies in its focus. From the mountain you see the mountain. We animate what we can, and we see only what we animate. Nature and books belong to the eyes that see them. It depends on the mood of the man, whether he shall see the sunset or the fine poem. There are always sunsets, and there is always genius; but only a few hours so serene that we can relish nature or criticism. The more or less depends on structure or temperament. Temperament is the iron wire on which the beads are strung. Of what use is fortune or talent to a cold and defective nature? Who cares what sensibility or discrimination a man has at some time shown, if he falls asleep in his chair? or if he laugh and giggle? or if he apologize? or is infected with egotism? or thinks of his dollar? or cannot pass by food? or has gotten a child in his boyhood? Of what use is genius, if the organ is too convex or too concave, and cannot find a focal distance within the actual horizon of human life? Of what use, if the brain is too cold or too hot, and the man does not care enough for results, to stimulate him to experiment, and hold him up in it? or if the web is too finely woven, too irritable by pleasure and pain, so that life stagnates from too much reception, without due outlet? Of what use to make heroic vows of amendment, if the same old law-breaker is to keep them? What cheer can the religious sentiment yield, when that is suspected to be secretly dependent on the seasons of the year, and the state of the blood? I knew a witty physician who found the creed in the biliary duct, and

24    *Handsome* can mean easy to handle, useful, apt, imposing, or of good quality. Emerson relies most on the first of these meanings, but the others seem present as well. Compare his description, later in "Experience," of the man who "can take hold anywhere." Emerson asks what it means to grasp experience; how it slips from us; how we receive it.

25    Note the theme of nature's "game" announced in the prefatory poem and continued in the essay's later image of the kitten chasing its tail. "Casual" (from the Latin *casus*, "fall") also suggests *casualty:* the death of little Waldo mentioned in Emerson's preceding paragraph. In his Journal (January–February 1842), Emerson wrote, "Our experience would teach us that we thrive by casualties. Our capital experiences have been casual" (J 8:317); and he said of nature, "Surprise & casualty are the apples of her eyes" (J 10:383).

The Old Manse, home of Emerson's step-grandfather Ezra Ripley, where Emerson stayed as a child on family visits to Concord.

26     Gamaliel Bradford (1795–1839), super-
intendent of Massachusetts General Hospital.
Emerson commented in his Journal (May 15,
1842), "Calvinism seems complexional merely:
as Gam. Bradford said, 'The Calvinists have
the liver complaint: the Unitarians have not'"
(J 8:173). (Emerson alludes here to melancholy,
associated with the liver; the biliary, or bile,
ducts are located in the liver.) The Calvinists
were the followers of the Protestant Reformer
John Calvin (1509–1564), known for their emphasis on predestination and original sin; the
Unitarians were the far more liberal sect of Emerson's own day, dominating both his community and his university, Harvard.

27     See the later references in "Experience"
to Galileo's discoveries, to Columbus's finding
America, and to "this new yet unapproachable
America I have found in the West."

28     In the essay "Self-Reliance" Emerson remarked, "I suppose no man can violate his nature. All the sallies of his will are rounded in by
the law of his being"; and in "Worship," "Use
what language you will, you can never say anything but what you are." In a Journal entry from
December 1827, Emerson quoted the novel
*Vivian Grey* (1827) by the British statesman and
writer Benjamin Disraeli (1804–1881): "A man's
Fate is his temper" (J 6:69).

29     Back of the head.

30     See Hebrews 11:1: "Faith is the evidence
of things not seen." In the essay "Worship,"
Emerson wrote, "In our definitions, we grope
after the *spiritual* by describing it as invisible.
The true meaning of *spiritual* is real; that law
which executes itself, which works without
means . . ."

used to affirm that if there was disease in the liver, the man became a Calvinist, and if that organ was sound, he became a Unitarian.[26] Very mortifying is
the reluctant experience that some unfriendly excess or imbecility neutral-
izes the promise of genius. We see young men who owe us a new world,[27]
so readily and lavishly they promise, but they never acquit the debt; they
die young and dodge the account: or if they live, they lose themselves in
the crowd.

Temperament also enters fully into the system of illusions, and shuts us
in a prison of glass which we cannot see. There is an optical illusion about
every person we meet. In truth, they are all creatures of given temperament,
which will appear in a given character, whose boundaries they will never
pass:[28] but we look at them, they seem alive, and we presume there is impulse
in them. In the moment, it seems impulse; in the year, in the lifetime, it turns
out to be a certain uniform tune which the revolving barrel of the music-box
must play. Men resist the conclusion in the morning, but adopt it as the evening wears on, that temper prevails over everything of time, place, and condition, and is inconsumable in the flames of religion. Some modifications the
moral sentiment avails to impose, but the individual texture holds its dominion, if not to bias the moral judgments, yet to fix the measure of activity and
of enjoyment.

I thus express the law as it is read from the platform of ordinary life,
but must not leave it without noticing the capital exception. For temperament is a power which no man willingly hears any one praise but himself. On
the platform of physics, we cannot resist the contracting influences of so-
called science. Temperament puts all divinity to rout. I know the mental proclivity of physicians. I hear the chuckle of the phrenologists. Theoretic kid-
nappers and slave-drivers, they esteem each man the victim of another, who
winds him round his finger by knowing the law of his being, and by such
cheap signboards as the color of his beard, or the slope of his occiput,[29] reads
the inventory of his fortunes and character. The grossest ignorance does not
disgust like this impudent knowingness. The physicians say, they are not materialists; but they are:—Spirit is matter reduced to an extreme thinness: O *so
thin!*—But the definition of *spiritual* should be, *that which is its own evidence.*[30]
What notions do they attach to love! what to religion! One would not willingly pronounce these words in their hearing, and give them the occasion to

profane them. I saw a gracious gentleman who adapts his conversation to the form of the head of the man he talks with![31] I had fancied that the value of life lay in its inscrutable possibilities; in the fact that I never know, in addressing myself to a new individual, what may befall me. I carry the keys of my castle in my hand, ready to throw them at the feet of my lord, whenever and in what disguise soever he shall appear. I know he is in the neighborhood, hidden among vagabonds.[32] Shall I preclude my future, by taking a high seat, and kindly adapting my conversation to the shape of heads? When I come to that, the doctors shall buy me for a cent.—'But, sir, medical history; the report to the Institute; the proven facts!'—I distrust the facts and the inferences. Temperament is the veto or limitation-power in the constitution, very justly applied to restrain an opposite excess in the constitution, but absurdly offered as a bar to original equity. When virtue is in presence, all subordinate powers sleep. On its own level, or in view of nature, temperament is final. I see not, if one be once caught in this trap of so-called sciences, any escape for the man from the links of the chain of physical necessity. Given such an embryo, such a history must follow. On this platform, one lives in a sty of sensualism, and would soon come to suicide. But it is impossible that the creative power should exclude itself. Into every intelligence there is a door which is never closed, through which the creator passes. The intellect, seeker of absolute truth, or the heart, lover of absolute good, intervenes for our succor, and at one whisper of these high powers, we awake from ineffectual struggles with this nightmare. We hurl it into its own hell, and cannot again contract ourselves to so base a state.

*　*　*

The secret of the illusoriness is in the necessity of a succession of moods or objects. Gladly we would anchor, but the anchorage is quicksand. This onward trick of nature is too strong for us: *Pero si muove*.[33] When, at night, I look at the moon and stars, I seem stationary, and they to hurry. Our love of the real draws us to permanence, but health of body consists in circulation, and sanity of mind in variety or facility of association. We need change of objects. Dedication to one thought is quickly odious. We house with the insane, and must humor them;[34] then conversation dies out. Once I took such

31    Emerson may have had in mind the popular Scottish phrenologist George Combe (1788–1858), who undertook a lecture tour of the United States in 1838–1839. Phrenology (the study of human character based on the shape of the head) was a serious discipline in the nineteenth century. Emerson wrote in his Journal for August 6, 1838, "Lidian wonders what the phrenologists would pronounce on little Waldo's head. I reply, that, his head pronounces upon phrenology" (J 7:270).

32    Emerson alludes to the Gospels' association of Jesus with the common and disreputable (see Matthew 11:19 and note 51, below). In the poem "Redemption" (1633) by the English poet George Herbert (1593–1633) the speaker finds his heavenly lord on earth, unexpectedly "among thieves and murderers." By "my lord" Emerson means, not Jesus, but rather any temporary master able to afford him inspiration.

33    Emerson meant *Eppur si muove*, "Yet it moves": According to (doubtful) legend, Galileo Galilei (1564–1642) made this comment after recanting before the Inquisition his belief that the earth moves around the sun.

34    Emerson derives these ideas in part from a major precursor, the French writer Michel de Montaigne (1533–1592), who stresses in his essay "Of Experience" the importance of change —and the affectionate recognition that the world is made up of fools, including oneself.

35    Plotinus (ca. 204–270), philosopher of Neoplatonism; Francis Bacon (1561–1626), English scientist and essayist; J. W. von Goethe (1749–1832), German thinker and man of letters. *Goethe's Letters to and from a Child* (1835), by Elisabeth (Bettina) Brentano von Arnim (1785–1859), was very popular among the New England Transcendentalists. Emerson in an 1842 letter commented that Bettina had produced "the most remarkable book ever written by a woman" (L 3:77).

36    In the essay "Uses of Great Men," Emerson advised against "look[ing] in men for completeness," and urged his audience to accept instead "their social and delegated quality": the way they represent, for a certain time, the provocative and essential. In "The American Scholar" he wrote, "The man has never lived that can feed us ever"; and in "Circles," "Men cease to interest us when we find their limitations."

37    Compare Emerson's statement in his essay "The Poet": "On the brink of the waters of life and truth, we are miserably dying."

38    A grayish stone that, when the light falls on it, shows a variety of colors: blue, green, and, at times, yellow and red. In the next paragraph, Emerson alters the image to a "parti-colored wheel."

delight in Montaigne, that I thought I should not need any other book; before that, in Shakspeare; then in Plutarch; then in Plotinus; at one time in Bacon; afterwards in Goethe; even in Bettine;[35] but now I turn the pages of either of them languidly, whilst I still cherish their genius. So with pictures; each will bear an emphasis of attention once, which it cannot retain, though we fain would continue to be pleased in that manner. How strongly I have felt of pictures, that when you have seen one well, you must take your leave of it; you shall never see it again. I have had good lessons from pictures, which I have since seen without emotion or remark. A deduction must be made from the opinion, which even the wise express of a new book or occurrence. Their opinion gives me tidings of their mood, and some vague guess at the new fact, but is nowise to be trusted as the lasting relation between that intellect and that thing. The child asks, 'Mamma, why don't I like the story as well as when you told it me yesterday?' Alas, child, it is even so with the oldest cherubim of knowledge. But will it answer thy question to say, Because thou wert born to a whole, and this story is a particular? The reason of the pain this discovery causes us (and we make it late in respect to works of art and intellect), is the plaint of tragedy which murmurs from it in regard to persons, to friendship and love.

That immobility and absence of elasticity which we find in the arts, we find with more pain in the artist. There is no power of expansion in men. Our friends early appear to us as representatives of certain ideas, which they never pass or exceed.[36] They stand on the brink of the ocean of thought and power, but they never take the single step that would bring them there.[37] A man is like a bit of Labrador spar,[38] which has no lustre as you turn it in your hand, until you come to a particular angle; then it shows deep and beautiful colors. There is no adaptation or universal applicability in men, but each has his special talent, and the mastery of successful men consists in adroitly keeping themselves where and when that turn shall be oftenest to be practised. We do what we must, and call it by the best names we can, and would fain have the praise of having intended the result which ensues. I cannot recall any form of man who is not superfluous sometimes. But is not this pitiful? Life is not worth the taking, to do tricks in.

Of course, it needs the whole society, to give the symmetry we seek. The parti-colored wheel must revolve very fast to appear white. Something is learned too by conversing with so much folly and defect. In fine, whoever loses, we are always of the gaining party. Divinity is behind our failures and follies also. The plays of children are nonsense, but very educative nonsense. So is it with the largest and solemnest things, with commerce, government, church, marriage, and so with the history of every man's bread, and the ways by which he is to come by it. Like a bird which alights nowhere, but hops perpetually from bough to bough, is the Power which abides in no man and in no woman, but for a moment speaks from this one, and for another moment from that one.

* * *

But what help from these fineries or pedantries? What help from thought? Life is not dialectics. We, I think, in these times, have had lessons enough of the futility of criticism. Our young people have thought and written much on labor and reform, and for all that they have written, neither the world nor themselves have got on a step. Intellectual tasting of life will not supersede muscular activity. If a man should consider the nicety of the passage of a piece of bread down his throat, he would starve. At Education-Farm,[39] the noblest theory of life sat on the noblest figures of young men and maidens, quite powerless and melancholy. It would not rake or pitch a ton of hay; it would not rub down a horse; and the men and maidens it left pale and hungry. A political orator wittily compared our party promises to western roads, which opened stately enough, with planted trees on either side, to tempt the traveller, but soon became narrow and narrower, and ended in a squirrel-track, and ran up a tree.[40] So does culture with us; it ends in headache. Unspeakably sad and barren does life look to those, who a few months ago were dazzled with the splendor of the promise of the times. "There is now no longer any right course of action, nor any self-devotion left among the Iranis."[41] Objections and criticism we have had our fill of. There are objections to every course of life and action, and the practical wisdom infers an indifferency, from the omnipresence of objection. The whole frame of things preaches indifferency. Do not craze yourself[42] with thinking, but go about your business anywhere. Life is not intellectual or critical, but sturdy. Its chief good is for well-mixed[43] people who can enjoy what they find, without

39  In 1840 Emerson was invited to become a member of Brook Farm, a small utopian community then being founded by George and Sophia Ripley. In a letter to Emerson, George Ripley (1802–1880) wrote that at Brook Farm "thought would preside over the operations of labor, and labor would contribute to the expansion of thought; we should have industry without drudgery, and true equality without its vulgarity." Writing in December 1840 to Margaret Fuller, Emerson described himself as "so unpromising a candidate for any society. At the name of a society all my repulsions play, all my quills rise & sharpen" (L 2:364). Predictably, Emerson declined the invitation to join Brook Farm. (The community was dissolved in 1847.)

40  Emerson remembered the orator's speech, a denunciation of the presidency of Martin van Buren (1782–1862, president 1837–1841), from the spring of 1840 (J 7:492). The American philosopher William James (1842–1910), probably thinking of this passage, began his book *Pragmatism* (1907) with an anecdote about a squirrel running around a tree (a philosophical argument results).

41  A sentence from a (probably spurious) book of ancient Persian scriptures, *The Desatir*, that the Transcendentalist reformer Amos Bronson Alcott (1799–1888) presented to Emerson in 1842.

42  In addition to its obvious meaning (to go insane), to craze means "to produce fine cracks." The phrase therefore reflects Emerson's sense of life in the next sentence as "not intellectual or critical, but sturdy" (robust, vigorous, and durable).

43  In the *Nicomachean Ethics* of the Greek philosopher Aristotle (384–322 BCE) the temperate man is said to be *eukratês* (well-mixed).

question. Nature hates peeping, and our mothers speak her very sense when they say, "Children, eat your victuals, and say no more of it." To fill the hour,—that is happiness; to fill the hour, and leave no crevice for a repentance or an approval. We live amid surfaces, and the true art of life is to skate well on them. Under the oldest mouldiest conventions, a man of native force prospers just as well as in the newest world, and that by skill of handling and treatment. He can take hold anywhere. Life itself is a mixture of power and form, and will not bear the least excess of either. To finish the moment, to find the journey's end in every step of the road, to live the greatest number of good hours, is wisdom. It is not the part of men, but of fanatics, or of mathematicians, if you will, to say, that, the shortness of life considered, it is not worth caring whether for so short a duration we were sprawling in want, or sitting high. Since our office is with moments, let us husband them. Five minutes of today are worth as much to me, as five minutes in the next millennium. Let us be poised, and wise, and our own, today. Let us treat the men and women well: treat them as if they were real: perhaps they are. Men live in their fancy, like drunkards whose hands are too soft and tremulous for successful labor. It is a tempest of fancies, and the only ballast I know, is a respect to the present hour. Without any shadow of doubt, amidst this vertigo of shows and politics, I settle myself ever the firmer in the creed, that we should not postpone and refer and wish, but do broad justice where we are, by whomsoever we deal with, accepting our actual companions and circumstances, however humble or odious, as the mystic officials to whom the universe has delegated its whole pleasure for us. If these are mean and malignant, their contentment, which is the last victory of justice, is a more satisfying echo to the heart, than the voice of poets and the casual sympathy of admirable persons. I think that however a thoughtful man may suffer from the defects and absurdities of his company, he cannot without affectation deny to any set of men and women, a sensibility to extraordinary merit. The coarse and frivolous have an instinct of superiority, if they have not a sympathy, and honor it in their blind capricious way with sincere homage.

The fine young people despise life, but in me, and in such as with me are free from dyspepsia, and to whom a day is a sound and solid good, it is a great excess of politeness to look scornful and to cry for company. I am grown by sympathy a little eager and sentimental, but leave me alone, and I should relish every hour and what it brought me, the potluck of the day, as heartily as the oldest gossip in the bar-room. I am thankful for small mercies. I compared notes with one of my friends who expects everything of the universe, and is disappointed when anything is less than the best, and I found that I begin at the other extreme, expecting nothing, and am always full of thanks for moderate goods. I accept the clangor and jangle of contrary tendencies. I find my account in sots and bores also. They give a reality to the circumjacent picture, which such a vanishing meteorous appearance can ill spare. In the morning I awake, and find the old world, wife, babes, and mother, Concord and Boston, the dear old spiritual world, and even the dear old devil not far off. If we will take the good we find, asking no questions, we shall have heaping measures. The great gifts are not got by analysis. Everything good is on the highway. The middle region of our being is the temperate zone. We may climb into the thin and cold realm of pure geometry and lifeless science, or sink into that of sensation. Between these extremes is the equator of life, of thought, of spirit, of poetry,—a narrow belt. Moreover, in popular experience, everything good is on the highway. A collector peeps into all the picture-shops of Europe, for a landscape of Poussin, a crayon-sketch of Salvator; but the Transfiguration, the Last Judgment, the Communion of St. Jerome,[44] and what are as transcendent as these, are on the walls of the Vatican, the Uffizi, or the Louvre,[45] where every footman may see them; to say nothing of nature's pictures in every street, of sunsets and sunrises every day, and the sculpture of the human body never absent. A collector recently bought at public auction, in London, for one hundred and fifty-seven guineas, an autograph of Shakspeare: but for nothing a school-boy can read Hamlet, and can detect secrets of highest concernment yet unpublished therein. I think I will never read any but the commonest books,—the Bible, Homer, Dante, Shakspeare, and Milton.[46] Then we are impatient of so public a life and planet, and run hither and thither for nooks and secrets. The imagination delights in the wood-craft of Indians, trappers, and bee-hunters. We fancy that we are strangers, and not so intimately domesticated in the planet as the wild man, and the wild beast and bird. But the exclusion reaches them also; reaches the climbing, flying, gliding, feathered and four-footed

44    The landscapes of the French artist Nicolas Poussin (1594–1665) and the Italian artist Salvator Rosa (1615–1673) were enormously popular in Emerson's day. The Italian paintings that Emerson refers to are the *Transfiguration of Christ* by Raphael Sanzio (1483–1520), the *Last Judgment* by Michelangelo Buonarroti (1475–1564), and the *Last Communion of St. Jerome*, then a highly esteemed painting, by Domenichino (Domenico Zampieri; 1581–1641). Emerson saw all three during his visit to Rome in 1833.

45    Famous museums in (respectively) Rome, Florence, and Paris.

46    Homer, legendary author of Greek epics the *Iliad* and the *Odyssey* (9th century BCE); Dante Alighieri (ca. 1265–1321), greatest of Italian poets; the English poet John Milton (1608–1674), author of *Paradise Lost* (1667).

47    "Snipe, and bittern": varieties of wading birds.

48    "Nature all outside. Inside is the Nameless," Emerson wrote in his Journal (J 8:471).

49    Sages and moralists often prefer the "middle way." Emerson's favorite essayist, Montaigne, states such a preference in "Of Experience." Emerson, in his essay on Montaigne, saw the latter as "contented, self-respecting, and keeping the middle of the road."

50    "Lights" are luminaries; "Gentoos," Hindus. By "corn-eaters" Emerson means Grahamites, vegetarian followers of Sylvester Graham (1794–1851), who invented the Graham cracker. In an entry headed "Lethe" in his Journal, Emerson wrote, "It seemed strange to men that they should thus forget so fast, that they became suspicious that there was some treachery, and began to suspect their food that perhaps the bread they eat or the flesh was narcotic. Hence rose Graham societies" (1842; J 8:314).

51    See Matthew 11:19: "The Son of man came eating and drinking, and they say, Behold a man gluttonous, and a winebibber, a friend of publicans and sinners."

52    Allusion to Matthew 24:6: "and ye shall hear of wars and rumors of wars: see that ye be not troubled: for all these things must come to pass, but the end is not yet."

53    Shakespeare wrote in *The Tempest* (4.1.156–158), "We are such stuff / As dreams are made on, and our little life / Is rounded with a sleep."

man. Fox and woodchuck, hawk and snipe, and bittern,[47] when nearly seen, have no more root in the deep world than man, and are just such superficial tenants of the globe. Then the new molecular philosophy shows astronomical interspaces betwixt atom and atom, shows that the world is all outside: it has no inside.[48]

The mid-world is best.[49] Nature, as we know her, is no saint. The lights of the church, the ascetics, Gentoos and corn-eaters,[50] she does not distinguish by any favor. She comes eating and drinking and sinning.[51] Her darlings, the great, the strong, the beautiful, are not children of our law, do not come out of the Sunday School, nor weigh their food, nor punctually keep the commandments. If we will be strong with her strength, we must not harbor such disconsolate consciences, borrowed too from the consciences of other nations. We must set up the strong present tense against all the rumors of wrath,[52] past or to come. So many things are unsettled which it is of the first importance to settle,—and, pending their settlement, we will do as we do. Whilst the debate goes forward on the equity of commerce, and will not be closed for a century or two, New and Old England may keep shop. Law of copyright and international copyright is to be discussed, and, in the interim, we will sell our books for the most we can. Expediency of literature, reason of literature, lawfulness of writing down a thought, is questioned; much is to say on both sides, and, while the fight waxes hot, thou, dearest scholar, stick to thy foolish task, add a line every hour, and between whiles add a line. Right to hold land, right of property, is disputed, and the conventions convene, and before the vote is taken, dig away in your garden, and spend your earnings as a waif or godsend to all serene and beautiful purposes. Life itself is a bubble and a skepticism, and a sleep within a sleep.[53] Grant it, and as much more as they will,—but thou, God's darling! heed thy private dream: thou wilt not be missed in the scorning and skepticism: there are enough of them: stay there in thy closet, and toil, until the rest are agreed what to do about it. Thy sickness, they say, and thy puny habit, require that thou do this or avoid that, but know that thy life is a flitting state, a tent for a night, and do thou, sick or well, finish that stint. Thou art sick, but shalt not be worse, and the universe, which holds thee dear, shall be the better.

Human life is made up of the two elements, power and form, and the proportion must be invariably kept, if we would have it sweet and sound. Each of these elements in excess makes a mischief as hurtful as its defect. Everything runs to excess: every good quality is noxious, if unmixed, and, to carry the danger to the edge of ruin, nature causes each man's peculiarity to superabound. Here, among the farms, we adduce the scholars as examples of this treachery. They are nature's victims of expression. You who see the artist, the orator, the poet, too near, and find their life no more excellent than that of mechanics or farmers, and themselves victims of partiality, very hollow and haggard, and pronounce them failures,—not heroes, but quacks,—conclude very reasonably, that these arts are not for man, but are disease. Yet nature will not bear you out. Irresistible nature made men such, and makes legions more of such, every day. You love the boy reading in a book, gazing at a drawing, or a cast: yet what are these millions who read and behold, but incipient writers and sculptors? Add a little more of that quality which now reads and sees, and they will seize the pen and chisel. And if one remembers how innocently he began to be an artist, he perceives that nature joined with his enemy. A man is a golden impossibility. The line he must walk is a hair's breadth. The wise through excess of wisdom is made a fool.

*   *   *

How easily, if fate would suffer it, we might keep forever these beautiful limits, and adjust ourselves, once for all, to the perfect calculation of the kingdom of known cause and effect. In the street and in the newspapers, life appears so plain a business, that manly resolution and adherence to the multiplication-table through all weathers, will insure success. But ah! presently comes a day—or is it only a half-hour, with its angel-whispering—which discomfits the conclusions of nations and of years! Tomorrow again, everything looks real and angular, the habitual standards are reinstated, common sense is as rare as genius,—is the basis of genius, and experience is hands and feet to every enterprise;—and yet, he who should do his business on this understanding, would be quickly bankrupt. Power keeps quite another road than the turnpikes of choice and will, namely, the subterranean and invisible

54    This image is comparable to the earlier one of the squirrel track running up the tree: both passages depict an oblique, adventurous path rather than an orderly succession.

55    Leaping.

56    Short bouts (as in the expression "fits and starts").

57    In a letter printed in the *Dial* in October 1842, the English agitator and vegetarian James Pierrepont Greaves (1777–1842) was described as "a great apostle of the Newness to many, even when neither he nor they knew very clearly what was going forward."

58    See Luke 17:20–21: "The kingdom of God cometh not with observation . . . for, behold, the kingdom of God is within you."

59    Hiddenness: a transformation of the Lethe image from the beginning of "Experience."

tunnels and channels of life.[54] It is ridiculous that we are diplomatists, and doctors, and considerate people: there are no dupes like these. Life is a series of surprises, and would not be worth taking or keeping, if it were not. God delights to isolate us every day, and hide from us the past and the future. We would look about us, but with grand politeness he draws down before us an impenetrable screen of purest sky, and another behind us of purest sky. 'You will not remember,' he seems to say, 'and you will not expect.' All good conversation, manners, and action, come from a spontaneity which forgets usages, and makes the moment great. Nature hates calculators; her methods are saltatory[55] and impulsive. Man lives by pulses; our organic movements are such; and the chemical and ethereal agents are undulatory and alternate; and the mind goes antagonizing on, and never prospers but by fits.[56] We thrive by casualties. Our chief experiences have been casual. The most attractive class of people are those who are powerful obliquely, and not by the direct stroke: men of genius, but not yet accredited: one gets the cheer of their light, without paying too great a tax. Theirs is the beauty of the bird, or the morning light, and not of art. In the thought of genius there is always a surprise; and the moral sentiment is well called "the newness,"[57] for it is never other; as new to the oldest intelligence as to the young child,—"the kingdom that cometh without observation."[58] In like manner, for practical success, there must not be too much design. A man will not be observed in doing that which he can do best. There is a certain magic about his properest action, which stupefies your powers of observation, so that though it is done before you, you wist not of it. The art of life has a pudency,[59] and will not be exposed. Every man is an impossibility, until he is born; every thing impossible, until we see a success. The ardors of piety agree at last with the coldest skepticism,—that nothing is of us or our works,—that all is of God. Nature will not spare us the smallest leaf of laurel. All writing comes by the grace of God, and all doing and having. I would gladly be moral, and keep due metes and bounds, which I dearly love, and allow the most to the will of man, but I have set my heart on honesty in this chapter, and I can see nothing at last, in success or failure, than more or less of vital force supplied from the Eternal. The results of life are uncalculated and uncalculable. The years teach much which the days never know. The persons who compose our company, converse, and come and go, and design and execute many things, and somewhat comes of it all, but an unlooked-for result. The individual is always mistaken. He designed many things, and drew in other persons as coadjutors, quarrelled with some or all, blundered much, and something is done; all are a little advanced, but the individual is always mistaken. It turns out somewhat new, and very unlike what he promised himself.

\*   \*   \*

The ancients, struck with this irreducibleness of the elements of human life to calculation, exalted Chance into a divinity, but that is to stay too long at the spark,—which glitters truly at one point,—but the universe is warm with the latency of the same fire. The miracle of life which will not be expounded, but will remain a miracle, introduces a new element. In the growth of the embryo, Sir Everard Home, I think, noticed that the evolution was not from one central point, but coactive from three or more points.[60] Life has no memory. That which proceeds in succession might be remembered, but that which is coexistent, or ejaculated from a deeper cause, as yet far from being conscious, knows not its own tendency. So is it with us, now skeptical, or without unity, because immersed in forms and effects all seeming to be of equal yet hostile value, and now religious, whilst in the reception of spiritual law. Bear with these distractions, with this coetaneous[61] growth of the parts: they will one day be *members*, and obey one will.[62] On that one will, on that secret cause, they nail our attention and hope. Life is hereby melted into an expectation or a religion. Underneath the inharmonious and trivial particulars, is a musical perfection, the Ideal journeying always with us, the heaven without rent or seam. Do but observe the mode of our illumination. When I converse with a profound mind, or if at any time being alone I have good thoughts, I do not at once arrive at satisfactions, as when, being thirsty, I drink water, or go to the fire, being cold: no! but I am at first apprised of my vicinity to a new and excellent region of life. By persisting to read or to think, this region gives further sign of itself, as it were in flashes of light, in sudden discoveries of its profound beauty and repose, as if the clouds that covered it parted at intervals, and showed the approaching traveller the in-

60    According to Home (1756–1832) in his *Lectures on Comparative Anatomy* (1814–1828), the ovum forms centers within itself shortly after impregnation. The embryo, mentioned earlier in "Experience," will becomes a mature globe or sphere later in the essay.

61    Roughly simultaneous, of the same age.

62    Allusion to St. Paul's vision of the "whole body" made of "many members" in I Corinthians 12:11–20.

63    A transformation of the essay's images of the "little man" (from the prefatory poem to "Experience") and of Emerson's beloved son, little Waldo. Here Emerson himself, with child-like glee, takes the place of little Waldo: with a glance, perhaps, at the opening of Wordsworth's *Immortality Ode* ("the child is father to the man").

64    Mecca, the holy city of Islam and goal of Muslim pilgrims, stands in the middle of the Saudi Arabian desert.

65    Here Emerson seems to enter the promised land that was denied to him earlier in "Experience," when he wished to be "introduce[d] . . . into the reality." He passes beyond the friends who (like the lover in Plato's *Symposium* gazing on "the great sea of beauty" [210d] but unable to fully enter it) "stand on the brink of the ocean of thought and power, but . . . never take the single step that would bring them there," as Emerson puts it. (In his essay "The Poet," Emerson's judgment was more drastic: "On the brink of the waters of life and truth, we are miserably dying.") Emerson's new world is still "unapproachable": and he himself becomes less approachable here, abandoning us as he enters his own vision (or, possibly, mirage). Thoreau in his *Walden* (1854) exhorted the reader: "Be a Columbus to whole new continents and worlds within you." Emerson gives us a more playfully qualified vision than Thoreau's: though sublime, his hand-clapping enthusiasm also seems faintly silly. As with the comparison a few pages later of Columbus and America to "puss with her tail," Emerson here juxtaposes solitary play and exalted discovery, radical transformation and fond delusion. Like the kitten he describes, Emerson remains wrapped up in his own imaginative performance.

land mountains, with the tranquil eternal meadows spread at their base, whereon flocks graze, and shepherds pipe and dance. But every insight from this realm of thought is felt as initial, and promises a sequel. I do not make it; I arrive there, and behold what was there already. I make! O no! I clap my hands in infantine joy and amazement,[63] before the first opening to me of this august magnificence, old with the love and homage of innumerable ages, young with the life of life, the sunbright Mecca of the desert.[64] And what a future it opens! I feel a new heart beating with the love of the new beauty. I am ready to die out of nature, and be born again into this new yet unapproachable America I have found in the West.[65]

> "Since neither now nor yesterday began
> These thoughts, which have been ever, nor yet can
> A man be found who their first entrance knew."[66]

If I have described life as a flux of moods, I must now add, that there is that in us which changes not, and which ranks all sensations and states of mind. The consciousness in each man is a sliding scale,[67] which identifies him now with the First Cause, and now with the flesh of his body; life above life, in infinite degrees. The sentiment from which it sprung determines the dignity of any deed, and the question ever is, not, what you have done or forborne, but, at whose command you have done or forborne it.

Fortune, Minerva,[68] Muse, Holy Ghost,—these are quaint names, too narrow to cover this unbounded substance. The baffled intellect must still kneel before this cause, which refuses to be named,—ineffable cause, which every fine genius has essayed to represent by some emphatic symbol, as, Thales by water, Anaximenes by air, Anaxagoras by (Νοῦς) thought, Zoroaster by fire,[69] Jesus and the moderns by love: and the metaphor of each has become a national religion. The Chinese Mencius[70] has not been the least successful in his generalization. "I fully understand language," he said, "and nourish well my vast-flowing vigor."—"I beg to ask what you call vast-flowing vigor?" said his companion. "The explanation," replied Mencius, "is difficult. This vigor is supremely great, and in the highest degree unbending. Nourish it correctly, and do it no injury, and it will fill up the vacancy between heaven and earth. This vigor accords with and assists justice and reason, and leaves no hunger." In our more correct writing, we give to this generalization the name of Being, and thereby confess that we have arrived as far as we can go. Suffice it for the joy of the universe, that we have not arrived at a wall, but at interminable oceans. Our life seems not present, so much as prospective; not for the affairs on which it is wasted, but as a hint of this vast-flowing vigor. Most of life seems to be mere advertisement of faculty: information is given us not to sell ourselves cheap; that we are very great. So, in particulars, our greatness is always in a tendency or direction, not in an action. It is for us to believe in the rule, not in the exception. The noble are thus known from the ignoble. So in accepting the leading of the sentiments, it is not what we believe concerning the immortality of the soul, or the like, but *the universal impulse to believe*,[71] that is the material circumstance, and is the principal fact in the history of the globe. Shall we describe this cause as that which works directly? The spirit is not helpless or needful of mediate organs. It has plentiful powers and direct effects. I am explained without explaining, I am felt without acting, and where I am not. Therefore all just persons are satisfied with their own praise. They refuse to explain themselves, and are content that new actions should do them that office. They believe that we communicate without speech, and above speech, and that no right action of ours is quite unaffecting to our friends, at whatever distance; for the influence of action is not to be measured by miles. Why should I fret myself, because a circumstance has occurred, which hinders my presence where I was expected? If I am not at the meeting, my presence where I am should be as useful to the commonwealth of friendship and wisdom, as would be my presence in that place. I exert the same quality of power in all places. Thus journeys the mighty Ideal before us; it never was known to fall into the rear. No man ever came to an experience which was satiating, but his good is tidings of a better. Onward and onward! In liberated moments, we know that a new picture of life and duty is already possible; the elements already exist in many minds around you, of a doctrine of life which shall transcend any written record we have. The new statement will comprise the skepticisms, as well as the faiths of society, and out of unbeliefs a creed shall be formed. For, skepticisms are not gratuitous or lawless, but are

66   Lines 455–457 from *Antigone* by the Greek playwright Sophocles (ca. 496–406 BCE), quoted by Plutarch in a discussion of the soul's immortality (in his essay "Of Common Conception against the Stoics").

67   Revises the image of the stairs at the beginning of "Experience."

68   Fortune (in Greek, *Tukhê*; in Latin, Fortuna) was a divinity among the Greeks and Romans; Minerva is the Roman goddess equivalent to Athena.

69   The first three are pre-Socratic Greek philosophers (Thales and Anaximenes lived in the seventh and sixth centuries BCE, Anaxagoras in the fifth century); the last, the legendary founder of Zoroastrianism, the ancient Persian religion (ca. 11th century BCE).

70   Chinese philosopher (4th century BCE) whom Emerson read with great admiration in 1843, probably at the instigation of Bronson Alcott.

71   William James adapted Emerson's phrase as the title of his lecture "The Will to Believe" (1897).

72    The Emerson scholar Barbara Packer argues that the Fall described here is "'self-distrust,' the self's ignorance or denial of its own divinity": what Emerson calls, later in "Experience," our "ill-concealed deity," which makes us "believe in ourselves, as we do not believe in others." When we fall into adult circumspection and conformity (that is, "consciousness"), we lose sight of the visionary ruthlessness of the "great and crescive self" outlined in the next few pages of the essay.

73    Growing, increasing.

limitations of the affirmative statement, and the new philosophy must take them in, and make affirmations outside of them, just as much as it must include the oldest beliefs.

\* \* \*

It is very unhappy, but too late to be helped, the discovery we have made, that we exist. That discovery is called the Fall of Man. Ever afterwards, we suspect our instruments.[72] We have learned that we do not see directly, but mediately, and that we have no means of correcting these colored and distorting lenses which we are, or of computing the amount of their errors. Perhaps these subject-lenses have a creative power; perhaps there are no objects. Once we lived in what we saw; now, the rapaciousness of this new power, which threatens to absorb all things, engages us. Nature, art, persons, letters, religions,—objects, successively tumble in, and God is but one of its ideas. Nature and literature are subjective phenomena; every evil and every good thing is a shadow which we cast. The street is full of humiliations to the proud. As the fop contrived to dress his bailiffs in his livery, and make them wait on his guests at table, so the chagrins which the bad heart gives off as bubbles, at once take form as ladies and gentlemen in the street, shopmen or bar-keepers in hotels, and threaten or insult whatever is threatenable and insultable in us. 'Tis the same with our idolatries. People forget that it is the eye which makes the horizon, and the rounding mind's eye which makes this or that man a type or representative of humanity with the name of hero or saint. Jesus the "providential man," is a good man on whom many people are agreed that these optical laws shall take effect. By love on one part, and by forbearance to press objection on the other part, it is for a time settled, that we will look at him in the centre of the horizon, and ascribe to him the properties that will attach to any man so seen. But the longest love or aversion has a speedy term. The great and crescive[73] self, rooted in absolute nature, supplants all relative existence, and ruins the kingdom of mortal friendship and love. Marriage (in what is called the spiritual world) is impossible, because of the inequality between every subject and every object. The subject is the receiver of Godhead, and at every comparison must feel his being enhanced by that cryptic might. Though not in energy, yet by presence, this magazine of substance cannot be otherwise than felt: nor can any force of intellect attribute to the object the proper deity which sleeps or wakes forever in every subject. Never can love make consciousness and ascription equal in force. There will be the same gulf between every me and thee, as between the original and the picture. The universe is the bride of the soul. All private sympathy is partial. Two human beings are like globes, which can touch only in a point, and, whilst they remain in contact, all other points of each of the spheres are inert; their turn must also come, and the longer a particular union lasts, the more energy of appetency the parts not in union acquire.

Life will be imaged, but cannot be divided nor doubled. Any invasion of its unity would be chaos. The soul is not twin-born, but the only begotten, and though revealing itself as child in time, child in appearance, is of a fatal and universal power, admitting no co-life. Every day, every act betrays the ill-concealed deity. We believe in ourselves, as we do not believe in others. We permit all things to ourselves, and that which we call sin in others, is experiment for us.[74] It is an instance of our faith in ourselves, that men never speak of crime as lightly as they think: or, every man thinks a latitude safe for himself, which is nowise to be indulged to another. The act looks very differently on the inside, and on the outside; in its quality, and in its consequences. Murder in the murderer is no such ruinous thought as poets and romancers will have it; it does not unsettle him, or fright him from his ordinary notice of trifles: it is an act quite easy to be contemplated, but in its sequel, it turns out to be a horrible jangle and confounding of all relations. Especially the crimes that spring from love, seem right and fair from the actor's point of view, but, when acted, are found destructive of society. No man at last believes that he can be lost, nor that the crime in him is as black as in the felon. Because the intellect qualifies in our own case the moral judgments. For there is no crime to the intellect. That is antinomian or hypernomian, and judges law as well as fact. "It is worse than a crime, it is a blunder," said Napoleon, speaking the language of the intellect.[75] To it, the world is a problem in mathematics or the science of quantity, and it leaves out praise and blame, and all weak emotions. All stealing is comparative. If you come to absolutes, pray who does not steal? Saints are sad, because they behold sin, (even when they speculate,) from the point of view of the conscience, and not of the

74    An idea reminiscent of Goethe's *Faust* (1808–1832), whose hero restlessly incarnates the will to experiment, even when it proves morally damaging. "America, from the circumstances of its late discovery and natural advantages has been a land of experiments," Emerson observed in a Journal entry of 1821 (J 1:297).

75    In 1804 the French emperor Napoleon Bonaparte (1769–1821), fearing assassination, had the duc d'Enghien kidnapped and killed, causing a scandal. The words Emerson attributes to Napoleon himself were probably spoken by his former minister of police, Joseph Fouché (1759–1820; as reported by the Scottish novelist Sir Walter Scott [1771–1832] in his *Life of Napoleon* [1827]): "the duke's execution was worse than a moral crime—it was a political blunder."

76    In this and the following sentences Emerson engages theological arguments concerning evil: is evil merely the absence of good, or does it have a substance, and a will, of its own?

77    The phrase "fall into place" recalls, and revises, Emerson's image of the Fall of Man earlier in "Experience." "As I am, so I see" might be Emerson's answer to the motto of the philosopher René Descartes (1596–1650), "Cogito, ergo sum" (I think, therefore I am). Compare, as well, Emerson's later statement, "I am and I have, but I do not get."

78    Hermes was the Greek messenger god; Cadmus, the legendary founder of Thebes. Emerson joins to them the scientist Sir Isaac Newton (1642–1727), the explorer Christopher Columbus (1451–1506), and Napoleon.

79    Hard coal that burns with a clean, pure flame.

80    "When I play with my cat," Montaigne wrote in his "Apology for Raymond Sebond," "who knows if I am not a pastime to her more than she is to me?" Johannes Kepler (1571–1630), the German astronomer, discovered in 1604 that Mars travels around the sun. In a notebook Emerson remarked, "Eternity. Identity Past Kitty & her tail" (J 12:417).

81    From Emerson's Journal (1845): "Ah we busybodies! Cannot we be a little abstemious? We talk too much, & act too much, & think too much. Cannot we cease doing, & gravitate only to our ends? Cannot we let the morning be?" (J 9:186). In 1850–1851, he added, "We are wasted with our versatility; with the eagerness to grasp on every possible side, we all run to nothing" (J 11:319).

82    Emerson wrote in his Journal in May 1843, "A man should not be able to look except
*(continued)*

intellect; a confusion of thought. Sin seen from the thought, is a diminution or *less:* seen from the conscience or will, it is pravity or *bad.* The intellect names it shade, absence of light, and no essence.[76] The conscience must feel it as essence, essential evil. This it is not: it has an objective existence, but no subjective.

Thus inevitably does the universe wear our color, and every object fall successively into the subject itself. The subject exists, the subject enlarges; all things sooner or later fall into place. As I am, so I see;[77] use what language we will, we can never say anything but what we are; Hermes, Cadmus, Columbus, Newton, Bonaparte,[78] are the mind's ministers. Instead of feeling a poverty when we encounter a great man, let us treat the new comer like a travelling geologist, who passes through our estate, and shows us good slate, or limestone, or anthracite,[79] in our brush pasture. The partial action of each strong mind in one direction, is a telescope for the objects on which it is pointed. But every other part of knowledge is to be pushed to the same extravagance, ere the soul attains her due sphericity. Do you see that kitten chasing so prettily her own tail? If you could look with her eyes, you might see her surrounded with hundreds of figures performing complex dramas, with tragic and comic issues, long conversations, many characters, many ups and downs of fate,—and meantime it is only puss and her tail. How long before our masquerade will end its noise of tambourines, laughter, and shouting, and we shall find it was a solitary performance?—A subject and an object,—it takes so much to make the galvanic circuit complete, but magnitude adds nothing. What imports it whether it is Kepler and the sphere; Columbus and America; a reader and his book; or puss with her tail?[80]

It is true that all the muses and love and religion hate these developments, and will find a way to punish the chemist, who publishes in the parlor the secrets of the laboratory. And we cannot say too little of our constitutional necessity of seeing things under private aspects, or saturated with our humors. And yet is the God the native of these bleak rocks. That need makes in morals the capital virtue of self-trust. We must hold hard to this poverty, however scandalous, and by more vigorous self-recoveries, after the sallies of action, possess our axis more firmly. The life of truth is cold, and so far mournful; but it is not the slave of tears, contritions, and perturbations. It does not attempt another's work, nor adopt another's facts. It is a main lesson of wisdom to know your own from another's. I have learned that I cannot dispose of other people's facts; but I possess such a key to my own, as persuades me against all their denials, that they also have a key to theirs. A sympathetic person is placed in the dilemma of a swimmer among drowning men, who all catch at him, and if he give so much as a leg or a finger, they will drown him. They wish to be saved from the mischiefs of their vices, but not from their vices. Charity would be wasted on this poor waiting on the symptoms. A wise and hardy physician will say, *Come out of that*, as the first condition of advice.

In this our talking America, we are ruined by our good nature and listening on all sides.[81] This compliance takes away the power of being greatly useful. A man should not be able to look other than directly and forthright.[82] A preoccupied attention is the only answer to the importunate frivolity of other people: an attention, and to an aim which makes their wants frivolous.[83] This is a divine answer, and leaves no appeal, and no hard thoughts. In Flaxman's drawing of the Eumenides of Æschylus, Orestes supplicates Apollo, whilst the Furies sleep on the threshold.[84] The face of the god expresses a shade of regret and compassion, but calm with the conviction of the irreconcilableness of the two spheres. He is born into other politics, into the eternal and beautiful. The man at his feet asks for his interest in turmoils of the earth, into which his nature cannot enter.[85] And the Eumenides there lying express pictorially this disparity. The god is surcharged with his divine destiny.

\* \* \*

Illusion, Temperament, Succession, Surface, Surprise, Reality, Subjectiveness,—these are threads on the loom[86] of time, these are the lords of life. I dare not assume to give their order, but I name them as I find them in my way. I know better than to claim any completeness for my picture. I am a fragment, and this is a fragment of me. I can very confidently announce one or another law, which throws itself into relief and form, but I am too young yet by some ages to compile a code. I gossip for my hour concerning the eternal politics. I have seen many fair pictures not in vain. A wonderful time I have lived in. I am not the novice I was fourteen, nor yet seven years ago.

directly. He should be the fool of his thought, mad with his action" (J 8:401). Emerson asks us to recognize such directness even when it occurs in the form of the "oblique and casual" (as "Experience" puts it).

83    In a passage noted by Emerson, the English Romantic author S. T. Coleridge (1772–1834) in *The Statesman's Manual* (1816) wrote, "An excess in our attachment to temporal and personal objects can be counteracted only by a pre-occupation of the intellect and the affections with permanent, universal, and eternal truths." In his Journal Emerson warned, "And if those seek you, whom you do not seek, hold them stiffly to their rightful claims. Give them your conversation; be to them a teacher, utter oracles, but admit them never into any infringement on your hours; keep state: be their priest not their companion . . ." (September 1836; J 5:209).

84    The British artist John Flaxman (1755–1826) illustrated the *Eumenides* (458 BCE) of the Greek tragic poet Aeschylus (ca. 525–ca. 456 BCE). In Aeschylus's play, the Furies, spirits of revenge and the persecutors of Orestes (who has killed his mother, Clytemnaestra) are transmuted into kindly guardians of Athens. As Emerson suggests, Apollo in fact plays only a small role in the defense of Orestes: it is Athena who argues for him. Emerson implies that we are to identify with Apollo's divine remoteness, rather than with Athena's civic involvement, her loyalty to Orestes and to Athens.

85    The ending of the essay "Illusions" takes up this Emersonian picture of solitary man alone with the gods.

86    Suggesting the thread of life spun, lengthened, and cut by the classical Parcae, or Fates. The sequence of presences beginning
(continued)

with "Illusion" differs from the earlier list of the lords of life in the prefatory poem to "Experience." Reality and Illusion have been added; Use, Dream, and Wrong dropped. The "inventor of the game" remains unnamed.

87    "Fruit" here means "profit"; it also suggests the essay's earlier image of the Fall of Man.

88    "Get" means "to beget" as well as "to grasp or possess." Compare, a few pages earlier, "I do not make it; I arrive there." In his essay "The Poet," Emerson emphasized the talent for creative reception: the poet receives "rays or appulses" broadcast by the cosmos.

89    Destiny or necessity. According to Plato, whose *Phaedrus* Emerson cites here, Adrastia rewards in their next lives souls who have caught a glimpse of truth, but punishes those who "take on a burden of forgetfulness and wrongdoing" (248c).

90    Manipular (that is, through manipulation), derived from the Latin *manus* (hand), recalls Emerson's earlier reference to "the most unhandsome part of our condition."

91    Emerson plays on the similarity of "success" and "succession"—and glances back at the essay's opening image of taking steps on a stairway.

92    In his introductory lecture to the series "Human Culture" (1837), Emerson boldly claimed, "Ideal is not opposed to Real, but to Actual. The Ideal is the Real. The Actual is but the apparent and the Temporary" (EL 2:217).

Let who will ask, where is the fruit? I find a private fruit sufficient.[87] This is a fruit,—that I should not ask for a rash effect from meditations, counsels, and the hiving of truths. I should feel it pitiful to demand a result on this town and county, an overt effect on the instant month and year. The effect is deep and secular as the cause. It works on periods in which mortal lifetime is lost. All I know is reception; I am and I have: but I do not get,[88] and when I have fancied I had gotten anything, I found I did not. I worship with wonder the great Fortune. My reception has been so large, that I am not annoyed by receiving this or that superabundantly. I say to the Genius, if he will pardon the proverb, *In for a mill, in for a million.* When I receive a new gift, I do not macerate my body to make the account square, for, if I should die, I could not make the account square. The benefit overran the merit the first day, and has overran the merit ever since. The merit itself, so-called, I reckon part of the receiving.

Also, that hankering after an overt or practical effect seems to me an apostasy. In good earnest, I am willing to spare this most unnecessary deal of doing. Life wears to me a visionary face. Hardest, roughest action is visionary also. It is but a choice between soft and turbulent dreams. People disparage knowing and the intellectual life, and urge doing. I am very content with knowing, if only I could know. That is an august entertainment, and would suffice me a great while. To know a little, would be worth the expense of this world. I hear always the law of Adrastia, "that every soul which had acquired any truth, should be safe from harm until another period."[89]

I know that the world I converse with in the city and in the farms, is not the world I *think*. I observe that difference, and shall observe it. One day, I shall know the value and law of this discrepance. But I have not found that much was gained by manipular attempts[90] to realize the world of thought. Many eager persons successively make an experiment in this way, and make themselves ridiculous. They acquire democratic manners, they foam at the mouth, they hate and deny. Worse, I observe, that, in the history of mankind, there is never a solitary example of success,—taking their own tests of success.[91] I say this polemically, or in reply to the inquiry, why not realize your world?[92] But far be from me the despair which prejudges the law by a paltry empiricism,—since there never was a right endeavor, but it succeeded. Patience and patience, we shall win at the last. We must be very suspicious of the deceptions of the element of time. It takes a good deal of time to eat or to sleep, or to earn a hundred dollars, and a very little time to entertain a hope and an insight which becomes the light of our life. We dress our garden, eat our dinners, discuss the household with our wives, and these things make no impression, are forgotten next week; but in the solitude to which every man is always returning, he has a sanity and revelations, which in his passage into new worlds he will carry with him. Never mind the ridicule, never mind the defeat: up again, old heart!—it seems to say,—there is victory yet for all justice; and the true romance which the world exists to realize,[93] will be the transformation of genius into practical power.[94]

93    "Romance" here means a fabulous fictional narrative (as opposed to a realistic work). Emerson remarked in his Journal (May–June 1843), "Reform, people hate the sound of, now that they have begun to think it is like reading novels, which, when they are done, leave them just where they were, carpenters, & merchants, & debtors, & poor ladies,—only, they disbelieved the novel & believed at first the reformer" (J 8:416).

In his lecture "The Spirit of the Times" (1848), Emerson exclaimed, "The life of man is the true romance which, when it is valiantly conducted and all the stops of the instrument opened, will go nigh to craze the beholder with anxiety, wonder, and love" (LL 1:124).

94    Emerson returns to his theme of genius (see note 5, above); the word occurs a number of times in "Experience."

Waldo Emerson.

# Politics

*"Politics" is the seventh essay in* Essays: Second Series *(1844). Emerson's essay began in 1837 as a lecture, "Politics," that he revised several times over the years. Emerson's aim in the essay is to make us see beyond the idea that politics exists to safeguard property. Instead, he argues, a society's politics stems from its character and is subject to continual change. Politics is meant to serve our hopes, and even a politics of love is therefore imaginable (as it was for the Hebrew prophets, or Jesus). Emerson is no mere dreamer: he knows that "persons and property must and will have their just sway." Through such worldly action, through the commerce of persons and property, principles take effect, and corruption becomes intolerable; the world's just character is revealed.*

1    Merlin, legendary magician from the tales of King Arthur; Napoleon Bonaparte (1769–1821), French emperor and conqueror of much of Europe.

2    Amphion, in ancient Greek myth, was supposed to have raised the walls of Thebes by

*(continued)*

Gold and iron are good
To buy iron and gold;
All earth's fleece and food
For their like are sold.
Hinted Merlin wise,
Proved Napoleon great,—[1]
Nor kind nor coinage buys
Aught above its rate.
Fear, Craft, and Avarice
Cannot rear a State.
Out of dust to build
What is more than dust,—
Walls Amphion piled
Phœbus[2] stablish must.
When the Muses nine
With the Virtues[3] meet,
Find to their design
An Atlantic seat,
By green orchard boughs
Fended from the heat,

Where the statesman ploughs
Furrow for the wheat;
When the Church is social worth,
When the state-house is the hearth,
Then the perfect State is come,
The republican at home.[4]

In dealing with the State, we ought to remember that its institutions are not aboriginal,[5] though they existed before we were born: that they are not superior to the citizen: that every one of them was once the act of a single man:[6] every law and usage was a man's expedient to meet a particular case: that they all are imitable, all alterable; we may make as good; we may make better. Society is an illusion to the young citizen. It lies before him in rigid repose,

playing music; Phoebus Apollo is the sun god, associated with poetry. Emerson sees Amphion as the practical builder, but Phoebus as the poet who truly establishes a city.

3    There are four cardinal virtues (justice, prudence, fortitude, and temperance).

4    A self-consciously utopian prefatory poem, recalling the Fool's prophecy in Shakespeare's *King Lear:* "When priests are more in word than matter; / When brewers mar their malt with water; / When nobles are their tailors' tutors; / . . . When every case in law is right; / No squire in debt, nor no poor knight . . ." (The Fool credits his prophecy to Merlin, whom Emerson mentions as well.)

5    Original.

6    "An institution is the lengthened shadow of one man," Emerson wrote in "Self-Reliance."

South side of Concord's main street, the Milldam.

7      Pisistratus or Peisistratus (d. 527 BCE), tyrant of Athens; Oliver Cromwell (1599–1658), Lord Protector of England. Emerson contrasts their brief rule to the long-lasting influence of the philosopher Plato (429–347 BCE) and the apostle Paul (ca. 5–ca. 67 CE): he esteems the power of the nonpolitician over that of the politician.

8      Edward Emerson, in his edition of his father's writings, supplied this footnote: "Students of the Black Art held that demons could be kept out of mischief by setting them at hopeless tasks, such as making ropes out of sand."

9      Reminder. Emerson rejects the idea, promoted in Plato's *Republic* and *Laws* as well as in the works of later thinkers, that laws imposed on a people can shape them, guiding the nation or city in a particular direction. Instead, he argues, laws stem from the character of a people; when that character changes, the laws will, too.

10      Emerson's friend Henry David Thoreau (1817–1862) wrote in his essay "Resistance to Civil Government" (1849; later known as "Civil Disobedience") that the government "can have no pure right over my person or property but what I concede to it."

11      Fine capacity to perceive and appreciate.

with certain names, men, and institutions, rooted like oak-trees to the centre, round which all arrange themselves the best they can. But the old statesman knows that society is fluid; there are no such roots and centres; but any particle may suddenly become the centre of the movement, and compel the system to gyrate round it, as every man of strong will, like Pisistratus, or Cromwell, does for a time, and every man of truth, like Plato, or Paul,[7] does forever. But politics rest on necessary foundations, and cannot be treated with levity. Republics abound in young civilians, who believe that the laws make the city, that grave modifications of the policy and modes of living, and employments of the population, that commerce, education, and religion, may be voted in or out; and that any measure, though it were absurd, may be imposed on a people, if only you can get sufficient voices to make it a law. But the wise know that foolish legislation is a rope of sand, which perishes in the twisting;[8] that the State must follow, and not lead the character and progress of the citizen; the strongest usurper is quickly got rid of; and they only who build on Ideas, build for eternity; and that the form of government which prevails, is the expression of what cultivation exists in the population which permits it. The law is only a memorandum.[9] We are superstitious, and esteem the statute somewhat: so much life as it has in the character of living men, is its force. The statute stands there to say, yesterday we agreed so and so, but how feel ye this article today?[10] Our statute is a currency, which we stamp with our own portrait: it soon becomes unrecognizable, and in process of time will return to the mint. Nature is not democratic, nor limited-monarchical, but despotic, and will not be fooled or abated of any jot of her authority, by the pertest of her sons: and as fast as the public mind is opened to more intelligence, the code is seen to be brute and stammering. It speaks not articulately, and must be made to. Meantime the education of the general mind never stops. The reveries of the true and simple are prophetic. What the tender poetic youth dreams, and prays, and paints today, but shuns the ridicule of saying aloud, shall presently be the resolutions of public bodies, then shall be carried as grievance and bill of rights through conflict and war, and then shall be triumphant law and establishment for a hundred years, until it gives place, in turn, to new prayers and pictures. The history of the State sketches in coarse outline the progress of thought, and follows at a distance the delicacy[11] of culture and of aspiration.

The theory of politics, which has possessed the mind of men, and which they have expressed the best they could in their laws and in their revolutions, considers persons and property as the two objects for whose protection government exists. Of persons, all have equal rights, in virtue of being identical in nature.[12] This interest, of course, with its whole power demands a democracy. Whilst the rights of all as persons are equal, in virtue of their access to reason, their rights in property are very unequal. One man owns his clothes, and another owns a county. This accident, depending, primarily, on the skill and virtue of the parties, of which there is every degree, and, secondarily, on patrimony, falls unequally, and its rights, of course, are unequal. Personal rights, universally the same, demand a government framed on the ratio of the census: property demands a government framed on the ratio of owners and of owning.[13] Laban, who has flocks and herds, wishes them looked after by an officer on the frontiers, lest the Midianites shall drive them off, and pays a tax to that end. Jacob has no flocks or herds, and no fear of the Midianites, and pays no tax to the officer. It seemed fit that Laban and Jacob should have equal rights to elect the officer, who is to defend their persons, but that Laban, and not Jacob, should elect the officer who is to guard the sheep and cattle. And, if question arise whether additional officers or watchtowers should be provided, must not Laban and Isaac, and those who must sell part of their herds to buy protection for the rest, judge better of this, and with more right, than Jacob, who, because he is a youth and a traveller, eats their bread and not his own?[14]

In the earliest society the proprietors made their own wealth, and so long as it comes to the owners in the direct way, no other opinion would arise in any equitable community, than that property should make the law for property, and persons the law for persons.

But property passes through donation or inheritance to those who do not create it. Gift, in one case, makes it as really the new owner's, as labor made it the first owner's: in the other case, of patrimony, the law makes an ownership, which will be valid in each man's view according to the estimate which he sets on the public tranquillity.

It was not, however, found easy to embody the readily admitted principle, that property should make law for property, and persons for persons: since persons and property mixed themselves in every transaction.[15] At last it

12    A severe though somewhat oblique comment on the Constitution's provision (in Article 1, Section 2) that slaves, euphemistically described as "all other Persons," count as three-fifths of "free Persons . . . excluding Indians not taxed" in the apportioning of representatives to Congress.

13    Under President Andrew Jackson (1767–1845), in office 1829–1837, voting rights for free white males were largely freed from property qualifications (a development that had begun earlier in the 1820s).

14    Emerson freely adapts Genesis 28–31. In the original narrative, Jacob—as Emerson and his readers well knew—asserts his rights against Laban through trickery, and finally flees from him.

15    The English philosopher John Locke (1632–1704) argued that property rights develop when people "mix" their labor with the land. Emerson, against Locke, asserts that person and property mix in "every transaction," and therefore that property rights are more fluid than Locke thought. Many Unitarians and Transcendentalists criticized Locke's elevation of empirical sense over aspiration and imagination.

16    Sparta, famously ascetic city-state in classical Greece; the quoted saying comes from the *Moralia* by the Greek writer Plutarch (ca. 46–ca. 122), one of Emerson's favorite authors.

17    This complex, paragraph-long sentence ends with a conditional: "if men can be educated . . . the moral sentiment will write the law of the land." Emerson acknowledges that such education is not easy, and that property may well retain its hold.

18    In his essay "Compensation," Emerson writes, "Things refuse to be mismanaged long. *Res nolunt diu male administrari*" (a Latin proverb, translated in the preceding phrase).

seemed settled, that the rightful distinction was, that the proprietors should have more elective franchise than non-proprietors, on the Spartan principle of "calling that which is just, equal; not that which is equal, just."[16]

That principle no longer looks so self-evident as it appeared in former times, partly, because doubts have arisen whether too much weight had not been allowed in the laws, to property, and such a structure given to our usages, as allowed the rich to encroach on the poor, and to keep them poor; but mainly, because there is an instinctive sense, however obscure and yet inarticulate, that the whole constitution of property, on its present tenures, is injurious, and its influence on persons deteriorating and degrading; that truly, the only interest for the consideration of the State, is persons: that property will always follow persons; that the highest end of government is the culture of men: and if men can be educated, the institutions will share their improvement, and the moral sentiment will write the law of the land.[17]

If it be not easy to settle the equity of this question, the peril is less when we take note of our natural defences. We are kept by better guards than the vigilance of such magistrates as we commonly elect. Society always consists, in greatest part, of young and foolish persons. The old, who have seen through the hypocrisy of courts and statesmen, die, and leave no wisdom to their sons. These believe their own newspaper, as their fathers did at their age. With such an ignorant and deceivable majority, States would soon run to ruin, but that there are limitations, beyond which the folly and ambition of governors cannot go. Things have their laws, as well as men; and things refuse to be trifled with.[18] Property will be protected. Corn will not grow, unless it is planted and manured; but the farmer will not plant or hoe it, unless the chances are a hundred to one, that he will cut and harvest it. Under any forms, persons and property must and will have their just sway. They exert their power, as steadily as matter its attraction. Cover up a pound of earth never so cunningly, divide and subdivide it; melt it to liquid, convert it to gas; it will always weigh a pound: it will always attract and resist other matter, by the full virtue of one pound weight;—and the attributes of a person, his wit and his moral energy, will exercise, under any law or extinguishing tyranny, their proper force,—if not overtly, then covertly; if not for the law, then against it; if not wholesomely, then poisonously; with right, or by might.

The boundaries of personal influence it is impossible to fix, as persons are organs of moral or supernatural force. Under the dominion of an idea, which possesses the minds of multitudes, as civil freedom, or the religious sentiment, the powers of persons are no longer subjects of calculation. A nation of men unanimously bent on freedom, or conquest, can easily confound the arithmetic of statists,[19] and achieve extravagant actions, out of all proportion to their means; as, the Greeks, the Saracens,[20] the Swiss, the Americans, and the French have done.

In like manner, to every particle of property belongs its own attraction. A cent is the representative of a certain quantity of corn or other commodity. Its value is in the necessities of the animal man. It is so much warmth, so much bread, so much water, so much land. The law may do what it will with the owner of property, its just power will still attach to the cent. The law may in a mad freak[21] say, that all shall have power except the owners of property: they shall have no vote. Nevertheless, by a higher law, the property will, year after year, write every statute that respects property. The non-proprietor will be the scribe of the proprietor. What the owners wish to do, the whole power of property will do, either through the law, or else in defiance of it. Of course, I speak of all the property, not merely of the great estates. When the rich are outvoted, as frequently happens, it is the joint treasury of the poor which exceeds their accumulations. Every man owns something, if it is only a cow, or a wheelbarrow, or his arms, and so has that property to dispose of.

The same necessity which secures the rights of person and property against the malignity or folly of the magistrate, determines the form and methods of governing, which are proper to each nation, and to its habit of thought, and nowise transferable to other states of society. In this country, we are very vain of our political institutions, which are singular in this, that they sprung, within the memory of living men, from the character and condition of the people, which they still express with sufficient fidelity,—and we ostentatiously prefer them to any other in history. They are not better, but only fitter for us. We may be wise in asserting the advantage in modern times of the democratic form, but to other states of society, in which religion consecrated the monarchical, that and not this was expedient. Democracy is better for us, because the religious sentiment of the present time accords better

19    Statisticians.

20    Muslims (term used by medieval Christians).

21    Whim.

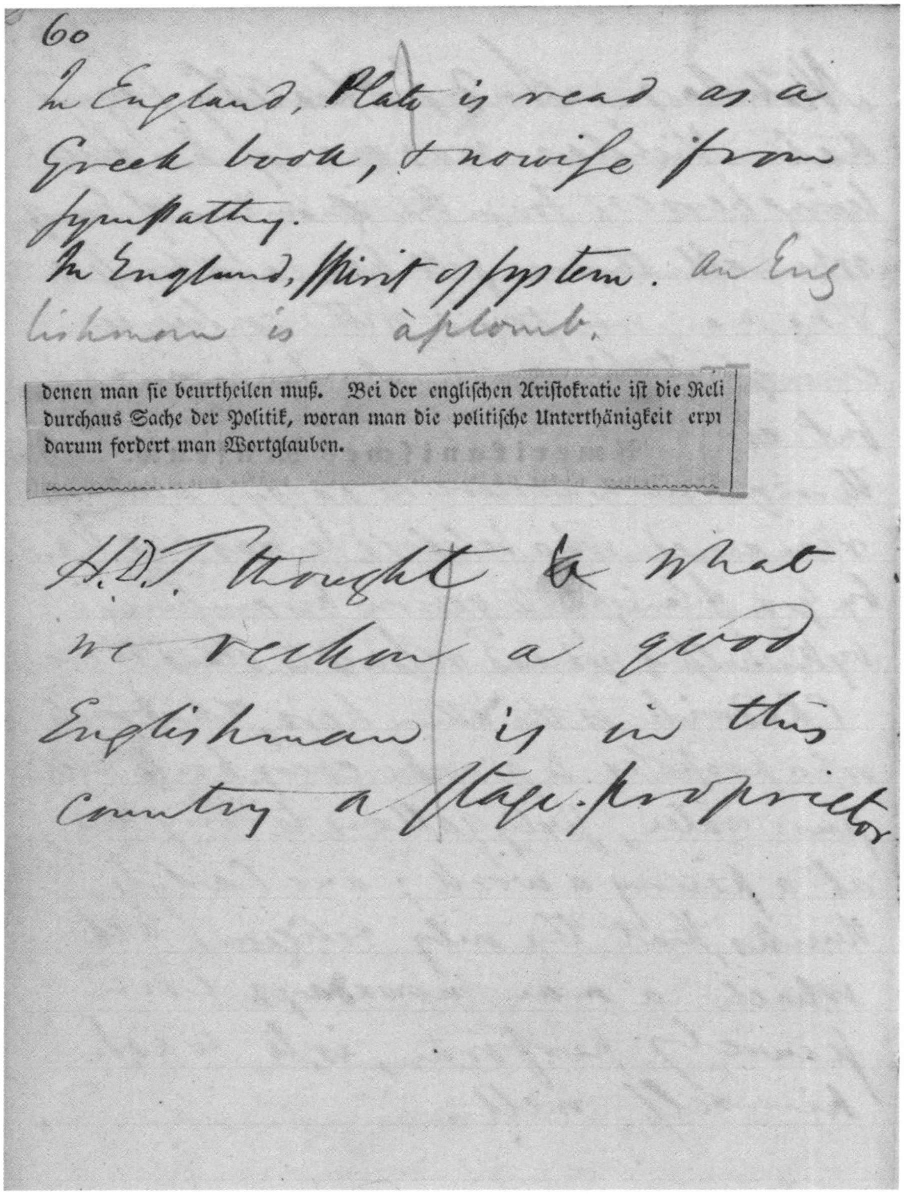

60

In England, Plato is read as a
Greek book, & nowise from
sympathy.

In England, Spirit of system. An Eng
lishman is  àplomb.

denen man sie beurtheilen muß.   Bei der englischen Aristokratie ist die Reli
durchaus Sache der Politik, woran man die politische Unterthänigkeit erpi
darum fordert man Wortglauben.

H.D.T. thought to what
we reckon a good
Englishman is in this
country a stage-proprietor

Page from Emerson's Journal written during his stay in London (1848).

with it. Born democrats, we are nowise qualified to judge of monarchy, which, to our fathers living in the monarchical idea, was also relatively right. But our institutions, though in coincidence with the spirit of the age, have not any exemption from the practical defects which have discredited other forms. Every actual State is corrupt. Good men must not obey the laws too well.[22] What satire on government can equal the severity of censure conveyed in the word *politic*, which now for ages has signified *cunning*, intimating that the State is a trick?[23]

The same benign necessity and the same practical abuse appear in the parties into which each State divides itself, of opponents and defenders of the administration of the government. Parties are also founded on instincts, and have better guides to their own humble aims than the sagacity of their leaders. They have nothing perverse in their origin, but rudely mark some real and lasting relation. We might as wisely reprove the east wind, or the frost, as a political party, whose members, for the most part, could give no account of their position, but stand for the defence of those interests in which they find themselves. Our quarrel with them begins, when they quit this deep natural ground at the bidding of some leader, and, obeying personal considerations, throw themselves into the maintenance and defence of points, nowise belonging to their system. A party is perpetually corrupted by personality. Whilst we absolve the association from dishonesty, we cannot extend the same charity to their leaders. They reap the rewards of the docility and zeal of the masses which they direct. Ordinarily, our parties are parties of circumstance, and not of principle; as, the planting interest in conflict with the commercial; the party of capitalists, and that of operatives; parties which are identical in their moral character, and which can easily change ground with each other, in the support of many of their measures. Parties of principle, as, religious sects, or the party of free-trade, of universal suffrage, of abolition of slavery, of abolition of capital punishment, degenerate into personalities, or would inspire enthusiasm. The vice of our leading parties in this country (which may be cited as a fair specimen of these societies of opinion) is, that they do not plant themselves on the deep and necessary grounds to which they are respectively entitled, but lash themselves to fury in the carrying of some local and momentary measure, nowise useful to the commonwealth. Of the two great parties, which, at this hour, almost share the nation

22    A radical assertion that the state has only a limited claim on its citizens—and that they, not the state, must decide the extent of this claim. Thoreau develops the idea in "Civil Disobedience."

23    In his "Ode, Inscribed to W. H. Channing," Emerson wrote, "If I refuse / My study for their politique, / Which at the best is trick, / The angry muse / Puts confusion in my brain."

24    Emerson wrote in his Journal (November–December 1842) that the "Whigs have the best men, Democrats the best cause. But the last are destructive, not constructive. What hope, what end have they?" (J 8:314). The Whigs were an American political party between 1833 and 1856, opposed to the Democratic party. Emerson seems to have voted Whig in the 1830s, but he decided not to vote in the 1840 election, in which the Whig William Henry Harrison (1773–1841) defeated the Democratic incumbent, Martin Van Buren (1782–1862). Emerson strongly disliked Van Buren and his predecessor, Andrew Jackson (1767–1845). In 1860, he was an enthusiastic supporter of Abraham Lincoln's (1809–1865) campaign.

25    Penal colony established by Britain in New South Wales, Australia, in 1788.

26    Perhaps the Frenchman Alexis de Tocqueville (1805–1859), author of the celebrated book *Democracy in America* (1835–1840).

27    Calvinism, a stringent variety of Protestantism especially influential in New England; Fisher Ames (1758–1808) was an American politician from the Federalist party.

between them, I should say, that, one has the best cause, and the other contains the best men.[24] The philosopher, the poet, or the religious man, will, of course, wish to cast his vote with the democrat, for free-trade, for wide suffrage, for the abolition of legal cruelties in the penal code, and for facilitating in every manner the access of the young and the poor to the sources of wealth and power. But he can rarely accept the persons whom the so-called popular party propose to him as representatives of these liberalities. They have not at heart the ends which give to the name of democracy what hope and virtue are in it. The spirit of our American radicalism is destructive and aimless: it is not loving; it has no ulterior and divine ends; but is destructive only out of hatred and selfishness. On the other side, the conservative party, composed of the most moderate, able, and cultivated part of the population, is timid, and merely defensive of property. It vindicates no right, it aspires to no real good, it brands no crime, it proposes no generous policy, it does not build, nor write, nor cherish the arts, nor foster religion, nor establish schools, nor encourage science, nor emancipate the slave, nor befriend the poor, or the Indian, or the immigrant. From neither party, when in power, has the world any benefit to expect in science, art, or humanity, at all commensurate with the resources of the nation.

I do not for these defects despair of our republic. We are not at the mercy of any waves of chance. In the strife of ferocious parties, human nature always finds itself cherished, as the children of the convicts at Botany Bay[25] are found to have as healthy a moral sentiment as other children. Citizens of feudal states are alarmed at our democratic institutions lapsing into anarchy; and the older and more cautious among ourselves are learning from Europeans to look with some terror at our turbulent freedom. It is said that in our license of construing the Constitution, and in the despotism of public opinion, we have no anchor; and one foreign observer[26] thinks he has found the safeguard in the sanctity of Marriage among us; and another thinks he has found it in our Calvinism. Fisher Ames[27] expressed the popular security more wisely, when he compared a monarchy and a republic, saying, "that a monarchy is a merchantman, which sails well, but will sometimes strike on a rock, and go to the bottom; whilst a republic is a raft, which would never sink, but then your feet are always in water." No forms can have any dangerous importance, whilst we are befriended by the laws of things. It makes no difference how many tons weight of atmosphere presses on our heads, so long as the same pressure resists it within the lungs. Augment the mass a thousand fold, it cannot begin to crush us, as long as reaction is equal to action. The fact of two poles, of two forces, centripetal and centrifugal, is universal, and each force by its own activity develops the other. Wild liberty develops iron conscience.[28] Want of liberty, by strengthening law and decorum, stupefies conscience. 'Lynch-law'[29] prevails only where there is greater hardihood and self-subsistency in the leaders. A mob cannot be a permanency: everybody's interest requires that it should not exist, and only justice satisfies all.

We must trust infinitely to the beneficent necessity which shines through all laws. Human nature expresses itself in them as characteristically as in statues, or songs, or railroads, and an abstract of the codes of nations would be a transcript of the common conscience. Governments have their origin in the moral identity of men. Reason for one is seen to be reason for another, and for every other. There is a middle measure which satisfies all parties, be they never so many, or so resolute for their own. Every man finds a sanction for his simplest claims and deeds in decisions of his own mind, which he calls Truth and Holiness. In these decisions all the citizens find a perfect agreement, and only in these; not in what is good to eat, good to wear, good use of time, or what amount of land, or of public aid, each is entitled to claim.[30] This truth and justice men presently endeavor to make application of, to the measuring of land, the apportionment of service, the protection of life and property. Their first endeavors, no doubt, are very awkward. Yet absolute right is the first governor; or, every government is an impure theocracy. The idea, after which each community is aiming to make and mend its law, is, the will of the wise man. The wise man, it cannot find in nature, and it makes awkward but earnest efforts to secure his government by contrivance; as, by causing the entire people to give their voices on every measure; or, by a double choice to get the representation of the whole; or, by a selection of the best citizens; or, to secure the advantages of efficiency and internal peace, by confiding the government to one, who may himself select his agents.[31] All forms of government symbolize an immortal government, common to all dynasties and independent of numbers, perfect where two men exist, perfect where there is only one man.

28 This is the law of compensation that Emerson addresses in his essay of that name.

29 A phrase first used by the Virginian Charles Lynch (1736–1796), who gave a summary trial to a group of Loyalists in 1780.

30 Emerson's near-prophetic sense of social justice derives from the Hebrew Bible and the Gospels; he insists on "Truth and Holiness" over the idea of entitlement that animates most political discussion.

31 Emerson is thinking of Plato's idea, in the *Republic*, that the just city will be possible only if the philosopher agrees to govern it. For Emerson, the people of the city themselves can become the philosopher or "wise man."

32    Emerson's version of the Golden Rule.

33    Foolishly idealistic (after the hero of *Don Quixote* [1605–1615] by the Spanish novelist Miguel de Cervantes Saavedra [1547–1616]).

34    Thoreau's "Civil Disobedience" begins, "I heartily accept the motto,—'That government is best which governs least;' and I should like to see it acted up to more rapidly and systematically."

35    Bring out.

36    Emerson's vision here is, as he realizes, extravagant, yet there is a hidden realism, too: the state will become unnecessary for the wise man, but not for everyone else.

37    Finished. Thought precedes the consulting of books.

38    Frankincense and myrrh were two precious aromatic gums derived from trees; they are mentioned together in the Bible's Song of Songs and in Matthew 2:11, where they are given by the wise men to the infant Jesus.

Every man's nature is a sufficient advertisement to him of the character of his fellows. My right and my wrong, is their right and their wrong.[32] Whilst I do what is fit for me, and abstain from what is unfit, my neighbor and I shall often agree in our means, and work together for a time to one end. But whenever I find my dominion over myself not sufficient for me, and undertake the direction of him also, I overstep the truth, and come into false relations to him. I may have so much more skill or strength than he, that he cannot express adequately his sense of wrong, but it is a lie, and hurts like a lie both him and me. Love and nature cannot maintain the assumption: it must be executed by a practical lie, namely, by force. This undertaking for another, is the blunder which stands in colossal ugliness in the governments of the world. It is the same thing in numbers, as in a pair, only not quite so intelligible. I can see well enough a great difference between my setting myself down to a self-control, and my going to make somebody else act after my views: but when a quarter of the human race assume to tell me what I must do, I may be too much disturbed by the circumstances to see so clearly the absurdity of their command. Therefore, all public ends look vague and quixotic[33] beside private ones. For, any laws but those which men make for themselves, are laughable. If I put myself in the place of my child, and we stand in one thought, and see that things are thus or thus, that perception is law for him and me. We are both there, both act. But if, without carrying him into the thought, I look over into his plot, and, guessing how it is with him, ordain this or that, he will never obey me. This is the history of governments,—one man does something which is to bind another. A man who cannot be acquainted with me, taxes me; looking from afar at me, ordains that a part of my labor shall go to this or that whimsical end, not as I, but as he happens to fancy. Behold the consequence. Of all debts, men are least willing to pay the taxes. What a satire is this on government! Everywhere they think they get their money's worth, except for these.

Hence, the less government we have, the better,—the fewer laws, and the less confided power.[34] The antidote to this abuse of formal Government, is, the influence of private character, the growth of the Individual; the appearance of the principal to supersede the proxy; the appearance of the wise man, of whom the existing government, is, it must be owned, but a shabby imitation. That which all things tend to educe,[35] which freedom, cultivation, intercourse, revolutions, go to form and deliver, is character; that is the end of nature, to reach unto this coronation of her king. To educate the wise man, the State exists; and with the appearance of the wise man, the State expires. The appearance of character makes the State unnecessary.[36] The wise man is the State. He needs no army, fort, or navy,—he loves men too well; no bribe, or feast, or palace, to draw friends to him; no vantage ground, no favorable circumstance. He needs no library, for he has not done[37] thinking; no church, for he is a prophet; no statute book, for he has the lawgiver; no money, for he is value; no road, for he is at home where he is; no experience, for the life of the creator shoots through him, and looks from his eyes. He has no personal friends, for he who has the spell to draw the prayer and piety of all men unto him, needs not husband and educate a few, to share with him a select and poetic life. His relation to men is angelic; his memory is myrrh to them; his presence, frankincense[38] and flowers.[39]

We think our civilization near its meridian, but we are yet only at the cock-crowing and the morning star. In our barbarous society the influence of character is in its infancy. As a political power, as the rightful lord who is to tumble all rulers from their chairs, its presence is hardly yet suspected. Malthus and Ricardo[40] quite omit it; the Annual Register[41] is silent; in the Conversations' Lexicon,[42] it is not set down; the President's Message, the Queen's Speech, have not mentioned it; and yet it is never nothing. Every thought which genius and piety throw into the world, alters the world.[43] The gladiators in the lists of power feel, through all their frocks[44] of force and simulation, the presence of worth. I think the very strife of trade and ambition are confession of this divinity; and successes in those fields are the poor amends, the fig-leaf with which the shamed soul attempts to hide its nakedness.[45] I find the like unwilling homage in all quarters. It is because we know how much is due from us, that we are impatient to show some petty talent as a substitute for worth. We are haunted by a conscience of this right to grandeur of character, and are false to it. But each of us has some talent, can do somewhat useful, or graceful, or formidable, or amusing, or lucrative. That we do, as an apology to others and to ourselves, for not reaching the mark of a good and equal life. But it does not satisfy *us*, whilst we thrust it on the notice of our companions. It may throw dust in their eyes, but does not smooth our own brow, or give us the tranquillity of the strong when we walk abroad.

39    This strange, idealized portrait of the wise man is comparable to Emerson's earlier depictions of the scholar (in "The American Scholar") and the poet (in "The Poet"). We know no such persons, and yet we are allured by Emerson's dream of them.

40    John Malthus (1766–1834) and David Ricardo (1772–1823), influential English political economists. Malthus studied population growth and poverty; Ricardo developed a labor theory of value. The English Romantic writer S. T. Coleridge (1772–1834) referred to Malthus's "monstrous practical sophism," and took him to be encouraging cruelty and selfishness. Many Victorian thinkers, from Emerson's friend Thomas Carlyle (1795–1881) to Charles Dickens (1812–1870) and John Ruskin (1819–1900), criticized the views of political economy as an inhumane reduction of social life to commerce and statistics. Instead they pursued, like Emerson, the influence of "character."

41    Almanac recording the year's major events, first issued in 1758.

42    German encyclopedia started in 1796.

43    A reminder of "Self-Reliance," in which Emerson underlines the unsuspected power of original thoughts to change the world—against conformity's endorsement of the way things are.

44    That is, "frocks of mail": coats of armor.

45    Like the newly self-conscious Adam and Eve in Genesis 3:7.

46    Capable of grasping objects. Emerson
implicitly and shrewdly asks us why we so suspect politicians: we must have another, better
idea about life than they do.

47    Dissenter. In his essay on Thoreau, Emerson describes him as a "born protestant."

We do penance as we go. Our talent is a sort of expiation, and we are constrained to reflect on our splendid moment, with a certain humiliation, as
somewhat too fine, and not as one act of many acts, a fair expression of our
permanent energy. Most persons of ability meet in society with a kind of
tacit appeal. Each seems to say, "I am not all here." Senators and presidents
have climbed so high with pain enough, not because they think the place
specially agreeable, but as an apology for real worth, and to vindicate their
manhood in our eyes. This conspicuous chair is their compensation to themselves for being of a poor, cold, hard nature. They must do what they can.
Like one class of forest animals, they have nothing but a prehensile[46] tail:
climb they must, or crawl. If a man found himself so rich-natured that he
could enter into strict relations with the best persons, and make life serene
around him by the dignity and sweetness of his behavior, could he afford to
circumvent the favor of the caucus and the press, and covet relations so hollow and pompous, as those of a politician? Surely nobody would be a charla-
tan, who could afford to be sincere.

The tendencies of the times favor the idea of self-government, and
leave the individual, for all code, to the rewards and penalties of his own
constitution, which work with more energy than we believe, whilst we depend on artificial restraints. The movement in this direction has been very
marked in modern history. Much has been blind and discreditable, but the
nature of the revolution is not affected by the vices of the revolters; for this is
a purely moral force. It was never adopted by any party in history, neither
can be. It separates the individual from all party, and unites him, at the same
time, to the race. It promises a recognition of higher rights than those of
personal freedom, or the security of property. A man has a right to be employed, to be trusted, to be loved, to be revered. The power of love, as the
basis of a State, has never been tried. We must not imagine that all things are
lapsing into confusion, if every tender protestant[47] be not compelled to bear
his part in certain social conventions: nor doubt that roads can be built, letters carried, and the fruit of labor secured, when the government of force is
at an end. Are our methods now so excellent that all competition is hopeless?
Could not a nation of friends even devise better ways? On the other hand, let
not the most conservative and timid fear anything from a premature surrender of the bayonet, and the system of force. For, according to the order of

nature, which is quite superior to our will, it stands thus; there will always be a government of force, where men are selfish; and when they are pure enough to abjure[48] the code of force, they will be wise enough to see how these public ends of the post-office, of the highway, of commerce, and the exchange of property, of museums and libraries, of institutions of art and science, can be answered.

We live in a very low state of the world, and pay unwilling tribute to governments founded on force. There is not, among the most religious and instructed men of the most religious and civil nations, a reliance on the moral sentiment, and a sufficient belief in the unity of things to persuade them that society can be maintained without artificial restraints, as well as the solar system; or that the private citizen might be reasonable, and a good neighbor, without the hint of a jail or a confiscation. What is strange too, there never was in any man sufficient faith in the power of rectitude,[49] to inspire him with the broad design of renovating the State on the principle of right and love. All those who have pretended this design, have been partial reformers, and have admitted in some manner the supremacy of the bad State. I do not call to mind a single human being who has steadily denied the authority of the laws, on the simple ground of his own moral nature. Such designs, full of genius and full of fate as they are, are not entertained except avowedly as air-pictures. If the individual who exhibits them, dare to think them practicable, he disgusts scholars and churchmen; and men of talent, and women of superior sentiments, cannot hide their contempt. Not the less does nature continue to fill the heart of youth with suggestions of this enthusiasm, and there are now men,—if indeed I can speak in the plural number,—more exactly, I will say, I have just been conversing with one man,[50] to whom no weight of adverse experience will make it for a moment appear impossible, that thousands of human beings might share and obey each with the other the grandest and truest sentiments, as well as a knot of friends, or a pair of lovers.

48    Renounce.

49    Emerson invokes a strict uprightness in contrast to the politician's postures ("climb they must, or crawl").

50    Perhaps Amos Bronson Alcott (1799–1888), the Transcendentalist reformer. Emerson holds back from endorsing Alcott's utopian dream; yet he does not discount it, even in the face of "adverse experience."

# Nominalist and Realist

*This is the eighth and penultimate essay in Emerson's* Essays: Second Series *(1844). The title is Emerson's reflection on two opposing perspectives: the nominalist dwells among surfaces and focuses on particular individuals; the realist aims for the universal. (Emerson adapts these terms from medieval philosophy.) Emerson scholar David Robinson remarks that "Nominalist and Realist" restates the dilemma of "Experience," in which Emerson saw a "lack of coherence between inner and outer experience," between the world we think and the actual world. In "Nominalist and Realist," the division falls between our experience of individuals, with their faults and exaggerations, and our faith in the greater reality that blends together, and surpasses, these individuals. We need both points of view: we must cling to persons and yet see beyond them.*

1    Followers of the Greek philosopher Plato (429–347 BCE), including such Neoplatonic philosophers of Alexandria as Plotinus (ca. 204–270), Proclus (412–485), and Porphyry (ca. 232–ca. 305)—all three of whom Emerson read avidly in translation.

> In countless upward-striving waves
> The moon-drawn tide-wave strives;
> In thousand far-transplanted grafts
> The parent fruit survives;
> So, in the new-born millions,
> The perfect Adam lives.
> Not less are summer-mornings dear
> To every child they wake,
> And each with novel life his sphere
> Fills for his proper sake.

I cannot often enough say, that a man is only a relative and representative nature. Each is a hint of the truth, but far enough from being that truth, which yet he quite newly and inevitably suggests to us. If I seek it in him, I shall not find it. Could any man conduct into me the pure stream of that which he pretends to be! Long afterwards, I find that quality elsewhere which he promised me. The genius of the Platonists,[1] is intoxicating to the student, yet how few particulars of it can I detach from all their books. The man momentarily stands for the thought, but will not bear examination; and a society of men will cursorily represent well enough a certain quality and culture, for example, chivalry or beauty of manners, but separate them, and there is no gentleman and no lady in the group. The least hint sets us on the pursuit of a character, which no man realizes. We have such exorbitant[2] eyes, that on seeing the smallest arc, we complete the curve, and when the curtain is lifted from the diagram which it seemed to veil, we are vexed to find that no more was drawn, than just that fragment of an arc which we first beheld. We are greatly too liberal in our construction of each other's faculty and promise. Exactly what the parties have already done, they shall do again; but that which we inferred from their nature and inception, they will not do. That is in nature, but not in them. That happens in the world, which we often witness in a public debate. Each of the speakers expresses himself imperfectly: no one of them hears much that another says, such is the preoccupation of mind of each; and the audience, who have only to hear and not to speak, judge very wisely and superiorly how wrongheaded and unskilful is each of the debaters to his own affair. Great men or men of great gifts you shall easily find, but symmetrical men never. When I meet a pure intellectual force, or a generosity of affection, I believe, here then is man; and am presently mortified by the discovery, that this individual is no more available to his own or to the general ends, than his companions; because the power which drew my respect, is not supported by the total symphony of his talents. All persons exist to society by some shining trait of beauty or utility, which they have. We borrow the proportions of the man from that one fine feature, and finish the portrait symmetrically; which is false; for the rest of his body is small or deformed.[3] I observe a person who makes a good public appearance, and conclude thence the perfection of his private character, on which this is based; but he has no private character. He is a graceful cloak or lay-figure[4] for holidays. All our poets, heroes, and saints, fail utterly in some one or in many parts to satisfy our idea, fail to draw our spontaneous interest, and so leave us without any hope of realization but in our own future. Our exaggeration of all fine characters arises from the fact, that we identify each in turn with the soul. But there are no such men as we fable; no Jesus, nor Pericles, nor Cæsar, nor Angelo, nor Washington,[5] such as we have made. We consecrate a great deal of nonsense, because it was allowed by great men. There is none without his foible. Must I believe that if an angel should come to chaunt the chorus of the moral law, he would eat too much gingerbread, or take liberties with private letters, or do some precious atroc-

2   A pun on "orb." Emerson points to the failure of vision—and to the compensatory acts of imagination that the failure leads to: we "finish the portrait symmetrically." In his essay "Illusions," Emerson shows how, when the imagination rounds off a deficient reality, we trust in its powers.

3   In his essay "Culture," Emerson wrote, "Nature usually in the instances where a marked man is sent into the world, overloads him with bias, sacrificing his symmetry to his working power."

4   Mannequin. Emerson may have had in mind the figures of saints paraded in Italian religious festivals.

5   Pericles (ca. 495–429 BCE), leader of classical Athens; Julius Caesar (100–44 BCE), Roman general and ruler; Michaelangelo Buonarroti (1475–1564), great painter and sculptor of the Italian Renaissance; George Washington (1732–1799), first president of the United States and commander of the Revolutionary army.

6     In Plato's dialogue *Ion*, Socrates says that the Muse of poetry resembles a magnet, and that the poet, the reciter of poetry, and the listening audience are like a chain of rings attracted by this magnetism. Mummery here means ridiculous ceremonial behavior.

7     Merely palpable.

8     "Foolish fire" (Latin): phosphorescent light glimpsed over swampy ground at night, and known to mislead travelers; it is also called will-o'-the-wisp.

9     Benjamin Franklin (1706–1790), American statesman and inventor.

10    Universal.

ity? It is bad enough, that our geniuses cannot do anything useful, but it is worse that no man is fit for society, who has fine traits. He is admired at a distance, but he cannot come near without appearing a cripple. The men of fine parts protect themselves by solitude, or by courtesy, or by satire, or by an acid worldly manner, each concealing, as he best can, his incapacity for useful association, but they want either love or self-reliance.

Our native love of reality joins with this experience to teach us a little reserve, and to dissuade a too sudden surrender to the brilliant qualities of persons. Young people admire talents or particular excellences; as we grow older, we value total powers and effects, as, the impression, the quality, the spirit of men and things. The genius is all. The man,—it is his system: we do not try a solitary word or act, but his habit. The acts which you praise, I praise not, since they are departures from his faith, and are mere compliances. The magnetism which arranges tribes and races in one polarity, is alone to be respected; the men are steel-filings. Yet we unjustly select a particle, and say, "O steel-filing number one! what heart-drawings I feel to thee! what prodigious virtues are these of thine! how constitutional to thee, and incommunicable!" Whilst we speak, the loadstone is withdrawn; down falls our filing in a heap with the rest, and we continue our mummery to the wretched shaving.[6] Let us go for universals; for the magnetism, not for the needles. Human life and its persons are poor empirical[7] pretensions. A personal influence is an *ignis fatuus*.[8] If they say, it is great, it is great; if they say, it is small, it is small; you see it, and you see it not, by turns; it borrows all its size from the momentary estimation of the speakers: the Will-of-the-wisp vanishes, if you go too near, vanishes if you go too far, and only blazes at one angle. Who can tell if Washington be a great man, or no? Who can tell if Franklin[9] be? Yes, or any but the twelve, or six, or three great gods of fame? And they, too, loom and fade before the eternal.

We are amphibious creatures, weaponed for two elements, having two sets of faculties, the particular and the catholic.[10] We adjust our instrument for general observation, and sweep the heavens as easily as we pick out a single figure in the terrestrial landscape. We are practically skilful in detecting elements, for which we have no place in our theory, and no name. Thus we are very sensible of an atmospheric influence in men and in bodies of men, not accounted for in an arithmetical addition of all their measurable properties. There is a genius of a nation, which is not to be found in the numerical citizens, but which characterizes the society. England, strong, punctual, practical, well-spoken England, I should not find, if I should go to the island to seek it. In the parliament, in the playhouse, at dinner-tables, I might see a great number of rich, ignorant, book-read, conventional, proud men,—many old women,—and not anywhere the Englishman who made the good speeches, combined the accurate engines, and did the bold and nervous[11] deeds. It is even worse in America, where, from the intellectual quickness of the race, the genius of the country is more splendid in its promise, and more slight in its performance. Webster cannot do the work of Webster.[12] We conceive distinctly enough the French, the Spanish, the German genius, and it is not the less real, that perhaps we should not meet in either of those nations, a single individual who corresponded with the type. We infer the spirit of the nation in great measure from the language, which is a sort of monument, to which each forcible[13] individual in a course of many hundred years has contributed a stone. And, universally, a good example of this social force, is the veracity of language, which cannot be debauched. In any controversy concerning morals, an appeal may be made with safety to the sentiments, which the language of the people expresses. Proverbs, words, and grammar inflections convey the public sense with more purity and precision, than the wisest individual.

In the famous dispute with the Nominalists, the Realists had a good deal of reason.[14] General ideas are essences. They are our gods: they round and ennoble the most partial and sordid way of living. Our proclivity to details cannot quite degrade our life, and divest it of poetry. The day-laborer is reckoned as standing at the foot of the social scale, yet he is saturated with the laws of the world. His measures are the hours; morning and night, solstice and equinox, geometry, astronomy, and all the lovely accidents of nature play through his mind. Money, which represents the prose of life, and which is hardly spoken of in parlors without an apology, is, in its effects and laws, as beautiful as roses. Property keeps the accounts of the world, and is always moral. The property will be found where the labor, the wisdom, and the virtue have been in nations, in classes, and (the whole life-time considered, with the compensations) in the individual also. How wise the world appears, when the laws and usages of nations are largely detailed, and the

11    Strong, vigorous (nerve in this sense means "muscle," from the Latin *nervus*).

12    Emerson was a great admirer of Daniel Webster (1782–1852), preeminent American orator and statesman from New Hampshire; but he later felt betrayed by Webster's advocacy of the Fugitive Slave Law of 1850 (see Introduction).

13    Powerful.

14    In medieval philosophy, the Realists maintained that universal ideas stand behind particular things; the Nominalists argued that such universals were mere names.

15    Government office where duties are paid.

16    Secretive religious cult of ancient Greece.

17    Pertaining to the Freemasons.

completeness of the municipal system is considered! Nothing is left out. If you go into the markets, and the custom-houses,[15] the insurers' and notaries' offices, the offices of sealers of weights and measures, of inspection of provisions,—it will appear as if one man had made it all. Wherever you go, a wit like your own has been before you, and has realized its thought. The Eleusinian mysteries,[16] the Egyptian architecture, the Indian astronomy, the Greek sculpture, show that there always were seeing and knowing men in the planet. The world is full of masonic[17] ties, of guilds, of secret and public legions of honor; that of scholars, for example; and that of gentlemen fraternizing with the upper class of every country and every culture.

Emerson's daughter, Edith Emerson.

I am very much struck in literature by the appearance, that one person wrote all the books; as if the editor of a journal planted his body of reporters in different parts of the field of action, and relieved some by others from time to time; but there is such equality and identity both of judgment and point of view in the narrative, that it is plainly the work of one all-seeing, all-hearing gentleman. I looked into Pope's Odyssey[18] yesterday: it is as correct and elegant after our canon of today, as if it were newly written. The modernness of all good books seems to give me an existence as wide as man. What is well done, I feel as if I did; what is ill done, I reck not of. Shakspeare's passages of passion (for example, in Lear and Hamlet) are in the very dialect of the present year. I am faithful again to the whole over the members in my use of books. I find the most pleasure in reading a book in a manner least flattering to the author. I read Proclus, and sometimes Plato, as I might read a dictionary, for a mechanical help to the fancy and the imagination. I read for the lustres,[19] as if one should use a fine picture in a chromatic experiment, for its rich colors. 'Tis not Proclus, but a piece of nature and fate that I explore. It is a greater joy to see the author's author, than himself. A higher pleasure of the same kind I found lately at a concert, where I went to hear Handel's Messiah.[20] As the master overpowered the littleness and incapableness of the performers, and made them conductors of his electricity, so it was easy to observe what efforts nature was making through so many hoarse, wooden, and imperfect persons, to produce beautiful voices, fluid and soul-guided men and women. The genius of nature was paramount at the oratorio.

This preference of the genius to the parts is the secret of that deification of art, which is found in all superior minds. Art, in the artist, is proportion, or, a habitual respect to the whole by an eye loving beauty in details. And the wonder and charm of it is the sanity in insanity which it denotes. Proportion is almost impossible to human beings. There is no one who does not exaggerate. In conversation, men are encumbered with personality, and talk too much.[21] In modern sculpture, picture, and poetry, the beauty is miscellaneous; the artist works here and there, and at all points, adding and adding, instead of unfolding the unit of his thought. Beautiful details we must have, or no artist: but they must be means and never other. The eye must not lose sight for a moment of the purpose. Lively boys write to their ear and

18   Translation (1726) of the *Odyssey* of Homer (ca. 9th century BCE) by the British poet Alexander Pope (1688–1744).

19   Gleams.

20   Oratorio (1742) by the German-born composer Georg Friedrich Handel (1685–1759), which Emerson heard in Boston on Christmas 1843.

21   In his essay "Experience" Emerson wrote, "In this our talking America we are ruined by our good nature and listening on all sides."

22    Subject-matter.

23    Phrenology, popular in Emerson's day, was the study of the shape of the head for clues to an individual's personality.

24    Health (Greek).

25    Franz Anton Mesmer (1734–1825), German inventor of "animal magnetism" (a form of hypnosis); Emanuel Swedenborg (1688–1772), Swedish mystic and philosopher; Charles Fourier (1768–1830), French utopian thinker. The Millennial Church was another name for the Shakers, a chaste religious cult known for the beautiful simplicity of their music, furniture, and architecture.

26    In the Journal entry on which this passage is based, Emerson added, "A metaphysician, a saint, a poet of God has nothing to do with them" (1843, J 9:6). In his essay "Experience," Emerson wrote, "Let us treat the men and women well: treat them as if they were real: perhaps they are."

27    Emerson may be thinking of Antony's speech in Shakespeare's *Antony and Cleopatra* (4.14.3–8), in which he compares himself to a shape-shifting cloud.

28    In his essay "The Transcendentalist," Emerson identifies the Buddhist with the Transcendentalist. "The oriental mind has always tended to this largeness. Buddhism is an expression of it."

29    In botany, distribution means classification; and section, a subgenus.

eye, and the cool reader finds nothing but sweet jingles in it. When they grow older, they respect the argument.[22]

We obey the same intellectual integrity, when we study in exceptions the law of the world. Anomalous facts, as the never quite obsolete rumors of magic and demonology, and the new allegations of phrenologists[23] and neurologists, are of ideal use. They are good indications. Homœopathy is insignificant as an art of healing, but of great value as criticism on the hygeia[24] or medical practice of the time. So with Mesmerism, Swedenborgism, Fourierism, and the Millennial Church;[25] they are poor pretensions enough, but good criticism on the science, philosophy, and preaching of the day. For these abnormal insights of the adepts, ought to be normal, and things of course.

All things show us, that on every side we are very near to the best. It seems not worth while to execute with too much pains some one intellectual, or æsthetical, or civil feat, when presently the dream will scatter, and we shall burst into universal power. The reason of idleness and of crime is the deferring of our hopes. Whilst we are waiting, we beguile the time with jokes, with sleep, with eating, and with crimes.

*　*　*

Thus we settle it in our cool libraries, that all the agents with which we deal are subalterns, which we can well afford to let pass, and life will be simpler when we live at the centre, and flout the surfaces. I wish to speak with all respect of persons, but sometimes I must pinch myself to keep awake, and preserve the due decorum. They melt so fast into each other, that they are like grass and trees, and it needs an effort to treat them as individuals.[26] Though the uninspired man certainly finds persons a conveniency in household matters, the divine man does not respect them: he sees them as a rack of clouds, or a fleet of ripples which the wind drives over the surface of the water.[27] But this is flat rebellion. Nature will not be Buddhist:[28] she resents generalizing, and insults the philosopher in every moment with a million of fresh particulars. It is all idle talking: as much as a man is a whole, so is he also a part; and it were partial not to see it. What you say in your pompous distribution only distributes you into your class and section.[29] You have not got rid of parts by denying them, but are the more partial. You are one thing, but nature is *one thing and the other thing*, in the same moment. She will not remain orbed in a thought, but rushes into persons; and when each person, inflamed to a fury of personality, would conquer all things to his poor crotchet,[30] she raises up against him another person, and by many persons incarnates again a sort of whole. She will have all. Nick Bottom cannot play all the parts, work it how he may:[31] there will be somebody else, and the world will be round. Everything must have its flower or effort at the beautiful, coarser or finer according to its stuff. They relieve and recommend each other, and the sanity of society is a balance of a thousand insanities. She punishes abstractionists, and will only forgive an induction which is rare and casual. We like to come to a height of land and see the landscape, just as we value a general remark in conversation. But it is not the intention of nature that we should live by general views. We fetch fire and water, run about all day among the shops and markets, and get our clothes and shoes made and mended, and are the victims of these details, and once in a fortnight we arrive perhaps at a rational moment. If we were not thus infatuated, if we saw the real from hour to hour, we should not be here to write and to read, but should have been burned or frozen long ago. She would never get anything done, if she suffered admirable Crichtons,[32] and universal geniuses. She loves better a wheelwright who dreams all night of wheels, and a groom who is part of his horse: for she is full of work, and these are her hands. As the frugal farmer takes care that his cattle shall eat down the rowen,[33] and swine shall eat the waste of his house, and poultry shall pick the crumbs, so our economical mother despatches a new genius and habit of mind into every district and condition of existence, plants an eye wherever a new ray of light can fall, and gathering up into some man every property in the universe, establishes thousandfold occult mutual attractions among her offspring, that all this wash and waste of power may be imparted and exchanged.

Great dangers undoubtedly accrue from this incarnation and distribution of the godhead, and hence nature has her maligners, as if she were Circe; and Alphonso of Castile fancied he could have given useful advice.[34] But she does not go unprovided; she has hellebore[35] at the bottom of the cup. Solitude would ripen a plentiful crop of despots. The recluse thinks of men as having his manner, or as not having his manner; and as having de-

30   Peculiar, idiosyncratic notion.

31   In Shakespeare's *Midsummer Night's Dream* (1.2), Nick Bottom the weaver wants to play all the parts in the mechanicals' interlude: the lovers Pyramus and Thisbe and the lion that terrorizes them.

32   James Crichton (1560–1582), a Scottish child prodigy and polymath whose career later fizzled.

33   Field left in stubble for grazing cattle.

34   Circe bewitched Odysseus's men in Homer's *Odyssey*. Alphonso the Wise of Castile (1221–1284) was known for remarking (on the complex subject of Ptolemaic astronomy) that if God had asked his advice at the Creation, he could have come up with a simpler plan. In Emerson's poem "Alphonso of Castile" (1847), Alphonso asks the "celestial fellows," "Men and gods are too extense; / Could you slacken and condense?"

35   Plant said to cure insanity.

36    Clever or deceptive device; peculiar, characteristic habit.

37    Thomas Paine (1737–1809), American radical pamphleteer and opponent of religion.

38    Superabundance, overflow.

39    The triangles measure the distance between the earth and various stars and planets.

40    Brook Farm was an experiment in collective living, started by Emerson's friends George Ripley (1802–1880) and his wife, Sophia Ripley (1803–1861), which Emerson declined to join in 1840. The Skaneateles Community was in upstate New York and Northampton, in Massachusetts; its members communally operated a silk factory.

41    The Essenes were an ascetic religious sect during the time of Jesus; the school at Port-Royal-des-Champs, near Paris, was the center for teaching the pious doctrines of Netherlandish Catholic theologian Cornelius Jansen (1585–1638).

grees of it, more and less. But when he comes into a public assembly, he sees that men have very different manners from his own, and in their way admirable. In his childhood and youth, he has had many checks and censures, and thinks modestly enough of his own endowment. When afterwards he comes to unfold it in propitious circumstance, it seems the only talent: he is delighted with his success, and accounts himself already the fellow of the great. But he goes into a mob, into a banking-house, into a mechanic's shop, into a mill, into a laboratory, into a ship, into a camp, and in each new place he is no better than an idiot: other talents take place, and rule the hour. The rotation which whirls every leaf and pebble to the meridian, reaches to every gift of man, and we all take turns at the top.

For nature, who abhors mannerism, has set her heart on breaking up all styles and tricks, and it is so much easier to do what one has done before, than to do a new thing, that there is a perpetual tendency to a set mode. In every conversation, even the highest, there is a certain trick, which may be soon learned by an acute person, and then that particular style continued indefinitely. Each man, too, is a tyrant in tendency, because he would impose his idea on others; and their trick[36] is their natural defence. Jesus would absorb the race; but Tom Paine[37] or the coarsest blasphemer helps humanity by resisting this exuberance[38] of power. Hence the immense benefit of party in politics, as it reveals faults of character in a chief, which the intellectual force of the persons, with ordinary opportunity, and not hurled into aphelion by hatred, could not have seen. Since we are all so stupid, what benefit that there should be two stupidities! It is like that brute advantage so essential to astronomy, of having the diameter of the earth's orbit for a base of its triangles.[39] Democracy is morose, and runs to anarchy, but in the state, and in the schools, it is indispensable to resist the consolidation of all men into a few men. If John was perfect, why are you and I alive? As long as any man exists, there is some need of him; let him fight for his own. A new poet has appeared; a new character approached us; why should we refuse to eat bread, until we have found his regiment and section in our old army-files? Why not a new man? Here is a new enterprise of Brook Farm, of Skeneateles, of Northampton:[40] why so impatient to baptize them Essenes, or Port-Royalists, or Shakers, or by any known and effete name?[41] Let it be a new way of living. Why have only two or three ways of life, and not thousands?

Every man is wanted, and no man is wanted much. We came this time for condiments, not for corn. We want the great genius only for joy; for one star more in our constellation, for one tree more in our grove. But he thinks we wish to belong to him, as he wishes to occupy us. He greatly mistakes us. I think I have done well, if I have acquired a new word from a good author; and my business with him is to find my own, though it were only to melt him down into an epithet or an image for daily use.

"Into paint will I grind thee, my bride!"[42]

To embroil the confusion, and make it impossible to arrive at any general statement, when we have insisted on the imperfection of individuals, our affections and our experience urge that every individual is entitled to honor, and a very generous treatment is sure to be repaid. A recluse sees only two or three persons, and allows them all their room; they spread themselves at large. The statesman looks at many, and compares the few habitually with others, and these look less. Yet are they not entitled to this generosity of reception? and is not munificence[43] the means of insight? For though gamesters say, that the cards beat all the players, though they were never so skilful, yet in the contest we are now considering, the players are also the game, and share the power of the cards. If you criticise a fine genius, the odds are that you are out of your reckoning, and, instead of the poet, are censuring your own caricature of him. For there is somewhat spheral and infinite in every man, especially in every genius, which, if you can come very near him, sports with all your limitations. For, rightly, every man is a channel through which heaven floweth, and, whilst I fancied I was criticising him, I was censuring or rather terminating[44] my own soul. After taxing Goethe as a courtier, artificial, unbelieving, worldly,—I took up this book of Helena,[45] and found him an Indian of the wilderness, a piece of pure nature like an apple or an oak, large as morning or night, and virtuous as a briar-rose.

But care is taken that the whole tune shall be played. If we were not kept among surfaces, every thing would be large and universal: now the excluded attributes burst in on us with the more brightness, that they have been excluded. "Your turn now, my turn next," is the rule of the game. The universality being hindered in its primary form, comes in the secondary form

42  Famous line from the poem "The Paint King" (1813) by the celebrated American painter Washington Allston (1779–1843). In Allston's fable, a fiendish artist soaks the unfortunate "fair Ellen" in oil and turns her into paint.

43  Lavish generosity.

44  Confining.

45  Part Two of *Faust* by the German author J. W. von Goethe (1749–1832) contains the story of Helen of Troy (published separately in 1827). In his Journal (August 13, 1836), Emerson wrote that Goethe sees "the value of truth," "but I am provoked with his Olympian self complacency . . . [he] merely went up & down, from object to object, lifting the veil from every one & did no more" (J 5:133). By the time of "Nominalist and Realist" Emerson had changed his mind: Goethe was now potent and real as nature.

46    Emerson may be thinking of Plato in his dialogue *Timaeus. Plenum* is Latin for fullness.

47    Emerson names two figures from early Christianity, St. John the Evangelist and St. Paul (ca. 5 BCE–ca. 67), along with the founder of Islam, Mahomet (Muhammad) (ca. 570–632), and the Greek philosopher Aristotle (384–322 BCE), who influenced much later thought.

of *all sides:* the points come in succession to the meridian, and by the speed of rotation, a new whole is formed. Nature keeps herself whole, and her representation complete in the experience of each mind. She suffers no seat to be vacant in her college. It is the secret of the world that all things subsist, and do not die, but only retire a little from sight, and afterwards return again. Whatever does not concern us, is concealed from us. As soon as a person is no longer related to our present well-being, he is concealed, or *dies*, as we say. Really, all things and persons are related to us, but according to our nature, they act on us not at once, but in succession, and we are made aware of their presence one at a time. All persons, all things which we have known, are here present, and many more than we see; the world is full. As the ancient said, the world is a *plenum* or solid;[46] and if we saw all things that really surround us, we should be imprisoned and unable to move. For, though nothing is impassable to the soul, but all things are pervious to it, and like highways, yet this is only whilst the soul does not see them. As soon as the soul sees any object, it stops before that object. Therefore, the divine Providence, which keeps the universe open in every direction to the soul, conceals all the furniture and all the persons that do not concern a particular soul, from the senses of that individual. Through solidest eternal things, the man finds his road, as if they did not subsist, and does not once suspect their being. As soon as he needs a new object, suddenly he beholds it, and no longer attempts to pass through it, but takes another way. When he has exhausted for the time the nourishment to be drawn from any one person or thing, that object is withdrawn from his observation, and though still in his immediate neighborhood, he does not suspect its presence. Nothing is dead: men feign themselves dead, and endure mock funerals and mournful obituaries, and there they stand looking out of the window, sound and well, in some new and strange disguise. Jesus is not dead: he is very well alive: nor John, nor Paul, nor Mahomet, nor Aristotle;[47] at times we believe we have seen them all, and could easily tell the names under which they go.

  If we cannot make voluntary and conscious steps in the admirable science of universals, let us see the parts wisely, and infer the genius of nature from the best particulars with a becoming charity. What is best in each kind is an index of what should be the average of that thing. Love shows me the

Emerson's grave in Sleepy Hollow Cemetery, Concord.

48    As stated in the atomic theory of the Croatian Jesuit mathematician R. J. Boscovich (1711–1787), which Emerson also refers to in "Experience."

49    The Roman god Janus had two opposing faces, directed toward past and future.

opulence of nature, by disclosing to me in my friend a hidden wealth, and I infer an equal depth of good in every other direction. It is commonly said by farmers, that a good pear or apple costs no more time or pains to rear, than a poor one; so I would have no work of art, no speech, or action, or thought, or friend, but the best.

The end and the means, the gamester and the game,—life is made up of the intermixture and reaction of these two amicable powers, whose marriage appears beforehand monstrous, as each denies and tends to abolish the other. We must reconcile the contradictions as we can, but their discord and their concord introduce wild absurdities into our thinking and speech. No sentence will hold the whole truth, and the only way in which we can be just, is by giving ourselves the lie; Speech is better than silence; silence is better than speech;—All things are in contact; every atom has a sphere of repulsion;[48]—Things are, and are not, at the same time;—and the like. All the universe over, there is but one thing, this old Two-Face,[49] creator-creature, mind-matter, right-wrong, of which any proposition may be affirmed or denied. Very fitly, therefore, I assert, that every man is a partialist, that nature

50    John Scott, first Earl of Eldon (1751–1838), politician and jurist.

51    Immovable.

52    The ancient Israelites carried the Ark of the Covenant, containing the tablets of the law, with them on their wanderings. A furlong is about one-eighth of a mile (or one-fifth of a kilometer).

secures him as an instrument by self-conceit, preventing the tendencies to religion and science; and now further assert, that, each man's genius being nearly and affectionately explored, he is justified in his individuality, as his nature is found to be immense; and now I add, that every man is a universalist also, and, as our earth, whilst it spins on its own axis, spins all the time around the sun through the celestial spaces, so the least of its rational children, the most dedicated to his private affair, works out, though as it were under a disguise, the universal problem. We fancy men are individuals; so are pumpkins; but every pumpkin in the field, goes through every point of pumpkin history. The rabid democrat, as soon as he is senator and rich man, has ripened beyond possibility of sincere radicalism, and unless he can resist the sun, he must be conservative the remainder of his days. Lord Eldon said in his old age, "that, if he were to begin life again, he would be damned but he would begin as agitator."[50]

We hide this universality, if we can, but it appears at all points. We are as ungrateful as children. There is nothing we cherish and strive to draw to us, but in some hour we turn and rend it. We keep a running fire of sarcasm at ignorance and the life of the senses; then goes by, perchance, a fair girl, a piece of life, gay and happy, and making the commonest offices beautiful, by the energy and heart with which she does them, and seeing this, we admire and love her and them, and say, "Lo! a genuine creature of the fair earth, not dissipated, or too early ripened by books, philosophy, religion, society, or care!" insinuating a treachery and contempt for all we had so long loved and wrought in ourselves and others.

If we could have any security against moods! If the profoundest prophet could be holden to his words, and the hearer who is ready to sell all and join the crusade, could have any certificate that tomorrow his prophet shall not unsay his testimony! But the Truth sits veiled there on the Bench, and never interposes an adamantine[51] syllable; and the most sincere and revolutionary doctrine, put as if the ark of God were carried forward some furlongs,[52] and planted there for the succor of the world, shall in a few weeks be coldly set aside by the same speaker, as morbid; "I thought I was right, but I was not," —and the same immeasurable credulity demanded for new audacities. If we were not of all opinions! if we did not in any moment shift the platform on which we stand, and look and speak from another! if there could be any reg-ulation, any "one-hour-rule,"[53] that a man should never leave his point of view, without sound of trumpet. I am always insincere, as always knowing there are other moods.[54]

How sincere and confidential we can be, saying all that lies in the mind, and yet go away feeling that all is yet unsaid, from the incapacity of the par-ties to know each other, although they use the same words! My companion assumes to know my mood and habit of thought, and we go on from expla-nation to explanation, until all is said which words can, and we leave matters just as they were at first, because of that vicious[55] assumption. Is it that every man believes every other to be an incurable partialist, and himself an univer-salist? I talked yesterday with a pair of philosophers:[56] I endeavored to show my good men that I liked everything by turns, and nothing long; that I loved the centre, but doated on the superficies; that I loved man, if men seemed to me mice and rats; that I revered saints, but woke up glad that the old pagan world stood its ground, and died hard; that I was glad of men of every gift and nobility, but would not live in their arms. Could they but once under-stand, that I loved to know that they existed, and heartily wished them God-speed, yet, out of my poverty of life and thought, had no word or welcome for them when they came to see me, and could well consent to their living in Oregon,[57] for any claim I felt on them, it would be a great satisfaction.

53   Limit imposed on speechmaking in New England legislatures.

54   By knowing his own partiality, Emerson here moves toward the universal.

55   Faulty.

56   Emerson's Journal entry for April 17, 1843, reveals that the two men were Charles Lane (1800–1870) and Amos Bronson Alcott (1799–1888), the reformers who in 1844 founded the utopian community of Fruitlands (J 8:386–387).

57   A vast immigration to the Oregon terri-tory occurred in 1843–1844, after the long dis-pute with Great Britain over its ownership was resolved. In this final sentence, Emerson asserts his liking for a panorama of different eras and individuals, his desire to keep men at a distance, and his distaste for the utopian project of Alcott and Lane: their desire to make different human types embrace one another and form a commu-nal whole. Emerson plays the role of spectator rather than participant, interested in persons, but not in love with them.

# New England Reformers

*Told by his publisher in the summer of 1844 that his manuscript of* Essays: Second Series *was not quite long enough for the physical shape of the book he wanted, Emerson decided to add this lecture. Along with other reformers and abolitionists, Emerson participated in the Society at Amory Hall (Boston), which substituted radical lectures for the traditional Sunday church service. Emerson's lecture on West Indian Emancipation, from August 1844, is a fiery statement of faith in the triumph of principles. "New England Reformers," which mentions antislavery only in passing, has misgivings about the reformers' strategies, in particular their push toward the forced solidarity of utopian community and their emphasis on particular evils. Emerson wants the reform movement to be more than it is, and to challenge us more intimately. The reformers do not look high enough for solutions; for Emerson, the individual must "come to himself" and be renewed so that society can be transformed. Emerson's earlier lecture "Reforms," from his series "The Present Age" (1840), gave similarly short shrift to the subject of slavery: "When the best hands shall work with love and honor there will be no slave" (EL 3:264).*

In the suburb, in the town,
On the railway, in the square,
Came a beam of goodness down
Doubling daylight everywhere:
Peace now each for malice takes,
Beauty for his sinful weeds,
For the angel Hope aye makes
Him an angel whom she leads.[1]

*A Lecture Read before the Society in Amory Hall,
on Sunday, 3 March, 1844*

Whoever has had opportunity of acquaintance with society in New England, during the last twenty-five years, with those middle and with those leading sections that may constitute any just representation of the character and aim of the community, will have been struck with the great activity of thought and experimenting. His attention must be commanded by the signs that the Church, or religious party, is falling from the church nominal,[2] and is appearing in temperance and non-resistance societies, in movements of abolitionists and of socialists, and in very significant assemblies, called Sabbath and Bible Conventions,—composed of ultraists, of seekers, of all the soul of the soldiery of dissent, and meeting to call in question the authority of the Sabbath, of the priesthood, and of the church.[3] In these movements, nothing was more remarkable than the discontent they begot in the movers. The spirit of protest and of detachment, drove the members of these Conventions to bear testimony against the church, and immediately afterward, to declare their discontent with these Conventions, their independence of their colleagues, and their impatience of the methods whereby they were working. They defied each other, like a congress of kings, each of whom had a realm to rule, and a way of his own that made concert unprofitable. What a fertility of projects for the salvation of the world! One apostle thought all men should go to farming; and another, that no man should buy or sell: that the use of money was the cardinal evil; another, that the mischief was in our diet, that we eat and drink damnation.[4] These made unleavened bread, and were foes to the death to fermentation. It was in vain urged by the housewife, that God made yeast, as well as dough, and loves fermentation just as dearly as he loves vegetation; that fermentation develops the saccharine element in the grain, and makes it more palatable and more digestible. No; they wish the pure wheat, and will die but it shall not ferment. Stop, dear nature, these incessant advances of thine; let us scotch[5] these ever-rolling wheels! Others attacked the system of agriculture, the use of animal manures in farming; and the tyranny of man over brute nature; these abuses polluted his food. The ox must be taken from the plough, and the horse from the cart, the hundred acres of the farm must be spaded, and the man must walk wherever boats and locomotives will not carry him.[6] Even the insect world was to be defended,—that had been too long neglected, and a society for the protection of ground-worms, slugs, and mosquitos was to be incorporated without delay.[7] With these appeared the adepts of homœopathy, of hydropathy, of mesmerism, of phrenology, and their wonderful theories of the Christian miracles![8] Others assailed particular vocations, as that of the lawyer, that of the merchant, of the manufacturer, of the clergyman, of the scholar. Others attacked the institution of marriage, as the fountain of social evils.[9] Others devoted themselves to the worrying of churches and meetings for public worship; and the fertile forms of antinomianism[10] among the elder

1   Emerson added these lines to "New England Reformers" in the 1850 edition of *Essays: Second Series*.

2   The church in name only; a play on phrases such as "the church militant" (that is, on earth) and "the church triumphant" (that is, in heaven).

3   Emerson alludes to the popularity in the 1840s of societies inveighing against alcohol, war, slavery, and capitalism. The ultraists sought religious truth outside any established church. In 1841–1842 the Friends of Universal Reform held several conventions in Boston to discuss the observance of the Sabbath and other church practices, as well as the authority of scripture. In a report for the *Dial*, Emerson described the crowd that attended: "Madmen, madwomen, men with beards . . . Quakers, Abolitionists, Calvinists, Unitarians, and Philosophers," all of them come "to chide, or pray, or preach, or protest."

4   Emerson himself in his 1841 lecture "Man the Reformer" lamented, "We eat and drink and wear perjury and fraud in a hundred commodities." The belief in the wholesomeness of farming was common in Emerson's circle; Edward Palmer (1802–1886) campaigned against the use of money; Sylvester Graham (1794–1851) was an influential vegetarian and apostle of bread, as well as the inventor of the Graham cracker.

5   Put blocks under.

6    An account of the principles behind Fruitlands, the utopian community that Emerson's friend Amos Bronson Alcott (1799–1888) and the English reformer Charles Lane (1800–1870) established in June 1843 in the town of Harvard, fifteen miles west of Concord. The members of Fruitlands never tried to produce more than they could consume; they ate a simple diet and avoided strenuous labor. But the community (eleven adults and a number of children) could not raise enough food to sustain itself. By the winter of 1843, only Alcott's and Lane's families remained at Fruitlands; the experiment ended completely in January 1844.

7    Bronson Alcott reportedly spared even the worms that infested Fruitlands' apples.

8    Hydropathists believed in the healing properties of water, mesmerists hypnotized their patients, and phrenologists studied the shape of the head. All three practices were fashionable in the 1840s, as was homeopathy. Some even claimed that Christian miracles were the effects of mesmeric processes.

9    The Shakers practiced chastity, convinced of the sinfulness of marriage. The Oneida community of upstate New York featured group marriage.

10   Abolitionists disrupted church services and Quaker meetings. Antinomianism is the belief that adherence to Christian moral law is unnecessary, since God demands faith alone. The early American religious leader Anne Hutchinson (1591–1643) was accused of antinomianism, among other offenses, and expelled from the Massachusetts Bay Colony. The apostle of tolerance Roger Williams (ca. 1603–1683) and the Quakers were labeled antinomian as well.

puritans, seemed to have their match in the plenty of the new harvest of reform.[11]

With this din of opinion and debate, there was a keener scrutiny of institutions and domestic life than any we had known, there was sincere protesting against existing evils, and there were changes of employment dictated by conscience. No doubt, there was plentiful vaporing,[12] and cases of backsliding might occur. But in each of these movements emerged a good result, a tendency to the adoption of simpler methods, and an assertion of the sufficiency of the private man. Thus it was directly in the spirit and genius of the age, what happened in one instance, when a church censured and threatened to excommunicate one of its members, on account of the somewhat hostile part to the church, which his conscience led him to take in the antislavery business; the threatened individual immediately excommunicated the church in a public and formal process.[13] This has been several times repeated: it was excellent when it was done the first time, but, of course, loses all value when it is copied. Every project in the history of reform, no matter how violent and surprising, is good, when it is the dictate of a man's genius and constitution, but very dull and suspicious when adopted from another. It is right and beautiful in any man to say, "I will take this coat, or this book, or this measure of corn of yours,"—in whom we see the act to be original, and to flow from the whole spirit and faith of him; for then that taking will have a giving as free and divine: but we are very easily disposed to resist the same generosity of speech, when we miss originality and truth to character in it.

There was in all the practical activities of New England, for the last quarter of a century, a gradual withdrawal of tender consciences from the social organizations. There is observable throughout, the contest between mechanical and spiritual methods, but with a steady tendency of the thoughtful and virtuous to a deeper belief and reliance on spiritual facts.[14]

In politics, for example, it is easy to see the progress of dissent. The country is full of rebellion; the country is full of kings. Hands off! let there be no control and no interference in the administration of the affairs of this kingdom of me. Hence the growth of the doctrine and of the party of Free Trade,[15] and the willingness to try that experiment, in the face of what appear incontestable facts. I confess, the motto of the Globe newspaper[16] is so

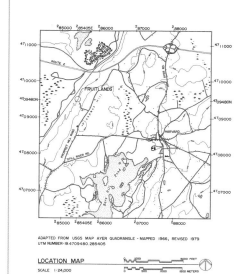

# FRUITLANDS

"FRUITLANDS," A TYPICAL RED-PAINTED EIGHTEENTH-CENTURY NEW ENGLAND FARMHOUSE WITH LATER NINETEENTH-CENTURY ADDITIONS AND MODIFICATIONS MADE AFTER 1914 FOR MUSEUM PURPOSES, STANDS ON ITS ORIGINAL SITE ON THE WESTERN SLOPE OF PROSPECT HILL OVERLOOKING THE NASHUA VALLEY WITH A DISTANT VIEW OF MT. WACHUSETT. IT IS NOW A PRINCIPAL FEATURE OF THE FRUITLANDS MUSEUMS, AN EARLY OUTDOOR MUSEUM COMPLEX FOUNDED IN 1914 BY CLARA ENDICOTT SEARS.

THE FARMHOUSE, CALLED "FRUITLANDS" SINCE 1843, IS NOTEWORTHY AS THE SCENE OF A UTOPIAN EXPERIMENT IN COMMUNAL LIVING CONDUCTED BY THE TRANSCENDENTALIST PHILOSOPHER BRONSON ALCOTT (FATHER OF LOUISA MAY ALCOTT) AND HIS ENGLISH PARTNER CHARLES LANE. THEY HAD A SMALL GROUP OF IDEALISTIC FOLLOWERS, INCLUDING ISAAC HECKER, WHO LATER FOUNDED THE PAULISTS, AN ORDER OF ROMAN CATHOLIC PRIESTS. THE UTOPIAN PROJECT LASTED LESS THAN A YEAR, FROM JUNE 1, 1843, UNTIL THE DEPARTURE OF THE ALCOTT FAMILY FOR STILL RIVER IN JANUARY, 1844. THE DEMISE OF THE REFORMIST COLONY RESULTED FROM A COMBINATION OF DOCTRINAL DISPUTES AND HOPELESSLY IMPRACTICAL FARMING METHODS. FRUITLANDS WAS MADE A NATIONAL HISTORIC LANDMARK ON SEPTEMBER 24, 1974.

THE DOCUMENTATION OF FRUITLANDS WAS UNDERTAKEN BY THE HISTORIC AMERICAN BUILDINGS SURVEY (HABS) OF THE NATIONAL PARK SERVICE'S NATIONAL ARCHITECTURAL AND ENGINEERING RECORD IN COOPERATION WITH THE FRUITLANDS MUSEUMS. UNDER THE DIRECTION OF KENNETH L. ANDERSON, ACTING CHIEF OF HABS, THE FIELD RECORDING WAS CONDUCTED BY RICHARD J. CRONENBERGER, PROJECT SUPERVISOR, DAVID T. MARSH JR. AND PAUL D. DOLINSKY (WASHINGTON D.C. OFFICE STAFF), DURING THE SPRING OF 1981. THE DRAWINGS WERE PRODUCED DURING THE SUMMER OF 1981 BY STUDENT ARCHITECT DOUGLAS R. TAYLOR (AUBURN UNIVERSITY).

ADAPTED FROM USGS MAP AYER QUADRANGLE - MAPPED 1966, REVISED 1979
UTM NUMBER:19.4709480.285405

LOCATION MAP
SCALE 1:24,000

Fruitlands, the utopian commune established by Amos Bronson Alcott and Charles Lane in Harvard, Massachusetts.

attractive to me, that I can seldom find much appetite to read what is below it in its columns, "The world is governed too much." So the country is frequently affording solitary examples of resistance to the government, solitary nullifiers, who throw themselves on their reserved rights;[17] nay, who have reserved all their rights; who reply to the assessor, and to the clerk of court, that they do not know the State; and embarrass the courts of law, by nonjuring, and the commander-in-chief of the militia, by non-resistance.[18]

The same disposition to scrutiny and dissent appeared in civil, festive, neighborly, and domestic society. A restless, prying, conscientious criticism broke out in unexpected quarters. Who gave me the money with which I

11  In his lecture "The Anglo-Saxon Race" (1843), Emerson asked, "What is this abolition, non-resistance, and temperance but the continuation of Puritanism, though it operate the destruction of the church in which it grew as the new is always making the old superfluous" (LL 1:12).

12  Bombast, idle boasting.

13  The Congregationalist Parker Pillsbury (1809–1898), excommunicated for his raucous opposition to slavery, proceeded in 1841 to "excommunicate" all proslavery ministers.

14  In his lecture "Historic Notes of Life and Letters in New England" (first delivered in 1868), Emerson described his generation of dissenters: "These reformers were a new class. Instead of the fiery souls of the Puritans, bent on hanging the Quaker, burning the witch and banishing the Romanist, these were gentle souls, with peaceful and even with genial dispositions, casting sheep's-eyes even on Fourier and his houris." (Charles Fourier, 1772–1837, French utopian who advocated sexual fulfillment along with cooperative, fair labor; houris are the virgins promised to the virtuous in the Islamic paradise.)

15  The Democrats.

16  Of Washington, D.C.

17  The 10th Amendment to the U.S. Constitution states that "powers not delegated" are "reserved . . . to the people."

18  Non-juring: refusal to take an oath. In 1843, Alcott and his disciple Charles Lane refused to pay the poll tax, since Massachusetts (they argued) supported slavery. After a similar refusal in July 1846, Henry David Thoreau

(continued)

(1817–1862) spent a famous night in jail. In 1838 the abolitionist William Lloyd Garrison (1807–1879) founded the New England Non-Resistance Society, which opposed all governments and all wars and advocated separation from the slaveholding South.

19    Office of accounts in a business.

20    Salons, drawing-rooms. In his lecture "Man the Reformer" (1841) Emerson said, "The trail of the serpent reaches into all the lucrative professions and practices of man. . . . Each requires of the practitioner a certain shutting of the eyes, a certain dapperness and compliance . . ."

21    This detail comes from the essay "Against Idleness" by Emerson's admired precursor Michel de Montaigne (1533–1592), who quotes the Roman philosopher Seneca (4 BCE–65).

22    Emerson read this advice in a letter by the English Puritan John Hampden (1594–1643).

23    An "artificial volcano" was a popular variety of fireworks; in the 1840s nitrous oxide ("laughing gas") was beginning to be used as an anesthetic, owing to the efforts of Emerson's brother-in-law Charles T. Jackson (1805–1880), among others.

bought my coat? Why should professional labor and that of the counting-house[19] be paid so disproportionately to the labor of the porter, and wood-sawyer? This whole business of Trade gives me to pause and think, as it constitutes false relations between men; inasmuch as I am prone to count myself relieved of any responsibility to behave well and nobly to that person whom I pay with money, whereas if I had not that commodity, I should be put on my good behavior in all companies, and man would be a benefactor to man, as being himself his only certificate that he had a right to those aids and services which each asked of the other. Am I not too protected a person? is there not a wide disparity between the lot of me and the lot of thee, my poor brother, my poor sister? Am I not defrauded of my best culture in the loss of those gymnastics which manual labor and the emergencies of poverty constitute? I find nothing healthful or exalting in the smooth conventions of society; I do not like the close air of saloons.[20] I begin to suspect myself to be a prisoner, though treated with all this courtesy and luxury. I pay a destructive tax in my conformity.

The same insatiable criticism may be traced in the efforts for the reform of Education. The popular education has been taxed with a want of truth and nature. It was complained that an education to things was not given. We are students of words: we are shut up in schools, and colleges, and recitation-rooms, for ten or fifteen years, and come out at last with a bag of wind, a memory of words, and do not know a thing. We cannot use our hands, or our legs, or our eyes, or our arms. We do not know an edible root in the woods, we cannot tell our course by the stars, nor the hour of the day by the sun. It is well if we can swim and skate. We are afraid of a horse, of a cow, of a dog, of a snake, of a spider. The Roman rule was, to teach a boy nothing that he could not learn standing.[21] The old English rule was, "All summer in the field, and all winter in the study."[22] And it seems as if a man should learn to plant, or to fish, or to hunt, that he might secure his subsistence at all events, and not be painful to his friends and fellow men. The lessons of science should be experimental also. The sight of the planet through a telescope, is worth all the course on astronomy; the shock of the electric spark in the elbow, outvalues all the theories; the taste of the nitrous oxide, the firing of an artificial volcano, are better than volumes of chemistry.[23]

One of the traits of the new spirit, is the inquisition it fixed on our scholastic devotion to the dead languages. The ancient languages, with great beauty of structure, contain wonderful remains of genius, which draw, and always will draw, certain likeminded men,—Greek men, and Roman men, in all countries, to their study; but by a wonderful drowsiness of usage, they had exacted the study of *all* men. Once (say two centuries ago), Latin and Greek had a strict relation to all the science and culture there was in Europe, and the Mathematics had a momentary importance at some era of activity in physical science. These things became stereotyped as *education*, as the manner of men is. But the Good Spirit never cared for the colleges, and though all men and boys were now drilled in Latin, Greek, and Mathematics, it had quite left these shells high and dry on the beach, and was now creating and feeding other matters at other ends of the world. But in a hundred high schools and colleges, this warfare against common sense still goes on. Four, or six, or ten years, the pupil is parsing Greek and Latin, and as soon as he leaves the University, as it is ludicrously styled, he shuts those books for the last time. Some thousands of young men are graduated at our colleges in this country every year, and the persons who, at forty years, still read Greek, can all be counted on your hand. I never met with ten. Four or five persons I have seen who read Plato.[24]

But is not this absurd, that the whole liberal talent of this country should be directed in its best years on studies which lead to nothing? What was the consequence? Some intelligent persons said or thought: "Is that Greek and Latin some spell to conjure with, and not words of reason? If the physician, the lawyer, the divine, never use it to come at their ends, I need never learn it to come at mine. Conjuring is gone out of fashion, and I will omit this conjugating, and go straight to affairs." So they jumped the Greek and Latin, and read law, medicine, or sermons, without it. To the astonishment of all, the self-made men took even ground at once with the oldest of the regular graduates, and in a few months the most conservative circles of Boston and New York had quite forgotten who of their gownsmen was college-bred, and who was not.

One tendency appears alike in the philosophical speculation, and in the rudest democratical movements, through all the petulance and all the pueril-

24 Greek philosopher (429–347 BCE) highly esteemed by Emerson, who usually read him in the English translation of Thomas Taylor (1758–1835). Criticism of the classical curriculum was increasing in Emerson's day, spurred by educational reformers such as Horace Mann (1796–1859).

25      Distasteful. Emerson remarked in his
Journal (September 1838), "Sympathy is a supporting atmosphere & in it we unfold easily &
well. But climb into this thin iced difficult air of
Andes of reform, & sympathy leaves you & hatred comes" (J 7:90).

26      Emerson's "Politics," also in *Essays: Second Series*, considers the meaning of property as
well: not merely how property ought to be distributed, but how its meaning has changed, and
will still change, in different social worlds.

ity, the wish, namely, to cast aside the superfluous, and arrive at short methods, urged, as I suppose, by an intuition that the human spirit is equal to all
emergencies, alone, and that man is more often injured than helped by the
means he uses.

I conceive this gradual casting off of material aids, and the indication of
growing trust in the private, self-supplied powers of the individual, to be the
affirmative principle of the recent philosophy: and that it is feeling its own
profound truth, and is reaching forward at this very hour to the happiest
conclusions. I readily concede that in this, as in every period of intellectual
activity, there has been a noise of denial and protest; much was to be resisted,
much was to be got rid of by those who were reared in the old, before they
could begin to affirm and to construct. Many a reformer perishes in his removal of rubbish,—and that makes the offensiveness of the class. They are
partial; they are not equal to the work they pretend. They lose their way; in
the assault on the kingdom of darkness, they expend all their energy on some
accidental evil, and lose their sanity and power of benefit. It is of little moment that one or two, or twenty errors of our social system be corrected, but
of much that the man be in his senses.

The criticism and attack on institutions which we have witnessed, has
made one thing plain, that society gains nothing whilst a man, not himself
renovated, attempts to renovate things around him: he has become tediously
good in some particular, but negligent or narrow in the rest; and hypocrisy
and vanity are often the disgusting result.[25]

It is handsomer to remain in the establishment better than the establishment, and conduct that in the best manner, than to make a sally against
evil by some single improvement, without supporting it by a total regenera-
tion. Do not be so vain of your one objection. Do you think there is only
one? Alas! my good friend, there is no part of society or of life better than
any other part. All our things are right and wrong together. The wave of evil
washes all our institutions alike. Do you complain of our Marriage? Our
marriage is no worse than our education, our diet, our trade, our social customs. Do you complain of the laws of Property? It is a pedantry to give such
importance to them. Can we not play the game of life with these counters, as
well as with those; in the institution of property, as well as out of it. Let into
it the new and renewing principle of love, and property will be universality.

No one gives the impression of superiority to the institution, which he must give who will reform it. It makes no difference what you say: you must make me feel that you are aloof from it; by your natural and supernatural advantages, do easily see to the end of it,—do see how man can do without it. Now all men are on one side. No man deserves to be heard against property. Only Love, only an Idea, is against property, as we hold it.[26]

I cannot afford to be irritable and captious,[27] nor to waste all my time in attacks. If I should go out of church whenever I hear a false sentiment, I could never stay there five minutes. But why come out?[28] the street is as false as the church, and when I get to my house, or to my manners, or to my speech, I have not got away from the lie. When we see an eager assailant of one of these wrongs, a special reformer, we feel like asking him, What right have you, sir, to your one virtue? Is virtue piecemeal? This is a jewel amidst the rags of a beggar.

In another way the right will be vindicated. In the midst of abuses, in the heart of cities, in the aisles of false churches, alike in one place and in another,—wherever, namely, a just and heroic soul finds itself, there it will do what is next at hand, and by the new quality of character it shall put forth, it shall abrogate that old condition, law or school in which it stands, before the law of its own mind.

If partiality was one fault of the movement party, the other defect was their reliance on Association. Doubts such as those I have intimated, drove many good persons to agitate the questions of social reform. But the revolt against the spirit of commerce, the spirit of aristocracy, and the inveterate abuses of cities, did not appear possible to individuals; and to do battle against numbers, they armed themselves with numbers, and against concert, they relied on new concert.

Following, or advancing beyond the ideas of St. Simon, of Fourier, and of Owen, three communities have already been formed in Massachusetts on kindred plans, and many more in the country at large.[29] They aim to give every member a share in the manual labor, to give an equal reward to labor and to talent, and to unite a liberal culture with an education to labor. The scheme offers, by the economies of associated labor and expense, to make every member rich, on the same amount of property, that, in separate families, would leave every member poor. These new associations are composed

27    Excessively fault-finding.

28    In New England radical reformers or religious dissidents were known as "come-outers," possibly after St. Paul's advice: "Come out from among them, and be ye separate . . . and touch not the unclean thing" (I Corinthians 6:17).

29    Like Fourier, Henri de Saint-Simon (1760–1825) and Robert Owen (1771–1858) were European socialist reformers. In his Journal in 1843 Emerson wrote, "Fourier carries a whole French revolution in his head, & much more. This is arithmetic with a vengeance. His ciphering goes where ciphering never went before, stars & atmospheres, & animals, & men, & women, & classes of every character" (J 9:8). Brook Farm, established by George Ripley (1802–1880) in West Roxbury, Massachusetts, followed the ideas of Fourier; the other communities mentioned might be ones at Northampton and Hopedale, or Alcott's Fruitlands. Owen sponsored a cooperative community in New Harmony, Indiana, in 1825 (it collapsed within a few years). In his lecture "Historic Notes of Life and Letters in New England," Emerson described Owen as "the most amiable, sanguine and candid of men," adding, "He had not the least doubt that he had hit on a right and perfect socialism, or that all mankind would adopt it." In his Journal (1845), Emerson protested, "You are very external with your evils, Mr Owen: let me give you some real mischiefs Living for show Losing the whole in the particular Indigence of vital power I am afraid these will appear in a phalanstery or in a tub" (J 9:327). (Fourierist communities were known as phalansteries.)

30    In "The American Scholar" and elsewhere, Emerson demands that we become
whole persons, rather than partial ones.

31    Invited by Ripley to join Brook Farm in
1840, Emerson declined, with some misgivings.
He wrote to Ripley (December 15, 1840), "I
think that all I shall solidly do, I must do
alone. . . . If the community is not good for me
neither am I good for it" (L 2:370). In "Historic
Notes of Life and Letters in New England,"
Emerson said of Brook Farm, "It was a perpetual picnic, a French Revolution in small, an Age
of Reason in a patty-pan"; he added, "Of course
every visitor found that there was a comic side
to this Paradise of shepherds and shepherdesses
. . . one man ploughed all day and one looked
out of the window all day, and perhaps drew his
picture, and both received at night the same
wages." In his Journal (1843) Emerson characterized Brook Farm as "an intellectual Sans-
culottism" (J 8:377; the extreme French Revo-
lutionaries were known as sans-culottes because
they wore full-length trousers rather than knee-
breeches [culottes]).

32    Term for the group of 1,620 people who
would make up the Fourierist commune (or
phalanstery); originally the Greek word for a
band of soldiers.

33    Common, shared.

34    In his lecture "The Spirit of the Times"
(1848), Emerson commented, "The arrangements of Owen and Fourier are enforced by
arithmetic: but all the heroism and all the scope
and play of thought cleave to the solitary house.
The Spartan broth, the hermit's cell, the lonely
farmer's life, are poetic; the phalanstery, the
patent village, are culinary and mean. . . . Individualism never was tried" (LL 1:119).

of men and women of superior talents and sentiments: yet it may easily be
questioned, whether such a community will draw, except in its beginnings,
the able and the good; whether those who have energy, will not prefer their
chance of superiority and power in the world, to the humble certainties of
the association; whether such a retreat does not promise to become an asy-
lum to those who have tried and failed, rather than a field to the strong; and
whether the members will not necessarily be fractions of men,[30] because each
finds that he cannot enter it, without some compromise.[31] Friendship and
association are very fine things, and a grand phalanx[32] of the best of the human race, banded for some catholic[33] object: yes, excellent; but remember
that no society can ever be so large as one man.[34] He in his friendship, in his
natural and momentary associations, doubles or multiplies himself; but in
the hour in which he mortgages himself to two or ten or twenty, he dwarfs
himself below the stature of one.

But the men of less faith could not thus believe, and to such, concert
appears the sole specific of strength. I have failed, and you have failed, but
perhaps together we shall not fail. Our housekeeping is not satisfactory to
us, but perhaps a phalanx, a community, might be. Many of us have differed
in opinion, and we could find no man who could make the truth plain, but
possibly a college, or an ecclesiastical council might. I have not been able either to persuade my brother or to prevail on myself, to disuse the traffic or
the potation[35] of brandy, but perhaps a pledge of total abstinence might ef-
fectually restrain us. The candidate my party votes for is not to be trusted
with a dollar, but he will be honest in the Senate, for we can bring public
opinion to bear on him. Thus concert[36] was the specific in all cases. But concert is neither better nor worse, neither more nor less potent than individual
force. All the men in the world cannot make a statue walk and speak, cannot
make a drop of blood, or a blade of grass, any more than one man can. But
let there be one man, let there be truth in two men, in ten men, then is concert for the first time possible, because the force which moves the world is a
new quality, and can never be furnished by adding whatever quantities of a
different kind. What is the use of the concert of the false and the disunited?
There can be no concert in two, where there is no concert in one. When the
individual is not *individual*,[37] but is dual; when his thoughts look one way,
and his actions another; when his faith is traversed by his habits; when his

35    Buying and selling or drinking.

36    Agreement, harmony.

37    Single, indivisible (the word's original meaning).

Charles Fourier (1772–1837).

38    Reversing a rowboat by holding one oar stationary.

39    In "The Spirit of the Times" Emerson asserted, "The importance of sound individuals cannot be overvalued. Whatever may be the cry in books of philosophy or in the public opinion of the hour against the dangers of egotism, the energy and wisdom of the universe express themselves through personalities. It is a power now in its beginning, and its power is not demonstrated. As every house that would be most solid and stable, must be built of square stones; so every society that can be depended on, must be composed of men that are themselves complete" (LL 1:119).

40    In his Journal (1842) Emerson alluded to this trick, which is more feasible than one would think (J 8:251).

41    In "Self-Reliance," Emerson announced, "I will have no covenants but proximities."

Brook Farm, 1844; painting by Josiah Wolcott (ca. 1815–1885). Brook Farm's founder, George Ripley, wrote to Emerson in November 1840, "I wish to see a society of educated friends, working, thinking, and living together, with no strife."

will, enlightened by reason, is warped by his sense; when with one hand he rows, and with the other backs water,[38] what concert can be?[39]

I do not wonder at the interest these projects inspire. The world is awaking to the idea of union, and these experiments show what it is thinking of. It is and will be magic. Men will live and communicate, and plough, and reap, and govern, as by added ethereal power, when once they are united; as in a celebrated experiment, by expiration and respiration exactly together, four persons lift a heavy man from the ground by the little finger only, and without sense of weight.[40] But this union must be inward, and not one of covenants,[41] and is to be reached by a reverse of the methods they use. The union is only perfect, when all the uniters are isolated. It is the union of friends who live in different streets or towns. Each man, if he attempts to

join himself to others, is on all sides cramped and diminished of his proportion; and the stricter the union, the smaller and the more pitiful he is. But
leave him alone, to recognize in every hour and place the secret soul, he will
go up and down doing the works of a true member, and, to the astonishment
of all, the work will be done with concert, though no man spoke. Government will be adamantine[42] without any governor. The union must be ideal in
actual individualism.[43]

I pass to the indication in some particulars of that faith in man, which
the heart is preaching to us in these days, and which engages the more regard, from the consideration, that the speculations of one generation are the
history of the next following.

In alluding just now to our system of education, I spoke of the deadness
of its details. But it is open to graver criticism than the palsy[44] of its members: it is a system of despair. The disease with which the human mind now
labors, is want of faith. Men do not believe in a power of education. We do
not think we can speak to divine sentiments in man, and we do not try. We
renounce all high aims. We believe that the defects of so many perverse and
so many frivolous people, who make up society, are organic, and society is a
hospital of incurables. A man of good sense but of little faith, whose compassion seemed to lead him to church as often as he went there, said to me, "that
he liked to have concerts, and fairs, and churches, and other public amuse-
ments go on."[45] I am afraid the remark is too honest, and comes from the
same origin as the maxim of the tyrant, "If you would rule the world quietly,
you must keep it amused."[46] I notice too, that the ground on which eminent
public servants urge the claims of popular education is fear: "This country is
filling up with thousands and millions of voters, and you must educate them
to keep them from our throats." We do not believe that any education, any
system of philosophy, any influence of genius, will ever give depth of insight
to a superficial mind. Having settled ourselves into this infidelity, our skill is
expended to procure alleviations, diversion, opiates. We adorn the victim
with manual skill, his tongue with languages, his body with inoffensive and
comely manners. So have we cunningly hid the tragedy of limitation and inner death we cannot avert. Is it strange that society should be devoured by
a secret melancholy, which breaks through all its smiles, and all its gayety
and games?[47]

42    Unbreakable.

43    A beautifully proportioned Emersonian
equation: actuality makes up the ideal.

44    Bodily tremor and weakness.

45    Compassion here means fellow-feeling
(and, by extension, gregariousness). Emerson's
tavern-keeper friend Eli Robbins is the man of
little faith (see Matthew 6:30); the quoted line is
close to one Emerson attributes to Robbins in a
Journal entry of 1843 (J 9:40).

46    The source of this sentence has not been
found. In a similar vein, the Roman poet Ju-
venal (55–127) writes in his Satire 10 that the
people "anxiously wishes" for two things, "bread
and circuses."

47    In this paragraph Emerson seems to lend
himself to the "infidelity" he decries; his words
are themselves melancholy.

48    Integrity, honesty.

49    Show.

50    A familiar anecdote, originally from a historical account of King Philip of Macedon (382–336 BCE) by the Roman author Valerius Maximus (fl. 30).

51    In his essay "Circles," Emerson noted, "Our moods do not believe in each other."

52    From Bk. 3 of the *Republic* (413a) by the Greek philosopher Plato (429–347 BCE).

But even one step farther our infidelity has gone. It appears that some doubt is felt by good and wise men, whether really the happiness and probity[48] of men is increased by the culture of the mind in those disciplines to which we give the name of education. Unhappily, too, the doubt comes from scholars, from persons who have tried these methods. In their experience, the scholar was not raised by the sacred thoughts amongst which he dwelt, but used them to selfish ends. He was a profane person, and became a showman, turning his gifts to a marketable use, and not to his own sustenance and growth. It was found that the intellect could be independently developed, that is, in separation from the man, as any single organ can be invigorated, and the result was monstrous. A canine appetite for knowledge was generated, which must still be fed, but was never satisfied, and this knowledge not being directed on action, never took the character of substantial, humane truth, blessing those whom it entered. It gave the scholar certain powers of expression, the power of speech, the power of poetry, of literary art, but it did not bring him to peace, or to beneficence.

When the literary class betray[49] a destitution of faith, it is not strange that society should be disheartened and sensualized by unbelief. What remedy? Life must be lived on a higher plane. We must go up to a higher platform, to which we are always invited to ascend; there, the whole aspect of things changes. I resist the skepticism of our education, and of our educated men. I do not believe that the differences of opinion and character in men are organic. I do not recognize, beside the class of the good and the wise, a permanent class of skeptics, or a class of conservatives, or of malignants, or of materialists. I do not believe in two classes. You remember the story of the poor woman who importuned King Philip of Macedon to grant her justice, which Philip refused: the woman exclaimed, "I appeal": the king, astonished, asked to whom she appealed: the woman replied, "from Philip drunk to Philip sober."[50] The text will suit me very well. I believe not in two classes of men, but in man in two moods, in Philip drunk and Philip sober.[51] I think, according to the good-hearted word of Plato, "Unwillingly the soul is deprived of truth."[52] Iron conservative, miser, or thief, no man is, but by a supposed necessity, which he tolerates by shortness or torpidity of sight. The soul lets no man go without some visitations and holydays of a diviner presence. It would be easy to show, by a narrow scanning of any man's biography, that we are not so wedded to our paltry performances of every kind, but that every man has at intervals the grace to scorn his performances, in comparing them with his belief of what he should do, that he puts himself on the side of his enemies, listening gladly to what they say of him, and accusing himself of the same things.

What is it men love in Genius, but its infinite hope, which degrades all it has done? Genius counts all its miracles poor and short. Its own idea it never executed. The Iliad, the Hamlet, the Doric column, the Roman arch, the Gothic minster, the German anthem,[53] when they are ended, the master casts behind him. How sinks the song in the waves of melody which the universe pours over his soul! Before that gracious Infinite, out of which he drew these few strokes, how mean they look, though the praises of the world attend them. From the triumphs of his art, he turns with desire to this greater defeat. Let those admire who will. With silent joy he sees himself to be capable of a beauty that eclipses all which his hands have done, all which human hands have ever done.

Well, we are all the children of genius, the children of virtue,—and feel their inspirations in our happier hours. Is not every man sometimes a radical in politics? Men are conservatives when they are least vigorous, or when they are most luxurious.[54] They are conservatives after dinner, or before taking their rest; when they are sick, or aged: in the morning, or when their intellect or their conscience has been aroused, when they hear music, or when they read poetry, they are radicals. In the circle of the rankest tories[55] that could be collected in England, Old or New, let a powerful and stimulating intellect, a man of great heart and mind, act on them, and very quickly these frozen conservators will yield to the friendly influence, these hopeless will begin to hope, these haters will begin to love, these immovable statues will begin to spin and revolve. I cannot help recalling the fine anecdote which Warton relates of Bishop Berkeley, when he was preparing to leave England, with his plan of planting the gospel among the American savages. "Lord Bathurst told me, that the members of the Scriblerus club, being met at his house at dinner, they agreed to rally Berkeley, who was also his guest, on his scheme at Bermudas.[56] Berkeley, having listened to the many lively things they had to say, begged to be heard in his turn, and displayed his plan with such an astonishing and animating force of eloquence and enthusiasm, that

53 Great achievements in literature (by Homer and Shakespeare), architecture, and music. A minster is a monastery church.

54 Devoted to sensual enjoyment.

55 Conservatives.

56 This anecdote occurs in a book on the English poet Alexander Pope (1688–1744) by Joseph Warton (1722–1800). The Anglo-Irish philosopher and Anglican priest George, Bishop Berkeley (1685–1753), espoused the described scheme in a pamphlet published in 1725; he came to America in 1728 but never visited Bermuda, where he had intended to convert the Indians. Allen Bathurst (1684–1775), poet and conservative politician; the Scriblerus Club was a group of satirical writers, including Pope.

57    In his essay "Experience," Emerson wrote, "Ghostlike we glide through nature, and should not know our place again."

58    Jean-Jacques Rousseau (1712–1778), French radical philosopher and reformer; Honoré Riqueti, Comte de Mirabeau (1749–1791), French revolutionary; Charles Fox (1749–1806), English abolitionist and supporter of the French Revolution; Napoleon Bonaparte (1769–1821), French emperor; George Gordon, Lord Byron (1788–1824), English Romantic poet and firebrand.

59    Phrase from the Greek poet Pindar (ca. 522–443 BCE), quoted by Plutarch (ca. 46–ca. 122) in his *Moralia*, one of Emerson's favorite books.

60    Emerson mentions three famous Athenian generals: Cimon (5th century BCE), who defeated the Persians; Themistocles (ca. 528–462 BCE), who was responsible for the long walls between Athens and its port, Piraeus; and Alcibiades (ca. 450–404 BCE), an iconoclastic strategist who advocated the Sicilian expedition during the Peloponnesian Wars between Athens and Sparta. Alexander the Great of Macedon (356–323 BCE), the most successful military leader of the ancient world, conquered an enormous domain from Greece to India. Julius Caesar (100–44 BCE) was a Roman general and dictator.

61    The story is told in a Latin epic, the *Pharsalia*, by Lucan (39–65); but in the original version Caesar offers to give up only the civil war against Pompey (106–48 BCE), not the Egyptian queen Cleopatra (69–30 BCE). In the battle of Pharsalus, or Pharsalia (48 BCE), Caesar defeated Pompey and the Roman senators allied with him.

they were struck dumb, and, after some pause, rose up all together with earnestness, exclaiming, 'Let us set out with him immediately.'" Men in all ways are better than they seem. They like flattery for the moment, but they know the truth for their own. It is a foolish cowardice which keeps us from trusting them, and speaking to them rude truth. They resent your honesty for an instant, they will thank you for it always. What is it we heartily wish of each other? Is it to be pleased and flattered? No, but to be convicted and exposed, to be shamed out of our nonsense of all kinds, and made men of, instead of ghosts and phantoms. We are weary of gliding ghostlike through the world, which is itself so slight and unreal.[57] We crave a sense of reality, though it come in strokes of pain. I explain so,—by this manlike love of truth,—those excesses and errors into which souls of great vigor, but not equal insight, often fall. They feel the poverty at the bottom of all the seeming affluence of the world. They know the speed with which they come straight through the thin masquerade, and conceive a disgust at the indigence of nature: Rousseau, Mirabeau, Charles Fox, Napoleon, Byron,[58]—and I could easily add names nearer home, of raging riders, who drive their steeds so hard, in the violence of living to forget its illusion: they would know the worst, and tread the floors of hell.[59] The heroes of ancient and modern fame, Cimon, Themistocles, Alcibiades, Alexander, Cæsar,[60] have treated life and fortune as a game to be well and skilfully played, but the stake not to be so valued, but that any time, it could be held as a trifle light as air, and thrown up. Cæsar, just before the battle of Pharsalia, discourses with the Egyptian priest, concerning the fountains of the Nile, and offers to quit the army, the empire, and Cleopatra, if he will show him those mysterious sources.[61]

The same magnanimity shows itself in our social relations, in the preference, namely, which each man gives to the society of superiors over that of his equals. All that a man has, will he give for right relations with his mates. All that he has, will he give for an erect demeanor in every company and on each occasion. He aims at such things as his neighbors prize, and gives his days and nights, his talents and his heart, to strike a good stroke, to acquit himself in all men's sight as a man. The consideration of an eminent citizen, of a noted merchant, of a man of mark in his profession; naval and military honor, a general's commission, a marshal's baton, a ducal coronet, the laurel of poets, and, anyhow procured, the acknowledgment of eminent merit, have

this lustre for each candidate, that they enable him to walk erect and unashamed, in the presence of some persons, before whom he felt himself inferior. Having raised himself to this rank, having established his equality with
class after class, of those with whom he would live well, he still finds certain
others, before whom he cannot possess himself, because they have somewhat
fairer, somewhat grander, somewhat purer, which extorts homage of him. Is
his ambition pure? then, will his laurels and his possessions seem worthless:
instead of avoiding these men who make his fine gold dim,[62] he will cast all
behind him, and seek their society only, woo and embrace this his humiliation and mortification, until he shall know why his eye sinks, his voice is
husky, and his brilliant talents are paralyzed in this presence. He is sure that
the soul which gives the lie to all things, will tell none. His constitution will
not mislead him. If it cannot carry itself as it ought, high and unmatchable
in the presence of any man, if the secret oracles whose whisper makes the
sweetness and dignity of his life, do here withdraw and accompany him no
longer, it is time to undervalue what he has valued, to dispossess himself of
what he has acquired, and with Cæsar to take in his hand the army, the empire, and Cleopatra, and say, "All these will I relinquish, if you will show me
the fountains of the Nile." Dear to us are those who love us, the swift moments we spend with them are a compensation for a great deal of misery;
they enlarge our life;—but dearer are those who reject us as unworthy, for
they add another life: they build a heaven before us, whereof we had not
dreamed, and thereby supply to us new powers out of the recesses of the
spirit, and urge us to new and unattempted performances.

As every man at heart wishes the best and not inferior society, wishes to
be convicted of his error, and to come to himself, so he wishes that the same
healing should not stop in his thought, but should penetrate his will or active power. The selfish man suffers more from his selfishness, than he from
whom that selfishness withholds some important benefit. What he most
wishes is to be lifted to some higher platform, that he may see beyond his
present fear the transalpine good, so that his fear, his coldness, his custom
may be broken up like fragments of ice, melted and carried away in the great
stream of good will. Do you ask my aid? I also wish to be a benefactor. I wish
more to be a benefactor and servant, than you wish to be served by me, and
surely the greatest good fortune that could befall me, is precisely to be so

62    Lamentations 4:1: "How is the gold become dim! How is the most fine gold
changed!"

63    In a letter of November 11(?), 1840, Emerson wrote to Caroline Sturgis (1819–1888)
about Brook Farm, "I wish a grand thought or a
Bleeding Heart or a fiery zeal to be at the bottom of it, shared thoroughly by all the members, melting them all into one. Then the circumstances will fall rightly, and a new line be
surely written in history. But this movement is
not yet commanding: has not yet enlisted either
my Conscience or my Imagination" (L 7:429–
430).

64    Emerson revealed in his Journal (1842,
J 8:261) that the man was his neighbor Edmund
Hosmer (1798–1881).

moved by you that I should say, "Take me and all mine, and use me and mine
freely to your ends!" for, I could not say it, otherwise than because a great
enlargement had come to my heart and mind, which made me superior to
my fortunes. Here we are paralyzed with fear; we hold on to our little properties, house and land, office and money, for the bread which they have in
our experience yielded us, although we confess, that our being does not flow
through them. We desire to be made great, we desire to be touched with that
fire which shall command this ice to stream, and make our existence a benefit.[63] If therefore we start objections to your project, O friend of the slave, or
friend of the poor, or of the race, understand well, that it is because we wish
to drive you to drive us into your measures. We wish to hear ourselves con-
futed. We are haunted with a belief that you have a secret, which it would
highliest advantage us to learn, and we would force you to impart it to us,
though it should bring us to prison, or to worse extremity.

Nothing shall warp me from the belief, that every man is a lover of
truth. There is no pure lie, no pure malignity in nature. The entertainment
of the proposition of depravity is the last profligacy and profanation. There
is no skepticism, no atheism but that. Could it be received into common belief, suicide would unpeople the planet. It has had a name to live in some
dogmatic theology, but each man's innocence and his real liking of his neighbor, have kept it a dead letter. I remember standing at the polls one day,
when the anger of the political contest gave a certain grimness to the faces of
the independent electors, and a good man at my side looking on the people,
remarked, "I am satisfied that the largest part of these men, on either side,
mean to vote right."[64] I suppose, considerate observers looking at the masses
of men, in their blameless, and in their equivocal actions, will assent, that in
spite of selfishness and frivolity, the general purpose in the great number of
persons is fidelity. The reason why any one refuses his assent to your opinion, or his aid to your benevolent design, is in you: he refuses to accept you
as a bringer of truth, because, though you think you have it, he feels that you
have it not. You have not given him the authentic sign.

If it were worth while to run into details this general doctrine of the
latent but ever soliciting Spirit, it would be easy to adduce illustration in particulars of a man's equality to the church, of his equality to the state, and of
his equality to every other man. It is yet in all men's memory, that, a few

years ago, the liberal churches complained, that the Calvinistic church denied to them the name of Christian.[65] I think the complaint was confession: a religious church would not complain. A religious man like Behmen, Fox, or Swedenborg,[66] is not irritated by wanting the sanction of the church, but the church feels the accusation of his presence and belief.

It only needs, that a just man should walk in our streets, to make it appear how pitiful and inartificial[67] a contrivance is our legislation. The man whose part is taken,[68] and who does not wait for society in anything, has a power which society cannot choose but feel. The familiar experiment, called the hydrostatic paradox, in which a capillary column of water balances the ocean,[69] is a symbol of the relation of one man to the whole family of men. The wise Dandamis, on hearing the lives of Socrates, Pythagoras, and Diogenes read, "judged them to be great men every way, excepting, that they were too much subjected to the reverence of the laws, which to second and authorize, true virtue must abate very much of its original vigor."[70]

And as a man is equal to the church, and equal to the state, so he is equal to every other man. The disparities of power in men are superficial; and all frank and searching conversation, in which a man lays himself open to his brother, apprizes[71] each of their radical unity. When two persons sit and converse in a thoroughly good understanding, the remark is sure to be made, See how we have disputed about words! Let a clear, apprehensive[72] mind, such as every man knows among his friends, converse with the most commanding poetic genius, I think, it would appear that there was no inequality such as men fancy between them; that a perfect understanding, a like receiving, a like perceiving, abolished differences, and the poet would confess, that his creative imagination gave him no deep advantage, but only the superficial one, that he could express himself, and the other could not; that his advantage was a knack, which might impose on indolent men, but could not impose on lovers of truth; for they know the tax of talent, or, what a price of greatness the power of expression too often pays. I believe it is the conviction of the purest men, that the net amount of man and man does not much vary. Each is incomparably superior to his companion in some faculty. His want of skill in other directions, has added to his fitness for his own work. Each seems to have some compensation yielded to him by his infirmity, and every hindrance operates as a concentration of his force.

65   Calvinistic congregations denied communion to Unitarians.

66   Behmen is Jacob Boehme (1575–1624), German mystic; George Fox (1624–1691), English dissenter and founder of the Society of Friends (Quakers); Emanuel Swedenborg (1688–1772), Swedish mystic popular in Emerson's circle. "Behmen is healthily and beautifully wise . . . Swedenborg is disagreeably wise," Emerson wrote in his Journal (1849; J 11:179).

67   Unskillful, inept.

68   Whose task is chosen (by him).

69   It seems that the smaller vessel (the sealed column) ought to have a higher water level than the ocean; but the water level in both bodies is the same. The paradox was resolved by the French mathematician and philosopher Blaise Pascal (1623–1662). Capillary: narrow (describes a vessel or tube).

70   From Montaigne's essay "Of Profit and Honesty." Dandamis was an Indian sage who, according to Plutarch's life of Alexander (cited by Montaigne), made this remark about the Greek philosophers Socrates (ca. 469–399 BCE), Pythagoras (6th century BCE) and Diogenes (ca. 404–323 BCE).

71   Instructs.

72   Perceptive.

73    The phrase "paid or unpaid" in this sentence is rather painful to read, given the bitter
dispute over slavery. "I am Defeated all the
time; yet to Victory am I born," Emerson wrote
in his Journal several months after the death
of his five-year-old son Waldo (April 1842,
J 8:228). In his essay "Worship" he remarked,
"Wherever work is done, victory is obtained."
Emerson's friend the Scottish author Thomas
Carlyle (1795–1881) influenced Emerson's gospel of work: "Genuine WORK alone, what
thou workest faithfully, that is eternal, as the
Almighty Founder and World-Builder himself"
(from Carlyle's *Past and Present* ([1843]).

74    The last sentence is from Seneca (as
quoted by Montaigne in "Of Glory").

These and the like experiences intimate, that man stands in strict connexion with a higher fact never yet manifested. There is power over and behind us, and we are the channels of its communications. We seek to say thus
and so, and over our head some spirit sits, which contradicts what we say. We
would persuade our fellow to this or that; another self within our eyes dis-
suades him. That which we keep back, this reveals. In vain we compose our
faces and our words; it holds uncontrollable communication with the enemy,
and he answers civilly to us, but believes the spirit. We exclaim, 'There's a
traitor in the house!' but at last it appears that he is the true man, and I am
the traitor. This open channel to the highest life is the first and last reality, so
subtle, so quiet, yet so tenacious, that although I have never expressed the
truth, and although I have never heard the expression of it from any other,
I know that the whole truth is here for me. What if I cannot answer your
questions? I am not pained that I cannot frame a reply to the question, What
is the operation we call Providence? There lies the unspoken thing, present,
omnipresent. Every time we converse, we seek to translate it into speech, but
whether we hit, or whether we miss, we have the fact. Every discourse is an
approximate answer: but it is of small consequence, that we do not get it into
verbs and nouns, whilst it abides for contemplation forever.

If the auguries of the prophesying heart shall make themselves good in
time, the man who shall be born, whose advent men and events prepare and
foreshow, is one who shall enjoy his connexion with a higher life, with the
man within man; shall destroy distrust by his trust, shall use his native but
forgotten methods, shall not take counsel of flesh and blood, but shall rely
on the Law alive and beautiful, which works over our heads and under our
feet. Pitiless, it avails itself of our success, when we obey it, and of our ruin,
when we contravene it. Men are all secret believers in it, else, the word justice would have no meaning: they believe that the best is the true; that right
is done at last; or chaos would come. It rewards actions after their nature,
and not after the design of the agent. 'Work,' it saith to man, 'in every hour,
paid or unpaid, see only that thou work, and thou canst not escape the reward: whether thy work be fine or coarse, planting corn, or writing epics, so
only it be honest work, done to thine own approbation, it shall earn a reward
to the senses as well as to the thought: no matter, how often defeated, you
are born to victory.[73] The reward of a thing well done, is to have done it.'[74]

As soon as a man is wonted to look beyond surfaces, and to see how this high will prevails without an exception or an interval, he settles himself into serenity. He can already rely on the laws of gravity, that every stone will fall where it is due; the good globe is faithful, and carries us securely through the celestial spaces, anxious or resigned: we need not interfere to help it on, and he will learn, one day, the mild lesson they teach, that our own orbit is all our task, and we need not assist the administration of the universe. Do not be so impatient to set the town right concerning the unfounded pretensions and the false reputation of certain men of standing. They are laboring harder to set the town right concerning themselves, and will certainly succeed. Suppress for a few days your criticism on the insufficiency of this or that teacher or experimenter, and he will have demonstrated his insufficiency to all men's eyes. In like manner, let a man fall into the divine circuits, and he is enlarged. Obedience to his genius[75] is the only liberating influence. We wish to escape from subjection, and a sense of inferiority,—and we make self-denying ordinances, we drink water, we eat grass, we refuse the laws, we go to jail: it is all in vain; only by obedience to his genius; only by the freest activity in the way constitutional to him, does an angel seem to arise before a man, and lead him by the hand out of all the wards of the prison.[76]

That which befits us, embosomed in beauty and wonder as we are, is cheerfulness and courage, and the endeavor to realize our aspirations. The life of man is the true romance, which, when it is valiantly conducted, will yield the imagination a higher joy than any fiction.[77] All around us, what powers are wrapped up under the coarse mattings[78] of custom, and all wonder prevented. It is so wonderful to our neurologists that a man can see without his eyes, that it does not occur to them, that it is just as wonderful, that he should see with them; and that is ever the difference between the wise and the unwise: the latter wonders at what is unusual, the wise man wonders at the usual. Shall not the heart which has received so much, trust the Power by which it lives? May it not quit other leadings,[79] and listen to the Soul that has guided it so gently, and taught it so much, secure that the future will be worthy of the past?

75 Ruling power. In his Journal (December 27, 1834), Emerson wrote, "There is in every man a determination of character to a peculiar end. . . . This is called his genius, or his nature, or his turn of mind. The object of education should be to remove all obstructions & let this natural force have free play & exhibit its peculiar product. It seems to be true that no man in this is deluded" (J 4:378).

76 In the New Testament book of Acts, an angel leads Peter out of Herod's prison: "And, behold, the angel of the Lord came upon him, and a light shined in the prison: and he smote Peter on the side, and raised him up, saying, Arise up quickly. And his chains fell off from his hands" (Acts 12:7).

77 Emerson announced in the last sentence of his essay "Experience" that "the true romance which the world exists to realize, will be the transformation of genius into practical power."

78 Coarse fabrics.

79 Inspirations (term used by Quakers).

## An Address . . . on . . . the Anniversary of the Emancipation of the Negroes in the British West Indies

*Emerson gave this speech on August 1, 1844, in the Concord courthouse. His wife Lidian had been a fervent abolitionist since 1837, as were his mother, his brother Charles, and his Aunt Mary. Emerson, long an opponent of slavery, was now prepared to take an active role in the movement. Relentless and steadily reliant on fact, this address is his first public denunciation of the horrors of slavery; it was followed by many more.*

*The Women's Anti-Slavery Society of Concord invited Emerson to address the August 1 meeting; he was the featured speaker. Among the others was Frederick Douglass (1818–1895), the former slave and abolitionist hero. Emerson scholar Len Gougeon reports that "the sexton of the First Parish Church refused to ring the town bell" to announce the meeting, so Henry David Thoreau (1817–1862) "rushed to the church and rang the bell himself." George Curtis (1824–1892), a member of the utopian community Brook Farm, wrote that Emerson's address "was not of that cold, clear, intellectual character that chills so many people, but full of ardent Life"; and the antislavery* Liberator *applauded Emerson's new devotion to the cause. This text, which Emerson*
*(continued)*

Friends and Fellow Citizens,

We are met to exchange congratulations on the anniversary of an event singular in the history of civilization; a day of reason; of the clear light; of that which makes us better than a flock of birds and beasts: a day, which gave the immense fortification of a fact,—of gross history,—to ethical abstractions. It was the settlement, as far as a great Empire was concerned, of a question on which almost every leading citizen in it had taken care to record his vote; one which for many years absorbed the attention of the best and most eminent of mankind. I might well hesitate, from other studies, and without the smallest claim to be a special laborer in this work of humanity, to undertake to set this matter before you; which ought rather to be done by a strict cooperation of many well-advised persons; but I shall not apologize for my weakness. In this cause, no man's weakness is any prejudice; it has a thousand sons; if one man cannot speak, ten others can; and whether by the wisdom of its friends, or by the folly of the adversaries; by speech and by silence; by doing and by omitting to do, it goes forward. Therefore I will speak, or,—not I, but the might of liberty in my weakness. The subject is said to have the property of making dull men eloquent.

It has been in all men's experience a marked effect of the enterprise in behalf of the African, to generate an over-bearing and defying spirit. The institution of slavery seems to its opponent to have but one side, and he feels that none but a stupid or a malignant person can hesitate on a view of the facts. Under such an impulse, I was about to say, If any cannot speak, or cannot hear the words of freedom, let him go hence,—I had almost said, Creep into your grave, the universe has no need of you! But I have thought better: let him not go.[1] When we consider what remains to be done for this interest, in this country, the dictates of humanity make us tender of such as are not yet persuaded. The hardest selfishness is to be borne with. Let us withhold every reproachful, and, if we can, every indignant remark. In this cause, we must renounce our temper, and the risings of pride. If there be any man who thinks the ruin of a race of men a small matter, compared with the last decoration and completions of his own comfort,—who would not so much as part with his ice-cream, to save them from rapine[2] and manacles, I think, I must not hesitate to satisfy that man, that also his cream and vanilla are safer and cheaper, by placing the negro nation on a fair footing, than by robbing them. If the Virginian piques[3] himself on the picturesque luxury of his vassalage, on the heavy Ethiopian manners of his house-servants, their silent obedience, their hue of bronze, their turbaned heads, and would not exchange them for the more intelligent but precarious hired-service of whites, I shall not refuse to show him, that when their free-papers are made out, it will still be their interest to remain on his estate, and that the oldest planters of Jamaica are convinced, that it is cheaper to pay wages, than to own the slave.

The history of mankind interests us only as it exhibits a steady gain of truth and right, in the incessant conflict which it records, between the material and the moral nature. From the earliest monuments, it appears, that one race was victim, and served the other races. In the oldest temples of Egypt, negro captives are painted on the tombs of kings, in such attitudes as to show that they are on the point of being executed; and Herodotus, our oldest historian, relates that the Troglodytes hunted the Ethiopians in four-horse-chariots.[4] From the earliest time, the negro has been an article of luxury to the commercial nations. So has it been, down to the day that has just dawned on the world. Language must be raked,[5] the secrets of slaughter-houses and infamous holes that cannot front the day, must be ransacked, to tell what negro-slavery has been. These men, our benefactors, as they are producers of corn and wine, of coffee, of tobacco, of cotton, of sugar, of rum, and brandy, gentle and joyous themselves, and producers of comfort and luxury

*substantially expanded between delivery and publication, is that of the first edition (published in Boston by James Munroe, September 1844).*

*In his account of his journey to Mt. Katahdin in Maine, Thoreau describes a "rude logger's camp" in which "lay an odd leaf of the Bible, some genealogical chapter out of the Old Testament; and, half buried by the leaves, we found Emerson's Address on West India Emancipation, which had been left here formerly by one of our company, and had made two converts to the Liberty party here, as I was told . . ."*

1   As the critic Neal Dolan remarks, Emerson is "not sure to whom he should speak": he banishes the advocate of slavery, then calls him back. Emerson will argue that abolishing slavery benefits those who value their "cream and vanilla," as well as those who care for justice—and that self-interest and justice in fact go together.

2   Being seized by force.

3   Congratulates.

4   Emerson misremembers the account given by the ancient Greek historian Herodotus (5th century BCE), who writes in his *Histories* (ca. 440 BCE) that the Garamantes ("a very powerful nation") "hunt the Ethiopian Troglodytes in four-horse chariots; for the Ethiopian Troglodytes are the swiftest of foot of all men of whom we have heard any account given. The Troglodytes feed upon serpents and lizards, and such kind of reptiles: they speak a language like no other, but screech like bats" (4.183).

5   The word perhaps calls to mind the torture of slaves: language must itself be "raked" (or wracked?) to convey the slaves' suffering.

6        Moods.

7        Practitioners of witchcraft in West Africa or the Caribbean.

8        White man (in black dialect): "In Black patois of Suriname, *bakra*, master . . . in language of Calabar coast, 'demon, powerful and superior being'" (OED).

9        Raw, as yet undeveloped.

10       Added to.

11       Large boiler for cooking or laundry, made of copper.

12       As Dolan notes, wincing may seem an inadequate response to the torture of slaves, and "they are not pleasant sights," in its understatement, emphasizes the distance between the slave's pain and the audience's relative comfort. But, Dolan adds, the wince is still a bodily reaction to bodily suffering. A form of involuntary and innate sympathy, it hints that "the blood is moral . . . the stomach rises with disgust, and curses slavery."

for the civilized world,—there seated in the finest climates of the globe, children of the sun,—I am heart-sick when I read how they came there, and how they are kept there. Their case was left out of the mind and out of the heart of their brothers. The prizes of society, the trumpet of fame, the privileges of learning, of culture, of religion, the decencies and joys of marriage, honor, obedience, personal authority, and a perpetual melioration into a finer civility, these were for all, but not for them. For the negro, was the slave-ship to begin with, in whose filthy hold he sat in irons, unable to lie down; bad food, and insufficiency of that; disfranchisement; no property in the rags that covered him; no marriage, no right in the poor black woman that cherished him in her bosom,—no right to the children of his body; no security from the humors,[6] none from the crimes, none from the appetites of his master: toil, famine, insult, and flogging; and, when he sunk in the furrow, no wind of good fame blew over him, no priest of salvation visited him with glad tidings: but he went down to death, with dusky dreams of African shadow-catchers and Obeahs[7] hunting him. Very sad was the negro tradition, that the Great Spirit, in the beginning, offered the black man, whom he loved better than the buckra[8] or white, his choice of two boxes, a big and a little one. The black man was greedy, and chose the largest. "The buckra box was full up with pen, paper, and whip, and the negro box with hoe and bill; and hoe and bill for negro to this day."

But the crude[9] element of good in human affairs must work and ripen, spite of whips, and plantation-laws, and West Indian interest. Conscience rolled on its pillow, and could not sleep. We sympathize very tenderly here with the poor aggrieved planter, of whom so many unpleasant things are said; but if we saw the whip applied to old men, to tender women; and, undeniably, though I shrink to say so,—pregnant women set in the treadmill for refusing to work, when, not they, but the eternal law of animal nature refused to work;—if we saw men's backs flayed with cowhides, and "hot rum poured on, superinduced[10] with brine or pickle, rubbed in with a corn-husk, in the scorching heat of the sun;"—if we saw the runaways hunted with blood-hounds into swamps and hills; and, in cases of passion, a planter throwing his negro into a copper[11] of boiling cane-juice,—if we saw these things with eyes, we too should wince. They are not pleasant sights.[12] The blood is moral: the blood is anti-slavery: it runs cold in the veins: the stomach rises with disgust, and curses slavery. Well, so it happened; a good man or woman, a country-boy or girl, it would so fall out, once in a while saw these injuries, and had the indiscretion to tell of them. The horrid story ran and flew; the winds blew it all over the world. They who heard it, asked their rich and great friends, if it was true, or only missionary lies. The richest and greatest, the prime minister of England, the king's privy council were obliged to say, that it was too true. It became plain to all men, the more this business was looked into, that the crimes and cruelties of the slave-traders and slave-owners could not be overstated. The more it was searched, the more shocking anecdotes came up,—things not to be spoken. Humane persons who were informed of the reports, insisted on proving them. Granville Sharp was accidentally made acquainted with the sufferings of a slave, whom a West Indian planter had brought with him to London, and had beaten with a pistol on his head so badly, that his whole body became diseased, and the man useless to his master, who left him to go whither he pleased. The man applied to Mr. William Sharp, a charitable surgeon,[13] who attended the diseases of the poor. In process of time, he was healed. Granville Sharp found him at his brother's, and procured a place for him in an apothecary's shop. The master accidentally met his recovered slave, and instantly endeavored to get possession of him again. Sharp protected the slave. In consulting with the lawyers, they told Sharp the laws were against him. Sharp would not believe it; no prescription on earth could ever render such iniquities legal. But the decisions are against you, and Lord Mansfield, now chief justice of England, leans to the decisions. Sharp instantly sat down and gave himself to the study of English law for more than two years, until he had proved that the opinions relied on of Talbot and Yorke,[14] were incompatible with the former English decisions, and with the whole spirit of English law. He published his book in 1769;[15] and he so filled the heads and hearts of his advocates, that when he brought the case of George Somerset, another slave, before Lord Mansfield,[16] the slavish decisions were set aside, and equity affirmed. There is a sparkle of God's righteousness in Lord Mansfield's judgment, which does the heart good. Very unwilling had that great lawyer been to reverse the late decisions; he suggested twice from the bench, in the course of the trial, how the question might be got rid of: but the hint was not taken; the case was adjourned again and again, and judgment delayed. At last judgment was

13    William Sharp (1729–1810) and his brother Granville (1735–1813), an important abolitionist, paid for four months of medical treatment for the slave, Jonathan Strong, and then found employment for him at a Quaker apothecary. In 1767 Strong's master, David Lisle, saw him in the street and had him kidnapped in order to sell him for thirty pounds.

14    The Yorke-Talbot opinion of 1722, written by Philip Yorke (1690–1764) and Charles Talbot (1685–1737), upheld the legality of slavery in England.

15    *A Representation of the Injustice and Dangerous Tendency of Tolerating Slavery*, the first English antislavery tract.

16    William Murray, first Earl of Mansfield (1705–1793), the lord chief justice. Mansfield decided Somerset's case in 1772, holding that neither common law nor any parliamentary law recognized slavery, and that it was therefore illegal. Moreover, Mansfield stated, no one could be bound (as slaves were) to a contract without his consent.

17    A phrase used by the counsel in Somerset's case, but not by Mansfield.

18    The Quakers were pioneering opponents of slavery in both England and America. In 1790 they petitioned the U.S. Congress to abolish slavery.

19    A Quaker law clerk, tailor, and traveling preacher (1720–1772). Woolman wrote in his *Journal* (publ. 1774) of another incident: "A neighbor received a bad bruise on his body and sent for me to bleed him, which having done he desired me to write his will. I took notes, and among other things he told me to which of his children he gave his young Negro. I considered the pain and distress he was in and knew not how it would end, so I wrote his will save only that part concerning his slave, and, carrying it to his bedside, read it to him. I then told him in a friendly way that I could not write any instruments by which my fellow creatures were made slaves without bringing trouble on my own mind. I let him know I charged nothing for what I had done, and desired to be excused from doing the other part in the way he had proposed. We then had a serious conference on the subject; he, at length, agreeing to set her free, I finished the will." Woolman spoke to many slave owners, attempting to convince them of the evil of the institution.

demanded, and on the 22d June, 1772, Lord Mansfield is reported to have decided in these words; "Immemorial usage preserves the memory of *positive law*, long after all traces of the occasion, reason, authority, and time of its introduction, are lost; and in a case so odious as the condition of slaves, must be taken strictly (tracing the subject to natural principles, the claim of slavery never can be supported.) The power claimed by this return never was in use here. We cannot say the cause set forth by this return is allowed or approved of by the laws of this kingdom; and therefore the man must be discharged."

William Wilberforce (1759–1833).

This decision established the principle that the air of England is too pure for any slave to breathe,[17] but the wrongs in the islands were not thereby touched. Public attention, however, was drawn that way, and the methods of the stealing and the transportation from Africa, became noised abroad. The Quakers got the story. In their plain meeting-houses; and prim dwellings, this dismal agitation got entrance. They were rich: they owned for debt, or by inheritance, island property; they were religious, tender-hearted men and women; and they had to hear the news, and digest it as they could. Six Quakers met in London on the 6th July, 1783; William Dillwyn, Samuel Hoar, George Harrison, Thomas Knowles, John Lloyd, Joseph Woods, "to consider what step they should take for the relief and liberation of the negro slaves in the West Indies," and for the discouragement of the slave-trade on the coast of Africa. They made friends and raised money for the slave; they interested their Yearly Meeting; and all English and all American Quakers.[18] John Woolman[19] of New Jersey, whilst yet an apprentice, was uneasy in his mind when he was set to write a bill of sale of a negro, for his master. He gave his testimony against the traffic, in Maryland and Virginia. Thomas Clarkson[20] was a youth at Cambridge, England, when the subject given out for a Latin prize dissertation, was, "Is it right to make slaves of others against their will?" He wrote an essay, and won the prize; but he wrote too well for his own peace; he began to ask himself, if these things could be true; and if they were, he could no longer rest. He left Cambridge; he fell in with the six Quakers. They engaged him to act for them. He himself interested Mr. Wilberforce in the matter. The shipmasters in that trade were the greatest miscreants,[21] and guilty of every barbarity to their own crews. Clarkson went to Bristol, made himself acquainted with the interior of the slave-ships, and the details of the trade. The facts confirmed his sentiment, "that Providence had never made that to be wise, which was immoral, and that the slave-trade was as impolitic as it was unjust;" that it was found peculiarly fatal to those employed in it. More seamen died in that trade, in one year, than in the whole remaining trade of the country in two. Mr. Pitt and Mr. Fox[22] were drawn into the generous enterprise. In 1788, the House of Commons voted Parliamentary inquiry. In 1791, a bill to abolish the trade was brought in by Wilberforce,[23] and supported by him, and by Fox, and Burke,[24] and Pitt, with the utmost ability and faithfulness; resisted by the planters, and the whole West

20    In the summer of 1844 Emerson read *History of the Abolition of the African Slave Trade* (1807) by the tireless English abolitionist Thomas Clarkson (1760–1846), who reportedly rode 35,000 miles on horseback collecting evidence of the slave trade's atrocities.

21    Depraved persons.

22    William Pitt the Younger (1759–1806) became British prime minister in 1783, at the age of twenty-four. The prominent Whig and antislavery advocate Charles James Fox (1749–1806) was Pitt's rival.

23    The British philanthropist and politician William Wilberforce (1759–1833), drawing on Clarkson's evidence, made his first abolitionist speech in the House of Commons in May 1789.

24    Edmund Burke (1729–1797), Anglo-Irish statesman and author. In his Journal (1852) Emerson remarked, "Pitt is nothing without his victory. Burke, on the other side, who had no victory, & nothing but defeat & disparagement, is an ornament of the human race; & Fox had essential manliness. . . . Always on the right side" (J 13:115).

25   Man-of-war: a naval warship. The incident Emerson refers to probably derives from Angelina Grimké (1805–1879), who with her sister and fellow abolitionist Sarah Grimké (1792–1873) arrived in Boston in 1837 and were influential in Emerson's circle (in September 1837, on a visit to Concord, they converted Emerson's wife Lidian to the antislavery cause). In her *Letters to Catherine E. Beecher, in Reply to an Essay on Slavery and Abolitionism* . . . (Boston, 1838; published the previous year in the *Liberator* and other newspapers), Grimké writes: "A friend of mine one evening last winter, heard a conversation between two men, one of whom had, until recently, been a slave trader. He . . . said that once his vessel was chased by an English man of war, and that, in order to avoid a search and the penalty of death, he threw every slave overboard; and when his companion expressed surprise and horror at such a wholesale murder, 'Why,' said the trader, 'it was the fault of the English; they had no business to make a law to hang a man on the yard arm, if they caught him with slaves in his ship'" (letter of June 23, 1837). In the same letter Grimké mentions that in 1833 two slave vessels, the *Hercule* and the *Regule*, "pitched overboard upwards of 500 human beings, chained together." Emerson seems to have conflated the two incidents.

26   Beating.

27   A hot pepper, more commonly known as cayenne or Guinea pepper.

Indian interest, and lost. During the next sixteen years, ten times, year after year, the attempt was renewed by Mr. Wilberforce, and ten times defeated by the planters. The king, and all the royal family but one, were against it. These debates are instructive, as they show on what grounds the trade was assailed and defended. Every thing generous, wise, and sprightly is sure to come to the attack. On the other part, are found cold prudence, barefaced selfishness, and silent votes. But the nation was aroused to enthusiasm. Every horrid fact became known. In 1791, three hundred thousand persons in Britain pledged themselves to abstain from all articles of island produce. The planters were obliged to give way; and in 1807, on the 25th March, the bill passed, and the slave-trade was abolished.

The assailants of slavery had early agreed to limit their political action on this subject to the abolition of the trade, but Granville Sharp, as a matter of conscience, whilst he acted as chairman of the London Committee, felt constrained to record his protest against the limitation, declaring that slavery was as much a crime against the Divine law, as the slave-trade. The trade, under false flags, went on as before. In 1821, according to official documents presented to the American government by the Colonization Society, 200,000 slaves were deported from Africa. Nearly 30,000 were landed in the port of Havana alone. In consequence of the dangers of the trade growing out of the act of abolition, ships were built sharp for swiftness, and with a frightful disregard of the comfort of the victims they were destined to transport. They carried five, six, even seven hundred stowed in a ship built so narrow as to be unsafe, being made just broad enough on the beam to keep the sea. In attempting to make its escape from the pursuit of a man-of-war, one ship flung five hundred slaves alive into the sea.[25] These facts went into Parliament. In the islands, was an ominous state of cruel and licentious society; every house had a dungeon attached to it; every slave was worked by the whip. There is no end to the tragic anecdotes in the municipal records of the colonies. The boy was set to strip and to flog his own mother to blood, for a small offence. Looking in the face of his master by the negro was held to be violence by the island courts. He was worked sixteen hours, and his ration by law, in some islands, was a pint of flour and one salt herring a day. He suffered insult, stripes,[26] mutilation, at the humor of the master: iron collars were riveted on their necks with iron prongs ten inches long; capsicum pepper[27] was rubbed

Thomas Clarkson (1760–1846).

28    The Moravian Church was founded in Bohemia in 1457 by followers of the early Reformer Jan Hus (ca. 1369–1415). In England, the Moravians had an influence on John Wesley (1703–1791) and his brother Charles Wesley (1707–1788), founders of the Methodist (Wesleyan) movement. William Carey (1761–1834) and William Ward (1769–1823), also influenced by the Moravians, were Baptist missionaries in the East Indies. Along with Joshua Marshman (1768–1837) and Hannah Marshman (1767–1847), they founded in 1800 the mission at Serampore, West Bengal. They established schools and a college and were active in the effort to ban widow-burning (suttee) in Bengal (it was abolished in 1829).

in the eyes of the females; and they were done to death with the most shocking levity between the master and manager, without fine or inquiry. And when, at last, some Quakers, Moravians, and Wesleyan and Baptist missionaries, following in the steps of Carey and Ward[28] in the East Indies, had been moved to come and cheer the poor victim with the hope of some reparation, in a future world, of the wrongs he suffered in this, these missionaries were

# Slave Trade.

*Am not I a MAN, and a BROTHER!*

◆

Why was I ravish'd from my native strand?
  What savage race protects this *impious gain*?
Shall foreign plagues infest our teeming land,
  And more than sea-born monsters plow the main?

There, the dire *Locust's* horrid-swarms prevail,
  There the *blue Asps* with livid poisons swell,
There the dry *Dipsa*, writhes his sinuous mail;
  Could we not there, secure from envy dwell?

When the grim *Lion* urged his cruel chace,
  When the stern *Panther* sought his midnight prey,
What fate reserved me for this CHRISTIAN RACE:
  O race, more polish'd, more severe than they!

◆

A MEETING of the inhabitants of DUNBAR was held last Thursday,
when it was resolved, that a petition should be presented to both Houses of
Parliament, praying them to use their influence that the SLAVE TRADE
may be universally abolished. The petitions are lying upon the *Council
House* table, for the signature of the inhabitants of the Town and its Vicinity.

  It is requested that every well wisher to the melioration of the poor
*Africans*, and those who, from motives of humanity, are inclined to give
their dissenting vote to

## THE REVIVAL OF THE BLOODY TRAFFIC,

will come forward without delay.

DUNBAR, *July 1st*, 1814.

G. Miller and Son, Printers, Haddington.

English announcement of a petition against the slave trade (1814).

persecuted by the planters, their lives threatened, their chapels burned, and the negroes furiously forbidden to go near them. These outrages rekindled the flame of British indignation. Petitions poured into Parliament: a million persons signed their names to these; and in 1833, on the 14th May, Lord Stanley,[29] minister of the colonies, introduced into the House of Commons his bill for the Emancipation.

The scheme of the minister, with such modification as it received in the legislature, proposed gradual emancipation; that on 1st August, 1834, all persons now slaves should be entitled to be registered as apprenticed laborers, and to acquire thereby all the rights and privileges of freemen, subject to the restriction of laboring under certain conditions. These conditions were, that the prædials[30] should owe three fourths of the profits of their labor to their masters for six years, and the non-prædials for four years. The other fourth of the apprentice's time was to be his own, which he might sell to his master, or to other persons; and at the end of the term of years fixed, he should be free. With these provisions and conditions, the bill proceeds, in the twelfth section, in the following terms. "Be it enacted, that all and every person who, on the 1st August, 1834, shall be holden in slavery within any such British colony as aforesaid, shall upon and from and after the said 1st August, become and be to all intents and purposes free, and discharged of and from all manner of slavery, and shall be absolutely and forever manumitted;[31] and that the children thereafter born to any such persons, and the offspring of such children, shall, in like manner, be free from their birth; and that from and after the 1st August, 1834, slavery shall be and is hereby utterly and forever abolished and declared unlawful throughout the British colonies, plantations, and possessions abroad."

The ministers, having estimated the slave products of the colonies in annual exports of sugar, rum, and coffee, at 1,500,000 per annum, estimated the total value of the slave-property at 30,000,000 pounds sterling, and proposed to give the planters, as a compensation for so much of the slaves' time as the act took from them, 20,000,000 pounds sterling, to be divided into nineteen shares for the nineteen colonies, and to be distributed to the owners of slaves by commissioners, whose appointment and duties were regulated by the Act. After much debate, the bill passed by large majorities.

29    Edward Stanley (1799–1869), later prime minister of Great Britain, was secretary of state for war and the colonies in 1833–1834.

30    Slaves (or, in this case, serfs) who work the land.

31    Freed.

32    Henry Peter Brougham (pronounced "broom") (1778–1868), lord chancellor of England, 1830–1834.

33    William Ellery Channing (1780–1842), antislavery advocate, reformer, and influential Unitarian; author of *Slavery* (1835) and *Emancipation* (1840), on the freeing of the slaves in the West Indies. Like many Americans who condemned slavery, Channing recoiled from the stridency of abolitionism, and asserted in *Emancipation* that he had "no desire to force emancipation on the South." He remarked that, like "all noble enthusiasms," abolitionism had become over time less vehement, "wiser and more serene." Channing still warned the abolitionists not to become a political party: "now, then, when associations are waning, it is time for the individual to be heard, time for a free, solemn protest against wrong."

The apprenticeship system is understood to have proceeded from Lord Brougham,[32] and was by him urged on his colleagues, who, it is said, were inclined to the policy of immediate emancipation. The colonial legislatures received the act of Parliament with various degrees of displeasure, and, of course, every provision of the bill was criticised with severity. The new relation between the master and the apprentice, it was feared, would be mischievous; for the bill required the appointment of magistrates, who should hear every complaint of the apprentice, and see that justice was done him. It was feared that the interest of the master and servant would now produce perpetual discord between them. In the island of Antigua, containing 37,000 people, 30,000 being negroes, these objections had such weight, that the legislature rejected the apprenticeship system, and adopted absolute emancipation. In the other islands the system of the ministry was accepted.

The reception of it by the negro population was equal in nobleness to the deed. The negroes were called together by the missionaries and by the planters, and the news explained to them. On the night of the 31st July, they met everywhere at their churches and chapels, and at midnight, when the clock struck twelve, on their knees, the silent, weeping assembly became men; they rose and embraced each other; they cried, they sung, they prayed, they were wild with joy, but there was no riot, no feasting. I have never read anything in history more touching than the moderation of the negroes. Some American captains left the shore and put to sea, anticipating insurrection and general murder. With far different thoughts, the negroes spent the hour in their huts and chapels. I will not repeat to you the well-known paragraph, in which Messrs. Thome and Kimball, the commissioners sent out in the year 1837 by the American Anti-slavery Society, describe the occurrences of that night in the island of Antigua. It has been quoted in every newspaper, and Dr. Channing[33] has given it additional fame. But I must be indulged in quoting a few sentences from the pages that follow it, narrating the behavior of the emancipated people on the next day.

"The first of August came on Friday, and a release was proclaimed from all work until the next Monday. The day was chiefly spent by the great mass of the negroes in the churches and chapels. The clergy and missionaries throughout the island were actively engaged, seizing the opportunity to enlighten the people on all the duties and responsibilities of their new relation, and urging them to the attainment of that higher liberty with which Christ maketh his children free. In every quarter, we were assured, the day was like a sabbath. Work had ceased. The hum of business was still: tranquility pervaded the towns and country. The planters informed us, that they went to the chapels where their own people were assembled, greeted them, shook hands with them, and exchanged the most hearty good wishes. At Grace Hill, there were at least a thousand persons around the Moravian Chapel who could not get in. For once the house of God suffered violence, and the violent took it by force. At Grace Bay, the people, all dressed in white, formed a procession, and walked arm in arm into the chapel. We were told that the dress of the negroes on that occasion was uncommonly simple and modest. There was not the least disposition to gaiety. Throughout the island, there was not a single dance known of, either day or night, nor so much as a fiddle played."[34]

On the next Monday morning, with very few exceptions, every negro on every plantation was in the field at his work. In some places, they waited to see their master, to know what bargain he would make; but, for the most part, throughout the islands, nothing painful occurred. In June, 1835, the ministers, Lord Aberdeen and Sir George Grey,[35] declared to the Parliament, that the system worked well; that now for ten months, from 1st August, 1834, no injury or violence had been offered to any white, and only one black had been hurt in 800,000 negroes: and, contrary to many sinister predictions, that the new crop of island produce would not fall short of that of the last year.

But the habit of oppression was not destroyed by a law and a day of jubilee. It soon appeared in all the islands, that the planters were disposed to use their old privileges, and overwork the apprentices; to take from them, under various pretences, their fourth part of their time; and to exert the same licentious despotism as before. The negroes complained to the magistrates, and to the governor. In the island of Jamaica, this ill blood continually grew worse. The governors, Lord Belmore, the Earl of Sligo, and afterwards Sir Lionel Smith,[36] (a governor of their own class, who had been sent out to gratify the planters,) threw themselves on the side of the oppressed, and are at constant quarrel with the angry and bilious island legislature. Nothing can exceed the ill humor and sulkiness of the addresses of this assembly.

34    "Emancipation in the West Indies: a Six Months Tour in Antigua, Barbadoes, and Jamaica, in the year 1837. By J. A. Thome and J. H. Kimball. New York, 1838."—pp. 146, 147 (Emerson's note). The book's description of a solemn, even sacred, turning point in history provides a sabbath in the lecture: a moment of rest before Emerson turns to the new difficulties that faced the ex-slaves.

35    George Hamilton-Gordon, the Earl of Aberdeen (1784–1860), was secretary of state for war and the colonies in 1834–1835; George Grey (1799–1882) was under-secretary of state for war and the colonies (1835–1839).

36    The Anglo-Irish nobelman Somerset Lowry-Corry, Earl of Belmore (1774–1841), governed Jamaica 1829–1832. Howe Peter Browne, the Marquess of Sligo (1788–1845), was governor from 1834 to 1836. Lionel Smith (1778–1842) was governor of Tobago (1833) and Barbados (1833–1836), as well as Jamaica (1836–1839). In Jamaica, Smith tried to ease conditions for ex-slave apprentices: he proposed a law restricting the work day to nine hours and mandating that each worker be given a sufficient amount of food (the law was not passed).

37    Addictive pleasure.

38    Unlike some other abolitionists, Emerson depicts the planters as "spoiled child[ren]," rather than as evil monsters; but their addiction to "absolute control" over other human beings is far from innocent.

39    Paid officers.

40    Thomas Fowell Buxton (1786–1845), British politician, brewer, and abolitionist.

I may here express a general remark, which the history of slavery seems to justify, that it is not founded solely on the avarice of the planter. We sometimes say, the planter does not want slaves, he only wants the immunities and the luxuries which the slaves yield him; give him money, give him a machine that will yield him as much money as the slaves, and he will thankfully let them go. He has no love of slavery, he wants luxury, and he will pay even this price of crime and danger for it. But I think experience does not warrant this favorable distinction, but shows the existence, beside the covetousness, of a bitterer element, the love of power, the voluptuousness[37] of holding a human being in his absolute control. We sometimes observe, that spoiled children contract a habit of annoying quite wantonly those who have charge of them, and seem to measure their own sense of well-being, not by what they do, but by the degree of reaction they can cause. It is vain to get rid of them by not minding them: if purring and humming is, not noticed, they squeal and screech; then if you chide and console them, they find the experiment succeeds, and they begin again. The child will sit in your arms contented, provided you do nothing. If you take a book and read, he commences hostile operations. The planter is the spoiled child of his unnatural habits, and has contracted in his indolent and luxurious climate the need of excitement by irritating and tormenting his slave.[38]

Sir Lionel Smith defended the poor negro girls, prey to the licentiousness of the planters; they shall not be whipped with tamarind rods, if they do not comply with their masters will; he defended the negro women; they should not be made to dig the cane-holes, (which is the very hardest of the field-work;) he defended the Baptist preachers and the stipendiary magistrates,[39] who are the negroes' friends, from the power of the planter. The power of the planters, however, to oppress, was greater than the power of the apprentice and of his guardians to withstand. Lord Brougham and Mr. Buxton[40] declared that the planter had not fulfilled his part in the contract, whilst the apprentices had fulfilled theirs; and demanded that the emancipation should be hastened, and the apprenticeship abolished. Parliament was compelled to pass additional laws for the defence and security of the negro, and in ill humor at these acts, the great island of Jamaica, with a population of half a million, and 300,000 negroes, early in 1838, resolved to throw up the two remaining years of apprenticeship, and to emancipate absolutely on the 1st August, 1838 in British Guiana, in Dominica, the same resolution had been earlier taken with more good will; and the other islands fell into the measure; so that on the 1st August, 1838, the shackles dropped from every British slave. The accounts which we have from all parties, both from the planters, and those too who were originally most opposed to the measure, and from the new freemen, are of the most satisfactory kind. The manner in which the new festival was celebrated, brings tears to the eyes. The First of August, 1838, was observed in Jamaica as a day of thanksgiving and prayer. Sir Lionel Smith, the governor, writes to the British Ministry, "It is impossible for me to do justice to the good order, decorum, and gratitude, which the whole laboring population manifested on that happy occasion. Though joy beamed on every countenance, it was throughout tempered with solemn thankfulness to God, and the churches and chapels were everywhere filled with these happy people in humble offering of praise."

The Queen,[41] in her speech to the Lords and Commons, praised the conduct of the emancipated population: and, in 1840, Sir Charles Metcalfe,[42] the new governor of Jamaica, in his address to the Assembly, expressed himself to that late exasperated body in these terms. "All those who are acquainted with the state of the island, know that our emancipated population are as free, as independent in their conduct, as well-conditioned, as much in the enjoyment of abundance, and as strongly sensible of the blessings of liberty, as any that we know of in any country. All disqualifications and distinctions of color have ceased; men of all colors have equal rights in law, and an equal footing in society, and every man's position is settled by the same circumstances which regulate that point in other free countries, where no difference of color exists. It may be asserted, without fear of denial, that the former slaves of Jamaica are now as secure in all social rights, as freeborn Britons." He further describes the erection of numerous churches, chapels, and schools, which the new population required, and adds that more are still demanded. The legislature, in their reply, echo the governor's statement, and say, "The peaceful demeanor of the emancipated population redounds to their own credit, and affords a proof of their continued comfort and prosperity."

I said, this event is signal in the history of civilization. There are many styles of civilization, and not one only. Ours is full of barbarities. There are

41    Queen Victoria (1819–1901) had ascended the throne in 1837.

42    Charles Metcalfe (1785–1846) was governor of Jamaica from 1839 to 1842; he then became governor general of Canada.

Emancipation festival in Barbados, 1834.

43    The Spartans were admired for their discipline and civic virtue, though they produced no great works of art. They traced their origins to the Dorians, one of the original tribes of Greece.

44    Emerson expands his criticism of British materialism in *English Traits:* "the Englishman has pure pride in his wealth, and esteems it a final certificate."

45    A mocking reference. In Shakespeare's *Othello* (3.3.155–156), Iago tells Othello, "Good name in man and woman, dear my lord, / Is the immediate jewel of their souls."

many faculties in man, each of which takes its turn of activity, and that faculty which is paramount in any period, and exerts itself through the strongest nation, determines the civility of that age; and each age thinks its own the perfection of reason. Our culture is very cheap and intelligible. Unroof any house, and you shall find it. The well-being consists in having a sufficiency of coffee and toast, with a daily newspaper; a well-glazed parlor, with marbles, mirrors, and centre-table; and the excitement of a few parties and a few rides in a year. Such as one house, such are all. The owner of a New York manor imitates the mansion and equipage of the London nobleman; the Boston merchant rivals his brother of New York; and the villages copy Boston. There have been nations elevated by great sentiments. Such was the civility of Sparta and the Dorian race,[43] whilst it was defective in some of the chief elements of ours. That of Athens, again, lay in an intellect dedicated to beauty. That of Asia Minor in poetry, music, and arts; that of Palestine in piety; that of Rome in military arts and virtues, exalted by a prodigious magnanimity; that of China and Japan in the last exaggeration of decorum and etiquette. Our civility, England determines the style of, inasmuch as England is the strongest of the family of existing nations, and as we are the expansion of that people. It is that of a trading nation; it is a shop-keeping civility.[44] The English lord is a retired shopkeeper, and has the prejudices and timidities of that profession. And we are shopkeepers, and have acquired the vices and virtues that belong to trade. We peddle, we truck, we sail, we row, we ride in cars, we creep in teams, we go in canals,—to market, and for the sale of goods. The national aim and employment streams into our ways of thinking, our laws, our habits, and our manners. The customer is the immediate jewel of our souls.[45] Him we flatter, him we feast, compliment, vote for, and will not contradict. It was or it seemed the dictate of trade, to keep the negro down. We had found a race who were less warlike, and less energetic shopkeepers than we; who had very little skill in trade. We found it very convenient to keep them at work, since, by the aid of a little whipping, we could get their work for nothing but their board and the cost of whips. What if it cost a few unpleasant scenes on the coast of Africa? That was a great way off; and the scenes could be endured by some sturdy, unscrupulous fellows, who could go for high wages and bring us the men, and need not trouble our ears with the disagreeable particulars. If any mention was made of homicide, madness, adultery, and intolerable tortures, we would let the church-bells ring louder, the church-organ swell its peal, and drown the hideous sound. The sugar they raised was excellent: nobody tasted blood in it.[46] The coffee was fragrant; the tobacco was incense; the brandy made nations happy, the cotton clothed the world. What! all raised by these men, and no wages? Excellent! What a convenience! They seemed created by providence to bear the heat and the whipping, and make these fine articles.

But unhappily, most unhappily, gentlemen, man is born with intellect, as well as with a love of sugar, and with a sense of justice, as well as a taste for strong drink.[47] These ripened, as well as those. You could not educate him, you could not get any poetry, any wisdom, any beauty in woman, any strong and commanding character in man, but these absurdities would still come flashing out, these absurdities of a demand for justice, a generosity for the weak and oppressed. Unhappily too, for the planter, the laws of nature are in harmony with each other: that which the head and the heart demand, is found to be, in the long run, for what the grossest calculator calls his advantage. The moral sense is always supported by the permanent interest of the parties.[48] Else, I know not how, in our world, any good would ever get done. It was shown to the planters that they, as well as the negroes, were slaves; that though they paid no wages, they got very poor work; that their estates were ruining them, under the finest climate; and that they needed the severest monopoly laws at home to keep them from bankruptcy. The oppression of the slave recoiled on them. They were full of vices; their children were lumps of pride, sloth, sensuality and rottenness. The position of woman was nearly as bad as it could be, and, like other robbers, they could not sleep in security. Many planters have said, since the emancipation, that, before that day, they were the greatest slaves on the estates. Slavery is no scholar, no improver; it does not love the whistle of the railroad; it does not love the newspaper, the mailbag, a college, a book, or a preacher who has the absurd whim of saying what he thinks; it does not increase the white population; it does not improve the soil; everything goes to decay. For these reasons, the islands proved bad customers to England. It was very easy for manufacturers less shrewd than those of Birmingham and Manchester[49] to see, that if the state of things in the islands was altered, if the slaves had wages, the slaves would be clothed, would build houses, would fill them with tools, with

46    A bitter and effective thrust.

47    In *Emancipation*, Channing condemned the idea that "emancipation is a curse, because the civilized world must pay a few cents more to bring tea or coffee to the due degree of sweetness. . . . What is the great end of civilized society? Not coffee and sugar . . . but the protection of the rights of all its members."

48    Emerson often insists that self-interest and the moral sense go hand in hand: he looks forward to, he sees already, the victory of justice and of moral principle.

49    English industrial cities, both of them with an impoverished and desperate working class. "Shrewd" here means depraved or malicious: Emerson refers to the shocking oppression of the British factory system.

50    Who sold their people, or those of other tribes, as slaves.

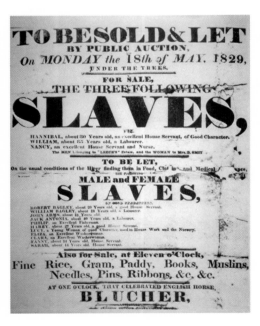

Poster for a slave auction (1829).

pottery, with crockery, with hardware; and negro women love fine clothes as well as white women. In every naked negro of those thousands, they saw a future customer. Meantime, they saw further, that the slave-trade, by keeping in barbarism the whole coast of eastern Africa, deprives them of countries and nations of customers, if once freedom and civility, and European manners could get a foothold there. But the trade could not be abolished, whilst this hungry West Indian market, with an appetite like the grave, cried, More, more, bring me a hundred a day; they could not expect any mitigation in the madness of the poor African war-chiefs.[50] These considerations opened the eyes of the dullest in Britain. More than this, the West Indian estate was owned or mortgaged in England, and the owner and the mortgagee had very plain intimations that the feeling of English liberty was gaining every hour new mass and velocity, and the hostility to such as resisted it, would be fatal. The House of Commons would destroy the protection of island produce, and interfere on English politics in the island legislation: so they hastened to make the best of their position, and accepted the bill.

These considerations, I doubt not, had their weight, the interest of trade, the interest of the revenue, and, moreover, the good fame of the action. It was inevitable that men should feel these motives. But they do not appear to have had an excessive or unreasonable weight. On reviewing this history, I think the whole transaction reflects infinite honor on the people and parliament of England. It was a stately spectacle, to see the cause of human rights argued with so much patience and generosity, and with such a mass of evidence before that powerful people. It is a creditable incident in the history, that when, in 1789, the first privy-council report of evidence on the trade, a bulky folio, (embodying all the facts which the London Committee had been engaged for years in collecting, and all the examinations before the council,) was presented to the House of Commons, a late day being named for the discussion, in order to give members time,—Mr. Wilberforce, Mr. Pitt, the prime minister, and other gentlemen, took advantage of the postponement, to retire into the country, to read the report. For months and years the bill was debated, with some consciousness of the extent of its relations by the first citizens of England, the foremost men of the earth; every argument was weighed, every particle of evidence was sifted, and laid in the scale; and, at last, the right triumphed, the poor man was vindicated, and the

"The Abolition of the Slave Trade" (1792), antislavery etching by George Cruikshank (1792–1878).

oppressor was flung out. I know that England has the advantage of trying the question at a wide distance from the spot where the nuisance exists the planters are not, excepting in rare examples, members of the legislature. The extent of the empire, and the magnitude and number of other questions crowding into court, keep this one in balance, and prevent it from obtaining that ascendency, and being urged with that intemperance, which a question of property tends to acquire. There are causes in the composition of the British legislature, and the relation of its leaders to the country and to Europe, which exclude much that is pitiful and injurious in other legislative assemblies. From these reasons, the question was discussed with a rare independence and magnanimity. It was not narrowed down to a paltry electioneering trap, and, I must say, a delight in justice, an honest tenderness for the poor negro, for man suffering these wrongs, combined with the national pride, which refused to give the support of English soil, or the protection of the English flag, to these disgusting violations of nature.

51     Merchants of New York (in 1842) and Boston (in 1843) had petitioned Congress against the Southern practice of seizing African-American crew members and passengers while ships were docked in port cities, and demanding a fee for their release.

Abolitionist concern with kidnapping of free persons of color increased with the publication of *Chronicles of Kidnapping* (1834) by Elizur Wright (1804–1885). In 1836 in Massachusetts, Chief Justice Lemuel Shaw (1781–1861) decided the case of *Commonwealth v. Aves;* he ruled that slaves who entered the state were free men while they remained in Massachusetts, and therefore could not be reclaimed by their masters. By contrast, the Fugitive Slave Law of 1850 appalled antislavery advocates, including Emerson, because it allowed Southern slave-owners to repossess their slaves who had fled to the North, and even commanded Northerners to arrest such fugitives.

52     On March 6, 1839, George Bradburn of Nantucket reported to the state legislature that he had, "during the last six years . . . by the aid of various benevolent individuals, procured the deliverance from jail of six citizens of Massachusetts, who had been arrested and imprisoned as runaway slaves." Bradburn mentioned in his speech the prominent businessman Jacob Barker (1779–1871) of Nantucket, who moved to New Orleans in 1834, and who worked with Rowland Hazard (1801–1888) to liberate men imprisoned as slaves. Barker described (in a letter to Samuel Jenks of Nantucket, August 19, 1837) his successful efforts to buy the freedom of several men who had been enslaved in New Orleans, including Eral Lonnon, a Nantucket Indian employed in the whaling industry: "he *(continued)*

Forgive me, fellow citizens, if I own to you, that in the last few days that my attention has been occupied with this history, I have not been able to read a page of it, without the most painful comparisons. Whilst I have read of England, I have thought of New England. Whilst I have meditated in my solitary walks on the magnanimity of the English Bench and Senate, reaching out the benefit of the law to the most helpless citizen in her world-wide realm, I have found myself oppressed by other thoughts. As I have walked in the pastures and along the edge of woods, I could not keep my imagination on those agreeable figures, for other images that intruded on me. I could not see the great vision of the patriots and senators who have adopted the slaves' cause:—they turned their backs on me. No: I see other pictures—of mean men: I see very poor, very ill-clothed, very ignorant men, not surrounded by happy friends,—to be plain,—poor black men of obscure employment as mariners, cooks, or stewards, in ships, yet citizens of this our Commonwealth of Massachusetts,—freeborn as we,—whom the slave-laws of the States of South Carolina, Georgia, and Louisiana, have arrested in the vessels in which they visited those ports, and shut up in jails so long as the vessel remained in port, with the stringent addition, that if the shipmaster fails to pay the costs of this official arrest, and the board in jail, these citizens are to be sold for slaves, to pay that expense.[51] This man, these men, I see, and no law to save them. Fellow citizens, this crime will not be hushed up any longer. I have learned that a citizen of Nantucket, walking in New Orleans, found a freeborn citizen of Nantucket, a man, too, of great personal worth, and, as it happened, very dear to him, as having saved his own life, working chained in the streets of that city, kidnapped by such a process as this. In the sleep of the laws, the private interference of two excellent citizens of Boston has, I have ascertained, rescued several natives of this State from these southern prisons.[52] Gentlemen, I thought the deck of a Massachusetts ship was as much the territory of Massachusetts, as the floor on which we stand. It should be as sacred as the temple of God. The poorest fishing-smack, that floats under the shadow of an iceberg in the northern seas, or hunts the whale in the southern ocean, should be encompassed by her laws with comfort and protection, as much as within the arms of Cape Ann and Cape Cod. And this kidnapping is suffered within our own land and federa-

tion, whilst the fourth article of the Constitution of the United States ordains in terms, that, "The citizens of each State shall be entitled to all privileges and immunities of citizens in the several States." If such a damnable
outrage can be committed on the person of a citizen with impunity, let the
Governor break the broad seal of the State; he bears the sword in vain. The
Governor of Massachusetts is a trifler: the State-house in Boston is a playhouse: the General Court is a dishonored body: if they make laws which they
cannot execute. The great-hearted Puritans have left no posterity. The rich
men may walk in State-street, but they walk without honor; and the farmers
may brag their democracy in the country, but they are disgraced men. If the
State has no power to defend its own people in its own shipping, because it
has delegated that power to the Federal Government, has it no representation in the Federal Government? Are those men dumb? I am no lawyer, and
cannot indicate the forms applicable to the case, but here is something which
transcends all forms. Let the senators and representatives of the State, containing a population of a million freemen, go in a body before the Congress,
and say, that they have a demand to make on them so imperative, that all
functions of government must stop, until it is satisfied. If ordinary legislation
cannot reach it, then extraordinary must be applied. The Congress should
instruct the President to send to those ports of Charleston, Savannah, and
New Orleans, such orders and such force, as should release, forthwith, all
such citizens of Massachusetts as were holden in prison without the allegation of any crime, and should set on foot the strictest inquisition to discover
where such persons, brought into slavery by these local laws, at any time
heretofore, may now be. That first;—and then, let order be taken to indem-
nify all such as have been incarcerated. As for dangers to the Union, from
such demands!—the Union is already at an end, when the first citizen of
Massachusetts is thus outraged.[53] Is it an union and covenant in which the
State of Massachusetts agrees to be imprisoned, and the State of Carolina to
imprison? Gentlemen, I am loath to say harsh things, and perhaps I know
too little of politics for the smallest weight to attach to any censure of mine,
—but I am at a loss how to characterize the tameness and silence of the two
senators and the ten representatives of the State at Washington. To what
purpose, have we clothed each of those representatives with the power of

prefers to encounter the leviathan of the deep, rather than the turnkeys of New Orleans," wrote Barker (from *American Slavery As It Is: Testimony of a Thousand Witnesses* [1839]).

53    Emerson here voices his dissent from Daniel Webster's (1782–1852) emphasis on pre-serving the Union. In his Channing Ode, Emerson balks at the prospect of a Northern seces-sion from the slaveholding South. Later on he was willing to entertain the idea in his Journal, in his revulsion at the passage of the Fugitive Slave Law of 1850. Here Emerson exclaimed, "Union is a delectable thing, & so is wealth, & so is life, but they may *all* cost too much, if they cost honour" (1851; J 11:360).

NOTICE.—Was committed to the jail of Frederick county, on the 29th day of July last, as a runaway, a negro man, who calls himself THOMAS RANKIN. He is about 27 years of age, 5 feet 6 inches high, has no visible mark about him; had on when committed linen pantaloons, and an old black hat; he says he is free and last from Washington city. The owner, if any, is hereby requested to come forward and have him released; he will otherwise be discharged according to law.

HENRY HOUCK,

aug 8 — law4t          Sheriff of Frederick county, Md.

---

200 DOLLARS REWARD.—Ran away from the subscriber's residence, about 4 miles from Bryantown, Charles county, Maryland, on Thursday morning, the 11th June, my negro man CHARLES, calls himself Charles Dyson, about 23 years old, 5 feet 6 or 7 inches high; a bright mulatto, and has a scar on the right or left side of his lower jaw bone, occasioned several years ago by a burn. The above reward will be paid i taken in a non-slaveholding State, and fifty dollars if taken within the States of Virginia and Maryland, or the District of Columbia.

july 10—2awcptf          J. ED. KEECH.

---

50 DOLLARS REWARD.—Ran away, on the 21st of July, from the subscriber, living near Chaptico, St. Mary's county, Md., negro WILLIAM. His wearing apparel cannot be accurately described, as he took with him a variety. William is about five feet six inches high, and well built, and so bright a mulatto that at first sight he would be taken for a white man. His hair is brown, and nearly straight; he has a wide mouth, and a very fine set of teeth. His voice is coarse, and when spoken to his eyes, though generally turned towards the ground, are rolled suddenly upwards, so as to display the balls considerably. William, having left home without cause, is doubtless making his way to a free State.

I will give the above reward to any person who will bring him home, or secure him in jail so that I get him again.

THOMAS W. GARDINER,

july 28—w2m      Near Chaptico, St. Mary's co. Md.

Rewards for runaway slaves, advertised in the Washington, D.C., *Intelligencer* (1840).

seventy thousand persons, and each senator with near half a million, if they are to sit dumb at their desks, and see their constituents captured and sold;—perhaps to gentlemen sitting by them in the hall? There is a scandalous rumor that has been swelling louder of late years, perhaps it is wholly false,—that members are bullied into silence by southern gentlemen. It is so easy to omit to speak, or even to be absent when delicate things are to be handled. I may as well say what all men feel, that whilst our very amiable and very innocent representatives and senators at Washington, are accomplished lawyers and merchants, and very eloquent at dinners and at caucuses, there is a disastrous want of *men* from New England. I would gladly make exceptions, and you will not suffer me to forget one eloquent old man, in whose veins the blood of Massachusetts rolls, and who singly has defended the freedom of speech, and the rights of the free, against the usurpation of the slaveholder.[54] But the reader of Congressional debates, in New England, is perplexed to see with what admirable sweetness and patience the majority of the free States, are schooled and ridden by the minority of slave-holders. What if we should send thither representatives who were a particle less amiable and less innocent? I entreat you, sirs, let not this stain attach, let not this misery accumulate any longer. If the managers of our political parties are too prudent and too cold;—if, most unhappily, the ambitious class of young men and political men have found out, that these neglected victims and without weight that are poor, that they have no graceful hospitalities to offer; no valuable business to throw into any man's hands, no strong vote to cast at the elections; and therefore may with impunity be left in their chains or to the chance of chains, then let the citizens in their primary capacity take tip their cause on this very ground, and say to the government of the State, and of the Union, that government exists to defend the weak and the poor and the injured party; the rich and the strong can better take care of themselves. And as an omen and assurance of success, I point you to the bright example which England set you, on this day, ten years ago.

There are other comparisons and other imperative duties which come sadly to mind,—but I do not wish to darken the hours of this day by crimination;[55] I turn gladly to the rightful theme, to the bright aspects of the occasion.

This event was a moral revolution. The history of it is before you. Here was no prodigy, no fabulous hero, no Trojan horse, no bloody war, but all

54    Former President John Quincy Adams (1767–1848) was a member of the U.S. House of Representatives from Massachusetts (1831–1848). During his time in the House, Adams, a staunch abolitionist, denounced the "gag rule" passed in May 1836, which prevented petitions against slavery from being heard. On December 3, 1844, Adams finally succeeded in overturning the "gag rule" (he had the date engraved on the top of his cane). In 1841 Adams successfully represented the Amistad Africans, who had seized control of a ship that was transporting them as slaves, in a case before the Supreme Court.

Emerson conspicuously fails to commend a man he otherwise admired: Daniel Webster, senator from Massachusetts from 1827 to 1841 and 1845 to 1850, and earlier a representative from the state, denounced slavery as "one of the greatest evils, both moral and political," during his 1830 debate with Robert Y. Hayne (1791–1839) of South Carolina and on other occasions—but Webster was no abolitionist.

55    Accusation of a crime.

56    Robert Henley, Earl of Northington (1708–1772), made this comment in 1762 about the British slave case *Shanley v. Harvey*.

57    Richard Grenville (1776–1839), the playwright Richard Brinsley Sheridan (1751–1816), Charles Grey (1764–1845), and George Canning (1770–1827) were antislavery members of Parliament; the English poet William Cowper (1731–1800) was author of *The Task* (1785).

58    During the parliamentary debate on the bill for the abolition of the slave trade, introduced by Wilberforce (February 28, 1805), John Huddleston (member of Parliament for Bridgewater, Somersetshire) argued, "Even supposing human blood should be pronounced, as it was by some, the best manure, did it follow that the blood of man should be shed for such a purpose; and was it not as well to bleed men to death at once, as to sweat the poor negroes to death in our colonies?"

was achieved by plain means of plain men, working not under a leader, but under a sentiment. Other revolutions have been the insurrection of the oppressed; this was the repentance of the tyrant. It was the masters revolting from their mastery. The slave-holder said, I will not hold slaves. The end was noble, and the means were pure. Hence, the elevation and pathos of this chapter of history. The lives of the advocates are pages of greatness, and the connexion of the eminent senators with this question, constitutes the immortalizing moments of those men's lives. The bare enunciation of the theses, at which the lawyers and legislators arrived, gives a glow to the heart of the reader. Lord Chancellor Northington[56] is the author of the famous sentence, "As soon as any man puts his foot on English ground, he becomes free." "I was a slave," said the counsel of Somerset, speaking for his client, "for I was in America: I am now in a country, where the common rights of mankind are known and regarded." Granville Sharp filled the ear of the judges with the sound principles, that had from time to time been affirmed by the legal authorities. "Derived power cannot be superior to the power from which it is derived." "The reasonableness of the law is the soul of the law." "It is better to suffer every evil, than to consent to any." Out it would come, the God's truth, out it came, like a bolt from a cloud, for all the mumbling of the lawyers. One feels very sensibly in all this history that a great heart and soul are behind there, superior to any man, and making use of each, in turn, and infinitely attractive to every person according to the degree of reason in his own mind, so that this cause has had the power to draw to it every particle of talent and of worth in England, from the beginning. All the great geniuses of the British senate, Fox, Pitt, Burke, Grenville, Sheridan, Grey, Canning, ranged themselves on its side; the poet Cowper[57] wrote for it: Franklin, Jefferson, Washington, in this country, all recorded their votes. All men remember the subtlety and the fire of indignation, which the *Edinburgh Review* contributed to the cause; and every liberal mind, poet, preacher, moralist, statesman, has had the fortune to appear somewhere for this cause. On the other part, appeared the reign of pounds and shillings, and all manner of rage and stupidity; a resistance which drew from Mr. Huddleston[58] in Parliament the observation, "That a curse attended this trade even in the mode of defending it. By a certain fatality, none but the vilest arguments were brought forward, which corrupted the very persons who used

them. Every one of these was built on the narrow ground of interest, of pecuniary profit, of sordid gain, in opposition to every motive that had reference to humanity, justice, and religion, or to that great principle which comprehended them all."—This moral force perpetually reinforces and dignifies
the friends of this cause. It gave that tenacity to their point which has insured
ultimate triumph; and it gave that superiority in reason, in imagery, in eloquence, which makes in all countries anti-slavery meetings so attractive to
the people, and has made it a proverb in Massachusetts, that, "eloquence is
dog-cheap at the anti-slavery chapel?"

I will say further, that we are indebted mainly to this movement, and to
the continuers of it, for the popular discussion of every point of practical
ethics, and a reference of every question to the absolute standard. It is notorious, that the political, religious, and social schemes, with which the minds
of men are now most occupied, have been matured, or at least broached, in
the free and daring discussions of these assemblies. Men have become aware
through the emancipation, and kindred events, of the presence of powers,
which, in their days of darkness, they had overlooked. Virtuous men will not
again rely on political agents. They have found out the deleterious effect of
political association. Up to this day, we have allowed to statesmen a paramount social standing, and we bow low to them as to the great. We cannot
extend this deference to them any longer. The secret cannot be kept, that
the seats of power are filled by underlings, ignorant, timid, and selfish, to a
degree to destroy all claim, excepting that on compassion, to the society of
the just and generous. What happened notoriously to an American ambas-
sador in England, that he found himself compelled to palter, and to disguise
the fact that he was a slave-breeder, happens to men of state. Their vocation
is a presumption against them, among well-meaning people. The superstition respecting power and office, is going to the ground. The stream of human affairs flows its own way, and is very little affected by the activity of
legislators. What great masses of men wish done, will be done; and they do
not wish it for a freak, but because it is their state and natural end. There are
now other energies than force, other than political, which no man in future
can allow himself to disregard. There is direct conversation and influence. A
man is to make himself felt, by his proper force. The tendency of things runs
steadily to this point, namely, to put every man on his merits, and to give

59    Farmers (a yeoman is an independent farmer or countryman).

60    Insurers. On November 29, 1781, Captain Luke Collingwood of the slave ship *Zong* threw 132 sick slaves overboard so that the ship's insurers would pay their cost (if they died on board, the owners would bear the cost). The incident became a court case in March 1783 (*Gregson v. Gilbert*). The owners won, but the decision was reversed on appeal. No one was ever charged for the murder of the slaves. The case galvanized antislavery opinion in Britain. The great, terrifying painting *Slave Ship* (1840) by the British artist J. M. W. Turner (1775–1851) was inspired by the massacre.

him so much power as he naturally exerts—no more, no less. Of course, the timid and base persons, all who are conscious of no worth in themselves, and who owe all their place to the opportunities which the old order of things allowed them to deceive and defraud men, shudder at the change, and would fain silence every honest voice, and lock up every house where liberty and innovation can be pleaded for. They would raise mobs, for fear is very cruel. But the strong and healthy yeomen and husbands[59] of the land, the self-sustaining class of inventive and industrious men, fear no competition or superiority. Come what will, their faculty cannot be spared.

The First of August marks the entrance of a new element into modern politics, namely, the civilization of the negro. A man is added to the human family. Not the least affecting part of this history of abolition, is, the annihilation of the old indecent nonsense about the nature of the negro. In the case of the ship Zong, in 1781, whose master had thrown one hundred and thirty-two slaves alive into the sea, to cheat the underwriters,[60] the first jury gave a verdict in favor of the master and owners: they had a right to do what they had done. Lord Mansfield is reported to have said on the bench, "The matter left to the jury is,—Was it from necessity? For they had no doubt,—though it shocks one very much,—that the case of slaves was the same as if horses had been thrown overboard. It is a very shocking case. But a more enlightened and humane opinion began to prevail. Mr. Clarkson, early in his career, made a collection of African productions and manufactures as specimens of the arts and culture of the negro; comprising cloths and loom, weapons, polished stones and woods, leather, glass, dyes, ornaments, soap, pipe-bowls, and trinkets. These he showed to Mr. Pitt, who saw and handled them with extreme interest. On sight of these, says Clarkson, many sublime thoughts seemed to rush at once into his mind, some of which he expressed; and hence appeared to arise a project which was always dear to him, of the civilization of Africa,—a dream which forever elevates his fame. In 1791, Mr. Wilberforce announced to the House of Commons, We have already gained one victory we have obtained for these poor creatures the recognition of their human nature, which, for a time, was most shamefully denied them. It was the sarcasm of Montesquieu, "it would not do to suppose that negroes were men, lest it should turn out that whites were not;" for, the white has, for ages, done what he could to keep the negro in that hoggish state. His

*Slave Ship (Slavers Throwing Overboard the Dead and Dying, Typhoon Coming On)* (1840), by J. M. W. Turner.

61    Channing wrote in *Emancipation* that "the negro is more susceptible of civilization from abroad than any other race of men."

62    Joseph Sturge (1793–1859), English Quaker abolitionist who visited Jamaica and wrote several books about the aftermath of the August 1 decree; James Thome (1813–1873) and Horace Kimball (1813–1838), American antislavery activists and authors of *Emancipation in the West Indies* (1838); Joseph John Gurney (1788–1847), English Quaker who wrote *A Winter in the West Indies* (1840); James Phillippo (1798–1879), English antislavery missionary to Jamaica, author of *Jamaica, Its Past and Present State* (1843).

laws have been furies. It now appears, that the negro race is, more than any other, susceptible of rapid civilization.[61] The emancipation is observed, in the islands, to have wrought for the negro a benefit as sudden as when a thermometer is brought out of the shade into the sun. It has given him eyes and ears. If, before, he was taxed with such stupidity, or such defective vision, that he could not set a table square to the walls of an apartment, he is now the principal, if not the only mechanic, in the West Indies; and is, besides, an architect, a physician, a lawyer, a magistrate, an editor, and a valued and increasing political power. The recent testimonies of Sturge, of Thome and

Sailors throwing slaves overboard, from the antislavery tract *American Slave Trade* (1822), by Jesse Torrey.

Kimball, of Gurney, of Phillippo,[62] are very explicit on this point, the capacity and the success of the colored and the black population in employments of skill, of profit, and of trust; and, best of all, is the testimony to their moderation. They receive hints and advances from the whites, that they will be gladly received as subscribers to the Exchange, as members of this or that committee of trust. They hold back, and say to each other, that "social position is not to be gained by pushing."

I have said that this event interests us because it came mainly from the concession of the whites; I add, that in part it is the earning of the blacks. They won the pity and respect which they have received, by their powers and native endowments. I think this a circumstance of the highest import. Their whole future is in it. Our planet, before the age of written history, had its races of savages, like the generations of sour paste, or the animalcules that wriggle and bite in a drop of putrid water. Who cares for these or for their wars? We do not wish a world of bugs or of birds; neither afterward of Scythians, Caraibs, or Feejees.[63] The grand style of nature, her great periods, is all we observe in them. Who cares for oppressing whites, or oppressed blacks, twenty centuries ago, more than for bad dreams? Eaters and food are in the harmony of nature; and there too is the germ forever protected, unfolding gigantic leaf after leaf, a newer flower, a richer fruit, in every period, yet its next product is never to be guessed. It will only save what is worth saving; and it saves not by compassion, but by power. It appoints no police to guard the lion, but his teeth and claws; no fort or city for the bird, but his wings; no rescue for flies and mites, but their spawning numbers, which no ravages can overcome. It deals with men after the same manner. If they are rude and foolish, down they must go. When at last in a race, a new principle appears, an idea,—*that* conserves it; ideas only save races. If the black man is feeble, and not important to the existing races, not on a parity with the best race, the black man must serve, and be exterminated. But if the black man carries in his bosom an indispensable element of a new and coming civilization, for the sake of that element, no wrong, nor strength, nor circumstance, can hurt him: he will survive and play his part. So now, the arrival in the world of such men as Toussaint, and the Haytian heroes, or of the leaders of their race in Barbadoes and Jamaica,[64] outweighs in good omen all the English and American humanity. The anti-slavery of the whole world, is dust in the balance

63   In ancient Greece the Scythians, who inhabited the Caucasus and the surrounding areas, were legendary for their barbarous ferocity. The Amerindian Carib Islanders of the West Indies were similarly warlike. Christian missionaries arrived in the South Pacific island of Fiji in the 1830s, and Charles Wilkes (1798–1877) reported on the "Feejee cannibals" in his *Narrative of the United States Exploring Expedition during the Years 1838–42* (1844).

64   Toussaint L'Ouverture (1743–1803), a former slave and brilliant strategist, led the Haitian revolution from 1791. The Jamaican fight against slavery was led by a slave, Samuel "Daddy" Sharpe, in 1831 and then by Edward Jordon (1800–1869), a free mulatto who became a member of the Jamaican Assembly in 1835 (and, in the 1860s, colonial secretary). In 1834 in Barbados, Samuel Jackman Prescod (1806–1871), whose mother was of African descent, became the first "colored" person to enter the island's Parliament; he made heroic efforts to expand voting rights.

In his essay "Character," Emerson wrote, "Suppose a slaver on the coast of Guinea should take on board a gang of negroes, which should contain persons of the stamp of Toussaint L'Ouverture: or, let us fancy, under these swarthy masks he has a gang of Washingtons in chains. When they arrive at Cuba, will the relative order of the ship's company be the same? Is there nothing but rope and iron? Is there no love, no reverence? Is there never a glimpse of right in a poor slave-captain's mind; and cannot these be supposed available to break, or elude, or in any manner overmatch the tension of an inch or two of iron ring?"

65    Strident abuse, blame.

66    The English Maritime Insurance Law governing slave ships spoke of cases "when the captive destroys himself through despair, which often happens." In such cases the insurers were not liable, as they were when slaves were thrown overboard "to quell an insurrection" (the "jettison clause"). During the *Zong* massacre, ten slaves threw themselves overboard.

before this,—is a poor squeamishness and nervousness: the might and the right are here: here is the anti-slave: here is man: and if you have man, black or white is an insignificance. The intellect,—that is miraculous! Who has it, has the talisman: his skin and bones, though they were of the color of night, are transparent, and the ever-lasting stars shine through, with attractive beams. But a compassion for that which is not and cannot be useful or lovely, is degrading and futile. All the songs, and news papers, and money-subscriptions, and vituperation[65] of such as do not think with us, will avail nothing against a fact. I say to you, you must save yourself, black or white, man or woman; other help is none. I esteem the occasion of this jubilee to be the proud discovery, that the black race can contend with the white; that, in the great anthem which we call history, a piece of many parts and vast compass, after playing a long time a very low and subdued accompaniment, they perceive the time arrived when they can strike in with effect, and take a masters part in the music. The civility of the world has reached that pitch, that their more moral genius is becoming indispensable, and the quality of this race is to be honored for itself. For this, they have been preserved in sandy deserts, in rice-swamps, in kitchens and shoe-shops, so long: now let them emerge, clothed and in their own form.

There remains the very elevated consideration which the subject opens, but which belongs to more abstract views than we are now taking, this namely, that the civility of no race can be perfect whilst another race is degraded. It is a doctrine alike of the oldest, and of the newest philosophy, that, man is one, and that you cannot injure any member, without a sympathetic injury to all the members. America is not civil, whilst Africa is barbarous.

These considerations seem to leave no choice for the action of the intellect and the conscience of the country. There have been moments in this, as well as in every piece of moral history, when there seemed room for the infusions of a skeptical philosophy; when it seemed doubtful, whether brute force would not triumph in the eternal struggle. I doubt not, that sometimes a despairing negro, when jumping over the ships sides to escape from the white devils who surrounded him, has believed there was no vindication of right;[66] it is horrible to think of, but it seemed so. I doubt not, that sometimes the negro's friend, in the face of scornful and brutal hundreds of traders and drivers, has felt his heart sink. Especially, it seems to me, some degree of despondency is pardonable, when he observes the men of conscience and of intellect, his own natural allies and champions,—those whose attention should be nailed to the grand objects of this cause, so hotly offended by whatever incidental petulances or infirmities of indiscreet defenders of the negro, as to permit themselves to be ranged with the enemies of the human race; and names which should be the alarums of liberty and the watchwords of truth, are mixed up with all the rotten rabble of selfishness and tyranny. I assure myself that this coldness and blindness will pass away. A single noble wind of sentiment will scatter them forever. I am sure that the good and wise elders, the ardent and generous youth will not permit what is incidental and exceptional to withdraw their devotion from the essential and permanent characters of the question. There have been moments, I said, when men might be forgiven, who doubted. Those moments are past. Seen in masses, it cannot be disputed, there is progress in human society. There is a blessed necessity by which the interest of men is always driving them to the right; and, again, making all crime mean and ugly. The genius of the Saxon race, friendly to liberty;[67] the enterprise, the very muscular vigor of this nation, are inconsistent with slavery. The Intellect, with blazing eye, looking through history from the beginning onward, gazes on this blot, and it disappears. The sentiment of Right, once very low and indistinct, but ever more articulate, because it is the voice of the universe, pronounces Freedom. The Power that built this fabric of things affirms it in the heart; and in the history of the First of August, has made a sign to the ages, of his will.

67    The Saxons were early settlers of Britain (from the 5th century on). In *English Traits*, Emerson wrote that, after the Norman Conquest in 1066, "It came out, that the Saxon had the most bottom and longevity, had managed to make the victor speak the language and accept the law and usage of the victim; forced the baron to dictate Saxon terms to Norman kings; and, step by step, got all the essential securities of civil liberty invented and confirmed" (in the Magna Carta of 1215).

# Montaigne; or, the Skeptic

*"Montaigne; or, the Skeptic," is the fourth essay in Emerson's* Representative Men *(1850). The book was born on the lecture platform: in 1845 Emerson gave a lecture series "On the Uses of Great Men," and repeated it often over the next few years. Unlike his friend Thomas Carlyle (1795–1881) in* On Heroes, Hero-Worship, and the Heroic in History *(1841), Emerson is no worshipper of greatness: he values his representative men for their "temporary and prospective" quality, and he refuses them godlike completeness. As the critics Andrew Delbanco and Judith Shklar note, Emerson in* Representative Men *agrees with Jacksonian America's principle of "rotation": "the idea that no man, no matter how imposing, should be accorded permanent authority." Emerson's heroes—Plato, Swedenborg, Montaigne, Shakespeare, Napoleon, and Goethe— are democratic heroes: they demand that we participate in their lives, and that we see their limits as well as their brilliance. Conspicuously, Emerson selects no American and resists his era's adulation of the Revolutionary War giants.*

*Michel de Montaigne (1533–1592), the French essayist and moral philosopher, was one of Emerson's*
*(continued)*

Every fact is related on one side to sensation, and, on the other, to morals. The game of thought is, on the appearance of one of these two sides, to find the other: given the upper, to find the under side. Nothing so thin, but has these two faces, and, when the observer has seen the obverse, he turns it over to see the reverse. Life is a pitching of this penny,—heads or tails. We never tire of the game, because there is still a slight shudder of astonishment at the exhibition of the other face, at the contrast of the two faces. A man is flushed with success, and bethinks himself what this good luck signifies. He drives his bargain in the street, but it occurs, that he also is bought and sold. He sees the beauty of a human face, and searches the cause of that beauty, which must be more beautiful. He builds his fortunes, maintains the laws, cherishes his children, but he asks himself, Why? and Whereto? This head and this tail are called in the language of philosophy, Infinite and Finite; Relative and Absolute; Apparent and Real; and many fine names beside.

Each man is born with a predisposition to one or the other of these sides of nature, and, it will easily happen that men will be found devoted to one or the other. One class has the perception of Difference, and is conversant with facts and surfaces;[1] cities and persons; and the bringing certain things to pass;—the men of talent and action. Another class have the perception of Identity, and are men of faith and philosophy, men of genius.

Michel de Montaigne (1533–1592).

*favorite authors. Emerson esteemed Montaigne for his honest, self-aware vigor, and for the frank way he confronts his reader: who touches Montaigne's book touches a man. In his Journal, in 1843, Emerson recalled, "In Roxbury, in 1825, I read Cotton's translation of Montaigne. It seemed to me as if I had written the book myself in some former life . . . No book before or since was ever so much to me as that" (J 8:376); Emerson read Montaigne in the translation of the English writer Charles Cotton (1630–1687).*

1    Emerson wrote in his Journal in 1845, "Surfaces are safe. There are no improprieties, no perturbations, no risks, no questions hard to be solved. Ah! Let us live there" (J 9:190).

2     The Man of Difference and the Man of Identity: the skeptic, Emerson will argue, rides between these two.

3     Plotinus (ca. 204–270), ancient thinker devoted to the works of the Greek philosopher Plato (429–347 BCE); François de Fénelon (1651–1715), French priest and writer; Pindar (ca. 522–443 BCE), Greek poet; George Gordon, Lord Byron (1788–1824), English Romantic poet and adventurer. In his Journal (1845), Emerson commented, "Byron, because his poetic talent was surpassing, could ruin his poem . . . a human wisdom should have assisted at the birth" (J 9:268–269).

4     Emerson concludes his essay "Plato: New Readings" (also in *Representative Men*) by claiming that "Plato plays Providence a little with the baser sort, as people allow themselves with their dogs and cats." In his Journal (1841), Emerson announced, "Away with your prismatics, I want a spermatic book. Plato, Plotinus, & Plutarch are such" (J 7:547; Plutarch [ca. 46–ca. 122] was a Greek moralist and biographer esteemed by both Emerson and Montaigne).

5     Alexander Pope (1688–1744) and Jonathan Swift (1667–1745), acid-tongued satirists from (respectively) England and Ireland; J. W. von Goethe (1749–1832) and Friedrich Schiller (1759–1805), the most renowned German authors of Emerson's day. *Representative Men* concludes with an essay on Goethe.

6     Here and in "Self-Reliance," Emerson refers to the folk-tale motif of the beggar who dreams that he is a prince.

Each of these riders[2] drives too fast. Plotinus believes only in philosophers; Fénelon, in saints; Pindar and Byron,[3] in poets. Read the haughty language in which Plato and the Platonists speak of all men who are not devoted to their own shining abstractions: Other men are rats and mice.[4] The literary class is usually proud and exclusive. The correspondence of Pope and Swift describes mankind around them as monsters; and that of Goethe and Schiller,[5] in our own time, is scarcely more kind.

It is easy to see how this arrogance comes. The genius is a genius by the first look he casts on any object. Is his eye creative? Does he not rest in angles and colours, but beholds the design; he will presently undervalue the actual object. In powerful moments, his thought has dissolved the works of art and nature into their causes, so that the works appear heavy and faulty. He has a conception of beauty, which the sculptor cannot embody. Picture, statue, temple, railroad, steamengine, existed first in an artist's mind, without flaw, mistake, or friction, which impair the executed models. So did the church, the state, college, court, social circle, and all the institutions. It is not strange that these men, remembering what they have seen and hoped of ideas, should affirm disdainfully the superiority of ideas. Having at some time seen that the happy soul will carry all the arts in power, they say, Why cumber ourselves with superfluous realizations? And, like dreaming beggars,[6] they assume to speak and act as if these values were already substantiated.

On the other part, the men of toil and trade and luxury, the animal world, including the animal in the philosopher and poet also,—and the practical world, including the painful drudgeries which are never excused to philosopher or poet any more than to the rest, weigh heavily on the other side. The trade in our streets believes in no metaphysical causes, thinks nothing of the force which necessitated traders and a trading planet to exist; no, but sticks to cotton, sugar, wool, and salt. The ward-meetings on election-days are not softened by any misgiving of the value of these ballotings. Hot life is streaming in a single direction. To the men of this world, to the animal strength and spirits, to the men of practical power whilst immersed in it, the man of ideas appears out of his reason. They alone have reason.

Things always bring their own philosophy with them, that is, prudence. No man acquires property without acquiring with it a little arithmetic also.

In England, the richest country that ever existed, property stands for more compared with personal ability, than in any other. After dinner, a man believes less, denies more: verities have lost some charm. After dinner, arithmetic is the only science: Ideas are disturbing, incendiary, follies of young men, repudiated by the solid portion of society: and a man comes to be valued by his athletic and animal qualities. Spence relates, that Mr Pope was with Sir Godfrey Kneller, one day, when his nephew, a Guinea trader, came in. "Nephew," said Sir Godfrey, "you have the honour of seeing the two greatest men in the world."—"I don't know how great men you may be," said the Guinea man, "but I don't like your looks. I have often bought a man much better than both of you, all muscles and bones, for ten guineas."[7] Thus the men of the senses revenge themselves on the professors, and repay scorn for scorn. The first had leaped to conclusions not yet ripe, and say more than is true; the others make themselves merry with the philosopher, and weigh man by the pound. They believe that mustard bites the tongue, that pepper is hot, friction-matches are incendiary, revolvers to be avoided, and suspenders hold up pantaloons; that there is much sentiment in a chest of tea; and a man will be eloquent if you give him good wine. Are you tender and scrupulous, you must eat more mince-pie. They hold that Luther had milk in him when he said,

Wer nicht liebt Wein, Weib, und Gesang,
Der bleibt ein Narr sein Leben lang,[8]

and when he advised a young scholar perplexed with foreordination and free-will, to get well drunk.[9] "The nerves," says Cabanis, "they are the man."[10] My neighbor, a jolly farmer in the tavern bar-room, thinks that the use of money is sure and speedy spending. "For his part," he says, "he puts his down his neck, and gets the good of it."[11]

The inconvenience of this way of thinking is that it runs into indifferentism, and then into disgust. Life is eating us up. We shall be fables presently.[12] Keep cool: It will be all one a hundred years hence. Why should we fret and drudge? Our meat will taste tomorrow as it did yesterday, and we may at last have had enough of it. "Ah," said my languid gentleman at Oxford, "there's nothing new, or true,—and no matter."[13]

7 From *Anecdotes, Observations, and Characters* (1820) by Joseph Spence (1699–1768). Sir Godfrey Kneller (1646–1723) was a painter and friend of Pope. The Guinea man is a slave trader.

8 "Who doesn't love wine, women and song, / Remains a fool his whole life long."

9 The German Reformer Martin Luther (1483–1546) wrote a letter to Hieronymus (Jerome) Weller (1499–1572), a depressed student of theology, counseling him to drink, be merry, or even commit a minor sin in contempt of the devil, in order to cure himself. The German verse is inscribed in Luther's study at Wartburg Castle, where he sought refuge. Emerson's admirer Friedrich Nietzsche (1844–1900), in the third essay of *Toward a Genealogy of Morals* (1887), emphasizes the sensuality of Luther.

10 The French scientist, philosopher, and revolutionary Jean George Cabanis (1757–1808) argued that consciousness is a product of the nervous system (J 6:367).

11 Possibly John Hosmer (J 11:46 [1848] attributes the sentence to "J. H.").

12 Satire 5.151–153 by the Roman poet Persius (34–62) announces "cinis et manes et fabula fies" ("you will become ashes, a ghost, a tale").

13 Attributed to a "country gentleman" during Emerson's 1848 trip to England (J 10:246).

14    In his Journal Emerson credited this observation to "the wise Queen of Sheba," that is,
his wife Lidian (J 9:201 [1845]).

15    Moved by his friend Pope's impending
death, Henry St. John (1678–1751), first Vis-
count Bolingbroke, made this remark (as reported in Spence's *Anecdotes*).

16    The "philosopher" was Emerson's neighbor in Concord, John L. Tuttle (J 9:30 [1843]).

17    The ancient skeptics rejected dogmatic
thinking and argued that one should suspend
judgment since one cannot, by definition, grasp
the real nature of things.

18    Map, navigational chart.

19    In the book of Joshua, the men of Gibeon,
afraid because Joshua has destroyed the cities of
Jericho and Ai, pretend to be ragged wanderers
"from a far country." They make a treaty with
Joshua and his Israelites but are discovered and
punished for their deception, condemned to
be "hewers of wood and drawers of water"
(Joshua 9).

20    Imaginary stone of impenetrable hardness.

21    Allusion to "Affliction (I)" by the English
poet George Herbert (1593–1633): "Thou didst
betray me to a lingring book, / and wrap me in
a gown." In a letter to his aunt, Mary Moody
Emerson (December 25, 1831), Emerson exclaimed that Montaigne was "wild & savory as
sweetfern . . . it is exhilarating once in a while to
come across a genuine Saxon stump, a wild virtuous man who knows books, but gives them
their right place in his mind, lower than his reason. Books are apt to turn reason out of doors"
(L 7:201).

With a little more bitterness the cynic moans, Our life is like an ass led to market by a bundle of hay being carried before him; he sees nothing but the bundle of hay.[14] "There is so much trouble in coming into the world," said Lord Bolingbroke, "and so much more, as well as meanness, in going out of it, that 'tis hardly worth while to be here at all."[15] I knew a philosopher of this kidney who was accustomed briefly to sum up his experience of human nature, in saying, "Mankind is a damned rascal."[16] And the natural corollary is pretty sure to follow, "The world lives by humbug, and so will I."

The abstractionist and the materialist thus mutually exasperating each other, and the scoffer expressing the worst of materialism, there arises a third party to occupy the middle ground between these two, the skeptic,[17] namely. He finds both wrong by being in extremes. He labours to plant his feet, to be the beam of the balance. He will not go beyond his card.[18] He sees the onesidedness of these men of the street; he will not be a Gibeonite;[19] he stands for the intellectual faculties, a cool head, and whatever serves to keep it cool: no unadvised industry, no unrewarded selfdevotion, no loss of the brains in toil. Am I an ox or a dray?—You are both in extremes, he says. You who will have all solid, and a world of piglead, deceive yourselves grossly. You believe yourselves rooted and grounded on adamant,[20] and yet if we uncover the last facts of our knowledge, you are spinning like bubbles in a river, you know not whither or whence, and you are bottomed and capped and wrapped in delusions.

Neither will he be betrayed to a book, and wrapped in a gown.[21] The studious class are their own victims: they are thin and pale, their feet are cold, their heads are hot, the night is without sleep, the day a fear of interruption, pallor, squalor, hunger, and egotism. If you come near them, and see what conceits they entertain,—they are abstractionists, and spend their days and nights in dreaming some dream; in expecting the homage of society to some precious scheme built on a truth, but destitute of proportion in its presentment, of justness in its application, and of all energy of will in the schemer to embody and vitalize it.

But I see plainly, he says, that I cannot see. I know that human strength is not in extremes, but in avoiding extremes. I, at least, will shun the weakness of philosophizing beyond my depth. What is the use of pretending to powers we have not? What is the use of pretending to assurances we have not, respecting the other life? Why exaggerate the power of virtue? Why be an angel before your time? These strings wound up too high will snap. If there is a wish for immortality, and no evidence, why not say just that? If there are conflicting evidences, why not state them? If there is not ground for a candid thinker to make up his mind, yea or nay,—why not suspend the judgment? I weary of these dogmatizers. I tire of these hacks of routine, who deny the dogmas. I neither affirm nor deny. I stand here to try the case. I am here to consider, *skeptein*[22] to consider how it is. I will try to keep the balance true. Of what use to take the chair, and glibly rattle off theories of society, religion, and nature, when I know that practical objections lie in the way insurmountable by me and by my mates? Why so talkative in public, when each of my neighbors can pin me to my seat by arguments I cannot refute? Why pretend that life is so simple a game, when we know how subtle and elusive the Proteus is? Why think to shut up all things in your narrow coop, when we know there are not one or two only, but ten, twenty, a thousand things, and unlike. Why fancy that you have all the truth in your keeping? There is much to say on all sides.

Who shall forbid a wise skepticism, seeing that there is no practical question on which anything more than an approximate solution can be had. Is not marriage an open question, when it is alleged, from the beginning of the world, that such as are in the institution wish to get out; and such as are out, wish to get in?[23] And the reply of Socrates to him who asked whether he should choose a wife, still remains reasonable, "That, whether he should choose one or not, he would repent it."[24] Is not the State a question? All society is divided in opinion on the subject of the State. Nobody loves it, great numbers dislike it, and suffer conscientious scruples to allegiance. And the only defence set up, is, the fear of doing worse in disorganizing. Is it otherwise with the Church? Or to put any of the questions which touch mankind nearest, Shall the young man aim at a leading part in law, in politics, in trade? It will not be pretended that a success in either of these kinds is quite coincident with what is best and inmost in his mind. Shall he, then, cutting the stays that hold him fast to the social state, put out to sea with no guidance but his genius?[25] There is much to say on both sides. Remember the open question between the present order of "competition," and the friends of "attractive and associated Labour."[26] The generous minds embrace the proposi-

22    This Greek verb, *skeptein*, means to consider; "skeptic" derives from it.

23    "It happens, as with cages, the birds without despair to get in, and those within despair of getting out" (from Montaigne's "Upon Some Verses of Virgil," also the source of the next sentence, about Socrates).

24    Montaigne derived the anecdote from the life of Socrates by the Dutch humanist Diogenes Laertius (3rd century). In "Upon Some Verses of Virgil," he goes on to apply to marriage the adage of Desiderius Erasmus (1466–1536), *Homo homini, aut deus, aut lupus* ("man is either a god or a wolf to man"—a variation on the phrase from the Roman playwright Plautus [254–184 BCE], *homo homini lupus* ["man is a wolf to man]).

25    Guiding power or daemon. Defined by the Neoplatonist Iamblichus (ca. 250–ca. 330), in a passage marked by Emerson: "the peculiar daemon" of a soul "directs its peculiar life, and imparts to us the principles of all our thoughts and reasonings. . . . There is one daemon who is the guardian and governor of every thing that is in us."

26    "Attractive industry" was a key concept of Charles Fourier (1772–1837), the French socialist who was much in vogue in Emerson's circle. Each worker would be allowed to choose his or her own work, transforming toil into pleasure.

27    In his Journal (March 19, 1837), Emerson commented, "I shall never believe that any book is so good to read as that which sets the reader into a working mood, makes him feel his strength, & inspires hilarity. Such as Plutarch, & Montaigne & Wordsworth" (J 5:289; William Wordsworth, 1770–1850, English Romantic poet). In "Upon Some Verses of Virgil," Montaigne wrote, "I can hardly be without a Plutarch, he is so universal, and so full, that upon all Occasions, and what extravagant Subject so ever you take in hand, he will still intrude himself into your Business. . . . I can no sooner cast an Eye upon him, but I purloyn either a Leg or a Wing." Emerson noted the passage in his copy of the essay.

28    Unidentified quotation.

29    Imaginary things (after a fanciful fire-breathing monster made from parts of a lion, a goat, and a serpent).

30    Again from Spence's *Anecdotes.*

31    Wasteful, dissolute.

32    Managing, cultivating. Emerson makes it clear that the skeptic is not a doubter but an adroit believer in circumstances and character.

33    Vain, conceited person; fop.

34    Sparta was famous in antiquity for its rigorous and ascetic practices. The Stoics, a philosophical sect founded by Zeno in Athens about 300 BCE, argued that pleasure is not a good; rather, one should strive to live in harmony with nature, which operates according to reasonable laws. The Stoics insisted that changes of fortune, however disastrous, do not affect the wise man's happiness. Montaigne discusses Stoicism in his essays "On Constancy," "Of Physiognomy," and "Of Cruelty."

tion of labour shared by all; it is the only honesty; nothing else is safe. It is from the poor man's hut alone, that strength and virtue come: and yet, on the other side, it is alleged, that labour impairs the form and breaks the spirit of man, and the labourers cry unanimously, 'We have no thoughts.' Culture, how indispensable! I cannot forgive you the want of accomplishments: and yet culture will instantly impair that chiefest beauty of spontaneousness. Excellent is culture for a savage; but once let him read in the book, and he is no longer able not to think of Plutarch's[27] heroes. In short, since true fortitude of understanding consists "in not letting what we know be embarrassed by what we do not know,"[28] we ought to secure those advantages which we can command, and not risk them by clutching after the airy and unattainable. Come, no chimæras![29] Let us go abroad, let us mix in affairs, let us learn, and get, and have, and climb. "Men are a sort of moving plants, and, like trees, receive a great part of their nourishment from the air. If they keep too much at home, they pine."[30] Let us have a robust manly life, let us know what we know for certain. What we have, let it be solid, and seasonable, and our own. A world in the hand is worth two in the bush. Let us have to do with real men and women, and not with skipping ghosts.

This, then, is the right ground of the skeptic, this of consideration, of selfcontaining, not at all of unbelief, not at all of universal denying, nor of universal doubting, doubting even that he doubts; least of all, of scoffing, and profligate[31] jeering at all that is stable and good. These are no more his moods, than are those of religion and philosophy. He is the Considerer, the prudent, taking in sail, counting stock, husbanding[32] his means, believing that a man has too many enemies, than that he can afford to be his own foe; that we cannot give ourselves too many advantages, in this unequal conflict, with powers so vast and unweariable ranged on one side, and this little conceited vulnerable popinjay[33] that a man is, bobbing up and down into every danger, on the other. It is a position taken up for better defence, as of more safety, and one that can be maintained, and it is one of more opportunity and range; as, when we build a house, the rule is, to set it not too high nor too low, under the wind, but out of the dirt.

The philosophy we want is one of fluxions and mobility. The Spartan and Stoic[34] schemes are too stark and stiff for our occasion. A theory of Saint John, and of nonresistance,[35] seems, on the other hand, too thin and aerial.

We want some coat woven of elastic steel, stout as the first, and limber as the second. We want a *ship*, in these billows we inhabit. An angular dogmatic house would be rent to chips and splinters, in this storm of many elements. No, it must be tight, and fit to the form of man, to live at all; as a shell must dictate the architecture of a house founded on the sea. The soul of man must be the type of our scheme, just as the body of man is the type after which a dwellinghouse is built. Adaptiveness is the peculiarity of human nature. We are golden averages, volitant[36] stabilities, compensated or periodic errours,[37] houses founded on the sea.

The wise skeptic wishes to have a near view of the best game, and the chief players, what is best in the planet, art and nature, places and events, but mainly men. Every thing that is excellent in mankind, a form of grace, an arm of iron, lips of persuasion, a brain of resources, every one skilful to play and win, he will see and judge.

The terms of admission to this spectacle, are, that he have a certain solid and intelligible way of living of his own, some method of answering the inevitable needs of human life; proof that he has played with skill and success: that he has evinced the temper, stoutness, and the range of qualities which, among his contemporaries and countrymen, entitle him to fellowship and trust. For, the secrets of life are not shown except to sympathy and likeness. Men do not confide themselves to boys, or coxcombs,[38] or pedants, but to their peers. Some wise limitation, as the modern phrase is; some condition between the extremes, and having itself a positive quality, some stark and sufficient man, who is not salt or sugar, but sufficiently related to the world to do justice to Paris and London, and, at the same time, a vigorous and original thinker, whom cities cannot overawe, but who uses them,—is the fit person to occupy this ground of speculation. These qualities meet in the character of Montaigne. And yet, since the personal regard which I entertain for Montaigne may be unduly great, I will, under the shield of this prince of egotists, offer as an apology for electing him as the representative of Skepticism, a word or two to explain how my love began and grew for this admirable gossip.

A single odd volume of Cotton's translation of the Essays remained to me from my father's library, when a boy. It lay long neglected, until, after many years, when I was newly escaped from college, I read the book, and

35    Obedience to authority.

36    Fluttering, flying.

37    Compensated: counterbalanced; periodic: occurring at predictable intervals.

38    Fools (after the fool's characteristic rooster-like hat).

39    The actual inscription on the grave of Collignon also mentions the fables of the French writer Jean de la Fontaine (1621–1695), along with Montaigne's essays, as aids to his efforts to do good and lead a "sweet and happy" life.

40    Emerson corresponded with John Sterling (1806–1844), a young friend of Thomas Carlyle who reported on the many "mottoes and pithy sentences" from the ancients and from Ecclesiastes inscribed on the rafters of Montaigne's study. As Emerson notes, there is also an account of these inscriptions in Hazlitt's edition of Montaigne—see note 41. Montaigne's village, Castellan, is in Périgord (currently called the Dordogne).

41    William Hazlitt (1811–1893), son of the famous essayist.

42    The translation of Montaigne by John Florio (ca. 1533–1625) was known to Shakespeare, who echoes passages from it in several of his plays; but the Shakespeare autograph is of doubtful status.

43    Ben Jonson (1572–1637), English playwright, friend and rival of Shakespeare; Leigh Hunt (1784–1859), English Romantic poet and editor.

Emerson's eldest daughter, Ellen Emerson.

procured the remaining volumes. I remember the delight and wonder in which I lived with it. It seemed to me as if I had myself written the book in some former life, so sincerely it spoke to my thought and experience. It happened, when in Paris, in 1833, that, in the Cemetery of Père Lachaise, I came to a tomb of Auguste Collignon, who died in 1830, aged sixty-eight years, and who, said the monument, "lived to do right, and had formed himself to virtue on the Essays of Montaigne."[39] Some years later, I became acquainted with an accomplished English poet, John Sterling, and, in prosecuting my correspondence, I found that, from a love of Montaigne, he had made a pilgrimage to his chateau, still standing near Castellan, in Périgord, and, after two hundred and fifty years, had copied from the walls of his library the inscriptions which Montaigne had written there.[40] That Journal of Mr Sterling's, published in the (London) Westminster Review, Hazlitt[41] has reprinted in the Prolegomena to his edition of the Essays. I heard with pleasure that one of the newly discovered autographs of William Shakspeare was in a copy of Florio's translation of Montaigne.[42] It is the only book which we certainly know to have been in the poet's library. And oddly enough, the duplicate copy of Florio which the British Museum purchased with a view of protecting the Shakspeare autograph, (as I was informed in the Museum,) turned out to have the autograph of Ben Jonson in the flyleaf. Leigh Hunt[43] relates of Lord Byron, that Montaigne was the only great writer of past times whom he read with avowed satisfaction. Other coincidences not needful to be mentioned here, concurred to make this old Gascon[44] still new and immortal for me.

In 1571, on the death of his father, Montaigne, then thirty-eight years old, retired from the practice of law at Bordeaux, and settled himself on his estate. Though he had been a man of pleasure, and sometimes a courtier, his studious habits now grew on him, and he loved the compass, staidness, and independence, of the country gentleman's life. He took up his economy in good earnest, and made his farms yield the most. Downright and plaindealing, and abhorring to be deceived or to deceive, he was esteemed in the country for his sense and probity. In the civil wars of the League, which converted every house into a fort, Montaigne kept his gates open, and his house without defence.[45] All parties freely came and went, his courage and honour being universally esteemed. The neighboring lords and gentry brought jewels and papers to him for safe-keeping. Gibbon[46] reckons in these bigoted times but two men of liberality in France, Henry IV and Montaigne.[47]

Montaigne is the frankest and honestest of all writers.[48] His French freedom runs into grossness, but he has anticipated all censure by the bounty of his own confessions. In his times, books were written to one sex only, and almost all were written in Latin; so that, in a humourist, a certain nakedness of statement was permitted, which our manners of a literature addressed equally to both sexes, do not allow. But, though a biblical plainness coupled with a most uncanonical levity, may shut his pages to many sensitive readers, yet the offence is superficial. He parades it: he makes the most of it: nobody can think or say worse of him, than he does. He pretends to most of the

44    Montaigne was born in Bordeaux, in Gascony (southwest France, near the Spanish border).

45    Civil war between Catholic and Protestant began in France in 1562. In 1576 the Catholic Holy League was formed; the league warred against the Protestant Henri of Navarre (1553–1610) until the latter defeated it in 1594 and became King Henri IV (and converted to Catholicism). Montaigne asserted in his essay "Difficulties Augment Our Desires" that "the facility of entring my House" was his means of defense: "It is never shut to any one that knocks."

46    The English historian Edward Gibbon (1737–1794) found sixteenth-century France a "general ferment of fanaticism, discord, and faction," with "two singular exceptions": Montaigne and Henri IV.

47    In his Journal (1845), Emerson noted, more critically, "Montaigne good against bigots as cowage against worms acts mechanically But there is a higher muse there sitting where he durst not soar. A muse that follows the flowing power a 'Dialectic' that respects results" (J 9:326).

48    In his Journal (1848), Emerson named Montaigne (along with two English authors, John Milton [1608–1674] and Sir Thomas Browne [1605–1682]) one of the "old writers" who, "when they had put down their thoughts, jumped into their book bodily themselves, so that we have all that is left of them in our shelves; there is not a pinch of dust beside" (J 10:350).

49    Montaigne in his essay "Of Presumption" wrote that he was "guilty of the meanest and most popular Defects."

50    From Montaigne's essay "Of Three Commerces" (paraphrased). In the same essay Montaigne wrote, "Others study how to raise and elevate their minds; I, how to humble mine and to bring it low."

51    From "That we Tast nothing pure." The passage continues: "Man is wholly and throughout but patch't and motly."

52    Flash: showy display. In his Journal (March 1838) Emerson noted, "Montaigne is spiced throughout with rebellion, as much as Alcott or my young Henry Thoreau" (J 5:460). Amos Bronson Alcott (1799–1888) and Henry David Thoreau (1817–1862) were important Transcendentalist authors and close companions of Emerson.

53    Montaigne wrote an essay "Of Cannibals" in which he compared cannibals favorably (in some respects) to civilized Europeans.

54    Invented. Montaigne in "Upon Some Verses of Virgil": "My philosophy is in action, in natural and present use, very little in fancy."

55    In his essay "Of Experience," Montaigne gives a virtuosic and rather excruciating description of the passing of his gallstones.

56    Montaigne emblazoned this motto (in English, "What do I know?"), accompanied by a pair of scales, on the walls of his house.

57    Justice Poz is a complacent and foolish old judge in a popular play for children, "Old Poz, the Mimic," by the Irish writer Maria Edgeworth (1767–1849).

vices, and, if there be any virtue in him, he says, it got in by stealth.[49] There is no man, in his opinion, who has not deserved hanging five or six times; and he pretends no exception in his own behalf. "Five or six as ridiculous stories," too, he says, "can be told of me, as of any man living."[50] But, with all this really superfluous frankness, the opinion of an invincible probity grows into every reader's mind.

"When I the most strictly and religiously confess myself, I find that the best virtue I have has in it some tincture of vice; and I am afraid that Plato, in his purest virtue, (I, who am as sincere and perfect a lover of virtue of that stamp as any other whatever,) if he had listened, and laid his ear close to himself, would have heard some jarring sound of human mixture; but faint and remote, and only to be perceived by himself."[51]

Here is an impatience and fastidiousness about colour or pretence of any kind. He has been in courts so long as to have conceived a furious disgust at appearances, he will indulge himself with a little cursing and swearing, he will talk with sailors and gipsies, use flash and streetballads: he has stayed in doors, till he is deadly sick; he will to the open air, though it rain bullets.[52] He has seen too much of Gentlemen of the long robe, until he wishes for cannibals;[53] and is so nervous by factitious[54] life, that he thinks the more barbarous man is, the better he is. He likes his saddle. You may read theology and grammar and metaphysics elsewhere. Whatever you get here, shall smack of the earth and of real life, sweet or smart or stinging. He makes no hesitation to entertain you with the records of his disease;[55] and his journey to Italy is quite full of that matter. He took and kept this position of equilibrium. Over his name, he drew an emblematic pair of scales, and wrote *Que sçais je?* under it.[56] As I look at his effigy opposite the title page, I seem to hear him say, You may play Old Poz,[57] if you will; you may rail and exaggerate. I stand here for truth, and will not, for all the states and churches and revenues and personal reputations of Europe, overstate the dry fact, as I see it; I will rather mumble and prose about what I certainly know; my house and barns; my father, my wife and my tenants; my old lean bald pate; my knives and forks; what meats I eat; and what drinks I prefer; and a hundred straws, just as ridiculous; than I will write with a fine crowquill a fine romance. I like gray days and autumn and winter weather. I am gray and autumnal myself,[58] and think an undress, and old shoes that do not pinch my feet, and old friends who do not constrain me, and plain topics where I do not need to strain myself and pump my brains, the most suitable. Our condition as men is risky and ticklish enough. One cannot be sure of himself and his fortune an hour, but he may be whisked off into some pitiable or ridiculous plight. Why should I vapour and play the philosopher, instead of ballasting the best I can this dancing balloon. So, at least, I live within compass, keep myself ready for action, and can shoot the gulf, at last, with decency. If there be anything farcical in such a life, the blame is not mine: let it lie at Fate's and nature's door.

The Essays, therefore, are an entertaining soliloquy on every random topic that comes into his head, treating everything without ceremony, yet with masculine sense. There have been men with deeper insight, but, one would say, never a man with such abundance of thoughts. He is never dull, never insincere, and has the genius to make the reader care for all that he cares for.

The sincerity and marrow of the man reaches to his sentences. I know not anywhere the book that seems less written. It is the language of conversation transferred to a book. Cut these words, and they would bleed; they are vascular and alive.[59] One has the same pleasure in it that we have in listening to the necessary speech of men about their work, when any unusual circumstance gives momentary importance to the dialogue. For blacksmiths and teamsters do not trip in their speech; it is a shower of bullets; it is Cambridge men who correct themselves, and begin again at every half sentence, and moreover will pun, and refine too much, and swerve from the matter to the expression. Montaigne talks with shrewdness, knows the world, and books, and himself, and uses the positive degree: never shrieks, or protests, or prays; no weakness, no convulsion, no superlative: does not wish to jump out of his skin, or play any antics, or annihilate space or time, but is stout and solid; tastes every moment of the day; likes pain, because it makes him feel himself, and realize things; as we pinch ourselves to know that we are awake. He keeps the plain; he rarely mounts or sinks; likes to feel solid ground, and the stones underneath. His writing has no enthusiasms, no aspiration; contented, selfrespecting, and keeping the middle of the road.[60] There is but one exception,—in his love for Socrates. In speaking of him, for once his cheek flushes, and his style rises to passion.[61]

58    In 1841 Emerson wrote in his Journal, "For me, what I may call the autumnal style of Montaigne keeps all its old attraction" (J 8:43).

59    The American religious author Sampson Reed (1800–1880) in *The Growth of the Mind* (1826), which Emerson admired, remarked, "We desire language neither extravagant nor cold, but blood warm." Emerson commented in his Journal (1843), "In Montaigne, man & thinker are inseparable: you cannot insert the blade of a pen knife betwixt the man & his book" (J 9:41).

60    In his Journal (May–July 1847), Emerson noted that Montaigne "easily & habitually attain[s] . . . an utterance whole, generous, sustained, equal, graduated-at-will" (J 10:68).

61    Montaigne writes about the great Greek philosopher Socrates (ca. 469–399 BCE) most notably in his essay "Of Physiognomy."

62    Throat inflammation.

63    From Montaigne's "Upon Some Verses of Virgil."

64    Emerson remarked in a Journal entry (August 1847–January 1848), "What is Europe but the chance of meeting with such a man as Montaigne?" (J 10:138).

65    Emerson wrote in his Journal (October 5, 1838), "I read today a horrid story of murder; it fills one with glooms, bludgeons & gibbets: then it turns out to be a systematic long-sought accurately-measured revenge: instantly the gloom clears up; for in a degree the light of law & of cause & effect shines in" (J 7:98).

Montaigne died of a quinsy,[62] at the age of sixty, in 1592. When he came to die, he caused the mass to be celebrated in his chamber. At the age of thirty-three, he had been married. "But," he says, "might I have had my own will, I would not have married Wisdom herself, if she would have had me: but 'tis to much purpose to evade it, the common custom and use of life will have it so. Most of my actions are guided by example, not choice."[63] In the hour of death he gave the same weight to custom. *Que sçais je?* What do I know?

This book of Montaigne the world has endorsed, by translating it into all tongues, and printing seventy-five editions of it in Europe: and that, too, a circulation somewhat chosen, namely, among courtiers, soldiers, princes, men of the world, and men of wit and generosity.[64]

Shall we say that Montaigne has spoken wisely, and given the right and permanent expression of the human mind on the conduct of life?

\*    \*    \*

We are natural believers. Truth or the connection of cause and effect alone interests us.[65] We are persuaded that a thread runs through all things: all worlds are strung on it as beads: and men and events and life come to us only because of that thread: they pass and repass only that we may know the direction and continuity of that line. A book or statement which goes to show that there is no line, but random and chaos; a calamity out of nothing, a prosperity and no account of it, a hero born from a fool, a fool from a hero,— dispirits us. Seen or unseen, we believe the tie exists. Talent makes counterfeit ties; Genius finds the real ones. We hearken to the man of science, because we anticipate the sequence in natural phenomena which he uncovers. We love whatever affirms, connects, preserves, and dislike what scatters or pulls down. One man appears whose nature is to all men's eyes conserving and constructive: His presence supposes a well-ordered society, agriculture, trade, large institutions, and empire. If these did not exist, they would begin to exist through his endeavours. Therefore he cheers and comforts men, who feel all this in him very readily. The non-conformist and the rebel say all manner of unanswerable things against the existing republic, but discover to our sense no plan of house or state of their own. Therefore, though the town and state and way of living which our counsellor contemplated, might be a very modest or musty prosperity, yet men rightly go for him, and reject the Reformer, so long as he comes only with axe and crowbar.

But though we are natural conservers and causationists, and reject a sour dumpish unbelief, the skeptical class which Montaigne represents, have reason, and every man, at some time, belongs to it. Every superior mind will pass through this domain of equilibration,—I should rather say, will know how to avail himself of the checks and balances in nature, as a natural weapon against the exaggeration and formalism[66] of bigots and blockheads.

Skepticism is the attitude assumed by the student in relation to the particulars which society adores, but which he sees to be reverend only in their tendency and spirit. The ground occupied by the skeptic is the vestibule of the temple. Society does not like to have any breath of question blown on the existing order. But the interrogation of custom at all points is an inevitable stage in the growth of every superior mind, and is the evidence of its perception of the flowing power which remains itself in all changes.

The superior mind will find itself equally at odds with the evils of society, and with the projects that are offered to relieve them. The wise skeptic is a bad citizen; no conservative; he sees the selfishness of property and the drowsiness of institutions. But neither is he fit to work with any democratic party that ever was constituted; for parties wish every one committed, and he penetrates the popular patriotism. His politics are those of the "Soul's Errand" of Sir Walter Raleigh; or of Krishna, in the Bhagavat, "There is none who is worthy of my love or hatred;"[67] whilst he sentences law, physic, divinity, commerce, and custom. He is a Reformer; yet he is no better member of the philanthropic association. It turns out that he is not the champion of the operative, the pauper, the prisoner, the slave. It stands in his mind, that our life in this world is not of quite so easy interpretation as churches and schoolbooks say. He does not wish to take ground against these benevolences, to play the part of devil's attorney, and blazon every doubt and sneer that darkens the sun for him. But he says, There are doubts.

I mean to use the occasion and celebrate the calendar-day of our Saint Michel de Montaigne, by counting and describing these doubts or negations.

66 Relying on forms and ceremonies, especially in religion, without spiritual conviction.

67 Walter Ralegh (or Raleigh, 1552–1618), the English poet, courtier, and explorer; in his poem "Soul's Errand" (more commonly known as "The Lie"), Raleigh directs the reader to defy various worldly powers, from the court and the church to fortune, justice, and law. Emerson read about Krishna, the Hindu god and principal avatar of Vishnu, in a Sanskrit scripture, the *Bhagavad-Gita.* In "Swedenborg, or the Mystic," which precedes the essay on Montaigne in *Representative Men*, Emerson remarks on "the generous spirit of the Indian Vishnu," and quotes him as saying "'I am the same to all mankind. There is not one who is worthy of my love or hatred. They who serve me with adoration—I am in them, and they in me.'"

68    That is, the herd's.

69    Edward Emerson writes that his father had in mind the Providence Transcendentalist Charles King Newcomb (1820–1894), who was "of a sensitive and beautiful character, a mystic, but with the Hamlet temperament" and therefore "paralyzed for all action by the tenderness of his conscience and the power with which all sides of a question presented themselves to him in turn."

70    Devoted follower.

71    In ancient Israel, according to the Hebrew Bible, the Ark of the Covenant contained the Tablets of the Law (the commandments received by Moses on Mount Sinai).

72    Devil in *Faust* (1808–1832) by the German writer and thinker J. W. von Goethe (1749–1832).

73    Bogey; impish, iconoclastic force of mischief.

74    Imaginary causes of terror or worry.

I wish to ferret them out of their holes, and sun them a little. We must do with them as the police do with old rogues, who are shown up to the public at the Marshal's office. They will never be so formidable, when once they have been identified and registered. But I mean honestly by them, that justice shall be done to their terrors. I shall not take Sunday objections, made up on purpose to be put down. I shall take the worst I can find, whether I can dispose of them, or they of me.

I do not press the skepticism of the materialist. I know, the quadruped[68] opinion will not prevail. 'Tis of no importance what bats and oxen think. The first dangerous symptom I report is the levity of intellect, as if it were fatal to earnestness to know much. Knowledge is the knowing that we cannot know. The dull pray; the geniuses are light mockers. How respectable is earnestness on every platform! but intellect kills it. Nay, San Carlo, my subtle and admirable friend,[69] one of the most penetrating of men, finds that all direct ascension, even of lofty piety, leads to this ghastly insight and sends back the votary[70] orphaned. My astonishing San Carlo thought the lawgivers and saints infected. They found the ark empty,[71] saw and would not tell; and tried to choke off their approaching followers, by saying, 'Action, action, my dear fellows, is for you!' Bad as was to me this detection by San Carlo, this frost in July, this blow from a bride, there was still a worse, namely, the cloy or satiety of the saints. In the mount of vision, ere they have yet risen from their knees, they say, We discover that this our homage and beatitude is partial and deformed. We must fly for relief to the suspected and reviled Intellect, to the Understanding, the Mephistopheles,[72] to the gymnastics of talent.

This is Hobgoblin[73] the first, and though it has been the subject of much elegy in our nineteenth century from Byron, Goethe, and other poets of less fame, not to mention many distinguished private observers, I confess, it is not very affecting to my imagination. For it seems to concern the shattering of babyhouses and crockery shops. What flutters the Church of Rome or of England or of Geneva or of Boston, may yet be very far from touching any principle of faith. I think that the intellect and moral sentiment are unanimous; and that though philosophy extirpates bugbears,[74] yet it supplies the natural checks of vice, and polarity to the soul. I think that the wiser a man is, the more stupendous he finds the natural and moral economy, and lifts himself to a more absolute reliance.

There is the power of moods, each setting at nought all but its own tissue of facts and beliefs.[75] There is the power of complexions—obviously modifying the dispositions and sentiments. The beliefs and unbeliefs appear to be structural, and, as soon as each man attains the poise and vivacity which allow the whole machinery to play, he will not need extreme examples, but will rapidly alternate all opinions in his own life. Our life is March weather, savage and serene in one hour. We go forth austere, dedicated, believing in the iron links of Destiny, and will not turn on our heel to save our life: but a book, or a bust, or only the sound of a name, shoots a spark through the nerves, and we suddenly believe in will; my finger-ring shall be the seal of Solomon;[76] Fate is for imbeciles. All is possible to the resolved mind. Presently, a new experience gives a new turn to our thoughts; commonsense resumes its tyranny. We say, 'Well, the army, after all, is the gate to fame, manners, and poetry: and, look you, on the whole selfishness plants best, prunes best, makes the best commerce, and the best citizen.' Are the opinions of a man on right and wrong, on fate and causation, at the mercy of a broken sleep, or an indigestion? Is his belief in God and Duty no deeper than a stomach evidence? And what guaranty for the permanence of his opinions? I like not the French celerity,[77] a new church and state once a week. This is the second negation; and I shall let it pass for what it will. As far as it asserts rotation of states of mind, I suppose it suggests its own remedy, namely, in the record of larger periods. What is the mean of many states; of all the states? Does the general voice of ages affirm any principle, or is no community of sentiment discoverable in distant times and places? And when it shows the power of selfinterest, I accept that as part of the divine law and must reconcile it with aspiration the best I can.

The word Fate or Destiny expresses the sense of mankind in all ages that the laws of the world do not always befriend, but often hurt and crush us. Fate in the shape of *Kinde* or Nature, grows over us like grass.[78] We paint Time with a scythe; Love and Fortune blind; and Destiny, deaf. We have too little power of resistance against this ferocity which champs us up. What front can we make against these unavoidable, victorious, maleficent forces?

75    In "Experience," Emerson wrote, "Our moods do not believe in each other."

76    A magical signet ring possessed, according to medieval legend, by the Israelite King Solomon (10th century BCE).

77    Speed.

78    "*Kinde* was the old English, which however only filled half the range of our fine Latin word, with its delicate future tense, *Natura, About to be born*" (J 11:118 [1849]). Emerson's later essay "Fate" elaborates the theme.

79   Tuberculosis of the neck, shown by swelling of the lymph nodes.

80   Rude, surly person.

81   Emerson wrote in his Journal (1845), "The East is grand,—& makes Europe appear the land of trifles. Identity, identity! friend & foe are of one stuff, and the stuff is such & so much that the variations of surface are unimportant. All is for the soul, & the soul is Vishnu; & animals & stars are transient paintings; & light is whitewash; & durations are deceptive; and form is imprisonment and heaven itself a decoy" (J 9:322).

What can I do against the influence of *Race* in my history? What can I do against hereditary and constitutional habits, against scrofula,[79] lymph, impotence? against climate, against barbarism, in my country? I can reason down or deny everything except this perpetual Belly: feed he must and will, and I cannot make him respectable.

\* \* \*

But the main resistance which the affirmative impulse finds and one including all others is in the doctrine of the Illusionists. There is a painful rumour in circulation that we have been practised upon in all the principal performances of life, and free agency is the emptiest name. We have been sopped and drugged with the air, with food, with woman, with children, with customs, with sciences, with events; which leave us exactly where they found us. The mathematics, 'tis complained, leave the mind where they find it: so do all sciences, and so do all events and actions. I find a man who has passed through all the sciences the churl[80] he was, and through all the offices, learned, civil, social, I can detect the child. We are not the less necessitated to dedicate life to them. In fact we may come to accept it as the fixed rule and theory of our state of education that God is a substance, and his method is illusion. The eastern sages owned the Goddess Yoganidra, the great illusory energy of Vishnu by whom as utter ignorance the whole world is beguiled.[81]

Or, shall I state it thus? The astonishment of life, is, the absence of any appearance of reconciliation between the theory and practice of life. Reason, the prized reality, the Law, is apprehended now and then for a serene and profound moment amidst the hubbub of cares and works which have no direct bearing on it;—is then lost, for months or years, and again found, for an interval, to be lost again. If we compute it in time, we may, in fifty years, have half a dozen reasonable hours. But what are these cares and works the better? A method in the world we do not see, but this parallelism of great and little, which never react on each other, nor discover the smallest tendency to converge. Experiences, fortunes, governings, readings, writings, are nothing to the purpose; as when a man comes into the room, it does not appear whether he has been fed on yams or buffalo,—he has contrived to get so much bone and fibre as he wants, out of rice or out of snow. So vast is the

I feel the longevity of the mind: I admit the
evidence of the immortality of the soul. Well as
I said, I am afraid the season of this rare fruit's
irrecoverably past; that the earth has made
such a mutation of its nodes, that the heat has will
never reach again that Hesperian garden in
which alone these apricots & pomegranates
grew.

Concord N. H. Dec. 21, 1828. I have now been four
days engaged to Ellen Louisa Tucker. Will my Father in
Heaven regard us with kindness, and as he hath, as
we trust, made us for each other, will he be pleased
to strengthen & purify & prosper & eternize our affection!
Sunday morning.

She has the purity & confiding religion of an
angel. Are the words common? the words are
true. Will God forgive me my sins & aid me
to deserve this gift of his mercy. Jan. 17. 1829

Page from Emerson's Journal announcing his engagement to Ellen Tucker (December 21, 1828).

82    Ant.

83    Drunkard.

84    Principles of Christianity summarized in question and answer form.

85    Trusting in the evidence of the senses.

disproportion between the sky of law and the pismire[82] of performance under it, that, whether he is a man of worth or a sot,[83] is not so great a matter as we say. Shall I add, as one juggle of this enchantment, the stunning non-intercourse law which makes cooperation impossible. The young spirit pants to enter society. But all the ways of culture and greatness lead to solitary imprisonment. He had been often balked. He did not expect a sympathy with his thought from the village, but he went with it to the chosen and intelligent, and found no entertainment for it, but mere misapprehension, distaste, and scoffing. Men are strangely mistimed and misapplied, and the excellence of each is an inflamed individualism which separates him more.

There are these and more than these diseases of thought, which our ordinary teachers do not attempt to remove. Now shall we, because a good nature inclines us to Virtue's side, say, There are no doubts,—and lie for the right? Is life to be led in a brave, or in a cowardly manner? and is not the satisfaction of the doubts essential to all manliness? Is the name of Virtue to be a barrier to that which is Virtue? Can you not believe that a man of earnest and burly habit may find small good in tea, essays, and catechism,[84] and want a rougher instruction, want men, labour, trade, farming, war, hunger, plenty, love, hatred, doubt, and terror, to make things plain to him, and has he not a right to insist on being convinced in his own way? When he is convinced, he will be worth the pains.

Belief consists in accepting the affirmations of the soul; Unbelief, in denying them. Some minds are incapable of skepticism. The doubts they profess to entertain are rather a civility or accommodation to the common discourse of their company. They may well give themselves leave to speculate, for they are secure of a return. Once admitted to the heaven of thought, they see no relapse into night, but infinite invitation on the other side. Heaven is within heaven, and sky over sky, and they are encompassed with divinities. Others there are, to whom the heaven is brass, and it shuts down to the surface of the earth. It is a question of temperament, or of more or less immersion in nature. The last class must needs have a reflex or parasitic faith; not a sight of realities, but an instinctive reliance on the seers and believers of realities. The manners and thoughts of believers astonish them and convince them that these have seen something which is hid from themselves. But their sensual[85] habit would fix the believer to his last position, whilst he as inevitably advances: and presently the unbeliever for love of belief burns the believer.

Great believers are always reckoned infidels, impracticable, fantastic, atheistic, and really men of no account. The spiritualist finds himself driven to express his faith by a series of skepticisms. Charitable souls come with their projects, and ask his cooperation. How can he hesitate? It is the rule of mere comity[86] and courtesy, to agree where you can, and to turn your sentence with something auspicious and not sneering and sinister. But he is forced to say, 'O these things will be as they must be; what can you do? These particular griefs and crimes are the foliage and fruit of such trees as we see growing. It is vain to complain of the leaf or the berry: cut it off, it will bear another just as bad. You must begin your cure lower down.' The generosities of the day prove an intractable element for him. The people's questions are not his; their methods are not his; and against all the dictates of good nature, he is driven to say, he has no pleasure in them.

Even the doctrines dear to the hope of man, of the divine Providence, and of the immortality of the Soul, his neighbours cannot put the statement so, that he shall affirm it. But he denies out of more faith, and not less. He denies out of honesty. He had rather stand charged with the imbecility of skepticism, than with untruth. I believe, he says, in the moral design of the universe; it exists hospitably for the weal[87] of souls; but your dogmas seem to me caricatures. Why should I make believe them?—Will any say this is cold and infidel? The wise and magnanimous will not say so. They will exult in his farsighted goodwill, that can abandon to the adversary all the ground of tradition and common belief, without losing a jot of strength. It sees to the end of all transgression. George Fox saw that there was "an ocean of darkness and death but withal an infinite ocean of light and love which flowed over that of darkness."[88]

The final solution in which Skepticism is lost, is, in the moral sentiment, which never forfeits its supremacy. All moods may be safely tried, and their weight allowed to all objections: the moral sentiment as easily outweighs them all, as any one. This is the drop which balances the sea. I play with the miscellany of facts and take those superficial views which we call Skepticism but I know that they will presently appear to me in that order which makes Skepticism impossible. A man of thought must feel the

86    Friendly association.

87    Well-being.

88    George Fox (1624–1691), founder of the Society of Friends (or "Quakers"). Emerson found the sentence paraphrased by William Sewell (1650–ca. 1726) in his *History of the People Called Quakers* (1722, written with John Gough).

89    Slogan written on Fourier's tomb in the Paris cemetery of Montmartre.

90    In October 1840, Emerson recorded a dream in his Journal: "I dreamed that I floated at will in the great Ether, and I saw this world floating also not far off, but diminished to the size of an apple. Then an angel took it in his hand and brought it to me and said, 'This must thou eat.' And I ate the world" (J 7:525). In "Uses of Great Men," the first essay in *Representative Men*, he wrote (referring to Buddhist myth), "In the legends of the Gautama, the first men ate the earth, and found it deliciously sweet."

91    Emerson remembers God's spectacular challenge to Job in the Bible's book of Job (38:4–7): "Where wast thou when I laid the foundations of the earth? . . . When the morning stars sang together, and all the sons of God shouted for joy?"

92    Beautiful females, tempting and fatal, who lure mariners to their death by singing praise of their heroism (in the *Odyssey* by Homer [ca. 9th century BCE]).

thought that is parent of the universe: that the masses of nature do undulate and flow.

This faith avails to the whole emergency of life and objects. The world is saturated with deity and with law. He is content with just and unjust, with sots and fools, with the triumph of folly and fraud. He can behold with serenity, the yawning gulf between the ambition of man and his power of performance, between the demand and supply of power which makes the tragedy of all souls.

Charles Fourier announced that "the attractions of man are proportioned to his destinies;"[89] in other words, that every desire predicts its own satisfaction. Yet all experience exhibits the reverse of this; the incompetency of power is the universal grief of young and ardent minds. They accuse the divine Providence of a certain parsimony. It has shown the heaven and earth to every child, and filled him with a desire for the whole; a desire raging, infinite, a hunger as of space to be filled with planets; a cry of famine as of devils for souls. Then for the satisfaction;—to each man is administered a single drop, a bead of dew of vital power, *per day*,—a cup as large as space, and one drop of the water of life in it. Each man woke in the morning with an appetite that could eat the solar system like a cake;[90] a spirit for action and passion without bounds; he could lay his hand on the morningstar; he could try conclusions with gravitation or chemistry; but on the first motion to prove his strength, hands, feet, senses, gave way, and would not serve him.[91] He was an emperor deserted by his states, and left to whistle by himself or thrust into a mob of emperors all whistling: and still the sirens[92] sung, "The attractions are proportioned to the destinies." In every house, in the heart of each maiden and of each boy, in the soul of the soaring saint, this chasm is found,—between the largest promise of ideal power, and the shabby experience.

The expansive nature of truth comes to our succour, elastic, not to be surrounded. Man helps himself by larger generalizations. The lesson of life is practically to generalize, to believe what the years and the centuries say against the hours; to resist the usurpation of particulars; to penetrate to their catholic sense. Things seem to say one thing, and say the reverse. The appearance is immoral; the result is moral. Things seem to tend downward, to justify despondency, to promote rogues, to defeat the just; and by knaves, as by martyrs, the just cause is carried forward. Although knaves win in every political struggle, although society seems to be delivered over from the hands of one set of criminals into the hands of another set of criminals, as fast as the government is changed, and the march of civilization is a train of felonies, yet, general ends are somehow answered. We see now, events forced on, which seem to retard or retrograde the civility of ages. But the world spirit is a good swimmer, and storms and waves cannot drown him. He snaps his finger at laws: and so, throughout history, heaven seems to affect low and poor means. (The needles are nothing; the magnetism is all.) Through the years and the centuries, through evil agents, through toys and atoms, a great and beneficent tendency irresistibly streams.

Let a man learn to look for the permanent in the mutable and fleeting; let him learn to bear the disappearance of things he was wont to reverence, without losing his reverence; let him learn that he is here not to work, but to be worked upon, and, that, though abyss open under abyss, and opinion displace opinion, all are at last contained in the eternal Cause.

"If my bark sink, 'tis to another sea."[93]

93    Final line of "A Poet's Hope" by William Ellery Channing (1817–1901), friend of Emerson (and nephew of the more famous Unitarian minister of the same name).

# Shakspeare; or, the Poet

*Emerson used the spelling "Shakspeare" for the man more commonly known as William Shakespeare (1564–1616). Emerson had earlier discussed Shakespeare in his 1835–1836 lecture series on the history of English literature. This is Chapter V of Emerson's* Representative Men *(1850).*

1    In *The Battle of the Books* (1704) by the Anglo-Irish satirist Jonathan Swift (1667–1745), the bee, come from roving the fields, confronts a proud spider engorged with flies. The spider, mechanical, systematic, and ingenious, represents the moderns, who worship their own originality. The bee, reliant on nature for his food, represents the ancients, the superior party in Swift's view. Emerson's Shakespeare resembles the bee rather than the spider.

Great men are more distinguished by range and extent, than by originality. If we require the originality which consists in weaving like a spider their web from their own bowels,[1] in finding clay, and making bricks, and building the house, no great men are original. Nor does valuable originality consist in unlikeness to other men. The hero is in the press of knights, and the thick of events, and, seeing what men want, and sharing their desire, he adds the needful length of sight and of arm to come at the desired point. The greatest genius is the most indebted man. A poet is no rattlebrain saying what comes uppermost, and, because he says everything, saying, at last, something good; but a heart in unison with his time and country. There is nothing whimsical and fantastic in his production, but sweet and sad earnest, freighted with the weightiest convictions and pointed with the most determined aim which any man or class knows of in his times.

The genius of our life is jealous of individuals, and will not have any individual great, except through the general. There is no choice to genius. A great man does not wake up on some fine morning, and say, I am full of life, I will go to sea, and find an Antarctic continent: today, I will square the circle: I will ransack botany, and find a new food for man: I have a new architecture in my mind: I foresee a new mechanic power: no; but he finds himself in the river of the thoughts and events, forced onward by the ideas and necessities of his contemporaries. He stands where all the eyes of men look one way, and their hands all point in the direction in which he should go. The Church has reared him amidst rites and pomps, and he carries out the advice which her music gave him, and builds a cathedral needed by her chants and processions. He finds a war raging; it educates him by trumpet in barracks, and he betters the instruction. He finds two counties groping to bring coal, or flour, or fish, from the place of production to the place of consumption, and he hits on a railroad. Every master has found his materials collected, and his power lay in his sympathy with his people, and in his love of the materials he wrought in. What an economy of power! and what a compensation for the shortness of life! All is done to his hand. The world has brought him thus far on his way. The human race has gone out before him, sunk the hills, filled the hollows, and bridged the rivers. Men, nations, poets, artisans, women, all have worked for him, and he enters into their labours. Choose any other thing, out of the line of tendency, out of the national feeling and history, and he would have all to do for himself: his powers would be expended in the first preparations. Great genial[2] power, one would almost say, consists in not being original at all; in being altogether receptive; in letting the world do all, and suffering the spirit of the hour to pass unobstructed through the mind.[3]

Shakspeare's youth fell in a time when the English people were importunate for dramatic entertainments. The court took offence easily at political allusions, and attempted to suppress them. The Puritans, a growing and energetic party, and the religious within the Anglican Church would suppress them.[4] But the people wanted them. Innyards, houses without roofs, or extemporaneous enclosures at country fairs, were the ready theatres of strolling players.[5] The people had tasted this new joy, and, as we could not hope to suppress newspapers now, no, not by the strongest party, neither then, could king, prelate,[6] or puritan, alone or united, suppress an organ, which was ballad, epic, newspaper, caucus, lecture, Punch,[7] and library, at the same time. Probably king, prelate, and puritan, all found their own account in it. It had become by all causes a national interest,—by no means conspicuous, so that some great scholar would have thought of treating it in an English history,—but not a whit less considerable because it was cheap, and of no account, like a baker's shop. The best proof of its vitality is the crowd of writers

2    Inborn, native.

3    In his essay "Self-Reliance," Emerson wrote, "We lie in the lap of immense intelligence, which makes us receivers of its truth and organs of its activity. When we discern justice, when we discern truth, we do nothing of ourselves, but allow a passage to its beams."

4    Plays were censored, and sometimes even suppressed, in Shakespeare's England, under the reigns of Elizabeth I (1533–1603, ruled 1558–1603) and James I (1566–1625, ruled 1603–1625). Puritans, dour and strict, denounced the theater as "Satan's chapel."

5    Before the building of the Theatre in 1576 (the first large, open-air venue for plays), plays were performed in inns and courtyards.

6    High-ranking cleric (usually a bishop or abbot).

7    Not the violent puppet Punch of Punch and Judy shows, but the British satirical magazine of Emerson's day.

8      Emerson's ample list describes a flood of Elizabethan and Jacobean dramatists: Thomas Kyd (1558–1594), author of *The Spanish Tragedy* (1592), a revenge play that influenced Shakespeare; Christopher Marlowe (1564–1593), Shakespeare's contemporary whose heroic dramas were another key influence; the minor playwright Robert Greene (1558–1592); Ben Jonson (1572–1637), known for his comedies, and a drinking companion of Shakespeare. George Chapman (ca. 1559–1634) wrote comedies and heroic tragedies, Thomas Dekker (ca. 1570–ca. 1641), domestic comedies, and John Webster (ca. 1580–ca. 1625), gruesome Jacobean revenge tragedies; Thomas Heywood (ca. 1574–1641), Thomas Middleton (ca. 1570–1627), and George Peele (ca. 1558–1598) were minor authors for the stage; John Ford (ca. 1586–ca. 1640), a distinguished Jacobean playwright; Philip Massinger (1583–1640), Francis Beaumont (ca. 1584–1616), and John Fletcher (1579–1625) collaborated on a number of plays. Fletcher co-wrote *The Two Noble Kinsmen*, Shakespeare's last play.

9      Shakespeare drew on the biographies of famous Greeks and Romans by Plutarch (ca. 46–ca. 122) for several of his tragedies, along with the stories of Troy and the accounts of Henry IV, Henry V, and Henry VI in the English histories of Raphael Holinshed (d. ca. 1580). Brut was the legendary founder of Britain, described in the chronicles of Geoffrey of Monmouth (ca. 1100–ca. 1154). Arthurian tales were also popular fodder for stage drama, though not important to Shakespeare.

10     Apprentices.

11     Scholars in Emerson's time made the same argument for Shakespeare's own plays: they claimed that the texts of the dramas in-
*(continued)*

which suddenly broke into this field; Kyd, Marlow, Greene, Jonson, Chapman, Dekker, Webster, Heywood, Middleton, Peele, Ford, Massinger, Beaumont, and Fletcher.[8]

The secure possession by the stage of the public mind is of the first importance to the poet who works for it. He loses no time in idle experiments. Here is audience and expectation prepared. In the case of Shakspeare, there is much more. At the time when he left Stratford, and went up to London, a great body of stage plays of all dates and writers existed in manuscript, and were in turn produced on the boards. Here is the Tale of Troy, which the audience will bear hearing some part of, every week: the Death of Julius Cæsar, and other stories out of Plutarch, which they never tire of: a shelf full of English history, from the Chronicles of Brut and Arthur, down to the royal Henries,[9] which men hear eagerly: and a string of doleful tragedies, merry Italian tales, and Spanish voyages, which all the London prentices[10] know. All the mass has been treated with more or less skill by every playwright, and the prompter has the soiled and tattered manuscripts. It is now no longer possible to say who wrote them first. They have been the property of the Theatre so long, and so many rising geniuses have enlarged or altered them, inserting a speech, or a whole scene, or adding a song, that no man can any longer claim copyright in this work of numbers.[11] Happily, no man wishes to. They are not yet desired in that way. We have few readers, many spectators and hearers. They had best lie where they are.

Shakspeare, in common with his comrades, esteemed the mass of old plays waste stock, in which any experiment could be freely tried. Had the *prestige* which hedges about a modern tragedy existed, nothing could have been done. The rude warm blood of the living England circulated in the play, as in street ballads, and gave body which he wanted to his airy and majestic fancy.[12] The poet needs a ground in popular tradition on which he may work, and which, again, may restrain his art within the due temperance. It holds him to the people, supplies a foundation for his edifice, and in furnishing so much work done to his hand, leaves him at leisure, and in full strength for the audacities of his imagination. In short, the poet owes to his legend, what Sculpture owed to the temple. Sculpture in Egypt, and in Greece, grew up in subordination to architecture. It was the ornament of the temple wall: at first, a rude relief carved on pediments, then the relief became bolder, and a head or arm was projected from the wall, the groups being still arranged with reference to the building, which serves also as a frame to hold the figures, and when, at last, the greatest freedom of style and treatment was reached, the prevailing genius of architecture still enforced a certain calmness and continence in the statue. As soon as the statue was begun for itself, and with no reference to the temple or palace, the art began to decline: freak, extravagance, and exhibition, took the place of the old temperance. This balance-wheel which the sculptor found in architecture, the perilous irritability of poetic talent found in the accumulated dramatic materials to which the people were already wonted, and which had a certain excellence, which no single genius, however extraordinary, could hope to create.

In point of fact it appears that Shakspeare did owe debts in all directions, and was able to use whatever he found; and the amount of indebtedness may be inferred from Malone's laborious computations in regard to the second and third parts of Henry VI, in which, "out of 6043 lines, 1771 were written by some author preceding Shakspeare; 2373 by him on the foundation laid by his predecessors, and 1899 were entirely his own." And the proceeding investigation hardly leaves a single drama of his absolute invention.[13] Malone's sentence is an important piece of external history. In Henry VIII, I think I see plainly the cropping out of the original rock on which his own finer stratum was laid. The first play was written by a superior thoughtful man, with a vicious ear.[14] I can mark his lines, and know well their cadence. See Wolsey's soliloquy and the following scene with Cromwell, where, instead of the metre of Shakspeare, whose secret is, that the thought constructs the tune, so that reading for the sense will best bring out the rhythm, here the lines are constructed on a given tune, and the verse has even a trace of pulpit eloquence.[15] But the play contains through all its length unmistakeable traits of Shakspeare's hand, and some passages, as the account of the Coronation, are like autographs. What is odd, the compliment to Queen Elizabeth is in the bad rhythm.

Shakspeare knew that tradition supplies a better fable than any invention can. If he lost any credit of design, he augmented his resources, and, at that day, our petulant demand for originality was not so much pressed. There was no literature for the million. The universal reading, the cheap press, were unknown. A great poet who appears in illiterate times, absorbs into his

cluded many interpolations by actors or by other writers. We now believe they exaggerated the extent of such additions (although there were some).

12    In *A Midsummer Night's Dream*, Shakspeare's character Theseus says that the "poet's pen" "bodies forth / The forms of things unknown" and "gives to airy nothing / A local habitation and a name" (5.1.14–17).

13    Scholars have since discredited the efforts of the Irish scholar Edmund Malone (1741–1812) to undermine Shakespeare's authorship of his plays. In the late 1580s, early in his career, Shakespeare wrote a trilogy of plays about King Henry VI of England (1421–1471, ruled 1422–1461 and 1470–1471).

14    "Vicious" here means defective. Shakespeare probably wrote his play about Henry VIII (1491–1547), who ruled England 1509–1547, in collaboration with John Fletcher: Emerson's hunch that Shakespeare was revising another man's work is unlikely.

15    Cardinal Thomas Wolsey (ca. 1475–1530) was chief advisor to Henry VIII; he fell from favor after he failed to secure Henry's divorce from Catherine of Aragon, his first wife, in 1529. Thomas Cromwell (ca. 1485–1540) was first Wolsey's secretary and then his successor at Henry's court.

16    Homer (ca. 9th century BCE), Greek author of the *Iliad* and the *Odyssey*, relied on earlier versions of the epic stories; Geoffrey Chaucer (ca. 1343–1400) alludes abundantly to his
literary precursors in *The Canterbury Tales*
(1387–1400) and *Troilus and Criseyde* (ca. 1384).
Emerson valued Saadi (1184–ca. 1292), the
great Persian poet, very highly.

17    Lines (slightly misquoted) from "Il Penseroso" (ca. 1631) by the English poet John
Milton (1608–1674). Milton here refers to
Greek tragedy: Thebes is the city ruled by Oedipus; Pelops was the ancestor of Agamemnon.
His poem also invokes an atmosphere of romance, the literary genre concerned with
quests, knightly adventures, distressed damsels,
and magical enemies.

18    Alexander Pope (1688–1744) and John
Dryden (1631–1700), dominant British poets of
their time.

19    Emerson is confused and partly inaccurate here. John Lydgate (ca. 1370–ca. 1451) imitated Chaucer, rather than the reverse; William
Caxton (ca. 1422–1491) also came after Chaucer. Guido di Colonna, better known as Guido
delle Colonne, was a Sicilian writer of the thirteenth century; a Latin history of the destruction of Troy is attributed to him. Another Latin
history of the Trojan war (5th or 6th century),
attributed to the legendary Dares Phrygius (a
Trojan priest), was much read in the Middle
Ages; Ovid (43 BCE–17) and Statius (ca. 50–ca.
96) were Latin epic poets. The works of
Petrarch (Francesco Petrarca, 1304–1374) and
Giovanni Boccaccio (1313–1375) were sources
for Chaucer, but it is doubtful that he copied
Marie de France (fl. ca. 1200); and Chaucer
translated the thirteenth-century *Romance of the*
*(continued)*

sphere all the light which is anywhere radiating. Every intellectual jewel, every flower of sentiment, it is his fine office to bring to his people; and he
comes to value his memory, equally with his invention. He is therefore little
solicitous whence his thoughts have been derived, whether through translation, whether through tradition, whether by travel in distant countries,
whether by inspiration: from whatever source, they are equally welcome to
his uncritical audience. Nay, he borrows very near home. Other men say
wise things as well as he; only they say a good many foolish things, and do
not know when they have spoken wisely. He knows the sparkle of the true
stone, and puts it in high place, wherever he finds it.

Such is the happy position of Homer, perhaps; of Chaucer, of Saadi.[16]
They felt that all wit was their wit. And they are librarians and historiogra-
phers as well as poets. Each romancer was heir and dispenser of all the hundred tales of the world,—

"Presenting Thebes' and Pelops' line,
And the tale of Troy divine."[17]

The influence of Chaucer is conspicuous in all our early literature: and, more
recently, not only Pope and Dryden[18] have been beholden to him, but in the
whole society of English writers a large unacknowledged debt is easily traced.
One is charmed with the opulence which feeds so many pensioners. But
Chaucer is a huge borrower. Chaucer, it seems, drew continually through
Lydgate and Caxton, from Guido di Colonna, whose Latin romance of the
Trojan War was in turn a compilation from Dares Phrygius, Ovid, and Statius. Then Petrarch, Boccaccio, and the Provençal poets are his benefactors:
the Romaunt of the Rose is only judicious translation from William of Lorris and John of Meun: Troilus and Creseide, from Lollius of Urbino: The
Cock and the Fox, from the *Lais* of Marie: The House of Fame, from the
French or Italian: and poor Gower he uses, as if he were only a brickkiln or
stonequarry, out of which to build his house.[19] He steals by this apology, that
what he takes has no worth where he finds it, and the greatest where he
leaves it. It has come to be practically a sort of rule in literature, that a man
having once shown himself capable of original writing, is entitled thenceforth to steal from the writings of others at discretion. Thought is the prop-

erty of him who can entertain it; and of him who can adequately place it. A certain awkwardness marks the use of borrowed thoughts; but as soon as we have learned what to do with them, they become our own.

Thus all originality is relative. Every thinker is retrospective. The learned member of the legislature at Westminster or at Washington, speaks and votes for thousands. Show us the constituency, and the now invisible channels by which the senator is made aware of their wishes, the crowd of practical and knowing men, who, by correspondence or conversation, are feeding him with evidence, anecdotes, and estimates, and it will bereave his fine attitude and resistance of something of their impressiveness. As Sir Robert Peel and Mr Webster vote, so Locke and Rousseau think for thousands; and so there were fountains all around Homer, Menu, Saadi, or Milton,[20] from which they drew; friends, lovers, books, traditions, proverbs,—all perished,—which, if seen, would go to reduce the wonder. Did the bard speak with authority? did he feel himself overmatched by any companion? The appeal is to the consciousness of the writer. Is there at last in his breast a Delphi[21] whereof to ask concerning any thought or thing, whether it be verily so, yea or nay? and to have answer, and to rely on that? All the debts which such a man could contract to other wit, would never disturb his consciousness of originality: for the ministrations of books and of other minds are a whiff of smoke to that most private reality with which he has conversed.

It is easy to see that what is best written or done by genius in the world was no man's work, but came by wide social labour, when a thousand wrought like one, sharing the same impulse. Our English Bible is a wonderful specimen of the strength and music of the English language. But it was not made by one man or at one time; but centuries and churches brought it to perfection.[22] There never was a time when there was not some translation existing. The Liturgy, admired for its energy and pathos, is an anthology of the piety of ages and nations, a translation of the prayers and forms of the Catholic Church,—these selected, too, in long periods, from the prayers and meditations of every saint and sacred writer, all over the world. Grotius[23] makes the like remark in respect to the Lord's Prayer, that the single clauses of which it is composed, were already in use, in the time of Christ, in the Rabbinical forms. He picked out the grains of gold. The nervous[24] language of the Common Law, the impressive forms of our courts, and the precision and substan-

*Rose* by Guillaume de Lorris (ca. 1215–ca. 1278) and Jean de Meun (ca. 1250–ca. 1305). (Lollius of Urbino, named by Chaucer, never actually existed.) John Gower (ca. 1325–1408), Chaucer's friend, wrote *Confessio Amantis* (ca. 1383).

20   Sir Robert Peel (1788–1850), British prime minister; Daniel Webster (1782–1852), American statesman and orator; John Locke (1632–1704) and Jean-Jacques Rousseau (1712–1778), influential philosophers; Menu, legendary lawgiver of ancient India.

21   Ancient site of the oracle of Apollo, presided over by a priestess.

22   John Wycliff (ca. 1328–1384) produced the first substantial translation of the Bible into English; he was followed by William Tyndale (ca. 1494–1536), whose brilliant work provided the foundation for later translators, culminating in the King James Bible of 1611.

23   Hugo Grotius (1583–1645), Dutch jurist who wrote a commentary on the Christian gospels.

24   Sinewy.

25   Greek historian (ca. 46–ca. 122) greatly admired by Emerson. His English translators relied on other translations, not just Plutarch's Greek.

26   The Vedas are sacred books of ancient India, the *Iliad* and the *Song of the Cid*, European epics, and the rest, popular tales (Scottish ballads, stories of Robin Hood, the Arabian Nights, and the Greek fables of Aesop [ca. 6th century BCE]). Pilpay (or Bidpai) was the legendary Indian author of a series of tales and proverbs, circulated in Arabic and Persian and translated into English in the eighteenth century.

27   Common, universal.

28   The Medieval mystery plays were based on biblical narratives; originally played in churches, they moved to marketplaces and public squares, where they became more humorous and more marked by everyday life.

29   Ferrex and Porrex are characters in *Gorboduc* (1561–1565), a primitive English tragedy by Thomas Sackville (1536–1608) and Thomas Norton (1532–1584). Its plot influenced Shakespeare's *King Lear. Gammer Gurton's Needle* (performed 1566): an English comic play of disputed authorship, probably known to Shakespeare.

30   Emerson rehearses some of the better-known speculations about Shakespeare's life during his "lost years," for which no documentation exists (1585–1592): that he was a poacher, an ostler (handler of horses), or a schoolteacher. The bequest to Shakespeare's wife, Anne Hathaway (ca. 1556–1623), remains enigmatic.

31   The Tudors ruled England from 1485 to 1603. Emerson mentions a number of famous
*(continued)*

tial truth of the legal distinctions, are the contribution of all the sharpsighted strongminded men who have lived in the countries where these laws govern. The translation of Plutarch[25] gets its excellence by being translation on translation. There never was a time when there was none. All the truly idiomatic and national phrases are kept, and all others successively picked out and thrown away. Something like the same process had gone on long before with the originals of these books. The world takes liberties with worldbooks. Vedas, Æsop's Fables, Pilpay, Arabian Nights, Cid, Iliad, Robin Hood, Scottish Minstrelsy,[26] are not the work of single men. In the composition of such works, the time thinks, the market thinks, the mason, the carpenter, the merchant, the farmer, the fop, all think for us. Every book supplies its time with one good word; every municipal law, every trade, every folly of the day; and the generic catholic[27] genius, who is not afraid or ashamed to owe his originality to the originality of all, stands with the next age as the recorder and embodiment of his own.

We have to thank the researches of antiquaries and the Shakspeare Society, for ascertaining the steps of the English Drama, from the Mysteries[28] celebrated in churches and by churchmen, and the final detachment from the church, and the completion of secular plays, from Ferrex and Porrex, and Gammer Gurton's Needle,[29] down to the possession of the stage by the very pieces which Shakspeare altered, remodelled, and finally made his own. Elated with success, and piqued by the growing interest of the problem, they have left no bookstall unsearched, no chest in a garret unopened, no file of old yellow accounts to decompose in damp and worms, so keen was the hope to discover whether the boy Shakspeare poached or not, whether he held horses at the theatre door, whether he kept school, and why he left in his will only his second best bed to Ann Hathaway his wife.[30]

There is somewhat touching in the madness with which the passing age mischooses the object on which all candles shine, and all eyes are turned; the care with which it registers every trifle touching Queen Elizabeth and King James and the Essexes, Leicesters, Burleighs, and Buckinghams, and lets pass without a single valuable note the founder of another dynasty, which alone will cause the Tudor dynasty[31] to be remembered,—the man who carries the Saxon race[32] in him by the inspiration which feeds him, and on whose thoughts the foremost people of the world are now for some ages to be nourished, and minds to receive this, and not another bias.[33] A popular player, nobody suspected he was the poet of the human race: and the secret was kept as faithfully from poets and intellectual men, as from courtiers and frivolous people. Bacon, who took the inventory of the human understanding for his times, never mentioned his name. Ben Jonson, though we have strained his few words of regard and panegyric, had no suspicion of the elastic fame whose first vibrations he was attempting.[34] He, no doubt, thought the praise he has conceded to him generous, and esteemed himself, out of all question, the better poet of the two.

If it need wit to know wit, according to the proverb, Shakspeare's time should be capable of recognizing it. Sir Henry Wotton was born four years after Shakspeare, and died twenty-three years after him, and I find among

court figures: Robert Devereux, Earl of Essex (1567–1601); Robert Dudley, Earl of Leicester (ca. 1532–1588); and William Cecil, Lord Burleigh (or Burghley, 1520–1598), all three at the court of Elizabeth I; and George Villiers, Duke of Buckingham (1592–1628), the favorite of King James I.

32    The Saxons (along with the Angles) were the Germanic tribes who colonized Britain.

33    Emerson wrote in his Journal (December 1835), "In Shakspear I actually shade my eyes as I read for the splendor of the thoughts" (J 5:112).

34    Francis Bacon (1561–1626), renowned scientist and politician; Ben Jonson wrote a famous dedicatory poem praising Shakespeare, included in the First Folio of Shakespeare's works (1623).

Emerson's mother,
Ruth Haskins Emerson.

35    Henry Wotton (1568–1639) was an English writer and diplomat, from whom Emerson
takes a cascade, rather miscellaneous, of Renaissance names: Theodore Beza (1519–1605),
French Protestant theologian; Isaac Casaubon
(1559–1614), classical scholar born in Geneva;
Philip Sidney (1554–1586) and Walter Raleigh
(ca. 1552–1618), courtiers and poets of the
Elizabethan Age; Henry Vane (1613–1662),
governor of Massachusetts and an important
Puritan politician in England. Izaak Walton
(1593–1683) became famous for his book on
fishing, *The Compleat Angler* (1653); John
Donne (1572–1631) and Abraham Cowley
(1618–1667) were English poets. Robert Bellarmine (1542–1621) was an Italian Jesuit religious writer, and Charles Cotton (1630–1687)
an English poet and translator. Emerson also
mentions John Pym (ca. 1583–1643), a politician opposed to King Charles I (1600–1649,
ruled 1625–1649); John Hales (1584–1656),
an English religious writer; Johannes Kepler
(1571–1630), the great German astronomer;
François Vieta, or Viète (1540–1603), the
French mathematician who developed algebra;
Alberto Gentili (1552–1608), Italian-born jurist; Paolo Sarpi (1552–1623), Venetian religious historian. The Dutch theologian Jaco-
bus Arminius (1560–1609) was the influential
founder of Arminianism, which challenged rigid
Calvinist ideas of predestination.

36    Edmund Spenser (ca. 1552–1599), author
of the spectacular epic romance *The Faerie
Queene* (1590–1596), a probable influence on
Shakespeare. George Herbert (1593–1633) was
a remarkable poet; his lesser-known brother,
Edward, Lord Herbert of Cherbury (1583–
1648), was also a writer.

37    Brilliant general and leader of Athens in
its days of glory, Pericles died in 429 BCE.

38    G. E. Lessing (1729–1781), C. M. Wieland (1733–1813), and A. W. von Schlegel
(1767–1845) all translated plays of Shakespeare
into German—Schlegel with great brilliance.

39    Emerson will return at the end of his essay to a comparison between Shakespeare and
Christianity. In his Journal (October 1841) he
noted that "only a few are the fixed stars which
have no parallax, or none for us; Plato & Jesus
& Shakespeare. These are the gracious marks
of our own growth" (J 8:127). The German
writer and polymath J. W. von Goethe (1749–
1832) and the English poet and philosopher
S. T. Coleridge (1772–1834) both wrote influential interpretations of Shakespeare. In his
copy of Coleridge's *Letters, Conversations and
Recollections* (1836), Emerson noted his remark
about "the wonderful faculty which Shakspeare
above all other men possessed, or rather the
power which possessed him in the highest degree, of anticipating everything" (May 4–5,
1820).

    In an 1851 passage in his Journal, Emer-
son contrasted Shakespeare's greater influence
over his audience to the lesser powers of Goethe
and the English poet William Wordsworth
(1770–1850): "to Shakspeare alone God granted
the power to dispense with the humours of his
company: They must needs all take *his*. He is
always good. . . . I looked through the first part
of Faust today, & find it a little too modern &
intelligible . . . it wants . . . the cheerful, radiant,
profuse beauty of which Shakspeare, of which
Chaucer, had the secret.—The Faust on the
contrary abounds in the disagreeable. The vice
is prurient, learned, Parisian" (J 11:426).

his correspondents and acquaintances, the following persons: Theodore Beza, Isaac Casaubon, Sir Philip Sidney, Earl of Essex, Lord Bacon, Sir Walter Raleigh, John Milton, Sir Henry Vane, Isaak Walton, Dr Donne, Abraham Cowley, Bellarmine, Charles Cotton, John Pym, John Hales, Kepler, Vieta, Albericus Gentilis, Paul Sarpi, Arminius;[35] with all of whom exists some token of his having communicated, without enumerating many others whom doubtless he saw,—Shakspeare, Spenser, Jonson, Beaumont, Massinger, two Herberts, Marlow, Chapman,[36] and the rest. Since the constellation of great men who appeared in Greece, in the time of Pericles,[37] there was never any such society;—yet their genius failed them to find out the best head in the universe. Our poet's mask was impenetrable. You cannot see the mountain near. It took a century to make it suspected; and not until two centuries had passed, after his death, did any criticism which we think adequate begin to appear. It was not possible to write the history of Shakspeare till now; for he is the father of German literature: it was on the introduction of Shakspeare into German, by Lessing, and the translation of his works by Wieland and Schlegel,[38] that the rapid burst of German literature was most intimately connected. It was not until the nineteenth century, whose speculative genius is a sort of living Hamlet, that the tragedy of Hamlet could find such wondering readers. Now, literature, philosophy, and thought are Shakspearized. His mind is the horizon beyond which at present we do not see. Our ears are educated to music by his rhythm. Coleridge and Goethe are the only critics who have expressed our convictions with any adequate fidelity; but there is in all cultivated minds a silent appreciation of his superlative power and beauty, which, like Christianity, qualifies the period.[39]

The Shakspeare Society[40] have inquired in all directions, advertised the missing facts, offered money for any information that will lead to proof;—and with what result? Beside some important illustration of the history of the English stage to which I adverted, they have gleaned a few facts touching the property and dealings in regard to property of the Poet. It appears that from year to year he owned a larger share in the Blackfriars Theatre:[41] its wardrobe and other appurtenances were his; that he bought an estate in his native village with his earnings as writer and shareholder; that he lived in the best house in Stratford; was intrusted by his neighbours with their commis-

40  London's Shakespeare Society was founded in 1840.

41  An indoor theater, much smaller than the Globe; used by Shakespeare's company, the King's Men, after 1609.

42    In the *Theogony*, by the Greek poet He-
siod (8th century BCE), Rainbow (Iris) is the
daughter of Wonder (Thaumas).

43    The English bishop and critic William
Warburton (1698–1779) published an edition
of Shakespeare's plays, as did the Scot Alexander Dyce (1798–1869) and John Payne Collier
(1789–1883), founding director of the Shakespeare Society (and forger of Shakespeare manuscripts).

44    Renowned London theaters. Thomas
Betterton (ca. 1635–1710), David Garrick
(1717–1779), J. P. Kemble (1757–1823), Edmund Kean (1787–1833), and William C. Macready (1793–1873) were all acclaimed British
Shakespearean actors.

45    *Hamlet* 1.4.51–53. In his Journal (1845)
Emerson wrote, "I remember I came to the city
once to hear Macready's Hamlet and all I now
remember of that master was . . . simply the
magical expression, Revisit'st now the glimpses
of the Moon" (J 9:315). Macready was famous
for his portrayals of Shakespeare's tragic heroes,
including Hamlet.

46    Room. Emerson is thinking of Hamlet's
boast (and lament), "Oh God, I could be
bounded in a nutshell and count myself a king
of infinite space, were it not that I have bad
dreams" (2.2.258–260).

sions in London, as of borrowing money, and the like; that he was a veritable farmer. About the time when he was writing Macbeth, he sues Philip Rogers, in the borough-court of Stratford, for thirty-five shillings, tenpence, for corn delivered to him at different times; and, in all respects, appears as a good husband, with no reputation for eccentricity or excess. He was a good-natured sort of man, an actor and shareholder in the theatre, not in any strik-ing manner distinguished from other actors and managers. I admit the im-portance of this information. It was well worth the pains that have been taken to procure it.

But whatever scraps of information concerning his condition these re-searches may have rescued, they can shed no light upon that infinite inven-tion which is the concealed magnet of his attraction for us. We are very clumsy writers of history. We tell the chronicle of parentage, birth, birth-place, schooling, schoolmates, earning of money, marriage, publication of books, celebrity, death, and when we have come to an end of this gossip, no ray of relation appears between it and the goddess-born; and it seems as if, had we dipped at random into the "Modern Plutarch," and read any other life there, it would have fitted the poems as well. It is the essence of poetry to spring like the rainbow daughter of Wonder[42] from the invisible, to abolish the past, and refuse all history. Malone, Warburton, Dyce, and Collier[43] have wasted their oil. The famed theatres Covent Garden, Drury Lane, the Park, and Tremont, have vainly assisted. Betterton, Garrick, Kemble, Kean, and Macready[44] dedicate their lives to this genius; him they crown, elucidate, obey, and express. The Genius knows them not. The recitation begins; one golden word leaps out immortal from all this painted pedantry, and sweetly torments us with invitations to its own inaccessible homes. I remember I went once to see the Hamlet of a famed performer, the pride of the Eng-lish stage, and all I then heard and all I now remember of the tragedian, was that in which the tragedian had no part, simply Hamlet's question to the ghost,—

"What may this mean,
That thou, dead corse, again in complete steel
Revisit'st thus the glimpses of the moon?"[45]

That imagination which dilates the closet[46] he writes in to the world's dimension, crowds it with agents in rank and order, as quickly reduces the big reality to be the glimpses of the moon. These tricks of his magic spoil for us the illusions of the green room.[47] Can any biography shed light on the localities into which the Midsummer Night's Dream admits me? Did Shakspeare confide to any notary or parish Recorder, sacristan, or surrogate in Stratford,[48] the genesis of that delicate creation? The forest of Arden, the nimble air of Scone Castle, the moonlight of Portia's villa, "the antres vast and desarts idle" of Othello's captivity,[49]—where is the third cousin or grandnephew, the chancellor's file of accounts, or private letter, that has kept one word of those transcendant secrets? In fine, in this drama, as in all great works of art,—in the Cyclopæan architecture of Egypt and India; in the Phidian sculpture; the Gothic minsters;[50] the Italian painting; the Ballads of Spain and Scotland;—the Genius draws up the ladder after him, when the creative age goes up to heaven,[51] and gives way to a new, which sees the works, and asks in vain for a history.

Shakspeare is the only biographer of Shakspeare, and even he can tell nothing except to the Shakspeare in us, that is, to our most apprehensive and sympathetic hour. He cannot step from off his tripod, and give us anecdotes of his inspirations. Read the antique documents extricated, analyzed, and compared, by the assiduous Dyce and Collier; and now read one of those skiey sentences,—aerolites,[52]—which seem to have fallen out of heaven, and which, not your experience, but the man within the breast has accepted as words of fate, and tell me if they match: if the former account in any manner for the latter, or which gives the most historical insight into the man.

Hence, though our external history is so meagre, yet with Shakspeare for biographer, instead of Aubrey and Rowe,[53] we have really the information which is material, that which describes character and fortune, that which, if we were about to meet the man and deal with him, would most import us to know. We have his recorded convictions on those questions which knock for answer at every heart, on life and death, on love, on wealth, and poverty, on the prizes of life, and the ways whereby we come at them, on the characters of men, and the influences occult and open which affect their fortunes, and on those mysterious and demoniacal powers which defy our sci-

47  The green room is an offstage waiting room for actors (or other performers). In his *Journal* (1845) Emerson lamented, "Shakspeare's fault that the world appears so empty. He has educated you with his painted world, & this real one seems a huckster's shop" (J 9:342).

48  A sacristan is an officer charged with the care of a church and its ceremonies; a surrogate is the deputy of a bishop or ecclesiastical judge. Stratford, in the English Midlands, was Shakespeare's home town.

49  From (in order) *As You Like It*, *Macbeth*, *The Merchant of Venice*, and *Othello*.

50  Cyclopean architecture involves the use of massive, irregularly shaped stones; Phidias (5th century BCE), the most famous sculptor of Greece, contributed to the Parthenon; minsters are cathedrals, usually attached to a monastery.

51  In Milton's *Paradise Lost* (1667) Satan sees a magnificent set of stairs leading up to heaven, "let down, whether to dare / The fiend by easy ascent or aggravate / His sad exclusion from the doors of bliss" (3.523–525); Milton here alludes to Genesis 28:10–17, when Jacob, fleeing from his brother Esau, sees a ladder reaching to heaven, with angels ascending and descending on it.

52  Meteorites.

53  The English antiquary John Aubrey (1626–1697) includes a biographical sketch of Shakespeare in his *Brief Lives*; Nicholas Rowe (1674–1718) was another English editor of Shakespeare.

54    Published in 1609, probably without Shakespeare's consent.

55    From *Timon of Athens, Henry VI* (Parts 2 and 3), and *The Merchant of Venice*.

56    In his Journal (October 1832), Emerson wrote, "And thus is Shakspear moral not of set purpose but by elevating the soul to a nobler pitch. So too are all great exciters of man moral; in war & plague & shipwreck greatest virtues appear" (J 4:55).

57    François Talma (1763–1826), a stage actor and friend of the French emperor Napoleon Bonaparte (1769–1821).

58    Under the heading "Large utterance!" Emerson wrote in his Journal (May–July 1847), "Shakspeare sweats like a haymaker,—all pores" (J 10:68).

59    In his Journal (May–July 1847) Emerson described Shakespeare as "a wonderful symbolizer & expressor who has no rival in all ages, in his way, & has thrown an accidental lustre over his time & subject" (J 10:91).

ence, and which yet interweave their malice and their gift in our brightest hours. Who ever read the volume of the "Sonnets,"[54] without finding that the Poet had there revealed, under masks that are no masks to the intelligent, the lore of friendship and of love; the confusion of sentiments in the most susceptible, and, at the same time, the most intellectual of men? What trait of his private mind has he hidden in his dramas? One can discern in his ample pictures of the gentleman and the king, what forms and humanities pleased him; his delight in troops of friends, in large hospitality, in cheerful giving. Let Timon, let Warwick, let Antonio the merchant,[55] answer for his great heart. So far from Shakspeare's being the least known, he is the one person in all modern history known to us. What point of morals, of manners, of economy, of philosophy, of religion, of taste, of the conduct of life, has he not settled?[56] What mystery has he not signified his knowledge of? What office or function or district of man's work has he not remembered? What king has he not taught state, as Talma taught Napoleon?[57] What maiden has not found him finer than her delicacy? What lover has he not outloved? What sage has he not outseen? What gentleman has he not instructed in the rudeness of his behaviour?

Some able and appreciating critics think no criticism on Shakspeare valuable that does not rest purely on the dramatic merit; that he is falsely judged as poet and philosopher. I think as highly as these critics of his dramatic merit, but still think it secondary. He was a full man who liked to talk; a brain exhaling thoughts and images which seeking vent, found the drama next at hand.[58] Had he been less, we should have had to consider how well he filled his place, how good a dramatist he was, and he is the best in the world. But it turns out, that what he has to say is of that weight, as to withdraw some attention from the vehicle; and he is like some saint whose history is to be rendered into all languages, into verse and prose, into songs and pictures, and cut up into proverbs, so that the occasion which gave the saint's meaning the form of a conversation or of a prayer or of a code of laws is immaterial, compared with the universality of its application.[59] So it fares with the wise Shakspeare and his book of life. He wrote the airs for all our modern music. He wrote the text of modern life; the text of manners: he drew the man of England and Europe; the father of the man in America: he drew the man, and described the day, and what is done in it: he read the hearts of men and women, their probity, and their second thought and wiles; the wiles of innocence, and the transitions by which virtues and vices slide into their contraries: he could divide the mother's part from the father's part in the face of the child, or draw the fine demarcations of freedom and of fate: he knew the laws of repression, which make the police of nature: and all the sweets and all the terrors of human lot lay in his mind as truly but as softly as the landscape lies on the eye.[60] And the importance of this wisdom of life sinks the form, as of Drama or Epic, out of notice. 'Tis like making a question concerning the paper on which a king's message is written.

Shakspeare is as much out of the category of eminent authors, as he is out of the crowd. He is inconceivably wise, the others conceivably. A good reader can in a sort nestle into Plato's brain, and think from thence, but not into Shakspeare's. We are still out of doors.[61] For executive faculty, for creation, Shakspeare is unique. No man can imagine it better.[62] He was the farthest reach of subtlety compatible with an individual self,—the subtlest of authors, and only just within the possibility of authorship. With this wisdom of life, is the equal endowment of imaginative and of lyric power. He clothed the creatures of his legend with form and sentiments, as if they were people who had lived under his roof, and few real men have left such distinct characters as these fictions. And they spoke in language as sweet as it was fit. Yet his talents never seduced him into an ostentation, nor did he harp on one string.[63] An omnipresent humanity coordinates all his faculties. Give a man of talents a story to tell, and his partiality will presently appear. He has certain observations, opinions, topics, which have some accidental prominence, and which he disposes all to exhibit. He crams this part, and starves that other part, consulting not the fitness of the thing, but his fitness and strength. But Shakspeare has no peculiarity, no importunate topic, but all is duly given; no veins, no curiosities; no cowpainter, no birdfancier, no mannerist is he: he has no discoverable egotism: the great he tells greatly, the small subordinately. He is wise without emphasis or assertion; he is strong as nature is strong, who lifts the land into mountain slopes without effort, and by the same rule as she floats a bubble in the air, and likes as well to do the one as the other. This makes that equality of power in farce, tragedy, narrative, and

60    A stunning and enigmatic sentence. "Police" here means government or regulation.

61    In his Journal (1843) Emerson commented (with reference to the Greek philosopher Plato [429–347 BCE]), "I confess that Plato seems to me greatly more literary than strong—weak inasmuch as he is literary. Shakespeare is not literary, but the strong earth itself" (8:369).

62    Emerson commented in a Journal entry from 1850–1851 that "Shakspeare's fancy never flagged. He never appears the anatomist, never with a mere outline, which is to be filled up in a happier hour, but always gorgeous with new & shining draperies. As a dry thinker, too, he is one of the best in the world" (J 11:318–319).

63    In his Journal (1851), Emerson remarked of Shakespeare, "One would say, he must have been a thousand years old, when he wrote his first piece, so thoroughly is his thought familiar to him, so solidly worded, as if it were already a proverb, & not only hereafter to become one" (J 11:437–438).

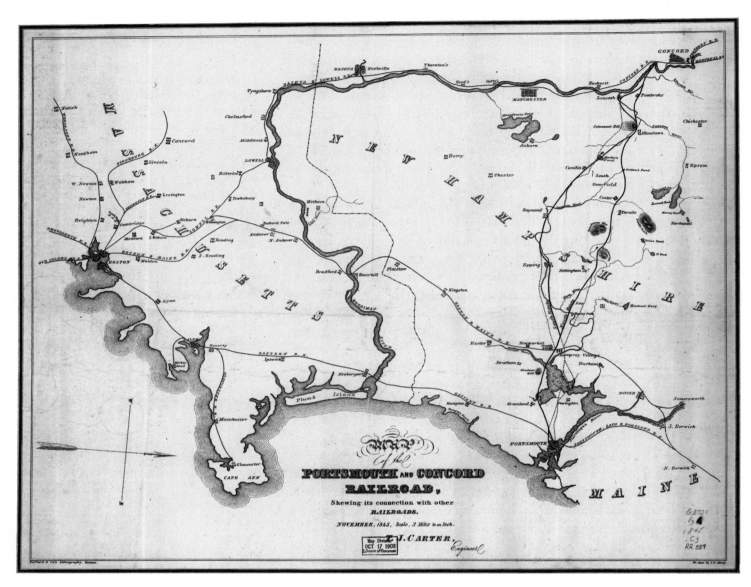

Portsmouth-Concord Railroad, 1845.

lovesongs; a merit so incessant, that each reader is incredulous of the perception of other readers.

This power of expression, or of transferring the inmost truth of things into music and verse, makes him the type of the poet, and has added a new problem to metaphysics. This is that which throws him into natural history as a main production of the globe, and as announcing new eras and ameliorations. Things were mirrored in his poetry without loss or blur;[64] he could paint the fine with precision, the great with compass; the tragic and the comic indifferently, and without any distortion or favour.[65] He carried his powerful execution into minute details to a hair point; finishes an eyelash or a dimple as firmly as he draws a mountain; and yet these, like nature's, will bear the scrutiny of the solar microscope. In short, he is the chief example to prove that more or less of production, more or fewer pictures is a thing indifferent. He had the power to make one picture. Daguerre[66] learned how to let one flower etch its image on his plate of iodine; and then proceeds at leisure to etch a million. There are always objects; but there was never representation. Here is perfect representation, at last, and now let the world of figures sit for their portraits. No recipe can be given for the making of a Shakspeare; but the possibility of the translation of things into song, is demonstrated.

His lyric power lies in the genius of the piece. The sonnets, though their excellence is lost in the splendour of the dramas, are as inimitable as they: and it is not a merit of lines, but a total merit of the piece; like the tone of voice of some incomparable person, so is this a speech of poetic beings, and any clause as unproducible now, as a whole poem. Though the speeches in the plays, and single lines have a beauty which tempts the ear to pause on them for their euphuism,[67] yet the sentence is so loaded with meaning, and so linked with its foregoers and followers, that the logician is satisfied. His means are as admirable as his ends; every subordinate invention by which he helps himself to connect some irreconcileable opposites, is a poem too. He is not reduced to dismount and walk, because his horses are running off with him in some distant direction: he always rides.

The finest poetry was first experience: but the thought has suffered a transformation since it was an experience. Cultivated men often attain a

64 Hamlet tells the players to "hold a mirror up to nature" (3.2.22). In his Journal (April 10, 1835) Emerson wrote that "the true genius the Shakspear & Goethe sees the tree & sky & man as they are, enters into them whilst the inferior writer dwells evermore with himself 'twinkling restlessly'" (J 5:27; the last phrase is from Wordsworth's *Excursion* of 1814).

65 From Emerson's Journal (1849): "The impartiality of Shakespeare is like that of the light itself, which is no aristocrat, but shines as mellowly on gipsies as on emperors, on bride & corpse, on city & swamp" (J 11:172).

66 The French artist and chemist Louis Daguerre (1789–1851) invented the daguerreotype, an early, and vastly popular, form of photography.

67 Elaborate, fluid style: from *Euphues* (1578–1580) by the English writer John Lyly (ca. 1554–1606).

68    The sloughed skin of an animal (a snake, for example).

69    Epicurus, Greek philosopher (ca. 341–270 BCE); a mistaken attribution.

70    From *Saadi's Gulistan or Rose Garden*, a book that Emerson treasured by the Persian poet Saadi (1184–ca. 1291).

71    Dante Alighieri (1265–1321), the great Italian poet, author of the *Divine Comedy* (1308–1321).

good degree of skill in writing verses, but it is easy to read through their poems their personal history: any one acquainted with parties, can name every figure: this is Andrew, and that is Rachel. The sense thus remains prosaic. It is a caterpillar with wings, and not yet a butterfly. In the poet's mind, the fact has gone quite over into the new element of thought, and has lost all that is exuvial.[68] This generosity abides with Shakspeare. We say, from the truth and closeness of his pictures, that he knows the lesson by heart. Yet there is not a trace of egotism.

One more royal trait properly belongs to the Poet, I mean his cheerfulness, without which no man can be a poet, for beauty is his aim. He loves virtue, not for its obligation, but for its grace: he delights in the world, in man, in woman, for the lovely light which sparkles from them. Beauty, the spirit of joy and hilarity, he sheds over the universe. Epicurus[69] says that poetry hath such charms that a lover might forsake his mistress to partake of them. And the true bards have been noted for their firm and cheerful temper. Homer lies in sunshine, Chaucer is glad and erect; and Saadi says, "it was rumoured abroad that I was penitent, but what had I to do with repentance?"[70] Not less sovereign and cheerful,—much more sovereign and cheerful is the tone of Shakspeare. His name suggests joy and emancipation to the heart of men. If he should appear in any company of human souls, who would not march in his troop? He touches nothing that does not borrow health and longevity from his festal style.

\*   \*   \*

And now how stands the account of man with this bard and benefactor, when in solitude, shutting our ears to the reverberations of his fame, we seek to strike the balance? Solitude has austere lessons, it can teach us to spare both heroes and poets; and it weighs Shakspeare also, and finds him to share the halfness and imperfection of humanity.

Shakspeare, Homer, Dante,[71] Chaucer, saw the splendour of meaning that plays over the visible world; knew that a tree had another use than for apples, and corn another than for meal, and the ball of the earth than for tillage and roads: that these things bore a second and finer harvest to the mind, being emblems of its thoughts, and conveying in all their natural history a certain mute commentary on human life. Shakspeare employed them as colours to compose his picture. He rested in their beauty; and never took the step which seemed inevitable to such genius, namely, to explore the virtue which resides in these symbols, and imparts this power,—What is that which they themselves say? He converted the elements which waited on his command, into entertainments. He was master of the revels[72] to mankind. Is it not as if one should have, through majestic powers of science, the comets given into his hand or the planets and their moons, and should draw them from their orbits to glare with the municipal fireworks on a holiday night, and advertise in all towns *very superior pyrotechny this evening?*[73] Are the agents of nature and the power to understand them, worth no more than a street serenade or the breath of a cigar? One remembers again the trumpet text in the Koran,—"The Heavens and the earth and all that is between them, think ye we have created them in jest?" As long as the question is of talent and mental power, the world of men has not his equal to show. But when the question is to life, and its materials, and its auxiliaries, how does he profit me? What does it signify? It is but a Twelfth night, or Midsummer's night's dream, or a Winter evening's tale:[74] What signifies another picture more or less? The Egyptian verdict of the Shakspeare Societies comes to mind, that he was a jovial actor and manager. I cannot marry this fact to his verse: Other admirable men have led lives in some sort of keeping with their thought, but this man in wide contrast. Had he been less, had he reached only the common measure of great authors, of Bacon, Milton, Tasso, Cervantes,[75] we might leave the fact in the twilight of human fate; but that this man of men, he who gave to the science of mind a new and larger subject than had ever existed, and planted the standard of humanity some furlongs forward into Chaos,—that he should not be wise for himself,—it must even go into the world's history, that the best poet led an obscure and profane life, using his genius for the public amusement.

Well, other men, priest and prophet, Israelite, German, and Swede, beheld the same objects: they also saw through them that which was contained. And to what purpose? The beauty straightway vanished, they read commandments, all-excluding mountainous duty; an obligation, a sadness,

72    The master of the revels was the Elizabethan official charged with overseeing, and sometimes censoring, stage plays.

73    Emerson marked this passage in his copy of Coleridge's *Table Talk* (April 7, 1833): "In Shakespeare one sentence begets the next naturally; the meaning is all inwoven. He goes on kindling like a meteor through the dark atmosphere; yet, when the creation in its outline is once perfect, then he seems to rest from his labour, and to smile upon his work, and tell himself that it is very good": then, Coleridge concludes, we see Shakespeare "disporting himself in joyous triumph and vigorous fun."

74    Three Shakespeare plays: two early comedies and a late romance *(The Winter's Tale).*

75    Torquato Tasso (1544–1595), Italian epic and lyric poet; Miguel de Cervantes Saavedra (1547–1616), Spanish author of *Don Quixote* (1605, 1615)—a book probably known to Shakespeare.

76    The gloomy Emanuel Swedenborg (1688–1772), Swedish mystic, is the subject of another essay in *Representative Men*. Rather surprisingly, Emerson ends by noting Shakespeare's partial nature: he is a player (actor) and a poet, not a poet-priest who can harmonize the cheerful and the mournful. In each of *Representative Men*'s essays, Emerson underlines the limitations of the man he focuses on. In this case, the naming of Shakespeare's fault ("trifl[ing]") seems unconvincing. Shakespeare is more the definitive "poet-priest" than Emerson is willing to admit.

77    Emerson remarked in his Journal (1846), "Thoreau objected to my 'Shakspeare,' that the eulogy impoverished the race. Shakspeare ought to be praised, as the sun is, so that all shall be rejoiced" (J 9:365).

as of piled mountains fell on them, and life became ghastly, joyless, a pilgrim's progress, a probation, beleaguered round with doleful histories of Adam's fall and curse, behind us; with Doomsdays and purgatorial and penal fires before us; and the heart of the seer and the heart of the listener sunk in them.

It must be conceded that these are halfviews of halfmen. The world still wants its poet-priest, a reconciler who shall not trifle, with Shakspeare the player, nor shall grope in graves, with Swedenborg[76] the mourner, but who shall see, speak, and act, with equal inspiration. For knowledge will brighten the sunshine; right is more beautiful than private affection, and love is compatible with universal wisdom.[77]

Emerson's son Edward
and daughter Edith.

# First Visit to England

I have been twice in England. In 1833, on my return from a short tour in Sicily, Italy, and France, I crossed from Boulogne, and landed in London at the Tower stairs. It was a dark Sunday morning; there were few people in the streets; and I remember the pleasure of that first walk on English ground, with my companion, an American artist, from the Tower up through Cheapside and the Strand, to a house in Russell Square,[1] whither we had been recommended to good chambers. For the first time for many months we were forced to check the saucy[2] habit of travellers' criticism, as we could no longer speak aloud in the streets without being understood. The shop-signs spoke our language; our country names were on the door-plates; and the public and private buildings wore a more native and wonted front.

Like most young men at that time, I was much indebted to the men of Edinburgh, and of the Edinburgh Review,—to Jeffrey, Mackintosh, Hallam, and to Scott, Playfair, and De Quincey;[3] and my narrow and desultory reading had inspired the wish to see the faces of three or four writers,—Coleridge, Wordsworth, Landor, De Quincey, and the latest and strongest contributor to the critical journals, Carlyle;[4] and I suppose if I had sifted the reasons that led me to Europe, when I was ill and was advised to travel,[5] it was mainly the attraction of these persons. If Goethe[6] had been still living, I might have wandered into Germany also. Besides those I have named, (for Scott was dead,) there was not in Britain the man living whom I cared to be-

*This is Chapter 1 of Emerson's* English Traits *(1856). Emerson's second trip to England, in 1847–1848, formed the basis of the book, which began as a lecture series. At the time of his first journey, in 1833, Emerson was an unknown young man; he returned a celebrated American writer (during 1847–1848 he gave more than sixty public lectures in England and Scotland). Emerson was appalled by the poverty of England and its class divisions. He noted that "40 percent of the English people cannot write their names," as opposed to one-half of 1 percent in Massachusetts (J 10:251). He was ambivalent about England's cultural achievements as well as its proud domination of the world's industry: aspiring America, still incomplete, seemed to him preferable to an England that had grown self-satisfied and narrow. He was impressed by England's material grasp; but he noticed the partial character of such this-worldly common sense, its resistance to spiritual innovation. This first chapter expresses Emerson's disappointment when he met the English literary icons he admired. By implication, he announces a new American presence—Emerson himself—who can see through, and beyond, the old*

(continued)

*world. Yet Emerson values England's legacy, too, even as he separates England from America.*

1    Edward Emerson writes that the artist was William Wall (1801–1885), of New Bedford; Wall's copy of the Fates (Parcae) by Michelangelo Buonarroti (1475–1564) hung in Emerson's study. The Tower of London, near London Bridge, massive fortress used as a prison for centuries of British history; Cheapside, bustling London market street; the Strand, well-known street that was the home of many writers and intellectuals, and a center of nightlife; Russell Square, garden square in Bloomsbury, near the British Museum.

2    Impudent, pert.

3    The *Edinburgh Review* was an influential intellectual journal with Whiggish sympathies, read as avidly in America as in Scotland and England. The Scottish critic and jurist Francis Jeffrey (1773–1850) founded the *Review* in 1802. The journalist and lecturer James Mackintosh (1765–1832), the historian Henry Hallam (1777–1859), and the mathematician and geologist John Playfair (1748–1819) all wrote for the *Review*, as did (for a time) Sir Walter Scott, celebrated Scottish novelist (1771–1832). Thomas de Quincey (1785–1859), the remarkable essayist and critic, had no association with the *Review*.

4    Emerson first read the works of the Scottish writer Thomas Carlyle (1795–1881) in the late 1820s, when Carlyle was writing anonymously for the *Edinburgh Review*, and visited him on his first trip to Europe in 1833. On January 23, 1835, Emerson wrote to Benjamin Peter Hunt about Carlyle, "In Scotland eighteen months ago I sought & made the acquaintance of this gentleman . . . he seems to me one of the
*(continued)*

hold, unless it were the Duke of Wellington, whom I afterwards saw at Westminster Abbey, at the funeral of Wilberforce.[7] The young scholar fancies it happiness enough to live with people who can give an inside to the world; without reflecting that they are prisoners, too, of their own thought, and cannot apply themselves to yours. The conditions of literary success are almost destructive of the best social power, as they do not leave that frolic liberty which only can encounter a companion on the best terms. It is probable you left some obscure comrade at a tavern, or in the farms, with right mother-wit, and equality to life, when you crossed sea and land to play bopeep with celebrated scribes. I have, however, found writers superior to their books, and I cling to my first belief, that a strong head will dispose fast enough of these impediments, and give one the satisfaction of reality, the sense of having been met, and a larger horizon.

On looking over the diary of my journey in 1833, I find nothing to publish in my memoranda of visits to places.[8] But I have copied the few notes

Samuel Taylor Coleridge
(1772–1834).

Thomas Carlyle (1795–1881).

best, & since Coleridge is dead, I think, the best thinker of the age" (L 1:432). Samuel Taylor Coleridge (1772–1834), English poet and moral philosopher, was a strong influence on Emerson, as was Coleridge's friend the poet William Wordsworth (1770–1850). Walter Savage Landor (1775–1864) was an English poet and essayist.

5 Emerson had serious digestive troubles in late 1832, after his resignation from the Second Church.

6 J. W. von Goethe (1749–1832), the preeminent German man of letters, whom Emerson had been reading in 1832.

7 Arthur Wellesley, first Duke of Wellington (1769–1852), Anglo-Irish general and statesman, defeated Napoleon at the Battle of Waterloo; William Wilberforce (1759–1833) was a British abolitionist. Westminster Abbey contains the tombs of many famous Englishmen.

8 Emerson makes it clear that he is not writing a travel book (one of the most popular genres of the 1850s).

9 Greenough (1805–1852), the most renowned American sculptor of the day, lived in Florence for several decades. His Medora (1832) is a large, striking figure of a semi-nude, dead woman (a character from *The Corsair* [1814], a popular poem by George Gordon, Lord Byron [1788–1824]). In a letter to his brother Charles (May 16, 1833), Emerson said of Greenough's incomplete statue of Achilles, "it is colossal & it is good" (L 1:32).

I made of visits to persons, as they respect parties quite too good and too transparent to the whole world to make it needful to affect any prudery of suppression about a few hints of those bright personalities.

At Florence, chief among artists I found Horatio Greenough, the American sculptor.[9] His face was so handsome, and his person so well formed, that he might be pardoned, if, as was alleged, the face of his Medora, and the figure of a colossal Achilles in clay, were idealizations of his own. Greenough was a superior man, ardent and eloquent, and all his opinions had elevation and magnanimity. He believed that the Greeks had wrought in schools or fraternities,—the genius of the master imparting his design to his friends, and inflaming them with it, and when his strength was spent, a new hand, with equal heat, continued the work; and so by relays, until it was finished in

10    John Ruskin (1819–1900), the great British critic and art historian, championed Gothic, in contrast to Greenough's advocacy of the Neoclassical. But both espoused principles of organic harmony and function in art.

11    Emerson cites a letter that Greenough wrote to him on December 28, 1851.

12    Small village near Florence, with a spectacular view of the city. Antagonized by Emerson's account of their meeting in *English Traits*, Landor published in 1856 a thirty-two-page open letter in response.

13    The wrath of the Greek warrior Achilles is the subject of Homer's *Iliad* (ca. 9th century BCE).

14    Small flower with nodding white, pink, or purple petals.

15    On his trip to England Emerson also visited (and was disappointed by) Wordsworth, like Byron a major Romantic poet. Philip Massinger (1583–1640), like Francis Beaumont (ca. 1584–1616) and John Fletcher (1579–1625), was an English Renaissance dramatist.

16    An unconventional judgment. Philip II of Macedon (382–336 BCE) was the father of Alexander the Great (356–323 BCE).

17    Michelangelo and Giovanni were the most important sixteenth-century Italian sculptors; it was unusual to prefer Giovanni to Michelangelo.

18    Raphael Sanzio (1483–1520), brilliant Florentine painter and architect; Pietro Perugino (ca. 1446–1523), one of Raphael's influences, was from Umbria, near Tuscany.

every part with equal fire. This was necessary in so refractory a material as stone; and he thought art would never prosper until we left our shy jealous ways, and worked in society as they. All his thoughts breathed the same generosity. He was an accurate and a deep man. He was a votary of the Greeks, and impatient of Gothic art. His paper on Architecture, published in 1843, announced in advance the leading thoughts of Mr. Ruskin on the *morality* in architecture, notwithstanding the antagonism in their views of the history of art.[10] I have a private letter from him,—later, but respecting the same period,—in which he roughly sketches his own theory. "Here is my theory of structure: A scientific arrangement of spaces and forms to functions and to site; an emphasis of features proportioned to their *gradated* importance in function; color and ornament to be decided and arranged and varied by strictly organic laws, having a distinct reason for each decision; the entire and immediate banishment of all make-shift and make-believe."[11]

Greenough brought me, through a common friend, an invitation from Mr. Landor, who lived at San Domenica di Fiesole.[12] On the 15th May I dined with Mr. Landor. I found him noble and courteous, living in a cloud of pictures at his Villa Gherardesca, a fine house commanding a beautiful landscape. I had inferred from his books, or magnified from some anecdotes, an impression of Achillean wrath,—an untamable petulance.[13] I do not know whether the imputation were just or not, but certainly on this May day his courtesy veiled that haughty mind, and he was the most patient and gentle of hosts. He praised the beautiful cyclamen[14] which grows all about Florence; he admired Washington; talked of Wordsworth, Byron, Massinger, Beaumont and Fletcher.[15] To be sure, he is decided in his opinions, likes to surprise, and is well content to impress, if possible, his English whim upon the immutable past. No great man ever had a great son, if Philip and Alexander be not an exception; and Philip he calls the greater man.[16] In art, he loves the Greeks, and in sculpture, them only. He prefers the Venus to every thing else, and, after that, the head of Alexander, in the gallery here. He prefers John of Bologna to Michel Angelo;[17] in painting, Raffaelle; and shares the growing taste for Perugino and the early masters.[18] The Greek histories he thought the only good; and after them, Voltaire's.[19] I could not make him praise Mackintosh, nor my more recent friends; Montaigne very cordially,—and Charron also, which seemed undiscriminating. He thought Degerando indebted to "Lucas on Happiness" and "Lucas on Holiness"! He pestered me with Southey; but who is Southey?[20]

He invited me to breakfast on Friday. On Friday I did not fail to go, and this time with Greenough. He entertained us at once with reciting half a dozen hexameter lines of Julius Cæsar's!—from Donatus,[21] he said. He glorified Lord Chesterfield more than was necessary, and undervalued Burke, and undervalued Socrates;[22] designated as three of the greatest of men, Washington, Phocion, and Timoleon;[23] much as our pomologists, in their lists, select the three or the six best pears "for a small orchard;" and did not even omit to remark the similar termination of their names. "A great man," he said, "should make great sacrifices, and kill his hundred oxen, without knowing

Walter Savage Landor (1775–1864).

19    Voltaire (François-Marie Arouet; 1694–1778), French philosopher and critic, was exiled to England in 1726–1729; in 1723 he published an epic poem on King Henri IV of France (1553–1610) and in 1731, a prose history of Charles XII of Sweden (1682–1718).

20    Michel de Montaigne (1533–1592), the great French essayist. Pierre Charron (1541–1603), a friend of Montaigne, was a more minor figure; he wrote about religious quarrels. (Landor in his open letter denied having compared the two.) Joseph Marie de Gérando (1772–1842), French political philosopher; Richard Lucas (1648–1715), English writer of devotional works. Robert Southey (1774–1843), English poet laureate and close friend of Landor.

21    Aelius Donatus (4th century) was the author of the *Ars grammatica*, a book on rhetoric that contained examples from many authors, including Julius Caesar (100–44 BCE), the general, historian, and dictator of Rome.

22    Philip Stanhope, the fourth Earl of Chesterfield (1694–1773), British statesman, author of *Letters to His Son* (1774), and critic of King George II (1683–1760); Edmund Burke (1729–1797), Anglo-Irish author and politician; Socrates (ca. 469–399 BCE), Athenian philosopher condemned by the state. All three were contentious figures, and fierce in debate.

23    Emerson extravagantly admired Phocion (ca. 402–ca. 318 BCE), the iconoclastic Athenian general and statesman; Timoleon (ca. 411–337 BCE), like Phocion and George Washington a great military leader, fought for Greece against Carthage. A pomologist was an expert on fruit (Emerson was an enthusiastic cultivator of fruit trees.)

William Wordsworth (1770–1850).

whether they would be consumed by gods and heroes, or whether the flies would eat them." I had visited Professor Amici,[24] who had shown me his microscopes, magnifying (it was said) two thousand diameters; and I spoke of the uses to which they were applied. Landor despised entomology, yet, in the same breath, said, "the sublime was in a grain of dust." I suppose I teased him about recent writers, but he professed never to have heard of Herschel,[25] *not even by name.* One room was full of pictures, which he likes to show, especially one piece, standing before which, he said "he would give fifty guineas to the man that would swear it was a Domenichino."[26] I was more curious to see his library, but Mr. H—, one of the guests,[27] told me that Mr. Landor gives away his books, and has never more than a dozen at a time in his house.

Mr. Landor carries to its height the love of freak[28] which the English delight to indulge, as if to signalize their commanding freedom. He has a wonderful brain, despotic, violent, and inexhaustible, meant for a soldier, by what chance converted to letters, in which there is not a style nor a tint not known to him, yet with an English appetite for action and heroes. The thing done avails, and not what is said about it. An original sentence, a step forward, is worth more than all the censures. Landor is strangely undervalued in England; usually ignored; and sometimes savagely attacked in the Reviews. The criticism may be right, or wrong, and is quickly forgotten; but year after year the scholar must still go back to Landor for a multitude of elegant sentences—for wisdom, wit, and indignation that are unforgetable.

\* \* \*

From London, on the 5th August, I went to Highgate, and wrote a note to Mr. Coleridge,[29] requesting leave to pay my respects to him. It was near noon. Mr. Coleridge sent a verbal message, that he was in bed, but if I would call after one o'clock, he would see me. I returned at one, and he appeared, a short, thick old man, with bright blue eyes and fine clear complexion, leaning on his cane. He took snuff freely, which presently soiled his cravat and neat black suit. He asked whether I knew Allston,[30] and spoke warmly of his merits and doings when he knew him in Rome; what a master of the Titianesque[31] he was, &c., &c. He spoke of Dr. Channing.[32] It was an unspeak-

24   Giovanni Battista Amici (1786–1863), Italian engineer of microscopes and telescopes.

25   John Herschel (1792–1871), British scientist who sought unifying explanations for natural phenomena; his 1831 book on the philosophy of nature influenced Emerson.

26   Domenico Zampieri, Italian baroque painter (1581–1641).

27   Julius Charles Hare (1795–1855), English theologian.

28   Capricious notion, sudden fancy.

29   Coleridge played a crucial role in Emerson's intellectual development in the 1820s and 1830s. In a (failed) effort to overcome his addiction to opium, Coleridge moved to Highgate, in north London, in 1817, and remained there for the rest of his life.

30   The painter Washington Allston (1779–1843).

31   After the Venetian painter Titian (Tiziano Vecelli; ca. 1488–1576).

32   William Ellery Channing (1780–1842) was a central figure of Emerson's day, founder of the Unitarian movement and influential preacher. His nephews, William Ellery Channing (1817–1901) and William Henry Channing (1810–1884), the subject of Emerson's "Channing Ode," were important Transcendentalists; Ellery became close friends with Emerson in the early 1850s.

33   Bishop Daniel Waterland (1683–1740) wrote *A Vindication of Christ's Divinity* (1719). Coleridge's *Aids to Reflection* (1825), which Emerson read in 1829, was a crucial influence on him, despite the book's denunciation of Unitarianism. (Coleridge in his maturity was a Trinitarian, whereas Unitarians deny the doctrine of the Trinity, and claim that God has only one, rather than three, persons.)

34   Joseph Priestley (1733–1804), dissenting clergyman and scientist, was a founder of English Unitarianism; he emigrated to Philadelphia in 1794. Philo Judaeus of Alexandria (ca. 20 BCE–50 CE), the Hellenistic Jewish philosopher who may have influenced the followers of Jesus, stated in a commentary on Genesis 18:2 that God is accompanied by two powers (represented by angels), the creative and the royal. Philo was therefore later thought by Christians to presage the idea of the Trinity. Evidence of Paul's trinitarian inclination is customarily, if somewhat implausibly, sought in the sentence from II Corinthians 13:14: "The grace of the Lord Jesus Christ, and the love of God, and the communion of the Holy Ghost be with you all."

35   As an undergraduate at Cambridge, Coleridge supported Unitarianism, and preached in Unitarian chapels in the 1790s.

36   "Threeism" and "fourism" (reference to the number of aspects or persons contained by the deity).

37   During much of Christian history, heretics were burned at the stake (a fagot is a bundle of sticks used for kindling fire).

able misfortune that he should have turned out a Unitarian after all. On this, he burst into a declamation on the folly and ignorance of Unitarianism,—its high unreasonableness; and taking up Bishop Waterland's book, which lay on the table, he read with vehemence two or three pages written by himself in the fly-leaves,—passages, too, which, I believe, are printed in the "Aids to Reflection."[33] When he stopped to take breath, I interposed, that, "whilst I highly valued all his explanations, I was bound to tell him that I was born and bred a Unitarian." "Yes," he said, "I supposed so;" and continued as before. 'It was a wonder, that after so many ages of unquestioning acquiescence in the doctrine of St. Paul,—the doctrine of the Trinity, which was also, according to Philo Judæus, the doctrine of the Jews before Christ,—this handful of Priestleians[34] should take on themselves to deny it, &c., &c. He was very sorry that Dr. Channing,—a man to whom he looked up,—no, to say that he looked *up* to him would be to speak falsely; but a man whom he looked *at* with so much interest,—should embrace such views. When he saw Dr. Channing, he had hinted to him that he was afraid he loved Christianity for what was lovely and excellent,—he loved the good in it, and not the true; and I tell you, sir, that I have known ten persons who loved the good, for one person who loved the true; but it is a far greater virtue to love the true for itself alone, than to love the good for itself alone. He (Coleridge) knew all about Unitarianism perfectly well, because he had once been a Unitarian, and knew what quackery it was. He had been called "the rising star of Unitarianism."'[35] He went on defining, or rather refining: 'The Trinitarian doctrine was realism; the idea of God was not essential, but super-essential; talked of *trinism* and *tetrakism*,[36] and much more, of which I only caught this, that the will was that by which a person is a person; because, if one should push me in the street, and so I should force the man next me into the kennel, I should at once exclaim, "I did not do it, sir," meaning it was not my will.' And this also, 'that if you should insist on your faith here in England, and I on mine, mine would be the hotter side of the fagot.'[37]

I took advantage of a pause to say, that he had many readers of all religious opinions in America, and I proceeded to inquire if the "extract" from the Independent's pamphlet, in the third volume of the Friend, were a veritable quotation. He replied, that it was really taken from a pamphlet in his possession, entitled "A Protest of one of the Independents," or something to that effect. I told him how excellent I thought it, and how much I wished to see the entire work. "Yes," he said, "the man was a chaos of truths, but lacked the knowledge that God was a God of order. Yet the passage would no doubt strike you more in the quotation than in the original, for I have filtered it."[38]

When I rose to go, he said, "I do not know whether you care about poetry, but I will repeat some verses I lately made on my baptismal anniversary," and he recited with strong emphasis, standing, ten or twelve lines, beginning,

"Born unto God in Christ—"[39]

He inquired where I had been travelling; and on learning that I had been in Malta and Sicily,[40] he compared one island with the other, 'repeating what he had said to the Bishop of London when he returned from that country, that Sicily was an excellent school of political economy; for, in any town there, it only needed to ask what the government enacted, and reverse that to know what ought to be done; it was the most felicitously opposite legislation to any thing good and wise. There were only three things which the government had brought into that garden of delights, namely, itch, pox,[41] and famine. Whereas, in Malta, the force of law and mind was seen, in making that barren rock of semi-Saracen[42] inhabitants the seat of population and plenty.' Going out, he showed me in the next apartment a picture of Allston's,[43] and told me 'that Montague, a picture-dealer, once came to see him, and, glancing towards this, said, "Well, you have got a picture!" thinking it the work of an old master; afterwards, Montague, still talking with his back to the canvas, put up his hand and touched it, and exclaimed, "By Heaven! this picture is not ten years old:"—so delicate and skilful was that man's touch.'

I was in his company for about an hour, but find it impossible to recall the largest part of his discourse, which was often like so many printed paragraphs in his book,—perhaps the same,—so readily did he fall into certain commonplaces. As I might have foreseen, the visit was rather a spectacle

38    Coleridge reprinted a section of a tract by the Puritan William Sedgwick (ca. 1610–ca. 1669) in *The Friend*, vol. 3 (1818).

39    Variant of the first line of Coleridge's poem "My Baptismal Birthday" (1834): "God's child in Christ adopted,—Christ my all—" Coleridge exclaims later in the poem: "In Christ I live! In Christ I draw the breath / Of the true life! . . ."

40    These were Emerson's first stops on his trip to Europe.

41    Pox: syphilis. The itch was a contagious skin eruption, also known as scabies.

42    Half-Muslim. Coleridge had lived in Malta in 1804 and 1805.

43    Allston's copy (1817) of a section of Titian's *Adoration of the Magi*.

44    Estate of Carlyle's wife, Jane Welsh (1801–1866), in southern Scotland. Emerson arrived there on August 25, 1833. Unlike Wordsworth and Coleridge, Carlyle was not an old man when Emerson met him in 1833, but a vital thirty-seven-year-old prose prophet whose will to find creative truth inspired Emerson. During his 1847–1848 visit, Emerson had been disappointed by the later Carlyle's misanthropy and bitterness. "He talks like a very unhappy man," Emerson wrote of Carlyle on that trip (October 1847?), "profoundly solitary, displeased & hindered by all men & things about him, & plainly biding his time & meditating how to undermine & explode the whole world of nonsense that torments him" (J 10:541).

45    Household gods and spirits of the dead (Roman).

46    *Blackwood's* and *Fraser's* were Tory magazines, rivals to the Whiggish *Edinburgh Review*.

47    Flexible, resilient.

48    Nero (37–68), the flamboyant Roman emperor, committed suicide after he was overthrown; among his dying words were the ones Emerson gives here in Latin: "What an artist perishes!"

than a conversation, of no use beyond the satisfaction of my curiosity. He was old and preoccupied, and could not bend to a new companion and think with him.

\* \* \*

From Edinburgh I went to the Highlands. On my return, I came from Glasgow to Dumfries, and being intent on delivering a letter which I had brought from Rome, inquired for Craigenputtock.[44] It was a farm in Nithsdale, in the parish of Dunscore, sixteen miles distant. No public coach passed near it, so I took a private carriage from the inn. I found the house amid desolate heathery hills, where the lonely scholar nourished his mighty heart. Carlyle was a man from his youth, an author who did not need to hide from his readers, and as absolute a man of the world, unknown and exiled on that hill-farm, as if holding on his own terms what is best in London. He was tall and gaunt, with a cliff-like brow, self-possessed, and holding his extraordinary powers of conversation in easy command; clinging to his northern accent with evident relish; full of lively anecdote, and with a streaming humor, which floated every thing he looked upon. His talk playfully exalting the familiar objects, put the companion at once into an acquaintance with his Lars and Lemurs,[45] and it was very pleasant to learn what was predestined to be a pretty mythology. Few were the objects and lonely the man, "not a person to speak to within sixteen miles except the minister of Dunscore;" so that books inevitably made his topics.

He had names of his own for all the matters familiar to his discourse. "Blackwood's" was the "sand magazine;" "Fraser's" nearer approach to possibility of life was the "mud magazine;"[46] a piece of road near by that marked some failed enterprise was the "grave of the last sixpence." When too much praise of any genius annoyed him, he professed hugely to admire the talent shown by his pig. He had spent much time and contrivance in confining the poor beast to one enclosure in his pen, but pig, by great strokes of judgment, had found out how to let a board down, and had foiled him. For all that, he still thought man the most plastic[47] little fellow in the planet, and he liked Nero's death, *"Qualis artifex pereo!"* better than most history.[48] He worships a man that will manifest any truth to him. At one time he had inquired and read a good deal about America. Landor's principle was mere rebellion, and *that* he feared was the American principle. The best thing he knew of that country was, that in it a man can have meat for his labor. He had read in Stewart's book, that when he inquired in a New York hotel for the Boots, he had been shown across the street and had found Mungo in his own house dining on roast turkey.[49]

We talked of books. Plato he does not read, and he disparaged Socrates; and, when pressed, persisted in making Mirabeau a hero. Gibbon[50] he called the splendid bridge from the old world to the new. His own reading had been multifarious. Tristram Shandy was one of his first books after Robinson Crusoe, and Robertson's America an early favorite. Rousseau's Confessions[51] had discovered to him that he was not a dunce; and it was now ten years since he had learned German, by the advice of a man who told him he would find in that language what he wanted.[52]

He took despairing or satirical views of literature at this moment; recounted the incredible sums paid in one year by the great booksellers for puffing. Hence it comes that no newspaper is trusted now, no books are bought, and the booksellers are on the eve of bankruptcy.

He still returned to English pauperism, the crowded country, the selfish abdication by public men of all that public persons should perform. 'Government should direct poor men what to do. Poor Irish folk come wandering over these moors. My dame makes it a rule to give to every son of Adam bread to eat, and supplies his wants to the next house. But here are thousands of acres which might give them all meat, and nobody to bid these poor Irish go to the moor and till it. They burned the stacks,[53] and so found a way to force the rich people to attend to them.'

We went out to walk over long hills, and looked at Criffel,[54] then without his cap, and down into Wordsworth's country. There we sat down, and talked of the immortality of the soul. It was not Carlyle's fault that we talked on that topic, for he had the natural disinclination of every nimble spirit to bruise itself against walls, and did not like to place himself where no step can be taken. But he was honest and true, and cognizant of the subtile links that bind ages together, and saw how every event affects all the future. 'Christ died on the tree: that built Dunscore kirk yonder: that brought you and me together. Time has only a relative existence.'

49   A Boots is a boot-cleaner; Mungo, slang term for an African-American. James Stuart in *Three Years in North America* (1833) recalled entering a shoe-black's apartment and finding "him and his wife, both persons of colour," dining on "one of the fattest roast geese I have ever seen, with potatoes, and apple pie."

50   Plato (429–347 BCE), Athenian philosopher and chronicler of Socrates; Honoré, Comte de Mirabeau (1749–1791), statesman who took a moderate stance during the French Revolution; Edward Gibbon (1737–1794), provocative British historian of Rome.

51   *Tristram Shandy* (1759–1769), extravagant comic novel by the Anglo-Irish writer Laurence Sterne (1713–1768); *Robinson Crusoe* (1719), tale of a castaway's life by the English author Daniel Defoe (ca. 1660–1731); *Confessions* (1782), immensely popular, and notorious, autobiography by the French philosopher Jean-Jacques Rousseau (1712–1778).

52   Carlyle was an ardent reader, and advocate, of German philosophy and literature.

53   "Rick burning" was the workers' protest against unemployment caused by the use of industrial machines for spinning.

54   Mountain near Carlyle's home (close to Wordsworth's birthplace, Cockermouth, in West Cumberland, England).

55    Emerson's Journal entry from his initial visit to Carlyle (August 1833) reads, "London. Heart of the world. Wonderful only from the mass of human beings. Muffins" (J 4:220). Later on in *English Traits*, Emerson noted that "the Englishman . . . is materialist, economical, mercantile. He must be treated with sincerity and reality, with muffins, and not the promise of muffins."

56    Possibly the Scottish clergyman Edward Irving (1792–1834) or the British author and political economist John Stuart Mill (1806–1873).

57    House in the Lake District, home to Wordsworth from 1813 until his death.

58    Emerson in a June 1837 lecture, "Address on Education," asserted, "It is not, believe me, the chief end of man that he should make a fortune and beget children whose end is likewise to make a fortune, but it is, in few words, that he should explore himself" (EL 2:199).

He was already turning his eyes towards London with a scholar's appreciation. London is the heart of the world, he said, wonderful only from the mass of human beings. He liked the huge machine. Each keeps its own round. The baker's boy brings muffins to the window at a fixed hour every day, and that is all the Londoner knows or wishes to know on the subject.[55] But it turned out good men. He named certain individuals, especially one man of letters, his friend, the best mind he knew, whom London had well served.[56]

*  *  *

On the 28th August, I went to Rydal Mount,[57] to pay my respects to Mr. Wordsworth. His daughters called in their father, a plain, elderly, white-haired man, not prepossessing, and disfigured by green goggles. He sat down, and talked with great simplicity. He had just returned from a journey. His health was good, but he had broken a tooth by a fall, when walking with two lawyers, and had said, that he was glad it did not happen forty years ago; whereupon they had praised his philosophy.

He had much to say of America, the more that it gave occasion for his favorite topic,—that society is being enlightened by a superficial tuition, out of all proportion to its being restrained by moral culture. Schools do no good. Tuition is not education. He thinks more of the education of circumstances than of tuition. 'Tis not question whether there are offences of which the law takes cognizance, but whether there are offences of which the law does not take cognizance. Sin is what he fears, and how society is to escape without gravest mischiefs from this source—? He has even said, what seemed a paradox, that they needed a civil war in America, to teach the necessity of knitting the social ties stronger. 'There may be,' he said, 'in America some vulgarity in manner, but that's not important. That comes of the pioneer state of things. But I fear they are too much given to the making of money;[58] and secondly, to politics; that they make political distinction the end, and not the means. And I fear they lack a class of men of leisure,—in short, of gentlemen,—to give a tone of honor to the community. I am told that things are boasted of in the second class of society there, which, in England,—God knows, are done in England every day,—but would never be spoken of. In America I wish to know not how many churches or schools, but what newspapers? My friend, Colonel Hamilton, at the foot of the hill, who was a year in America, assures me that the newspapers are atrocious, and accuse members of Congress of stealing spoons!'[59] He was against taking off the tax on newspapers in England, which the reformers represent as a tax upon knowledge,[60] for this reason, that they would be inundated with base prints. He said, he talked on political aspects, for he wished to impress on me and all good Americans to cultivate the moral, the conservative, &c., &c., and never to call into action the physical strength of the people, as had just now been done in England in the Reform Bill,—a thing prophesied by Delolme.[61] He alluded once or twice to his conversation with Dr. Channing, who had recently visited him, (laying his hand on a particular chair in which the Doctor had sat.)[62]

The conversation turned on books. Lucretius he esteems a far higher poet than Virgil:[63] not in his system, which is nothing, but in his power of illustration. Faith is necessary to explain any thing, and to reconcile the foreknowledge of God with human evil. Of Cousin, (whose lectures we had all been reading in Boston,) he knew only the name.[64]

I inquired if he had read Carlyle's critical articles and translations. He said, he thought him sometimes insane. He proceeded to abuse Goethe's Wilhelm Meister heartily. It was full of all manner of fornication. It was like the crossing of flies in the air. He had never gone farther than the first part; so disgusted was he that he threw the book across the room.[65] I deprecated this wrath, and said what I could for the better parts of the book; and he courteously promised to look at it again. Carlyle, he said, wrote most obscurely. He was clever and deep, but he defied the sympathies of every body. Even Mr. Coleridge wrote more clearly, though he had always wished Coleridge would write more to be understood. He led me out into his garden, and showed me the gravel walk in which thousands of his lines were composed. His eyes are much inflamed. This is no loss, except for reading, because he never writes prose, and of poetry he carries even hundreds of lines in his head before writing them. He had just returned from a visit to Staffa, and within three days had made three sonnets on Fingal's Cave,[66] and

59    Captain (not Colonel) Thomas Hamilton (1780–1842) wrote *Men and Manners in America* (1833).

60    In 1834, the year after Wordsworth's remarks, the tax duty on newspapers was reduced from four pence to one penny.

61    The Reform Bill of 1832 vastly increased the size of the British electorate; even after it passed, though, only one in five adult males was able to vote. Jean Louis Delolme (1740–1806), a Swiss jurist, wrote on the English constitution.

62    William Ellery Channing visited Wordsworth in 1822, over ten years earlier.

63    Two Roman epic poets: Lucretius (ca. 98–55 BCE), author of *De Rerum Natura (On the Nature of Things)*; Virgil (70–19 BCE), author of the *Aeneid* (26–19 BCE). It was unusual to rank Lucretius higher than Virgil.

64    Victor Cousin (1792–1867), French historian of philosophy, renowned in his day (and especially in Emerson's circle).

65    Carlyle translated Goethe's novel *Wilhelm Meister's Apprenticeship* (1796) in 1824 and parts of the sequel, *Wilhelm Meister's Travels* (1821–1829), in 1827. In conversation with the journalist Henry Crabb Robinson (1775–1867), Wordsworth deplored what he considered Carlyle's *"inhumanity,"* his "scorn and irony."

66    Fingal's Cave, which produces strange, haunting echoes, is on the remote island of Staffa, in the Scottish Hebrides.

67    Indiscriminate, casual. Here is the third
sonnet that Emerson heard Wordsworth recite
("Flowers on the Top of the Pillar at the Entrance of the Cave"):

Hope smiled when your nativity was cast,
Children of Summer! Ye fresh flowers that
    brave
What summer here escapes not, the fierce
    wave,
And whole artillery of the western blast,
Battering the Temple's front, its long-drawn
    nave
Smiting, as if each moment were their last.
But ye, bright flowers, on frieze and
    architrave
Survive, and once again the Pile stands fast,
Calm as the Universe, from specular Towers
Of heaven contemplated by Spirits pure –
Suns and their systems, diverse yet sustained
In symmetry, and fashioned to endure,
Unhurt, the assault of time with all his
    hours,
As the supreme Artificer ordained.

68    "Tintern Abbey" (1798) is widely read
today; *The Excursion* (1814), popular in Wordsworth's lifetime, is less familiar.

69    The Greek phrase is the description by
the historian Thucydides (ca. 460–ca. 400 BCE)
of his *History of the Peloponnesian War*, near the
beginning of that book.

70    Minor poems by Wordsworth.

71    Two famed British scientists: Isaac Newton (1643–1727) produced revolutionary theories of gravitation and motion; John Dalton
(1766–1844) pioneered atomic theory. Wordsworth's skylark carries the poet's spirit into the
clouds, defying gravity.

was composing a fourth, when he was called in to see me. He said, "If you are interested in my verses, perhaps you will like to hear these lines." I gladly assented; and he recollected himself for a few moments, and then stood forth and repeated, one after the other, the three entire sonnets with great anima-tion. I fancied the second and third more beautiful than his poems are wont to be. The third is addressed to the flowers, which, he said, especially the oxeye daisy, are very abundant on the top of the rock. The second alludes to the name of the cave, which is "Cave of Music;" the first to the circumstance of its being visited by the promiscuous[67] company of the steamboat.

   This recitation was so unlooked for and surprising,—he, the old Words-worth, standing apart, and reciting to me in a garden-walk, like a schoolboy declaiming,—that I at first was near to laugh; but recollecting myself, that I had come thus far to see a poet, and he was chanting poems to me, I saw that he was right and I was wrong, and gladly gave myself up to hear. I told him how much the few printed extracts had quickened the desire to possess his unpublished poems. He replied, he never was in haste to publish; partly, be-cause he corrected a good deal, and every alteration is ungraciously received after printing; but what he had written would be printed, whether he lived or died. I said, "Tintern Abbey" appeared to be the favorite poem with the public, but more contemplative readers preferred the first books of the "Ex-cursion," and the Sonnets.[68] He said, "Yes, they are better." He preferred such of his poems as touched the affections, to any others; for whatever is didactic,—what theories of society, and so on,—might perish quickly; but whatever combined a truth with an affection was *ktêma es aei*, good to-day and good forever.[69] He cited the sonnet "On the feelings of a high-minded Spaniard," which he preferred to any other, (I so understood him,) and the "Two Voices;" and quoted, with evident pleasure, the verses addressed "To the Skylark."[70] In this connection, he said of the Newtonian theory, that it might yet be superseded and forgotten; and Dalton's atomic theory.[71]

   When I prepared to depart, he said he wished to show me what a com-mon person in England could do, and he led me into the enclosure of his clerk, a young man,[72] to whom he had given this slip of ground, which was laid out, or its natural capabilities shown, with much taste. He then said he would show me a better way towards the inn; and he walked a good part of a mile, talking, and ever and anon stopping short to impress the word or the verse, and finally parted from me with great kindness, and returned across the fields.

Wordsworth honored himself by his simple adherence to truth, and was very willing not to shine;[73] but he surprised by the hard limits of his thought. To judge from a single conversation, he made the impression of a narrow and very English mind; of one who paid for his rare elevation by general tameness and conformity. Off his own beat, his opinions were of no value. It is not very rare to find persons loving sympathy and ease, who expiate their departure from the common, in one direction, by their conformity in every other.[74]

72    John Carter (d. 1856), Wordsworth's secretary and gardener.

73    By contrast, a later chapter in *English Traits* emphasizes Wordsworth's self-conceit. Emerson recounts a story he heard about Wordsworth: when an acquaintance showed him Milton's pocket watch, Wordsworth responded by silently holding up his own watch.

74    In his Journal on September 1, 1833, Emerson summed up his impression of Landor, Coleridge, Carlyle, and Wordsworth: "they would be remembered as sensible well read earnest men—not more. Especially are they all deficient all these four—in different degrees but all deficient—in insight into religious truth." He added, "These men make you feel that fame is a conventional thing & that man is a sadly 'limitary' spirit. You speak to them as to children or persons of inferior capacity whom it is necessary to humor; adapting our tone & remarks to their known prejudices & not to our knowledge of the truth" (J 4:79).

# Stonehenge

*Stonehenge is an enigmatic prehistoric circle of ponderous stones on Salisbury Plain, in southern England. "Henge" means "hanging," in reference to the lintel-like horizontal slabs of the Stonehenge monument. Our understanding of Stonehenge's purpose has advanced far beyond that of Emerson's day. We now know that the site was a burial ground, perhaps for a single prominent family. The stones, erected between about 2500 and 1600 BCE, might be a monument to the dead, signposts for a sacred site of healing, or both.*

1    Thomas Carlyle (1795–1881), the iconoclastic Scottish author whom Emerson first visited on his trip to England and Scotland in 1833. In July 1848, just before the end of Emerson's visit to England, he and Carlyle made the journey to Stonehenge and nearby places described in this chapter (XVI) of *English Traits* (1856).

2    Stonehenge is located two miles west of Amesbury on Salisbury Plain, County Wiltshire, in southwest England.

3    County that adjoins Wiltshire.

It had been agreed between my friend Mr. C.[1] and me, that before I left England, we should make an excursion together to Stonehenge, which neither of us had seen; and the project pleased my fancy with the double attraction of the monument and the companion. It seemed a bringing together of extreme points, to visit the oldest religious monument in Britain, in company with her latest thinker, and one whose influence may be traced in every contemporary book. I was glad to sum up a little my experiences, and to exchange a few reasonable words on the aspects of England, with a man on whose genius I set a very high value, and who had as much penetration, and as severe a theory of duty, as any person in it. On Friday, 7th July, we took the South Western Railway through Hampshire to Salisbury, where we found a carriage to convey us to Amesbury.[2] The fine weather and my friend's local knowledge of Hampshire,[3] in which he is wont to spend a part of every summer, made the way short. There was much to say, too, of the travelling Americans, and their usual objects in London. I thought it natural, that they should give some time to works of art collected here, which they cannot find at home, and a little to scientific clubs and museums, which, at this moment, make London very attractive. But my philosopher was not contented. Art and 'high art' is a favorite target for his wit. "Yes, *Kunst* is a great delusion, and Goethe and Schiller wasted a great deal of good time on it:"—and he thinks he discovers that old Goethe found this out, and, in his later writings, changed his tone.[4] As soon as men begin to talk of art, architecture, and antiquities, nothing good comes of it. He wishes to go through the British Museum[5] in silence, and thinks a sincere man will see something, and say nothing. In these days, he thought, it would become an architect to consult only the grim necessity, and say, 'I can build you a coffin for such dead persons as you are, and for such dead purposes as you have, but you shall have no ornament.' For the science, he had, if possible, even less tolerance, and compared the savans of Somerset House[6] to the boy who asked Confucius "how many stars in the sky?" Confucius replied, "he minded things near him:" then said the boy, "how many hairs are there in your eyebrows?" Confucius said, "he didn't know and didn't care."[7]

Still speaking of the Americans, C. complained that they dislike the coldness and exclusiveness of the English, and run away to France, and go with their countrymen, and are amused, instead of manfully staying in London, and confronting Englishmen, and acquiring their culture, who really have much to teach them.

I told C. that I was easily dazzled, and was accustomed to concede readily all that an Englishman would ask; I saw everywhere in the country proofs of sense and spirit, and success of every sort: I like the people: they are as good as they are handsome; they have everything, and can do everything: but meantime, I surely know, that, as soon as I return to Massachusetts, I shall lapse at once into the feeling, which the geography of America inevitably inspires, that we play the game with immense advantage; that there and not here is the seat and centre of the British race; and that no skill or activity can long compete with the prodigious natural advantages of that country, in the hands of the same race; and that England, an old and exhausted island, must one day be contented, like other parents, to be strong only in her children. But this was a proposition which no Englishman of whatever condition can easily entertain.

We left the train at Salisbury, and took a carriage to Amesbury, passing by Old Sarum, a bare, treeless hill, once containing the town which sent two members to Parliament,[8]—now, not a hut;—and, arriving at Amesbury, stopped at the George Inn. After dinner, we walked to Salisbury Plain. On the broad downs, under the gray sky, not a house was visible, nothing but Stonehenge, which looked like a group of brown dwarfs in the wide expanse,

4    *Kunst* means art in German. J. W. von Goethe (1749–1832) and Friedrich Schiller (1759–1805), widely idolized German authors of Emerson's era. In a letter to his aunt, Mary Moody Emerson, Emerson describes Goethe as "the restorer of Faith & Love after the desolations of Hume & the French" (August 19, 1832, L 1:354; referring to the skeptical Scottish philosopher David Hume, 1711–1776).

5    Vast museum of history and culture in Bloomsbury, London.

6    Somerset House, in central London, was in 1848 the site of the Royal Society, with its brilliant scientists and thinkers. Savans, or savants, are wise men.

7    Confucius (551–479 BCE), Chinese sage and philosopher of society. Emerson attributed this anecdote to Carlyle (J 10:311), who probably remembered it from a German translation of Confucius's writings. Prominent eyebrows were a sign of long life in Confucian belief.

8    Old Sarum, site of an ancient settlement in Salisbury, was before the Reform Act of 1832 one of the "rotten boroughs" whose political representation was out of proportion to their small population. It had three houses and seven voters, but, since the time of King Edward II (1284–ca. 1327), had sent two representatives to Parliament.

9    Haystacks. Bosses are raised areas or swellings.

10    Traveling salesman.

11    William Stukeley (1687–1765), Emerson's source for much of his information about Stonehenge, argued that the innermost circle of stones was egg-shaped because "the ancients thought the world of an egg-like shape."

12    The stone laid across the tops of several Stonehenge monoliths, akin to the lintel of a door.

13    The Stonehenge barrows are burial mounds. In 1822 the Scottish writer Charles Maclaren (1782–1866) suggested that Hissarlik (near the Hellespont, the narrow strait that separates Greece and Turkey) was the site of ancient Troy. Homer's *Iliad* (ca. 9th century BCE) recounts the siege of the city and the struggle of the Greek warrior Achilles. The site was subsequently excavated by the Englishman Frank Calvert (1828–1908) and, in the 1870s and 1880s, the German amateur archaeologist Heinrich Schliemann (1822–1890).

14    Abury, or Avebury, is another neolithic site near Stonehenge in County Wiltshire, north of Salisbury Plain. The quoted phrase comes from *The Mythology and Rites of the British Druids* (1809) by the English scholar Edward Davies (1756–1831). Davies, like Emerson's other sources, ascribed the building of Stonehenge to the Druids, ancient Celtic priests described by the Roman historians. In fact, the monument was constructed long before the Druids appeared.

15    The sarsens, hard-grained sandstone, were probably brought from the Marlborough Downs, fifteen miles north of Stonehenge. The

*(continued)*

—Stonehenge and the barrows,—which rose like green bosses about the plain, and a few hayricks.[9] On the top of a mountain, the old temple would not be more impressive. Far and wide a few shepherds with their flocks sprinkled the plain, and a bagman[10] drove along the road. It looked as if the wide margin given in this crowded isle to this primeval temple were accorded by the veneration of the British race to the old egg out of which all their ecclesiastical structures and history had proceeded.[11] Stonehenge is a circular colonnade with a diameter of a hundred feet, and enclosing a second and a third colonnade within. We walked round the stones, and clambered over them, to wont ourselves with their strange aspect and groupings, and found a nook sheltered from the wind among them, where C. lighted his cigar. It was pleasant to see, that, just this simplest of all simple structures,—two upright stones and a lintel[12] laid across,—had long outstood all later churches, and all history, and were like what is most permanent on the face of the planet: these, and the barrows,—mere mounds, (of which there are a hundred and sixty within a circle of three miles about Stonehenge,) like the same mound on the plain of Troy, which still makes good to the passing mariner on Hellespont, the vaunt of Homer and the fame of Achilles.[13] Within the enclosure, grow buttercups, nettles, and, all around, wild thyme, daisy, meadowsweet, goldenrod, thistle, and the carpeting grass. Over us, larks were soaring and singing,—as my friend said, "the larks which were hatched last year, and the wind which was hatched many thousand years ago." We counted and measured by paces the biggest stones, and soon knew as much as any man can suddenly know of the inscrutable temple. There are ninety-four stones, and there were once probably one hundred and sixty. The temple is circular, and uncovered, and the situation fixed astronomically,—the grand entrances here, and at Abury, being placed exactly northeast, "as all the gates of the old cavern temples are."[14] How came the stones here? for these *sarsens* or Druidical sandstones, are not found in this neighborhood. The *sacrificial stone*, as it is called, is the only one in all these blocks, that can resist the action of fire, and as I read in the books, must have been brought one hundred and fifty miles.[15]

On almost every stone we found the marks of the mineralogist's hammer and chisel. The nineteen smaller stones of the inner circle are of granite. I, who had just come from Professor Sedgwick's Cambridge Museum of

Stonehenge (1801).

megatheria and mastodons,[16] was ready to maintain that some cleverer elephants or mylodonta[17] had borne off and laid these rocks one on another. Only the good beasts must have known how to cut a well-wrought tenon and mortise,[18] and to smooth the surface of some of the stones. The chief mystery is, that any mystery should have been allowed to settle on so remarkable a monument, in a country on which all the muses have kept their eyes now for eighteen hundred years. We are not yet too late to learn much more than is known of this structure. Some diligent Fellows or Layard will arrive, stone by stone, at the whole history, by that exhaustive British sense and perseverance, so whimsical in its choice of objects, which leaves its own Stonehenge or Choir Gaur to the rabbits, whilst it opens pyramids, and uncovers Nineveh.[19] Stonehenge, in virtue of the simplicity of its plan, and its good preservation, is as if new and recent; and, a thousand years hence, men will

monument's bluestones, igneous rocks, may have originated in Pembrokeshire, in Wales; how they were transported remains a mystery. Stonehenge's altar or "sacrificial" stone, sixteen feet long and three feet wide, is a sandstone rock from south Wales.

16    Adam Sedgwick (1785–1873), English geologist, researched fossils; the mastodon was a prehistoric, elephant-like creature, and megatheria were elephant-size ground sloths (also extinct).

17    The (extinct) mylodon was a giant ground sloth that lived in Patagonia, in South America. The great British scientist Charles Darwin (1809–1882) found its fossil remains during the voyage of the *H.M.S. Beagle*, in 1832.

18    Method of fitting together two pieces of wood or (in this case) stone: the tenon is a narrow, jutting section of one piece wedged into the hole (mortise) of another.

19    Fellows of the Royal Society included archeologists. Austen Henry Layard (1817–1894) was a British archeologist and traveler who, in the 1840s, excavated the monuments of the ancient Assyrian city of Nineveh, in present-day Iraq. In 1842–1843, Karl Richard Lepsius (1810–1884) undertook an extensive study of the Egyptian pyramids. Choir Gaur is another name for Stonehenge; Stukeley, in *Stonehenge, A Temple Restor'd to the British Druids* (1740), commented, "The ancient Britons call'd it *choir-gaur*, which the Monks latiniz'd into chorea gigantum, the giants dance; a name suited to the marvelous notion they had of the structure, or of the reports of magic, concern'd in raising it. But I had rather chuse to think choir gaur in Welsh, truly means, the great church."

20    Stonehenge is comparable to the Great Sphinx of Giza, in the Egyptian desert. An enormous stone lion with a human head, it is the largest and most mysterious monolith sculpture in the world.

21    *Acts of the Saints*, massive encyclopedia of saints' lives compiled by a Jesuit sect. The first fifty-three volumes were published between 1643 and 1794.

22    Saint Adomnán (ca. 627–704) of Iona, a small island in the Scottish Hebrides, wrote the *Life of Saint Columba* (521–597), who traveled to Iona from Ireland to convert the Picts to Christianity. The book is a vital source for medieval Scottish and Irish history, and was therefore of interest to Carlyle.

23    Row of cut or mowed hay.

24    A light carriage, often with just two wheels, drawn by a single horse.

25    Joseph Brown, the son of Henry Brown (ca. 1768–1839), published in 1849 a third edition of his father's guidebook, *An Illustration of Stonehenge and Abury*.

26    The upright or astronomical stone is more commonly known as the "heel stone," over which the sun rises during the summer solstice. John Smith's *Choir Gaur* (1771) argued that Stonehenge was "a TEMPLE erected . . . for observing the motions of the HEAVENLY BODIES." In 1846, the Rev. Edward Duke (1779–1852) published *Druidical Temples of the County of Wiltshire*, in which he argued that Stonehenge and other stone circles in Wiltshire, including one at Avebury, formed a gigantic orrery (a device for predicting the positions of the stars and planets).

thank this age for the accurate history it will yet eliminate. We walked in and out, and took again and again a fresh look at the uncanny stones. The old sphinx[20] put our petty differences of nationality out of sight. To these conscious stones we two pilgrims were alike known and near. We could equally well revere their old British meaning. My philosopher was subdued and gentle. In this quiet house of destiny, he happened to say, "I plant cypresses wherever I go, and if I am in search of pain, I cannot go wrong." The spot, the gray blocks, and their rude order, which refuses to be disposed of, suggested to him the flight of ages, and the succession of religions. The old times of England impress C. much: he reads little, he says, in these last years, but *"Acta Sanctorum,"*[21] the fifty-three volumes of which are in the London Library. He finds all English history therein. He can see, as he reads, the old saint of Iona[22] sitting there, and writing, a man to men. The *Acta Sanctorum* show plainly that the men of those times believed in God, and in the immortality of the soul, as their abbeys and cathedrals testify: now, even the puritanism is all gone. London is pagan. He fancied that greater men had lived in England, than any of her writers; and, in fact, about the time when those writers appeared, the last of these were already gone.

We left the mound in the twilight, with the design to return the next morning, and coming back two miles to our inn, we were met by little showers, and late as it was, men and women were out attempting to protect their spread wind-rows.[23] The grass grows rank and dark in the showery England. At the inn, there was only milk for one cup of tea. When we called for more, the girl brought us three drops. My friend was annoyed who stood for the credit of an English inn, and still more, the next morning, by the dog-cart,[24] sole procurable vehicle, in which we were to be sent to Wilton. I engaged the local antiquary, Mr. Brown, to go with us to Stonehenge, on our way, and show us what he knew of the "astronomical" and "sacrificial" stones.[25] I stood on the last, and he pointed to the upright, or rather, inclined stone, called the "astronomical," and bade me notice that its top ranged with the sky-line. "Yes." Very well. Now, at the summer solstice, the sun rises exactly over the top of that stone, and, at the Druidical temple at Abury, there is also an astronomical stone, in the same relative positions.[26]

In the silence of tradition, this one relation to science becomes an important clue; but we were content to leave the problem, with the rocks. Was this the "Giants' Dance" which Merlin brought from Killaraus, in Ireland, to be Uther Pendragon's monument to the British nobles whom Hengist slaughtered here, as Geoffrey of Monmouth relates?[27] or was it a Roman work, as Inigo Jones explained to King James; or identical in design and style with the East Indian temples of the sun, as Davies in the Celtic Researches maintains?[28] Of all the writers, Stukeley is the best. The heroic antiquary, charmed with the geometric perfections of his ruin, connects it with the oldest monuments and religion of the world, and, with the courage of his tribe, does not stick to say, "the Deity who made the world by the scheme of Stonehenge." He finds that the *cursus*[29] on Salisbury Plain stretches across the downs, like a line of latitude upon the globe, and the meridian line of Stonehenge passes exactly through the middle of this *cursus*. But here is the high point of the theory: the Druids had the magnet; laid their courses by it; their cardinal points in Stonehenge, Ambresbury, and elsewhere, which vary a little from true east and west, followed the variations of the compass. The Druids were Phœnicians.[30] The name of the magnet is *lapis Heracleus*,[31] and Hercules was the god of the Phœnicians. Hercules, in the legend, drew his bow at the sun, and the sun-god gave him a golden cup, with which he sailed over the ocean. What was this, but a compass-box?[32] This cup or little boat, in which the magnet was made to float on water, and so show the north, was probably its first form, before it was suspended on a pin. But science was an *arcanum*,[33] and, as Britain was a Phœnician secret, so they kept their compass a secret, and it was lost with the Tyrian commerce. The golden fleece, again, of Jason, was the compass,[34]—a bit of loadstone, easily supposed to be the only one in the world, and therefore naturally awakening the cupidity[35] and ambition of the young heroes of a maritime nation to join in an expedition to obtain possession of this wise stone. Hence the fable that the ship Argo was loquacious and oracular.[36] There is also some curious coincidence in the names. Apollodorus makes *Magnes* the son of *Æolus*, who married *Nais*.[37] On hints like these, Stukeley builds again the grand colonnade into historic harmony, and computing backward by the known variations of the compass, bravely assigns the year 406 before Christ, for the date of the temple.[38]

For the difficulty of handling and carrying stones of this size, the like is done in all cities, every day, with no other aid than horse power. I chanced to see a year ago men at work on the substructure of a house in Bowdoin

27   Geoffrey of Monmouth (ca. 1100–ca. 1155) in his chronicle history of British kings, describes the career of the legendary Uther Pendragon (father of King Arthur) and his conflict with Hengist, king of Kent. Geoffrey claims that Merlin the wizard transported Stonehenge (called the "giants' dance") from Ireland, where giants had built it on Mt. Killaraus, and that Uther was buried within the circle.

28   Davies wrote *Celtic Researches on the Origins, Traditions, and Language, of the Ancient Britons* (1804), in which he suggested "a connection between Druidism, and the religion of India." (He did not, however, despite Emerson's claim, argue that Stonehenge resembles Indian temples.) Inigo Jones (1573–1652) was an English architect prominent during the reign (1603–1625) of King James I (1566–1625).

29   "Connected with Stonehenge are an avenue and a cursus. The avenue is a narrow road of raised earth, extending 594 yards in a straight line from the grand entrance, then dividing into two branches, which lead, severally, to a row of barrows; and to the cursus,—an artificially formed flat tract of ground. This is half a mile northeast from Stonehenge, bounded by banks and ditches, 3036 yards long, by 110 broad" (Emerson's note).

30   Stukeley insisted that the Druids came to Britain "as a Phœnician colony, in the very earliest times, even as soon as Tyre was founded: during the life of the patriarch Abraham, or very soon after."

31   Herculean stone.

32   Stukeley wrote, "Lucian says, that Hercules sail'd in a sea-conch shell. What can we understand by all this, mention'd by so many

*(continued)*

grave authors, but a compass-box, which enabled him to sail the great ocean, and penetrate to our northern island . . ?" Lucian (2nd century) was an ancient Syrian author who wrote epigrams, essays, and satirical dialogues in Greek.

33    Secret knowledge.

34    Stukeley: "If we suppose this golden fleece to be a compass box, we see the reason why the choice youth of Greece set out upon that voyage: which, as all other matters of ancient history, among the Greeks, is so unaccountably puft up with the leaven of fable." The Hellenistic Greek author Apollonius Rhodius (3rd century BCE) narrated the expedition of Jason and his crew of legendary heroes to obtain the Golden Fleece in an epic poem, the *Argonautica*.

35    Greedy desire.

36    The prow of the *Argo* contained a piece of wood from the sacred forest of Dodona, which enabled it to speak and prophesy. Stukeley added that "the antient navigators took the hint of applying the figure of the ram to their compasses, however form'd, and gave it the name of the ram, or golden fleece . . . and hence their ships deriv'd their oracular quality. *Phrixus*'s ship, the golden ram, being said to speak on occasion, as well as the ship *argos*." Phrixus was rescued from his stepmother (Ino, who wanted to sacrifice him) by a flying ram with golden wool (identified with the golden-fleeced ram that Jason pursues).

37    Magnes was the first man to feel magnetic attraction (he walked over a stone mine while wearing shoes with iron nails). According to the Greek mythographer Apollodorus (2nd century BCE), he was the son of the god of the

(continued)

Square, in Boston, swinging a block of granite of the size of the largest of the Stonehenge columns with an ordinary derrick. The men were common masons, with paddies[39] to help, nor did they think they were doing anything remarkable. I suppose, there were as good men a thousand years ago. And we wonder how Stonehenge was built and forgotten. After spending half an hour on the spot, we set forth in our dog-cart over the downs for Wilton, C. not suppressing some threats and evil omens on the proprietors, for keeping these broad plains a wretched sheep-walk, when so many thousands of English men were hungry and wanted labor.[40] But I heard afterwards that it is not an economy to cultivate this land, which only yields one crop on being broken up and is then spoiled.

We came to Wilton and to Wilton Hall,—the renowned seat of the Earls of Pembroke, a house known to Shakspeare and Massinger, the frequent home of Sir Philip Sidney where he wrote the Arcadia; where he conversed with Lord Brooke, a man of deep thought, and a poet, who caused to be engraved on his tombstone, "Here lies Fulke Greville Lord Brooke, the friend of Sir Philip Sidney."[41] It is now the property of the Earl of Pembroke, and the residence of his brother, Sidney Herbert, Esq.,[42] and is esteemed a noble specimen of the English manor-hall. My friend had a letter from Mr. Herbert to his housekeeper, and the house was shown. The state drawing-room is a double cube, 30 feet high, by 30 feet wide, by 60 feet long: the adjoining room is a single cube, of 30 feet every way. Although these apartments and the long library were full of good family portraits, Vandykes[43] and

Concord ball program (1875) commemorating the one hundredth anniversary of the Battle of Concord.

winds, Aeolus, and he married the nymph Nais. (Stukeley wrote that Aeolus "was a great sailor, invented sails, and studied the winds," and was therefore deified.)

38    Stukeley's chronology is, we now know, off by at least 2,500 years.

39    Irish laborers. In his Journal (1860), Emerson wrote, "Now when I go . . . to Stonehenge, I find the sentiment of ancient peoples, their delight in their gods, & in the future, their humanity, expressed in this patience of labor that staggered under the toil of hewing & lifting these grey rocks into scientific symmetry" (J 14:359).

40    In many parts of England the enclosure of common land for sheep grazing, land previously used for farming, prevented agricultural laborers from earning a living.

41    William Herbert, the third Earl of Pembroke (1580–1630), was a patron of the dramatist Philip Massinger (1583–1640), among other writers. Shakespeare's company, the King's Men, gave a performance before the king at Wilton House in December 1603. Philip Sidney (ca. 1554–1586), poet, critic, and writer of prose romance, was related by marriage to the Herberts; Fulke Greville, Lord Brooke (1554–1628), was a lyric poet and biographer of Sidney.

42    Sidney Herbert, Baron Lea (1810–1901), English statesman and secretary-at-war during the Crimean War.

43    Sir Anthony van Dyck, or Vandyke (1599–1641), Flemish artist who became the leading portrait painter in England, at the court of King Charles I (1600–1649, reigned 1625–1649).

44    The bridge was not, in fact, built by Jones, but by one of the earls of Pembroke. In "Kubla Khan" (1816), the English Romantic poet Samuel Taylor Coleridge (1772–1834) writes, "Alph, the sacred river, ran / Through caverns measureless to man / Down to a sunless sea."

45    Smart, elegant.

46    The mullein has a towering, flowery stalk. In November 1940, German bombs destroyed the church of St. Michael at Coventry, which (despite Emerson's claim) was recognized as a beautiful instance of the Gothic Perpendicular style.

47    Salisbury Cathedral, consecrated in 1258, is a striking example of early English Gothic architecture (one of whose features is that flying buttresses, or half-arches, are exposed on the outside of the building).

48    A modern addition to the cathedral.

49    The Constitutions or Decrees of Clarendon, passed in 1164 by Henry II (1133–1189, ruled 1158–1189), restricted the powers of the church in England. Thomas à Becket (ca. 1118–1170), the archbishop of Canterbury, opposed Henry's decree, and as a result was murdered at the altar.

50    Bishopstoke is a town in Hampshire, southwest of London. There the English writer and court official Arthur Helps (1813–1875) met Emerson and Carlyle and drove them to the nearby town of Waltham.

other; and though there were some good pictures, and a quadrangle cloister full of antique and modern statuary,—to which C., catalogue in hand, did all too much justice,—yet the eye was still drawn to the windows, to a magnificent lawn, on which grew the finest cedars in England. I had not seen more charming grounds. We went out, and walked over the estate. We crossed a bridge built by Inigo Jones over a stream, of which the gardener did not know the name, (*Qu.* Alph?)[44] watched the deer; climbed to the lonely sculptured summer house, on a hill backed by a wood; came down into the Italian garden, and into a French pavilion, garnished with French busts; and so again, to the house, where we found a table laid for us with bread, meats, peaches, grapes, and wine.

On leaving Wilton House, we took the coach for Salisbury. The Cathedral, which was finished 600 years ago, has even a spruce[45] and modern air, and its spire is the highest in England. I know not why, but I had been more struck with one of no fame at Coventry, which rises 300 feet from the ground, with the lightness of a mullein-plant,[46] and not at all implicated with the church. Salisbury is now esteemed the culmination of the Gothic art in England, as the buttresses are fully unmasked, and honestly detailed from the sides of the pile.[47] The interior of the Cathedral is obstructed by the organ in the middle, acting like a screen.[48] I know not why in real architecture the hunger of the eye for length of line is so rarely gratified. The rule of art is that a colonnade is more beautiful the longer it is, and that *ad infinitum*. And the nave of a church is seldom so long that it need be divided by a screen.

We loitered in the church, outside the choir, whilst service was said. Whilst we listened to the organ, my friend remarked, the music is good, and yet not quite religious, but somewhat as if a monk were panting to some fine Queen of Heaven. C. was unwilling, and we did not ask to have the choir shown us, but returned to our inn, after seeing another old church of the place. We passed in the train Clarendon Park, but could see little but the edge of a wood, though C. had wished to pay closer attention to the birthplace of the Decrees of Clarendon.[49] At Bishopstoke we stopped, and found Mr. H., who received us in his carriage, and took us to his house at Bishops Waltham.[50]

INIGO JONES.

STUKELY.

WOOD.

SMITH.

View of Stonehenge.

51    *"Mais, Monseigneur, il faut que j'existe"*
(Emerson's note: But, Monseigneur, I need to
exist)—the sentence answered by the line that
Emerson quotes in his essay. Emerson attrib-
utes this line (meaning "Sir, I don't see the
need") to the French politician Charles de
Talleyrand-Perigord (1754–1838). In fact it de-
rives from the French philosopher Voltaire
(François-Marie Arouet; 1694–1778) in his play
*Alzire* (1736).

52    Sadness.

53    Bedraggled, unkempt.

On Sunday, we had much discourse on a very rainy day. My friends asked, whether there were any Americans?—any with an American idea,—any theory of the right future of that country? Thus challenged, I bethought myself neither of caucuses nor congress, neither of presidents nor of cabinet-ministers, nor of such as would make of America another Europe. I thought only of the simplest and purest minds; I said, "Certainly yes;—but those who hold it are fanatics of a dream which I should hardly care to relate to your English ears, to which it might be only ridiculous,—and yet it is the only true." So I opened the dogma of no-government and non-resistance, and anticipated the objections and the fun, and procured a kind of hearing for it. I said, it is true that I have never seen in any country a man of sufficient valor to stand for this truth, and yet it is plain to me, that no less valor than this can command my respect. I can easily see the bankruptcy of the vulgar musket-worship,—though great men be musket-worshippers;—and 'tis certain, as God liveth, the gun that does not need another gun, the law of love and justice alone, can effect a clean revolution. I fancied that one or two of my anecdotes made some impression on C., and I insisted, that the manifest absurdity of the view to English feasibility could make no difference to a gentleman; that as to our secure tenure of our mutton-chop and spinage in London or in Boston, the soul might quote Talleyrand, *"Monsieur, je n'en vois pas la nécessité."*[51] As I had thus taken in the conversation the saint's part, when dinner was announced, C. refused to go out before me,—"he was altogether too wicked." I planted my back against the wall, and our host wittily rescued us from the dilemma, by saying, he was the wickedest, and would walk out first, then C. followed, and I went last.

On the way to Winchester, whither our host accompanied us in the afternoon, my friends asked many questions respecting American landscape, forests, houses,—my house, for example. It is not easy to answer these queries well. There I thought, in America, lies nature sleeping, overgrowing, almost conscious, too much by half for man in the picture, and so giving a certain *tristesse*,[52] like the rank vegetation of swamps and forests seen at night, steeped in dews and rains, which it loves; and on it man seems not able to make much impression. There, in that great sloven[53] continent, in high Alleghany pastures, in the sea-wide, sky-skirted prairie, still sleeps and murmurs and hides the great mother, long since driven away from the trim hedge-rows and over-cultivated garden of England. And, in England, I am quite too sensible of this. Every one is on his good behavior, and must be dressed for dinner at six. So I put off my friends with very inadequate details, as best I could.

Just before entering Winchester, we stopped at the Church of Saint Cross, and, after looking through the quaint antiquity, we demanded a piece of bread and a draught of beer, which the founder, Henry de Blois, in 1136, commanded should be given to every one who should ask it at the gate.[54] We had both, from the old couple who take care of the church. Some twenty people, every day, they said, make the same demand. This hospitality of seven hundred years' standing did not hinder C. from pronouncing a malediction on the priest who receives £2000 a year, that were meant for the poor, and spends a pittance on this small beer and crumbs.

In the Cathedral, I was gratified, at least by the ample dimensions. The length of line exceeds that of any other English church; being 556 feet by 250 in breadth of transept.[55] I think I prefer this church to all I have seen, except Westminster and York. Here was Canute buried, and here Alfred the Great was crowned and buried, and here the Saxon kings: and, later, in his own church, William of Wykeham.[56] It is very old: part of the crypt into which we went down and saw the Saxon and Norman arches of the old church on which the present stands, was built fourteen or fifteen hundred years ago. Sharon Turner says, "Alfred was buried at Winchester, in the Abbey he had founded there, but his remains were removed by Henry I. to the new Abbey in the meadows at Hyde, on the northern quarter of the city, and laid under the high altar. The building was destroyed at the Reformation, and what is left of Alfred's body now lies covered by modern buildings, or buried in the ruins of the old."[57] William of Wykeham's shrine tomb was unlocked for us, and C. took hold of the recumbent statue's marble hands, and patted them affectionately, for he rightly values the brave man who built Windsor, and this Cathedral, and the School here, and New College at Oxford.[58] But it was growing late in the afternoon. Slowly we left the old house, and parting with our host, we took the train for London.

54 Henry of Blois (1101–1171), the bishop of Winchester, started the practice of the Wayfarer's Dole that Emerson describes.

55 Winchester Cathedral is, in fact, the longest church in Europe. The transept is the area of a church on either side of the altar. Emerson had visited Westminster Abbey and York Minster earlier on this same trip.

56 Canute the Great (ca. 994–1035), king of the English and the Danes; Alfred the Great (849–899), Anglo-Saxon king of Wessex from 871 to 899; and William of Wykeham, bishop of Winchester (1324–1404).

57 "History of the Anglo-Saxons," I.599 (Emerson's note). Sharon Turner (1768–1847), English historian; Emerson cites his *History of the Anglo-Saxons* (1836).

58 Wykeham redesigned parts of Windsor Castle and Winchester (both built centuries earlier). He planned and built Oxford's New College and the school at Winchester.

# John Brown

*Emerson gave this speech on January 6, 1860, in Salem, Massachusetts. It first appeared in James Redpath's book* Echoes of Harpers Ferry *(1860). Redpath used as his epigraph the first stanza of Emerson's Concord Hymn, implying that Brown's doomed antislavery raid on the United States Armory and Arsenal at Harpers Ferry, Virginia, in October 1859 was a "shot heard round the world." Emerson saw in Brown an ideal incarnate, an icon of successful will and pure virtue. In his speech "Courage," which he gave at Tremont Temple in Boston on November 8, several weeks after Harpers Ferry, Emerson called Brown a "new saint, than whom none purer or more brave was ever led by love of man into conflict and death; a new saint, waiting yet his martyrdom; and who, if he shall suffer, will make the gallows glorious like the cross." (Emerson adapted this line from Mattie Griffith, a Kentucky abolitionist who had freed her slaves: he quoted Griffith as saying, "If Brown is hung, the gallows will be sacred as the cross" [1859; J 14:333].) Emerson added, "I wish we should have health enough to know virtue when we see it, and not cry with the*
(continued)

Mr. Chairman: I have been struck with one fact, that the best orators who have added their praise to his fame—and I need not go out of this house to find the purest eloquence in the country—have one rival who comes off a little better, and that is John Brown. Every thing that is said of him leaves people a little dissatisfied; but as soon as they read his own speeches and letters they are heartily contented—such is the singleness of purpose which justifies him to the head and the heart of all. Taught by this experience, I mean, in the few remarks I have to make, to cling to his history, or let him speak for himself.

John Brown, the founder of liberty in Kansas,[1] was born in Torrington, Litchfield County, Connecticut, in 1800. When he was five years old his father emigrated to Ohio, and the boy was there set to keep sheep and to look after cattle and dress skins; he went bareheaded and bare-footed, and clothed in buckskin. He said that he loved rough play, could never have rough play enough; could not see a seedy hat without wishing to pull it off. But for this it needed that the playmates should be equal; not one in fine clothes and the other in buckskin;[2] not one his own master, hale and hearty, and the other watched and whipped. But it chanced that in Pennsylvania, where he was sent by his father to collect cattle, he fell in with a boy whom he heartily liked and whom he looked upon as his superior. This boy was a slave; he saw *fools and newspapers, 'Madman!' when a hero passes." In his Journal, Emerson wrote that Brown "was the rarest of heroes a pure idealist, with no by-ends of his own. He is therefore precisely what lawyers call crazy, being governed by ideas, & not by external circumstance" (1859; J 14:334).*

*In early 1857, Brown was in the East raising money. In the Pottawatomie (Kansas) Massacre of May 24, 1856, Brown and his allies had brutally murdered five unarmed members of pro-slavery families (including a father and his two sons, and a husband killed before his wife). Brown's supporters believed the antislavery press's version of Pottawatomie, which blamed pro-slavery men for the deaths. In February, Brown spoke at Town Hall in Concord. The journalist and political activist F. B. Sanborn (1831–1917), who was secretly supplying Brown with money and guns for his antislavery campaign, introduced Brown to Henry David Thoreau (1817–1862) in March 1857. Thoreau then introduced Brown to Emerson, who gave him fifty dollars. Emerson's son Edward Emerson remembered, "His clear-cut face, smooth-shaven and bronzed, his firmly shut mouth and mild but steady blue eyes, gave him the appearance of the best type of old New England farmers . . . very modest about his own part and leadership." But Edward continued, "The last time he came to Concord he was a changed man; all the pleasant look was gone. [He had] a wild, fierce expression. His speech in the Town Hall was excited . . ." On this occasion (May 8, 1859), Brown took out a huge sheath-knife and showed it to the crowd. He then "drew from his bosom a horse-chain and clanked it in air, telling that his son had been bound with this and led bare-headed under a burning sun beside their horses, by United States dragoons, and in the mania brought on by this inhuman treatment had worn the rusty chain bright . . ." Brown felt he "held a commission direct from God Almighty," Edward Emerson reported.*

*Brown raised about $2,000 on this trip. What followed was Brown's disastrous attack on Harpers Ferry on October 16. Brown commanded just twenty-one men, including two of his sons and five African Americans; his first casualty was a free black man, the baggage master at the Harpers Ferry train station. A court sentenced Brown to death on November 1; Emerson spoke at a meeting in Boston to give aid to Brown's family on November 18, two weeks before his execution.*

1    The Kansas-Nebraska Act of 1854 established the principle of popular sovereignty: the residents of a territory would decide whether it was to be a free or a slave state. Masses of both pro- and antislavery immigrants arrived in Kansas, and their violent conflicts led to the name "bleeding Kansas." In January 1861 Kansas entered the Union as a free state; the Civil War was only a few months away.

2    Leather made from deer or elk hide, popular with frontiersmen.

3    The incident is reminiscent of a forma-
tive event in the life of the young Moses. In
Exodus 2:11–12 Moses sees an Egyptian beating an Israelite slave, and kills the Egyptian.

4    Brown expected local slaves to rise up
and join his raid on Harpers Ferry (though he
had not informed them of his plan). Instead,
Marines commanded by Colonel Robert E. Lee
(1807–1870) captured Brown and his men. (Lee
later became commanding general of the Con-
federacy.) On December 2, 1859, Brown was
hanged. On the way to the scaffold, he remarked, "I, John Brown, am now quite certain
that the crimes of this guilty land will never be
purged away but with blood." On the day of
Brown's execution, Emerson read Brown's last
speech at a memorial service in Concord arranged by Thoreau and others.

5    Charlestown, Virginia (now West Virginia), the site of Brown's trial.

John Brown (1800–1859).

him beaten with an iron shovel, and otherwise maltreated;[3] he saw that this
boy had nothing better to look forward to in life, whilst he himself was pet-
ted and made much of; for he was much considered in the family where he
then stayed, from the circumstance that this boy of twelve years had conducted alone a drove of cattle a hundred miles. But the colored boy had no
friend, and no future. This worked such indignation in him that he swore an
oath of resistance to Slavery as long as he lived. And thus his enterprise to go
into Virginia and run off five hundred or a thousand slaves[4] was not a piece
of spite or revenge, a plot of two years or of twenty years, but the keeping
of an oath made to heaven and earth forty-seven years before. Forty-seven
years at least, though I incline to accept his own account of the matter at
Charlestown,[5] which makes the date a little older, when he said, "This was
all settled millions of years before the world was made."

He grew up a religious and manly person in severe poverty; a fair specimen of the best stock of New England; having that force of thought and that sense of right which are the warp and woof of greatness.[6] Our farmers were Orthodox Calvinists, mighty in the Scriptures; had learned that life was a preparation, a "probation," to use their word, for a higher world, and was to be spent in loving and serving mankind.[7]

Thus was formed a romantic character absolutely without any vulgar trait; living to ideal ends, without any mixture of self-indulgence or compromise, such as lowers the value of benevolent and thoughtful men we know; abstemious, refusing luxuries, not sourly and reproachfully, but simply as unfit for his habit; quiet and gentle as a child in the house. And, as happens usually to men of romantic character, his fortunes were romantic. Walter Scott[8] would have delighted to draw his picture and trace his adventurous career. A shepherd and herdsman, he learned the manners of animals, and knew the secret signals by which animals communicate.[9] He made his hard bed on the mountains with them; he learned to drive his flock through thickets all but impassable; he had all the skill of a shepherd by choice of breed and by wise husbandry to obtain the best wool, and that for a course of years. And the anecdotes preserved show a far-seeing skill and conduct which, in spite of adverse accidents, should secure, one year with another, an honest reward, first to the farmer, and afterwards to the dealer. If he kept sheep, it was with a royal mind; and if he traded in wool, he was a merchant prince, not in the amount of wealth, but in the protection of the interests confided to him.

I am not a little surprised at the easy effrontery with which political gentlemen, in and out of Congress, take it upon them to say that there are not a thousand men in the North who sympathize with John Brown. It would be far safer and nearer the truth to say that all people, in proportion to their sensibility and self-respect, sympathize with him. For it is impossible to see courage, and disinterestedness, and the love that casts out fear, without sympathy. All women are drawn to him by their predominance of sentiment. All gentlemen, of course, are on his side. I do not mean by "gentlemen," people of scented hair and perfumed handkerchiefs, but men of gentle blood and generosity, "fulfilled with all nobleness," who, like the Cid, give

6     In Thoreau's "Plea for Captain John Brown," a speech he first delivered in Concord on October 30, 1859 (the day before Brown's sentencing), and repeated on November 1 and 3, Thoreau said, "He was like the best of those who stood at Concord Bridge once, on Lexington Common, and on Bunker Hill, only he was firmer and higher principled than any that I have chanced to hear of as there."

7     Thoreau, in his "Plea," remarked that Brown "was one of that class of whom we hear a great deal, but, for the most part, see nothing at all—the Puritans." Most New England Puritans were strict Calvinists (after the French religious reformer John Calvin [1509–1564], who presided over the Christian community in Geneva).

8     The Scottish novelist (1771–1832) whose historical tales of adventure were wildly popular in Emerson's day.

9     Edward Emerson wrote, "I well remember the evening, in my school-boy days, when John Brown, in my father's house, told of his experiences as a sheep-farmer, and his eye for animals and power over them. He said he knew at once a strange sheep in his flock of many hundred, and that he could always make a dog or a cat so uncomfortable as to wish to leave the room, simply by fixing his eyes on it."

Arrest of Franklin B. Sanborn (1831–1917) in Concord by U.S. marshals (1860). Sanborn was one of the "Secret Six" who helped sponsor Brown's raid on Harpers Ferry.

the outcast leper a share of their bed; like the dying Sidney, pass the cup of cold water to the dying soldier who needs it more.[10] For what is the oath of gentle blood and knighthood? What but to protect the weak and lowly against the strong oppressor?

\* \* \*

Nothing is more absurd than to complain of this sympathy, or to complain of a party of men united in opposition to Slavery.—As well complain of gravity, or the ebb of the tide. Who makes the Abolitionist? The Slaveholder. The sentiment of mercy is the natural recoil which the laws of the universe provide to protect man-kind from destruction by savage passions. And our blind statesmen go up and down, with committees of vigilance and safety, hunting for the origin of this new heresy. They will need a very vigilant committee indeed to find its birthplace, and a very strong force to root it out. For the arch-abolitionist, older than Brown, and older than the Shenandoah Mountains,[11] is Love, whose other name is Justice, which was before Alfred, before Lycurgus,[12] before slavery, and will be after it.

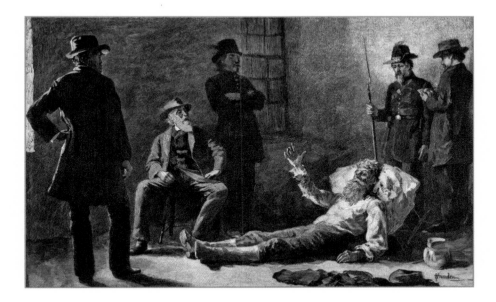

John Brown after his capture.

10    Rodrigo Díaz (1043–1099), the great Spanish hero known as El Cid, sheltered a leper under his cloak; in a dream, the leper revealed himself as St. Lazarus. The English poet and courtier Sir Philip Sidney (1554–1586) died at the battle of Zutphen in Holland; in his last moments, he gave his drink of water to a fellow soldier, also dying, "with these words, Thy necessity is greater than mine" (from the biography of Sidney by his fellow poet Fulke Greville [1554–1628]).

11    In Virginia, site of Brown's uprising (Harpers Ferry is in the Shenandoah River valley). In his brief poem "The Portent" (1859), the American author Herman Melville (1819–1891) wrote, "So your future veils its face, / Shenandoah! / But the streaming beard is shown / (Weird John Brown), / The meteor of the war."

12    Alfred the Great (849–899), king of Wessex, in southern England, issued an elaborate law code; Lycurgus (ca. 800–ca. 730 BCE) was the legendary lawgiver of ancient Sparta.

# Fate

"Fate" is the opening chapter in Emerson's Conduct of Life, *published in December 1860 (from a lecture series first delivered in Pittsburgh in March and April 1851); two later chapters of the book, "Power" and "Illusions," are also included in this selection. After reading* The Conduct of Life, *Emerson's friend Thomas Carlyle (1795–1881) remarked, "You have grown older, more pungent, piercing;—I never read from you before such lightning-gleams of meaning as are to be found here." It is often seen as Emerson's last definitive book, and the epitome of his most mature thinking. Emerson avoided the topical in* Conduct—*the book contained no chapter on politics or slavery—yet he confronted throughout the facts of power, studying how the individual argues a claim to the world.*

*By "Fate" Emerson means Necessity, the iron law of the universe—yet he also recognizes freedom. The essay falls into two movements: the first underlines the cruel constraint imposed on us by nature and circumstances; the second insists on the freedom that antagonizes fate, a freedom expressed in human will and duty.*

*(continued)*

Delicate omens traced in air
To the lone bard true witness bare;
Birds with auguries[1] on their wings
Chanted undeceiving things
Him to beckon, him to warn;
Well might then the poet scorn
To learn of scribe or courier[2]
Hints writ in vaster character;[3]
And on his mind, at dawn of day,
Soft shadows of the evening lay.[4]
For the prevision is allied
Unto the thing so signified;
Or say, the foresight that awaits
Is the same Genius that creates.

It chanced during one winter, a few years ago, that our cities were bent on discussing the theory of the Age. By an odd coincidence, four or five noted men were each reading a discourse to the citizens of Boston or New York, on the Spirit of the Times.[5] It so happened that the subject had the same prominence in some remarkable pamphlets and journals issued in London in the same season. To me, however, the question of the times resolved itself into a practical question of the conduct of life. How shall I live? We are incompetent to solve the times. Our geometry cannot span the huge orbits of the prevailing ideas, behold their return, and reconcile their opposition. We can only obey our own polarity. 'Tis fine[6] for us to speculate and elect our course, if we must accept an irresistible dictation.

In our first steps to gain our wishes, we come upon immovable limitations. We are fired with the hope to reform men. After many experiments, we find that we must begin earlier,—at school. But the boys and girls are not docile;[7] we can make nothing of them. We decide that they are not of good stock. We must begin our reform earlier still,—at generation: that is to say, there is Fate, or laws of the world.[8]

But if there be irresistible dictation, this dictation understands itself.[9] If we must accept Fate, we are not less compelled to affirm liberty, the significance of the individual, the grandeur of duty, the power of character. This is true, and that other is true. But our geometry cannot span these extreme points, and reconcile them. What to do? By obeying each thought frankly, by harping, or, if you will, pounding on each string, we learn at last its power.[10] By the same obedience to other thoughts, we learn theirs, and then comes some reasonable hope of harmonizing them. We are sure, that, though we know not how, necessity does comport with liberty, the individual with the world, my polarity with the spirit of the times.[11] The riddle of the age has for each a private solution.[12] If one would study his own time, it must be by this method of taking up in turn each of the leading topics which belong to our scheme of human life, and, by firmly stating all that is agreeable to experience on one, and doing the same justice to the opposing facts in the others, the true limitations will appear. Any excess of emphasis, on one part, would be corrected, and a just balance would be made.

But let us honestly state the facts. Our America has a bad name for superficialness. Great men, great nations, have not been boasters and buffoons, but perceivers of the terror of life, and have manned themselves to face it. The Spartan, embodying his religion in his country, dies before its majesty without a question. The Turk, who believes his doom is written on the iron leaf in the moment when he entered the world, rushes on the enemy's sabre with undivided will. The Turk, the Arab, the Persian, accepts the foreordained fate.[13]

*Years before the writing of "Fate," a few months after the death of his five-year-old son Waldo, Emerson had written in his Journal (1842), "I know that tomorrow will be as this day, I am a dwarf, & I remain a dwarf. That is to say, I believe in Fate. As long as I am weak, I shall talk of Fate; whenever the God fills me with his fulness, I shall see the disappearance of Fate.*

*"I am Defeated all the time; yet to Victory I am born" (J 8:228).*

1    Ancient Roman augurs interpreted the flights of birds in order to predict the future.

2    The poet learns directly from nature's rather ominous signs, rather than relying on copyist (scribe) or messenger (courier).

3    Larger letters.

4    Emerson here recalls the theme of the *Immortality Ode* (1807) by the English Romantic poet William Wordsworth (1770–1850).

5    In January 1850, Emerson delivered his lecture "The Spirit of the Times" in Albany, New York, and in New York City. The next month he remarked in his Journal that several other authors, including Carlyle and William Henry Channing (1810–1884), were addressing the same subject that winter in their lectures (J 11:228).

6    Polarity here means the magnetic attraction that directs a compass needle. Emerson wrote in his Journal, "Every mind has a polarity,—and that will finally guide us to the sea. I see no choice" (J 11:218). "'Tis fine" means "it's all very well (and a refined thought), but . . ."

7    Teachable.

8    In a letter of July 22, 1853, to Caroline Sturgis (1818–1888), Emerson wrote, "Friends
*(continued)*

are few, thoughts are few, facts few—only one: one only fact, now tragically, now tenderly, now exultingly illustrated in sky, in earth, in men & women, Fate, Fate. The universe is all chemistry . . ." (L 4:376). "Your fate is what you do, because first it is what you are," Emerson wrote in his Journal (1858; J 14:207).

9    Emerson's harping on the word *dictation* exposes its double meaning: giving orders (like a dictator) and dictating words or meanings (compare giving of written hints and omens in the prefatory poem of "Fate"). Can fate be interpreted, like writing, or are its commands fixed?

10   True to the "delicate omens" of his opening verse, Emerson harps (plucks) his theme—but he also hammers it home.

11   In the 1850 Journal passage that provided the basis for this passage, Emerson continued, "Goethe said, 'Every man loves to be distinguished, and loves also to be entirely melted into the crowd.' We men are necessary to each other, yet every one stands on the top of the world. Over the nadir, & under the zenith" (J 11:220). (Emerson refers to J. W. von Goethe [1749–1832], influential German man of letters.)

12   Emerson challenges each of us to reconcile the iron law of necessity with our conviction of individual freedom—by emphasizing these two aspects of life in turn, as he does in "Fate."

13   The citizens of Sparta, in ancient Greece, were renowned for their severe heroism. Many years earlier, Emerson noticed a phrase about "iron leaves" of fate's "dark book" in the play

*Tyrannic Love* (1669) by the English author John Dryden (1631–1700) (J 2:273). Muslems were often thought to be fatalists—an idea implied, to some degree, by the Koran's command to submit to the will of Allah. In his Journal (1857) Emerson asserted, "'Tis the best use of Fate to teach us courage like the Turk" (J 14:156).

14   Emerson's translation of a quatrain by a Persian poet, found by him in *Geschichte der schönen Redekunst Persiens* (1818), a collection of Persian poetry by the German scholar Joseph von Hammer-Purgstall (1774–1856) (J 11:103).

15   The Hindu is a self-immolating worshipper of Vishnu, who has thrown himself under the Juggernaut—a huge cart with seven-foot wheels carrying a statue of the god. The Calvinist, a follower of the French reformer John Calvin (1509–1564), believes in predestination, the idea that God has designated each individual even before birth for either salvation or damnation.

16   The Knight's Tale is a lavish chivalric narrative, the first story in *The Canterbury Tales* (1387–1400) by the English poet Geoffrey Chaucer (ca. 1343–1400). "Purveyance" here means "providence."

17   Ancient Greek tragedies often refer to Anankê, or Necessity. The words in quotation marks are Emerson's own. In his Journal (1845), Emerson commented that the Indian sense of fate outstripped the Greek: in Greece, "we are only at a more beautiful opera or at private theatricals. But in India, it is the dread reality, it is the cropping out in our planted gardens of the core of the world: it is the abysmal Force untameable & immense" (J 9:313).

"On two days, it steads not to run from thy grave,
   The appointed, and the unappointed day;
On the first, neither balm nor physician can save,
   Nor thee, on the second, the Universe slay."[14]

The Hindoo, under the wheel, is as firm. Our Calvinists, in the last generation, had something of the same dignity.[15] They felt that the weight of the Universe held them down to their place. What could *they* do? Wise men feel that there is something which cannot be talked or voted away,—a strap or belt which girds the world.

"The Destiny, minister general,
That executeth in the world o'er all,
The purveyance which God hath seen beforne,
So strong it is, that tho' the world had sworn
The contrary of a thing by yea or nay,
Yet sometime it shall fallen on a day
That falleth not oft in a thousand year;
For, certainly, our appetités here,
Be it of war, or peace, or hate, or love,
All this is ruléd by the sight above."

CHAUCER: The Knight's Tale.[16]

The Greek Tragedy expressed the same sense: "Whatever is fated, that will take place. The great immense mind of Jove is not to be transgressed."[17]

Savages cling to a local god of one tribe or town. The broad ethics of Jesus were quickly narrowed to village theologies, which preach an election or favoritism.[18] And, now and then, an amiable parson, like Jung Stilling, or Robert Huntington, believes in a pistareen-Providence,[19] which, whenever the good man wants a dinner, makes that somebody shall knock at his door, and leave a half-dollar. But Nature is no sentimentalist,—does not cosset[20] or pamper us. We must see that the world is rough and surly, and will not mind drowning a man or a woman; but swallows your ship like a grain of

18   Emerson thrusts against the Calvinist notion of the elect (those marked for salvation).

19   Johann Heinrich Jung (1740–1817) was not a parson but wrote a pious autobiographical book, *Heinrich Stilling's Life* (1806); Emerson was probably thinking of William Huntington, S. S. (Sinner Saved) (1745–1813), an eccentric English preacher. A pistareen was a small coin used in the Spanish West Indies.

20   Coddle, indulge. The abolitionist Moncure Daniel Conway (1832–1907) in *Emerson at Home and Abroad* (1882) wrote that for Emerson "[t]here is no evil in nature, in the theological sense of evil; each organization is fit for its own purpose, but when it is not fit for mine I call it evil. Cat is evil to mouse."

21      "Graceful" offers a dark irony: the way of providence is not colored by grace (in either a divine or a social sense), but is instead "rude," fierce, and wild. The races devoured here are both human (African-American slaves or Irish workers) and animal.

dust. The cold, inconsiderate of persons, tingles your blood, benumbs your feet, freezes a man like an apple. The diseases, the elements, fortune, gravity, lightning, respect no persons. The way of Providence is a little rude. The habit of snake and spider, the snap of the tiger and other leapers and bloody jumpers, the crackle of the bones of his prey in the coil of the anaconda,— these are in the system, and our habits are like theirs. You have just dined, and, however scrupulously the slaughter-house is concealed in the graceful distance of miles, there is complicity,—expensive races,—race living at the expense of race.[21] The planet is liable to shocks from comets, perturbations

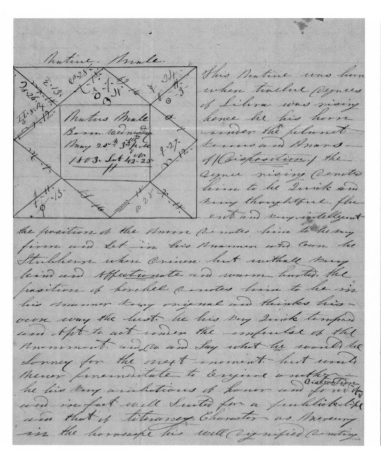

from planets, rendings from earthquake and volcano, alterations of climate, precessions of equinoxes. Rivers dry up by opening of the forest. The sea changes its bed. Towns and counties fall into it. At Lisbon, an earthquake killed men like flies.[22] At Naples, three years ago, ten thousand persons were crushed in a few minutes. The scurvy at sea; the sword of the climate in the west of Africa, at Cayenne,[23] at Panama, at New Orleans, cut off men like a massacre. Our western prairie shakes with fever and ague. The cholera, the small-pox, have proved as mortal to some tribes, as a frost to the crickets, which, having filled the summer with noise, are silenced by a fall of the tem-

22   The Great Lisbon Earthquake of 1755 killed about forty thousand people—an unprecedented disaster that drew much anguished commentary. Emerson marked a passage in *The Friend*, v. 3 (1818) by the English Romantic poet and thinker S. T. Coleridge (1772–1834): "Natural calamities that do indeed spread devastation wide . . . are almost without exception, voices of Nature in her all-intelligible language —do this! Or cease to do that!"

23   Cayenne is the capital of French Guiana; in 1852 the French government established penal colonies in the territory. Harsh treatment killed most of the prisoners at the Saint Georges colony, and many of the survivors committed suicide.

Emerson's horoscope, prepared by unknown person.

24    Silkworm.

25    Infusoria are microbes, invisible to the naked eye.

26    Two forms of reproduction employed by the same species.

27    Rather than labrus, Emerson probably meant labrax, a fierce predatory fish. A sea-wolf is a sea lion; a grampus is a killer whale. In Chapter 66 of *Moby-Dick* (1851) by the American novelist Herman Melville (1819–1891), a night of shark killing gives dangerous "new revelations of the incredible ferocity of the foe": "It was unsafe to meddle with the corpses and ghosts of these creatures. A sort of generic or Pantheistic vitality seemed to lurk in their very joints and bones, after what might be called the individual life had departed." Melville's reference to "pantheistic vitality" may mock what he saw as Emerson's overoptimism; but "Fate" fully answers Melville's charge (though it is doubtful that Emerson read *Moby-Dick*). Emerson's capacity to find life's purposes even in its most ruthless and predatory instances remains opposed to Melville's idea of a violent, meaningless abyss lurking behind the masks of worldly action.

28    Terrific here means "terrifying," paradoxically paired with "benefactor." In his first version of this passage (from his Journal, 1851), Emerson wrote of the "clean shirt & white neckloth of an Unitarian parson" (J 11:442).

29    The book of nature, praised in Emerson's early *Nature*, has now become a frightening bestiary.

30    In his Journal (1851), Emerson remarked, "Every spirit makes its house; but neither must
*(continued)*

perature of one night. Without uncovering what does not concern us, or counting how many species of parasites hang on a bombyx;[24] or groping after intestinal parasites, or infusory[25] biters, or the obscurities of alternate generation;[26]—the forms of the shark, the *labrus*, the jaw of the sea-wolf paved with crushing teeth, the weapons of the grampus, and other warriors hidden in the sea,[27]—are hints of ferocity in the interiors of nature. Let us not deny it up and down. Providence has a wild, rough, incalculable road to its end, and it is of no use to try to whitewash its huge, mixed instrumentalities, or to dress up that terrific benefactor in a clean shirt and white neckcloth of a student in divinity.[28]

Will you say, the disasters which threaten mankind are exceptional, and one need not lay his account for cataclysms every day? Aye, but what happens once, may happen again, and so long as these strokes are not to be parried by us, they must be feared.

But these shocks and ruins are less destructive to us, than the stealthy power of other laws which act on us daily. An expense of ends to means is fate;—organization tyrannizing over character. The menagerie, or forms and powers of the spine, is a book of fate: the bill of the bird, the skull of the snake, determines tyrannically its limits.[29] So is the scale of races, of temperaments; so is sex; so is climate; so is the reaction of talents imprisoning the vital power in certain directions. Every spirit makes its house; but afterwards the house confines the spirit.[30]

The gross lines are legible to the dull: the cabman is phrenologist so far: he looks in your face to see if his shilling is sure. A dome of brow denotes one thing; a pot-belly another; a squint, a pug-nose, mats of hair, the pigment of the epidermis, betray character. People seem sheathed in their tough organization.[31] Ask Spurzheim, ask the doctors, ask Quetelet,[32] if temperaments decide nothing? or if there be anything they do not decide? Read the description in medical books of the four temperaments,[33] and you will think you are reading your own thoughts which you had not yet told. Find the part which black eyes, and which blue eyes, play severally in the company. How shall a man escape from his ancestors, or draw off from his veins the black drop[34] which he drew from his father's or his mother's life? It often appears in a family, as if all the qualities of the progenitors were potted in several jars,—some ruling quality in each son or daughter of the house,—and sometimes the unmixed temperament, the rank unmitigated elixir, the family vice, is drawn off in a separate individual, and the others are proportionally relieved. We sometimes see a change of expression in our companion, and say, his father, or his mother, comes to the windows of his eyes, and sometimes a remote relative. In different hours, a man represents each of several of his ancestors, as if there were seven or eight of us rolled up in each man's skin,— seven or eight ancestors at least,—and they constitute the variety of notes for that new piece of music which his life is. At the corner of the street, you read the possibility of each passenger,[35] in the facial angle, in the complexion, in the depth of his eye. His parentage determines it. Men are what their mothers made them. You may as well ask a loom which weaves huckaback,[36] why it does not make cashmere, as expect poetry from this engineer, or a chemical discovery from that jobber. Ask the digger in the ditch to explain Newton's laws: the fine organs of his brain have been pinched by overwork and squalid poverty from father to son, for a hundred years. When each comes forth from his mother's womb, the gate of gifts closes behind him. Let him value his hands and feet, he has but one pair. So he has but one future, and that is already predetermined in his lobes, and described in that little fatty face, pig-eye, and squat form. All the privilege and all the legislation of the world cannot meddle or help to make a poet or a prince of him.

Jesus said, "When he looketh on her, he hath committed adultery."[37] But he is an adulterer before he has yet looked on the woman, by the superfluity of animal, and the defect of thought, in his constitution. Who meets him, or who meets her, in the street, sees that they are ripe to be each other's victim.

In certain men, digestion and sex absorb the vital force, and the stronger these are, the individual is so much weaker. The more of these drones perish, the better for the hive. If, later, they give birth to some superior individual, with force enough to add to this animal a new aim, and a complete apparatus to work it out, all the ancestors are gladly forgotten. Most men and most women are merely one couple more. Now and then, one has a new cell or camarilla[38] opened in his brain,—an architectural, a musical, or a philological knack, some stray taste or talent for flowers, or chemistry, or pigments, or story-telling, a good hand for drawing, a good foot for dancing, an athletic frame for wide journeying, &c.—which skill nowise alters rank in

the spirit's house cost too much any more than a merchant's who ruins himself to live on Beacon St" (a fashionable Boston location) (J 11:417).

31    In his Journal (1844–1845), Emerson wrote, "People seem to me often sheathed in their tough organization. I know those who are the charge each of their several Daemon, and in whom the Daemon at intervals appears at the gates of their eyes. They have intervals, God knows, of weakness & folly like other people. Of these I take no heed: I wait the reappearings of the Genius, which are sure and beautiful" (J 9:119–120; the daemon or genius is the guiding agent of inspiration in an individual).

32    Phrenologists, well known in Emerson's day, studied the shapes of heads to gain insight into human character; Johann Spurzheim (1776–1832) was one of them. Lambert Adolphe Quételet (1796–1874) was a Belgian astronomer and statistician who defined the *homme moyen*, or average individual.

33    The ancient doctrine of the four humors (sanguine, choleric, phlegmatic, and melancholic), popular in the Renaissance, lived on in Emerson's era.

34    Trace of melancholia (black bile).

35    Passerby.

36    Rough cotton or linen cloth, used for towels.

37    Matthew 6:28: "Whosoever looketh on a woman to lust after her hath committed adultery with her already in his heart."

38    Small room.

39    Joseph von Fraunhofer (1787–1826),
German inventor of microscopes and telescopes; William Carpenter (1813–1885), English physician, author of *The Microscope and Its
Revelations* (1856).

40    The Whigs, who supported the U.S.
Bank against the Democrats and advocated the
Compromise of 1850, last elected Zachary Taylor (1784–1850) to the presidency, in 1848. The
party dissolved in 1856. The Free-Soil Party
(1848–1854) opposed slavery in the territories. Emerson in his Journal (1845–1846) wrote,
"Whiggism, a feast of shells, idolatrous of the
forms of legislature; like a cat loving the house
not the inhabitant" (J 9:269).

41    Emerson's own rendition of the doctrine
of karma, familiar then as now.

42    From *Philosophical Studies on the Essence of
Human Freedom* (1809) by the German thinker
F. W. J. von Schelling (1775–1854).

43    The philosopher Stanley Cavell notes
that that etymology of "condition" suggests
"writing together," as opposed to the unilateral
"dictation," emphasized earlier in the essay.
"Account" implies an economic book-balancing,
as well as a narrative.

44    Emerson often thought of New Hampshire as the home of swaggering, wild heroic
spirits. Napoleon Bonaparte (1769–1821), emperor of France; Edmund Burke (1729–1797),
Anglo-Irish statesman and author; Henry Peter,
first Baron Brougham and Vaux (1778–1868),
Scottish politician, crusader against the English
slave trade and for education and voting rights;
Daniel Webster (1782–1852), American statesman and orator, much admired by Emerson until he announced his support for the Fugitive
Slave Law of 1850; and Lajos Kossuth (1802–
*(continued)*

the scale of nature, but serves to pass the time, the life of sensation going on as before. At last, these hints and tendencies are fixed in one, or in a succession. Each absorbs so much food and force, as to become itself a new centre. The new talent draws off so rapidly the vital force, that not enough remains for the animal functions, hardly enough for health; so that, in the second generation, if the like genius appear, the health is visibly deteriorated, and the generative force impaired.

People are born with the moral or with the material bias;—uterine brothers with this diverging destination: and I suppose, with high magnifiers, Mr. Frauenhofer or Dr. Carpenter[39] might come to distinguish in the embryo at the fourth day, this is a Whig, and that a Free-soiler.[40]

It was a poetic attempt to lift this mountain of Fate, to reconcile this despotism of race with liberty, which led the Hindoos to say, "Fate is nothing but the deeds committed in a prior state of existence."[41] I find the coincidence of the extremes of eastern and western speculation in the daring statement of Schelling, "there is in every man a certain feeling, that he has been what he is from all eternity, and by no means became such in time."[42] To say it less sublimely,—in the history of the individual is always an account of his condition, and he knows himself to be a party to his present estate.[43]

A good deal of our politics is physiological. Now and then, a man of wealth in the heyday of youth adopts the tenet of broadest freedom. In England, there is always some man of wealth and large connection planting himself, during all his years of health, on the side of progress, who, as soon as he begins to die, checks his forward play, calls in his troops, and becomes conservative. All conservatives are such from personal defects. They have been effeminated by position or nature, born halt and blind, through luxury of their parents, and can only, like invalids, act on the defensive. But strong natures, backwoodsmen, New Hampshire giants, Napoleons, Burkes, Broughams, Websters, Kossuths, are inevitable patriots, until their life ebbs, and their defects and gout, palsy and money, warp them.[44]

The strongest idea incarnates itself in majorities and nations, in the healthiest and strongest. Probably, the election goes by avoirdupois[45] weight, and, if you could weigh bodily the tonnage of any hundred of the Whig and the Democratic party in a town, on the Dearborn balance, as they passed the hayscales, you could predict with certainty which party would carry it.[46] On the whole, it would be rather the speediest way of deciding the vote, to put the selectmen or the mayor and aldermen at the hayscales.

In science, we have to consider two things: power and circumstance. All we know of the egg, from each successive discovery, is, *another vesicle*;[47] and if, after five hundred years, you get a better observer, or a better glass, he finds within the last observed another. In vegetable and animal tissue, it is just alike, and all that the primary power or spasm operates, is, still, vesicles, vesicles. Yes,—but the tyrannical Circumstance! A vesicle in new circumstances, a vesicle lodged in darkness, Oken thought, became animal; in light, a plant.[48] Lodged in the parent animal, it suffers changes, which end in unsheathing miraculous capability in the unaltered vesicle, and it unlocks itself to fish, bird, or quadruped, head and foot, eye and claw. The Circumstance is Nature. Nature is, what you may do. There is much you may not. We have two things,—the circumstance, and the life. Once we thought, positive power was all. Now we learn, that negative power, or circumstance, is half. Nature is the tyrannous circumstance, the thick skull, the sheathed snake, the ponderous, rock-like jaw; necessitated activity; violent direction; the conditions of a tool, like the locomotive, strong enough on its track, but which can do nothing but mischief off of it; or skates, which are wings on the ice, but fetters on the ground.[49]

The book of Nature is the book of Fate.[50] She turns the gigantic pages,—leaf after leaf,—never re-turning one. One leaf she lays down, a floor of granite; then a thousand ages, and a bed of slate; a thousand ages, and a measure of coal; a thousand ages, and a layer of marl and mud: vegetable forms appear; her first misshapen animals, zoophyte, trilobium, fish; then, saurians,[51]—rude forms, in which she has only blocked her future statue, concealing under these unwieldy monsters the fine type of her coming king. The face of the planet cools and dries, the races meliorate, and man is born. But when a race has lived its term, it comes no more again.[52]

The population of the world is a conditional population; not the best, but the best that could live now; and the scale of tribes, and the steadiness with which victory adheres to one tribe, and defeat to another, is as uniform as the superposition of strata. We know in history what weight belongs to race.[53] We see the English, French, and Germans planting themselves on every shore and market of America and Australia, and monopolizing the com-

1894), leader of the Hungarian Revolution of 1848, widely celebrated in America.

45     Measured in pounds and ounces.

46     The New England printer Benjamin Dearborn (1754–1838) invented the spring scales. Concord's Dearborn balance was large enough for a group of men to stand on.

47     Cell or sac.

48     Lorenz Oken (1779–1851), a German natural scientist, argued that all organisms originate from vesicles (cells) affected by differing conditions. Emerson noted in an 1851 Journal entry that "the naturalist can carry us no farther than the vesicle which has the capacity of change into oak, ape, man, & God" (J 11:425).

49     In his Journal (1851), Emerson wrote, "There is a thick skull, that is fate. The crustacia, the birds, the tortoises, are fatalists, yet amelioration must be assumed. These very walls & jails must be believed to be charity & protection; & meanness the preparation of magnificence: as madness is assumed to be a screen of a too much tempted soul" (J 11:393).

50     In Christian tradition, God was considered the author of the Book of Nature (the natural world).

51     Zoophyte: a primitive plant-like animal (such as a coral or sponge); trilobium: trilobite, a tiny extinct creature abundantly preserved in fossil remains; saurians: here, dinosaurs. In his Journal in March 1836, Emerson remarked, "We detect the brother of the human Hand in the fin of the whale & the flipper of the saurus" (J 5:137); in his essay "Works and Days" he referred to "the secular, refined, composite anatomy of man, which all strata go to form, which the prior races, from infusory and saurian, existed to ripen."

52    In his Journal (March–October 1848) Emerson wrote, "You cannot preserve races beyond their term" (J 10:357); and earlier in the 1840s, "It seems enough monument to any life to have thrown some thought into circulation, a line of verse, a new word. That is far more than the most have done. We are the madripores that build up the continents. What is the Past? We we we are the past or shall be so presently. And it is made up of just such indecisive melancholy pieces as we are overpowered all the while by the tide of tendency" (J 8:478; madripores are corals).

53    In a Journal entry of 1852 headed "Abolition," Emerson reflected on the relation between race and fate: "The argument of the slaveholder is one & simple: he pleads Fate. Here is an inferior race requiring wardship,— it is sentimentality to deny it. The argument of the abolitionist is, it is inhuman to treat a man thus." Emerson went on to denounce the Fugitive Slave Law of 1850: "If you cannot keep them without my help, let them go" (J 13:114).

54    Rough paraphrases from *The Races of Men: A Fragment* (1850) by Robert Knox (1791–1862), Scottish physician who believed in the strength of "pure" races, and warned against interracial marriage. He became notorious for buying corpses for dissection from the grave-robbers Burke and Hare. "Crab" here means "crab-apple" (devolved from the cultivated apple).

55    Guano began to be imported as a fertilizer from the Peruvian islands to England in the 1840s. The analogy suggests that the workers' bodies are like bird droppings, used to enrich the land.

56    Fagot: bundle of sticks or rods; adamantine bandages: unyielding bands or chains. "Adamantine Chains" hold the fallen angels in *Paradise Lost* (1667), 1.48, by the English poet John Milton (1608–1674). The Statistical Society of London was established in 1834.

57    Accidental.

58    The singer Jenny Lind (1820–1887), known as the Swedish nightingale, caused a sensation when she toured America in 1850–1852. Nathaniel Bowditch (1773–1838) was a talented mathematician and navigator, author of *The New American Practical Navigator* (1802), known as the Sailor's Bible.

59    "Everything which pertains to the human species, considered as a whole, belongs to the order of physical facts. The greater the number of individuals, the more does the influence of the individual will disappear, leaving predominance to a series of general facts dependent on causes by which society exists, and is preserved."—QUETELET (Emerson's note). Adolphe Quetelet (1796–1874) was a Belgian statistician and sociologist.

60    Homer, Greek epic poet (ca. 9th century BCE); Zoroaster, Iranian religious leader (ca. 11th century BCE); Menu or Manu, legendary Sanskrit lawgiver. In the Bible Tubal-Cain is credited with the invention of metallurgy (Genesis 4:22); Vulcan is the Roman metalsmith god. Cadmus of Tyre, according to legend, brought the Phoenician alphabet to Greece. Nicolas Copernicus (1473–1543) developed the modern idea of the solar system; Johann Fust (ca. 1400–1466), was the partner of the German blacksmith Johannes Gutenberg (1400–1468), who invented movable-type printing. The American engineer Robert Fulton (1765–1815) operated the first steamboat.

merce of these countries. We like the nervous and victorious habit of our own branch of the family. We follow the step of the Jew, of the Indian, of the Negro. We see how much will has been expended to extinguish the Jew, in vain. Look at the unpalatable conclusions of Knox, in his "Fragment of Races,"—a rash and unsatisfactory writer, but charged with pungent and unforgetable truths. "Nature respects race, and not hybrids." "Every race has its own *habitat*." "Detach a colony from the race, and it deteriorates to the crab."[54] See the shades of the picture. The German and Irish millions, like the Negro, have a great deal of guano in their destiny.[55] They are ferried over the Atlantic, and carted over America, to ditch and to drudge, to make corn cheap, and then to lie down prematurely to make a spot of green grass on the prairie.

One more fagot of these adamantine bandages, is, the new science of Statistics.[56] It is a rule, that the most casual[57] and extraordinary events—if the basis of population is broad enough—become matter of fixed calculation. It would not be safe to say when a captain like Bonaparte, a singer like Jenny Lind, or a navigator like Bowditch,[58] would be born in Boston: but, on a population of twenty or two hundred millions, something like accuracy may be had.[59]

'Tis frivolous to fix pedantically the date of particular inventions. They have all been invented over and over fifty times. Man is the arch machine, of which all these shifts drawn from himself are toy models. He helps himself on each emergency by copying or duplicating his own structure, just so far as the need is. 'Tis hard to find the right Homer, Zoroaster, or Menu; harder still to find the Tubal Cain, or Vulcan, or Cadmus, or Copernicus, or Fust, or Fulton, the indisputable inventor.[60] There are scores and centuries of them. "The air is full of men."[61] This kind of talent so abounds, this constructive tool-making efficiency, as if it adhered to the chemic atoms, as if the air he breathes were made of Vaucansons, Franklins, and Watts.[62]

Doubtless, in every million there will be an astronomer, a mathematician, a comic poet, a mystic. No one can read the history of astronomy, without perceiving that Copernicus, Newton, Laplace,[63] are not new men, or a new kind of men, but that Thales, Anaximenes, Hipparchus, Empedocles, Aristarchus, Pythagoras, Œnopides,[64] had anticipated them; each had the same tense geometrical brain, apt for the same vigorous computation and

61 From the poem "Death" (1843) by William Ellery Channing (1818–1901), Concord writer and friend of Emerson. Joseph Fouché (1763–1829), Napoleon's chief of police, warned, "The air is full of poniards" (that is, knives)—a saying well known in Emerson's time.

62 The French inventor Jacques de Vaucanson (1709–1782) developed machines used in textile- and metal-working, as well as colorful automata (mechanical puppets). Benjamin Franklin (1706–1790), the American statesman, brilliantly researched electricity; the Scottish engineer James Watt (1736–1819) developed a revolutionary steam engine.

63 The Englishman Sir Isaac Newton (1642–1727) and the Frenchman Pierre Laplace (1749–1827) revolutionized physics, mathematics, and astronomy.

64 A series of ancient Greek thinkers who anticipated modern discoveries. Thales (ca. 624–ca. 545 BCE) was thought to have founded geometry; Anaximenes (6th century BCE) produced theories of the physical elements; Hipparchus (2nd century BCE) accurately predicted the movements of the sun and moon and discovered the principle of the equinox; Empedocles (ca. 493–ca. 433 BCE) developed a sophisticated and influential theory of the cosmos, which he saw as inhabited by contrary forces, Love and Strife; Aristarchus (3rd century BCE) thought that the earth revolved around the sun; Pythagoras (6th century BCE) revealed the mathematical basis of musical scales; and Oenopides (5th century BCE) discovered the obliquity of the ecliptic in geometry.

65    Meridian: line showing longitude. The Roman mile (*milia passus*) consisted of a thousand five-foot paces. Emerson believed that sixty such miles equal one degree on the equator (see J 2:368). In fact, a Roman mile is about 1.47 kilometers, and one degree of equatorial longitude equals 111 kilometers. In Emerson's day it was widely believed that ancient units of measurement were derived from a calculation of the circumference of the earth.

66    In 1582, Pope Gregory XIII (1502–1585) introduced a reformed calendar that stabilized the occurrence of the vernal equinox (the point when the sun is at the zenith over the equator and night and day are equally long) and modified the cycle of leap years. Earlier, Muslim and ancient Chinese astronomers had made similar calendar reforms.

67    Cowry shells from the South Pacific were used as currency by New England traders in West Africa. The orange cowry (which Emerson calls orangia) was particularly valuable and rare.

68    Emerson remembers an observation about muffins credited to Carlyle in "First Visit to England," from *English Traits*; but he adds his sense of the beauty of casualty.

69    The British humor magazine *Punch* was first published in 1841.

70    Driving forward.

71    Emerson may be remembering the scene in "The Castaway" (1799) by the English poet William Cowper (1731–1800): "When snatch'd from all effectual aid, / We perish'd, each alone." He certainly remembers here the drowning death of his dear friend Margaret
(continued)

logic, a mind parallel to the movement of the world. The Roman mile probably rested on a measure of a degree of the meridian.[65] Mahometan and Chinese know what we know of leap-year, of the Gregorian calendar, and of the precession of the equinoxes.[66] As, in every barrel of cowries, brought to New Bedford, there shall be one *orangia*, so there will, in a dozen million of Malays and Mahometans, be one or two astronomical skulls.[67] In a large city, the most casual things, and things whose beauty lies in their casualty, are produced as punctually and to order as the baker's muffin for breakfast.[68] Punch makes exactly one capital joke a week;[69] and the journals contrive to furnish one good piece of news every day.

And not less work the laws of repression, the penalties of violated functions. Famine, typhus, frost, war, suicide, and effete races, must be reckoned calculable parts of the system of the world.

These are pebbles from the mountain, hints of the terms by which our life is walled up, and which show a kind of mechanical exactness, as of a loom or mill, in what we call casual or fortuitous events.

The force with which we resist these torrents of tendency[70] looks so ridiculously inadequate, that it amounts to little more than a criticism or a protest made by a minority of one, under compulsion of millions. I seemed, in the height of a tempest, to see men overboard struggling in the waves, and driven about here and there. They glanced intelligently at each other, but 'twas little they could do for one another; 'twas much if each could keep afloat alone. Well, they had a right to their eyebeams, and all the rest was Fate.[71]

\* \* \*

We cannot trifle with this reality, this cropping-out in our planted gardens of the core of the world. No picture of life can have any veracity that does not admit the odious facts. A man's power is hooped in by a necessity, which, by many experiments, he touches on every side, until he learns its arc.[72]

The element running through entire nature, which we popularly call Fate, is known to us as limitation. Whatever limits us, we call Fate. If we are brute and barbarous, the fate takes a brute and dreadful shape. As we refine, our checks become finer. If we rise to spiritual culture, the antagonism takes a spiritual form.[73] In the Hindoo fables, Vishnu follows Maya through all her ascending changes, from insect and crawfish up to elephant; whatever form she took, he took the male form of that kind, until she became at last woman and goddess, and he a man and a god.[74] The limitations refine as the soul purifies, but the ring of necessity is always perched at the top.

When the gods in the Norse heaven were unable to bind the Fenris Wolf with steel or with weight of mountains,—the one he snapped and the other he spurned with his heel,—they put round his foot a limp band softer than silk or cobweb, and this held him: the more he spurned it, the stiffer it drew.[75] So soft and so stanch is the ring of Fate. Neither brandy, nor nectar, nor sulphuric ether, nor hell-fire, nor ichor,[76] nor poetry, nor genius, can get rid of this limp band. For if we give it the high sense in which the poets use it, even thought itself is not above Fate: that too must act according to eternal laws, and all that is wilful and fantastic in it is in opposition to its fundamental essence.

And, last of all, high over thought, in the world of morals, Fate appears as vindicator, levelling the high, lifting the low, requiring justice in man, and always striking soon or late, when justice is not done. What is useful will last; what is hurtful will sink.[77] "The doer must suffer," said the Greeks: "you would soothe a Deity not to be soothed." "God himself cannot procure good for the wicked," said the Welsh triad. "God may consent, but only for a time," said the bard of Spain.[78] The limitation is impassable by any insight of man. In its last and loftiest ascensions, insight itself, and the freedom of the will, is one of its obedient members. But we must not run into generalizations too large, but show the natural bounds or essential distinctions, and seek to do justice to the other elements as well.

\* \* \*

Thus we trace Fate, in matter, mind, and morals,—in race, in retardations of strata, and in thought and character as well. It is everywhere bound or limitation. But Fate has its lord; limitation its limits; is different seen from above and from below; from within and from without. For, though Fate is im-

Fuller (1810–1850). Emerson critic Joel Porte notes that, several pages later, Emerson counteracts the image of the drowning men's eyebeams with that of the hero, writing that "the glance of his eye has the force of sunbeams"— but we still recall the grim shipwreck.

72    Compare Emerson's statement earlier in "Fate" that public opinion was suppressed "with clamps and hoops of castles, garrisons, and police. But, sometimes, the religious principle would get in, and burst the hoops . . ." Emerson no longer thinks of bursting free from bonds, but rather of learning their contours.

Many years earlier, in the introductory lecture of his series "Human Culture" (1837), Emerson noted that man's "power is straitly hooped in by a necessity which by constant experiments he touches on every side until at length he learns its arc, which is learning his own nature" (EL 2:221–222).

73    The emphasis on refinement, on an ascent from the brute to the sophisticated, characterizes *The Conduct of Life*. "We begin low with coarse masks, and rise to the subtle and beautiful," Emerson writes in "Illusions." Earlier in "Fate," he notes that the "impressionable man"—and, especially, woman—"yields to a current so feeble as can be felt only by a needle delicately poised."

74    The Hindu god Vishnu's incarnations are said to be innumerable in the Puranas (Sanskrit religious texts). The goddess Maya represents illusion.

75    In 1847 Emerson enthusiastically read an 1842 translation of the Icelandic *Prose Edda*, an account of Norse mythology by Snorri Sturluson (1179–1241). It describes the band that held
*(continued)*

the foot of the giant Fenris wolf as "made of six things, footfall of cat, beard of woman, root of stone, sinew of bear, breath of fish, & spittle of bird," all melded in a smithy "smooth & soft as a silken string" (J 10:108–109). In *English Traits*, Emerson declared, "The telegraph is a limp-band that will hold the Fenris-wolf of war."

76   Sulphuric ether (later known simply as ether) was an anesthetic, often used for its intoxicating effects (J 10:116); later in *The Conduct of Life* (the essay "Culture"), Emerson remarks on its "benign discovery." According to Homer, the Olympian gods have in their veins not blood but ichor.

77   A dramatic contrast to the shipwreck described earlier in "Fate."

78   Emerson refers to Greek tragedy; to the triads, or three-line stanzas, of Welsh bards, as described by Edward Davies (1756–1831) in his *Mythology and Rites of the British Druids* (1809), which Emerson read; and to a Spanish proverb of unknown origin.

79   Four-handed (used to describe apes and monkeys).

80   Variation on a sentence in *On Providence and Fate* by the Neoplatonic philosopher Proclus (412–485), translated by Thomas Taylor (1758–1835).

81   An inferior or impoverished (view of things).

82   The Journal entry (May–November 1851) that formed the basis for this passage continued: "Let him empty his breast of all that is superfluous & traditional, of all dependence on the accidental, on money, on false fame, falsehood of any kind; & speak wild truth, & by manners & actions as unaffected as the weather,
*(continued)*

mense, so is power, which is the other fact in the dual world, immense. If Fate follows and limits power, power attends and antagonizes Fate. We must respect Fate as natural history, but there is more than natural history. For who and what is this criticism that pries into the matter? Man is not order of nature, sack and sack, belly and members, link in a chain, nor any ignominious baggage, but a stupendous antagonism, a dragging together of the poles of the Universe. He betrays his relation to what is below him,—thick-skulled, small-brained, fishy, quadrumanous,[79]—quadruped ill-disguised, hardly escaped into biped, and has paid for the new powers by loss of some of the old ones. But the lightning which explodes and fashions planets, maker of planets and suns, is in him. On one side, elemental order, sandstone and granite, rock-ledges, peat-bog, forest, sea and shore; and, on the other part, thought, the spirit which composes and decomposes nature,—here they are, side by side, god and devil, mind and matter, king and conspirator, belt and spasm, riding peacefully together in the eye and brain of every man.

Nor can he blink the freewill. To hazard the contradiction,—freedom is necessary. If you please to plant yourself on the side of Fate, and say, Fate is all; then we say, a part of Fate is the freedom of man. Forever wells up the impulse of choosing and acting in the soul. Intellect annuls Fate. So far as a man thinks, he is free. And though nothing is more disgusting than the crowing about liberty by slaves, as most men are, and the flippant mistaking for freedom of some paper preamble like a "Declaration of Independence," or the statute right to vote, by those who have never dared to think or to act, yet it is wholesome to man to look not at Fate, but the other way: the practical view is the other. His sound relation to these facts is to use and command, not to cringe to them. "Look not on nature, for her name is fatal," said the oracle.[80] The too much contemplation of these limits induces meanness.[81] They who talk much of destiny, their birth-star, &c., are in a lower dangerous plane, and invite the evils they fear.

I cited the instinctive and heroic races as proud believers in Destiny. They conspire with it; a loving resignation is with the event. But the dogma makes a different impression, when it is held by the weak and lazy. 'Tis weak and vicious people who cast the blame on Fate. The right use of Fate is to bring up our conduct to the loftiness of nature. Rude and invincible except by themselves are the elements. So let man be.[82] Let him empty his breast of his windy conceits, and show his lordship by manners and deeds on the scale of nature. Let him hold his purpose as with the tug of gravitation. No power, no persuasion, no bribe shall make him give up his point.[83] A man ought to compare advantageously with a river, an oak, or a mountain. He shall have not less the flow, the expansion, and the resistance of these.

'Tis the best use of Fate to teach a fatal courage. Go face the fire at sea, or the cholera in your friend's house, or the burglar in your own, or what danger lies in the way of duty, knowing you are guarded by the cherubim of Destiny.[84] If you believe in Fate to your harm, believe it, at least, for your good.

For, if Fate is so prevailing, man also is part of it, and can confront fate with fate. If the Universe have these savage accidents, our atoms are as savage in resistance. We should be crushed by the atmosphere, but for the reaction of the air within the body. A tube made of a film of glass can resist the shock of the ocean, if filled with the same water. If there be omnipotence in the stroke, there is omnipotence of recoil.

1. But Fate against Fate is only parrying and defence: there are, also, the noble creative forces. The revelation of Thought takes man out of servitude into freedom. We rightly say of ourselves, we were born, and afterward we were born again, and many times. We have successive experiences so important, that the new forgets the old, and hence the mythology of the seven or the nine heavens.[85] The day of days, the great day of the feast of life, is that in which the inward eye opens to the Unity in things, to the omnipresence of law;—sees that what is must be, and ought to be, or is the best. This beatitude dips from on high down on us, and we see. It is not in us so much as we are in it. If the air come to our lungs, we breathe and live; if not, we die. If the light come to our eyes, we see; else not. And if truth come to our mind, we suddenly expand to its dimensions, as if we grew to worlds. We are as lawgivers; we speak for Nature; we prophesy and divine.[86]

This insight throws us on the party and interest of the Universe, against all and sundry; against ourselves, as much as others.[87] A man speaking from insight affirms of himself what is true of the mind: seeing its immortality, he says, I am immortal; seeing its invincibility, he says, I am strong. It is not in

let him be instead of God to men, full of God, new & astonishing . . ." (J 11:387).

83 In his Journal (1851), Emerson had written, "I believe so much in metamorphosis, that I think the man will find the type not only in kind, but in quantity, of all his moral & mental properties in the great world without. He is to hold to his purposes with the tough impracticability of gravitation itself: 'no power nor wheedling on earth could have made' him give up his point" (J 11:386). The phrase in quotation marks is from a letter by the English Romantic poet George Gordon, Lord Byron (1788–1824), to his publisher, John Murray (Venice, March 9, 1817).

84 In the Bible, cherubim, evidently mysterious winged creatures, guard the gates of Eden so that Adam and Eve cannot return to it (Genesis 3:24); they later appear prominently in the book of Ezekiel and elsewhere.

85 The Koran refers to seven heavens; Ptolemaic astronomy described nine concentric spheres.

86 In this astonishing paragraph, Emerson drops his previous idea that our nobility consists in seeing ourselves as pieces of fate, just as implacable and severe as fate itself. Instead, he produces a wild, ecstatic vision of rebirth—and, as the critic Harold Bloom suggests, of self-begetting. Emerson sees beyond fate, to a new best.

87 In October 1837 Emerson admonished himself in his Journal, "Keep the habit of the observer & as fast as you can, break off your association with your personality & identify yourself with the Universe. Be a football to time & chance the more kicks the better so that you inspect the whole game & know its uttermost law" (J 5:391).

88    Minuscule particles.

us, but we are in it. It is of the maker, not of what is made. All things are touched and changed by it. This uses, and is not used. It distances those who share it, from those who share it not. Those who share it not are flocks and herds. It dates from itself;—not from former men or better men,—gospel, or constitution, or college, or custom. Where it shines, Nature is no longer intrusive, but all things make a musical or pictorial impression. The world of men show like a comedy without laughter:—populations, interests, government, history;—'tis all toy figures in a toy house. It does not overvalue particular truths. We hear eagerly every thought and word quoted from an intellectual man. But, in his presence, our own mind is roused to activity, and we forget very fast what he says, much more interested in the new play of our own thought, than in any thought of his. 'Tis the majesty into which we have suddenly mounted, the impersonality, the scorn of egotisms, the sphere of laws, that engage us. Once we were stepping a little this way, and a little that way; now, we are as men in a balloon, and do not think so much of the point we have left, or the point we would make, as of the liberty and glory of the way.

Just as much intellect as you add, so much organic power. He who sees through the design, presides over it, and must will that which must be. We sit and rule, and, though we sleep, our dream will come to pass. Our thought, though it were only an hour old, affirms an oldest necessity, not to be separated from thought, and not to be separated from will. They must always have coëxisted. It apprises us of its sovereignty and godhead, which refuse to be severed from it. It is not mine or thine, but the will of all mind. It is poured into the souls of all men, as the soul itself which constitutes them men. I know not whether there be, as is alleged, in the upper region of our atmosphere, a permanent westerly current, which carries with it all atoms[88] which rise to that height, but I see, that when souls reach a certain clearness of perception, they accept a knowledge and motive above selfishness. A breath of will blows eternally through the universe of souls in the direction of the Right and Necessary. It is the air which all intellects inhale and exhale, and it is the wind which blows the worlds into order and orbit.

Thought dissolves the material universe, by carrying the mind up into a sphere where all is plastic. Of two men, each obeying his own thought, he whose thought is deepest will be the strongest character. Always one man more than another represents the will of Divine Providence to the period.

2. If thought makes free, so does the moral sentiment. The mixtures of spiritual chemistry refuse to be analyzed. Yet we can see that with the perception of truth is joined the desire that it shall prevail. That affection is essential to will. Moreover, when a strong will appears, it usually results from a certain unity of organization, as if the whole energy of body and mind flowed in one direction. All great force is real and elemental. There is no manufacturing a strong will. There must be a pound to balance a pound. Where power is shown in will, it must rest on the universal force. Alaric[89] and Bonaparte must believe they rest on a truth, or their will can be bought or bent. There is a bribe possible for any finite will. But the pure sympathy with universal ends is an infinite force, and cannot be bribed or bent. Whoever has had experience of the moral sentiment cannot choose but believe in unlimited power. Each pulse from that heart is an oath from the Most High. I know not what the word *sublime* means, if it be not the intimations in this infant of a terrific force. A text of heroism, a name and anecdote of courage, are not arguments, but sallies of freedom. One of these is the verse of the Persian Hafiz, "'Tis written on the gate of Heaven, 'Wo unto him who suffers himself to be betrayed by Fate!'"[90] Does the reading of history make us fatalists? What courage does not the opposite opinion show! A little whim of will to be free gallantly contending against the universe of chemistry.

But insight is not will, nor is affection will. Perception is cold, and goodness dies in wishes; as Voltaire said, 'tis the misfortune of worthy people that they are cowards; *"un des plus grands malheurs des honnêtes gens c'est qu'ils sont des lâches."*[91] There must be a fusion of these two to generate the energy of will. There can be no driving force, except through the conversion of the man into his will, making him the will, and the will him. And one may say boldly, that no man has a right perception of any truth, who has not been reacted on by it, so as to be ready to be its martyr.

The one serious and formidable thing in nature is a will. Society is servile from want of will, and therefore the world wants saviours and religions. One way is right to go: the hero sees it, and moves on that aim, and has the world under him for root and support. He is to others as the world. His

89   The Visigoth chieftain Alaric (ca. 370–410) sacked Rome in 410.

90   Hafiz (ca. 1325–ca. 1389), Persian poet much admired by Emerson, who read him in the German translation of von Hammer-Purgstall.

91   An aphorism of the French skeptical philosopher Voltaire (François-Marie Alouet, 1694–1778): "One of the greatest misfortunes of decent people is that they are cowards." In the original Journal passage (1859), Emerson added, "But strong will, perfect will is electricity, is unquenchable fire, & burns like the sun, & all creatures must conform themselves accordingly" (J 14:337).

92    Measure.

93    Later in *The Conduct of Life*, in the essay "Wealth," Emerson wrote, "Within doors, a system settles itself paramount and tyrannical over master and mistress, servant and child, cousin and acquaintance. 'Tis in vain that genius or virtue or energy of character strive and cry against it. This is fate."

94    That is, at the exchange or bourse, the place for trading stocks.

95    Morally unprincipled people.

approbation is honor; his dissent, infamy. The glance of his eye has the force of sunbeams. A personal influence towers up in memory only worthy, and we gladly forget numbers, money, climate, gravitation, and the rest of Fate.

\* \* \*

We can afford to allow the limitation, if we know it is the meter[92] of the growing man. We stand against Fate, as children stand up against the wall in their father's house, and notch their height from year to year. But when the boy grows to man, and is master of the house, he pulls down that wall, and builds a new and bigger. 'Tis only a question of time. Every brave youth is in training to ride and rule this dragon. His science is to make weapons and wings of these passions and retarding forces. Now whether, seeing these two things, fate and power, we are permitted to believe in unity? The bulk of mankind believe in two gods. They are under one dominion here in the house, as friend and parent,[93] in social circles, in letters, in art, in love, in religion: but in mechanics, in dealing with steam and climate, in trade, in politics, they think they come under another; and that it would be a practical blunder to transfer the method and way of working of one sphere, into the other. What good, honest, generous men at home, will be wolves and foxes on change![94] What pious men in the parlor will vote for what reprobates[95] at the polls! To a certain point, they believe themselves the care of a Providence. But, in a steamboat, in an epidemic, in war, they believe a malignant energy rules.

But relation and connection are not somewhere and sometimes, but everywhere and always. The divine order does not stop where their sight stops. The friendly power works on the same rules, in the next farm, and the next planet. But, where they have not experience, they run against it, and hurt themselves. Fate, then, is a name for facts not yet passed under the fire of thought;—for causes which are unpenetrated.

But every jet of chaos which threatens to exterminate us, is convertible by intellect into wholesome force. Fate is unpenetrated causes. The water drowns ship and sailor, like a grain of dust. But learn to swim, trim your bark, and the wave which drowned it, will be cloven by it, and carry it, like its own foam, a plume and a power. The cold is inconsiderate of persons, tingles your blood, freezes a man like a dew-drop.[96] But learn to skate, and the ice will give you a graceful, sweet, and poetic motion. The cold will brace your limbs and brain to genius, and make you foremost men of time. Cold and sea will train an imperial Saxon race, which nature cannot bear to lose, and, after cooping it up for a thousand years in yonder England, gives a hundred Englands a hundred Mexicos. All the bloods it shall absorb and domineer: and more than Mexicos,—the secrets of water and steam, the spasms of electricity, the ductility of metals, the chariot of the air, the ruddered balloon[97] are awaiting you.

The annual slaughter from typhus far exceeds that of war; but right drainage destroys typhus. The plague in the sea-service from scurvy is healed by lemon juice and other diets portable or procurable: the depopulation by cholera and small-pox is ended by drainage and vaccination; and every other pest is not less in the chain of cause and effect, and may be fought off. And, whilst art draws out the venom, it commonly extorts some benefit from the vanquished enemy. The mischievous torrent is taught to drudge for man: the wild beasts he makes useful for food, or dress, or labor; the chemic explosions are controlled like his watch. These are now the steeds on which he rides. Man moves in all modes, by legs of horses, by wings of wind, by steam, by gas of balloon, by electricity, and stands on tiptoe threatening to hunt the eagle in his own element. There's nothing he will not make his carrier.

Steam was, till the other day, the devil which we dreaded. Every pot made by any human potter or brazier had a hole in its cover, to let off the enemy, lest he should lift pot and roof, and carry the house away. But the Marquis of Worcester, Watt, and Fulton[98] bethought themselves, that, where was power, was not devil, but was God; that it must be availed of, and not by any means let off and wasted. Could he lift pots and roofs and houses so handily? he was the workman they were in search of. He could be used to lift away, chain, and compel other devils, far more reluctant and dangerous, namely, cubic miles of earth, mountains, weight or resistance of water, machinery, and the labors of all men in the world; and time he shall lengthen, and shorten space.

96    In the essay "Culture" (also in *The Conduct of Life*) Emerson wrote, "For performance, Nature has no mercy, and sacrifices the performer to get it done; makes a dropsy or a tympany of him."

97    Ductility: flexibility. The ruddered balloon, invented in 1872, was steered by a triangular sail.

98    Edward Somerset, Marquis of Worcester (ca. 1601–1667), invented a steam water pump. Imprisoned in the Tower of London in the 1650s, he observed the lid of a steaming pot rising and falling—his "Eureka" moment. Somerset wrote a book describing one hundred of his inventions, *Century of Inventions* (1663).

99    This physician, the Emerson scholar Joseph Slater suggests, may have been the American Oliver Wendell Holmes, Sr. (1809–1894), also a well-known poet.

100   In Shakespeare's *Merchant of Venice*, Shylock tells Antonio that "sufferance [that is, patience] is the badge of all our tribe" (1.3.111).

It has not fared much otherwise with higher kinds of steam. The opinion of the million was the terror of the world, and it was attempted, either to dissipate it, by amusing nations, or to pile it over with strata of society,—a layer of soldiers; over that, a layer of lords; and a king on the top; with clamps and hoops of castles, garrisons, and police. But, sometimes, the religious principle would get in, and burst the hoops, and rive every mountain laid on top of it. The Fultons and Watts of politics, believing in unity, saw that it was a power, and, by satisfying it, (as justice satisfies everybody,) through a different disposition of society,—grouping it on a level, instead of piling it into a mountain,—they have contrived to make of this terror the most harmless and energetic form of a State.

Very odious, I confess, are the lessons of Fate. Who likes to have a dapper phrenologist pronouncing on his fortunes? Who likes to believe that he has hidden in his skull, spine, and pelvis, all the vices of a Saxon or Celtic race, which will be sure to pull him down,—with what grandeur of hope and resolve he is fired,—into a selfish, huckstering, servile, dodging animal? A learned physician tells us, the fact is invariable with the Neapolitan, that, when mature, he assumes the forms of the unmistakable scoundrel.[99] That is a little overstated,—but may pass.

But these are magazines and arsenals. A man must thank his defects, and stand in some terror of his talents. A transcendent talent draws so largely on his forces, as to lame him; a defect pays him revenues on the other side. The sufferance, which is the badge of the Jew, has made him, in these days, the ruler of the rulers of the earth.[100] If Fate is ore and quarry, if evil is good in the making, if limitation is power that shall be, if calamities, oppositions, and weights are wings and means,—we are reconciled.

Fate involves the melioration. No statement of the Universe can have any soundness, which does not admit its ascending effort. The direction of the whole, and of the parts, is toward benefit, and in proportion to the health. Behind every individual, closes organization: before him, opens liberty,—the Better, the Best. The first and worst races are dead. The second and imperfect races are dying out, or remain for the maturing of higher. In the latest race, in man, every generosity, every new perception, the love and praise he extorts from his fellows, are certificates of advance out of fate into freedom.

Liberation of the will from the sheaths and clogs of organization which he has outgrown, is the end and aim of this world.[101] Every calamity is a spur and valuable hint; and where his endeavors do not yet fully avail, they tell as tendency. The whole circle of animal life,—tooth against tooth,—devouring war, war for food, a yelp of pain and a grunt of triumph, until, at last, the whole menagerie, the whole chemical mass is mellowed and refined for higher use,—pleases at a sufficient perspective.[102]

But to see how fate slides into freedom, and freedom into fate, observe how far the roots of every creature run, or find, if you can, a point where there is no thread of connection. Our life is consentaneous[103] and far-related. This knot of nature is so well tied, that nobody was ever cunning enough to find the two ends. Nature is intricate, overlapped, interweaved, and endless. Christopher Wren said of the beautiful King's College chapel, "that, if anybody would tell him where to lay the first stone, he would build such another." But where shall we find the first atom in this house of man, which is all consent, inosculation,[104] and balance of parts?

The web of relation is shown in *habitat*, shown in hybernation. When hybernation was observed, it was found, that, whilst some animals became torpid[105] in winter, others were torpid in summer: hybernation then was a false name.[106] The *long sleep* is not an effect of cold, but is regulated by the supply of food proper to the animal. It becomes torpid when the fruit or prey it lives on is not in season, and regains its activity when its food is ready.

Eyes are found in light; ears in auricular[107] air; feet on land; fins in water; wings in air; and, each creature where it was meant to be, with a mutual fitness. Every zone has its own *Fauna*. There is adjustment between the animal and its food, its parasite, its enemy. Balances are kept. It is not allowed to diminish in numbers, nor to exceed. The like adjustments exist for man. His food is cooked, when he arrives; his coal in the pit; the house ventilated; the mud of the deluge dried; his companions arrived at the same hour, and awaiting him with love, concert, laughter, and tears. These are coarse adjustments, but the invisible are not less. There are more belongings to every creature than his lair and his food. His instincts must be met, and he has predisposing power that bends and fits what is near him to his use. He is not

101   Emerson was here influenced by his reading of a Hindu sacred text, the *Vishnu Purana*. In 1845 he wrote in his Journal, "Emancipation from *existence*, they say, is the Indian beatitude. I think it intends emancipation from *organization*" (J 9:307).

102   Emerson wrote in his Journal (September 20, 1838), "The fact detached is ugly. Replace it in its series of cause & effect, and it is beautiful. Putrefaction is loathsome; but putrefaction seen as a step in the circle of nature, pleases. . . . The laws of disease are the laws of health masked" (J 7:81).

103   Consistent, concurrent.

104   In physiology, the flowing of blood vessels into one another; from the Latin *osculum*, a kiss.

105   Dormant, sluggish.

106   The epoch-making British scientist Charles Darwin (1809–1882) makes this same point in *The Voyage of the Beagle* (1839) and proposes the term "aestivation" (from the Latin *aestas*, summer, rather than *hibernus*, of winter).

107   Audible or, here, suited to the ear.

108    Dante Alighieri (1265–1321), Italian epic poet; Christopher Columbus (1451–1506), Genoese explorer and discoverer of the New World. Emerson wrote of Dante in his Journal (1849), "Here is an imagination that rivals in closeness & precision the senses. But we must prize him as we do a rainbow, we can appropriate nothing of him" (J 11:134).

109    Darting.

110    Nipples (or other small protuberances).

111    Seed vessel.

112    G. W. F. Hegel (1770–1831), German idealist philosopher; Prince Clemens Metternich (1773–1859), Austrian statesman who was the main architect of political repression throughout Europe after the Congress of Vienna in 1815; John Adams (1735–1826), second president of the United States, whose son, John Quincy Adams (1767–1848), was also president; John C. Calhoun (1782–1850), American statesman and champion of the slaveholding states; François Guizot (1787–1874), French historian and reactionary politician; Sir Robert Peel (1788–1850), English conservative politician; Richard Cobden (1804–1865), English advocate of free trade who campaigned against the Corn Laws and the Crimean War (1853–1856); Meyer Rothschild (1743–1812), German-born founder of a dynasty of Jewish bankers central to the workings of European politics; John Jacob Astor (1763–1848), German-born American financier, fur trader, and philanthropist; Isambard Brunel (1806–1859), English engineer and designer of public works, railways, and steamships.

possible until the invisible things are right for him, as well as the visible. Of what changes, then, in sky and earth, and in finer skies and earth, does the appearance of some Dante or Columbus apprise us![108]

How is this effected? Nature is no spendthrift, but takes the shortest way to her ends. As the general says to his soldiers, "if you want a fort, build a fort," so nature makes every creature do its own work and get its living,—is it planet, animal, or tree. The planet makes itself. The animal cell makes itself;—then, what it wants. Every creature,—wren or dragon,—shall make its own lair. As soon as there is life, there is self-direction, and absorbing and using of material. Life is freedom,—life in the direct ratio of its amount. You may be sure, the new-born man is not inert. Life works both voluntarily and supernaturally in its neighborhood. Do you suppose, he can be estimated by his weight in pounds, or, that he is contained in his skin,—this reaching, radiating, jaculating[109] fellow? The smallest candle fills a mile with its rays, and the papillæ[110] of a man run out to every star.

When there is something to be done, the world knows how to get it done. The vegetable eye makes leaf, pericarp,[111] root, bark, or thorn, as the need is; the first cell converts itself into stomach, mouth, nose, or nail, according to the want: the world throws its life into a hero or a shepherd; and puts him where he is wanted. Dante and Columbus were Italians, in their time: they would be Russians or Americans to-day. Things ripen, new men come. The adaptation is not capricious. The ulterior aim, the purpose beyond itself, the correlation by which planets subside and crystallize, then animate beasts and men, will not stop, but will work into finer particulars, and from finer to finest.

The secret of the world is, the tie between person and event. Person makes event, and event person. The "times," "the age," what is that, but a few profound persons and a few active persons who epitomize the times?— Goethe, Hegel, Metternich, Adams, Calhoun, Guizot, Peel, Cobden, Kossuth, Rothschild, Astor, Brunel,[112] and the rest. The same fitness must be presumed between a man and the time and event, as between the sexes, or between a race of animals and the food it eats, or the inferior races it uses. He thinks his fate alien, because the copula is hidden. But the soul contains the event that shall befall it, for the event is only the actualization of its thoughts; and what we pray to ourselves for is always granted. The event is the print of your form. It fits you like your skin. What each does is proper to him. Events are the children of his body and mind. We learn that the soul of Fate is the soul of us, as Hafiz sings,

> "Alas! till now I had not known,
> My guide and fortune's guide are one."[113]

All the toys that infatuate men, and which they play for,—houses, land, money, luxury, power, fame, are the selfsame thing, with a new gauze or two of illusion overlaid.[114] And of all the drums and rattles by which men are made willing to have their heads broke, and are led out solemnly every morning to parade,—the most admirable is this by which we are brought to believe that events are arbitrary, and independent of actions. At the conjuror's, we detect the hair by which he moves his puppet, but we have not eyes sharp enough to descry the thread that ties cause and effect.

Nature magically suits the man to his fortunes, by making these the fruit of his character. Ducks take to the water, eagles to the sky, waders to the sea margin, hunters to the forest, clerks to counting-rooms, soldiers to the frontier. Thus events grow on the same stem with persons; are sub-persons. The pleasure of life is according to the man that lives it, and not according to the work or the place. Life is an ecstasy. We know what madness belongs to love,—what power to paint a vile object in hues of heaven. As insane persons are indifferent to their dress, diet, and other accommodations, and, as we do in dreams, with equanimity, the most absurd acts, so, a drop more of wine in our cup of life will reconcile us to strange company and work. Each creature puts forth from itself its own condition and sphere, as the slug sweats out its slimy house on the pear-leaf, and the woolly aphides on the apple perspire their own bed, and the fish its shell. In youth, we clothe ourselves with rainbows, and go as brave as the zodiac. In age, we put out another sort of perspiration,—gout, fever, rheumatism, caprice, doubt, fretting, and avarice.

A man's fortunes are the fruit of his character. A man's friends are his magnetisms. We go to Herodotus and Plutarch[115] for examples of Fate; but

113  Emerson also read these lines in von Hammer-Purgstall's German translation.

114  Emerson prefaced the original version of this sentence in his Journal (1851) with a bitter sentiment: "Here & there were souls which saw through peaches & wine, politics, money, & women, saw that these as objects of desire were all alike, & all cheats; that the finest fruit is dirty" (J 11:439).

115  Herodotus (ca. 484–ca. 425 BCE), early Greek historian; Plutarch (ca. 46–ca. 122), Greek biographer and moralist. In his Journal entry of 1851, Emerson followed this sentence with: "Toss up a pebble & it falls. And the soaring of your mind & the magnanimity you indulge will fall. But cannot we ride the horse which now throws us?" (J 11:416).

116 "We each suffer our own manes," "manes" here meaning ghosts, fates, or ancestral powers. From the *Aeneid* (29–19 BCE), Latin epic by Virgil (70–19 BCE). The line is spoken by Anchises to his son Aeneas in the underworld (6.743).

117 As in *Oedipus Rex* by the Greek tragic poet Sophocles (ca. 496–406 BCE). By fleeing when an oracle predicts that he will kill his father and marry his mother, Oedipus fulfills the prophecy.

118 Sent forth.

119 Joseph Rotch (1704–1784) founded New Bedford and its whaling industry in 1765.

120 Melt.

121 Reveals.

we are examples. "*Quisque suos patimur manes.*"[116] The tendency of every man to enact all that is in his constitution is expressed in the old belief, that the efforts which we make to escape from our destiny only serve to lead us into it:[117] and I have noticed, a man likes better to be complimented on his position, as the proof of the last or total excellence, than on his merits.

A man will see his character emitted[118] in the events that seem to meet, but which exude from and accompany him. Events expand with the character. As once he found himself among toys, so now he plays a part in colossal systems, and his growth is declared in his ambition, his companions, and his performance. He looks like a piece of luck, but is a piece of causation;—the mosaic, angulated and ground to fit into the gap he fills. Hence in each town there is some man who is, in his brain and performance, an explanation of the tillage, production, factories, banks, churches, ways of living, and society, of that town. If you do not chance to meet him, all that you see will leave you a little puzzled: if you see him, it will become plain. We know in Massachusetts who built New Bedford,[119] who built Lynn, Lowell, Lawrence, Clinton, Fitchburg, Holyoke, Portland, and many another noisy mart. Each of these men, if they were transparent, would seem to you not so much men, as walking cities, and, wherever you put them, they would build one.

History is the action and reaction of these two,—Nature and Thought; —two boys pushing each other on the curb-stone of the pavement. Everything is pusher or pushed: and matter and mind are in perpetual tilt and balance, so. Whilst the man is weak, the earth takes up him. He plants his brain and affections. By and by he will take up the earth, and have his gardens and vineyards in the beautiful order and productiveness of his thought. Every solid in the universe is ready to become fluid on the approach of the mind, and the power to flux[120] it is the measure of the mind. If the wall remain adamant, it accuses[121] the want of thought. To a subtler force, it will stream into new forms, expressive of the character of the mind. What is the city in which we sit here, but an aggregate of incongruous materials, which have obeyed the will of some man? The granite was reluctant, but his hands were stronger, and it came. Iron was deep in the ground, and well combined with stone; but could not hide from his fires. Wood, lime, stuffs, fruit, gums, were dispersed over the earth and sea, in vain. Here they are, within reach of every man's day-labor,—what he wants of them. The whole world is the flux of matter over the wires of thought to the poles[122] or points where it would build. The races of men rise out of the ground preoccupied with a thought which rules them, and divided into parties ready armed and angry to fight for this metaphysical abstraction. The quality of the thought differences the Egyptian and the Roman, the Austrian and the American. The men who come on the stage at one period are all found to be related to each other. Certain ideas are in the air. We are all impressionable, for we are made of them;[123] all impressionable, but some more than others, and these first express them. This explains the curious contemporaneousness of inventions and discoveries. The truth is in the air, and the most impressionable brain will announce it first, but all will announce it a few minutes later. So women, as most susceptible, are the best index of the coming hour.[124] So the great man, that is, the man most imbued with the spirit of the time, is the impressionable man,—of a fibre irritable and delicate, like iodine to light. He feels the infinitesimal attractions. His mind is righter than others, because he yields to a current so feeble as can be felt only by a needle delicately poised.[125]

The correlation is shown in defects. Moller, in his Essay on Architecture, taught that the building which was fitted accurately to answer its end, would turn out to be beautiful, though beauty had not been intended.[126] I find the like unity in human structures rather virulent and pervasive; that a crudity in the blood will appear in the argument; a hump in the shoulder will appear in the speech and handiwork. If his mind could be seen, the hump would be seen. If a man has a seesaw in his voice, it will run into his sentences, into his poem, into the structure of his fable, into his speculation, into his charity. And, as every man is hunted by his own dæmon,[127] vexed by his own disease, this checks all his activity.

So each man, like each plant, has his parasites. A strong, astringent, bilious nature has more truculent enemies than the slugs and moths that fret my leaves. Such an one has curculios, borers, knife-worms: a swindler ate him first, then a client, then a quack, then smooth, plausible gentlemen, bitter and selfish as Moloch.[128]

122   Perhaps a telegraphic metaphor. Emerson varies his earlier image of polarity (see note 6).

123   Compare Emerson's earlier quotation from W. E. Channing: "'The air is full of men.'"

124   In the 1850 Journal passage that supplied the original version of this sentence, Emerson continued, "I am part of the solar system. Let the brain alone & it will keep time with that as the shell with the sea-tide. We are made of ideas. Let the river roll which way it will, cities will rise on its banks" (J 11:218).

125   In the paragraph in his Journal (1850) where the first version of these sentences appeared, Emerson continued, "He can orient himself. In the woods, I have one guide, namely, to follow the light,—to go where the woods are thinnest; then at last I am sure to come out" (J 11:240).

126   Georg Moller (1784–1852), architect and writer, wrote an *Essay on the Origin and Progress of Gothic Architecture* (1815–1821).

127   Guiding spirit or "genius."

128   A pagan god mentioned in the Hebrew Bible and Milton's *Paradise Lost*, associated with war and child sacrifice.

129 From the Proem to Chaucer's *House of Fame* (1379–1380).

130 An echo of the myth of the charioteer in the dialogue *Phaedrus*, by the Greek philosopher Plato (429–347 BCE), also alluded to in Emerson's "The Poet." In Plato, the soul's chariot is pulled by two horses, one raging and the other orderly. Emerson also invokes the double consciousness in "Montaigne, or the Skeptic" and in "Experience": we position ourselves between the world of action and the world of thought.

131 Like the end of the Bible's book of Job, with its celebration of the incommensurable might of a God who destroys as well as blesses, Emerson's assertion seems an affront to our powers of human sympathy. The perspective he recommends appears impossible, and for that very reason, a valid sublimity.

132 In Greek mythology, Pegasus was a winged horse; when he kicked Mt. Helicon, the mountain brought forth the waters of the Hippocrene, the fountain of the Muses that inspire poetry.

133 Emerson may be echoing Schelling's phrase in his *Human Freedom*, "heilige Nothwendigkeit" (holy necessity). In his Journal in 1848, Emerson wrote, "Our philosophy is to *wait*. . . . I obey the Beautiful Necessity. The powers that I want will be supplied, as *I* am supplied, and the philosophy of waiting is sustained by all the oracles of the Universe" (J 11:15). In contrast to this essay's praise of Necessity, Emerson's earlier essay "Self-Reliance" ended with a paean to Will.

This correlation really existing can be divined. If the threads are there, thought can follow and show them. Especially when a soul is quick and docile; as Chaucer sings,

"Or if the soul of proper kind
Be so perfect as men find,
That it wot what is to come,
And that he warneth all and some
Of every of their aventures,
By previsions or figures;
But that our flesh hath not might
It to understand aright
For it is warned too darkly."—[129]

Some people are made up of rhyme, coincidence, omen, periodicity, and presage: they meet the person they seek; what their companion prepares to say to them, they first say to him; and a hundred signs apprise them of what is about to befall.

Wonderful intricacy in the web, wonderful constancy in the design this vagabond life admits. We wonder how the fly finds its mate, and yet year after year we find two men, two women, without legal or carnal tie, spend a great part of their best time within a few feet of each other. And the moral is, that what we seek we shall find; what we flee from flees from us; as Goethe said, "what we wish for in youth, comes in heaps on us in old age," too often cursed with the granting of our prayer: and hence the high caution, that, since we are sure of having what we wish, we beware to ask only for high things.

One key, one solution to the mysteries of human condition, one solution to the old knots of fate, freedom, and foreknowledge, exists, the propounding, namely, of the double consciousness. A man must ride alternately on the horses of his private and his public nature, as the equestrians in the circus throw themselves nimbly from horse to horse, or plant one foot on the back of one, and the other foot on the back of the other.[130] So when a man is the victim of his fate, has sciatica in his loins, and cramp in his mind;

a club-foot and a club in his wit; a sour face, and a selfish temper; a strut in his gait, and a conceit in his affection; or is ground to powder by the vice of his race; he is to rally on his relation to the Universe, which his ruin benefits. Leaving the dæmon who suffers, he is to take sides with the Deity who secures universal benefit by his pain.[131]

To offset the drag of temperament and race, which pulls down, learn this lesson, namely, that by the cunning co-presence of two elements, which is throughout nature, whatever lames or paralyzes you, draws in with it the divinity, in some form, to repay. A good intention clothes itself with sudden power. When a god wishes to ride, any chip or pebble will bud and shoot out winged feet, and serve him for a horse.[132]

Let us build altars to the Blessed Unity which holds nature and souls in perfect solution, and compels every atom to serve an universal end. I do not wonder at a snow-flake, a shell, a summer landscape, or the glory of the stars; but at the necessity of beauty under which the universe lies; that all is and must be pictorial; that the rainbow, and the curve of the horizon, and the arch of the blue vault are only results from the organism of the eye. There is no need for foolish amateurs to fetch me to admire a garden of flowers, or a sun-gilt cloud, or a waterfall, when I cannot look without seeing splendor and grace. How idle to choose a random sparkle here or there, when the indwelling necessity plants the rose of beauty on the brow of chaos, and discloses the central intention of Nature to be harmony and joy.

Let us build altars to the Beautiful Necessity.[133] If we thought men were free in the sense, that, in a single exception one fantastical will could prevail over the law of things, it were all one as if a child's hand could pull down the sun.[134] If, in the least particular, one could derange the order of nature,— who would accept the gift of life?

Let us build altars to the Beautiful Necessity, which secures that all is made of one piece; that plaintiff and defendant, friend and enemy, animal and planet, food and eater, are of one kind.[135] In astronomy, is vast space, but no foreign system; in geology, vast time, but the same laws as to-day. Why should we be afraid of Nature, which is no other than "philosophy and theology embodied?"[136] Why should we fear to be crushed by savage elements, we who are made up of the same elements?[137] Let us build to the Beautiful

134 A potent simile. In his Journal (1859) Emerson wrote, "We grasp & pull down, & would pull down God if we could. . . . Excellence is lost sight of in this hunger for performance" (J 14:265).

135 In his Journal (1845–1846), Emerson identified this gospel with "the Indian teaching": "The East is grand,—& makes Europe appear the land of trifles. Identity, identity! friend & foe are of one stuff . . . form is imprisonment and heaven itself a decoy" (J 9:322). In another passage (July 1840) he asserted, "We are all boarders at one table,—White man, black man, ox and eagle, bee, & worm" (J 9:322).

136 The phrase is from the introduction to the 1845–1846 English edition of Emanuel Swedenborg's (1688–1772) *Economy of the Animal Kingdom*, by the London surgeon J. J. Garth Wilkinson (1812–1899). Emerson became friends with Wilkinson in London in 1848.

137 Emerson wrote in his Journal (July 31, 1835), "Spit at consequences; launch boldly forth into the pure element & that which you think will drown you, shall buoy you up" (J 5:73). The advice of the character Stein in *Lord Jim* (1900) by the Polish-born English novelist Joseph Conrad (1857–1924) is "in the destructive element immerse."

Emerson's first wife, Ellen Tucker Emerson.

Necessity, which makes man brave in believing that he cannot shun a danger that is appointed, nor incur one that is not; to the Necessity which rudely or softly educates him to the perception that there are no contingencies; that Law rules throughout existence, a Law which is not intelligent but intelligence,—not personal nor impersonal,—it disdains words and passes understanding; it dissolves persons; it vivifies nature; yet solicits the pure in heart to draw on all its omnipotence.

# Power

His tongue was framed to[1] music,
And his hand was armed with skill,
His face was the mould of beauty,[2]
And his heart the throne of will.

There is not yet any inventory of a man's faculties, any more than a bible of his opinions. Who shall set a limit to the influence of a human being? There are men, who, by their sympathetic attractions, carry nations with them, and lead the activity of the human race. And if there be such a tie, that, wherever the mind of man goes, nature will accompany him, perhaps there are men whose magnetisms are of that force to draw material and elemental powers, and, where they appear, immense instrumentalities organize around them. Life is a search after power; and this is an element with which the world is so saturated,—there is no chink or crevice in which it is not lodged,—that no honest seeking goes unrewarded. A man should prize events and possessions as the ore in which this fine mineral is found: he can well afford to let events and possessions, and the breath of the body go, if their value has been added to him in the shape of power.[3] If he have secured the elixir,[4] he can spare the wide gardens from which it was distilled. A cultivated man, wise to know and bold to perform, is the end to which nature works, and the education of the will is the flowering and result of all this geology and astronomy.

*"Power" is the second chapter of* The Conduct of Life *(1860). By "power" Emerson means not mere force but rather an innate potency of character or event that leads to wide influence. His study of power recognizes the "strict connection between every trifle and the principle of being." Emerson's stance, both abrasive and genial, strongly influenced the German philosopher Friedrich Nietzsche (1844–1900), who discovered Emerson as a teenager in boarding school and treasured his works for the rest of his life. Both Emerson and Nietzsche believe that existence is a grand antagonism of forces, that the individual is called to self-begetting, and that we are at our best when we become the representatives of creative possibility. They share an attraction to sharp paradoxes, gnomic statements, and seeming self-contradictions designed to test the reader.*

1    Suited for, adapted to.

2    Ophelia describes Hamlet as "the glass of fashion and the mould of form" (that is, beauty; 3.1.153). Emerson here pictures a Hamlet-like paragon of human powers, without Hamlet's destructive melancholy.

3    In his copy of the essay "Of Cruelty" by the French author Michel de Montaigne (1533–1592), Emerson marked this passage: "It is not enough to have the Soul seated in a good place, of a good temper, and well disposed to Vertue. . . . We are to covet pain, necessity and contempt, to contend with them, and to keep the Soul in Breath."

4    Curative potion.

5    Title of an early essay by Emerson, and a central idea in his work. According to "Compensation," "there is always this vindictive circumstance stealing in at unawares . . .—this back-stroke, this kick of the gun, certifying that the law is fatal; that in nature nothing can be given, all things are sold." Emerson connects the notions of compensation and power to show that power is an acknowledgment of law, not an attempt to override the ways of the universe.

6    This sentence from the French emperor Napoleon Bonaparte (1769–1821) has not been located.

7    A shocking turn in Emerson's essay. Imbecility here means frailty (not necessarily mental).

8    In his essay "Self-Reliance," Emerson describes the relation between self-reliance and originality: "The magnetism which all original action exerts is explained when we inquire the reason of self-trust."

9    From *The Animal Kingdom* by the Swedish thinker Emanuel Swedenborg (1688–1772).

10    Eric the Red, banished from Iceland, discovered Greenland; Thorfinn, Eric's son-in-law, spent a winter in what is often supposed to have been New England. Bjarni (Biorn) sighted Vinland (perhaps Labrador), later reached by Eric's son Leif.

All successful men have agreed in one thing;—they were *causationists*. They believed that things went not by luck, but by law; that there was not a weak or a cracked link in the chain that joins the first and last of things. A belief in causality, or strict connexion between every pulse-beat and the principle of being, and, in consequence, belief in compensation,[5] or, that nothing is got for nothing,—characterizes all valuable minds, and must control every effort that is made by an industrious one. The most valiant men are the best believers in the tension of the laws. "All the great captains," said Bonaparte, "have performed vast achievements by conforming with the rules of the art,—by adjusting efforts to obstacles."[6]

The key to the age may be this, or that, or the other, as the young orators describe;—the key to all ages is—Imbecility;[7] imbecility in the vast majority of men, at all times, and, even in heroes, in all but certain eminent moments; victims of gravity, custom, and fear. This gives force to the strong,—that the multitude have no habit of self-reliance or original action.[8]

We must reckon success a constitutional trait. Courage,—the old physiologists taught, (and their meaning holds, if their physiology is a little mythical,)—courage, or the degree of life, is as the degree of circulation of the blood in the arteries. "During passion, anger, fury, trials of strength, wrestling, fighting, a large amount of blood is collected in the arteries, the maintenance of bodily strength requiring it, and but little is sent into the veins. This condition is constant with intrepid persons."[9] Where the arteries hold their blood, is courage and adventure possible. Where they pour it unrestrained into the veins, the spirit is low and feeble. For performance of great mark, it needs extraordinary health. If Eric is in robust health, and has slept well, and is at the top of his condition, and thirty years old, at his departure from Greenland, he will steer west, and his ships will reach Newfoundland. But take out Eric, and put in a stronger and bolder man,—Biorn, or Thorfin,—and the ships will, with just as much ease, sail six hundred, one thousand, fifteen hundred miles further, and reach Labrador and New England.[10] There is no chance in results. With adults, as with children, one class enter cordially into the game, and whirl with the whirling world; the others have cold hands, and remain by-standers; or are only dragged in by the humor and vivacity of those who can carry a dead weight. The first wealth is health. Sickness is poor-spirited, and cannot serve any one: it must husband its resources to live. But health or fulness answers its own ends, and has to spare, runs over, and inundates the neighborhoods and creeks of other men's necessities.

All power is of one kind, a sharing of the nature of the world. The mind that is parallel with the laws of nature will be in the current of events, and strong with their strength.[11] One man is made of the same stuff of which events are made; is in sympathy with the course of things; can predict it. Whatever befals, befals him first; so that he is equal to whatever shall happen. A man who knows men, can talk well on politics, trade, law, war, religion. For, everywhere, men are led in the same manners.

The advantage of a strong pulse is not to be supplied by any labor, art, or concert. It is like the climate, which easily rears a crop which no glass, or irrigation, or tillage, or manures, can elsewhere rival. It is like the opportunity of a city like New York, or Constantinople, which needs no diplomacy to force capital or genius or labor to it. They come of themselves, as the waters flow to it. So a broad healthy massive understanding seems to lie on the shore of unseen rivers, of unseen oceans, which are covered with barks, that, night and day, are drifted to this point. That is poured into its lap, which other men lie plotting for. It is in everybody's secret; anticipates everybody's discovery; and if it does not command every fact of the genius and the scholar, it is, because it is large and sluggish, and does not think them worth the exertion which you do.

This affirmative force is in one, and is not in another, as one horse has the spring in him, and another in the whip. "On the neck of the young man," said Hafiz, "sparkles no gem so gracious as enterprize."[12] Import into any stationary district, as into an old Dutch population in New York or Pennsylvania, or among the planters of Virginia, a colony of hardy Yankees, with seething brains, heads full of steam-hammer, pulley, crank, and toothed wheel,—and every thing begins to shine with values. What enhancement to all the water and land in England, is the arrival of James Watt or Brunel![13] In every company, there is not only the active and passive sex, but, in both men and women, a deeper and more important *sex of mind*, namely, the inventive or creative class of both men and women, and the uninventive or accepting class.[14] Each *plus* man represents his set, and, if he have the accidental advantage of personal ascendency,—which implies neither more nor less of talent,

11    Emerson gives a different version in a Journal entry of 1852: "Souls with a certain quantity of light are in excess, & irrevocably belong to the moral class,—what animal force they may retain, to the contrary, notwithstanding. Souls with less light, it is chemically impossible that they be moral;—what talent or good they have, to the contrary, notwithstanding; & these belong to the world of Fate, or animal good: the youth of the universe; not yet twenty-one; not yet voters . . ." (J 13:75).

12    This line from the Persian poet Hafiz (ca. 1325–ca. 1389) has not been found in the German translation of Hafiz that Emerson used. In his Journal (1847–1848), Emerson remarked that Hafiz was "characterized by a perfect intellectual emancipation which also he provokes in the reader. Nothing stops him. He makes the daregod & daredevil experiment. He is not to be scared by a name, or a religion. He fears nothing" (J 10:165).

13    James Watt (1736–1819) manufactured steam engines; Marc Brunel (1769–1849) and his son Isambard Brunel (1806–1859) engineered bridges, ships, and tunnels.

14    Emerson frequently uses "manly" in a metaphorical sense; here he makes it clear that active, creative strength occurs in both men and women.

15    Charles Wilkes (1798–1877) explored
Antarctica in 1839–1840; Bertel Thorvaldsen
(1770–1844) was a Danish sculptor. Alexandre
Dumas Père (1802–1870) wrote, with the help
of about ninety collaborators, over a thousand
books.

but merely the temperamental or taming eye of a soldier or a schoolmaster,
(which one has, and one has not, as one has a black moustache and one a
blond,) then quite easily and without envy or resistance, all his coadjutors
and feeders will admit his right to absorb them. The merchant works by
bookkeeper and cashier; the lawyer's authorities are hunted up by clerks; the
geologist reports the surveys of his subalterns; Commander Wilkes appro-
priates the results of all the naturalists attached to the Expedition; Thor-
waldsen's statue is finished by stonecutters; Dumas[15] has journeymen; and
Shakspeare was theatre manager, and used the labor of many young men, as
well as the play books.

There is always room for a man of force, and he makes room for many.
Society is a troop of thinkers, and the best heads among them take the best
places. A feeble man can see the farms that are fenced and tilled, the houses
that are built. The strong man sees also the possible houses and farms. His
eye makes estates, as fast as the sun breeds clouds.

When a new boy comes into school, when a man travels, and encoun-
ters strangers every day, or, when into any old club a new comer is domesticated, that happens which befalls, when a strange ox is driven into a pen or
pasture where cattle are kept; there is at once a trial of strength between the
best pair of horns and the new comer, and it is settled thenceforth which is
the leader. So now, there is a measuring of strength, very courteous, but decisive, and an acquiescence thenceforward when these two meet. Each reads
his fate in the other's eyes. The weaker party finds, that none of his information or wit quite fits the occasion. He thought he knew this or that: he finds
that he omitted to learn the end of it. Nothing that he knows will quite hit
the mark, whilst all the rival's arrows are good, and well-thrown. But if he
knew all the facts in the encyclopædia, it would not help him: for this is an
affair of presence of mind, of attitude, of aplomb: the opponent has the sun
and wind, and, in every cast, the choice of weapon and mark; and, when he
himself is matched with some other antagonist, his own shafts fly well and
hit. 'Tis a question of stomach and constitution. The second man is as good
as the first,—perhaps better; but has not stoutness and stomach, as the first
has, and so his wit seems overfine or underfine.

Health is good, power, life, that resists disease, poison, and all enemies, and is conservative, as well as creative. Here is question, every spring,

whether to graft with wax, or whether with clay; whether to whitewash or to potash, or to prune; but the one point is the thrifty tree.[16] A good tree, that agrees with the soil, will grow in spite of blight, or bug, or pruning, or neglect, by night and by day, in all weathers and all treatments. Vivacity, leadership, must be had, and we are not allowed to be nice in choosing. We must fetch the pump[17] with dirty water, if clean cannot be had. If we will make bread, we must have contagion, yeast, emptyings,[18] or what not to induce fermentation into the dough: as the torpid[19] artist seeks inspiration at any cost,—by virtue or by vice, by friend or by fiend, by prayer or by wine.[20] And we have a certain instinct, that where is great amount of life, though gross and peccant,[21] it has its own checks and purifications, and will be found at last in harmony with moral laws.

We watch in children with pathetic[22] interest, the degree in which they possess recuperative force. When they are hurt by us, or by each other, or go to the bottom of the class, or miss the annual prizes, or are beaten in the game,—if they lose heart, and remember the mischance in their chamber at home, they have a serious check. But if they have the buoyancy and resistance that preoccupies them with new interest in the new moment,—the wounds cicatrize,[23] and the fibre is the tougher for the hurt.

One comes to value this *plus* health, when he sees that all difficulties vanish before it. A timid man listening to the alarmists in Congress, and in the newspapers, and observing the profligacy of party,—sectional interests urged with a fury which shuts its eyes to consequences, with a mind made up to desperate extremities, ballot in one hand, and rifle in the other,—might easily believe that he and his country have seen their best days, and he hardens himself the best he can against the coming ruin.[24] But, after this has been foretold with equal confidence fifty times, and government six per cents have not declined a quarter of a mill, he discovers that the enormous elements of strength which are here in play, make our politics unimportant. Personal power, freedom, and the resources of nature strain every faculty of every citizen. We prosper with such vigor, that, like thrifty trees, which grow in spite of ice, lice, mice, and borers, so we do not suffer from the profligate swarms that fatten on the national treasury. The huge animals nourish huge parasites, and the rancor of the disease attests the strength of the constitution. The same energy in the Greek *demos*[25] drew the remark, that the evils of

16  Emerson was an experienced orchard-keeper, and well acquainted with different ways of grafting (grafting wax was a relatively new-fangled invention, clay a traditional means). Fruit trees are whitewashed to repel insects; potash is used as a fertilizer.

17  Add water to it (so it can "fetch" the water already in the bottom).

18  Contagion: bacterial activity; emptyings: preparation of yeast for leavening.

19  Sluggish.

20  Emerson explores this theme in his essay "The Poet": "bards love wine, mead, narcotics, coffee, tea, opium, the fumes of sandalwood and tobacco"—but as for the true poet, "air should suffice for his inspiration, and he should be tipsy with water."

21  Sinning.

22  Passionate.

23  Create scars.

24  *The Conduct of Life* was published just four months before the Civil War began.

25  People.

26 One Judge Emmons, encountered by Emerson during a lecture tour of Michigan in 1856 (J 14:29).

27 Requirements.

28 The Admiralty Court had federal jurisdiction over commerce, but only on the high seas; Emerson envisions an interstate commerce authority for railroads and aviation. A "pond-hole" is small but precipitously deep.

29 Horse-breakers, tough cowboys—as in its later use as a name for the volunteer cavalry of Theodore Roosevelt (1858–1919).

30 Natives of Indiana, Illinois, Michigan, and Wisconsin (respectively).

31 Greedy desire.

32 The Whigs were a U.S. reform party during the years 1834–1856; they opposed the Jacksonian Democrats. In 1803 President Thomas Jefferson (1743–1826) engineered the Louisiana Purchase, vastly increasing the territory of the United States, and in 1818 General Andrew Jackson (1767–1845), later president, invaded Florida, then Spanish territory.

33 Senator Thomas Hart Benton of Missouri (1782–1858) opposed the conquering and annexation of Mexican territory (the Mexican War initiated by President James Polk [1795–1849] in 1846); so did John C. Calhoun of South Carolina (1782–1850). Daniel Webster of Massachusetts (1782–1852), like Calhoun a central political presence and orator, condemned the war, but he was absent from the Senate when it voted for the war in May. In December 1846, he voted in favor of a war appropriations bill that contained the Wilmot Proviso (which would have barred slavery from any new *(continued)*

popular government appear greater than they are; there is compensation for them in the spirit and energy it awakens. The rough and ready style which belongs to a people of sailors, foresters, farmers, and mechanics has its advantages. Power educates the potentate. As long as our people quote English standards they dwarf their own proportions. A western lawyer of eminence[26] said to me he wished it were a penal offense to bring an English law-book into a court in this country, so pernicious had he found in his experience our deference to English precedent. The very word 'commerce' has only an English meaning, and is pinched to the cramp exigences[27] of English experience. The commerce of rivers, the commerce of railroads, and who knows but the commerce of air balloons, must add an American extension to the pond-hole of admiralty.[28] As long as our people quote English standards they will miss the sovereignty of power, but let these rough riders,[29]—legislators in shirtsleeves—Hoosier, Sucker, Wolverine, Badger[30]—or whatever hard head Arkansaw, Oregon, or Utah sends, half-orator, half-assassin, to represent its wrath and cupidity[31] at Washington,—let these drive as they may; and the disposition of territories and public lands and the necessity of balancing and keeping at bay the snarling majorities of German, Irish, and of native millions, will bestow promptness, address, and reason, at last, on our buffalo-hunter, and authority and majesty of manners. The instinct of the people is right. Men expect from good whigs, put into office by the respectability of the country, much less skill to deal with Mexico, Spain, Britain, or with our own malcontent members, than from some strong transgressor, like Jefferson, or Jackson,[32] who first conquers his own government, and then uses the same genius to conquer the foreigner. The senators who dissented from Mr Polk's Mexican war, were not those who knew better, but those who from political position could afford it; not Webster, but Benton and Calhoun.[33]

This power, to be sure, is not clothed in satin. 'Tis the power of Lynch law,[34] of soldiers and pirates; and it bullies the peaceable and loyal. But it brings its own antidote; and here is my point,—that all kinds of power usually emerge at the same time; good energy, and bad; power of mind, with physical health; the ecstasies of devotion, with the exasperations of debauchery.[35] The same elements are always present, only sometimes these conspicuous, and sometimes those, what was yesterday foreground, being today background,—what was surface, playing now a not less effective part as basis. The longer the drought lasts, the more is the atmosphere surcharged with water. The faster the ball falls to the sun, the force to fly off is by so much augmented.[36] And, in morals, wild liberty breeds iron conscience; natures with great impulses have great resources, and return from far. In politics, the sons of democrats will be whigs; whilst red republicanism, in the father, is a spasm of nature to engender an intolerable tyrant in the next age.[37] On the other hand, conservatism, ever more timorous and narrow, disgusts the children, and drives them for a mouthful of fresh air into radicalism.

Those who have most of this coarse energy,—the 'bruisers,'[38] who have run the gauntlet of caucus and tavern through the county or the state, have their own vices, but they have the goodnature of strength and courage. Fierce and unscrupulous, they are usually frank and direct, and above falsehood. Our politics fall into bad hands, and churchmen and men of refinement, it seems agreed, are not fit persons to send to Congress. Politics is a deleterious profession, like some poisonous handicrafts. Men in power have no opinions, but may be had cheap for any opinion, for any purpose,— and if it be only a question between the most civil and the most forcible, I lean to the last. These Hoosiers and Suckers are really better than the snivelling opposition.[39] Their wrath is at least of a bold and manly cast. They see, against the unanimous declarations of the people, how much crime the people will bear; they proceed from step to step, and they have calculated but too justly upon their Excellencies, the New England governors, and upon their honors, the New England legislators. The messages of the governors and the Resolutions of the legislatures, are a proverb for expressing a sham virtuous indignation, which, in the course of events, is sure to be belied.[40]

In trade, also, this energy usually carries a trace of ferocity. Philanthropic and religious bodies do not commonly make their executive officers out of saints. The Communities hitherto founded by Socialists,—the Jesuits, the Port-Royalists, the American communities at New Harmony, at Brook Farm, at Zoar,[41] are only possible, by installing Judas as steward. The rest of the offices may be filled by good burgesses. The pious and charitable propri-

territories that the United States acquired from Mexico). The Wilmot Proviso was then removed from the bill. By the end of 1846 Webster's protests against the war, like those of many other Whigs, had become ineffective. "Mr. Webster," Emerson wrote in his Journal (1846), "told them how much the war cost, that was his protest, but voted the war, & sends his son to it. They calculated rightly on Mr. Webster" (J 9:445). (Webster's son Edward volunteered for the Mexican War: *pace* Emerson, against his father's wishes.)

34  Named for the Virginia planter and revolutionary Charles Lynch (1736–1796), who presided over the summary trials and hangings of those loyal to the English crown.

35  "Get energy, & you get all," Emerson added in the 1848 Journal passage on which this sentence is based (J 11:59).

36  Emerson marked this sentence in the English poet S. T. Coleridge's (1772–1834) *Friend* (1818), v. 3: "For all things by force compelled from their nature will fly back with the greater earnestness on the removal of that force."

37  Red was the color of revolution, and republicans, those determined to overthrow monarchy. Emerson alludes to Bks. VIII and IX of the *Republic* by the Greek philosopher Plato (429–347 BCE), who sees sons' rebellions against fathers as the reason for the transformation of political regimes (from aristocracy to oligarchy, then democracy, then tyranny).

38  Prize-fighters.

39  Emerson disdains the relatively polite ("snivelling") Whigs, preferring the Hoosiers (natives of Indiana or, more generally, rough-

*(continued)*

necks) and Suckers (natives of Illinois; miners from Illinois worked in Wisconsin during the summer, migrating like the sucker, a fish). In his lecture "The Poet" (1841), from his series "The Times," Emerson said that "we may detect the poetic genius . . . in Senates, when the forest has cast out some wild, black-browed bantling, some great boy, to show the same energy in the crowd of officials, which he had learned in driving cattle to the hills, or in scrambling through thickets in a winter forest, or through the swamp and river for his game" (EL 3:362). (A bantling is a child.)

40    In his lecture "The Present Age" (1837) from his series "The Philosophy of History," Emerson commented, "The reporters say in the newspapers that this and that great senator in the heat of debate screamed with passion at the outrage offered to the laws. They did not think so when they wrote it, and nobody believes it was anything else than a fine, wise, oratorical scream" (EL 2:162).

41    The Jesuits, a Catholic religious order founded by the Spanish religious leader Ignatius of Loyola (1491–1556), built schools throughout Europe; the community of Port-Royal near Paris was, in the seventeenth century, a center of Jansenism, a strict theology opposed to that of the Jesuits; New Harmony was a utopian community in Indiana, founded in 1814, and later directed by the Welsh reformer Robert Owen (1771–1858); Brook Farm, in West Roxbury, Massachusetts, was started by Emerson's friends George Ripley (1802–1880) and Sophia Ripley (1803–1861); Zoar, in Ohio, was founded by the agrarian Society of Separatists in 1817.

42    The Shakers, an intense spiritual community devoted to equality of the sexes and cel-
(continued)

etor has a foreman not quite so pious and charitable. The most amiable of country gentlemen has a certain pleasure in the teeth of the bull-dog which guards his orchard. Of the Shaker Society,[42] it was formerly a sort of proverb in the country, that they always sent the devil to market. And in representations of the Deity, painting, poetry, and popular religion have ever drawn the wrath from Hell. It is an esoteric doctrine of society, that a little wickedness is good to make muscle; as if conscience were not good for hands and legs, as if poor decayed formalists of law and order cannot run like wild goats, wolves, and conies;[43] that, as there is a use in medicine for poisons, so the world cannot move without rogues; that public spirit and the ready hand are as well found among the malignants.[44] 'Tis not very rare, the coincidence of sharp private and political practice, with public spirit, and good neighborhood.

I knew a burly Boniface[45] who for many years kept a public house in one of our rural capitals. He was a knave whom the town could ill spare. He was a social vascular[46] creature, grasping and selfish. There was no crime which he did not or could not commit. But he made good friends of the Selectmen;[47] served them with his best chop, when they supped at his house, and also with his honor the Judge, he was very cordial, grasping his hand. He introduced all the fiends, male and female, into the town, and united in his person the functions of bully, incendiary, swindler, barkeeper, burglar. He girdled the trees, and cut off the horses' tails of the Temperance people, in the night. He led the 'rummies'[48] and radicals in town meeting with a speech. Meantime, he was civil, fat, and easy, in his house, and precisely the most public-spirited citizen. He was active in getting the roads repaired and planted with shade-trees; he subscribed for the fountains, the gas, and the telegraph; he introduced the new horse-rake, the new scraper, the baby-jumper,[49] and what not, that Connecticut sends to the admiring citizens. He did this the easier, that the pedler stopped at his house, and paid his keeping, by setting up his new trap on the landlord's premises.

Whilst thus the energy for originating and executing work, deforms itself by excess, and so our axe chops off our own fingers,—this evil is not without remedy. All the elements whose aid man calls in, will sometimes become his masters, especially those of most subtle force. Shall he, then, renounce steam, fire and electricity, or, shall he learn to deal with them? The rule for this whole class of agencies is,—all *plus* is good; only put it in the right place.

Men of this surcharge of arterial blood, cannot live on nuts, herb-tea, and elegies; cannot read novels, and play whist; cannot satisfy all their wants at the Thursday Lecture, or the Boston Athenæum.[50] They pine for adventure, and must go to Pike's Peak; had rather die by the hatchet of a Pawnee

Friedrich Nietzsche (1844–1900). Nietzsche said of Emerson, "He does not know how old he is already, or how young he is still going to be."

ibacy, flourished in nineteenth-century America; they produced distinctive achievements in music, architecture, and design.

43  Rabbits.

44  In his essay "Considerations by the Way," Emerson wrote, "The first lesson of history is the good of evil. Good is a good doctor, but Bad is sometimes a better."

45  Innkeeper, after a character in *The Beaux' Stratagem* by the playwright George Farquhar (1677–1707).

46  Full of freely flowing blood, and therefore energetic and hearty—a peculiar Emersonian usage. In his lecture "Literary Ethics," Emerson wrote, "An able man is nothing else than a good, free, vascular organization, whereinto the universal spirit freely flows."

47  Members of the elected governing board of a New England town.

48  Opponents of the temperance party (who advocated prohibition).

49  The horse-rake, recently invented, was a toothed sickle that moved quickly back and forth on a frame; drawn by horses, it was used for mowing hay. Scraper: a scoop on wheels drawn by horses, used for clearing snow or earth; baby-jumper: a hoop or frame suspended by elastic, enabling the infant (in a harness) to bounce. Connecticut peddlers were famous for selling such newfangled devices.

50  Library and art collection founded in 1807 by the Anthology Club, which was organized by Emerson's father, Rev. William Emerson. From the 1820s on, the Athenaeum also sponsored lectures.

51    Pike's Peak, in present-day Colorado, was first climbed in 1820; its discoverer, Zebulon Pike (1779–1813), tried and failed to do so in 1806. The Pawnee were a Great Plains Indian tribe that clashed with settlers in Nebraska territory. A compting room, more often called a counting-house or counting-room, is a book-keeping or accounting office.

52    Uproarious, swaggering fellows.

53    Maelstrom: a deadly whirlpool off the coast of Norway, and by extension all dangerous whirlpools; Hellespont: strait between Greece and Turkey, swum only by the bold (like the legendary Leander, to reach his beloved Hero). George Henry Borrow (1803–1880), English traveler and writer who studied gypsies; Charles Waterton (1782–1865), an English traveler and naturalist; Sir Austen Henry Layard (1817–1894), a French-born British archaeologist who excavated monuments of ancient Mesopotamia, including the cities of Nimrud and Nineveh. A pacha, or pasha, was a high-ranking Ottoman Turkish official. Lancaster Sound, in present-day Nunavut, Canada, was explored twice by the Scottish admiral John Ross (1777–1856), in 1818 and 1829; on his second voyage, he was stranded for four years. The crease or kris is a distinctively shaped dagger used in Malaysia.

54    France's last Bourbon monarch, Charles X (1757–1836), was deposed in 1830 and was replaced by the Orleanist Louis-Philippe (1773–1850), who abdicated during the Revolution of 1848. Charles de Montalembert (1810–1870), a liberal intellectual, was a member of the French Chamber of Deputies; he was not the leader of a party or faction.

than sit all day and every day at a compting room desk.[51] They are made for war, for the sea, for mining, hunting, and clearing; for hairbreadth adventures, and huge risks, and the joy of eventful living. Some men cannot endure an hour of calm at sea. I remember a poor Malay cook, on board a Liverpool packet, who, when the wind blew a gale, could not contain his joy; "Blow!" he cried, "me do tell you, blow!" Their friends and governors must see that some vent for their explosive complexion is provided. The roisters[52] who are destined for infamy at home, if sent to Mexico, will "cover you with glory," and come back heroes and generals. There are Oregons, Californias, Exploring Expeditions enough appertaining to America, to find them in files to gnaw, and in crocodiles to eat. The young English are fine animals, full of blood, and when they have no wars to breathe their riotous valors in, they seek for travels as dangerous as war, diving into Mælstroms; swimming Hellesponts; wading up the snowy Himmaleh; hunting lion, rhinoceros, elephant, in South Africa; gipsying with Borrow in Spain and Algiers; riding alligators in South America with Waterton; utilizing Bedouin, Sheik, and Pacha, with Layard; yachting among the icebergs of Lancaster Sound; peeping into craters on the equator; or running on the creases of Malays in Borneo.[53]

The excess of virility has the same importance in general history, as in private and industrial life. Strong race or strong individual rests at last on natural forces, which are best in the savage, who, like the beasts around him, is still in reception of the milk from the teats of Nature. Cut off the connexion between any of our works, and this aboriginal source, and the work is shallow. The people lean on this, and the mob is not quite so bad an argument as we sometimes say, for it has this good side. "March without the people," said a French deputy from the tribune, "and you march into night: their instincts are a finger-pointing of Providence, always turned toward real benefit. But when you espouse an Orleans party, or a Bourbon, or a Montalembert party,[54] or any other but an organic party, though you mean well, you have a personality instead of a principle, which will inevitably drag you into a corner."

The best anecdotes of this force are to be had from savage life, in explorers, soldiers, and buccaneers. But who cares for fallings-out of assassins, and fights of bears, or grindings of icebergs? Physical force has no value, where there is nothing else. Snow in snowbanks, fire in volcanoes and solfa-taras[55] is cheap: the luxury of ice is in tropical countries, and midsummer days. The luxury of fire is, to have a little on our hearth: and of electricity, not volleys of the charged cloud, but the manageable stream on the battery-wires. So of spirit, or energy; the rests or remains of it in the civil and moral man, are worth all the cannibals in the Pacific.

In history, the great moment, is, when the savage is just ceasing to be a savage, with all his hairy Pelasgic strength directed on his opening sense of beauty:—and you have Pericles and Phidias,—not yet passed over into the Corinthian civility.[56] Everything good in nature and the world is in that moment of transition, when the swarthy juices still flow plentifully from nature, but their astringency or acridity is got out by ethics and humanity.[57]

The triumphs of peace have been in some proximity to war. Whilst the hand was still familiar with the sword-hilt, whilst the habits of the camp were still visible in the port[58] and complexion of the gentleman, his intellectual power culminated: the compression and tension of these stern conditions is a training for the finest and softest arts, and can rarely be compensated in tranquil times, except by some analogous vigor drawn from occupations as hardy as war.

We say that success is constitutional; depends on a *plus* condition of mind and body, on power of work, on courage; that it is of main efficacy in carrying on the world, and, though rarely found in the right state for an article of commerce, but oftener in the supersaturate or excess, which makes it dangerous and destructive, yet it cannot be spared, and must be had in that form, and absorbents provided to take off its edge.

The affirmative class monopolize the homage of mankind. They originate and execute all the great facts. What a force was coiled up in the skull of Napoleon! Of the sixty thousand men making his army at Eylau,[59] it seems, some thirty thousand were thieves and burglars. The men whom, in peaceful communities, we hold if we can, with iron at their legs, in prisons, under the muskets of sentinels, this man dealt with, hand to hand, dragged them to their duty, and won his victories by their bayonets.

This aboriginal[60] might gives a surprising pleasure when it appears under conditions of supreme refinement, as in the proficients in high art. When Michel Angelo was forced to paint the Sistine Chapel in fresco, of which art

55   Small, inactive volcanoes or holes in the earth that spew gas, named after Mt. Solfatara ("Sulphur Mountain"), near Naples.

56   The Pelasgi were mythical, primitive inhabitants of Greece, credited with buildings made of rough stones. Corinthian architecture, by contrast, was sophisticated, and Corinth's people had a reputation for decadent luxury. Pericles (ca. 495–429 BCE) was the leader of Athens during its golden age, and Phidias (ca. 480–430 BCE) its greatest sculptor. In the Journal entry that formed the basis for this passage (May–July 1847), Emerson originally wrote "Parisian civility" (J 10:82).

57   In the first version in his Journal, Emerson wrote, "Every thing good in nature & the world is in that moment of transition, the foam hangs but a moment on the wave . . ." (May–July 1847, J 10:82). Years earlier, he had noted, "Vices even in slight degree improve the expression. Malice & scorn add to beauty" (June 10, 1838, J 7:11).

58   Bearing.

59   On February 8, 1807, in frigid weather, Napoleon's army brilliantly fought a combined force of Russians and Prussians in Eylau, a town in East Prussia.

60   Primitive, original.

61 Earthy ores used as pigment.

62 Spectacular figures on the ceiling of the Sistine Chapel, in the Vatican, painted by Michelangelo Buonarroti (1475–1564) in 1508–1512. The story of Michelangelo digging in the pope's garden does not appear in the most authoritative early life of the painter, in *Lives of the Artists* (1550) by the Italian artist and writer Giorgio Vasari (1511–1574).

63 Vasari reports that Michelangelo, in his mid-seventies, no longer had the strength for painting, "and since he could not paint, he set to work upon a piece of marble, to bring out of it four figures larger than life, for his amusement and pastime, and as he said, because working with the hammer kept him healthy in body." The sculpture, the Florentine Pietà, was shattered by Michelangelo and later reconstructed.

64 Substitutes.

65 In European folklore, used to contain evil presences or ward off witchcraft.

he knew nothing, he went down into the Pope's gardens behind the Vatican, and with a shovel dug out ochres,[61] red and yellow, mixed them with glue and water with his own hands, and having, after many trials, at last suited himself, climbed his ladders, and painted away, week after week, month after month, the sibyls and prophets.[62] He surpassed his successors, in rough vigor, as much as in purity of intellect and refinement. He was not crushed by his one picture left unfinished at last.[63] Michel was wont to draw his figures first in skeleton, then to clothe them with flesh, and lastly to drape them. "Ah!" said a brave painter to me, thinking on these things, "if the man has failed, you will find he has dreamed instead of working. There is no way to success in our art, but to take off your coat, grind paint, and work like a digger on the railroad, all day and every day."

Success goes thus invariably with a certain *plus* or positive power: an ounce of power must balance an ounce of weight. And, though a man cannot return into his mother's womb, and be born with new amounts of vivacity, yet there are two economies, which are the best *succedanea*[64] which the case admits. The first is,—the stopping off decisively our miscellaneous activity, and concentrating our force on one or a few points; as the gardener, by severe pruning, forces the sap of the tree into one or two vigorous limbs, instead of suffering it to spindle into a sheaf of twigs.

"Enlarge not thy destiny," said the oracle: "endeavor not to do more than is given thee in charge." The one prudence in life is concentration; the one evil is dissipation: and it makes no difference whether our dissipations are coarse or fine; property and its cares, friends, and a social habit, or politics, or music, or feasting. Everything is good which takes away one plaything and delusion more, and drives us home to add one stroke of faithful work. Friends, books, pictures, lower duties, talents, flatteries, hopes,—all are distractions which cause oscillations in our giddy balloon, and make a good poise and a straight course, impossible. You must elect your work; you shall take what your brain can, and drop all the rest. Only so, can that amount of vital force accumulate, which can make the step from knowing to doing. No matter how much faculty of idle seeing a man has, the step from knowing to doing is rarely taken. 'Tis a step out of a chalk circle[65] of imbecility into fruitfulness. Many an artist lacking this, lacks all: he sees the masculine

Angelo or Cellini[66] with despair. He, too, is up to Nature and the First Cause in his thought. But the spasm to collect and swing his whole being into one act, he has not. The poet Campbell[67] said, that "a man accustomed to work was equal to any achievement he resolved on, and, that, for himself, necessity not inspiration was the prompter of his Muse."

Concentration is the secret of strength in politics, in war, in trade, in short, in all management of human affairs. One of the high anecdotes of the world is the reply of Newton to the inquiry "how he had been able to achieve his discoveries?"—"By always intending my mind."[68] Or if you will have a text from politics, take this from Plutarch;[69] "There was, in the whole city, but one street in which Pericles was ever seen, the street which led to the market-place and the council house. He declined all invitations to banquets, and all gay assemblies and company. During the whole period of his administration, he never dined at the table of a friend." Or if we seek an example from trade,—"I hope," said a good man to Rothschild, "your children are not too fond of money and business: I am sure you would not wish that."—"I am sure I should wish that: I wish them to give mind, soul, heart, and body to business,—that is the way to be happy. It requires a great deal of boldness and a great deal of caution, to make a great fortune; and when you have got it, it requires ten times as much wit to keep it. If I were to listen to all the projects proposed to me, I should ruin myself very soon. Stick to one business, young man. Stick to your brewery, (he said this to young Buxton,) and you will be the great brewer of London. Be brewer, and banker, and merchant, and manufacturer, and you will soon be in the Gazette."[70]

Many men are knowing, many are apprehensive and tenacious, but they do not rush to a decision. But in our flowing affairs a decision must be made,—the best, if you can; but any is better than none. There are twenty ways of going to a point, and one is the shortest; but set out at once on one. A man who has that presence of mind which can bring to him on the instant all he knows, is worth for action a dozen men who know as much, but can only bring it to light slowly. The good Speaker in the House is not the man who knows the theory of parliamentary tactics, but the man who decides off-hand. The good judge is not he who does hair-splitting justice to every allegation, but who, aiming at substantial justice, rules something intelligible for

66   Benvenuto Cellini (1500–1571), Florentine sculptor and autobiographer.

67   The Scottish author Thomas Campbell (1777–1844), a favorite poet of Emerson when he was a boy at Boston Latin School.

68   This quotation from the great British scientist and inventor Isaac Newton (1642–1727) has not been located.

69   From the life of Pericles by the Greek historian Plutarch (ca. 46–ca. 122 CE), who was among Emerson's best-loved authors.

70   The anecdote of a conversation between Nathan Mayer Rothschild (1777–1836), head of the Rothschild banking dynasty in England, and Edward Buxton (1812–1858), comes from the *Memoirs* (1848) by Edward's father, the philanthropist Sir Thomas Buxton (1786–1845), who was largely responsible for the emancipation of the slaves in the British West Indies. The brewery, Truman, Hanbury, and Buxton, still exists.

71    Emerson seems to be remembering, and considerably altering, a passage in *Rasselas* (1759), the prose fiction by the central English critic Dr. Samuel Johnson (1709–1784). In response to the young prince Rasselas's opinion that the most important factor in his choice of a wife will be "whether she be willing to be led by reason," his sister Nekayah responds, "There are a thousand familiar disputes which reason never can decide; questions that elude investigation, and make logic ridiculous; cases where something must be done, and where little can be said. . . . Wretched would be the pair above all names of wretchedness, who should be doomed to adjust by reason, every morning, all the minute detail of a domestic day."

72    Hack: ordinary saddle horse; Arab barb: the noble Barbary horse, famous for its grace, speed, and endurance, and prized in war.

73    Batteries produce galvanic currents by chemical means; they are weaker, but steadier, than the sparks created by friction. "Arts" here means useful processes.

74    Trunnions: pivots that allow a cannon to be raised or lowered. Colonel Napoleon Bonaparte Buford (1807–1883), who fought for the Union in the Civil War, was briefly an instructor at West Point.

75    Henry VIII (1491–1547), king of England 1509–1547. "Diligence surpasses judgment" is (as Emerson well knew) a better translation of the sentence, which has not been found in any writings by or history of Henry VIII.

76    The famous British Shakespearean actor (1757–1823), also a director and theater manager.

the guidance of suitors. The good lawyer is not the man who has an eye to every side and angle of contingency, and qualifies all his qualifications, but who throws himself on your part so heartily, that he can get you out of a scrape. Dr Johnson[71] said in one of his flowing sentences, "Miserable beyond all names of wretchedness is that unhappy pair, who are doomed to reduce beforehand to the principles of abstract reason all the details of each domestic day. There are cases when little can be said, and much must be done."

The second substitute for temperament is drill, the power of use and routine. The hack is a better roadster than the Arab barb.[72] In chemistry the galvanic stream, slow, but continuous, is equal in power to the electric spark, and is, in our arts, a better agent.[73] So in human action, against the spasm of energy, we offset the continuity of drill. We spread the same amount of force over much time, instead of condensing it into a moment. 'Tis the same ounce of gold here in a ball, and there in a leaf. At West Point, Col. Buford, the Chief Engineer, pounded with a hammer the trunnions of a cannon, until he broke them off. He fired a piece of ordnance some hundred times in swift succession, until it burst.[74] Now which stroke broke the trunnion? Every stroke. Which blast burst the piece? Every blast. *"Diligence passe sens,"* Henry VIII.[75] was wont to say, or, great is drill. John Kemble[76] said, that the worst provincial company of actors would go through a play better than the best amateur company. Basil Hall[77] likes to show that the worst regular troops will beat the best volunteers. Practice is nine tenths. A course of mobs is good practice for orators.[78] All the great speakers were bad speakers at first. Stumping it through England for seven years, made Cobden a consummate debater. Stumping it through New England for twice seven trained Wendell Phillips.[79] The way to learn German, is, to read the same dozen pages over and over a hundred times, till you know every word and particle in them, and can pronounce and repeat them by heart. No genius can recite a ballad at first reading, so well as mediocrity can at the fifteenth or twentieth reading. The rule for hospitality and Irish 'help,' is, to have the same dinner every day throughout the year. At last, Mrs O'Shaughnessy[80] learns to cook it to a nicety, the host learns to carve it, and the guests are well served. A humorous friend of mine thinks, that the reason why Nature is so perfect in her art, and gets up such inconceivably fine sunsets, is, that she has learned how, at last, by dint of doing the same thing so very often. Cannot one converse better on a topic on which he has experience, than on one which is new? Men whose opinion is valued on 'Change,[81] are only such as have a special experience, and off that ground their opinion is not valuable. "More are made good by exercitation, than by nature," said Democritus.[82] The friction in nature is so enormous that we cannot spare any power. It is not question to express our thought, to elect our way, but to overcome resistances of the medium and material in everything we do. Hence the use of drill, and the worthlessness of amateurs to cope with practitioners. Six hours every day at the piano, only to give facility of touch: six hours a day at painting, only to give command of the odious materials, oil, ochres and brushes. The masters say, that they know a master in music, only by seeing the pose of the hands on the keys; —so difficult and vital an act is the command of the instrument. To have learned the use of the tools, by thousands of manipulations; to have learned the arts of reckoning, by endless adding and dividing, is the power of the mechanic and the clerk.

I remarked in England, in confirmation of a frequent experience at home, that, in literary circles, the men of trust and consideration, bookmakers, editors, university deans and professors, bishops, too, were by no means men of the largest literary talent, but usually of a low and ordinary intellectuality, with a sort of mercantile activity and working talent. Indifferent hacks and mediocrities tower, by pushing their forces to a lucrative point, or by working power, over multitudes of superior men, in old as in New England.[83]

I have not forgotten that there are sublime considerations which limit the value of talent and superficial success. We can easily overpraise the vulgar hero. There are sources on which we have not drawn. I know what I abstain from. I adjourn what I have to say on this topic to the chapters on Culture and Worship. But this force or spirit being the means relied on by nature for bringing the work of the day about,—as far as we attach importance to household life, and the prizes of the world, we must respect that. And I hold, that an economy may be applied to it; it is as much a subject of exact law and arithmetic as fluids and gases are; it may be husbanded, or wasted; every man is efficient only as he is a container or vessel of this force, and never was any

77   Hall (1788–1844) was a captain in the British Royal Navy and travel writer.

78   "A course of mobs would do me much good," Emerson wrote in his Journal (March 25, 1847; J 10:28).

79   Both the British statesman Richard Cobden (1804–1865), the industrialist and free-trade champion, and the American orator Wendell Phillips (1811–1884), the renowned abolitionist, made many stump speeches in the 1840s and (in Phillips's case) later.

80   Typical Irish name.

81   Financial exchange.

82   Democritus, Greek philosopher (ca. 460–ca. 370 BCE). Exercitation: exercise; the word's meaning spans a range from artistic practice to religious devotion and meditation.

83   In the original Journal passages (J 11:81, 245) Emerson named the men he considered mediocrities: the American journalist and publisher Horace Greeley (1811–1872), the American editor Rufus Griswold (1815–1857), the Scottish geologist Charles Lyell (1797–1875), and the English religious apologist John Henry Newman (1801–1890).

84    Flimsy, shoddy.

signal act or achievement in history, but by this expenditure. This is not gold, but the gold-maker; not the fame, but the exploit.

If these forces and this husbandry are within reach of our will, and the laws of them can be read, we infer that all success, and all conceivable benefit for man, is also, first or last, within his reach, and has its own sublime economies by which it may be attained. The world is mathematical, and has no casualty, in all its vast and flowing curve. Success has no more eccentricity, than the gingham and muslin we weave in our mills. I know no more affecting lesson to our busy plotting New England brains, than to go into one of the factories with which we have lined all the watercourses in the States. A man hardly knows how much he is a machine, until he begins to make telegraph, loom, press, and locomotive, in his own image. Only in these, he is forced to leave out his follies and hindrances, so that when we go to the mill, the machine is more moral than we. Let a man dare go to a loom, and see if he be equal to it. Let machine confront machine, and see how they come out. The world-mill is more complex than the calico-mill, and the architect stooped less. In the gingham-mill, a broken thread or a shred spoils the web through a piece of a hundred yards, and is traced back to the girl that wove it, and lessens her wages. The stockholder, on being shown this, rubs his hands with delight. Are you so cunning, Mr Profitloss, and do you expect to swindle your master and employer, in the web you weave? A day is a more magnificent cloth than any muslin, the mechanism that makes it is infinitely cunninger, and you shall not conceal the sleezy[84] fraudulent rotten hours you have slipped into the piece, nor fear that any honest thread, or straighter steel, or more inflexible shaft, will not testify in the web.

# Illusions

Flow, flow the waves hated,
Accursed, adored,
The waves of mutation:
No anchorage is.
Sleep is not, death is not;
Who seem to die live.
House you were born in,
Friends of your spring-time,
Old man and young maid,
Day's toil and its guerdon,[1]
They are all vanishing,
Fleeing to fables,
Cannot be moored.
See the stars through them,
Through treacherous marbles.[2]
Know, the stars yonder,
The stars everlasting,
Are fugitive also,
And emulate, vaulted,
The lambent[3] heat-lightning,
And fire-fly's flight.

*This is the ninth chapter in* The Conduct of Life *(1860). Life, for Emerson, is about illusion because we deceive ourselves, via the "rounding . . . powers of the eye" and the imagination. There is something of us mixed in all we see; we bend the world to our vision. Our illusions are dreams or mysteries rather than simple lies, and they sustain us; but we also like to "lift a corner of the curtain," and show our awareness of the fiction. At the end of his essay Emerson tempts us with the thought that we can peer behind the veil and discern the law behind the appearances we live by. He returns from the skepticism that, in the course of the essay, has turned even the self into a fable. Yet such assurance offers (in the last sentence of "Illusions") only a momentary glimpse of rest, not an eternal home.*

1    Reward.

2    "Treacherous" because the human presences within the house cannot share the permanence of its marble roof.

3    Playing lightly (from Latin *lambere*, "to lick").

4     Entanglement.

5     Proteus was a shape-shifting Greek god; to ride him is to ride change. Emerson alludes here as elsewhere to the picture of the soul commanding a chariot with horses in the dialogue *Phaedrus* by the Greek philosopher Plato (429–347 BCE). In the essay "Fate," Emerson wrote, "A man must ride alternately on the horses of his private and his public nature."

6     During a lecture tour of the American West, in June 1850. Mammoth Cave is still a well-known tourist site.

7     The name recalls a pastoral episode in *The Faerie Queene* (1590–1596) by the English poet Edmund Spenser (ca. 1552–1599).

8     Rivers of the classical underworld.

9     Bengal lights are flares (Emerson and his group actually shot Roman candles; see L 4:212); groins are, in architecture, the intersections of two vaults; and "sparry" means dotted with spar (lustrous crystal rock).

10     Imitative.

When thou dost return
On the wave's circulation,
Beholding the shimmer,
The wild dissipation,
And, out of endeavor
To change and to flow,
The gas become solid,
And phantoms and nothings
Return to be things,
And endless imbroglio[4]
Is law and the world,—
Then first shalt thou know,
That in the wild turmoil,
Horsed on the Proteus,[5]
Thou ridest to power,
And to endurance.

Some years ago, in company with an agreeable party, I spent a long summer day in exploring the Mammoth Cave in Kentucky.[6] We traversed, through spacious galleries affording a solid masonry foundation for the town and country overhead, the six or eight black miles from the mouth of the cavern to the innermost recess which tourists visit,—a niche or grotto made of one seamless stalactite, and called, I believe, Serena's Bower.[7] I lost the light of one day. I saw high domes, and bottomless pits; heard the voice of unseen waterfalls; paddled three quarters of a mile in the deep Echo River, whose waters are peopled with the blind fish; crossed the streams "Lethe" and "Styx;"[8] plied with music and guns the echoes in these alarming galleries; saw every form of stalagmite and stalactite in the sculptured and fretted chambers,—icicle, orange-flower, acanthus, grapes, and snowball. We shot Bengal lights into the vaults and groins of the sparry[9] cathedrals, and examined all the masterpieces which the four combined engineers, water, limestone, gravitation, and time, could make in the dark.

The mysteries and scenery of the cave had the same dignity that belongs to all natural objects, and which shames the fine things to which we foppishly compare them. I remarked, especially, the mimetic[10] habit, with which Nature, on new instruments, hums her old tunes, making night to mimic day, and chemistry to ape vegetation. But I then took notice, and still chiefly remember, that the best thing which the cave had to offer was an illusion. On arriving at what is called the "Star-Chamber,"[11] our lamps were taken from us by the guide,[12] and extinguished or put aside, and, on looking upwards, I saw or seemed to see[13] the night heaven thick with stars[14] glimmering more or less brightly over our heads, and even what seemed a comet flaming among them. All the party were touched with astonishment and pleasure. Our musical friends sung with much feeling a pretty song, "The stars are in the quiet sky," &c.,[15] and I sat down on the rocky floor to enjoy the serene picture. Some crystal specks in the black ceiling high

[11]   Name of England's high judicial court in the Elizabethan Age.

[12]   The party used oil lamps; their guide was an accomplished slave named Stephen, a student of geology.

[13]   Reference to a phrase from the *Aeneid* (29–19 BCE) of Virgil (70–19 BCE). Virgil's hero Aeneas, in the underworld, "sees or thinks he sees" the Carthaginian queen Dido, who has killed herself for him. Virgil's words were imitated by John Milton (1608–1674) in his *Paradise Lost* (1667): Milton compares the deities of hell to "fairy elves, / Whose midnight revels . . . some belated peasant sees, / Or dreams he sees" (1.781–784).

[14]   In *Paradise Lost* (3.60–61), Milton says of God the Father, "About him all the sanctities of heaven / Stood thick as stars."

[15]   From *Ernest Maltravers* (1837) by the English novelist Edward Bulwer-Lytton (1803–1873).

Mammoth Cave, Kentucky.

.. 

16    Increasing, by using an expedient substitute.

17    Emerson's confidence at reading the Book of Nature in his first book, *Nature*, has been replaced by a sense of the world's, and our, reliance on trickery.

18    Emerson echoes the sense of childhood illuminations that fade later on, and that are linked to sunrise and sunset, in the *Immortality Ode* (1807) by the English poet William Wordsworth (1770–1850). Spheral: symmetrical, perfect.

19    Constitution.

20    Subtract.

21    This sentence appears as well in "Fate," the first essay in *The Conduct of Life*.

overhead, reflecting the light of a half-hid lamp, yielded this magnificent effect.

I own, I did not like the cave so well for eking out[16] its sublimities with this theatrical trick. But I have had many experiences like it, before and since; and we must be content to be pleased without too curiously analyzing the occasions. Our conversation with Nature is not just what it seems.[17] The cloud-rack, the sunrise and sunset glories, rainbows, and northern lights are not quite so spheral as our childhood thought them;[18] and the part our organization[19] plays in them is too large. The senses interfere everywhere, and

Lidian Emerson with son Waldo.

mix their own structure with all they report of. Once, we fancied the earth a plane, and stationary. In admiring the sunset, we do not yet deduct[20] the rounding, coördinating, pictorial powers of the eye.

The same interference from our organization creates the most of our pleasure and pain. Our first mistake is the belief that the circumstance gives the joy which we give to the circumstance. Life is an ecstasy.[21] Life is sweet as nitrous oxide;[22] and the fisherman dripping all day over a cold pond, the switchman at the railway intersection, the farmer in the field, the negro in the rice-swamp, the fop in the street, the hunter in the woods, the barrister with the jury, the belle at the ball, all ascribe a certain pleasure to their employment, which they themselves give it. Health and appetite impart the sweetness to sugar, bread, and meat. We fancy that our civilization has got on far, but we still come back to our primers.

We live by our imaginations, by our admirations, by our sentiments. The child walks amid heaps of illusions, which he does not like to have disturbed. The boy, how sweet to him is fancy! how dear the story of barons and battles! What a hero he is, whilst he feeds on his heroes! What a debt is his to imaginative books! He has no better friend or influence, than Scott, Shakspeare, Plutarch, and Homer.[23] The man lives to other objects, but who dare affirm that they are more real? Even the prose of the streets is full of refractions. In the life of the dreariest alderman,[24] fancy enters into all details, and colors them with rosy hue. He imitates the air and actions of people whom he admires, and is raised in his own eyes. He pays a debt quicker to a rich man than to a poor man. He wishes the bow and compliment of some leader in the state, or in society; weighs what he says; perhaps he never comes nearer to him for that, but dies at last better contented for this amusement of his eyes and his fancy.

The world rolls, the din of life is never hushed. In London, in Paris, in Boston, in San Francisco, the carnival, the masquerade is at its height. Nobody drops his domino.[25] The unities, the fictions of the piece it would be an impertinence to break. The chapter of fascinations is very long. Great is paint; nay, God is the painter; and we rightly accuse the critic who destroys too many illusions. Society does not love its unmaskers. It was wittily, if somewhat bitterly, said by D'Alembert, *"qu'un état de vapeur était un état très fâcheux, parcequ'il nous faisait voir les choses comme elles sont."*[26] I find men vic-

22    Then being used as an anesthetic in dentistry, as it still is today. Under the title "Lotos eaters," Emerson wrote in his Journal (fall 1841), "I suppose there is no more abandoned Epicure or opium eater than I. I taste every hour of these autumn days. Every light from the sky every shadow on the earth ministers to my pleasure. I love this gas" (J 8:47). In October of the same year, he exclaimed, "We wish to take the gas which allows us to break through your wearisome proprieties, to plant the foot, to set the teeth, to fling abroad the arms, & dance & sing" (J 8:117). And in 1856, Emerson described "the sweet nitrous oxide gas which the speakers seem to breathe" at public meetings: "Once they taste it, they cling like mad to the bladder, & will not let it go" (J 14:92).

23    Sir Walter Scott (1771–1832), Scottish novelist; Plutarch (ca. 46–ca. 122), Greek historian and moralist prized by Emerson; Homer (ca. 9th century BCE), author of the *Iliad* and the *Odyssey*. "Plutarch, the elixir of Greece & Rome, that is the book which nations went to compose," Emerson exclaimed in his Journal (1860): "— If the world's library were burning, I should as soon fly to rescue that, as Shakspeare & Plato, or next after" (J 14:356).

24    Ward officer, magistrate.

25    Black mask that covers the upper half of the face, often seen during carnival (the Venetian masquerade ball).

26    "A misty condition would be very annoying, since it would make us see things as they are." Saying attributed to the mathematician and philosopher Jean d'Alembert (1717–1783) by Denis Diderot (1713–1784). Both Diderot and d'Alembert were Enlightenment thinkers who uncovered the role of illusion in life.

27　From Emerson's Journal (1859): "As soon the intellect awakes, all things make a musical impression. It is comedy without laughter. Everything in the human world, fashionist, millionaire, presidents, academics, are toy people in a toy-house—" (J 14:301).

28　Yoganidra, also called Maya, is the Hindu goddess of illusion; Momus mocked the faults of the Greek gods; *Gylfi's Mocking* is a compendium of Norse myths, part of the *Prose Edda* by the Icelandic poet and politician Snorri Sturluson (1179–1242). Gylfi is left standing alone at the end of the story, after the palace he has been visiting vanishes, along with its mysterious inhabitants.

29　In his Journal (1851) Emerson commented, "I see plainly enough that ordinarily we take counters for gold, that our eating & trading & marrying & learning are mistaken by us for ends & realities, whilst they are only symbols of true life . . . 'tis a glimpse; 'tis a peeping through a chink; the dream in a dream. We play at Bo-peep with Truth, and cannot write the Chapter of Metaphysics" (J 11:438–439).

30　Raucous serenade, featuring the banging of pots and pans; used either to mock or celebrate a marriage, or to deride someone.

31　Emerson, an assiduous cultivator of pears, exhibited them at Concord's County Fair —but never, apparently, at the State Fair in Springfield.

32　Comfits: fruits or nuts coated with sugar; sweetmeat: confection. The youth, according to Emerson's son Edward, was the poet William Ellery Channing (1818–1901), his neighbor in Concord.

33　Chatter. The humorist was the Boston merchant G. W. Tyler (J 8:91).

34　Ability to laugh; sense of the ridiculous.

tims of illusion in all parts of life. Children, youths, adults, and old men, all are led by one bawble or another.[27] Yoganidra, the goddess of illusion, Proteus, or Momus, or Gylfi's Mocking,—for the Power has many names,—is stronger than the Titans, stronger than Apollo.[28] Few have overheard the gods, or surprised their secret. Life is a succession of lessons which must be lived to be understood. All is riddle, and the key to a riddle is another riddle. There are as many pillows of illusion as flakes in a snow-storm. We wake from one dream into another dream. The toys, to be sure, are various, and are graduated in refinement to the quality of the dupe. The intellectual man requires a fine bait; the sots are easily amused. But everybody is drugged with his own frenzy, and the pageant marches at all hours, with music and banner and badge.[29]

Amid the joyous troop who give in to the charivari,[30] comes now and then a sad-eyed boy, whose eyes lack the requisite refractions to clothe the show in due glory, and who is afflicted with a tendency to trace home the glittering miscellany of fruits and flowers to one root. Science is a search after identity, and the scientific whim is lurking in all corners. At the State Fair, a friend of mine complained that all the varieties of fancy pears in our orchards seem to have been selected by somebody who had a whim for a particular kind of pear, and only cultivated such as had that perfume; they were all alike.[31] And I remember the quarrel of another youth with the confectioners, that, when he racked his wit to choose the best comfits in the shops, in all the endless varieties of sweetmeat[32] he could only find three flavors, or two. What then? Pears and cakes are good for something; and because you, unluckily, have an eye or nose too keen, why need you spoil the comfort which the rest of us find in them? I knew a humorist, who, in a good deal of rattle,[33] had a grain or two of sense. He shocked the company by maintaining that the attributes of God were two,—power and risibility;[34] and that it was the duty of every pious man to keep up the comedy. And I have known gentlemen of great stake in the community, but whose sympathies were cold,— presidents of colleges, and governors, and senators,—who held themselves bound to sign every temperance pledge, and act with Bible societies, and missions, and peacemakers, and cry *Hist-a-boy!*[35] to every good dog. We must not carry comity[36] too far, but we all have kind impulses in this direction. When the boys come into my yard for leave to gather horsechestnuts, I own

I enter into Nature's game, and affect to grant the permission reluctantly, fearing that any moment they will find out the imposture of that showy chaff.[37] But this tenderness is quite unnecessary; the enchantments are laid on very thick. Their young life is thatched with them. Bare and grim to tears is the lot of the children in the hovel I saw yesterday; yet not the less they hung it round with frippery romance, like the children of the happiest fortune, and talked of "the dear cottage where so many joyful hours had flown."[38] Well, this thatching of hovels is the custom of the country. Women, more than all, are the element and kingdom of illusion. Being fascinated, they fascinate. They see through Claude–Lorraines.[39] And how dare any one, if he could, pluck away the *coulisses*,[40] stage effects, and ceremonies, by which they live? Too pathetic, too pitiable, is the region of affection, and its atmosphere always liable to *mirage*.[41]

We are not very much to blame for our bad marriages. We live amid hallucinations; and this especial trap is laid to trip up our feet with, and all are tripped up first or last. But the mighty Mother who had been so sly with us, as if she felt that she owed us some indemnity, insinuates into the Pandora-box[42] of marriage some deep and serious benefits, and some great joys. We find a delight in the beauty and happiness of children, that makes the heart too big for the body. In the worst-assorted connections there is ever some mixture of true marriage. Teague and his jade[43] get some just relations of mutual respect, kindly observation, and fostering of each other, learn something, and would carry themselves wiselier, if they were now to begin.

'Tis fine for us to point at one or another fine madman, as if there were any exempts. The scholar in his library is none. I, who have all my life heard any number of orations and debates, read poems and miscellaneous books, conversed with many geniuses, am still the victim of any new page; and, if Marmaduke, or Hugh, or Moosehead,[44] or any other, invent a new style or mythology, I fancy that the world will be all brave and right, if dressed in these colors, which I had not thought of. Then at once I will daub with this new paint; but it will not stick. 'Tis like the cement which the pedler sells at the door; he makes broken crockery hold with it, but you can never buy of him a bit of the cement which will make it hold when he is gone.

35  "Sic 'em": used to urge a dog to action.

36  Courteous understanding.

37  Directly across from the Emersons' house was the East Primary schoolhouse; the schoolchildren often came across the road for horse chestnuts and apples. Chaff is the unusable part of a wheat stalk.

38  Emerson wrote in his Journal (1846), "Great is paint! This poor child who has had no childhood, but a harsh hedgehog lot, talks of that grim farmhouse as the happiest days of her life" (J 9:444).

39  Small colored, convex mirrors named after the French painter Claude Lorraine (ca. 1600–1682) and used by travelers in Emerson's day to give a landscape tinted, soft effects like those in Lorraine's paintings.

40  Stage scenery, slid in and out from the wings.

41  A new word, invented by the soldiers of the French emperor Napoleon Bonaparte (1769–1821) during his North African campaign to describe the shimmering effects of the desert atmosphere.

42  In Greek myth, Jupiter bestowed on Pandora ("all gifts") a box to be given to whomever she married. Epimetheus, the brother of Prometheus, married Pandora and opened the box: it contained all evils, which have ever since plagued the world.

43  An Irishman and his rough or sharp-tongued woman.

44  Eccentric names, chosen apparently at random—though Emerson may be thinking of Moosehead Lake in Maine, "a suitably wild-looking sheet of water," as Henry David Thoreau (1817–1862) described it when he visited there in 1853.

45    Julius Caesar (100–44 BCE), Roman general and dictator, or Augustus Caesar (63 BCE–14 CE), Roman emperor.

46    Bedeviled. "The dragon" meant Satan.

47    In Cuba, messengers of Christopher Columbus (ca. 1451–1506) met Indians who introduced them to tobacco. In 1859 or 1860 Emerson wrote in his Journal, "The believing we do something when we do nothing, is the first illusion of tobacco" (J 14:338).

48    Straw (or strip of wood or ivory) used in a game: the jackstraws are thrown on a table in a heap, and one has to be picked out without disturbing the rest.

49    The starry cloud in the sword hilt of the constellation Orion; it takes 190,000 years for Mizar to revolve around Alcor, its fellow star in Ursa Major.

50    As in the destruction of Sodom and Gomorrah in the Bible (Genesis 19:1–29), or the swallowing up in the earth of Korah and his rebellious band (Numbers 16:1–40).

Men who make themselves felt in the world avail themselves of a certain fate in their constitution, which they know how to use. But they never deeply interest us, unless they lift a corner of the curtain, or betray never so slightly their penetration of what is behind it. 'Tis the charm of practical men, that outside of their practicality are a certain poetry and play, as if they led the good horse Power by the bridle, and preferred to walk, though they can ride so fiercely. Bonaparte is intellectual, as well as Cæsar;[45] and the best soldiers, sea-captains, and railway men have a gentleness, when off duty; a good-natured admission that there are illusions, and who shall say that he is not their sport? We stigmatize the cast-iron fellows, who cannot so detach themselves, as "dragon-ridden,"[46] "thunder-stricken," and fools of fate, with whatever powers endowed.

Since our tuition is through emblems and indirections, 'tis well to know that there is method in it, a fixed scale, and rank above rank in the phantasms. We begin low with coarse masks, and rise to the most subtle and beautiful. The red men told Columbus, "they had an herb which took away fatigue;" but he found the illusion of "arriving from the east at the Indies" more composing to his lofty spirit than any tobacco.[47] Is not our faith in the impenetrability of matter more sedative than narcotics? You play with jackstraws,[48] balls, bowls, horse and gun, estates and politics; but there are finer games before you. Is not time a pretty toy? Life will show you masks that are worth all your carnivals. Yonder mountain must migrate into your mind. The fine star-dust and nebulous blur in Orion, "the portentous year of Mizar and Alcor,"[49] must come down and be dealt with in your household thought. What if you shall come to discern that the play and playground of all this pompous history are radiations from yourself, and that the sun borrows his beams? What terrible questions we are learning to ask! The former men believed in magic, by which temples, cities, and men were swallowed up, and all trace of them gone.[50] We are coming on the secret of a magic which sweeps out of men's minds all vestige of theism and beliefs which they and their fathers held and were framed upon.

There are deceptions of the senses, deceptions of the passions, and the structural, beneficent illusions of sentiment and of the intellect. There is the illusion of love, which attributes to the beloved person all which that person shares with his or her family, sex, age, or condition, nay, with the human mind itself. 'Tis these which the lover loves, and Anna Matilda[51] gets the credit of them. As if one shut up always in a tower, with one window, through which the face of heaven and earth could be seen, should fancy that all the marvels he beheld belonged to that window. There is the illusion of time, which is very deep; who has disposed of it? or come to the conviction that what seems the *succession* of thought is only the distribution of wholes into causal series? The intellect sees that every atom carries the whole of Nature; that the mind opens to omnipotence; that, in the endless striving and ascents, the metamorphosis is entire, so that the soul doth not know itself in its own act, when that act is perfected. There is illusion that shall deceive even the elect. There is illusion that shall deceive even the performer of the miracle. Though he make his body, he denies that he makes it. Though the world exist from thought, thought is daunted in presence of the world. One after the other we accept the mental laws, still resisting those which follow, which however must be accepted. But all our concessions only compel us to new profusion. And what avails it that science has come to treat space and time as simply forms of thought, and the material world as hypothetical,[52] and withal our pretension of *property* and even of self-hood are fading with the rest, if, at last, even our thoughts are not finalities; but the incessant flowing and ascension reach these also, and each thought which yesterday was a finality, to-day is yielding to a larger generalization?

With such volatile elements to work in, 'tis no wonder if our estimates are loose and floating. We must work and affirm, but we have no guess of the value of what we say or do. The cloud is now as big as your hand, and now it covers a county.[53] That story of Thor, who was set to drain the drinking-horn in Asgard, and to wrestle with the old woman, and to run with the runner Lok, and presently found that he had been drinking up the sea, and wrestling with Time, and racing with Thought,[54] describes us who are contending, amid these seeming trifles, with the supreme energies of Nature. We fancy we have fallen into bad company and squalid condition, low debts, shoe-bills, broken glass to pay for, pots to buy, butcher's meat, sugar, milk, and coal. 'Set me some great task, ye gods! and I will show my spirit.' 'Not so,' says the good Heaven; 'plod and plough, vamp[55] your old coats and hats,

51 Pen name used by the English playwright and poet Hannah Cowley (1743–1809) for her sentimental poetry. As Anna Matilda she also wrote a Gothic novel, *The Italian Marauders, A Romance* (1810).

52 Emerson here alludes to the advances of German idealist philosophy, especially that of Immanuel Kant (1724–1804).

53 In 1 Kings 18:44, a servant tells the prophet Elijah, "Behold, there ariseth a little cloud out of the sea, like a man's hand"; soon, "the heaven was black with clouds and wind."

54 The tale is from Norse mythology; Emerson read it in *Gylfi's Mocking*, from Sturluson's *Prose Edda*.

55 Patch.

56    The starry heavens (firmament), in which we could read our destiny, have been replaced by an opaque eggshell, like the artificial roof of Mammoth Cave. Instead of reading nature, or discerning our fate, we wait for a fleeting glimpse of the order that lurks behind the scenes.

57    Emerson returns to his skeptical mood.

58    Recognized.

59    Brilliant effect.

60    "At the top or at the bottom" because the supreme or most basic illusion makes us work for illusions, even though we tell ourselves that "what we really are" matters most. Earlier on, Emerson argued that we cannot know what we are apart from illusion. Now, he says that we still desire clear sight of a reality based on fixed law, and a "face to face" acknowledgment of our true selves (see the next paragraph).

weave a shoestring; great affairs and the best wine by and by.' Well, 'tis all phantasm; and if we weave a yard of tape in all humility and as well as we can, long hereafter we shall see it was no cotton tape at all, but some galaxy which we braided, and that the threads were Time and Nature.

We cannot write the order of the variable winds. How can we penetrate the law of our shifting moods and susceptibility? Yet they differ as all and nothing. Instead of the firmament of yesterday, which our eyes require, it is to-day an eggshell which coops us in; we cannot even see what or where our stars of destiny are.[56] From day to day, the capital facts of human life are hidden from our eyes. Suddenly the mist rolls up, and reveals them, and we think how much good time is gone, that might have been saved, had any hint of these things been shown. A sudden rise in the road shows us the system of mountains, and all the summits, which have been just as near us all the year, but quite out of mind. But these alternations are not without their order, and we are parties to our various fortune. If life seems a succession of dreams, yet poetic justice is done in dreams also. The visions of good men are good; it is the undisciplined will that is whipped with bad thoughts and bad fortunes. When we break the laws, we lose our hold on the central reality. Like sick men in hospitals, we change only from bed to bed, from one folly to another; and it cannot signify much what becomes of such castaways,—wailing, stupid, comatose creatures,—lifted from bed to bed, from the nothing of life to the nothing of death.[57]

In this kingdom of illusions we grope eagerly for stays and foundations. There is none but a strict and faithful dealing at home, and a severe barring out of all duplicity or illusion there. Whatever games are played with us, we must play no games with ourselves, but deal in our privacy with the last honesty and truth. I look upon the simple and childish virtues of veracity and honesty as the root of all that is sublime in character. Speak as you think, be what you are, pay your debts of all kinds. I prefer to be owned[58] as sound and solvent, and my word as good as my bond, and to be what cannot be skipped, or dissipated, or undermined, to all the *éclat*[59] in the universe. This reality is the foundation of friendship, religion, poetry, and art. At the top or at the bottom of all illusions I set the cheat which still leads us to work and live for appearances, in spite of our conviction, in all sane hours, that it is what we really are that avails with friends, with strangers, and with fate or fortune.[60]

One would think from the talk of men, that riches and poverty were a great matter; and our civilization mainly respects it. But the Indians say, that they do not think the white man with his brow of care, always toiling, afraid of heat and cold, and keeping within doors, has any advantage of them. The permanent interest of every man is, never to be in a false position, but to have the weight of Nature to back him in all that he does. Riches and poverty are a thick or thin costume; and our life—the life of all of us—identical. For we transcend the circumstance continually, and taste the real quality of existence; as in our employments, which only differ in the manipulations, but express the same laws; or in our thoughts, which wear no silks, and taste no ice-creams. We see God face to face[61] every hour, and know the savour of Nature.

The early Greek philosophers Heraclitus and Xenophanes measured their force on this problem of identity. Diogenes of Apollonia[62] said, that unless the atoms were made of one stuff, they could never blend and act with one another. But the Hindoos, in their sacred writings, express the liveliest feeling, both of the essential identity, and of that illusion which they conceive variety to be. "The notions, 'I am,' and 'This is mine,' which influence mankind, are but delusions of the mother of the world. Dispel, O Lord of all creatures! the conceit of knowledge which proceeds from ignorance." And the beatitude of man they hold to lie in being freed from fascination.[63]

The intellect is stimulated by the statement of truth in a trope,[64] and the will by clothing the laws of life in illusions. But the unities of Truth and of Right are not broken by the disguise. There need never be any confusion in these. In a crowded life of many parts and performers, on a stage of nations, or in the obscurest hamlet in Maine or California, the same elements offer the same choices to each new comer, and, according to his election, he fixes his fortune in absolute nature. It would be hard to put more mental and moral philosophy than the Persians have thrown into a sentence:—

"Fooled thou must be, though wisest of the wise:
Then be the fool of virtue, not of vice."[65]

61    In Genesis 32:30, Jacob, after his struggle with a mysterious being at the Jabbok ford, says, "I have seen God face to face, and my life is preserved"; in Exodus 33:20, God tells Moses, "Thou canst not see my face: for there shall no man see me, and live"; in I Corinthians 13:12, St. Paul (ca. 5–ca. 67) writes (referring to a future revelation), "For now we see through a glass, darkly; but then face to face: now I know in part; but then shall I know even as also I am known."

62    Heraclitus, Xenophanes, and Diogenes of Apollonia all lived in the 5th century BCE: all three were speculative cosmologists.

63    Emerson's summary of Hinduism derives in part from his reading of a Sanskrit scripture, the *Vishnu Purana*, in an 1840 translation by Horace Wilson; in 1845, he quoted this book frequently in his Journal (J 9:258).

64    A turn of thought or phrase (in Greek, *trephein* means "to turn"). In his late compilation "Poetry and Imagination," Emerson wrote, "The value of a trope is that the hearer is one: and indeed Nature itself is a vast trope and all particular natures are tropes." Some of Emerson's central tropes in his work are: the Book of Nature, the circle, the wave, the representative man, ascent and descent, the spark or daemon within us, and Anankê (Necessity).

65    Emerson found these lines in *Practical Philosophy of the Mohammadan People* (1839), a fifteenth-century Persian compilation translated by W. F. Thompson.

66    Word used for the sky or heavens in the creation account in Genesis (1:6–8).

67    In Emerson's Divinity School Address, he describes a bad sermon in winter: "A snow storm was falling around us. The snow storm was real; the preacher merely spectral; and the eye felt the sad contrast in looking at him, and then out of the window behind him, into the beautiful meteor of the snow."

There is no chance, and no anarchy, in the universe. All is system and gradation. Every god is there sitting in his sphere. The young mortal enters the hall of the firmament:[66] there is he alone with them alone, they pouring on him benedictions and gifts, and beckoning him up to their thrones. On the instant, and incessantly, fall snow-storms of illusions.[67] He fancies himself in a vast crowd which sways this way and that, and whose movement and doings he must obey: he fancies himself poor, orphaned, insignificant. The mad crowd drives hither and thither, now furiously commanding this thing to be done, now that. What is he that he should resist their will, and think or act for himself? Every moment, new changes, and new showers of deceptions, to baffle and distract him. And when, by and by, for an instant, the air clears, and the cloud lifts a little, there are the gods still sitting around him on their thrones,—they alone with him alone.

# From *Memoirs of Margaret Fuller Ossoli*

She was everywhere a welcome guest. The houses of her friends in town and country were open to her, and every hospitable attention eagerly offered. Her arrival was a holiday, and so was her abode. She stayed a few days, often a week, more seldom a month, and all tasks that could be suspended were put aside to catch the favorable hour, in walking, riding, or boating, to talk with this joyful guest, who brought wit, anecdotes, love-stories, tragedies, oracles with her, and, with her broad web of relations to so many fine friends, seemed like the queen of some parliament of love,[1] who carried the key to all confidences, and to whom every question had been finally referred.

Persons were her game, specially, if marked by fortune, or character, or success;—to such was she sent. She addressed them with a hardihood,—almost a haughty assurance,—queen-like. Indeed, they fell in her way, where the access might have seemed difficult, by wonderful casualties; and the inveterate recluse, the coyest maid, the waywardest poet, made no resistance, but yielded at discretion, as if they had been waiting for her, all doors to this imperious dame. She disarmed the suspicion of recluse scholars by the absence of bookishness. The ease with which she entered into conversation made them forget all they had heard of her; and she was infinitely less interested in literature than in life.[2] They saw she valued earnest persons, and Dante, Petrarch, and Goethe,[3] because they thought as she did, and gratified her with high portraits, which she was everywhere seeking. She drew her

*Emerson's memoir of Margaret Fuller Ossoli, excerpted here, was published in 1852; also included with it, in two volumes, were memoirs of Fuller by William Henry Channing (1810–1884) and James Freeman Clarke (1810–1888), both Unitarian ministers. Fuller first visited Emerson at his home in Concord in 1835. Emerson reported (in his memoir), "I remember that she made me laugh more than I liked; for I was, at that time, an eager scholar of ethics, and had tasted the sweets of solitude and stoicism . . ."*

*Fuller, who learned Latin and Greek by age six, was a formidable intellectual and a polemical feminist. Among Emerson's friends, she was, along with Thoreau, the mind he responded to most strongly. She and Emerson both edited the* Dial, *the short-lived Transcendentalist journal. She was the author of the feminist tract* Woman in the Nineteenth Century (1845) *and* Summer on the Lakes, in 1843 (1844), *a meditative account of a journey to the Great Lakes. She became the first woman to write for the* New York Tribune. *In addition to influencing Emerson's views on a range of literary and philosophical subjects, Fuller made him more*
(continued)

*sympathetic to the feminist movement. He wrote about women in his Journal (1851), "I think that, as long as they have not equal rights of property & right of voting, they are not on a right footing . . . I find the Evils real & great" (J 11:444–445).*

*The text of this excerpt from Emerson's memoir is taken from the Boston edition of 1857, published by Sampson and Company.*

1     Emerson has in mind the medieval courts of love presided over by powerful women, such as Eleanor of Aquitaine (ca. 1122–1204) and her daughter Marie, Countess of Champagne (1145–1198); the "parliament" was the contest of poets that took place at these courts.

Women were important intellectual influences in Emerson's early life, especially Sarah Alden Bradford Ripley (1793–1867) and his aunt Mary Moody Emerson. In later years, Caroline Sturgis (1819–1888), Sophia Ripley (1803–1861), Elizabeth Hoar (1814–1878), and Elizabeth Palmer Peabody (1804–1894) played central roles in Emerson's Transcendentalist circle; Sturgis was one of Emerson's closest friends.

2     In his Journal (1842) Emerson credited Fuller with "the most entertaining conversation in America" (J 8:369).

3     Dante Alighieri (1265–1321) and Francesco Petrarca, known as Petrarch (1304–1374), great Italian poets and humanists; J. W. von Goethe (1749–1832), preeminent German man of letters. Emerson wrote in his Journal (1851), "Goethe is the pivotal man of the old and new times with us. He shuts up the old, he opens the new" (J 11:430).

4     As in "The Rime of the Ancient Mariner" (1798) by the English Romantic poet S. T. Coleridge (1772–1834).

companions to surprising confessions. She was the wedding-guest, to whom the long-pent story must be told;[4] and they were not less struck, on reflection, at the suddenness of the friendship which had established, in one day, new and permanent covenants. She extorted the secret of life, which cannot be told without setting heart and mind in a glow; and thus had the best of those she saw. Whatever romance, whatever virtue, whatever impressive experience,—this came to her; and she lived in a superior circle; for they suppressed all their commonplace in her presence.

She was perfectly true to this confidence. She never confounded relations, but kept a hundred fine threads in her hand, without crossing or entangling any. An entire intimacy, which seemed to make both sharers of the whole horizon of each others' and of all truth, did not yet make her false to any other friend; gave no title to the history that an equal trust of another friend had put in her keeping. In this reticence was no prudery and no effort. For, so rich her mind, that she never was tempted to treachery, by the desire of entertaining. The day was never long enough to exhaust her opulent memory; and I, who knew her intimately for ten years,—from July, 1836, till August, 1846, when she sailed for Europe,[5]—never saw her without surprise at her new powers.

Of the conversations above alluded to, the substance was whatever was suggested by her passionate wish for equal companions, to the end of making life altogether noble.

\*    \*    \*

Her ready sympathies endeared her to my wife and my mother, each of whom highly esteemed her good sense and sincerity. She suited each, and all. Yet, she was not a person to be suspected of complaisance, and her attachments, one might say, were chemical.[6]

She had so many tasks of her own, that she was a very easy guest to entertain, as she could be left to herself, day after day, without apology. According to our usual habit, we seldom met in the forenoon. After dinner, we read something together, or walked, or rode. In the evening, she came to the library, and many and many a conversation was there held, whose details, if they could be preserved, would justify all encomiums.[7] They interested me in every manner;—talent, memory, wit, stern introspection, poetic play, religion, the finest personal feeling, the aspects of the future, each followed each in full activity, and left me, I remember, enriched and sometimes astonished by the gifts of my guest. Her topics were numerous, but the cardinal points of poetry, love, and religion, were never far off. She was a student of art, and, though untravelled, knew, much better than most persons who had been abroad, the conventional reputation of each of the masters. She was familiar with all the field of elegant criticism in literature. Among the problems of the day, these two attracted her chiefly, Mythology and Demonology; then, also, French Socialism, especially as it concerned woman; the whole prolific family of reforms, and, of course, the genius and career of each remarkable person.[8]

\* \* \*

It was soon evident that there was somewhat a little pagan about her; that she had some faith more or less distinct in a fate, and in a guardian genius; that her fancy, or her pride, had played with her religion. She had a taste for gems, ciphers, talismans, omens, coincidences, and birth-days. She had a special love for the planet Jupiter, and a belief that the month of September was inauspicious to her. She never forgot that her name, Margarita, signified a pearl. "When I first met with the name Leila," she said, "I knew, from the very look and sound, it was mine; I knew that it meant night,[9]—night, which brings out stars, as sorrow brings out truths." Sortilege she valued. She tried *sortes biblicae*,[10] and her hits were memorable. I think each new book which interested her, she was disposed to put to this test, and know if it had somewhat personal to say to her. As happens to such persons, these guesses were justified by the event. She chose carbuncle[11] for her own stone, and when a dear friend was to give her a gem, this was the one selected. She valued what she had somewhere read, that carbuncles are male and female. The female casts out light, the male has his within himself. "Mine," she said, "is the male." And she was wont to put on her carbuncle, a bracelet, or some selected gem, to write letters to certain friends. One of her friends she coupled

5     Fuller visited England, where she met famous authors, including William Wordsworth (1770–1850) and Emerson's friend Thomas Carlyle (1795–1881), and observed dismal industrial conditions; she then went on to France and Italy, where she became involved in the Italian revolution. She met an Italian, Giovanni Angelo, Marquis Ossoli (1821–1850), had a son by him, and later apparently married him. On July 19, 1850, on the way to America, all three were drowned off Long Island; Fuller's manuscript history of the Italian revolution was lost in the shipwreck.

6     Having the irresistible force of a chemical bond between atoms.

7     Praises.

8     Fuller's ambition was remarkable (Emerson reported that she said, "I now know all the people worth knowing in America, and I find no intellect comparable to my own"). Her self-confidence was originally fostered by her father, Timothy Fuller (1778–1835), who imposed strenuous lessons on her when she was a small child. Fuller wrote to Susan Prescott (July 11, 1825), "I have learned to believe that nothing, no! not perfection, is unattainable. I am determined on distinction . . . I am wanting in that intuitive tact and polish, which was bestowed upon some, but which I must acquire."

9     In Arabic and Hebrew, Leila means "night."

10     The practice of opening the Bible at random and taking as decisive the passage that appears.

11     Red precious stone (such as a ruby).

12　"Dragon's cliff," site of a ruined castle near Bonn, Germany. In German legend, recounted in the *Nibelungenlied* (ca. 1200), there the hero Siegfried killed and then bathed in the blood of the dragon Fafnir.

13　Acknowledge.

14　Presaging.

with the onyx, another in a decided way with the amethyst. She learned that the ancients esteemed this gem a talisman to dispel intoxication, to give good thoughts and understanding.

＊　＊　＊

[Emerson quotes from one of Fuller's letters.]

"As to the Daemoniacal, I know not that I can say to you anything more precise than you find from Goethe. There are no precise terms for such thoughts. The word instinctive indicates their existence. I intimated it in the little piece on the Drachenfels.[12] It may be best understood, perhaps, by a symbol. As the sun shines from the serene heavens, dispelling noxious exhalations, and calling forth exquisite thoughts on the surface of earth in the shape of shrub or flower, so gnome-like works the fire within the hidden caverns and secret veins of earth, fashioning existences which have a longer share in time, perhaps, because they are not immortal in thought. Love, beauty, wisdom, goodness are intelligent, but this power moves only to seize its prey. It is not necessarily either malignant or the reverse, but it has no scope beyond demonstrating its existence. When conscious, self-asserting, it becomes (as power working for its own sake, unwilling to acknowledge love for its superior, must) the devil. That is the legend of Lucifer, the star that would not own[13] its centre. Yet, while it is unconscious, it is not devilish, only daemoniac. In nature, we trace it in all volcanic workings, in a boding[14] position of lights, in whispers of the wind, which has no pedigree; in deceitful invitations of the water, in the sullen rock, which never shall find a voice, and in the shapes of all those beings who go about seeking what they may devour. We speak of a mystery, a dread; we shudder, but we approach still nearer, and a part of our nature listens, sometimes answers to this influence, which, if not indestructible, is at least indissolubly linked with the existence of matter.

"In genius, and in character, it works, as you say, instinctively; it refuses to be analyzed by the understanding, and is most of all inaccessible to the person who possesses it. We can only say, I have it, he has it. You have seen it often in the eyes of those Italian faces you like. It is most obvious in the eye. As we look on such eyes, we think on the tiger, the serpent, beings who lurk,

15   Simultaneous.

16   The association of mother (in Latin, *mater*) with matter was a familiar one.

Margaret Fuller (1810–1850).

glide, fascinate, mysteriously control. For it is occult by its nature, and if it could meet you on the highway, and be familiarly known as an acquaintance, could not exist. The angels of light do not love, yet they do not insist on exterminating it.

"It has given rise to the fables of wizard, enchantress, and the like; these beings are scarcely good, yet not necessarily bad. Power tempts them. They draw their skills from the dead, because their being is coeval[15] with that of matter, and matter is the mother of death."[16]

In later days, she allowed herself sometimes to dwell sadly on the resistances which she called her fate, and remarked, that "all life that has been or could be natural to me, is invariably denied."
She wrote long afterwards:—

"My days at Milan were not unmarked. I have known some happy hours, but they all lead to sorrow, and not only the cups of wine, but of milk,

17    Sappho (ca. 620–ca. 570 BCE), the great Greek lyric poet, became a model for woman writers; sibyl: prophetess (in the ancient world) and, by extension, an intuitive, sagacious woman with mystic pretensions.

18    Known.

19    The French philosopher Jean-Jacques Rousseau (1712–1778), who analyzed, and chastised, himself in his *Confessions* (1769).

20    "Fair Annie of Lochroyan" is a famous, tragic Scots ballad; Annie is barred from her lover's door and dies in a shipwreck.

21    Emerson's biographer Robert Richardson writes that Fuller "gave him new standards for friendship and for a kind of social openness that he found attractive but difficult"; Emerson's difficulty is apparent in this passage. Fuller instructed Emerson, as well, about the situation of women, about Goethe, art, and mythology, and she introduced him to the French novelist George Sand (1804–1876).

seem drugged with poison, for me. It does not seem to be my fault, this destiny. I do not court these things,—they come. I am a poor magnet, with power to be wounded by the bodies I attract."

\* \* \*

She had great energy of speech and action, and seemed formed for high emergencies.

Her life concentrated itself on certain happy days, happy hours, happy moments. The rest was a void. She had read that a man of letters must lose many days, to work well in one. Much more must a Sappho or a sibyl.[17] The capacity of pleasure was balanced by the capacity of pain. "If I had wist![18]—" she writes, "I am a worse self-tormentor than Rousseau,[19] and all my riches are fuel to the fire. My beautiful lore, like the tropic clime, hatches scorpions to sting me. There is a verse, which Annie of Lochroyan[20] sings about her ring, that torments my memory, 't is so true of myself."

When I found she lived at a rate so much faster than mine, and which was violent compared with mine, I foreboded rash and painful crises, and had a feeling as if a voice cried, *Stand from under!*—as if, a little further on, this destiny was threatened with jars and reverses, which no friendship could avert or console. This feeling partly wore off, on better acquaintance, but remained latent; and I had always an impression that her energy was too much a force of blood, and therefore never felt, the security for her peace which belongs to more purely intellectual natures. She seemed more vulnerable. For the same reason, she remained inscrutable to me; her strength was not my strength,—her powers were a surprise. She passed into new states of great advance, but I understood these no better.[21] It were long to tell her peculiarities. Her childhood was full of presentiments. She was then a somnambulist. She was subject to attacks of delirium, and, later, perceived that she had spectral illusions. When she was twelve, she had a determination of blood to the head. "My parents," she said, "were much mortified to see the fineness of my complexion destroyed. My own vanity was for a time wounded; but I recovered, and made up my mind to be bright and ugly."

She was all her lifetime the victim of disease and pain. She read and wrote in bed, and believed that she could understand anything better when

The Margaret Fuller house in Cambridge, Mass. Fuller lived here with her father.

22   In 1224, St. Francis of Assisi (ca. 1181–1226) saw a beautiful winged seraph (angel) on a cross; when it disappeared, St. Francis was marked with the stigmata (wounds of crucifixion).

23   Early form of hypnosis with an attendant theory of "animal magnetism," developed by the German physician Franz Anton Mesmer (1734–1815).

she was ill. Pain acted like a girdle, to give tension to her powers. A lady, who was with her one day during a terrible attack of nervous headache, which made Margaret totally helpless, assured me that Margaret was yet in the finest vein of humor, and kept those who were assisting her in a strange, painful excitement, between laughing and crying, by perpetual brilliant sallies. There were other peculiarities of habit and power. When she turned her head on one side, she alleged she had second sight, like St. Francis.[22] These traits or predispositions made her a willing listener to all the uncertain science of mesmerism and its goblin brood, which have been rife in recent years.[23]

She had a feeling that she ought to have been a man, and said of herself, "A man's ambition with a woman's heart, is an evil lot." In some verses which she wrote "To the Moon," occur these lines:—

24    "The Mystic Book," an 1835 collection by Honoré de Balzac (1799–1850), the French novelist, included his *Louis Lambert*, a fervent autobiographical fiction about a brilliant young man, fascinated by mysticism, who goes mad.

25    Attica is the Greek province where Athens, home of classical Greece's greatest achievements, is located; Thessaly, in northern Greece, is traditionally associated with magic.

26    Typhon, a gigantic monster in Greek mythology, was identified with the malevolent Egyptian god Set, who kills and dismembers his brother, the wise and merciful Osiris. The Greek author Plutarch (ca. 46–ca. 122) in "Of Isis and Osiris" writes that "everything harmful and destructive that Nature contains . . . is to be set down as a part of Typhon."

27    The Inferno is the first book of Dante's *Divine Comedy* (1308–1321).

28    Most mischievous.

But if I steadfast gaze upon thy face,
A human secret, like my own, I trace;
For, through the woman's smile looks the male eye.

And she found something of true portraiture in a disagreeable novel of Balzac's, *"Le Livre Mystique,"*[24] in which an equivocal figure exerts alternately a masculine and a feminine influence on the characters of the plot.

Of all this nocturnal element in her nature she was very conscious, and was disposed, of course, to give it as fine names as it would carry, and to draw advantage from it. "Attica," she said to a friend, "is your province, Thessaly is mine: Attica produced the marble wonders of the great geniuses; but Thessaly is the land of magic."[25]

"I have a great share of Typhon to the Osiris,[26] wild rush and leap, blind force for the sake of force."

"Dante, thou didst not describe, in all thy apartments of Inferno,[27] this tremendous repression of an existence half unfolded; this swoon as the soul was ready to be born."

"Every year I live, I dislike routine more and more, though I see that society rests on that, and other falsehoods. The more I screw myself down to hours, the more I become expert at giving out thought and life in regulated rations,—the more I weary of this world, and long to move upon the wing, without props and sedan chairs."

TO R. W. E.

*Dec.* 26, 1839.—If you could look into my mind just now, you would send far from you those who love and hate. I am on the Drachenfels, and cannot get off; it is one of my naughtiest[28] moods. Last Sunday, I wrote a long letter, describing it in prose and verse, and I had twenty minds to send it you as a literary curiosity; then I thought, this might destroy relations, and I might not be able to be calm and chip marble with you any more, if I talked to you in magnetism and music; so I sealed and sent it in the due direction.

"I remember you say, that forlorn seasons often turn out the most profitable. Perhaps I shall find it so. I have been reading Plato all the week, because I could not write. I hoped to be tuned up thereby. I perceive, with gladness, a keener insight in myself, day by day; yet, after all, could not make a good statement this morning on the subject of beauty."

She had, indeed, a rude strength, which, if it could have been supported by an equal health, would have given her the efficiency of the strongest men. As it was, she had great power of work. The account of her reading in Groton is at a rate like Gibbon's,[29] and, later, that of her writing, considered with the fact that writing was not grateful[30] to her, is incredible. She often proposed to her friends, in the progress of intimacy, to write every day. "I think less than a daily offering of thought and feeling would not content me, so much seems to pass unspoken." In Italy, she tells Madame Arconati,[31] that she has "more than a hundred correspondents;" and it was her habit there to devote one day of every week to those distant friends. The facility with which she assumed stints of literary labor, which veteran feeders of the press would shrink from,—assumed and performed,—when her friends were to be served, I have often observed with wonder, and with fear, when I considered the near extremes of ill-health, and the manner in which her life heaped itself in high and happy moments, which were avenged by lassitude[32] and pain.

"As each task comes," she said, "I borrow a readiness from its aspect, as I always do brightness from the face of a friend. Yet, as soon as the hour is past, I sink."

I think most of her friends will remember to have felt, at one time or another, some uneasiness, as if this athletic soul craved a larger atmosphere than it found; as if she were ill-timed and mis-mated, and felt in herself a tide of life, which compared with the slow circulation of others as a torrent with a rill.

\* \* \*

She *had* a sound judgment, on which, in conversation, she could fall back, and anticipate and speak the best sense of the largest company. But, left to herself, and in her correspondence, she was much the victim of Lord Bacon's *idols of the cave*,[33] or self-deceived by her own phantasms. I have looked over volumes of her letters to me and others. They are full of probity, talent, wit, friendship, charity, and high aspiration. They are tainted with a mysticism, which to me appears so much an affair of constitution, that it claims no more respect than the charity or patriotism of a man who has dined well, and feels

29  In 1833 Timothy Fuller, Margaret's father, moved his family to a farm in Groton, Massachusetts; there Margaret read widely, translated Goethe, and wrote a number of essays. Edward Gibbon (1737–1794), the English historian, read prodigiously as he researched his *History of the Decline and Fall of the Roman Empire* (1776–1788).

30  Pleasing.

31  The Marchioness Costanza Arconati Visconti (d. 1870), a cultured Italian patriot, was one of Fuller's friends in Milan, and friend of the renowned women of letters Bettina von Arnim (1785–1859) and Rahel Varnhagen (1771–1833).

32  Weariness.

33  According to the English author and scientist Francis Bacon (1561–1626), "idols of the cave" are ideas closely held by an individual as a result of personal experience; they are unfounded and obstruct the search for knowledge.

34    *Muscae volitantes:* fluttering flies (Latin). The legendary phoenix was famed for rising from its own ashes; "phoenixes" here means "imaginary creatures."

35    Various arcane references. Magna Dea: the Great Goddess.

36    James Macpherson (1736–1796), the Scottish poet, published a series of poems that he claimed he had translated from the works of a third-century Gaelic bard named Ossian. The poems, rhapsodic and bold (and largely Macpherson's own work), were a sensational success, even after the hoax was detected.

37    Emerson is here the rude pragmatist, opposed to Fuller's extravagance and her theatrical ways: for all Emerson's trust in imagination, he demanded an adherence to reality. Fuller, for her part, wrote to Emerson early on in their friendship (March 1, 1838), "I want to see you and still more to hear you. I must kindle my torch again." But she also remarked to Caroline Sturgis (1819–1888) in 1840, "Yet Waldo is still only a small and secluded part of Nature, secluded by a doubt, secluded by a sneer"; and she addressed Emerson in a letter (May 9, 1843), "O Waldo, most unteachable of men."

38    From "Eleanora" (1692), an elegy for the Countess of Abingdon, by the English poet John Dryden (1631–1700); slightly misquoted.

better for it. One sometimes talks with a genial *bon vivant*, who looks as if the omelet and turtle have got into his eyes. In our noble Margaret, her personal feeling colors all her judgment of persons, of books, of pictures, and even of the laws of the world. This is easily felt in ordinary women, and a large deduction is civilly made on the spot by whosoever replies to their remark. But when the speaker has such brilliant talent and literature as Margaret, she gives so many fine names to these merely sensuous and subjective phantasms, that the hearer is long imposed upon, and thinks so precise and glittering nomenclature cannot be of mere *muscae volitantes*, phoenixes[34] of the fancy, but must be of some real ornithology, hitherto unknown to him. This mere feeling exaggerates a host of trifles into a dazzling mythology. But when one goes to sift it, and find if there be a real meaning, it eludes search. Whole sheets of warm, florid writing are here, in which the eye is caught by "sapphire," "heliotrope," "dragon," "aloes," "Magna Dea," "limboes," "stars," and "purgatory,"[35] but can connect all this, or any part of it, with no universal experience. In short, Margaret often loses herself in sentimentalism. That dangerous vertigo nature in her case adopted, and was to make respectable. As it sometimes happens that a grandiose style, like that of the Alexandrian Platonists, or like Macpherson's Ossian,[36] is more stimulating to the imagination of nations, than the true Plato, or than the simple poet, so here was a head so creative of new colors, of wonderful gleams,—so iridescent, that it piqued curiosity, and stimulated thought, and communicated mental activity to all who approached her; though her perceptions were not to be compared to her fancy, and she made numerous mistakes. Her integrity was perfect, and she was led and followed by love, and was really bent on truth, but too indulgent to the meteors of her fancy.[37]


FRIENDSHIP.

"Friends she must have, but in no one could find
A tally fitted to so large a mind."[38]

It is certain that Margaret, though unattractive in person, and assuming in manners, so that the girls complained that "she put upon them," or, with her burly masculine existence, quite reduced them to satellites, yet inspired an enthusiastic attachment. I hear from one witness, as early as 1829, that "all the girls raved about Margaret Fuller," and the same powerful magnetism wrought, as she went on, from year to year, on all ingenuous[39] natures. "The loveliest and the highest endowed women were eager to lay their beauty, their grace, the hospitalities of sumptuous homes, and their costly gifts, at her feet. When I expressed, one day, many years afterwards, to a lady who knew her well, some surprise at the homage paid her by men in Italy,—offers of marriage having there been made her by distinguished parties,—she replied: 'There is nothing extraordinary in it. Had she been a man, any one of those fine girls of sixteen, who surrounded her here, would have married her: they were all in love with her, she understood them so well.' She had seen many persons, and had entire confidence in her own discrimination of characters. She saw and foresaw all in the first interview. She had certainly made her own selections with great precision, and had not been disappointed. When pressed for a reason, she replied, in one instance, "I have no good reason to give for what I think of—. It is a daemoniacal intimation. Everybody at—praised her, but their account of what she said gave me the same unfavorable feeling. This is the first instance in which I have not had faith, if you liked a person. Perhaps I am wrong now; perhaps, if I saw her, a look would give me a needed clue to her character, and I should change my feeling. Yet I have never been mistaken in these intimations, as far as I recollect. I hope I am now."

I am to add, that she gave herself to her friendships with an entireness not possible to any but a woman, with a depth possible to few women. Her friendships, as a girl with girls, as a woman with women, were not unmingled with passion, and had passages of romantic sacrifice and of ecstatic fusion, which I have heard with the ear, but could not trust my profane[40] pen to report. There were, also, the ebbs and recoils from the other party,—the mortal unequal to converse with an immortal,—ingratitude, which was more truly incapacity, the collapse of overstrained affections and powers. At all events, it is clear that Margaret, later, grew more strict, and values herself with her friends on having the tie now "redeemed from all search after Eros." So much, however, of intellectual aim and activity mixed with her alliances, as to breathe a certain dignity and myrrh[41] through them all. She and her

39   Innocent, frank. Fuller gave lessons to young women. In a letter of July 3, 1837 (probably to Emerson), she described her teaching: "Activity of mind, accuracy in processes, constant looking for principles, and search after the good and beautiful, 'that's the ground I go upon' as Mr S says in Vivian Gray" (novel, published in 1827, by the English author, and later prime minister, Benjamin Disraeli [1804–1881]).

40   Uninitiated (in a religious rite); mundane.

41   A precious aromatic balm, used as incense; mentioned in the Bible's Song of Songs, and offered by the magi to the infant Jesus (Matthew 2:11).

42     Fuller wrote to Emerson on September 29, 1840, "I am no usurper. I ask only mine own inheritance . . . I felt that you did not for me the highest office of friendship, by offering me the clue of the labyrinth of mine own being. Yet I thought you appreciated the fearlessness which shrinks from no truth in myself & others, & trusted me, believing that I knew the path for myself."

friends are fellow-students with noblest moral aims. She is there for help and for counsel. "Be to the best thou knowest ever true!" is her language to one. And that was the effect of her presence. Whoever conversed with her felt challenged by the strongest personal influence to a bold and generous life.

\*     \*     \*

Of course, she made large demands on her companions, and would soon come to sound their knowledge, and guess pretty nearly the range of their thoughts. There yet remained to command her constancy, what she valued more, the quality and affection proper to each. But she could rarely find natures sufficiently deep and magnetic. With her sleepless curiosity, her magnanimity, and her diamond-ring, like Annie of Lochroyan's, to exchange for gold or for pewter, she might be pardoned for her impatient questionings. To me, she was uniformly generous; but neither did I escape. Our moods were very different; and I remember, that, at the very time when I, slow and cold, had come fully to admire her genius, and was congratulating myself on the solid good understanding that subsisted between us, I was surprised with hearing it taxed by her with superficiality and halfness. She stigmatized our friendship as commercial. It seemed, her magnanimity was not met, but I prized her only for the thoughts and pictures she brought me;—so many thoughts, so many facts yesterday,—so many to-day;—when there was an end of things to tell, the game was up: that, I did not know, as a friend should know, to prize a silence as much as a discourse,—and hence a forlorn feeling was inevitable; a poor counting of thoughts, and a taking the census of virtues, was the unjust reception so much love found. On one occasion, her grief broke into words like these: "The religious nature remained unknown to you, because it could not proclaim itself, but claimed to be divined. The deepest soul that approached you was, in your eyes, nothing but a magic lantern, always bringing out pretty shows of life."[42]

But as I did not understand the discontent then,—of course, I cannot now. It was a war of temperaments, and could not be reconciled by words; but, after each party had explained to the uttermost, it was necessary to fall back on those grounds of agreement which remained, and leave the differences henceforward in respectful silence. The recital may still serve to show to sympathetic persons the true lines and enlargements of her genius. It is certain that this incongruity never interrupted for a moment the intercourse, such as it was, that existed between us.

I ought to add here, that certain mental changes brought new questions into conversation. In the summer of 1840, she passed into certain religious states, which did not impress me as quite healthy, or likely to be permanent; and I said, "I do not understand your tone; it seems exaggerated. You are one who can afford to speak and to hear the truth. Let us hold hard to the commonsense, and let us speak in the positive degree."

Giovanni Angelo Ossoli (1821–1850).

# Thoreau

*Emerson first met Henry David Thoreau (1817–1862) in 1838; on September 1 he wrote to his aunt, Mary Moody Emerson, "a brave fine youth he is" (L 2:154). Thoreau lived for two years in Emerson's house (1841–1843) and served as handyman to the Emersons. Thoreau later built a cabin on property owned by Emerson near Walden Pond, and lived there during 1845–1847, the experience that led to his best-known book, Walden (1854). Walden, one of the monuments of American letters, is a consummately strange and inventive text written in Thoreau's peculiar voice, at once attractive and aloof. Thoreau would never have discovered that voice had it not been for Emerson's influence; but his eloquent stubbornness and his careful devotion to nature are all his own.*

*Thoreau died of tuberculosis at age forty-four, on May 6, 1862; the next day, Emerson delivered the eulogy at the funeral. One listener, the journalist and reformer F. B. Sanborn (1831–1917), reported that Emerson recited it in a "broken, tender voice." This address, an expanded version of the eulogy, was first published in the* Atlantic Monthly *in 1862. It was reprinted as the "Biographical Sketch"*
*(continued)*

It seemed as if the breezes brought him,[1]
It seemed as if the sparrows taught him,
As if by secret sign he knew
Where in far fields the orchis[2] grew.

Henry David Thoreau was the last male descendant of a French ancestor who came to this country from the Isle of Guernsey.[3] His character exhibited occasional traits drawn from this blood in singular combination with a very strong Saxon genius.

He was born in Concord, Massachusetts, on the 12th of July, 1817. He was graduated at Harvard College in 1837, but without any literary distinction. An iconoclast in literature, he seldom thanked colleges for their service to him, holding them in small esteem, whilst yet his debt to them was important.[4] After leaving the University, he joined his brother in teaching a private school, which he soon renounced.[5] His father was a manufacturer of lead-pencils, and Henry applied himself for a time to this craft, believing he could make a better pencil than was then in use. After completing his experiments, he exhibited his work to chemists and artists in Boston, and having obtained their certificates to its excellence and to its quality with the best London manufacturer, he returned home contented.[6] His friends congratulated him that he had now opened his way to fortune. But he replied, that he should never make another pencil. "Why should I? I would not do again what I have done once." He resumed his endless walks and miscellaneous studies, making every day some new acquaintance with Nature, though as yet never speaking of zoology or botany, since, though very studious of natural facts, he was incurious of technical and textual science.

At this time, a strong, healthy youth, fresh from college, while all his companions were choosing their profession, or eager to begin some lucrative employment, it was inevitable that his thoughts should be exercised on the same conditions, and it required rare decision to refuse all the accustomed paths, and keep his solitary freedom at the cost of disappointing the natural expectations of his family and friends: all the more difficult that he had a

*prefacing* Excursions *(1863), a collection of Thoreau's essays edited by Emerson and Thoreau's sister Sophia. This edition is the source of the text reproduced here.*

1    In *Walden* ("The Ponds"), Thoreau wrote of Walden Pond, "I am its stony shore, / And the breeze that passes o'er."

2    A colorful flower of the orchid family, seen in the eastern United States.

3    Island off the coast of Normandy, France. Henry's grandfather, Jean Thoreau (1754–1801), who came to America in 1773, was a French Protestant.

4    Thoreau wrote in *Walden*, "To my astonishment I was informed on leaving college that I had studied navigation! –why, if I had taken one turn down the harbor I should have known more about it."

5    Thoreau lasted for only two weeks as a teacher in Concord's Center Grammar School, resigning in September 1837; he went on to open a private school for a few pupils with his brother (it closed in 1841).

6    For his improved pencil, Thoreau mixed graphite with clay rather than wax, and developed a new grinding mill for the graphite. He also invented a new method of baking the leads and cutting them, and of drilling a hole in the wood for the lead.

Henry David Thoreau (1817–1862).

7    Dissenter.

8    Thoreau taught Emerson the art of grafting plants. "We work together day by day in my garden," Emerson reported in a letter (May 30, 1841) to the Scottish author Thomas Carlyle (1795–1881). In the same letter, Emerson described Thoreau as "a noble manly youth full of melodies & inventions" (CEC 300).

9    Measuring.

10   To an extreme degree.

11   Croesus, king of Lydia (6th century BCE) famous for his wealth.

12   In *Walden*, Thoreau remarked, "I cannot but perceive that this so called rich and refined life is a thing jumped at, and I do not get on in the enjoyment of the *fine* arts which adorn it, my attention being wholly occupied with the jump."

13   According to F. B. Sanborn, in his eulogy for Thoreau Emerson said that the three people who had "made a profound impression" on Thoreau were "John Brown, Joe Polis, his Indian guide, and *another person not known to this audience.*" The third person was the poet Walt Whitman (1819–1892), Emerson later told Sanborn. (For John Brown, see note 29, below.) Emerson remarked about Thoreau in his Journal (February 1862) that "perhaps his fancy for Walt Whitman grew out of his taste for wild nature, for an otter, a woodchuck, or a loon. He loved sufficiency, hated a sum that would not prove: loved Walt and hated Alcott" (J 9:401; Emerson refers to a member of the Concord circle, the long-winded reformer Amos Bronson Alcott [1799–1888]).

perfect probity, was exact in securing his own independence, and in holding every man to the like duty. But Thoreau never faltered. He was a born protestant.[7] He declined to give up his large ambition of knowledge and action for any narrow craft or profession, aiming at a much more comprehensive calling, the art of living well. If he slighted and defied the opinions of others, it was only that he was more intent to reconcile his practice with his own belief. Never idle or self-indulgent, he preferred, when he wanted money, earning it by some piece of manual labor agreeable to him, as building a boat or a fence, planting, grafting, surveying, or other short work, to any long engagement.[8] With his hardy habits and few wants, his skill in wood-craft, and his powerful arithmetic, he was very competent to live in any part of the world. It would cost him less time to supply his wants than another. He was therefore secure of his leisure.

A natural skill for mensuration,[9] growing out of his mathematical knowledge, and his habit of ascertaining the measures and distances of objects which interested him, the size of trees, the depth and extent of ponds and rivers, the height of mountains, and the air-line distance of his favorite summits,—this, and his intimate knowledge of the territory about Concord, made him drift into the profession of land-surveyor. It had the advantage for him that it led him continually into new and secluded grounds, and helped his studies of Nature. His accuracy and skill in this work were readily appreciated, and he found all the employment he wanted.

He could easily solve the problems of the surveyor, but he was daily beset with graver questions, which he manfully confronted. He interrogated every custom, and wished to settle all his practice on an ideal foundation. He was a protestant à l'outrance,[10] and few lives contain so many renunciations. He was bred to no profession; he never married; he lived alone; he never went to church; he never voted; he refused to pay a tax to the State; he ate no flesh, he drank no wine, he never knew the use of tobacco; and, though a naturalist, he used neither trap nor gun. He chose, wisely, no doubt, for himself, to be bachelor of thought and Nature. He had no talent for wealth, and knew how to be poor without the least hint of squalor or inelegance. Perhaps he fell into his way of living without forecasting it much, but approved it with later wisdom. "I am often reminded," he wrote in his journal, "that, if I had bestowed on me the wealth of Croesus,[11] my aims must be still the same, and my means essentially the same." He had no temptations to fight against, —no appetites, no passions, no taste for elegant trifles.[12] A fine house, dress, the manners and talk of highly cultivated people were all thrown away on him. He much preferred a good Indian,[13] and considered these refinements as impediments to conversation, wishing to meet his companion on the simplest terms.[14] He declined invitations to dinner-parties, because there each was in every one's way, and he could not meet the individuals to any purpose. "They make their pride," he said, "in making their dinner cost much; I make my pride in making my dinner cost little." When asked at table what dish he preferred, he answered, "The nearest." He did not like the taste of wine, and never had a vice in his life. He said,—"I have a faint recollection of pleasure derived from smoking dried lily-stems, before I was a man. I had commonly a supply of these. I have never smoked anything more noxious."

He chose to be rich by making his wants few, and supplying them himself. In his travels, he used the railroad only to get over so much country as was unimportant to the present purpose, walking hundreds of miles, avoiding taverns, buying a lodging in farmers and fishermen's houses, as cheaper, and more agreeable to him, and because there he could better find the men and the information he wanted.

There was something military in his nature not to be subdued, always manly and able, but rarely tender, as if he did not feel himself except in opposition. He wanted a fallacy to expose, a blunder to pillory,[15] I may say required a little sense of victory, a roll of the drum, to call his powers into full exercise. It cost him nothing to say No; indeed, he found it much easier than to say Yes.[16] It seemed as if his first instinct on hearing a proposition was to controvert it, so impatient was he of the limitations of our daily thought.[17] This habit, of course, is a little chilling to the social affections; and though the companion would in the end acquit him of any malice or untruth, yet it mars conversation. Hence, no equal companion stood in affectionate relations with one so pure and guileless. "I love Henry," said one of his friends, "but I cannot like him; and as for taking his arm, I should as soon think of taking the arm of an elm-tree."[18]

14 In his Journal (1852) Emerson wrote, "Henry Thoreau's idea of the men he meets, is, that they are his old thoughts walking. It is all affectation to make much of them, as if he did not long since know them thoroughly" (J 13:29).

15 Hold up for public ridicule.

16 Traveling in Italy in May 1833, Emerson noted in his Journal, "I like the sayers of No better than the sayers of Yes" (J 4:73). In his *English Traits*, Emerson attributes the same preference to the English.

17 "Resistance," wrote Thoreau in his Journal (1841), "is a very wholesome and delicious morsel at times." In a Notebook entry, Emerson remarked, "If I knew only Thoreau, I should think cooperation of good men impossible. Must we always talk for victory, & never once for truth, for comfort, & joy? Centrality he has, & penetration, strong understanding, & the higher gifts [but] Always some weary captious paradox to fight you with, & the time & temper wasted" (J 13:54).

18 Elizabeth Hoar (1814–1878) remarked to Emerson, "I love Henry, but do not like him"; in summer 1848, Emerson wrote in his Journal, "I spoke of friendship, but my friends & I are fishes in their habit. As for taking T.'s arm, I should as soon take the arm of an elm tree" (J 10:343).

19    The Stoics were an ancient philosophical sect known for advocating impassive, self-respecting conduct; they preached a hardy indifference to worldly chances, pleasures, and pains.

20    Novel (1720) by the English author Daniel Defoe (1660–1731). The discussion occurred in early December 1853 (J 13:270).

21    The young girl was Emerson's daughter Edith, twelve years old at the time (J 13:270). Thoreau's lecture, "Journey to Moose Head Lake," took place on December 14, 1853. Along with Emerson, Thoreau was a curator of the Concord Lyceum, founded in 1828; the Lyceum hosted debates and lectures. Emerson was its most frequent speaker, and Thoreau gave several important speeches there, including, in January 1848, the lecture that would become his famous essay "Resistance to Civil Government" (more widely known as "Civil Disobedience").

22    Emerson recorded an exchange between Thoreau and the Rev. Joseph Lovejoy (1805–1871): "Here's the chap who camped in the woods," Lovejoy remarked; Thoreau's response was, "And here's the chap who camps in a pulpit" (J 13:68). In a Notebook entry from 1852, Emerson confessed, "Thoreau gives me in flesh & blood & pertinacious Saxon belief, my own ethics. He is far more real, & daily practically obeying them, than I; and fortifies my memory at all times with an affirmative experience which refuses to be set aside" (J 13:66).

23    Charge.

24    It is not known who bailed Thoreau out of jail, though many have speculated (his aunt? his sister? Emerson?). After Thoreau's arrest, Emerson wrote disapprovingly in his Journal (July–August 1846), "Don't run amuck against
*(continued)*

Yet, hermit and stoic[19] as he was, he was really fond of sympathy, and threw himself heartily and childlike into the company of young people whom he loved, and whom he delighted to entertain, as he only could, with the varied and endless anecdotes of his experiences by field and river. And he was always ready to lead a huckleberry party or a search for chestnuts or grapes. Talking, one day, of a public discourse, Henry remarked, that whatever succeeded with the audience was bad. I said, "Who would not like to write something which all can read, like Robinson Crusoe?[20] and who does not see with regret that his page is not solid with a right materialistic treatment, which delights everybody?" Henry objected, of course, and vaunted the better lectures which reached only a few persons. But, at supper, a young girl, understanding that he was to lecture at the Lyceum,[21] sharply asked him, "whether his lecture would be a nice, interesting story, such as she wished to hear, or whether it was one of those old philosophical things that she did not care about." Henry turned to her, and bethought himself, and, I saw, was trying to believe that he had matter that might fit her and her brother, who were to sit up and go to the lecture, if it was a good one for them.

He was a speaker and actor of the truth,—born such,—and was ever running into dramatic situations from this cause.[22] In any circumstance, it interested all bystanders to know what part Henry would take, and what he would say; and he did not disappoint expectation, but used an original judgment on each emergency. In 1845 he built himself a small framed house on the shores of Walden Pond, and lived there two years alone, a life of labor and study. This action was quite native and fit for him. No one who knew him would tax[23] him with affection. He was more unlike his neighbors in his thought than in his action. As soon as he had exhausted the advantages of that solitude, he abandoned it. In 1847, not approving some uses to which the public expenditure was applied, he refused to pay his town tax, and was put in jail. A friend paid the tax for him, and he was released.[24] The like annoyance was threatened the next year. But, as his friends paid the tax, notwithstanding his protest, I believe he ceased to resist. No opposition or ridicule had any weight with him. He coldly and fully stated his opinion without affecting to believe that it was the opinion of the company. It was of no consequence, if every one present held the opposite opinion. On one occasion he went to the University Library to procure some books. The librarian refused to lend them. Mr. Thoreau repaired to the President, who stated to him the rules and usages, which permitted the loan of books to resident graduates, to clergymen who were alumni, and to some other residents within a circle of ten miles radius from the College. Mr. Thoreau explained to the President that the railroad had destroyed the old scale of distances,—that the library was useless, yes, and President and College useless, on the terms of his rules,—that the one benefit he owed to the College was its library,—that, at this moment, not only his want of books was imperative, but he wanted a large number of books, and assured him that he, Thoreau, and not the librarian, was the proper custodian of these. In short, the President found the petitioner so formidable, and the rules getting to look so ridiculous, that he ended by giving him a privilege which in his hands proved unlimited thereafter.

No truer American existed than Thoreau. His preference of his county and condition was genuine, and his aversation[25] from English and European manners and tastes almost reached contempt. He listened impatiently to news or bonmots[26] gleaned from London circles; and though he tried to be civil, these anecdotes fatigued him. The men were all imitating each other, and on a small mould. Why can they not live as far apart as possible, and each be man by himself?[27] What he sought was the most energetic nature; and he wished to go to Oregon, not to London. "In every part of Great Britain," he wrote in his diary, "are discovered traces of the Romans, their funereal urns, their camps, their roads, their dwellings. But New England, at least, is not based on any Roman ruins. We have not to lay the foundations of our houses on the ashes of a former civilization."

But, idealist as he was, standing for abolition of slavery, abolition of tariffs, almost for abolition of government, it is needless to say he found himself not only unrepresented in actual politics, but almost equally opposed to every class of reformers.[28] Yet he paid the tribute of his uniform respect to the Anti-Slavery Party. One man, whose personal acquaintance he had formed, he honored with exceptional regard. Before the first friendly word had been spoken for Captain John Brown, after the arrest, he sent notices to most houses in Concord, that he would speak in a public ball on the condition and character of John Brown, on Sunday evening, and invited all people to come.[29] The Republican Committee, the Abolitionist Committee, sent

the world . . . wait until you have a good difference to join issue upon. Thus Socrates was told he should not teach. 'Please God, but I will.' And he could die well for that. And Jesus had a cause. You will get one by & by. But now I have no sympathy" (J 9:446).

25    Aversion.

26    Witty remarks.

27    "I seek a garret," was Thoreau's first entry in his Journal.

28    In his lecture "Historic Notes of Life and Letters in New England" (1880), Emerson said, "Thoreau was in his own person a practical answer, almost a refutation, to the theories of the socialists. He required no Phalanx, no Government, no society, almost no memory. He lived extempore from hour to hour, like the birds and the angels; brought every day a new proposition, as revolutionary as that of yesterday, but different: the only man of leisure in his town; and his independence made all others look like slaves." (The Phalanx was the communal form advocated by the French socialist Charles Fourier [1772–1837], who influenced New England's utopian experiments.)

29    John Brown (1800–1859) was an antislavery militant who warred against slavery supporters in Kansas and, when he raided the federal armory at Harpers Ferry, Virginia, was captured, tried, and executed. In a lecture at Tremont Temple in Boston (November 11, 1859), Emerson said that Brown would "make the gallows as glorious as the cross." Thoreau met Brown in 1847, when Brown was an overnight guest in the Emersons' house (where Thoreau was living). Thoreau delivered his "Plea for Captain John Brown" on October 30, 1859. (See "John Brown" in this volume.)

30    The *Life* of the Neoplatonic philosopher
Plotinus (ca. 204–270) by Porphyry (ca. 232–ca.
305) begins with the remark that Plotinus
seemed ashamed of being in his body.

Thoreau's Cove, near his cabin on Walden Pond.

him word that it was premature and not advisable. He replied,—"I did not
send to you for advice, but to announce that I am to speak." The hall was
filled at an early hour by people of all parties, and his earnest eulogy of the
hero was heard by all respectfully, by many with a sympathy that surprised
themselves.

It was said of Plotinus that he was ashamed of his body,[30] and 'tis very
likely he had good reason for it,—that his body was a bad servant, and he had
not skill in dealing with the material world, as happens often to men of abstract intellect. But Mr. Thoreau was equipped with a most adapted and ser-
viceable body. He was of short stature, firmly built, of light complexion, with
strong, serious blue eyes, and a grave aspect,—his face covered in the late
years with a becoming beard. His senses were acute, his frame well-knit and
hardy, his hands strong and skillful in the use of tools. And there was a wonderful fitness of body and mind. He could pace sixteen rods more accurately

than another man could measure them with rod and chain.[31] He could find his path in the woods at night, he said, better by his feet than his eyes. He could estimate the measure of a tree very well by his eyes; he could estimate the weight of a calf or a pig, like a dealer. From a box containing a bushel or more of loose pencils, he could take up with his hands fast enough just a dozen pencils at every grasp. He was a good swimmer, runner, skater,[32] boatman, and would probably outwalk most countrymen in a day's journey. And the relation of body to mind was still finer than we have indicated. He said he wanted every stride his legs made. The length of his walk uniformly made the length of his writing. If shut up in the house, he did not write at all.

He had a strong common sense, like that which Rose Flammock, the weaver's daughter, in Scott's romance,[33] commends in her father, as resembling a yardstick, which, whilst it measures dowlas and diaper,[34] can equally

Site of Thoreau's cabin at Walden Pond.

31 In Emerson's Journal, the description of Thoreau's ability to measure distances is followed by: "The man of men, the only man you have ever seen—(if you have seen one,) is he who is immovably centred" (J 11:438).

32 Sophia Hawthorne (1809–1871), wife of the author Nathaniel Hawthorne (1804–1864), described the winter afternoon Hawthorne, Emerson, and Thoreau went skating on the Concord River, and revealed something of the personalities of the three skaters: "Henry Thoreau is an experienced skater, and was figuring dithyrambic dances and Bacchic leaps on the ice—very remarkable, but very ugly, methought. Next him followed Mr. Hawthorne who, wrapped in his cloak, moved like a self-impelled Greek statue, stately and grave. Mr. Emerson closed the line, evidently too weary to hold himself erect, pitching headforemost, half lying on the air."

33 *The Betrothed* (1825) by Sir Walter Scott (1771–1832), Scottish novelist.

34 Dowlas: coarse linen cloth; diaper: soft fabric with a distinctive pattern.

35    Forceful, cutting.

36    Sylvester Graham (1794–1851) was a di-
etary reformer who promoted vegetarianism
and invented the Graham cracker. His followers were "Grahamites."

37    In the White Mountains of New Hampshire.

38    "Hairy arnica," herb with yellow flowers.

well measure tapestry and cloth of gold. He had always a new resource.
When I was planting forest-trees, and had procured half of a peck of acorns,
he said that only a small portion of them would be sound, and proceeded to examine them, and select the sound ones. But finding this took
time, he said, "I think, if you put them all into water, the good ones will
sink;" which experiment we tried with success. He could plan a garden, or a
house, or a barn; would have been competent to lead a "Pacific Exploring Expedition;" could give judicious counsel in the gravest private or public
affairs.

He lived for the day, not cumbered and mortified by his memory. If he
brought you yesterday a new proposition, he would bring you to-day another not less revolutionary. A very industrious man, and setting, like all
highly organized men, a high value on his time, he seemed the only man of
leisure in town, always ready for any excursion that promised well, or for
conversation prolonged into late hours. His trenchant[35] sense was never
stopped by his rules of daily prudence, but was always up to the new occasion. He liked and used the simplest food, yet, when some one urged a vegetable diet, Thoreau thought all diets a very small matter, saying that "the
man who shoots the buffalo lives better than the man who boards at the Graham House."[36] He said,—"You can sleep near the railroad, and never be disturbed: Nature knows very well what sounds are worth attending to, and has
made up her mind not to hear the railroad-whistle. But things respect the
devout mind, and a mental ecstasy was never interrupted." He noted, what
repeatedly befell him, that, after receiving from a distance a rare plant,
he would presently find the same in his own haunts. And those pieces of
luck which happen only to good players happened to him. One day, walking
with a stranger, who inquired where Indian arrow-heads could be found,
he replied, "Everywhere," and, stooping forward, picked one on the instant from the ground. At Mount Washington, in Tuckerman's Ravine,[37]
Thoreau had a bad fall, and sprained his foot. As he was in the act of getting up from his fall, he saw for the first time the leaves of the Arnica
mollis.[38]

His robust common sense, armed with stout hands, keen perceptions,
and strong will, cannot yet account for the superiority which shone in his
simple and hidden life. I must add the cardinal fact, that there was an excel-

lent wisdom in him, proper to a rare class of men, which showed him the material world as a means and symbol. This discovery, which sometimes yields to poets a certain casual and interrupted light, serving for the ornament of their writing, was in him an unsleeping insight; and whatever faults or obstructions of temperament might cloud it, he was not disobedient to the heavenly vision. In his youth, he said, one day, "The other world is all my art; my pencils will draw no other; my jack-knife will cut nothing else; I do not use it as a means." This was the muse and genius[39] that ruled his opinions, conversation, studies, work, and course of life. This made him a searching judge of men. At first glance he measured his companion, and, though insensible to some fine traits of culture, could very well report his weight and calibre.[40] And this made the impression of genius which his conversation often gave.

He understood the matter in hand at a glance, and saw the limitations and poverty of those he talked with, so that nothing seemed concealed from such terrible eyes. I have repeatedly known young men of sensibility converted in a moment to the belief that this was the man they were in search of, the man of men, who could tell them all they should do. His own dealing with them was never affectionate, but superior, didactic.[41]—scorning their petty ways,—very slowly conceding, or not conceding at all, the promise of his society at their houses, or even at his own. "Would he not walk with them?" "He did not know. There was nothing so important to him as his walk; he had no walks to throw away on company." Visits were offered him from respectful parties, but he declined them. Admiring friends offered to carry him at their own cost to the Yellow-Stone River,—to the West Indies, —to South America. But though nothing could be more grave or considered than his refusals, they remind one in quite new relations of that fop Brummel's[42] reply to the gentlemen who offered him his carriage in a shower, "But where will you ride, then?"—and what accusing silences, and what searching and irresistible speeches, battering down all defences, his companions can remember![43]

Mr. Thoreau dedicated his genius with such entire love to the fields, hills, and waters of his native town, that he made them known and interesting to all reading Americans, and to people over the sea. The river on whose banks he was born and died he knew from its springs to its confluence with

39   Guiding spirit.

40   Diameter of the bore of a firearm; by extension, worth or quality.

41   In his Journal (March–April 1847) Emerson remarked, "Novels, Poetry, Mythology must be well allowed for an imaginative being. You do us great wrong, Henry T. in railing at the novel reading" (J 10:48).

42   Beau (George Bryan) Brummel (1778–1840), the influential English dandy and wit.

43   Emerson cut the following sentence from his manuscript: "When a man for whom he once had a great regard, but who had become intemperate, came to see him on some business, Thoreau perceived that he had been drinking, & declined to deal with him, but advised him to go home & cut his throat, & that speedily."

44    The Concord River joins the Merrimack near Lowell, MA. Thoreau and his brother traveled on the two rivers in 1839, an experience that led to Thoreau's first book, *A Week on the Concord and Merrimack Rivers* (1849).

45    Mayflies, tiny insects with brief lifespans.

46    Excessive fullness.

47    The hyla is the tree frog; the sheldrake, a diving duck; the osprey, a fish-eating hawk. In *Walden*, Thoreau wrote that the loon's call is "perhaps the wildest sound that is ever heard here, making the woods ring far and wide."

48    In his Journal in 1864, Emerson remarked, "Henry pitched his tone very low in his love of nature,—not on stars & suns . . . but tortoises, crickets, muskrats, suckers, toads & frogs" (J 15:487).

49    Used in chemistry to collect alcohol after distillation or condensation.

50    Elisha Kane (1820–1857), the explorer, wrote *Arctic Explorations* (1853–1855). Though Thoreau enjoyed reading travelers' accounts, he preferred the local—as did Emerson. In late April 1838, Emerson went to a local cliff with Thoreau. He reported in his Journal, "A crow's voice filled all the miles of air with sound. . . . At night I went out into the dark & saw a glimmering star & heard a frog & Nature seemed to say Well do not these suffice? Here is a new scene a new experience. Ponder it, Emerson, & not like the foolish world hanker after thunders & multitudes & vast landscapes the sea or Niagara" (J 5:480).

51    A hill in Concord.

52    Water lily present in South America.

the Merrimack.[44] He had made summer and winter observations on it for many years, and at every hour of the day and the night. The result of the recent survey of the Water Commissioners appointed by the State of Massachusetts he had reached by his private experiments, several years earlier. Every fact which occurs in the bed, on the banks, or in the air over it; the fishes, and their spawning and nests, their manners, their food; the shad-flies[45] which fill the air on a certain evening once a year, and which are snapped at by the fishes so ravenously that many of these die of repletion[46]; the conical heaps of small stones on the river-shallows, one of which heaps will sometimes overfill a cart,—these heaps the huge nests of small fishes; the birds which frequent the stream, heron, duck, sheldrake, loon, osprey; the snake, musk-rat, otter, woodchuck, and fox, on the banks; the turtle, frog, hyla, and cricket, which make the banks vocal,[47]—were all known to him, and, as it were, townsmen and fellow-creatures; so that he felt an absurdity or violence in any narrative of one of these by itself apart, and still more of its dimensions on an inch-rule, or in the exhibition of its skeleton, or the specimen of a squirrel or a bird in brandy.[48] He liked to speak of the manners of the river, as itself a lawful creature, yet with exactness, and always to an observed fact. As he knew the river, so the ponds in this region.

One of the weapons he used, more important than microscope or alcohol-receiver[49] to other investigators, was a whim which grew on him by indulgence, yet appeared in gravest statement, namely, of extolling his own town and neighborhood as the most favored centre for natural observation. He remarked that the Flora of Massachusetts embraced almost all the important plants of America,—most of the oaks, most of the willows, the best pines, the ash, the maple, the beech, the nuts. He returned Kane's "Arctic Voyage" to a friend of whom he had borrowed it, with the remark, that "most of the phenomena noted might be observed in Concord."[50] He seemed a little envious of the Pole, for the coincident sunrise and sunset, or five minutes' day after six months: a splendid fact, which Annursnuc[51] had never afforded him. He found red snow in one of his walks, and told me that he expected to find yet the Victoria regia[52] in Concord. He was the attorney of the indigenous plants, and owned to a preference of the weeds to the imported plants, as of the Indian to the civilized man,—and noticed, with pleasure, that the willow bean-poles of his neighbor had grown more than his beans. "See these weeds," he said, "which have been hoed at by a million farmers all spring and summer, and yet have prevailed, and just now come out triumphant over all lanes, pastures, fields, and gardens, such is their vigor. We have insulted them with low names, too,—as Pigweed, Wormwood, Chickweed, Shad-Blossom." He says, "They have brave names, too,—Ambrosia, Stellaria, Amelanchia, Amaranth, etc."

I think his fancy for referring everything to the meridian[53] of Concord did not grow out of any ignorance or depreciation of other longitudes or latitudes, but was rather a playful expression of his conviction of the indifferency[54] of all places, and that the best place for each is where he stands. He expressed it once in this wise:—"I think nothing is to be hoped from you, if this bit of mould under your feet is not sweeter to you to eat than any other in this world, or in any world."

The other weapon with which he conquered all obstacles in science was patience. He knew how to sit immovable, a part of the rock he rested on, until the bird, the reptile, the fish, which had retired from him, should come back, and resume its habits, nay, moved by curiosity, should come to him and watch him.

It was a pleasure and a privilege to walk with him. He knew the country like a fox or a bird, and passed through it as freely by paths of his own. He knew every track in the snow or on the ground, and what creature had taken this path before him. One must submit abjectly[55] to such a guide, and the reward was great. Under his arm he carried an old music-book to press plants; in his pocket, his diary and pencil, a spy-glass for birds, microscope, jack-knife, and twine. He wore straw hat, stout shoes, strong gray trousers, to brave shrub-oaks and smilax,[56] and to climb a tree for a hawk's or a squirrel's nest. He waded into the pool for the water-plants, and his strong legs were no insignificant part of his armor. On the day I speak of he looked for the Menyanthes,[57] detected it across the wide pool, and, on examination of the florets, decided that it had been in flower five days. He drew out of his breast-pocket his diary, and read the names of all the plants that should bloom on this day, whereof he kept account as a banker when his notes[58] fall due. The Cypripedium[59] not due till to-morrow. He thought, that, if waked

[53] Special, distinct place (with a glance at another of its meanings, longitude).

[54] Lack of meaningful difference.

[55] In a lowly (and therefore submissive) way.

[56] A slender vine.

[57] Buckbean: plant with long stalks and white flowers, growing in marshes and bogs.

[58] Promissory notes, to be paid to a bank on specified dates. In his Journal (May 21, 1856), Emerson recounted the previous day's walk with Thoreau: "Having found his flowers, he drew out of his breast pocket his diary & read the names of all the plants that should bloom on this day, 20 May; whereof he keeps account as a banker when his notes fall due" (J 14:91).

[59] Member of the flamboyant "lady's slipper" orchid subfamily.

*Henry rightly said, the other evening, talking of lightning-rods, that the only rod of safety was in the vertebrae of his own spine. GO 22.*

"Henry rightly said, the other evening, talking of lightning-rods, that the only rod of safety was in the vertebrae of his own spine" (page from Emerson's Journal, July 1852).

up from a trance, in this swamp, he could tell by the plants what time of the year it was within two days. The redstart was flying about, and presently the fine grosbeaks, whose brilliant scarlet "makes the rash gazer wipe his eye," and whose fine clear note Thoreau compared to that of a tanager[60] which has got rid of its hoarseness. Presently he heard a note which he called that of the night-warbler, a bird he had never identified, had been in search of twelve years, which always, when he saw it, was in the act of diving down into a tree or bush, and which it was vain to seek; the only bird that sings indifferently by night and by day. I told him he must beware of finding and booking[61] it, lest life should have nothing more to show him. He said, "What you seek in vain for, half your life, one day you come full upon all the family at dinner. You seek it like a dream, and as soon as you find it you become its prey."

His interest in the flower or the bird lay very deep in his mind, was connected with Nature,—and the meaning of Nature was never attempted to be defined by him. He would not offer a memoir of his observations to the Natural History Society. "Why should I? To detach the description from its connections in my mind would make it no longer true or valuable to me: and they do not wish what belongs to it." His power of observation seemed to indicate additional senses. He saw as with microscope, heard as with eartrumpet,[62] and his memory was a photographic register of all he saw and heard. And yet none knew better than he that it is not the fact that imports, but the impression or effect of the fact on your mind. Every fact lay in glory in his mind, a type of the order and beauty of the whole. His determination on Natural History was organic. He confessed that he sometimes felt like a hound or a panther, and, if born among Indians, would have been a fell[63] hunter. But, restrained by his Massachusetts culture he played out the game in this mild form of botany and ichthyology.[64] His intimacy with animals suggested what Thomas Fuller records of Butler the apiologist, that "either he had told the bees things or the bees had told him."[65] Snakes coiled round his leg; the fishes swam into his hand, and he took them out of the water; he pulled the woodchuck out of its hole by the tail, and took the foxes under his protection from the hunters. Our naturalist had perfect magnanimity; he had no secrets; he would carry you to the heron's haunt, or even to his most

60    Emerson alludes to the poem "Virtue" (1633) by the English poet George Herbert (1593–1633), which contains the lines, "Sweet rose, whose hue angry and brave / Bids the rash gazer wipe his eye." The tanager (described by Thoreau later in Emerson's essay) is a bright scarlet migratory songbird present in the New England summer. The redstart has orange-red patches; the rose-breasted grosbeak is a colorful songbird with a short, thick bill.

61    Recording. The elusive night-warbler has a loud, varied, and cheerful song.

62    Device used as a hearing aid.

63    Fierce.

64    The study of fish.

65    Charles Butler (1560–1647) was an early English apiologist (researcher of bees) and author of *The Feminine Monarchie* (1609), on beekeeping. The English historian Thomas Fuller (1608–1661) discussed Butler in his *History of the Worthies of England* (1662), where he wrote that Butler's "Book of Bees" showed him "most knowing in the state mysteries of their commonwealth," and recorded a poem addressed to Butler with the line "bees counsel thee, or else thou counsellest bees."

66   In one Journal entry Emerson was less admiring: "Henry Thoreau is like the woodgod who solicits the wandering poet & draws him into antres vast & desarts idle, & bereaves him of his memory, & leaves him naked, plaiting vines & with twigs in his hand. Very seductive are the first steps from the town to the woods, but the End is want & madness" (March–October 1848, J 10:344). (Antres are caves: "antres vast & desarts idle" is quoted from Shakespeare's *Othello* 1.3.140.)

67   Inclination toward.

68   Tools for grinding.

69   Emerson wrote to W. H. Furness (1802–1896) (August 6, 1847) that "Henry D. Thoreau is a great man in Concord, a man of original genius & character who knows Greek & knows Indian also,—not the language quite as well as John Eliot—but the history monuments & genius of the Sachems, being a pretty good Sachem himself, master of all woodcraft, & an intimate associate of the birds, beasts, & fishes of this region" (L 8:121). John Eliot (ca. 1604–1690) was an English Puritan missionary to the Indians of Massachusetts; a sachem is an Indian chief.

70   Thoreau's last audible words on his deathbed were "moose" and "Indian."

71   Questioning methodically.

prized botanical swamp,—possibly knowing that you could never find it again, yet willing to take his risks.[66]

* * *

No college ever offered him a diploma, or a professor's chair; no academy made him its corresponding secretary, its discoverer, or even its member. Perhaps these learned bodies feared the satire of his presence. Yet so much knowledge of Nature's secret and genius few others possessed, none in a more large and religious synthesis. For not a particle of respect had he to the opinions of any man or body of men, but homage solely to the truth itself; and as he discovered everywhere among doctors some leaning of[67] courtesy, it discredited them. He grew to be revered and admired by his townsmen, who had at first known him only as an oddity. The farmers who employed him as a surveyor soon discovered his rare accuracy and skill, his knowledge of their lands, of trees, of birds, of Indian remains, and the like, which enabled him to tell every farmer more than he knew before of his own farm; so that he began to feel as if Mr. Thoreau had better rights in his land than he. They felt, too, the superiority of the character which addressed all men with a native authority.

Indian relics abound in Concord,—arrow-heads, stone chisels, pestles,[68] and fragments of pottery; and on the river-bank, large heaps of clam-shells and ashes mark spots which the savages frequented. These, and every circumstance touching the Indian, were important in his eyes.[69] His visits to Maine were chiefly for love of the Indian.[70] He had the satisfaction of seeing the manufacture of the bark-canoe, as well as of trying his hand in its management on the rapids. He was inquisitive about the making of the stone arrow-head, and in his last days charged a youth setting out for the Rocky Mountains to find an Indian who could tell him that: "It was well worth a visit to California to learn it." Occasionally, a small party of Penobscot Indians would visit Concord, and pitch their tents for a few weeks in summer on the river-bank. He failed not to make acquaintance with the best of them; though he well knew that asking questions of Indians is like catechizing[71] beavers and rabbits. In his last visit to Maine he had great satisfaction from

Joseph Polis, an intelligent Indian of Oldtown, who was his guide for some weeks.

He was equally interested in every natural fact. The depth of his perception found likeness of law throughout Nature, and I know not any genius who so swiftly inferred universal law from the single fact. He was no pedant of a department. His eye was open to beauty, and his ear to music. He found these, not in rare conditions, but wheresoever he went.[72] He thought the best of music was in single strains; and he found poetic suggestion in the humming of the telegraph-wire.

His poetry might be bad or good; he no doubt wanted a lyric facility and technical skill; but he had the source of poetry in his spiritual perception.[73] He was a good reader and critic, and his judgment on poetry was to the ground of it. He could not be deceived as to the presence or absence of the poetic element in any composition, and his thirst for this made him negligent and perhaps scornful of superficial graces. He would pass by many delicate rhythms, but he would have detected every live stanza or line in a volume, and knew very well where to find an equal poetic charm in prose. He was so enamored of the spiritual beauty that he held all actual written poems in very light esteem in the comparison. He admired Æschylus and Pindar; but, when some one was commending them, he said that "Æschylus and the Greeks, in describing Apollo and Orpheus,[74] had given no song, or no good one. They ought not to have moved trees, but to have chanted to the gods such a hymn as would have sung all their old ideas out of their heads, and new ones in." His own verses are often rude and defective. The gold does not yet run pure, is drossy and crude. The thyme and marjoram[75] are not yet honey. But if he want[76] lyric fineness and technical merits, if he have not the poetic temperament, he never lacks the causal thought, showing that his genius was better than his talent. He knew the worth of the Imagination for the uplifting and consolation of human life, and liked to throw every thought into a symbol. The fact you tell is of no value, but only the impression. For this reason his presence was poetic, always piqued the curiosity to know more deeply the secrets of his mind. He had many reserves, an unwillingness to exhibit to profane eyes what was still sacred in his own, and knew well how to throw a poetic veil over his experience. All

72   In his Journal (August 1847–January 1848) Emerson remembered, "H. D. T when you talked of art, blotted a paper with ink, then doubled it over, & safely defied the artist to surpass his effect" (J 10:151).

73   In February 1839 Emerson wrote to Margaret Fuller, "In the lecturing season I hate a pen & have nothing to say. My Henry Thoreau has broke out into good poetry & better prose; he, my protester" (L 2:182); and to Mary Moody Emerson he remarked, "Then we have Henry Thoreau here who writes genuine poetry that rarest product of New England wit" (December 22, 1839; L 2:244). In a notebook, though, Emerson remarked, "H. D. T.'s poetry; poetry pre-written; mass a compensation for quality" (J 12:350).

74   Aeschylus (ca. 525–ca. 456 BCE) and Pindar (ca. 522–443 BCE), renowned Greek poets. Apollo is the god of poetry, and Orpheus a legendary poet credited with moving trees and rocks through the power of his song.

75   Plants favored by bees.

76   Lack.

77    A mysterious and much-interpreted passage from *Walden*. In a letter of March 20, 1854,
to Richard Bentley on *Walden*, then about to be
published, Emerson wrote, "Mr Thoreau is a
man of rare ability: he is a good scholar, & a
good naturalist, and he is a man of genius, &
writes always with force, & sometimes with
wonderful depth & beauty" (L 8:399).

78    Simonides, Greek poet (ca. 556–ca.
468 BCE).

readers of "Walden" will remember his mythical record of his disappoint-
ments:—

"I long ago lost a hound, a bay horse, and a turtle-dove, and am
still on their trail. Many are the travellers I have spoken concerning them, describing their tracks, and what calls they answered to.
I have met one or two who had heard the hound, and the tramp of
the horse, and even seen the dove disappear behind a cloud; and
they seemed an anxious to recover them as if they had lost them
themselves."[77]

His riddles were worth the reading, and I confide, that, if at any time I
do not understand the expression, it is yet just. Such was the wealth of his
truth that it was not worth his while to use words in vain. His poem entitled
"Sympathy" reveals the tenderness under that triple steel of stoicism, and
the intellectual subtilty it could animate. His classic on "Smoke" suggests
Simonides,[78] but is better than any poem of Simonides. His biography is in
his verses. His habitual thought makes all his poetry a hymn to the Cause of
causes, the Spirit which vivifies and controls his own:—

"I hearing get, who had but ears,
And sight, who had but eyes before;
I moments live, who lived but years,
And truth discern, who knew but learning's lore."

And still more in these religious lines:—

"Now chiefly is my natal hour,
And only now my prime of life;
I will not doubt the love untold,
Which not my worth or want hath bought,
Which wooed me young, and woos me old,
And to this evening hath me brought."

Whilst he used in his writings a certain petulance of remark in reference to churches or churchmen, he was a person of a rare, tender, and abso-

lute religion, a person incapable of any profanation, by act or by thought. Of course, the same isolation which belonged to his original thinking and living detached him from the social religious forms. This is neither to be censured nor regretted. Aristotle long ago explained it, when he said, "One who surpasses his fellow-citizen in virtue is no longer a part of the city. Their law is nor for him, since he is a law to himself."[79]

Thoreau was sincerity itself, and might fortify the convictions of prophets in the ethical laws by his holy living.[80] It was an affirmative experience which refused to be set aside. A truth-speaker he, capable of the most deep and strict conversation; a physician to the wounds of any soul; a friend, knowing not only the secret of friendship, but almost worshipped by those few persons who resorted to him as their confessor and prophet, and knew the deep value of his mind and great heart.[81] He thought that without religion or devotion of some kind nothing great was ever accomplished; and he thought that the bigoted sectarian[82] had better bear this in mind.

His virtues, of course, sometimes ran into extremes. It was easy to trace to the inexorable demand in all for exact truth that austerity which made this willing hermit more solitary even than he wished. Himself of a perfect probity,[83] he required not less of others. He had a disgust at crime, and no worldly success could cover it. He detected paltering[84] as readily in dignified and prosperous persons as in beggars, and with equal scorn. Such dangerous frankness was in his dealing that his admirers called him "that terrible Thoreau," as if he spoke when silent, and was still present when he had departed. I think the severity of his ideal interfered to deprive him of a healthy sufficiency of human society.[85]

The habit of a realist to find things the reverse of their appearance inclined him to put every statement in a paradox. A certain habit of antagonism defaced his earlier writings,—a trick of rhetoric not quite outgrown in his later, of substituting for the obvious word and thought its diametrical opposite. He praised wild mountains and winter forests for their domestic air, in snow and ice he would find sultriness, and commended the wilderness for resembling Rome and Paris. "It was so dry, that you might call it wet."

The tendency to magnify the moment, to read all the laws of Nature in the one object or one combination under your eye, is of course comic to those who do not share the philosopher's perception of identity. To him

79    Aristotle (384–322 BCE), Greek philosopher. The passage is from Aristotle's *Politics* (3.9).

80    In a letter to an English friend, John Abraham Heraud (January 31, 1847), Emerson described Thoreau as "a man of profound & symmetrical nature, who, if he lives, will certainly be heard from in this country, & I think in yours also" (L 3:370).

81    Emerson speaks of himself. In a Journal entry from October 27, 1851, Emerson reported "last night's talk with H. T.": "We stated over again, to sadness, almost, the Eternal loneliness . . . how insular & pathetically solitary, are all the people we know! . . . It is hard to believe that all times are alike & that the present is also rich." Emerson added, "I am struck with a feeling of great poverty; my bareness! my bareness! Seems America to say" (J 9:447–448).

82    Narrow-minded adherent to a sect or group.

83    Integrity.

84    Insincerity.

85    In a Journal entry (August 5, 1864), Emerson noted, "I see the Thoreau poison working today in many valuable lives, in some for good, in some for harm" (J 15:487).

86    Savans (or savants): experts; sepals: parts of the calyx, the green cup-like part of a flower that envelopes the blossom. Emerson wrote to Henry James, Sr. (May 6, 1843), that "Thoreau is a profound mind and a person of true magnanimity, and if it should happen that there is some village pedantry & tediousness of facts, it will easily be forgotten when you come at what is better" (L 7:23).

87    Nine-Acre Corner: the site of White Pond, about two and a half miles west of Walden; Bateman's Pond and Becky Stow's Swamp (or Hole), about a mile from Emerson's house between the Bedford Road and the Lexington Road, are other local landmarks. Emerson wrote in his Journal (1864), "Yesterday with Ellery walked through 'Becky Stow's Hole,' dry-shod, hitherto a feat for a muskrat alone" (J 15:438). (William Ellery Channing [1818–1901], the Concord poet.) Thoreau described in his Journal (June 10, 1853) the area around Bateman's Pond: "It is a paradise for walkers in the fall. There are also boundless huckleberry pastures, as well as many blueberry swamps . . . It would make a princely estate in Europe."

88    Engineering: planning, supervising. This is Emerson's most famous characterization of Thoreau, and a frowning one at that. Thoreau, who did in fact enjoy organizing searches for huckleberries, might have smiled. Emerson, however, drastically underestimates Thoreau's ambition, and ignores his insistence that the most circumscribed and local life has wide, even momentous, implications. Emerson here marks the difference between his own practical commitment to influence, to discussing the questions of the day with a large audience, and Thoreau's refusal of such commitment.

there was no such thing as size. The pond was a small ocean; the Atlantic, a large Walden Pond. He referred every minute fact to cosmical laws. Though he meant to be just, he seemed haunted by a certain chronic assumption that the science of the day pretended completeness, and he had just found out that the savans had neglected to discriminate a particular botanical variety, had failed to describe the seeds or count the sepals.[86] "That is to say," we replied, "the blockheads were not born in Concord; but who said they were? It was their unspeakable misfortune to be born in London, or Paris, or Rome; but, poor fellows, they did what they could, considering that they never saw Bateman's Pond, or Nine-Acre Corner, or Becky-Stow's Swamp.[87] Besides, what were you sent into the world for, but to add this observation?"

Had his genius been only contemplative, he had been fitted to his life, but with his energy and practical ability he seemed born for great enterprise and for command; and I so much regret the loss of his rare powers of action, that I cannot help counting it a fault in him that he had no ambition. Wanting this, instead of engineering for all America, he was the captain of a huckleberry party.[88] Pounding beans is good to the end of pounding empires one of these days; but if, at the end of years, it is still only beans![89]

But these foibles, real or apparent, were fast vanishing in the incessant growth of a spirit so robust and wise, and which effaced its defeats with new triumphs. His study of Nature was a perpetual ornament to him, and inspired his friends with curiosity to see the world through his eyes, and to hear his adventures. They possessed every kind of interest.

He had many elegances of his own, whilst he scoffed at conventional elegance. Thus, he could not bear to hear the sound of his own steps, the grit of gravel; and therefore never willingly walked in the road, but in the grass, on mountains and in woods. His senses were acute, and he remarked that by night every dwelling-house gives out bad air, like a slaughter-house. He liked the pure fragrance of melilot.[90] He honored certain plants with special regard, and, over all, the pondlily,—then the gentian, and the Mikania scandens,[91] and "life-everlasting," and a bass-tree[92] which he visited every year when it bloomed, in the middle of July. He thought the scent a more oracular inquisition[93] than the sight,—more oracular and trustworthy. The scent, of course, reveals what is concealed from the other senses. By it he detected

The Thoreau-Alcott house in Concord. Thoreau lived here from 1850 to 1862; Louisa May Alcott (1832–1888) later bought the house and lived in it along with her sister and her father, Amos Bronson Alcott.

89　Emerson wryly echoes Thoreau's line in *Walden*, "I was determined to know beans."

90　Sweet clover.

91　Climbing hempweed. The gentian is a hardy flowering plant, usually with blue petals, whose roots have medicinal uses.

92　A large, spreading, vigorously growing tree.

93　That is, a searching test, with solemn import (like the words of an oracle).

94　In *Walden*, Thoreau depicts himself in a boat on Walden Pond: "When, as was commonly the case, I had none to commune with, I used to raise the echoes by striking with a paddle on the side of my boat, filling the surrounding woods with circling and dilating sound, stirring them up as the keeper of a menagerie his wild beasts, until I elicited a growl from every wooded vale and hillside." *Walden*'s chapter "Sounds" describes a spectrum of echoing animal calls.

earthiness. He delighted in echoes, and said they were almost the only kind of kindred voices that he heard.[94] He loved Nature so well, was so happy in her solitude, that he became very jealous of cities, and the sad work which their refinements and artifices made with man and his dwelling. The axe was always destroying his forest. "Thank God," he said, "they cannot cut down the clouds!" "All kinds of figures are drawn on the blue ground with this fibrous white paint." I subjoin a few sentences taken from his unpublished manuscripts, not only as records of his thought and feeling, but for their power of description and literary excellence.

\* \* \*

95    *Solanum stelligerum*, a prickly evergreen shrub.

96    The chipping sparrow, small songbird with a bright orange-rust or red cap.

97    Surface.

98    Trunk.

99    Church officer charged with ringing the bells.

"Some circumstantial evidence is very strong, as when you find a trout in the milk."

"The chub is a soft fish, and tastes like boiled brown paper salted."

"The youth gets together his materials to build a bridge to the moon, or, perchance, a palace or temple on the earth, and at length the middle-aged man concludes to built a wood-shed with them."

"The locust z-ing."

"Devil's-needles[95] zigzagging along the Nut-Meadow brook."

"Sugar is not so sweet to the palate as sound to the healthy ear."

"I put on some hemlock-boughs, and the rich salt crackling of their leaves was like mustard to the ear, the crackling of uncountable regiments. Dead trees love the fire."

"The bluebird carries the sky on his back."

"The tanager flies through the green foliage as if it would ignite the leaves."

"If I wish for a horse-hair for my compass-sight, I must go to the stable; but the hair-bird,[96] with her sharp eyes, goes to the road."

"Immortal water, alive even to the superficies."[97]

"Fire is the most tolerable third party."

"Nature made ferns for pure leaves, to show what she could do in that line."

"No tree has so fair a bole[98] and so handsome an instep as the beech."

"How did these beautiful rainbow-tints get into the shell of the fresh-water clam, buried in the mud at the bottom of our dark river?"

"Hard are the times when the infant's shoes are second-foot."

"We are strictly confined to our men to whom we give liberty."

"Nothing is so much to be feared as fear. Atheism may comparatively be popular with God himself."

"Of what significance the things you can forget? A little thought is sexton[99] to all the world."

"How can we expect a harvest of thought who have not had a seed-time of character?"

"Only he can be trusted with gifts who can present a face of bronze to expectations."

"I ask to be melted. You can only ask of the metals that they be tender to the fire that melts them. To nought else can they be tender."

\*　\*　\*

There is a flower known to botanists, one of the same genus with our summer plant called "Life-Everlasting," a Gnaphalium like that, which grows on the most inaccessible cliffs of the Tyrolese mountains, where the chamois[100] dare hardly venture, and which the hunter, tempted by its beauty, and by his love, (for it is immensely valued by the Swiss maidens,) climbs the cliffs to gather, and is sometimes found dead at the foot, with the flower in his hand. It is called by botanists the Gnaphalium leontopodium, but by the Swiss Edelweisse, which signifies Noble Purity.[101] Thoreau seemed to me living in the hope to gather this plant, which belonged to him of right. The scale on which his studies proceeded was so large as to require longevity, and we were the less prepared for his sudden disappearance. The country knows not yet, or in the least part, how great a son it has lost. It seems an injury that he should leave in the midst his broken task, which none else can finish,—a kind of indignity to so noble a soul, that it should depart out of Nature before yet he has been really shown to his peers for what he is. But he, at least, is content. His soul was made for the noblest society; he had in a short life exhausted the capabilities of this world;[102] wherever there is knowledge, wherever there is virtue, wherever there is beauty, he will find a home.[103]

100   Agile European goat-antelope that lives in high, rocky terrain.

101   The Edelweiss ("noble white") is a European flower covered with white hairs, growing in rocky alpine regions; as Emerson notes, it symbolizes purity.

102   In a letter to George Stewart, Jr. (January 22, 1877), Emerson wrote, "Thoreau was a superior genius. I read his books & manuscripts always with new surprise at the range of his topics & the novelty & depth of his thought. A man of large reading, of quick perception, of great practical courage & ability,—who grew greater every day, &, had his short life been prolonged would have found few equals to the power & wealth of his mind" (L 10:303).

103   Emerson ended his brief obituary for Thoreau, in the *Boston Daily Advertiser* (May 8, 1862), "As he was incapable of any the least dishonesty or untruth, he had nothing to hide, and kept his haughty independence to the end. And when we now look back at the solitude of his erect and spotless person, we lament that he did not live long enough for all men to know him."

   In his last years, when his memory had faded, Emerson would ask his wife Lidian, "What was the name of my best friend?" "Henry Thoreau," she would answer. "Oh, yes, Henry Thoreau," he would respond.

# Poetry Selections

# The Sphinx

The Sphinx is drowsy,
    Her wings are furled;
Her ear is heavy,
    She broods on the world.[1]
"Who'll tell me my secret,
    The ages have kept?—
I awaited the seer,
    While they slumbered and slept;—

"The fate of the man-child;
    The meaning of man;
Known fruit of the unknown;
    Dædalian[2] plan;
Out of sleeping a waking,
    Out of waking a sleep;
Life death overtaking;
    Deep underneath deep?[3]

"Erect as a sunbeam,
    Upspringeth the palm;
The elephant browses,
    Undaunted and calm;
In beautiful motion
    The thrush plies his wings;

The poem was written in 1840 and published in the Dial. Near the beginning of his essay "History," Emerson alludes to "that old fable of the Sphinx, who was said to sit in the roadside and put riddles to every passenger. If the man could not answer she swallowed him alive. If he could solve the riddle, the Sphinx was slain." The Sphinx had the body of a lion, the wings of an eagle, and a woman's head and breasts. Oedipus finally solved her riddle, and she dashed herself against a stone and killed herself.

The great American novelist Herman Melville (1819–1891) in Chapter 70 of Moby-Dick (1851) depicts the "black and hooded head" of a decapitated whale that "seemed the Sphynx's in the desert": "'Speak, thou vast and venerable head,' muttered Ahab, '. . . speak, mighty head, and tell us the secret thing that is in thee. Of all divers, thou hast dived the deepest. . . . O head! Thou hast seen enough to split the planets and make an infidel of Abraham, and not one syllable is thine!'"

Henry David Thoreau (1817–1862) wrote a detailed commentary on Emerson's poem in a manuscript (repeated with variation in his Journal for March 7–10, 1841, 1:279–286). Thoreau remarked that "the Sphinx is the pure intellect . . . it is man's insatiable and questing spirit, which still, as of old, stands by the road side in us, and puts the

(continued)

*riddle of life to every passer . . . She had no distinct existence, but brooded over all . . . for we live by confidence, and our bravery is 'in' some moment when we have a glimpse of the end of time . . ."*

1    The English poet John Milton (1608–1674) at the beginning of *Paradise Lost* (1667) addresses the Spirit that "dove-like satst brooding on the vast Abyss / And mad'st it pregnant" (1.21–22). (To brood is to hover over, to meditate on, to nurse or incubate.) Thoreau commented on this first stanza, "We must look on the world with drowsy and half shut eye, that it may not be too much in our eye, and rather stand aloof from, than within it . . ."

2    From Daedalus, the legendary Greek artificer whose work was brilliant and intricate. He built the labyrinth of Crete for King Minos, and then escaped from Crete with the aid of the wings he constructed for himself. (Daedalus's son Icarus wore a similar set of wings; they melted when he flew too close to the sun.)

3    Thoreau wrote that this stanza "hints generally at man's mystery. He knows only that he is, not how, nor whence. . . . He is 'lost in' himself as in a labyrinth . . ."

4    An animal departs from its lair.

5    The picture of the infant, and the contrast between childhood peace and adult guilt, owes a debt to one of Emerson's favorite poems, the *Immortality Ode* (1807) by the English Romantic poet William Wordsworth (1770–1850).

6    Equivocates, talks misleadingly.

Kind leaves of his covert,[4]
   Your silence he sings.

"The waves, unashamed,
   In difference sweet,
Play glad with the breezes,
   Old playfellows meet;
The journeying atoms,
   Primordial wholes,
Firmly draw, firmly drive,
   By their animate poles.

"Sea, earth, air, sound, silence,
   Plant, quadruped, bird,
By one music enchanted,
   One deity stirred,—
Each the other adorning,
   Accompany still;
Night veileth the morning,
   The vapor the hill.

"The babe by its mother
   Lies bathed in joy;
Glide its hours uncounted,—
   The sun is its toy;
Shines the peace of all being,
   Without cloud, in its eyes;
And the sum of the world
   In soft miniature[5] lies.

"But man crouches and blushes,
   Absconds and conceals;
He creepeth and peepeth,
   He palters[6] and steals;
Infirm, melancholy,
   Jealous glancing around,

An oaf, an accomplice,
    He poisons the ground.

"Out spoke the great mother,
    Beholding his fear;—
At the sound of her accents
    Cold shuddered the sphere:—
'Who has drugged my boy's cup?[7]
    Who has mixed my boy's bread?
Who, with sadness and madness,
    Has turned my child's head?'"

I heard a poet answer,[8]
    Aloud and cheerfully,
"Say on, sweet Sphinx! thy dirges
    Are pleasant songs to me.
Deep love lieth under
    These pictures of time;
They fade in the light of
    Their meaning sublime.

"The fiend that man harries
    Is love of the Best;
Yawns the pit of the Dragon,
    Lit by rays from the Blest.
The Lethe[9] of nature
    Can't trance him again,
Whose soul sees the perfect,
    Which his eyes seek in vain.

"Profounder, profounder,
    Man's spirit must dive;
To his aye[10]—rolling orbit
    No goal will arrive;
The heavens that now draw him
    With sweetness untold,

7    In his essay "Experience," Emerson writes that "the Genius which, according to the old belief, stands at the door by which we enter, and gives us the lethe to drink, that we may tell no tales, mixed the cup too strongly, and we cannot shake off the lethargy now at noonday."

8    As in *Nature* and "The Poet," Emerson imagines an ideal bard who sees beyond earthly tricks and limitations.

9    River of forgetfulness in Hades.

10    Ever.

11    There is a longstanding tradition that Satan and his cohort fell through pride; the most familiar dramatization of the theme occurs in Bk. 6 of Milton's *Paradise Lost.*

12    Rue: a bitter evergreen leaf used as medicine; myrrh: an aromatic resin; cummin (or cumin): an aromatic plant.

13    Partner.

14    Man is the true Sphinx, an unanswerable riddle because ever-changing and yet eternally whole. Each human attempt to solve existence is a "lie," yet because it forms part of the truth (the Sphinx's panorama of illusions), it gives mastery as well. The American composer Charles Ives (1874–1954), an admirer of Emerson, wrote his orchestral piece *The Unanswered Question* in 1906.

15    Make your way (with implications of pliancy or yielding, and of "ply," meaning "fold").

Once found,—for new heavens
    He spurneth the old.

"Pride ruined the angels,[11]
    Their shame them restores;
And the joy that is sweetest
    Lurks in stings of remorse.
Have I a lover
    Who is noble and free?—
I would he were nobler
    Than to love me.

"Eterne alternation
    Now follows, now flies;
And under pain, pleasure,—
    Under pleasure, pain lies.
Love works at the centre,
    Heart-heaving alway;
Forth speed the strong pulses
    To the borders of day.

"Dull Sphinx, Jove keep thy five wits!
    Thy sight is growing blear;
Rue, myrrh, and cummin[12] for the Sphinx—
    Her muddy eyes to clear!"—
The old Sphinx bit her thick lip,—
    Said, "Who taught thee me to name?
I am thy spirit, yoke-fellow,[13]
    Of thine eye I am eyebeam.

"Thou art the unanswered question;[14]
    Couldst see thy proper eye,
Alway it asketh, asketh;
    And each answer is a lie.
So take thy quest through nature,
    It through thousand natures ply;[15]

Ask on, thou clothed eternity;
    Time is the false reply."

Uprose the merry Sphinx,
    And crouched no more in stone;
She melted into purple cloud,
    She silvered in the moon;
She spired into a yellow flame;
    She flowered in blossoms red;
She flowed into a foaming wave;
    She stood Monadnoc's[16] head.

Thorough a thousand voices
    Spoke the universal dame:
"Who telleth one of my meanings,
    Is master of all I am."[17]

16     Mountain in New Hampshire, subject of a poem by Emerson written in 1846. It was the last peak that Thoreau climbed before he died, in 1862.

17     Emerson may be remembering the oracular judgment of Dame Nature at the end of the Mutabilitie Cantos (1596) by the English poet Edmund Spenser (ca. 1552–1599): that "all things . . . By their change their being doe dilate" (7.58.2–5). In a notebook entry of 1859, Emerson wrote, "I have often been asked the meaning of the 'Sphinx.' It is this,—The perception of identity unites all things and explains one by another, and the most rare and strange is equally facile as the most common. But if the mind live only in particulars, and see only differences (wanting the power to see the whole —all in each), then the world addresses to the mind a question it cannot answer, and each new fact tears it in pieces, and it is vanquished by the distracting variety" (quoted by Edward Emerson in his edition of his father's works).

# Uriel

Uriel is an archangel named in the apocryphal books of the Bible. He also appears in Milton's Paradise Lost, where as "regent of the sun" he is "held / The sharpest sighted spirit of all in heaven," but is nevertheless fooled by Satan (3.648–692). Emerson sent "Uriel" to his friend the poet Caroline Sturgis (1819–1888) in 1845 or 1846, with this note: "You have heard news from Saadi, that the most baleful heresy has been broached in heaven at some Epoch not fixed. It seems some body said words like these, that Geometers might say what they pleased, but in Uranometry there was no right line." (Saadi [1184–ca. 1292], called Said in the poem itself, was the great Persian poet cherished by Emerson. Uranometry is the measurement of the heavens.) What seems straight on earth is, in the heavens, curved; the heretic announces to shortsighted humans the true shape of things. Emerson did exactly this in his Divinity School Address of July 15, 1838, and was accused of heresy.

1    A constellation, called the "seven sisters." Emerson mentioned in his Journal (1859) the popular notion that there are now only six stars rather than seven in the constellation, and asked, "What is the poetic interest of the lost Pleiad for so many minds? . . . each nun or her-
(continued)

It fell in the ancient periods
    Which the brooding soul surveys,
Or ever the wild Time coined itself
    Into calendar months and days.

This was the lapse of Uriel,
Which in Paradise befell.
Once, among the Pleiads[1] walking,
SAID[2] overheard the young gods talking;
And the treason, too long pent,
To his ears was evident.
The young deities discussed
Laws of form, and metre just,
Orb, quintessence,[3] and sunbeams,
What subsisteth, and what seems.
One, with low tones that decide,
And doubt and reverend use defied,
With a look that solved the sphere,
And stirred the devils everywhere,
Gave his sentiment divine
Against the being of a line.
'Line in nature is not found;
Unit and universe are round;
In vain produced, all rays return;

Evil will bless, and ice will burn.'
As Uriel spoke with piercing eye,
A shudder ran around the sky;
The stern old war-gods shook their heads;
The seraphs[4] frowned from myrtle-beds;
Seemed to the holy festival
The rash word boded ill to all;
The balance-beam of Fate was bent;[5]
The bounds of good and ill were rent;
Strong Hades could not keep his own,
But all slid to confusion.[6]

A sad self-knowledge, withering, fell
On the beauty of Uriel;
In heaven once eminent, the god
Withdrew, that hour, into his cloud;
Whether doomed to long gyration
In the sea of generation,
Or by knowledge grown too bright
To hit the nerve of feebler sight.[7]
Straightway, a forgetting wind
Stole over the celestial kind,
And their lips the secret kept,
If in ashes the fire-seed slept.
But now and then, truth-speaking things
Shamed the angels' veiling wings;
And, shrilling from the solar course,
Or from fruit of chemic[8] force,
Procession of a soul in matter,
Or the speeding change of water,
Or out of the good of evil born,[9]
Came Uriel's voice of cherub scorn,[10]
And a blush tinged the upper sky,
And the gods shook, they knew not why.[11]

mit is struck with the circumstance & writes solitary verses about it. What is the charm of the incident? I think because it is to each a symbol of lost thoughts" (J 14:310).

2   See "Song of Seid Nimetollah of Kuhistan," below. The great Persian poet is probably intended by Emerson as a self-representation (or representation of the poet in general).

3   Fifth element (along with earth, air, fire, and water), thought by ancient and medieval thinkers to constitute the celestial realm.

4   Sublime, six-winged angels (Isaiah 6); their name means "afire."

5   In the *Iliad* by Homer (ca. 9th century BCE), Zeus, father of the gods, holds a pair of scales to determine the decisions of Fate.

6   Emerson wrote in his journal on October 30, 1838, "At the first entering ray of light, society is shaken with fear & anger from side to side. Who opened that shutter? they cry, Wo to him! They belie it, they call it darkness that comes in, affirming that they were in light before. Before the man who has spoken to them the dread word, they tremble & flee" (J 7:126).

7   Milton, in "Il Penseroso," writes that Melancholy's "saintly visage is too bright / To hit the sense of human sight."

8   Chemical or alchemical. Fruit: product.

9   Satan in *Paradise Lost* exults "evil be thou my good" (4.110), but his is a sterile claim; Emerson's point is closer to those of his inheritor Friedrich Nietzsche (1844–1900) or the poet William Blake (1757–1827): there is an irreplaceable, provocative, and even "divine" power in what we call evil.

10    Cherubim (cherubs) are angels in the
Hebrew Bible; they are traditionally associated
with knowledge. Cherubim guard the gates of
Eden in Genesis 3:24. The English Romantic
poet S. T. Coleridge (1772–1834) wrote in his
*Aids to Reflection* (1825), which Emerson read
avidly, that "it is on the wings of the CHERU-
BIM, i.e . . . the *intellectual* powers and energies,
that we must first be borne up to the 'pure empyrean'" (Aphorism XV).

11    The American poet Robert Frost (1874–
1963) in his dramatic poem "A Masque of
Reason" (1945) called "Uriel" "the greatest
Western poem yet." (Uriel's judgment, with its
perception that "evil will bless, and ice will
burn," sounds particularly Frostian.) In a talk at
Bread Loaf, Vermont (1959), Frost described
Emerson's opposition to "the old guard": "They
deserve cherubic scorn, Emersonian scorn. He
stayed cherubic all his days; he knew it; he knew
that he had the feeling of contempt for a person
that had aged to the point where he had given
up newness, betterness, you know."

Emerson with his son Edward and grandson Charles Lowell Emerson.

# The Rhodora: On Being Asked, Whence Is the Flower?

In May, when sea-winds pierced our solitudes,[1]
I found the fresh Rhodora in the woods,
Spreading its leafless blooms in a damp nook,
To please the desert and the sluggish brook.
The purple petals, fallen in the pool,
Made the black water with their beauty gay;
Here might the red-bird come his plumes to cool,
And court the flower that cheapens his array.[2]
Rhodora! if the sages ask thee why
This charm is wasted on the earth and sky,[3]
Tell them, dear, that if eyes were made for seeing,
Then Beauty is its own excuse for being:
Why thou wert there, O rival of the rose!
I never thought to ask, I never knew;
But, in my simple ignorance, suppose
The self-same Power that brought me there brought you.[4]

*This poem was written in 1834 in Newton, Massachusetts, where Emerson stayed in the late spring and summer at the home of his Aunt Mary. "In this still Newton we have seven Sabbaths in a week. The day is as calm as Eternity," he noted in his Journal (May 1, 1834; J 4:287). Emerson took long walks in the woods and studied botany. Emerson's knowledge of nature was far more casual, and less practical, than Thoreau's. But Emerson in this poem forecasts Thoreau's careful descriptions of flora. The rhodora is* Rhododendron canadense, *a flower characteristic of New England, with bright pinkish-purple flowers.*

1     A plangent and direct first line. "Our solitudes" are matched by the solitude of the Rhodora, which expends itself in a secluded place, not intending to rival bird or rose, but silent and sweet in its integrity. The poem's simple parabolic point resists the sentimental.

2     That is, outshines his costume.

3     Emerson remembers lines from "Elegy Written in a Country Churchyard" (1751) by the English poet Thomas Gray (1716–1771):
(continued)

"Full many a flower is born to blush unseen, / And waste its sweetness on the desert air."

4      Emerson's plainspoken address to the flower owes a debt to William Wordworth's poems to the daisy (1807) and presages the work of Emily Dickinson (1830–1886) ("Pink—small —and punctual—," "There is a flower that bees prefer—"), as well as Robert Frost's "Rose Pogonias" (1913). Frost's "Design" (1922) presents an infernal response to "The Rhodora": "What had that flower to do with being white, / The wayside blue and innocent heal-all?" (Frost's version of Emerson's "Power" is "design of darkness to appal.")

The rhodora.

# The Snow-Storm

Announced by all the trumpets of the sky,
Arrives the snow, and, driving o'er the fields,
Seems nowhere to alight: the whited air
Hides hills and woods, the river, and the heaven,
And veils the farm-house at the garden's end.
The sled and traveller stopped, the courier's feet
Delayed, all friends shut out, the housemates sit
Around the radiant fireplace, enclosed
In a tumultuous privacy of storm.[1]

    Come see the north wind's masonry.
Out of an unseen quarry evermore
Furnished with tile, the fierce artificer
Curves his white bastions[2] with projected roof
Round every windward stake, or tree, or door.
Speeding, the myriad-handed, his wild work[3]
So fanciful, so savage, nought cares he
For number or proportion. Mockingly,
On coop or kennel he hangs Parian[4] wreaths;
A swan-like form invests the hidden thorn;
Fills up the farmer's lane from wall to wall,
Maugre[5] the farmer's sighs; and, at the gate,
A tapering turret overtops the work.

*There was a heavy snowfall in Concord on December 29, 1834. Emerson saw and felt it from the upstairs of the Old Manse, the home of his step-grandfather Ezra Ripley (1751–1841)—and described it in his Journal: "The great willowtree over my roof is the trumpet & accompaniment of the storm & gives due importance to every caprice of the gale and the trees in the avenue announce the same facts with equal din to the front tenants. Hoarse concert: they roar like the rigging of a ship in a tempest" (J 4:384). Soon after the blizzard, Emerson wrote "The Snow-Storm," first in prose (J 6:246).*

1    These first nine lines became the epigraph of *Snow-Bound* (1866) by the American poet John Greenleaf Whittier (1807–1892).

2    Projecting parts of a fortification; ramparts.

3    In *Paradise Lost* (6.698), Milton describes the war between loyal and rebellious angels as "wild work in heaven."

4    The Greek island of Paros supplied a resplendent marble.

5    Despite.

6     Full of pranks or sport.

And when his hours are numbered, and the world
Is all his own, retiring, as he were not,
Leaves, when the sun appears, astonished Art
To mimic in slow structures, stone by stone,
Built in an age, the mad wind's night-work,
The frolic[6] architecture of the snow.

# Ode, Inscribed to W. H. Channing

Though loath to grieve[1]
The evil time's sole patriot,[2]
I cannot leave
My honied thought
For the priest's cant,
Or statesman's rant.[3]

If I refuse
My study for their politique,
Which at the best is trick,[4]
The angry Muse
Puts confusion in my brain.[5]

But who is he that prates[6]
Of the culture of mankind,
Of better arts and life?
Go, blindworm,[7] go,
Behold the famous States
Harrying Mexico
With rifle and with knife![8]

Or who, with accent bolder,
Dare praise the freedom-loving mountaineer?
I found by thee, O rushing Contoocook!

*Emerson wrote this brilliantly provocative political poem in June 1846, during a journey to Mt. Monadnoc in New Hampshire. William Henry Channing (1810–1884) was a Unitarian minister and abolitionist, as well as a member of the Transcendental Club (he was the nephew of the more famous William Ellery Channing [1780–1842], a central Unitarian thinker). Channing shared the stage with Emerson at an abolitionist rally in 1845, but there was some friction between them. Emerson wrote to Margaret Fuller (1810–1850) on May 29, 1842, that Channing "charges me with universal homicide, no less" because of Emerson's inadequate commitment to social reform. On May 19, 1846, Channing spoke at the funeral of abolitionist minister Charles Turner Torrey (1813–1846), who had been imprisoned for aiding escaped slaves and had died in jail. Emerson was troubled by what he saw as the theatrical anger of the speakers at the funeral (they "make believe to be enraged," he noted in his Journal; J 9:410). He also commented, "At the funeral of Torrey, it seems almost too late to say anything for freedom,—the battle is already won. You are a superserviceable echo. Yet when you come out & see the apathy & incredulity, the wood & the stone of the people, their supple neck, their appetite for pine apple & ice cream" (J 9:400).*

1    Vex, trouble.

2    Channing.

3    Emerson remarked in his Journal in 1844, "I do not & can not forsake my vocation for abolitionism" (J 9:64n).

4    In his essay "Politics," Emerson wrote, "What satire on government can equal the severity of censure conveyed in the word *politic*, which now for ages has signified *cunning*, intimating that the State is a trick?"

5    In "Self-Reliance," Emerson commented that "at times the whole world seems to be in conspiracy to importune you with emphatic trifles. . . . But keep thy state; come not into their confusion."

6    Chatters irrelevantly.

7    A small, feeble lizard.

8    The United States declared war on Mexico on May 13, 1846. Northern antislavery opinion denounced the war as an attempt to expand slavery and an illegitimate attack on a sovereign nation. Opposition to the war was strong in the Whig party; most Democrats, southern and northern, supported it.

9    The Contoocook is a New Hampshire river; Agiochook or Agiocochook is the Algonquin name for Mt. Washington, also in New Hampshire. New Hampshire had voted for the pro-slavery Democratic party in the 1844 presidential elections.

10    In his Journal Emerson, describing his trip to the region in September 1839, remarked, "In New Hampshire the dignity of the landscape made more obvious the meanness [that is, lowness] of the tavern-haunting men" (J 7:236).

Emerson was probably also thinking of his still-admired Daniel Webster (1782–1852), originally of New Hampshire. Emerson was disappointed in what he saw as Webster's eventual acquiescence in the Mexican War (as he suggests in his essay "Politics"). At the Whig convention of 1846, Webster refused to align himself with the abolitionist program of Senator Charles Sumner (1811–1874). In his Journal (1846) Emerson remarked, "Webster is a man by himself of the great mould, but he also underlies the American blight, & wants [that is, lacks] the power of the initiative, the affirmative talent . . . his great proportions only exposing his defect. America seems to have immense resources . . . but it is a village littleness;—village squabble & rapacity characterizes its policy" (J 9:444–445). In the notes for his May 3, 1851, address at Concord on the Fugitive Slave Law, Emerson mentioned "the deep servility of New Hampshire politics," excepting only Senator John P. Hale (1806–1873).

11    The crocodile famously cries false tears. Lines 7–31 seem to be derived from Isaiah 2:19–21, which predicts what will happen on the day when God "ariseth to shake terribly the earth": "In that day a man shall cast his idols of silver, and his idols of gold . . . to the moles and to the bats; To go into the clefts of the rocks, and into the tops of the ragged rocks . . ."

12    A reference to Torrey's funeral. The critic David Bromwich remarks that Emerson speaks the first two stanzas of the Ode and Channing the next three, concluding with this line. Now Emerson's voice returns.

13    Profits.

14    Angry.

And in thy valleys, Agiochook!
The jackals of the negro-holder.[9]

The God who made New Hampshire
Taunted the lofty land
With little men;[10]—
Small bat and wren
House in the oak:—
If earth-fire cleave
The upheaved land, and bury the folk,
The southern crocodile would grieve.[11]

Virtue palters; Right is hence;
Freedom praised, but hid;
Funeral eloquence
Rattles the coffin-lid.[12]

What boots[13] thy zeal,
O glowing[14] friend,
That would indignant rend
The northland from the south?[15]
Wherefore? to what good end?
Boston Bay and Bunker Hill
Would serve things still;—
Things are of the snake.[16]

The horseman serves the horse,
The neatherd serves the neat,[17]
The merchant serves the purse,
The eater serves his meat;
'Tis the day of the chattel,[18]
Web to weave, and corn to grind;
Things are in the saddle,
And ride mankind.[19]

There are two laws discrete,
Not reconciled,—

15    In a speech he gave on May 29, 1846, in Boston, Channing advocated the North's secession from the slaveholding South. Emerson opposes the idea here, but he shows more sympathy for it after the passage of the Fugitive Slave Law of 1850. In a letter to Oliver Wendell Holmes (1809–1894) in March 1856, he proclaimed, "And for the Union with Slavery no manly person will suffer a day to go by without discrediting disintegrating & finally exploding it. The 'union' they talk of is dead & rotten" (L 5:17–18).

16    That is, seductively evil, like the serpent in Genesis 3:1–5.

17    Cow.

18    Piece of property; also, slave.

19    Emerson's Harvard editors Albert von Frank and Thomas Wortham cite a passage from the New England Puritan Urian Oakes (*A Seasonable Discourse*, 1682): "Man is dethroned, and become a servant and slave to those things that were made to serve him, and he puts those things in his heart, that God hath put under his feet." The idea is a familiar one in Christian tradition since St. Augustine (354–430); Emerson uses it in this stanza to criticize a capitalist nation's priorities. Thoreau in *Walden* (1854) turns Emerson's point in an uncompromising direction: "We do not ride on the railroad; it rides upon us." Emerson, unlike Thoreau, does not develop a gospel of refusal: by the end of the ode, he accepts the law of things.

20    Land.

21    Benefit.

22    The rest of the Greek gods (ruled by Jove, or Zeus).

23    See Emerson's earlier mention of "ho-nied thought." Samson, in the Bible's book of Judges (14:14), tells a riddle: "Out of the eater came forth meat, and out of the strong came forth sweetness" (a dead lion with a honeycomb within). Emerson's God turns "dark to light" but "exterminates" races and nations (Poland, Mexico) in the process. Bromwich points to Wordsworth's frightening lines addressed to the God who "guides the Pestilence" in his "Ode: 1815": "But Thy most dreaded instrument / Is working out a pure intent, / Is Man—arrayed for mutual slaughter, / Yea, Carnage is thy daughter." Emerson returns to the "working out" of light from destruction in his essay "Fate."

Law for man, and law for thing;
The last builds town and fleet,
But it runs wild,
And doth the man unking.

'Tis fit the forest fall,
The steep be graded,
The mountain tunnelled,
The sand shaded,
The orchard planted,
The glebe[20] tilled,
The prairie granted,
The steamer built.

William Henry Channing
(1810–1884).

Let man serve law for man;
Live for friendship, live for love,
For truth's and harmony's behoof;[21]
The state may follow how it can,
As Olympus[22] follows Jove.

    Yet do not I implore
The wrinkled shopman to my sounding woods,
Nor bid the unwilling senator
Ask votes of thrushes in the solitudes.
Every one to his chosen work;—
Foolish hands may mix and mar;
Wise and sure the issues are.
Round they roll till dark is light,
Sex to sex, and even to odd;—
The over-god
Who marries Right to Might,
Who peoples, unpeoples,—
He who exterminates
Races by stronger races,
Black by white faces,—
Knows to bring honey
Out of the lion;[23]
Grafts gentlest scion
On pirate and Turk.[24]

The Cossack eats Poland,
Like stolen fruit;
Her last noble is ruined,
Her last poet mute:[25]
Straight,[26] into double band
The victors divide;
Half for freedom strike and stand;—
The astonished Muse finds thousands at her side.[27]

24    Part of a plant used for grafting. Turks, like pirates, had a warlike reputation. Emerson violates the image of this line (the gentle, growing plant) with the next stanza's "stolen fruit."

25    For over thirty years Russia ("the Cossack") had ruled most of Poland; in 1830 the Poles revolted in the November Uprising but were defeated by Russia. In his Journal (1846) Emerson struck a different note: "Nature is always gainer, & reckons surely on our sympathy. The Russians eat up the Poles. What then? when the last Polander is gone, the Russians are men, are ourselves, & the Pole is forgotten in our identification with Russian parties. A philosopher is no philosopher unless he takes lively part with the thief who picks his pocket and with the bully that insults or strikes him" (J 9:383).

26    Instantly.

27    The Muse is no longer angry at being deserted, as at the poem's beginning, but astonished that so many flock to her—to the cause of solitary imaginative work—rather than to Channing's militant advocacy of freedom. The quarrel between political battle and artistic creation becomes a silent scene of division, in which neither side overwhelms the other. Both are victorious—and separate. The conclusion is abrupt and surprising, and it sets a permanent distance between Emerson and Channing.

# Merlin (I)

*Emerson finished both parts of "Merlin" in July 1846; the idea for the poem had been with him for some time. He wrote in his Journal in late June 1839, "Rhyme; not tinkling rhyme but grand Pindaric strokes as firm as the tread of a horse. Rhyme that vindicates itself as an art, the stroke of the bell of a cathedral. Rhyme which knocks at prose & dulness with the stroke of a cannon ball. Rhyme which builds out into Chaos & Old night a splendid architecture to bridge the impassable, & call aloud on all the children of morning that the Creation is recommencing. I wish to write such rhymes as shall not suggest a restraint but contrariwise the wildest freedom" (J 7:219; the entry invokes* Paradise Lost *with its mention of "Chaos & old Night" [1.543] and divine creation).*

*Merlin is the magician in King Arthur's circle, described in the* Histories of the Kings of Britain *by Geoffrey of Monmouth (ca. 1100–ca. 1155), Edmund Spenser's (ca. 1552–1599)* Faerie Queene *(1590–1596), and elsewhere. In* Idylls of the King *(1859) by the English poet Alfred, Lord Tennyson (1809–1892), Merlin figures prominently; in "Merlin and the Gleam" (1889), Tennyson identifies the magician with the poet. Emerson may also have in mind the legendary Welsh bard Myrrdhin (6th century), whose verse was thought to be archaic, free, and authentic.*

Thy trivial harp will never please
Or fill my craving ear;
Its chords should ring as blows the breeze,
Free, peremptory, clear.
No jingling serenader's art,
Nor tinkle of piano strings,
Can make the wild blood start
In its mystic springs.
The kingly bard
Must smite the chords rudely and hard,
As with hammer or with mace;
That they may render back
Artful thunder, which conveys
Secrets of the solar track,
Sparks of the supersolar blaze.
Merlin's blows are strokes of fate,
Chiming with the forest tone,
When boughs buffet boughs in the wood;
Chiming with the gasp and moan
Of the ice-imprisoned flood;
With the pulse of manly hearts;
With the voice of orators;
With the din of city arts;

With the cannonade of wars;
With the marches of the brave;
And prayers of might from martyrs' cave.

Great is the art,
Great be the manners, of the bard.
He shall not his brain encumber
With the coil[1] of rhythm and number;
But, leaving rule and pale forethought,
He shall aye[2] climb
For his rhyme.
'Pass in, pass in,' the angels say,
'In to the upper doors,
Nor count compartments of the floors,
But mount to paradise
By the stairway of surprise.'[3]

Blameless master of the games,
King of sport that never shames,
He shall daily joy dispense
Hid in song's sweet influence.
Things more cheerly live and go,
What time the subtle mind
Sings aloud the tune whereto
Their pulses beat,
And march their feet,
And their members are combined.

By Sybarites[4] beguiled,
He shall no task decline;
Merlin's mighty line[5]
Extremes of nature reconciled,—
Bereaved a tyrant of his will,[6]
And made the lion mild.
Songs can the tempest still,
Scattered on the stormy air,

1    Restraint.

2    Always.

3    In Genesis 28:10–17, Jacob, fleeing from his brother Esau, sees a visionary ladder reaching to heaven, with angels going up and down on it.

4    Inhabitants of the ancient Greek city of Sybaris, famous for luxury.

5    Shakespeare's friend and fellow dramatist Ben Jonson (1572–1637) referred to "Marlowe's mighty line" (Christopher Marlowe, English playwright [1564–1593]) in "To the Memory of My Beloved, Mr. William Shakespeare" (1623).

6    In "Alexander's Feast" (1697) by the English poet John Dryden (1631–1700), the conqueror Alexander the Great (356–323 BCE) is freely manipulated by a bard whose verse and music "could swell the soul to rage, or kindle soft desire."

7 In his Journal (1835) Emerson wrote, "But suddenly in any place, in the street, in the chamber, will the heaven open, and the regions of wisdom be uncovered, as if to show how thin the veil, how null the circumstances. As quickly, a Lethean stream washes through us and bereaves us of ourselves" (J 5:275).

Mould the year to fair increase,
And bring in poetic peace.

He shall not seek to weave,
In weak, unhappy times,
Efficacious rhymes;
Wait his returning strength.
Bird, that from the nadir's floor
To the zenith's top can soar,
The soaring orbit of the muse exceeds that journey's length.
Nor profane affect to hit
Or compass that, by meddling wit,
Which only the propitious mind
Publishes when 'tis inclined.
There are open hours
When the God's will sallies free,
And the dull idiot might see
The flowing fortunes of a thousand years;—
Sudden, at unawares,
Self-moved, fly-to the doors,
Nor sword of angels could reveal
What they conceal.[7]

# Merlin (II)

The rhyme of the poet
Modulates the king's affairs;
Balance-loving Nature
Made all things in pairs.
To every foot its antipode;
Each color with its counter glowed;
To every tone beat answering tones,
Higher or graver;
Flavor gladly blends with flavor;
Leaf answers leaf upon the bough;
And match the paired cotyledons.[1]
Hands to hands, and feet to feet,
In one body grooms and brides;
Eldest rite, two married sides
In every mortal meet.
Light's far furnace shines,
Smelting balls and bars,
Forging double stars,
Glittering twins and trines.
The animals are sick with love,
Lovesick with rhyme;
Each with all propitious time
Into chorus wove.

1    Seed-bearing leaves.

2    Pledge.

3    The classical goddess of retribution.

4    Interval.

Like the dancers' ordered band,
Thoughts come also hand in hand;
In equal couples mated,
Or else alternated;
Adding by their mutual gage,[2]
One to other, health and age.
Solitary fancies go
Short-lived wandering to and fro,
Most like to bachelors,
Or an ungiven maid,
Not ancestors,
With no posterity to make the lie afraid,
Or keep truth undecayed.

Perfect-paired as eagle's wings,
Justice is the rhyme of things;
Trade and counting use
The self-same tuneful muse;
And Nemesis,[3]
Who with even matches odd,
Who athwart space redresses
The partial wrong,
Fills the just period,[4]
And finishes the song.

Subtle rhymes, with ruin rife,
Murmur in the house of life,
Sung by the Sisters as they spin;
In perfect time and measure they
Build and unbuild our echoing clay,
As the two twilights of the day
Fold us music-drunken in.

# Bacchus

Bring me wine, but wine which never grew
In the belly of the grape,
Or grew on vine whose tap-roots, reaching through
Under the Andes to the Cape,[1]
Suffered no savor of the earth to scape.

Let its grapes the morn salute
From a nocturnal root,
Which feels the acrid juice
Of Styx and Erebus;[2]
And turns the woe of Night,
By its own craft, to a more rich delight.

We buy ashes for bread;[3]
We buy diluted wine;
Give me of the true,[4]—
Whose ample leaves and tendrils curled
Among the silver hills of heaven,
Draw everlasting dew;
Wine of wine,
Blood of the world,[5]
Form of forms, and mould of statures,
That I intoxicated,
And by the draught assimilated,

*Emerson wrote this poem in July 1846, partly in imitation of drinking songs by the Persian poet Hafiz (ca. 1325–ca. 1389), which he had just been reading in Joseph von Hammer-Purgstall's German translation. (For the Sufi Hafiz as for Emerson, the intoxication is metaphorical, a God-given ecstasy.)*

*Bacchus is the Roman name for Dionysus, the Greek god of wine and intoxicated revelry. Emerson wrote in his Journal (1846), "O Bacchus, make them drunk, drive them mad, this multitude of vagabonds, hungry for eloquence, hungry for poetry" (J 9:441). "I take many stimulants & often make an art of my inebriation," he remarked in an 1843 Journal entry. "I read Proclus for my opium; it excites my imagination to let sail before me the pleasing & grand figures of gods & daemons and demoniacal men" (J 8:378; Proclus [412–485], Greek Neoplatonic philosopher).*

*Emerson's friend Margaret Fuller (1810–1850) was an enthusiast of Bacchus: she praised the god as "not severe in youthful beauty, like Apollo; but exuberant,—and liable to excess" (conversation reported by Elizabeth Palmer Peabody [1804–1894]).*

*Emerson later added an epigraph to "Bacchus" from the Phaedrus of the Greek philosopher Plato (429–347 BCE): "The man who is his own master knocks in vain at the doors of poetry."*

1    Cape Horn, the southernmost tip of South America.

2    Erebus: the lower part of Hades, the Greek underworld; Styx: a river that the dead were compelled to cross in order to enter Hades.

3    Instead of bread.

4    Emerson echoes lines from the "Ode to a Nightingale" (1819) by the English Romantic poet John Keats (1795–1821): "O for a beaker full of the warm South, / Full of the true, the blushful Hippocrene" (a fountain on Mt. Helicon sacred to the Muses).

5    Alludes to the Catholic idea of transubstantiation: during the Christian Eucharist the wine and wafer are transformed into the blood and body of Christ.

6    In Milton's "Il Penseroso," the speaker hopes to "rightly spell / Of every star that heaven doth show, / And every herb that sips the dew."

7    Enlivened. The last two lines of this stanza emulate, in their meter and mood, speeches by Puck in Shakespeare's *Midsummer Night's Dream* and Ariel in his *Tempest*, as well as Milton's "L'Allegro" and "Il Penseroso."

May float at pleasure through all natures;
The bird-language rightly spell,[6]
And that which roses say so well.

Wine that is shed
Like the torrents of the sun
Up the horizon walls,
Or like the Atlantic streams, which run
When the South Sea calls.

Water and bread,
Food which needs no transmuting,
Rainbow-flowering, wisdom-fruiting
Wine which is already man,
Food which teach and reason can.
Wine which Music is,—
Music and wine are one,—
That I, drinking this,
Shall hear far Chaos talk with me;
Kings unborn shall walk with me;
And the poor grass shall plot and plan
What it will do when it is man.
Quickened[7] so, will I unlock
Every crypt of every rock.

I thank the joyful juice
For all I know;—
Winds of remembering
Of the ancient being blow,
And seeming-solid walls of use
Open and flow.

Pour, Bacchus! the remembering wine;
Retrieve the loss of me and mine!
Vine for vine be antidote,

And the grape requite the lote![8]
Haste to cure the old despair,—
Reason in Nature's lotus drenched,
The memory of ages quenched;
Give them again to shine;
Let wine repair what this undid;
And where the infection slid,
A dazzling memory revive;
Refresh the faded tints,
Recut[9] the aged prints,
And write my old adventures with the pen
Which on the first day drew,
Upon the tablets blue,[10]

The dancing Pleiads[11] and eternal men.

8    Emerson renews his interest in forgetting and remembering, seen in "Experience," "Illusions," and elswhere. The lotus, a food eaten by Odysseus's mariners in Homer's *Odyssey* (9th century BCE), causing them to languish and forget their home (Emerson's Bacchic wine, the antidote, makes him remember). The lotus instills a pleasant but dangerous and drug-like oblivion in the *Odyssey* and in "The Lotos-Eaters" (1833) by Alfred, Lord Tennyson. The wild lote tree actually bears cherry-like but inedible fruit, and is therefore a symbol of uselessness. In the Koran (34:16), the lush Garden of Arabia is transformed into a wasteland with tamarisks and lote trees.

9    Re-engrave.

10   The American poet Wallace Stevens's (1879–1955) "Large Red Man Reading" (1950) begins, "There were ghosts that returned to earth to hear his phrases, / As he sat there reading, aloud, the great blue tabulae." (Blue is the color of the sky and, traditionally, of hope.)

11   The seven daughters of Atlas and Pleione in Greek mythology, who lend their name to a constellation, the Pleiades; also, a group of seven famous poets in Hellenistic Greece and in Renaissance France.

## Concord Hymn, Sung at the Completion of the Battle Monument, July 4, 1837

On April 19, 1775, Emerson's grandfather William Emerson (d. 1776), the pastor of Concord Church, wanted to join the minutemen defending Concord's North Bridge against British troops; they refused, and so he watched the battle between the redcoats and the minutemen from an upstairs window of his house, the Old Manse, with rifle at the ready. The battle was the first of the Revolutionary War.

1    Rude: primitive. Concord's North Bridge (demolished in 1793) was a simple structure, with moveable oak planks. Emerson's step-grandfather Ezra Ripley, who had published a *History of the Fight at Concord* in 1827, campaigned for a memorial at the site of the North Bridge. The monument was ready in 1837, and the town asked Emerson, who had given an account of the Concord battle in his "Historical Discourse" in 1835, to supply a hymn for the dedication of the monument (an impressive obelisk). In preparation for his 1835 speech on the occasion of Concord's bicentennial, Emerson had interviewed survivors of the battle; and during the speech, he mentioned "the presence
*(continued)*

By the rude bridge that arched the flood,[1]
    Their flag to April's breeze unfurled,
Here once the embattled farmers[2] stood,
    And fired the shot heard round the world.[3]

The foe long since in silence slept;
    Alike the conqueror silent sleeps;
And Time the ruined bridge has swept
    Down the dark stream which seaward creeps.

Monument Square, Concord.

On this green bank, by this soft stream,
    We set today a votive[4] stone,
That memory may their deed redeem,
    When, like our sires, our sons are gone.

Spirit, that made those heroes dare
    To die, and leave their children free,
Bid Time and Nature gently spare
    The shaft we raise to them and thee.

of these aged men who were in arms on that day
. . . the invincible men of old." Two years later,
Emerson emphasizes, by contrast, the notion
that "our sires" are "gone," like their British
oppressors. (The last remaining founding father, James Madison, had died in 1836.) At the
dedication ceremony a choir of townspeople,
including Thoreau, sang Emerson's verses to
the tune of Old Hundredth, a traditional hymn
melody.

2    In his 1835 speech, Emerson said, "Those
poor farmers who came up, that day, to defend
their native soil, acted from the simplest instincts. They did not know it was a deed of fame
they were doing."

3    One of the most famous lines by any
American. It is inscribed at the base of Daniel
Chester French's (1850–1931) statue of a min-
uteman in Concord, erected in 1875. The
twenty-two-year-old Ebenezer Munroe is
thought to have fired the first colonial shot in
the skirmish with the British.
    Emerson's line has been applied to a
number of historical and sporting events, from
the home run by Bobby Thomson (1923–2010)
that won the National League pennant for the
New York Giants, to the assassination of the
Austrian archduke Franz Ferdinand (1863–
1914) by the Bosnian Serb Gavrilo Princip
(1894–1918), an event that triggered World
War I.

4    Consecrated, vowed.

Concord Monument to the battle at Old North Bridge.

# Hafiz

*This poem of 1855 is from Emerson's* May-Day and Other Pieces *(1867). It is an imitation of the Persian poet Hafiz.*

Her passions the shy violet
From Hafiz never hides;
Love-longings of the raptured bird
The bird to him confides.

# The Exile

from the persian of kermani.
In Farsistan[1] the violet spreads
Its leaves to the rival sky;
I ask how far is the Tigris flood,
And the vine that grows thereby?
Except the amber morning wind,
Not one saluted me here;
There is no lover in all Bagdad
To offer the exile cheer.
I know that thou, O morning wind!
O'er Kerman's[2] meadow blowest,
And thou, heart-warming nightingale!
My father's orchard knowest.
The merchant hath stuffs of price,
And gems from the sea-washed strand,
And princes offer me grace
To stay in the Syrian land;[3]
But what is gold *for*, but for gifts?
And dark, without love, is the day;
And all that I see in Bagdad
Is the Tigris to float me away.[4]

*"The Exile," from* May-Day and Other Pieces, *is based on a poem by Khwaju Kermani (1280–1352) that Emerson found in Joseph von Hammer-Purgstall's German anthology of Persian poetry (1818). Emerson changes the poem considerably, and begins it with a few lines of Hafiz.*

1    Region in southern Persia whose city Shiraz, famous for art and culture, is the burial place of both Kermani and Hafiz.

2    Kerman is a city and province east of Farsistan, the homeland of Kermani.

3    Damascus, the Syrian city, was ruled from Baghdad.

4    The river Tigris runs from Baghdad to the vicinity of Farsistan. The Mongols sacked Baghdad in 1258 and massacred its people; the city remained in ruins during Kermani's lifetime. The conquering of Baghdad marked the end of the Islamic golden age.

# From Hafiz

This is a free translation of a poem by Hafiz (Book 25, Ode 10), from Emerson's May-Day and Other Pieces (1867).

1     Pleiades: the constellation of the "seven sisters" (see p. 519, n. 11).

2     Because the Pleiades set in November (and rise in May), they are associated with the just-concluded harvest; the Persian poets compare them to a sheaf.

I said to heaven that glowed above,
O hide yon sun-filled zone,
Hide all the stars you boast;
For, in the world of love
And estimation true,
The heaped-up harvest of the moon
Is worth one barley-corn at most,
The Pleiads'[1] sheaf[2] but two.

# [They say, through patience, chalk]

They say, through patience, chalk
Becomes a ruby stone;
Ah, yes! but by the true heart's blood
The chalk is crimson grown.

*A translation of Hafiz (Book 8, Ode 76), from May-Day and Other Pieces (1867).*

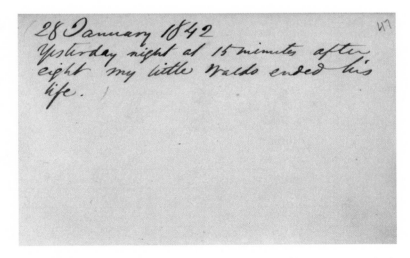

Page from Emerson's Journal on the death of his son Waldo (January 28, 1842).

# Song of Seid Nimetollah of Kuhistan

*This poem is from Emerson's* May-Day and Other Pieces *(1867). Sayyid Ni'matu'llâh of Kirman, who died in 1431, was a Persian poet and mystic, known as "the king of the dervishes." Emerson's poem is adapted from Joseph von Hammer-Purgstall's German translation. Von Hammer-Purgstall describes Seid Nimetollah as "a great sheikh and a mystical poet" and "a traveller in the valley of truth."*

1    The Sufi dervishes whirl in dances, and their ecstasy is often compared to drunkenness, though their movements are precise. The dance enables the transcendence of the ego and the God-given embrace of unity.

In a manuscript translation, probably from Hafiz, Emerson wrote, "Drink till the turbans are all unbound, / Drink till the house like the world turns round" (Emerson alludes to Shakespeare's *Antony and Cleopatra* [2.7.124]: "Cup us till the world go round").

2    King Solomon in the Bible was thought by later tradition to know the secret force of gems. The Sufi poets often mention Solomon's stone, which has magic powers. The Harvard
*(continued)*

[Among the religious customs of the dervishes is an astronomical dance, in which the dervish imitates the movements of the heavenly bodies, by spinning on his own axis, whilst at the same time he revolves round the Sheikh in the centre, representing the sun; and, as he spins, he sings the Song of Seid Nimetollah of Kuhistan.]

Spin the ball! I reel, I burn,
Nor head from foot can I discern,[1]
Nor my heart from love of mine,
Nor the wine-cup from the wine.
All my doing, all my leaving,
Reaches not to my perceiving;
Lost in whirling spheres I rove,
And know only that I love.
I am seeker of the stone,
Living gem of Solomon;[2]
From the shore of souls arrived,
In the sea of sense I dived;
But what is land, or what is wave,
To me who only jewels crave?
Love is the air-fed fire intense,
And my heart the frankincense;

As the rich aloes[3] flames, I glow,
Yet the censer cannot know.
I'm all-knowing, yet unknowing;
Stand not, pause not, in my going.
Ask not me, as Muftis can,
To recite the Alcoran;
Well I love the meaning sweet,—
I tread the book beneath my feet.[4]
Lo! the God's love blazes higher,
Till all difference expire.
What are Moslems? what are Giaours?[5]
All are Love's, and all are ours.
I embrace the true believers,
But I reck[6] not of deceivers.
Firm to Heaven my bosom clings,
Heedless of inferior things;
Down on earth there, underfoot,
What men chatter know I not.

editors of Emerson's poems cite an 1856 book by the Boston Unitarian William Rounseville Alger, *The Poetry of the East* (an inscribed copy was in Emerson's library). Alger wrote, "Such were the incredible virtues of [Solomon's] little talisman, that the touch of it exorcised all evil spirits, commanded the instant presence and services of the Genii, laid every secret bare, and gave its possessor almost unlimited powers of knowledge, dominion, and performance."

3    Sweet-smelling wood of an Asian tree, *Aquilaria agallocha*.

4    A mufti is a Muslim scholar. The Sufis (the sect of the dervishes) had a controversial relationship to Islam and its holy book, the Koran (or Alcoran).

5    Non-Muslims.

6    Consider.

Acknowledgments

Credits

# ACKNOWLEDGMENTS

For his constant encouragement and discernment I thank my editor, John Kulka; Matthew Hills of Harvard University Press was invaluable, too. I owe a tremendous amount, as always, to Harold Bloom, who has done so much to return Emerson to us. The late Barbara Packer, a great reader and scholar of Emerson who will be much missed, deserves special thanks. I would like to thank the editors of Harvard's *Collected Works of Ralph Waldo Emerson*, from whose ongoing efforts Emerson scholarship and this book in particular have benefited. The Concord Museum and the librarians at Harvard's Houghton Library and Concord's Free Public Library were very helpful in my search for illustrations for this volume. I am grateful to Christine Thorsteinsson and David LaRocca for copyediting, and to David for hosting, along with Horst Mewes, a Liberty Fund colloquium on Emerson and Nietzsche in Big Sky, Montana, in 2009; the conversations in Big Sky proved essential to my thinking about Emerson. The Houstoun Family Fund of the University of Houston generously assisted the completion of this project, like so many others; Jay Barksdale of the New York Public Library was consistently helpful. I also thank Jenn Lewin, Wendy Scheir, Lewis J. Mikics, and Larry and Edith Malkin. Victoria Malkin made this, like every book, possible. And to Ariel: *baruch ha-ba*.

# CREDITS

TEXT

*Nature*, Chapters I–VIII, v. 1, pp. 8–45
*The American Scholar*, v. 1, pp. 49–70
*The Divinity School Address*, v. 1, pp. 71–94
*Literary Ethics*, v. 1, 95–116

Reprinted by permission of the publisher from *The Collected Works of Ralph Waldo Emerson*, vol. 1: *Nature, Addresses and Lectures*, Introductions and Notes by Robert E. Spiller, Text established by Alfred R. Ferguson. Cambridge, Mass.: The Belknap Press of Harvard University Press, Copyright © 1971 by the President and Fellows of Harvard College.

*History*, v. 2, pp. 1–24
*Self-Reliance*, v. 2, pp. 25–52
*Circles*, v. 2, pp. 177–190

Reprinted by permission of the publisher from *The Collected Works of Ralph Waldo Emerson*, vol. 2: *Essays: First Series*, Introduction and Notes by Joseph Slater, Text established by Alfred R. Ferguson and Jean Ferguson Carr. Cambridge, Mass.: The Belknap Press of Harvard University Press, Copyright © 1979 by the President and Fellows of Harvard College.

"The Sphinx," v. 9, pp. 5–9

"Uriel," v. 9, pp. 33–35

"The Rhodora: On Being Asked, Whence Is the Flower?" v. 9, p. 79

"The Snow-Storm," v. 9, p. 90

"Ode, Inscribed to W. H. Channing," v. 9, pp. 146–149

"Merlin I," v. 9, pp. 223–225

"Merlin II," v. 9, pp. 228–229

"Bacchus," v. 9, pp. 232–234

"Concord Hymn, Sung at the Completion of the Battle Monument, July 4, 1837," v. 9, p. 307

"Hafiz," v. 9, p. 547

"The Exile," v. 9, p. 555

"From Hafiz," v. 9, p. 557

["They Say . . ."], v. 9, p. 561

"Song of Seid Nimetollah of Kuhistan," v. 9, pp. 578–579

Reprinted by permission of the publisher from *The Collected Works of Ralph Waldo Emerson*, vol. 9: *Poems: A Variorum Edition*, Historical Introduction, Textual Introduction, and Poem Headnotes by Albert J. von Frank, Text established by Albert J. von Frank and Thomas Wortham. Cambridge, Mass.: The Belknap Press of Harvard University Press, Copyright © 2011 by the President and Fellows of Harvard College.

### ADDITIONAL SOURCES

rwe.org

*Letter to Martin Van Buren, President of the United States, Concord, Mass., April 23, 1838*

*Thoreau*

libertyfund.org

*An Address . . . on . . . the Anniversary of the Emancipation of the Negroes in the British West Indies*

*John Brown*

archive.org

From *Memoirs of Margaret Fuller Ossoli*

ILLUSTRATIONS

Brook Farm, 1844. Painting by Josiah Wolcott (ca. 1815–1885). Oil on panel. Massachusetts Historical Society, Boston / Bridgeman Art Library International. *frontispiece, 286*

Ralph Waldo Emerson, 1857. Courtesy of George Eastman House, International Museum of Photography and Film.   *xxx*

Tickets to Emerson's lectures. Courtesy Houghton Library, Harvard University.   *28*

Silhouette of Emerson's aunt, Mary Moody Emerson. Courtesy Concord Free Public Library.   *29*

Caricature of Emerson by Christopher Cranch (1813–1892). Original owned by Harvard.   *32*

First page of Emerson's 1855 letter to Walt Whitman. Library of Congress, Manuscript Division, 20540 USA dcu.   *34*

Amos Bronson Alcott (1799–1888). Courtesy Concord Free Public Library.   *35*

Page from the seventeen-year-old Emerson's Journal. Courtesy Houghton Library, Harvard University.   *38*

Emerson's study. Courtesy Concord Free Public Library.   *43*

Lidian Emerson with son Edward. Courtesy Houghton Library, Harvard University.   *52*

Boston Latin School. © Bettmann / CORBIS.   *54*

Louis Agassiz (1807–1873). Harvard University Archives, call # HUP Agassiz, Louis (17).   *55*

Certificate issued after the Hungarian Revolution of 1848. Courtesy Houghton Library, Harvard University.   *62*

Emerson's father, Reverend William Emerson. Harvard College Library, Widener Library, P321.5, vol. 1, 1812.   *73*

Emerson in lecturing stance, 1869. Courtesy Concord Free Public Library.   *78*

Caricature, the Panic of 1837. Library of Congress, Prints and Photographs Division, LC-USZC4-12948.   *85*

Ralph Waldo Emerson. Courtesy Houghton Library, Harvard University.   *86*

First Parish Meeting House, engraving by George Girdler Smith, 1836, after drawing by Eliza Susan Quincy, 1836. From Josiah Quincy, *The History of Harvard University* (Cambridge, Mass.: J. Owen, 1840).   *92*

Sequoyah (1776–1843). Color litho, American School, 19th century. Private collection / Peter Newark American Pictures / Bridgeman Art Library International.   *94*

Antiremoval tract by the Cherokee Nation, 1831. Litho, American School, 19th century. Private collection / Peter Newark American Pictures / Bridgeman Art Library International.   *95*

President Martin Van Buren (1782–1862). Colored engraving, American School, 19th century. Private collection / Peter Newark American Pictures / Bridgeman Art Library International.   *97*

Front page of the *Cherokee Phoenix*, 1828. Print, American School, 19th century. American Antiquarian Society, Worcester, Mass. / Bridgeman Art Library International.   *99*

Concord in 1830. Courtesy Concord Free Public Library.   *103*

Oliver Wendell Holmes (1809–1894). Harvard University Archives, call # HUP Holmes, Oliver Wendell AB 1829 (6).   *113*

Map of Concord Village, 1852. Courtesy Concord Free Public Library.   *118*

Title page of Amos Bronson Alcott's *Conversations with Children on the Gospels.* Courtesy Houghton Library, Harvard University.   *126*

Emerson, 1847. Courtesy Concord Free Public Library.   *127*

East Boston, 1879. Library of Congress, Geography and Maps Division, G3764. B6:2E2A3 1879 .B3.   *133*

Senator Henry Clay speaking to Congress, 1850. Litho, Peter Fred Rothermel (1817–1895) (after). Private collection / Stapleton Collection / Bridgeman Art Library International.   *139*

Ralph Waldo and Lidian Emerson with children and grandchildren, 1879. Courtesy Concord Free Public Library.   *144*

Announcement of a reception for Emerson, 1873. Courtesy Houghton Library, Harvard University.   *153*

Page from "The Border Ruffian Code in Kansas," 1856. Published by the *New York Tribune* Office. Litho, American School, 19th century. Newberry Library, Chicago / Bridgeman Art Library International.   *161*

City of Boston, 1873. Library of Congress, Geography and Maps Division, G3764.B6.A3 1873 .P3.   *172*

Thomas Carlyle (1795–1881). Courtesy Houghton Library, Harvard University   *185*

Article on Emerson by Henry Sylvester Nash, 1881. Courtesy Houghton Library, Harvard University.   *187*

Map of Concord, 1852. Courtesy Concord Free Public Library.   *194*

Walt Whitman (1819–1892). Frontispiece to *Leaves of Grass*, 1855. Engraving, American School, 19th century. Private collection / Bridgeman Art Library International.   *201*

Funeral notice for Emerson's brother Edward. Courtesy Houghton Library, Harvard University.   *208*

Rewards for runaway slaves, 1840. Advertised in the Washington D.C. Intelligencer, 1840. Newsprint, American photographer, 19th century. Private collection / Peter Newark American Pictures / Bridgeman Art Library International.  *316*

*Slave Ship (Slavers Throwing Overboard the Dead and Dying, Typhoon Coming On)* (1840), by J. M. W. Turner (1775–1851). Oil on canvas. Museum of Fine Arts, Boston / Henry Lillie Pierce Fund / Bridgeman Art Library International.  *321*

Sailors throwing slaves overboard (1822), by Jesse Torrey. From Torrey's *American Slave Trade*, 1822. Engraving, black and white photo, American School, 19th century. Private collection / Bridgeman Art Library International.  *322*

Michel de Montaigne (1533–1592). Oil on canvas, French School, 17th century. Private collection / Giraudon / Bridgeman Art Library International.  *327*

Ellen Emerson, Emerson's eldest daughter. Courtesy Houghton Library, Harvard University.  *334*

Page from Emerson's Journal announcing his engagement to Ellen Tucker, 1828. Courtesy Houghton Library, Harvard University.  *343*

Emerson's mother, Ruth Haskins Emerson. Courtesy Houghton Library, Harvard University.  *355*

Portsmouth-Concord Railroad, 1845. Library of Congress, Geography and Maps Division, G3721.P3 1845 .C3 RR 539.  *362*

Emerson's son Edward and daughter Edith. Courtesy Concord Free Public Library.  *366*

Samuel Taylor Coleridge (1772–1834). Portrait study, 1818, pencil, charcoal and chalk on blue/gray paper, Charles Robert Leslie (1794–1859). Private collection / Photo © Philip Mould Ltd., London / Bridgeman Art Library International.  *368*

Thomas Carlyle (1795–1881). Black and white photo, Elliott & Fry Studio (fl.1860–1890). Copyright © Trustees of the Watts Gallery, Compton, Surrey, UK / Bridgeman Art Library International.  *369*

Walter Savage Landor (1775–1864). Pencil on paper, black and white photo, Alfred d'Orsay (1801–1852). Private collection / Bridgeman Art Library International.  *371*

William Wordsworth (1770–1850). Oil on canvas, 1840, Henry William Pickersgill (1782–1875). Wordsworth Trust / Bridgeman Art Library International.  *372*

Stonehenge, 1801. Engraving, John Britton (1771–1857). Salisbury and South Wiltshire Museum / Bridgeman Art Library International.  *385*

Concord ball program, 1875. Courtesy Concord Free Public Library.  *388, 493 (detail)*